# Census Substitutes & State Census Records

## 2nd Edition

### Substitute Name Lists for 50 States & State Censuses for 38 States

by

**William Dollarhide**

# Volume Two
## Central States

Family Roots Publishing Co.

Published by Family Roots Publishing Co., LLC
PO Box 1682
Orting, WA 98360-1682
**www.familyrootspublishing.com**

Library of Congress Control Number: 2016911714

ISBN: 978-1-62859-083-8

Recommended Citation:
***Census Substitutes & State Census Records, 2nd Edition, Volume 2 – Central States***,
by William Dollarhide, published by Family Roots Publishing Co., LLC, Orting, WA, 2016,
278 pages.

*Printed in the United States of America*

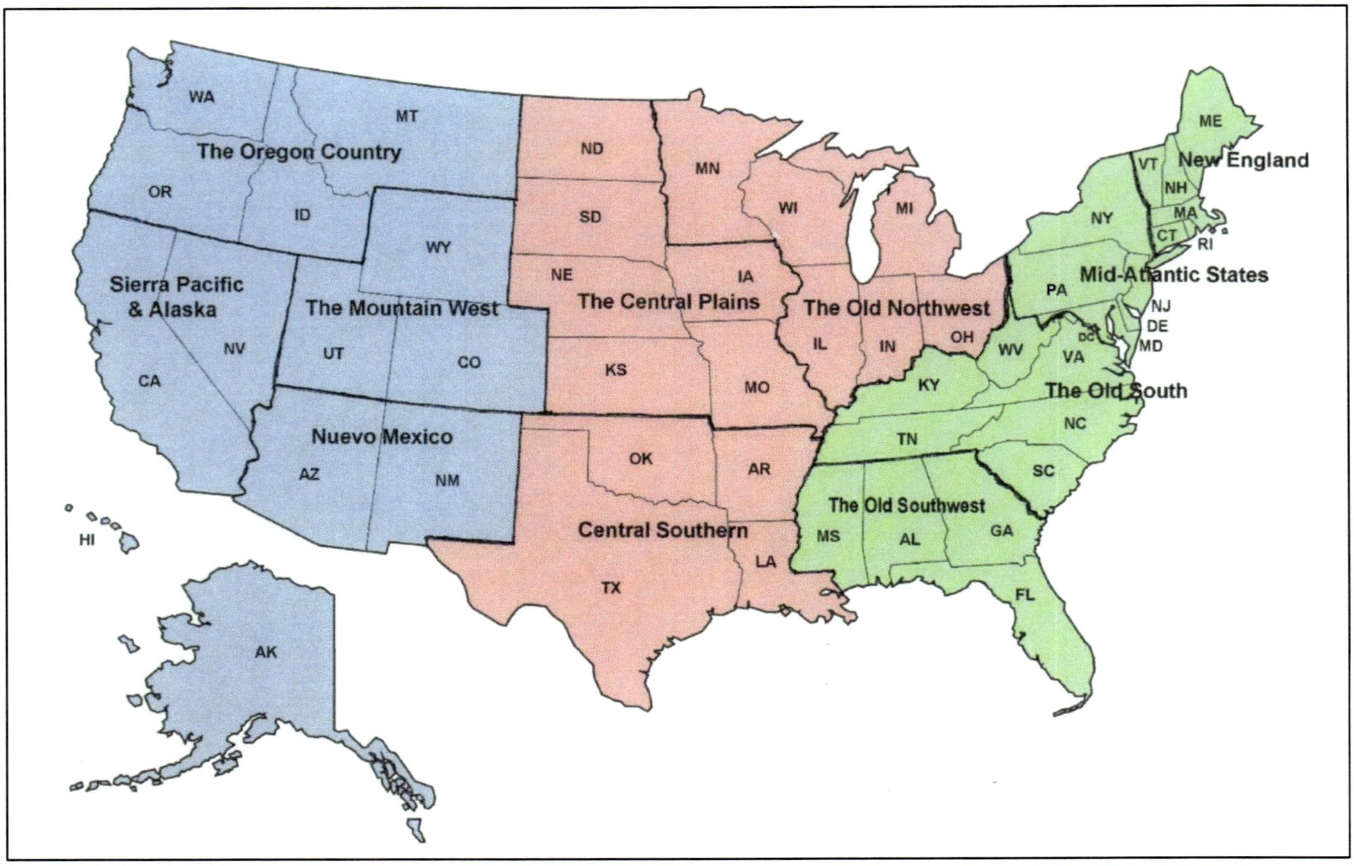


## Volume 3
**13 Western States / Nationwide**

**Chapter 1W – Sierra Pacific & Alaska** California, Nevada, Hawaii & Alaska

**Chapter 2W – Nuevo Mexico** Arizona & New Mexico

**Chapter 3W – The Mountain West** Colorado, Utah & Wyoming

**Chapter 4W – The Oregon Country** Idaho, Montana, Oregon & Washington

**Chapter 5W – National Name Lists** Federal Censuses, & National Substitute Name Lists

## Volume 2
**16 Central States**

**Chapter 1C – The Old Northwest**: Illinois, Indiana, Michigan, Minnesota, Ohio & Wisconsin

**Chapter 2C – The Central Plains** Iowa, Kansas, Missouri, Nebraska, Dakota Territory - North Dakota - South Dakota

**Chapter 3C – Central Southern** Arkansas, Louisiana, Oklahoma & Texas

## Volume 1
**22 Eastern States**

**Chapter 1E – The Old Southwest**: Alabama, Florida, Georgia, & Mississippi

**Chapter 2E – New England** Connecticut, Maine, Massachusetts, New Hampshire, Rhode Island & Vermont

**Chapter 3E – Mid-Atlantic States** Delaware, District of Columbia, Maryland, New Jersey, New York & Pennsylvania

**Chapter 4E – The Old South** Kentucky, North Carolina, South Carolina, Tennessee, Virginia & West Virginia

# Contents
## Volume Two

# Foreword

by Leland K. Meitzler

In late 2003 Bill Dollarhide came by my office and asked if I had any ideas for *Genealogy Bulletin* articles. As it turned out, I had just finished organizing materials for a lecture on state and territorial census records and had a file folder full of data I had collected over the years on my desk. I suggested he put something together on that subject and gave him the file to review. After looking through my file, Bill decided that we needed to identify the many substitutes to censuses (statewide tax lists, voter registration lists, and such), as he quickly noted that a number of states didn't take any state or territorial censuses at all. Bill began compiling a bibliography of not only extant state and territorial censuses, but substitute lists as well.

Researched and compiled by region, he added timelines of historical references to show the jurisdictions in place at the time of each census. Compiling the material by region was a stroke of genius on Bill's part, as we quickly realized that in most cases, it would have been very difficult to write about one state without writing about those surrounding it.

Much of the data found in the First Edition was initially published in serial form in the old *Genealogy Bulletin* (1983-2006). That said, the District of Columbia, for which there are many excellent sources, was never published. However, it is included in Vol. 1 - Eastern States. Also never published was The Oregon Country chapter (ID, MT, OR, WA), which is now included in Vol 3 – Western States. Numerous online sources have been added to the Second Edition, reflecting the ongoing efforts of both public and private companies to digitize relevant records.

And, in this new Second Edition, the Western States volume now includes extensive *Federal Censuses and National Substitute Name Lists,* and adds *US Maps* for the census years, 1790-1940.

Bill also spent countless hours compiling tabulated charts that may be worth the cost of this book all by themselves. The first, found on page 15, is a chart for the non-state census states. There happens to be 13 of them (including the District of Columbia). This chart lists the states and the years covered by census substitutes. The second chart, found on pages 16-17, lists the 38 states that have extant colonial, pre-statehood, territorial, and state censuses, complete with the census year, and an indication if the census is available online as of the date of publication. The third chart, found on page 18, shows in graphic form the states that had censuses taken in common years – "on the fives." Census dates for some states are within a range. The fourth chart, on page 19, shows the availability of federal censuses for all states, 1790-1940.

Note that the title of this series of volumes is *Census Substitutes & State Census Records,* which reflects the fact that the volumes really contain a list of census substitutes, with state censuses turning out to be in the minority. Substitutes outnumber censuses by a factor of ten to one! However, the state censuses identified in this series are by far the most complete lists of Colonial, Territorial, or State Censuses published to date.

State and Territorial Censuses have long fascinated me. Many were taken in order to get congress to allow statehood. Some territories would take censuses on a nearly annual basis, in the attempt to show that they had the population base necessary to justify statehood.

Other states, like New York, had authorization of non-federal censuses written into their state constitutions. New York was one of the most prolific when it came to state censuses, as it produced numerous schedules, most falling on the ubiquitous "fives." Today we have extant New York censuses for 1825, 1835, 1845, 1855, 1865, 1875, 1892, 1905, 1915, and 1925. Some of the early years are not complete, but what is available is certainly useful. The 1925 New York census was taken as well as any other, and the population returns are largely legible and complete. However, the census was wrought with scandal, leaving New Yorkers with a taste of bitterness for such things. To make a long story short, it seems that the New York Secretary of State, a former Dean of Home Economics at Syracuse University, Florence Elizabeth Smith Knapp, took nepotism to a whole new level. As the state official in charge of the 1925 census, she put family and friends on the payroll, and while this wasn't illegal, most of these folks did little or nothing to earn their salaries. Even her 74-year old mother, Ella Smith, enjoyed a non-working stint as an assistant supervisor. Florence's step-daughter, Clara Blanche Knapp, a professor at Middlebury College in Vermont, was on the payroll for over $5,000 in income, while never leaving the state of Vermont. Moreover, checks written to both Ella and Blanche seemed to have been endorsed into Florence E.S. Knapp's bank account. Numerous other family members and friends were paid substantial sums for non-work. In 1928, Mrs. Knapp finally went on trial for her misdeeds, and found guilty of first-degree grand larceny for misappropriation of state funds. She served 30 days in the Albany Jail. She could have gotten 10 years. So ended the brief political career of the first woman ever to be elected to state-wide office in New York. So also ended the state censuses of New York State.

Iowa, Kansas, Rhode Island, Florida, North Dakota, and South Dakota also took censuses up through 1925. South Dakota and Florida even took censuses in 1935 and 1945! The real value of state censuses is found in the numerous schedules enumerated in the mid-nineteenth century. Thirty-eight states took non-federal censuses that are still extant today.

And then there are the substitutes. They are of prime importance, since 12 states, as well as the District of Columbia, took no state censuses at all. And even if your ancestors lived in a state where censuses were taken "on the fives," census substitutes are helpful, especially if the family was on the move.

Although Mr. Dollarhide has used all kinds of substitutes throughout this volume, more attention has been given to tax lists, voter registration rolls, vital records, directories, statewide probate indexes, land records, and even military censuses, than most others. These records are often easily accessible and using this guide, you will be able to quickly find them for your own use. You are in for a treat, so sit back and look up the states of your ancestors. You will find information on records you never knew existed. Then… go get the records, and happy hunting!

Leland K. Meitzler
Publisher

# Introduction

## Census Substitutes & State Census Records

Census substitutes are those name lists derived from tax lists, directories, military lists, land ownership lists, voter registrations, and other compilations of names of residents for an entire state, or part of a state. A census substitute can be used to determine the names of residents in a given area when a federal or state census is missing. Moreover, a census substitute can be used as an alternative name list; confirming, contradicting, or adding to information found in a federal or state census.

This book identifies at least ten times the number of Census Substitute titles than any previous work ever published. All states are represented with significant alternative name lists – name lists that stop time for a certain year and place, and name the residents of a certain place. Since all of these name lists are specific to a certain year, they are listed within each state category in chronological order. Incorporated into the lists are any State Census titles – a reference to a state census taken for a specific year.

### Federal vs. State Censuses

Federal censuses have their origins in the constitutional provision for apportionment of the U.S. House of Representatives. The first federal census was taken in 1790, and beginning about the same time, state censuses were conducted for the same reason, that is, apportionment of the various state legislatures.

Although the primary purpose of all censuses was to simply count the population, beginning with the first federal census of 1790, more information than a simple tally was added. This included the name and age of a person and progressively more details about a household for each subsequent census year. State censuses followed this same pattern.

State censuses usually add even more information than the federal censuses, and as a result, they are premier genealogical resources. Except in cases where a federal census is lost, state census records are not substitutes for the federal censuses – state censuses were almost always taken between federal census years, and usually add unique information and details about a household not found in a federal census. If a state census exists between federal census years, it may add marginally to the knowledge one gains about a family. But, more often, it will add critical information, such as more exact dates of birth, marriages, deaths; plus additional children, different residences, other relatives living with a family; and more.

### Non-State Census States

Thirteen (13) states (including DC) have never conducted a state-sponsored census. For these Non-State Census States, this review attempts to identify as many census substitutes as possible. In some cases, the census substitutes are for a single county within a state, and by listing multiple county name lists for about the same time period, regional coverage is achieved.

For an overview of the Non-State Census States, see Table 1 (page 15) showing the years for which census substitutes exist. More detail for each census substitute year indicated on the table is covered in the bibliographic sections.

## State Census States

Thirty-eight (38) states have conducted censuses separate from the federal censuses. The number of censuses taken by each of the State Census States ranges from one (1) census year, e.g., the 1852 California; to twenty-four (24) census years, e.g., the 1792-1866 Mississippi territorial/state censuses. For this review, all of the state-sponsored censuses are identified, plus, to a lesser degree than the non-state census states, census substitutes available. See Table 2 (pages 16-17) for an overview of the State Census States, the year for each surviving census for a state; and an indication of which specific years are now available online as digitized databases.

## Locating the Extant State Census Records

Generally, state censuses were conducted from the time of territorial status or early statehood up until about 1905, but a few continued until 1925, 1935, or 1945. The last state censuses taken by any of the states was in 1945 (Florida and South Dakota). Due to budget restraints, the Depression Era of the 1930s was a contributing factor to states ending their census-taking endeavors. Eventually, all states of the Union stopped using the population figures from state censuses, and began using the federal census figures for apportionment of their state legislatures.

While the surviving federal census manuscripts are all located mostly in one repository (the National Archives), state census manuscripts are spread across the country in the various state archives or local repositories. The accessibility of state censuses may be just as good as federal censuses – but one needs to know where they are located first.

Beginning in 1941, the U.S. Bureau of the Census issued a bibliographic report identifying all known state censuses, those undertaken by the various states separate from the federal censuses since 1790.[1] As a project of the Library of Congress led by Henry J. Dubester, the report was the first known attempt to research all of the state constitutions and subsequent laws related to state censuses for all of the states. The Dubester report sought, first, to identify what state censuses had ever been authorized by a state constitution or legislature; and second, to identify what census manuscripts still survive. The identification of extant state censuses was very incomplete, due to the war and under-funding of the project.

However, Dubester's review of each state's constitutional provisions for taking state censuses still stands as the best overview of what state censuses were ever authorized. The report cites the specific articles of the state constitutions or the actual state laws relating to censuses for all states.

Unfortunately, the fact that a state legislature authorized a state census does not mean one was actually taken. For example, the State Constitution of California of 1849 authorized a census in the years 1852 and 1855 and each ten years thereafter, all for the purpose of apportionment of its state legislature. Yet, only one was ever taken, that for 1852. Later, the California Constitution of 1879 provided that the decennial national census serve as the basis for legislative apportionment.[2]

This was fairly typical of all states. Even in those states for which several decades of state censuses now survive, they eventually got out of the census business, turning to the federal decennial censuses to determine apportionment. For example, New York took state censuses from 1825 and every ten years thereafter until 1925, yet, in 1938, New York decided to use the federal decennial censuses thereafter.[3]

Since the Dubester report, there have been several attempts to list all known state censuses, where they are located, and the contents of the census name lists. All of these attempts differ dramatically, because some of the lists rely on the Dubester report, which may have been accurate in identifying which state censuses were ever authorized, but was not nearly complete in identifying the extant manuscripts of state census records. For example, Table 4-8 of *The Source,*[4] seems to use the census years cited in the Dubester report for "authorized state censuses" rather than those actually extant. There are lists of state censuses for each state in *The Red Book,*[5] but are only a slight improvement over those found in *The Source*. And, several Internet sites offer lists of state censuses, all of which seem to take data previously published in the *Source* or *The Red Book*, and similar publications.

Based on survey results from all states, the Family History Library prepared a two-volume publication, *U.S. State and Special Census Register: A Listing of Family History Library Microfilm Numbers,* compiled by G. Eileen Buckway and Fred Adams, a revised edition published by the FHL in 1992 (FHL book 973 X2 v. 1 & 2, and fiche #6104851 (vol. 1) and #6104852 (vol. 2). This is a very good guide to military censuses, school censuses, and special censuses of American Indian tribes. As a guide to state censuses, however, the list is incomplete. Since the results of the surveys from each of the states were only partially successful, there are many omissions.

Clearly, the best list of state censuses to date is Ann S. Lainhart, *State Census Records*, published by Genealogical Publishing Co., Inc., Baltimore, in 1992. The book identifies state censuses in 43 states, including 5 states without state censuses (but have major state-wide census substitutes available). For the 38 state census states, the lists generally do not include colonial or pre-territorial censuses. With a few exceptions, census substitutes such as those compiled from tax lists, voter registration lists, military lists, or other name sources, are also not included. Still, Lainhart's book stands as the most complete list ever done.

At the time when most of the previous state census lists were put together, there were some research tools unavailable to the authors. Today, the Internet as a resource for finding place-specific records is overwhelming. And, special tools such as the Periodical Source Index (PERSI)[6] which indexes articles in over 11,000 different genealogical periodicals (by subject, place, and surname) gives a big boost to the task of finding references to relevant articles using keywords such as "state census," "territorial census," or "tax list." In addition, the State Archives and/or State Libraries where obscure census originals and substitute name lists reside often have a website with an online searchable catalog.

For any genealogical research project, it helps to be close to the Family History Library (FHL) in Salt Lake City. But from any place where a researcher has access to the Internet, the FamilySearch™ online catalog as a genealogical research tool has no equal. Searching for published state censuses and census substitutes in the FHL catalog will not bring up every extant resource, but it is more complete than any other library in the world.

## Regional Chapter Organization

For this nationwide review, we decided to start with the areas of the United States that had the earliest census/name list records. That meant moving from the East Coast to the West Coast. The first chapter of Volume Two – Central States is for Census Substitutes and State Censuses available for the states of Illinois, Indiana, Michigan, Minnesota, Ohio, and Wisconsin. This area could be called "The Old Northwest."

A timeline for the region was prepared to put the area into a historical perspective from a genealogist's point of view. This grouping of states and a common timeline for each group was continued in two of the chapters, but timelines specific to certain states were also prepared.

Due to the addition of many online databases at the main genealogical websites, there is now a new arrangement of online and published resources in this Second Edition. For example, for each state section, there are now six separate listings for online and published censuses & substitutes at **1)** the main **State Resource Centers** (state archives, state library, and/or state historical society), **2)** the **Ancestry.com** website, **3)** the **FamilySearch.org** website, and **4) Other Online Databases** at various websites. And, a selection of pertinent articles found in genealogical periodicals are now grouped together for some states, with a reference to **5) PERSI** (the PERiodical Source Index) for a researcher to find even more articles. Published censuses and substitutes in the form of 6) **FHL Books and Microfilms** are still listed as a group within each state section, citing a FHL book or film number.

## Federal Censuses & National Substitute Name Lists

In the First Edition, the bibliography of Census Substitutes and State Censuses cited references to the location of statewide databases, but not generally all of the federal censuses. Federal censuses may have been mentioned in the chronological timelines or bibliographic lists, mainly to assist in locating census substitutes for a missing federal census year. For several of the western states, federal censuses were included to fill in the lack of state censuses and substitutes. For all states, in the case of lost federal censuses which have been reconstructed for a state or part of a state, any book titles or articles that could be found were included.

In this Second Edition, citations to the schedules and indexes to all federal censuses, 1790-1940, have been added as part of the last chapter of Volume 3 – Western States / Nationwide. Also added are *National Substitute Name Lists* and *U.S. Maps* for each federal census year, 1790 through 1940, showing the evolution of the state boundaries. And, a new Table 4 (page 19) was added to show the availability of federal censuses for each state, 1790-1940.

To review the federal censuses in more detail, refer to *The Census Book*[7] for each census year, and a review of published federal census indexes.

The maps of the changing county boundaries for all of the states shown in *Map Guide to the U.S. Federal Census, 1790-1920*[8] should also be helpful for reviewing substitute or state census years between federal census years.

- Wm. D.

---

**Notes:**

1. *State Censuses: An Annotated Bibliography of Censuses of Population Taken After the Year 1790 by States and Territories of the United States*, prepared by Henry J. Dubester, Chief, Census Library Project, Library of Congress, published Washington, DC, by United States Department of Commerce, Bureau of the Census, 1941, rev. 1948.

2. Dubester, *State Censuses*, p. 3.

3. Dubester, *State Censuses*, p. 50.

4. *The Source: A Guidebook of American Genealogy*, first edition, edited by Arlene Eakle and Johni Cerny, published by Ancestry, Inc., Salt Lake City, 1984.

5. *The Red Book: American State, County & Town Sources*, edited by Alice Eichholz, rev. ed., published by Ancestry, Inc., Salt Lake City, UT, 1992.

6. Allen County Public Library, *Periodical Source Index (PERSI)*, updated semi-annually. [database online at various contracted websites] Original data: Allen County Public Library. Periodical Source Index, Fort Wayne, IN: Allen County Public Library Foundation, 1985- .

7. *The Census Book: A Genealogist's Guide to Federal Census Facts, Schedules and Indexes*, by William Dollarhide, published by Heritage Quest, North Salt Lake, UT, 2000. The book is out of print, but may be available at various online book sites, such as Google Books, Amazon.com or eBay.com.

8. *Map Guide to the U.S. Federal Censuses, 1790-1920*, by William Thorndale and William Dollarhide, published by Genealogical Publishing Co., Inc., Baltimore, 1987-2016.

**Table 1 – Non-State Census States.** The following 13 states (including DC) have never conducted a state-sponsored census (or no state census survives). Census Substitutes for each state are shown for a range of years. Refer to the bibliographic listings for details about each.

| State | Terr. | State | Years for which Census Substitutes are Available |
|---|---|---|---|
| **Alaska** | 1912 | 1959 | 1870, 1873, 1878, 1885, 1887, 1890-1895, 1902-1912, 1905, 1908-1914, 1910- 1929, 1913-1916, 1917-1918, 1947, 1950, 1959-1986, and 1960-1985. |
| **Delaware** | — | 1787 | 1609-1888, 1646-1679, 1680-1934, 1682-1759, 1684-1693, 1726, 1755, 1759, 1779, 1782, 1785, 1790, 1800, 1807, 1850-1860, and 1862-1872. |
| **District of Columbia** | — | 1791 | 1803, 1807, 1818, 1867, 1878, 1885, 1888, 1894, 1897, 1905-1909, 1912-1913, 1915, 1917, 1919, and 1925. |
| **Idaho** | 1863 | 1890 | 1863, 1865-1874, 1871-1881, 1880, 1890, 1911-1937, 1911-1950, and 1930. |
| **Kentucky** | — | 1792 | 1773-1780, 1774-1796, 1780-1909, 1781-1839, 1782-1787, 1782-1875, 1787, 1787-1811, 1787-1875, 1788-1875, 1789-1882, 1792-1830, 1792-1913, 1792-1796, 1793-1836, 1794-1805, 1794-1817, 1795, 1796-1808, 1797-1866, 1800, 1820-1900, 1851-1900, 1859-1860, 1860-1936, 1861-1865, 1862-1866, and 1895- 1896. |
| **Montana** | 1864 | 1889 | 1860, 1856-1993, 1864-1872, 1868-1869, 1868-1929, 1870, 1880, 1870-1957, 1872- 1900, 1879-1880, 1881-1928, 1881-2000, 1891-1929, 1894, 1913, 1906- 1917, 1909- 1910, 1917-1918, 1921, and 1930-1975. |
| **New Hampshire** | — | 1788 | 1648, 1709. 1723, 1736, 1740, 1763, 1767, 1775, 1776, 1779, 1789, 1795-1816, 1797, 1802, 1803, 1821, 1826, 1833, 1836, 1838, 1849, 1855 & 1865 MA, 1860, 1862-1866, 1903, and 1902-1921 |
| **Ohio** | 1787 | 1803 | 1787-1840, 1787-1871, 1788-1799, 1788-1820, 1790, 1800-1803, 1801-1814, 1801-1824, 1802, 1803-1827, 1804, 1807, 1810, 1812, 1816-1838, 1816-1838, 1825, 1827, 1832-1850, 1833-1994, 1835, 1846-1880, 1851-1900, 1851-1907, and 1907. |
| **Pennsylvania** | — | 1787 | 1682-1950, 1759, 1680-1938, 1680s-1900s, 1760s-1790s, 1700s, 1780, 1798, 1740- 1900, 1887-1893, and 1870. |
| **Texas** | — | 1845 | 1736-1838, 1700s-1800s, 1756-1830s, 1782-1836, 1809-1836, 1814-1909, 1821-1846, 1826, 1826-1835, 1820s-1846, 1820-1829, 1826-1836, 1829-1836, 1830-1839, 1835, 1835-1846, 1836, 1836-1935, 1837-1859, 1840-1849, 1840, 1846, 1837-1910, 1851-1900, 1858, 1861-1865, 1863, 1865-1866, 1867, 1874, 1882-1895, 1884, 1889-1894, 1890, 1914, 1917-1918, 1896-1948, and 1964-1968. |
| **Vermont** | — | 1791 | 1770s-1780s, 1700s-1800s, 1654-1800, 1710-1753, 1721-1800, 1770-1832, 1771, 1782, 1788, 1793, 1796-1959, 1800s-1870, 1807, 1813, 1815, 1816, 1827-1833, 1828, 1832, 1843, 1852-1959, 1855-1860, 1861-1866, 1865, 1869, 1871-1908, 1874, 1880-1881, 1881-1882, 1882-1883, 1883-1884, 1884, 1887-1888, 1888, 1889, and 1895-1924. |
| **Virginia** | — | 1788 | 1600s-1700s, 1600s, 1619-1930, 1623-1990, 1623-1800, 1632-1800, 1654-1800, 1704-1705, 1720, 1736-1820, 1740, 1744-1890, 1760, 1769-1800, 1779, 1779-1978, 1779-1860, 1782-1785, 1785, 1787, 1809-1848, 1810, 1815, 1828-1938, 1835, 1835-1941, 1840, 1861, 1861-1865, 1852, 1853-1896, and 1889-1890. |
| **West Virginia** | — | 1863 | 1600s-1900s, 1777-1850, 1787, 1782-1907, 1782-1850, 1782-1860, 1782, 1783-1900, 1783-1850, 1785-1850, 1787,1850, 1789-1850, 1792-1850, 1797-1899, 1797-1851, 1799-1850, 1800, 1801-1850, 1810, 1811-1850, 1862-1866, 1863-1900, and 1899-1900. |

From ***Census Substitutes & State Census Records*** by William Dollarhide, published by Family Roots Publishing Co., Orting WA

### Table 2 – State Census States – Alabama to Michigan

The following 38 states have state-sponsored censuses available:

| State | Year a Terr. | Year a State | Years for which State Censuses are available (underlined year = an online database is available) | Notes |
|---|---|---|---|---|
| Alabama | 1817 | 1819 | **Colony:** 1706 1721 1764 1785 1786-1803 **AL Territory:** 1801* 1808* 1809* 1810* 1816* 1818 **State:** 1820** 1821 1823 1832 1838 1844 1850** 1855 1866. State copy of federal (index): 1870 | * as part of MS Terr. ** separate from federal. |
| Arizona | 1863 | 1912 | **AZ Territory:** 1864 1866 | |
| Arkansas | 1819 | 1836 | **Colony:** 1686 1723 1749 1791 1802 **AR Territory:** 1814* 1823 1827 1829 1833 1835 **State:** 1838 1854 1865 | * as part of MO Terr. |
| California | — | 1850 | **Colony:** 1790 **State:** 1852 only | |
| Colorado | 1861 | 1876 | **CO Territory:** 1861 1866* **State:** 1885 | * 2 counties only |
| Connecticut | -- | 1788 | **Colony:** 1762 **State:** 1917* | * Military census, males over 16 |
| Florida | 1822 | 1845 | **Colony:** 1759 1763-1779 1783-1814 **FL Territory:** 1825 1838 **State:** 1845** 1855 1864* 1867 1875 1885 1895 1935 1945 | * Military census ** Statehood census |
| Georgia | — | 1788 | 1800 federal* **State:** Partial lists only: 1827 1838 1845 1852 1859 1879 1890 federal** 1890 (statewide reconstruction). | * Oglethorpe Co only ** Washington Co only |
| Hawaii | 1900 | 1959 | **Kingdom of Hawaii:** 1840-1866 1878 1890 1896 | |
| Illinois | 1809 | 1818 | **IL Territory:** 1810 **State:** 1818 1820* 1825 1830* 1835 1840* 1845 1855 1865. | * separate from federal |
| Indiana | 1800 | 1816 | **IN Territory:** 1807. **State:** A few townships only: 1857 1871 1877 1883 1889 1901 1913 1919 1931 | |
| Iowa | 1838 | 1846 | As part of **WI Territory:** 1836 **IA Territory:** 1838 **State:** 1844 1845 1847 1849 1851 1852 1853 1854 1856 1859 1873 1875 1885 1888 1893 1895 1896 1897 1905 1915 1925 | |
| Kansas | 1854 | 1861 | **KS Territory:** 1855 1856 1857 1858 1859 **State:** 1865 1875 1885 1895 1905 1915 1925 | |
| Louisiana | 1809 | 1812 | **Colony:** 1699-1732 1706-1741 1791 **State:** 1833 1837 1890 federal* | *Ascension Parish only |
| Maine | — | 1820 | 1837 only. | |
| Maryland | — | 1788 | 1776 1778 1783* | * Tax list |
| Massachusetts | — | 1788 | 1855 1865 | |
| Michigan | 1805 | 1837 | **MI Territory:** 1827 1834 **State:** 1837 1845 1854 1864 1874 1884 1894 | |

From ***Census Substitutes & State Census Records*** by William Dollarhide, published by Family Roots Publishing Co., Orting WA

## Table 2 – State Census States – Minnesota to Wyoming

Continuation of states with state-sponsored censuses available:

| State | Year a Terr. | Year a State | Years for which State Censuses are available (underlined year = an online database is available) | Notes |
|---|---|---|---|---|
| Minnesota | 1849 | 1858 | **MN Territory:** 1849 1853 1855 1857* **State:** 1865 1875 1885 1895 1905 | * special federal. |
| Mississippi | 1798 | 1817 | **Colony:** 1792** **MS Territory:** 1801 1805 1809 1810 1813 1815 1816 1817 **State:** 1818 1820* 1822 1823 1824 1825 1830* 1837 1840* 1841 1845 1850* 1853 1857 1866 | * separate from federal ** Natchez District only |
| Missouri | 1805 | 1821 | **Colony:** 1752 1791 1797 **MO Territory:** 1817 1818 1819 **State:** 1844* 1845* 1846* 1852* 1856* 1864* 1868* 1876** | * 1-2 counties only ** 28 counties |
| Nebraska | 1854 | 1867 | **NE Territory**: 1854 1855 1856 1865 **State:** Lancaster & Cass Co Only: 1874 1875 1876 1877 1878 1881 1882 1883 1884 1885 | |
| Nevada | 1861 | 1864 | **NV Territory:** 1861 1862 1863 **State:** 1864 1875 | |
| New Jersey | — | 1787 | 1855 1865 1875* 1885 1895 1905 1915 | * a few townships only |
| New Mexico | 1850 | 1912 | **Colony:** 1600 **Territory:** 1885 | |
| New York | — | 1788 | 1825 1835 1845 1855 1865 1875 1892 1905 1915 1925 | |
| North Carolina | — | 1789 | **Pre-statehood:** 1784 -1787. | |
| North Dakota | 1861* | 1889 | **Dakota Territory:** 1885 **State:** 1905 (statistics only) 1915 1925 | * Dakota Territory |
| Oklahoma | 1890 | 1907 | **OK Territory**: 1890* **State:** 1907 federal (Seminole Co. only) | * separate from federal |
| Oregon | 1848 | 1859 | **OR Provisional Territory:** 1842 1843 1844 1846 **OR Territory:** 1849 1853 1854 1855 1856 1857 1858 1859 **State:** 1865* 1875* 1885* 1895* 1905 | * indexes for a few counties only |
| Rhode Island | — | 1790 | 1865 1875 1885 1905 1915 1925 1935 | |
| South Carolina | — | 1788 | 1829 1839 1869 1875 | |
| South Dakota | 1861* | 1889 | **Dakota Territory:** 1885 **State:** 1895 1905 1915 1925 1935 1945 | * Dakota Territory |
| Tennessee | 1790* | 1796 | **Southwest Territory:** 1790 (Reconstructed) **State:** 1891 (partial) | |
| Utah | 1850 | 1896 | **UT Territory:** 1856 only. | |
| Washington | 1853 | 1889 | **WA Territory:** 1851* 1856 1857 1858 1859 1861 1871 1879 1881 1883 1885 1887 **State:** 1889 1892 1894 | * As part of Oregon Territory. |
| Wisconsin | 1836 | 1848 | **WI Territory:** 1836 1838 1842 1846 1847 **State:** 1855 1865 1875 1885 1895 1905 | |
| Wyoming | 1868 | 1890 | **WY Territory:** 1869 only. | |

From ***Census Substitutes & State Census Records*** by William Dollarhide, published by Family Roots Publishing Co., Orting, WA

**Table 3 – State Censuses Taken in Common Years.** As a means of comparing state censuses taken by the 38 state census states, this table shows the common years for which many states conducted a state census. Many were done in years ending in "5." Census dates for some states are within a range, e.g., within 3 years of 1825, are indicated in the 1825 column.

| | 1815 | 1825 | 1835 | 1845 | 1855 | 1865 | 1875 | 1885 | 1895 | 1905 | 1915 | 1925 | 1935 | 1945 |
|---|---|---|---|---|---|---|---|---|---|---|---|---|---|---|
| **Alabama** | ● | ● | ● | ● | ● | ● | | | | | | | | |
| **Arizona** | | | | | | ● | | | | | | | | |
| **Arkansas** | ● | ● | ● | | ● | ● | | | | | | | | |
| **California** | | | | | ● | | | | | | | | | |
| **Colorado** | | | | | | ● | | ● | | | | | | |
| **Connecticut** | | | | | | | | | | | ● | | | |
| **Florida** | | ● | | | ● | | ● | ● | ● | | | ● | ● | ● |
| **Georgia** | | ● | ● | ● | ● | | ● | | | | | | | |
| **Hawaii** | | | | ● | | ● | ● | | ● | | | | | |
| **Illinois** | | ● | ● | ● | ● | | | | | | | | | |
| **Indiana** | | | | | ● | | | ● | ● | | ● | | | |
| **Iowa** | | | ● | ● | ● | | ● | ● | ● | ● | ● | ● | | |
| **Kansas** | | | | | ● | ● | ● | ● | ● | ● | ● | ● | | |
| **Louisiana** | | | ● | | | | | | | | | | | |
| **Maine** | | | ● | | | | | | | | | | | |
| **Maryland** | | | | | | | | | | | | | | |
| **Massachusetts** | | | | | ● | ● | | | | | | | | |
| **Michigan** | | | ● | ● | ● | ● | ● | ● | ● | | | | | |
| **Minnesota** | | | | ● | ● | ● | ● | ● | ● | ● | | | | |
| **Mississippi** | ● | ● | ● | ● | ● | ● | | | | | | | | |
| **Missouri** | | | | ● | ● | ● | ● | | | | | | | |
| **Nebraska** | | | | | ● | ● | ● | ● | | | | | | |
| **Nevada** | | | | | | ● | ● | | | | | | | |
| **New Jersey** | | | | | ● | ● | ● | ● | ● | ● | ● | | | |
| **New Mexico** | | | | | | | | ● | | | | | | |
| **New York** | | ● | ● | ● | ● | ● | ● | | ● | ● | ● | ● | | |
| **No. Carolina** | | | | | | | | | | | | | | |
| **No. Dakota** | | | | | | | | ● | | ● | ● | ● | | |
| **Oklahoma** | | | | | | | | | ● | ● | | | | |
| **Oregon** | | | | ● | ● | ● | ● | ● | ● | ● | | | | |
| **Rhode Island** | | | | | | ● | ● | ● | ● | ● | ● | ● | ● | |
| **So. Carolina** | | ● | ● | | | ● | ● | | | | | | | |
| **So. Dakota** | | | | | | | | ● | ● | ● | ● | ● | ● | ● |
| **Tennessee** | | | | | | | | | ● | | | | | |
| **Utah** | | | | | ● | | | | | | | | | |
| **Washington** | | | | | ● | | ● | ● | ● | | | | | |
| **Wisconsin** | | | ● | | ● | ● | ● | ● | ● | ● | | | | |
| **Wyoming** | | | | | | ● | | | | | | | | |
| *No. of States:* | 3 | 8 | 12 | 11 | 21 | 20 | 17 | 16 | 16 | 11 | 9 | 7 | 3 | 2 |

From ***Census Substitutes & State Census Records*** by William Dollarhide, published by Family Roots Publishing Co., Orting WA

| State | Year a Terr. | Year a State | Federal Census Years 1790 | 1800 | 1810 | 1820 | 1830 | 1840 | 1850 | 1860 | 1870 | 1880 | 1890 | 1900 | 1910 | 1920 | 1930 | 1940 |
|---|---|---|---|---|---|---|---|---|---|---|---|---|---|---|---|---|---|---|
| Alabama | 1817 | 1819 | | | | lost | ● | ● | ● | ● | ● | ● | Lost | ● | ● | ● | ● | ● |
| Alaska (to US, 1867) | 1912 | 1959 | No census taken, District of Alaska, 1870, 1880, or 1890 → | | | | | | | | -- | -- | -- | ● | ● | ● | ● | ● |
| Arizona | 1863 | 1912 | AZ Territory had a special federal census in 1864 → | | | | | | | | ● | ● | lost | ● | ● | ● | ● | ● |
| Arkansas | 1819 | 1836 | | | | lost | ● | ● | ● | ● | ● | ● | lost | ● | ● | ● | ● | ● |
| California (to US, 1848) | — | 1850 | | | | | | | ● | ● | ● | ● | lost | ● | ● | ● | ● | ● |
| Colorado | 1861 | 1876 | | | | | | | | | | ● | lost | ● | ● | ● | ● | ● |
| Connecticut | — | 1788 | ● | ● | ● | ● | ● | ● | ● | ● | ● | ● | lost | ● | ● | ● | ● | ● |
| Delaware | — | 1787 | ● | ● | ● | ● | ● | ● | ● | ● | ● | ● | lost | ● | ● | ● | ● | ● |
| Distr. of Columbia | — | 1791 | | ● | ● | ● | ● | ● | ● | ● | ● | ● | lost | ● | ● | ● | ● | ● |
| Florida | 1822 | 1845 | | | | | | | ● | ● | ● | ● | lost | ● | ● | ● | ● | ● |
| Georgia | — | 1788 | lost | lost | lost | ● | ● | ● | ● | ● | ● | ● | lost | ● | ● | ● | ● | ● |
| Hawaii (to US, 1898) | 1900 | 1959 | | | | | | | | | | | | ● | ● | ● | ● | ● |
| Idaho | 1863 | 1890 | | | | | | | | | ● | ● | lost | ● | ● | ● | ● | ● |
| Illinois | 1809 | 1818 | | | part | ● | ● | ● | ● | ● | ● | ● | lost | ● | ● | ● | ● | ● |
| Indiana | 1800 | 1816 | | lost | lost | ● | ● | ● | ● | ● | ● | ● | lost | ● | ● | ● | ● | ● |
| Iowa (* part of WI Terr.) | 1838 | 1846 | | | | | | ●* | ● | ● | ● | ● | lost | ● | ● | ● | ● | ● |
| Kansas | 1854 | 1861 | | | | | | | | ● | ● | ● | lost | ● | ● | ● | ● | ● |
| Kentucky (VA in 1790) | — | 1791 | lost | lost | ● | ● | ● | ● | ● | ● | ● | ● | lost | ● | ● | ● | ● | ● |
| Louisiana (*Orleans Tr) | 1804 | 1812 | | | ●* | ● | ● | ● | ● | ● | ● | ● | lost | ● | ● | ● | ● | ● |
| Maine (*Distr. of MA) | — | 1820 | ●* | ●* | ●* | ● | ● | ● | ● | ● | ● | ● | lost | ● | ● | ● | ● | ● |
| Maryland | — | 1788 | ● | ● | ● | ● | ● | ● | ● | ● | ● | ● | lost | ● | ● | ● | ● | ● |
| Massachusetts | — | 1788 | ● | ● | ● | ● | ● | ● | ● | ● | ● | ● | lost | ● | ● | ● | ● | ● |
| Michigan | 1805 | 1837 | | | lost | ● | ● | ● | ● | ● | ● | ● | lost | ● | ● | ● | ● | ● |
| Minnesota | 1849 | 1858 | MN Terr. had a special federal census in 1857 → | | | | | | ● | ● | ● | ● | lost | ● | ● | ● | ● | ● |
| Mississippi | 1798 | 1817 | | lost | lost | ● | ● | ● | ● | ● | ● | ● | lost | ● | ● | ● | ● | ● |
| Missouri | 1805 | 1821 | | | lost | lost | ● | ● | ● | ● | ● | ● | lost | ● | ● | ● | ● | ● |
| Montana | 1864 | 1889 | | | | | | | | | ● | ● | lost | ● | ● | ● | ● | ● |
| Nebraska | 1854 | 1867 | | | | | | | | ● | ● | ● | lost | ● | ● | ● | ● | ● |
| Nevada | 1861 | 1864 | | | | | | | | | ● | ● | lost | ● | ● | ● | ● | ● |
| New Hampshire | — | 1788 | ● | ● | ● | ● | ● | ● | ● | ● | ● | ● | lost | ● | ● | ● | ● | ● |
| New Jersey | — | 1787 | lost | lost | lost | lost | ● | ● | ● | ● | ● | ● | lost | ● | ● | ● | ● | ● |
| New Mexico | 1850 | 1912 | | | | | | | ● | ● | ● | ● | lost | ● | ● | ● | ● | ● |
| New York | — | 1788 | ● | ● | ● | ● | ● | ● | ● | ● | ● | ● | lost | ● | ● | ● | ● | ● |
| North Carolina | — | 1789 | ● | ● | ● | ● | ● | ● | ● | ● | ● | ● | lost | ● | ● | ● | ● | ● |
| North Dakota* | 1861* | 1889 | *1860, 1870, 1880 as part of Dakota Territory → | | | | | | | ● | ● | ● | lost | ● | ● | ● | ● | ● |
| Ohio | 1787 | 1803 | | | lost | ● | ● | ● | ● | ● | ● | ● | lost | ● | ● | ● | ● | ● |
| Oklahoma | 1890 | 1907 | OK had a special federal census in 1907 → | | | | | | | | | | lost | ● | ● | ● | ● | ● |
| Oregon | 1848 | 1859 | | | | | | | ● | ● | ● | ● | lost | ● | ● | ● | ● | ● |
| Pennsylvania | — | 1787 | ● | ● | ● | ● | ● | ● | ● | ● | ● | ● | lost | ● | ● | ● | ● | ● |
| Rhode Island | — | 1790 | ● | ● | ● | ● | ● | ● | ● | ● | ● | ● | lost | ● | ● | ● | ● | ● |
| South Carolina | — | 1788 | ● | ● | ● | ● | ● | ● | ● | ● | ● | ● | lost | ● | ● | ● | ● | ● |
| South Dakota* | 1861* | 1889 | *1860, 1870, 1880 as part of Dakota Territory → | | | | | | | ● | ● | ● | lost | ● | ● | ● | ● | ● |
| Tennessee (*SW Terr) | 1790* | 1796 | | lost | lost | part | ● | ● | ● | ● | ● | ● | lost | ● | ● | ● | ● | ● |
| Texas (to US, 1845) | — | 1845 | | | | | | | ● | ● | ● | ● | lost | ● | ● | ● | ● | ● |
| Utah | 1850 | 1896 | | | | | | | ● | ● | ● | ● | lost | ● | ● | ● | ● | ● |
| Vermont | — | 1791 | ● | ● | ● | ● | ● | ● | ● | ● | ● | ● | lost | ● | ● | ● | ● | ● |
| Virginia | — | 1788 | lost | lost | ● | ● | ● | ● | ● | ● | ● | ● | lost | ● | ● | ● | ● | ● |
| Washington | 1853 | 1889 | | | | | | | | ● | ● | ● | lost | ● | ● | ● | ● | ● |
| West Virginia | — | 1863 | | | | | | | | | ● | ● | lost | ● | ● | ● | ● | ● |
| Wisconsin | 1836 | 1848 | | | | | | ● | ● | ● | ● | ● | lost | ● | ● | ● | ● | ● |
| Wyoming | 1868 | 1890 | | | | | | | | | ● | ● | lost | ● | ● | ● | ● | ● |

From *Census Substitutes & State Census Records* by William Dollarhide, published by Family Roots Publishing Co., Orting WA

# Chapter 1C

# The Old Northwest

## Illinois, Indiana, Michigan, Minnesota, Ohio & Wisconsin

### Historical Timeline for the Old Northwest

**1614-1615. Ohio Country.** Samuel de Champlain, governor of New France and the founder of Québec, was the first of the French explorers to visit the Ohio country via Lake Erie. He is believed to have entered the Maumee River in 1614 or 1615.

**1668. Great Lakes region.** French Jesuit missionaries Jacques Marquette and Claude Dablon established the first mission at Sault Sainte Marie.

**1670. Great Lakes region.** René-Robert Cavelier (Sieur La Salle) explored and claimed the Ohio country for France.

**1673. Mississippi River.** French explorers Jacques Marquette and Louis Jolliet descended the Illinois River to discover the Mississippi River. They floated down the Mississippi as far as the mouth of the Arkansas River before returning to the Great Lakes.

**1675. Illinois Country.** Jacques Marquette founded a mission at the Great Village of the Illinois River, near present Utica, Illinois.

**1680**. French explorer René-Robert Cavelier (Sieur de LaSalle) and trader Henri deTonti built Fort Crève Coeur on the Illinois River, near present-day Peoria.

**1682.** René-Robert Cavelier (Sieur de LaSalle) erected a cross near the confluence of the Mississippi River and the Gulf of Mexico, after floating down river from the Illinois Country. He claimed the entire Mississippi Basin for Louis XIV of France, for whom Louisiana was named. All of the rivers and streams flowing into the Mississippi were part of the Mississippi Basin and included in the Louisiana claim.

**1696. Illinois Country.** Jesuit priest Pierre François Pinet established a mission at present-day Chicago.

**1699 Illinois Country.** Québec priests founded a mission at Cahokia, the first permanent settlement in the Illinois country.

**1717. French Louisiana.** The Illinois Country was officially added to the French Louisiana jurisdiction within New France. At that time *la Louisiane Française* extended from the Wabash River, down the Ohio and Mississippi Rivers to include several ports on the Gulf of Mexico. Any trading posts or forts north of the Highlands (Terra Haute) were considered part of French Québec.

**1721. Indiana.** Fort Philippe, later called Fort Miami, was built on the St. Mary's River, near present Fort Wayne, where the St. Mary's, St. Joseph's and Maumee Rivers meet.

**1732. Indiana.** Vincennes was established, the first permanent settlement in present Indiana.

**1754-1763. French and Indian War.** The Ohio Company of Virginia asserted the British claim to the Ohio region and began sending fur trading parties to the area. The British encroachment into "New France" and the French encroachment into "Virginia" led to a war between Britain and France. The first French Fort in the area was at the Forks of the Ohio, Fort Duquesne (now Pittsburgh) which became the focus of British forays into the western wilderness of colonial America for the first time. After the war, two wagon roads emerged (Braddock's Road and Forbes' Road) that provided overland migration routes to the Ohio River.

**1763. Treaty of Paris.** This was the end of the French and Indian war. (In Europe it was called the "Seven Years War.") At the Treaty of Paris of 1763, the French surrendered all their claims in North America. Spain acquired the former French areas west of the Mississippi, renamed *Spanish Louisiana*. Great Britain gained all of Québec, which they immediately renamed the *Province of Canada*. Britain also gained control of the rest of North America east of the Mississippi River. They named their entire area *British North America*.

**1764. Wisconsin Country.** Charles Langlade settled at Green Bay, the first permanent British settlement in present-day Wisconsin.

**1774. Québec Act.** In response to increased American colonial rebellions, the British sought to solidify loyalty from their French communities in British Canada. The British Parliament passed the Québec Act, which restored the name Québec, allowed the French Canadians to retain French laws and customs, and permitted the Catholic Church to maintain all of its rights. The early French settlements in present-day Michigan, Indiana, Illinois and Wisconsin, were by the act included in the Province of Québec, under British rule.

**1778-1779.** During the Revolutionary War, General George Rogers Clark of the Virginia Militia led the American forces to celebrated victories over the British, with the capture of Kaskaskia in 1778 and Vincennes in 1779. Because the British ceded the entire Northwest Territory to the U.S. in the 1783 treaty of Paris, Clark was often hailed as the "Conqueror of the Old Northwest."

**1783.** The Treaty of Paris recognized the United States of America as an independent nation and defined its borders from the Atlantic Ocean to the Mississippi River. Although the settlements in the Great Lakes region (formerly part of the Province of Québec) were to be included within the United States, British military forces continued to maintain control over parts of the Great Lakes area for several years after the Revolution. Notably, Fort Detroit remained in British control until 1796. And, Prairie du Chien, on the Mississippi River at the mouth of the Wisconsin River, was a strategic post that did not become American until after the War of 1812. The Isle Royale in Lake Superior was a mustering point for the British and their allied Indians, and also remained in British control until after the War of 1812.

**1784. Ohio Country.** Connecticut, Virginia and Massachusetts relinquished their claim to lands in the Ohio Country. Title transferred to the "public domain" of the United States Government. Connecticut retained ownership of the "Western Reserve" on Lake Erie, then sold the tract to the Connecticut Land Company in 1795.

**1787.** Jul 13. **Northwest Territory.** The Ordinance of 1787 established the "Territory Northwest of the River Ohio," and defined the procedure for any territory to obtain statehood. Present states carved out of the original area of the Northwest Territory include Ohio, Indiana, Illinois, Michigan, Wisconsin, and that part of Minnesota east of the Mississippi River.

**1787-1815. Flatboat Era.** The main family transportation on the Ohio River (usually beginning at Brownsville, Pittsburgh, or Wheeling) was by a flatboat designed for a one-way trip. The large, steerable rafts were constructed of lumber and nails that could be disassembled by migrating families when they arrived at their new homesites along the Ohio River and tributaries. The flatboat era continued until the classic flat-bottomed steamboats were introduced on the Ohio River in 1815.

**1788. Ohio Country.** Marietta was Ohio's first permanent settlement. It was founded in 1788 by General Rufus Putnam and named in honor of Marie Antoinette. Putman's Ohio Company of Associates purchased a large tract of land above the Ohio River and sold parcels to the first settlers of Ohio, most of whom arrived at Marietta by flatboat via Pittsburgh.

**1795.** The **Treaty of Greenville** ended the Indian Wars in Ohio. The "Greenville Line" defined the extent of areas opened to settlement by whites (about three-fourths of present-day Ohio).

**1796. Great Lakes Region.** The British evacuated Fort Detroit and surrounding areas, British hold-outs in the Old Northwest.

**1800. Indiana Territory** was established from the Northwest Territory with William Henry Harrison as the first Governor and Vincennes the capital. The area included all of present Indiana, Illinois, Wisconsin, and the western half of Michigan. The Northwest Territory was reduced to the present-day area of Ohio and the eastern half of Michigan.

**1800-1803. Louisiana.** In 1800, Napoleon defeated the Spanish in battle and gained title to Louisiana again after trading them a couple of duchies in Italy. However, Napoleon's troops in the Caribbean were under siege and unable to provide any help in establishing a French government in Louisiana. Several months later, when American emissaries showed up trying to buy New Orleans, Napoleon offered the entire tract to them. In 1803, President Thomas Jefferson urged Congress to vote in favor, and the U.S. purchased the huge tract from France, doubling the size of the United States.

**1803.** Mar 1. **Ohio** was admitted to the Union as the 17th state, with Chillicothe as the state capital. The portion of Michigan included in the Northwest Territory 1800-1803 became part of Indiana Territory. Upon Ohio's statehood, the name Northwest Territory was dropped.

**1804. Louisiana District (Minnesota Portion).** The United States had purchased Louisiana from France in 1803, land described as "the drainage of the Mississippi and Missouri Rivers." The Louisiana District, created in 1804, included that portion of present-day Minnesota west of the Mississippi River.

**1805.** Jun 30. **Michigan Territory** was created, taken from the Indiana Territory. The original area was between Lake Michigan and Lake Huron, as today, but included just the eastern tip of the Upper Peninsula (Sault Ste. Marie area).

**1809.** Mar 1. **Illinois Territory** was created, taken from Indiana Territory, with Kaskaskia the capital. The original area included present-day Illinois, Wisconsin, a portion of the Upper Peninsula of Michigan, and that portion of Minnesota east of the Mississippi River.

**1810. Ohio.** The state capital was moved from Chillicothe to Zanesville.

**1811. Indiana.** Tecumseh's forces were defeated at the Battle of Tippecanoe. American forces were led by Gov. William Henry Harrison, who later gained the presidential nickname "Tippecanoe." The victory over a large force of Indians opened up much of Indiana for settlement.

**1812. Ohio.** Fort Meigs was constructed to protect Ohio from invasion during the War of 1812. The fort was the largest walled fortification in North America, and successfully defended the Maumee River gateway to Ohio and Indiana from two major invasions of the British and allied Indians in 1813.

**1812-1815. Steamboats.** First introduced in 1812, by 1815 steamboats had quickly become the main mode of transportation on the Ohio and Mississippi Rivers.

**1813. Indiana Territory.** The capital was moved from Vincennes to Corydon.

**1814. Treaty of Ghent.** The War of 1812 ended, freeing up American settlement of the Old Northwest.

**1816. Ohio.** The state capital was moved from Zanesville to Columbus.

**1816. Wisconsin Country.** Fort Howard was established at Green Bay and Fort Shelby was rebuilt at Prairie du Chien (renamed Fort Crawford).

**1816.** Dec 11. **Indiana** became the 19th state with the same boundaries as today. The state capital was at Corydon.

**1818.** Dec 3. **Illinois** became the 21st state, with the same boundaries as today. Kaskaskia continued as the first state capital, but the capital was moved to Vandalia in 1820.

**1818. Minnesota Country.** By treaty with Britain, the northern boundary of Minnesota was set at the 49th parallel.

**1825. Indiana.** The state capital was moved from Corydon to Indianapolis.

**1825. Erie Canal** opened. This New York route from the Hudson River to Lake Erie provided direct access to the Ohio Country. Western New York and the State of Ohio were impacted the most, with many settlements attributed to the early Erie Canal travelers.

**1830s. Wisconsin Country.** Heavy settlement began along the Lake Michigan shoreline at the sites of present-day Milwaukee, Racine, and Kenosha.

**1835. Toledo War.** Michigan Territory's drive for statehood created heated arguments in Congress over the Michigan-Ohio boundary. Michigan was not admitted to the Union because she would not surrender her claim to the Toledo strip. As an adjoining state, Ohio asserted its veto power over the first attempt for statehood for Michigan Territory.

**1836-1838. Wisconsin Territory** was created in 1836, including ands west of the Mississippi River to the Missouri River. In 1838, after the creation of Iowa Territory, Wisconsin's western line ended at the Mississippi River. The first territorial capital was at Belmont.

**1837.** Jan 26. **Michigan** was admitted to the Union as the 26th state, after the Toledo Strip was finally surrendered in exchange for the remainder of the Upper Peninsula. Ohio gained the Toledo strip from Michigan, and Michigan gained the Upper Peninsula, extended to its present border with Wisconsin.

**1839. Illinois.** The state capital was moved from Vandalia to Springfield. Also in this year, the National Road was completed from Cumberland, Maryland, to Vandalia, Illinois. It became the most heavily traveled highway in America. (The National Road followed the same general line that Interstate 70 follows today).

**1846. Mormons** left Nauvoo, Illinois for the Great Salt Lake Basin of Utah.

**1846. The Donner Party** left Springfield, Illinois by wagon train for California; forty-two perished in Sierra-Nevada Mountains snowstorms.

**1848.** May 29. **Wisconsin** was admitted into the union as the 30th state, leaving residents of the area between the Mississippi and St. Croix rivers (present-day eastern Minnesota) without a territorial government or legal system for nearly a year.

**1849.** Mar 3. **Minnesota Territory** was created. The original area included the area of present Minnesota, extending west to the Missouri River, including that portion of present North and South Dakota east of the Missouri River.

**1858.** May 11. **Minnesota** became the 32nd state admitted to the Union.

**1908. Detroit, Michigan.** The first Ford Model T was manufactured.

**1911. Indianapolis, Indiana.** The first Indy 500 car race took place.

**1945.** The Chicago Cubs won the National League pennant, but lost the World Series to the Detroit Tigers.

# ILLINOIS
## Censuses & Substitutes, 1678-2009

Original documents still exist today with the names of residents of the Illinois country, from both the French and British eras. Some of the colonial records reside in the county courthouses for the first two counties of Illinois: both St. Clair and Randolph County have surviving French and British land records created prior to the Revolutionary War. More colonial records from the French and British eras are located at the State Archives in Springfield.

The first American census taken in what was to become Illinois was the 1807 Indiana territorial census. Illinois' two original counties were inherited from Indiana Territory when Illinois Territory was established in 1809. In the 1810 Illinois Territory federal census, St. Clair County was lost, Randolph County survives. The only territorial census taken in Illinois was in 1818, a census taken mainly to determine if Illinois Territory had the minimum residents required for statehood. In just a few weeks after the 1818 territorial census, Illinois became a state.

After statehood, the Illinois legislature authorized state censuses for 1820, 1825, 1830, 1835, 1840, 1845, 1855, and 1865, all separate from the federal censuses. Unfortunately only the 1820, 1855, and 1865 state censuses have survived reasonably intact. Most of the county returns for 1825, 1830, 1835, and 1845 are missing and nearly half of the 1840 state census was lost.

Since Illinois chose to conduct several of its state censuses in the same years as the federal censuses, it may not be obvious to genealogists that there are potentially two statewide name lists available for 1820, 1830, and 1840 (although the state versions are not nearly as complete).

## Online Databases at the Illinois State Archives and IRAD

The Illinois State Archives is the official depository for records of governments within the state of Illinois, including state, county, and local records. Statewide government records are housed at the State Archives (Norton) Building in Springfield; while county and local records are held at regional facilities. IRAD (Illinois Regional Archives Depositories), is a system administered by the State Archives, with regional depositories located at various state universities in Illinois. The main State Archives website has searchable databases for the statewide records as well as from each of the regional depositories. To see the complete list of online databases at the state archives as well as each of the regional archives websites, see **www.cyberdriveillinois.com/departments/archives/databases/.** Included are the following:

**Records in the Illinois State Archives:**

- Transcription Policy
- Global Database Search
- Illinois Servitude and Emancipation Records
- Public Domain Land Tract Sales Database
- 1929 Illinois Roll of Honor
- Illinois Black Hawk War Veterans
- Illinois Civil War Muster and Descriptive Rolls
- Illinois Civil War Veterans of Missouri Units
- Illinoi s Civil War Veterans Serving in the U.S. Navy
- Illinois Mexican War Veterans
- Illinois Soldiers' and Sailors' Home Residents
- Illinois Spanish–American War Veterans
- Illinois Veterans' History Project
- Illinois War of 1812 Veterans
- Illinois Winnebago War Veterans

**Illinois Statewide Vital Records Databases:**

- Illinois Statewide Death Index (1916–1950) An index created by the Illinois Department of Public Health
- Illinois Statewide Death Index, Pre–1916 An Ongoing Project of the Illinois State Archives
- Illinois Statewide Marriage Index, 1763–1900 An Ongoing Project of the Illinois State Archives & the Illinois State Genealogical Society

**Records in the Illinois Regional Archives Depositories (IRAD)**

- Local Governmental Records in the IRAD System
- Name Index to Illinois Local Governments
- **Records at Eastern Illinois University**(Charleston, IL): Databases from Arthur, Mattoon, Shelby Co, and Wayne Co IL.
- **Records at Illinois State University:** (Normal, IL): Databases from DeWitt Co, Livingston Co, Logan Co, McLean Co, Vermilion Co, and Woodford Co IL.
- **Records at Northeastern Illinois University** (Chicago, IL): Databases from Chicago and Cook Co IL.
- **Records at Northern Illinois University** (DeKalb, IL): Databases from Carroll Co, JoDaviess Co, Kane Co, Lake Co, and Ogle Co IL.
- **Records at Southern Illinois University** (Edwardsville, IL): Databases from East St. Louis City, Madison Co, and St. Clair Co IL.
- **Records at the University of Illinois at Springfield:** Databases from Macon Co, Macoupin Co, Morgan Co, and Sangamon Co IL.
- **Records at Western Illinois University** (Macomb, IL): Databases from Adams Co, Brown Co, Fulton Co, McDonough Co, Mercer Co, Peoria Co, Rock Island, and Stark Co IL.

---

## Illinois Databases Online at Ancestry.com

The Ancestry.com subscription website allows free access to all indexes, but to view any particular record requires a membership. Ancestry offers trial memberships and subscriptions for short periods and reduced rates. The following databases at the Ancestry.com website are unique to Illinois under the categories, Census & Voter Lists, Vital Records, Military, Immigrations, et al.

■ **1720-1865.** See ***Illinois Servitude and Emancipation Records, 1720-1865* [Online Database],** indexed at the FamilySearch.org website. Source: IL State Archives. Governed by the French, English and United States, some residents of the area were owned by others. This database is an index of servitude records held by the Illinois State Archives. It contains the names of over 2,000 persons who were bought, sold, or emancipated between 1720 and 1865. Included is a name, sex, race, and county of residence for the slave. This database has 2,055 records. See **http://search.ancestry.com/search/db.aspx?dbid=3749.**

■ **1772-1999.** See ***Illinois, Wills and Probate Records, 1772-1999* [Online Database],** indexed at the Ancestry.com website. Source: Ancestry extractions from Illinois county, district, and probate courts. In most cases, probate file can provide the names and residences of beneficiaries and their relationship to the decedent. An inventory of the estate assets can reveal personal details about the deceased's occupation and lifestyle. There may also be references to debts, deeds, and other documents related to the settling of the estate. This database has 897,153 records. See **http://search.ancestry.com/search/db.aspx?dbid=9048.**

■ **1775-1995.** See ***Web: Illinois, Databases of Illinois Veterans Index, 1775-1995*** **[Online Database],** indexed at the Ancestry.com website. This database is also accessible at the IL State Archives website. This veterans index is for all wars for which Illinois supplied soldiers. For example, the civil war soldiers each have detailed information, including name, rank, age at enlistment, unit, height, hair color, eye color, complexion, occupation, birth date, birth place, place where enlisted, period of service, and more. This database has 414,835 records. See **http://search.ancestry.com/search/db.aspx?dbid=9759.**

■ **1790-1850.** See ***Illinois Marriages to 1850*** **[Online Database],** indexed at the Ancestry.com website. Source: Jordan Dodd, editor, Liahona Research, Orem, UT, extracted from county records on microfilm at the Family History Library. This index includes the names of the brides and grooms in a single alpha listing, so each marriage date/place is shown twice. This database has 158,233 records. See **http://search.ancestry.com/search/db.aspx?dbid=2086.**

■ **1790-1860.** See ***Illinois Marriages, 1790-1860*** **[Online Database],** indexed at the Ancestry.com website. Source: Jordan Dodd, editor, Liahona Research, Orem, UT, extracted from county records on microfilm at the Family History Library. This index includes the names of the brides and grooms in a single alpha listing, so each marriage date/place is shown twice. This database has 163,917 records. See **http://search.ancestry.com/search/db.aspx?dbid=7851.**

■ **1790-1917.** See ***Illinois Revolutionary War Veteran Burials*** **[Online Database],** indexed at the Ancestry.com website. Source: *Revolutionary Soldiers Buried in Illinois,* by Mrs. Harriet J. Walker, publ. 1917. This database has 833 pages. See **http://search.ancestry.com/search/db.aspx?dbid=48613.**

■ **1800-1999.** See ***DeKalb County, Illinois Naturalizations, 1800-1999*** **[Online Database],** indexed at the Ancestry.com website. Source: DeKalb Co Clerk, Sycamore, IL. This database is an index to naturalizations for immigrants in DeKalb County, Illinois, between 1800-1999. For each entry you will find: name, naturalization date, link to purchase a copy of the record from DeKalb County Clerk and Recorder. This database has 22,521 records. See **http://search.ancestry.com/search/db.aspx?dbid=5392.**

■ ***1810 and 1818 Illinois (Territory) Census Returns*** **[Online Database],** digitized and indexed at the Ancestry.com website. Source: *Illinois Census Returns, 1810-1818,* edited by Margaret Cross Norton (1st IL State Archivist), publ. 1935, Springfield, reprinted, Genealogical Pub. Co., 1969. This database has 363 pages. See **http://search.ancestry.com/search/db.aspx?dbid=48327.**

■ **1810-1890.** See ***Illinois, Compiled Census and Census Substitutes Index, 1810-1890*** **[Online Database],** indexed at the Ancestry.com website. Originally edited by Ronald Jackson, Accelerated Indexing Systems, Salt Lake City, UT. This collection contains the following indexes: 1810 Randolph County Census; 1818 State (Terr.) Census Index; 1820 Federal Census Index; 1820 State Census Index; 1825 State Census Index; 1830 Federal Census Index; 1830 Morgan County Federal Census Index; 1835 State Census Index; 1840 Federal Census Index; 1840 State Census Index; 1840 Pensioners List; 1850 Federal Census Index; 1855 State Census Index; 1860 Federal Census Index; 1870 Federal Census Index; 1880 Cook County Census; and 1890 Veterans Schedule. This database has 47,577 records. See **http://search.ancestry.com/search/db.aspx?dbid=3545.**

■ **1811-1990.** See ***Illinois, Compiled Records from Lockport Area Genealogical and Historical Society, 1811-1990*** **[Online Database],** indexed at the Ancestry.com website. Browse the collection to see the types of records included. This database has 99,767 records. See **http://search.ancestry.com/search/db.aspx?dbid=61104.**

■ **1813-1909.** See ***Illinois, Public Land Purchase Records, 1813-1909*** **[Online Database],** indexed at the Ancestry.com website. Source: IL State Archives. Land sales from the Illinois public domain were recorded by federal, state or local governments. The records in this database were transferred to the Illinois State Archives and detail the sale of over 54,000 square miles of public land. Each entry includes the purchaser's name, purchase date, amount paid, number of acres, section, township, and range, and often more information. This database has 546,064 records. See **http://search.ancestry.com/search/db.aspx?dbid=3780.**
**Note 1 - Public Land Purchase Records:** The above database has detailed information about a public land purchase. But, the name of the county wherein the land is located today may not be given. For convenience, the IL State Archives website has a PDF map of all Illinois Counties, Townships and Ranges. For a free download, see **https://cyberdriveillinois.com/departments/archives/databases/pubdom.pdf.**

**Note 2 – Public Land Purchase Records:** The names of land purchasers may also appear on a land ownership map. Ancestry has digitized and indexed the largest collection of land ownership maps and atlases from the Library of Congress. A search of the index covers all states with land ownerships maps. See ***U.S., Indexed County Land Ownership Maps, 1860-1918*** **[Online Database].** See
**http://search.ancestry.com/search/db.aspx?dbid=1127.**
**Note 3 – Public Land Purchase Records:** A series of land ownership maps for Illinois, 1814-1925, was compiled by Greg Boyd and published by Arphax Publishing Co., Norman, OK. For more information, see **www.arphax.com.**

■ **1820.** See ***Illinois Census Returns, 1820*** **[Online Database],** digitized and indexed at the Ancestry.com website. Source: *Illinois Census Returns of 1820,* edited by Margaret Cross Norton, Illinois State Library, publ. 1934. This database has 471 pages. See
**http://search.ancestry.com/search/db.aspx?dbid=48328.**
Another edition of this work was published. See ***Illinois Census, 1820*** **[Online Database],** indexed at the Ancestry.com website. Source: Theodore Calvin Pease's *IL Census Returns of 1820*, publ. IL State Hist. Society. This is a companion work to the 1810 Federal and the 1818 Territorial censuses published in the Illinois Historical Collections. This Illinois state census lists the population by counties in 1820 and contains notes comparing discrepancies between names as written in the 1818 Territorial, the 1820 State, and the 1820 Federal censuses. There are over 25,000 records which indicate the following information: the name of the head of the family, number of males under 21, number of males age 21 and up, number of females under 18, and number of females age 18 and up. This database has 26,763 records. See
**http://search.ancestry.com/search/db.aspx?dbid=3110.**

■ **1824-2009.** See ***Illinois, Select United Methodist Church Records, 1824-2009*** **[Online Database],** indexed at the Ancestry.com website. Source: Illinois Great Rivers United Methodist Conference. Baptism, marriage, and death registers. Illinois Great Rivers United Methodist Conference Archives, Pfeiffer Library, MacMurray College, Jacksonville, Illinois. Browse the collections for the list of congregations included. This database has 112,750 records. See
**http://search.ancestry.com/search/db.aspx?dbid=9062.**

■ **1825-1865.** See ***Illinois, State Census Collection, 1825-1865*** **[Online Database],** indexed at the Ancestry.com website. Source: IL State Archives. This combined database includes state census population schedules for the years 1825, 1830, 1835, 1845, 1855, and 1865; plus the 1865 agriculture. This database does not include the 1820 IL State Census (indexed separately), or the 1840 IL State Census (indexed in the 1810-1890 database). State censuses, 1825-1865, recorded only the names of the heads of household, with other individuals in a household numbered in age and race categories. Counties included for each census year: **1825:** (3) Edwards, Fulton, and Randolph Cos. **1830:** (1) Morgan Co. **1835:** (4) Fayette, Fulton, Jasper, and Morgan Cos. **1845:** (3) Case, Putnam, and Tazewell Cos. **1855:** (87) missing counties: Carroll, Champaign, Franklin, Gallatin, Henry, Jefferson, Jo Davies, Lake, Stark, Will and Woodford. **1865:** (99) Missing counties: Gallatin, Mason, Monroe and most of Tazewell.) **Note:** Missing counties noted here are related to the files at the IL State Archives. There may be certain surviving county lists elsewhere. This database has 690,833 records. See
**http://search.ancestry.com/search/db.aspx?dbid=1079.**

■ **1833-1889.** See ***Cook County, Illinois, Marriage and Death Indexes, 1833-1889*** **[Online Database],** indexed at the Ancestry.com website. Source: Sam Fink's *Chicago Marriage and Death Index.* Sam Fink compiled these indexes from marriage and death notices in Chicago newspapers, plus Cook County death records. Marriages cover the years 1833–1871. Death records are extracted from newspapers for the years 1856–1889 and from Cook County death records as well for 1878–1884. Marriage entries include names, marriage date, and source. Death entries extracted from newspapers include name, death date, and source. Fink's indexes were extracted from 10 newspapers. This database has 182,100 records. See
**http://search.ancestry.com/search/db.aspx?dbid=2433.**

■ **1851-1900.** See **Illinois, Marriages, 1851-1900 [Online Database],** indexed at the Ancestry.com website. Source: Jordan Dodd, editor, Liahona Research, Orem, UT, extracted from county records on microfilm at the Family History Library. This index includes the names of the brides and grooms in a single alpha listing, so each marriage date/place is shown twice. This database has 659,028 records. See
**http://search.ancestry.com/search/db.aspx?dbid=7857.**

■ **1860-1920.** See ***Illinois, Marriage Index, 1860-1920*** **[Online Database],** indexed at the Ancestry.com website. Source: IL State Public Record offices. Each record includes the full names of the

bride and groom, as well as the marriage date and where the marriage took place. This database has 2,294,483 records. See
**http://search.ancestry.com/search/db.aspx?dbid=60984.**

■ **1877-1916.** See ***Web: Illinois, Select Deaths Index, 1877-1916* [Online Database],** indexed at the Ancestry.com website. This database is also accessible at the IL State Archives website. Each record contains a name, age, date, and place of death, and source (book/vol. of county record). This database has 1,162,513 records. See
**http://search.ancestry.com/search/db.aspx?dbid=9758.**

■ **1914-2007.** See ***Tazewell County, Illinois, Obituary Card Index from the Pekin Times, 1914-2007* [Online Database],** digitized at the Ancestry.com website. Source: FamilySearch. This is a digitized version of a library card index arranged in alphabetical order. Browse the images by surname range. This database has 91,928 records. See
**http://search.ancestry.com/search/db.aspx?dbid=60279.**

■ **1916-1947.** See ***Illinois, Deaths and Stillbirths Index, 1916-1947* [Online Database],** indexed at the Ancestry.com website. Source: FamilySearch indexing project, extracted from microfilm of county records at the Family History Library. Entries in this index may list name, gender, race/ethnicity, birth date, birthplace, age, occupation, residence, street address, marital status, spouse, date of death, place of death, place of burial, date of burial, cemetery name, father's name and birthplace, mother's name and birthplace, And FHL film number. This database has 2,881,376 records. See
**http://search.ancestry.com/search/db.aspx?dbid=2542.**

■ **1925-1977.** See ***Illinois, Order Sons of Italy in America, Lodge Records, 1925-1977* [Online Database],** indexed at the Ancestry.com website. Information included in the records varies by document type, but you may find details such as death date, place of death, name, age at death, gender, birth date, place of birth, spouse's name, father's name, mother's name, age, and residence date. This database has 1,805 records. See
**http://search.ancestry.com/search/db.aspx?dbid=1915.**

■ **1935-1970.** See ***U.S., Chicago and North Western Railroad Employment Records, 1935-1970* [Online Database],** indexed at the Ancestry.com website. Source: Chicago and North Western Railroad Employee Records, and Chicago, St. Paul, Minneapolis & Omaha Railway Employee Records, at the Chicago & North Western Historical Society, Berwyn, Illinois. The employment records include employee names, occupations within the company, with dates and locations of service, residences, Social Security numbers (redacted for those born after 1912), birth dates, death dates, start dates with the company, employee signatures, absences from service of the company, and parents' names (on Social Security applications).This database has 1,095,646 records. See
**http://search.ancestry.com/search/db.aspx?dbid=6944.**

■ **1938-1939.** See ***Genealogical Records, Illinois, 1938-1939* [Online Database],** indexed at the Ancestry.com website. Source: Illinois Society, DAR, publ.1939. Includes cemetery records, church records, family records, marriages, lists of soldiers, and more. This database has 1,178 pages. See
**http://search.ancestry.com/search/db.aspx?dbid=29768.**

■ **1943-1963.** See ***Illinois, Passenger and Crew Lists, 1943-1963* [Online Database],** indexed at the Ancestry.com website. Source: National Archives microfilm series A3716. These passenger and crew lists from both ships and aircraft were recorded on a variety of forms that were then turned over to the Immigration and Naturalization Service. Details requested on the forms varied, but they typically include the name of the vessel and arrival date, ports of departure and arrival (as well as future destinations on a ship's itinerary), dates of departure and arrival, shipmaster, full name, age, gender, physical description, military rank (if any), occupation, birthplace, citizen of what country, and residence. For military transports, you may find the next of kin, relationships, and address listed as well. Later manifests may include visa or passport numbers. This database has 273,301 records. See
**http://search.ancestry.com/search/db.aspx?dbid=9122.**

## Illinois Databases Online at the FamilySearch.org Website

The following databases are available for free at the FamilySearch.org website. To see the current list, visit the Illinois Indexed Historical Records and Illinois Image Only Historical Records webpage. Both lists are updated periodically. See
**https://familysearch.org/search/collection/location/14.**

■ **1729-1956.** See ***Illinois, Diocese of Belleville, Catholic Parish Records, 1729-1956*** **[Online Database],** digitized at the FamilySearch.org website. This FamilySearch image only database includes parish registers recording the events of baptism, first communion, confirmation (to 1907), marriage (to 1930) or death (to 1956) in the Diocese of Belleville (Illinois), Roman Catholic Church. In addition to traditional parish registers, this collection includes a small number of census, church history, family and financial records. Browse the records, organized by county, then town/village within a county. This database has 34,135 records. See **https://familysearch.org/search/collection/1388122.**

■ **1774-1974.** See ***Illinois Soldier Burial Places, 1774-1974*** **[Online Database],** indexed at the FamilySearch.org website. Source: IL State Archives. Index from a card file of soldiers buried in the state of Illinois. Most of these soldiers served from 1774 to 1898. This database has 144,735 records. See **https://familysearch.org/search/collection/2171435.**

■ **1800-1962.** See ***Illinois, County Naturalization Records, 1800-1962*** **[Online Database],** digitized at the FamilySearch.org website. Source: FamilySearch indexing from county records on microfilm at the Family History Library. Images of naturalization records from county courthouses in Illinois. The content and time period varies by county. Few counties have records after 1945. Browse through the records, organized by county, then by Declarations of Intentions, Petitions, Petition Evidence, and Naturalizations, each for a range of years. This database has 144,834 records. See **https://familysearch.org/search/collection/1989159.**

■ **1805-1985.** See ***Illinois, Church Marriages, 1805-1985*** **[Online Database],** indexed at the FamilySearch.org website. Source: FamilySearch extractions, unknown origin. Each record may contain the following information for both bride and groom: Name, Age, Birth year, Birth place, Parents' names, Marriage date, Marriage place, Marital status, Race, Previous spouse, Title, Page/Volume/Entry/Certificate number. This database has 9,190 records. See **https://familysearch.org/search/collection/2534491.**

■ **1810-1934.** See ***Illinois, County Marriages, 1810-1934*** **[Online Database],** indexed at the FamilySearch.org website. Source: FamilySearch extractions from county records on microfilm at the Family History Library. This database has 1,712,426 records. See **https://familysearch.org/search/collection/1803970.**

■ **1815-1935.** See ***Illinois Marriages, 1815-1935*** **[Online Database],** indexed at the FamilySearch.org website. Source: FamilySearch name index to marriage records from microfilm at the Family History Library. This database has 636,536 records. See **https://familysearch.org/search/collection/1680829.**

■ **1817-1990.** See ***Illinois, Adams County, Card Index to Deaths, 1877-1990*** **[Online Database],** indexed at the FamilySearch.org website. Source: Card index to death records in Adams County from the courthouse in Quincy, Illinois. The cards show a name of a person and a date (and nothing else). This database has 95,523 records. See **https://familysearch.org/search/collection/2174942.**

■ **1819-1988.** See ***Illinois Probate Records, 1819-1988*** **[Online Database],** digitized at the FamilySearch.org website. Source: FamilySearch extractions from county records on microfilm at the Family History Library. This is a collection of probate records, which includes wills, indexes, and other documents related too the estates of deceased individuals. Probates were generally recorded in the county of residence. This collection covers probate records created by Illinois courts, 1819-1970, but the content and time period of the records will vary by county. Some county probate courts also include guardianship, naturalization, and/or military records. Browse the records, organized by county, then record type, volume, and year range. This database has 1,316,299 records. See **https://familysearch.org/search/collection/1834344.**

■ **1824-1940.** See ***Illinois Births and Christenings, 1824-1940*** **[Online Database],** indexed at the FamilySearch.org website. Source: FamilySearch name index to birth, baptism and christening records from microfilm at the Family History Library. This database has 507,005 records. See **https://familysearch.org/search/collection/1676968.**

■ **1830-1954.** See ***Illinois, Lee County Records, 1830-1954*** **[Online Database],** digitized at the FamilySearch.org website. Naturalization and probate records from the Lee County courthouse in Dixon, Illinois. Browse through the records, organized by

Volume Title and Year. This database has 274,879 records. See
**https://familysearch.org/search/collection/2068938.**

■ **1833-1889.** See ***Illinois, Civil Marriages, 1833-1889*** **[Online Database],** indexed at the FamilySearch.org website. Source: DAR Records. Index to selected civil marriages from published transcripts for the counties of Boone, Champaign, Christian, Cook, DeKalb, DuPage, and Hancock. This database has 8,975 records. See
**https://familysearch.org/search/collection/2515894.**

■ **1833-1925.** See ***Illinois, Chicago, Catholic Church Records, 1833-1925*** **[Online Database],** indexed at the FamilySearch.org website. Source: Images of catholic church records from the Bishop of Chicago. The collection contains the following records: Births/Christenings (1833-1899; Deaths/Burials (1845-1899); and Marriages (1833-1899). The Archdiocese of Chicago covers parishes in Cook and Lake counties. The records are 95% in English with the remaining 5% distributed in Czech, Latin, and German. This database has 107,678 records. See
**https://familysearch.org/search/collection/1452409.**

■ **1838-1927.** See ***Illinois, DeKalb County Land Records, 1838-1927*** **[Online Database],** digitized at the FamilySearch.org website. Source: DeKalb County Clerk, Sycamore, IL. Digital images of deed books, grantor indexes, and grantee indexes from the courthouse in Sycamore, Illinois. Browse through the records, organized by Record Type, Volume, and Year Range. This database has 68,258 records. See
**https://familysearch.org/search/collection/2043772.**

■ **1840-1950.** See ***Illinois, Northern District Naturalization Index, 1840-1950*** **[Online Database],** indexed at the FamilySearch.org website. Source: National Archives microfilm series M1285. This card file is an index to petitions for residents of northern Illinois, northwestern Indiana, southern and eastern Wisconsin, and eastern Iowa. Filed by Soundex codes the entries prior to 1906 differ from those after 1906. After 1906 the entries generally include the name of petitioner; address; name of the court in which naturalization occurred; certificate, petition, or other identifying document number; country and date of birth; date and place of arrival in the United States; date of naturalization; and name and address of witnesses. Index cards for naturalizations taking place prior to 1906 typically contain only the name of the petitioner, the name of the court in which naturalization occurred, document number, country of origin, and the date. This database has 1,491,586 records. See
**https://familysearch.org/search/collection/1838804.**

■ **1850-1880.** See ***Illinois, Non-Population Census Schedules, 1850-1880*** **[Online Database],** digitized at the FamilySearch.org website. Source: National Archives microfilm series T1133. Images of federal (non-population) census schedules for Illinois: 1860 Industry, 1860 Social Statistics, 1870 Industry, 1870 Social Statistics, 1880 Manufactures, 1850 Agriculture, 1860 Agriculture, 1865 Agriculture (IL State Census?), 1870 Agriculture, and 1880 Agriculture. This database has 33,726 records. Browse the records, organized by census schedule, then county. See
**https://familysearch.org/search/collection/2287447.**

■ **1853-2009.** See ***Illinois Cemetery Transcriptions, 1853-2009*** **[Online Database],** digitized at the FamilySearch.org website. Source: Unknown. This FamilySearch image only database was intended to contain cemetery inscriptions from all over Illinois. Currently, the only cemetery is Elmwood Cemetery in Centralia, Illinois. Browse the images, which consist of both interment cards, and index cards for a range of years. This database has 5,040 records. See
**https://familysearch.org/search/collection/2043817.**

■ **1855.** See **Illinois State Census, 1855 [Online Database],** indexed at the FamilySearch.org website. Source: IL State Archives. The 1855 state census is a heads of household listing with the numbers of males and females in a household. This census is complete for 87 of 98 counties in Illinois in 1855. Missing counties: Carroll, Champaign, Franklin, Gallatin, Henry, Jefferson, Jo Davies, Lake, Stark, Will and Woodford. This database has 256,004 records. See
**https://familysearch.org/search/collection/1803969.**

■ **1865.** See **Illinois State Census, 1865 [Online Database],** indexed at the FamilySearch.org website. Source: IL State Archives. The 1865 state census is a heads of household listing with the numbers of males and females in a household. This census is complete for 98 of 102 counties in Illinois in 1865. Missing counties: Gallatin, Mason, Monroe and most of Tazewell. This database has 380,262 records. See
**https://familysearch.org/search/collection/1803971.**

■ **1871-1915.** See ***Illinois, Cook County Birth Registers, 1871-1915*** **[Online Database],** indexed at the FamilySearch.org website. Source: Cook County Clerk, Chicago. Name index of birth registers as recorded at Cook County, Illinois – including the City of Chicago. This database has 962,515 records. See **https://familysearch.org/search/collection/1463129.**

■ **1871-1920.** See ***Illinois, Cook County Marriages, 1871-1920*** **[Online Database],** indexed at the FamilySearch.org website. Source: Cook County Clerk, Chicago, IL. Name index of marriage licenses and returns recorded at Cook County, Illinois - including the City of Chicago. This database has 865,669 records. See **https://familysearch.org/search/collection/1463145.**

■ **1871-1940.** See ***Illinois, Cook County, Birth Certificates, 1871-1940*** **[Online Database],** indexed at the FamilySearch.org website. Source: Cook County Clerk, Chicago, IL. Index of birth records as recorded at Cook County, Illinois, including the city of Chicago. Contains delayed birth records. This database has 2,859,465 records. See **https://familysearch.org/search/collection/1462519.**

■ **1878-1994.** See ***Illinois, Cook County Deaths, 1878-1994*** **[Online Database],** indexed at the FamilySearch.org website. Source: Cook County Clerk, Chicago, IL. Index of deaths recorded at Cook County, Illinois - including the City of Chicago. Deaths for Cook County (excluding the City of Chicago) are missing for the years 1910-1915. This database has 6,527,955 records. See **https://familysearch.org/search/collection/1463134.**

■ **1879-2007.** See ***Illinois, Macon County, Decatur Public Library Collections, 1879-2007*** **[Online Database],** indexed at the FamilySearch.org website. Source: Decatur Public Library, Decatur, IL. The records include: Obituary indexes (1879-2007) - Arranged by year. Military indexes (1917-1919). This database has 64,268 records. See **https://familysearch.org/search/collection/1447337.**

■ **1885-2002.** See ***Illinois, Cook County, Maywood, Maywood Herald Obituary Card Index, 1885-2002*** **[Online Database],** indexed at the FamilySearch.org website. Source: Maywood Public Library, Maywood, IL. Images of a surname card index from the Maywood Public Library. The index is largely comprised of obituaries, as well as a list of "Maywoodians" (residents of the city of Maywood), from the "Maywood Herald" newspaper. This database has 61,565 records. See **https://familysearch.org/search/collection/1929848.**

■ **1906-1994.** See ***Illinois, Northern District Petitions for Naturalization, 1906-1994*** **[Online Database],** digitized at the FamilySearch.org website. Source: Naturalization petitions from the District Court for the Chicago Division of the Northern District of Illinois, filmed at the Great Lakes Region of NARA at Chicago. Corresponds with NARA ARC #593882. The current images are all related to Cook County, organized by Petitions/Years. This database has 2,046,215 records. See **https://familysearch.org/search/collection/2212212.**

■ **1914-2007.** See ***Illinois, Tazewell County, Obituary Card Index from the "Pekin Times," 1914-2007*** **[Online Database],** indexed at the FamilySearch.org website. Source: Pekin Public Library, Pekin, IL. This database has 91,822 records. See **https://familysearch.org/search/collection/1447328.**

■ **1916-1947.** See ***Illinois Deaths and Stillbirths, 1916-1947*** **[Online Database],** indexed at the FamilySearch.org website. Source: IL Public Board of Health. Each record includes a name, date of birth, date of death, place of death, date of burial, name of spouse, name of father, and name of mother. This database has 2,879,598 records. See **https://familysearch.org/search/collection/1438856.**

■ **1926-1979.** See ***Illinois, Northern District (Eastern Division), Naturalization Index, 1926-1979*** **[Online Database],** indexed at the FamilySearch.org website. This collection consists of a card index to naturalization records for the U.S. District Court for the Eastern Division of the Northern District of Illinois, in Chicago, ARC Identifier 1165908. This database has 550,932 records. See **https://familysearch.org/search/collection/2040533.**

## Illinois Databases Online At Various Websites

■ **1700s-2000s.** See ***Illinois GenWeb Archives*** **[Online Database].** The ILGenWeb site offers free genealogical databases with searchable statewide name lists and for all Illinois counties. Databases may include Bibles, Biographies, Cemeteries, Censuses, Court Records, Deaths, Deeds, Directories, Histories,

Marriages, Military, Newspapers, Obituaries, Photos, Schools, Tax Lists, Wills, and more. See **http://usgwarchives.net/il/ilfiles.htm.**

■ **1700s-2000s.** See ***Linkpendium – Illinois: Family History & Genealogy, Census, Birth, Marriage, Death Vita Records & More*** **[Online Databases].** Linkpendium is a genealogical portal site with links to state, county, town, and local databases. Currently listed are selected sites for Illinois statewide resources (991), Adams County (983), Alexander County (464), Bond County (633), Boone County (536), Brown County (324), Bureau County (982) and 95 more Illinois counties. See **www.linkpendium.com/il-genealogy.**

■ ***1732 Census of Fort De Chartres*** **[Online Database],** indexed at the GenealogyTrails.com site for Illinois. See **http://genealogytrails.com/ill/1732census.html.**

■ **1787.** See ***Census of Kaskaskia, 1787*** **[Online Database],** indexed at the GenealogyTrails.com site for Illinois. See **www.genealogytrails.com/ill/1787kaskcensus.html.**

■ **1790-1809.** See ***Names of Early Illinois Settlers*** **[Online Database],** extracts from American State Papers, 1790, 1791, and 1809 lists of early residents. Indexed at the GenealogyTrails.com site for Illinois. See **www.genealogytrails.com/ill/ILSettlers.html.**

■ ***1807 Indiana Territory Census Randolph County (now Illinois)*** **[Online Database],** indexed at the GenealogyTrails.com site for Illinois. See **www.genealogytrails.com/ill/randolph/1807census.html.**

■ ***1807 Election Results (Election held at Kaskaskia in the county of Randolph to elect a Representative to the assembly of Indiana Territory on 02 Feb 1807*** **[Online Database],** indexed at the GenealogyTrails.com site for Illinois. See **www.genealogytrails.com/ill/randolph/election1807.htm.**

■ **1814-1925 Illinois Original Land Owners.** See the ***Family Maps*** series for Illinois counties, maps of all original land patents, compiled by Greg Boyd and published by Arphax Publishing Co., Norman, OK. These privately-produced computer-generated maps show the first property owners for an entire county, produced as a book of maps, each map laid out on the federal township grid, and includes indexes to help you locate a person, place-name, or cemetery. Additional maps are added for each county to show roads, waterways, railroads, selected city centers, and cemeteries within a county. At this writing, *Family Maps* books have been published for the following Illinois counties: Adams, Bond, Brown, Clinton, Cook, Cumberland, DeKalb, DuPage, Edwards, Effingham, Fayette, Ford, Franklin, Fulton, Greene, Grundy, Hamilton, Hancock, Jackson, Jasper, Jefferson, Jersey, Johnson, Kane, Kendall, Knox, LaSalle, Lawrence, Lee, Macoupin, Massac, McDonough, McHenry, Montgomery, Morgan, Randolph, Richland, Rock Island, Saline, Sangamon, Shelby, Stark, Stephenson, Union, Vermilion, Warren, White, Williamson, and Winnebago counties. Visit the publisher's information and ordering website for more details and updated county coverage. See **www.arphax.com/.** Arphax's entire *Family Maps* series is also available as a subscription service online. See **www.historygeo.com.**

■ **1818-2010.** See ***Illinois Newspaper Archives, 1818-2010*** **[Online Databases],** digitized and indexed newspapers at the GenealogyBank website, for Belleville, Centralia, Chicago, East Moline, Edwardsville, Freeport, Kaskaskia, Nauvoo, Peoria, Quincy, Rockford, Springfield, and Vandalia. See **www.genealogybank.com/explore/newspapers/all/usa/illinois.**

■ **1985-Current.** See ***Illinois Recent Newspaper Obituaries (1985-Current)*** **[Online Database],** digitized and indexed newspaper obituaries at the GenealogyBank website, including newspapers for Abingdon, Avon, St. Augustine Addison Aledo Algonquin Alton Antioch Arlington Heights, and 220 more cities. See **www.genealogybank.com/explore/obituaries/all/usa/illinois.**

---

## Illinois Periodical Articles

### Censuses & Substitute Name Lists in Genealogical Periodicals

PERSI (PERiodical Source Index) is a digitized database project of the Allen County Public Library (ACPL), Fort Wayne, IN. Since 1986, the PERSI extractors have indexed article titles, places, and surnames from over 11,000 genealogical & historical periodicals. The PERSI database is currently available online through the FindMyPast.com subscription website. The Genealogy Center of the ACPL in Fort Wayne IN holds all 11,000 periodicals and will make copies of any article by special request. To obtain an order form for requesting a printed copy of any article indexed in the PERSI database, see **http://genealogycenter.org/docs/default-source/resources/articlerequest.pdf?sfvrsn=2.**

**Illinois PERSI Search:** Using the FindMyPast.com website, the keywords "Illinois Tax" had 595 results. The IL 1835 state census at the Ancestry.com website includes only Fayette, Fulton, Jasper, and Morgan Counties. A PERSI search for "1835 Census" revealed more counties, apparently not at the state archives, but at local repositories:

■ **"1835 Illinois State Census, Cass, Morgan, Scott Counties" [Printed Article],** in *Jacksonville, Illinois Genealogical Society Journal,* Vol. 26, No. 1 (Mar 1998).

■ **"1835 Illinois State Census, Edwards County" [Printed Article],** in *Edwards County Historical Society Newsletter,* Vol. 4, No. 2-3 (Summer 1983).

■ **"1835 Illinois State Census, Iroquois County" [Printed Article],** in *Iroquois Stalker*, Vol. 31, No. 2 (2001).

■ **"1835 Illinois State Census, Union County" [Printed Article],** in *Saga of Southern Illinois*, Vol. 5, No. 1 (Spring 1978), and Vol. 23, No. 3 (Fall 1996).

## Illinois Books & Microfilms at the Family History Library

The most important of Illinois' statewide census substitutes are cited below in chronological order. Each item includes a FHL book number or FHL film number, which can be used to search the FHL catalog for more details. To review an item, start at the FamilySearch catalog search page. See **https://familysearch.org/search/catalog/results.** Select "Search by Place" then "United States, Illinois" to see a list of catalog categories. Or, select "Call Number" then type an FHL book number; or select "Film/Fiche Number" to view a specific title.

■ **1678-1814.** See ***Consolidated Index for the Raymond H. Hammes Collection at the Illinois State Archives* [Microfilm],** from the original manuscripts at the Illinois State Archives, Springfield, IL. This is a comprehensive alphabetical surname index of the principal individuals involved in land transfers as well as cited individuals who were neighbors or witnesses to transactions. Filmed by the Genealogical Society of Utah, 1988, 1 roll, FHL film #1543598. See Genealogical Research Series Pamphlet No. 1, a downloadable PDF file at the Illinois State Archives for more information on the Hammes Collection and how to use this index to access the records. See **www.cyberdriveillinois.com/publications/pdf_publications/ard124.pdf.**

■ ***1722-1784 Land Records* [Microfilm],** from the original records at the Illinois State Archives, Springfield, IL, part of the Raymond H. Hammes Collection. This volume contains abstracts of Illinois land transactions, 1722-1784, translated from the original French. Includes a general index by transaction number. Some personal names are found under "Occupations" in the index. Lists of military & religious personnel are also found in the index. Filmed by the Genealogical Society of Utah, 1988, 1 roll, FHL film #1543598, Item 1 (Land Records).

■ **1722-1812.** See ***Miscellaneous Land Records: Insinuations, Grants, Confirmations, Lists of Inhabitants, Lists of Militia Men Entitled to Land, Etc., 1722-1812* [Microfilm],** from the original manuscript at the Illinois State Archives, Springfield, IL, part of the Raymond H. Hammes Collection. Indexed in the Consolidated Index, Hammes Collection. Filmed by the Genealogical Society of Utah, 1988, 1 roll, FHL film #1543598.

■ ***1763-1916 Illinois Marriage Records Index* [Microfilm],** compiled by the Illinois State Genealogical Society, from records located at the Illinois State Archives, Springfield, IL. This index is an ongoing project of the Illinois State Archives and the Illinois State Genealogical Society to produce an index of Illinois marriages prior to 1901. Filmed by the Archives and the Society, 1994, 94 microfiche, beginning with FHL fiche #6334564 (Unknown/incomplete names - Adams, David). For a complete list of fiche and contents of each, see the online FHL catalog page for this title: **https://familysearch.org/search/catalog/705931.**

■ **1778-1790.** See ***Cahokia Records, 1778-1790* [Printed Book],** edited by Clarence Walworth Alvord, publ. IL State Historical Library, 1907, 663 pages, FHL book 977.3 B4i v.2. Also on microfilm, FHL film #978492.

■ **1778-1790.** See ***Kaskaskia Records, 1778-1790* [Printed Book],** edited by Clarence Walworth Alvord, publ. IL State Historical Library, 1909.

See FHL book 977.3 B4i v.5. Also on microfilm, FHL film #978493. To access a digital version of this title, see the online FHL catalog page. See **https://familysearch.org/search/catalog/289327.**

■ **1790-1857.** See ***Indexes to Court Records (St. Clair County, IL), by Plaintiff and Defendant, 1790-1857* [Microfilm],** from originals at the Illinois State Archives, Springfield, IL. Filmed by the archives, 1986, 1 roll, FHL film #1689038.

■ **1791-1810.** See ***St. Clair County, Illinois, Book A, Marriage Certificates and Licenses, Feb. 1807-July 1810: Some Additional Records from Deed Book A & Loose Papers, 1791-1801* [Printed Book],** by Peggy Lathrop Sapp. Includes surname index. Published by Folk Works Research, Springfield, IL, 1993, 23 pages, FHL book 977.389 V2sp.

■ **1796-1814.** See ***St. Clair County, Illinois Court Records, Marks and Brands, 1807-1831 and 1796-1797, Tavern Licenses Granted 1808-1814* [Printed Book],** by Peggy Lathrop Sapp. Includes surname index. Published by Folk Works Research, Springfield, IL, 1993, 45 pages, FHL book 977.389 R2s.

■ ***1799-1813 Land and Property Records, St. Clair County, Illinois* [Microfilm],** from the original manuscripts at the Illinois State Archives, Springfield, IL. St. Clair (with Randolph) was one of the two original counties of Illinois, and covered the northern 3/4ths of the present state of Illinois. These records are mostly for the first settled areas along the Mississippi River north of Fort Kaskaskia. Some marriage information may be found among the deeds. Filmed by the state archives, 1985, 1 roll, FHL film #1689031.

■ **1800-1820.** See ***Cahokia Books B & C, Land Records (1800-1820)* [Microfilm],** vols. 4-5 of the Raymond H. Hammes Collection. Text mostly in English, some in French. All entries pertain to St. Clair County as it existed in the late 1700s and early 1800s, and to the inhabitants of the villages then within its borders: Cahokia (the county seat), Prairie du Pont, Harrison, Peoria, Michillimackinac, and Bellefontaine. Filmed by the Genealogical Society of Utah, 1988, 1 roll, FHL film #1543598.

■ **1800-1850.** See ***Randolph County, Where Illinois Began* [Printed Book],** FHL title: *Randolph County, Illinois Information, 1800-1850,* compiled by the Randolph County Genealogical Society, Chester, IL, 369 pages. Includes surname index. Includes: 1807, 1825 & 1840 censuses; marriages; deeds; court cases (participants only); deaths from administrators' lists, 1844-1848; cemetery records (those born before 1851); and probate index. FHL book 977.392 V3r.

■ **1804-1814.** See ***Kaskaskia French and English Deed Records, 1804-1814* [Microfilm],** from the original records at the Randolph County Courthouse, Chester, IL (1977). Kaskaskia was the first capital of Illinois Territory, and these records provide names of land owners during the transition from the early French to the English; and later American settlements in Illinois. Filmed by the Genealogical Society of Utah, 1977, 3 rolls, as follows:

- Deeds vol. A45-B46 1804-1806, FHL film #1012401.
- Deeds vol. C47-D48 1804-1814, FHL film #1012402.
- Translation of French deeds in vol. A-D, vol. 49 1804-1814, FHL film #1012403.

■ **1807.** See **Colonial and Territorial Research Collection of Illinois: Land Sales, Squatters [Microfilm],** vol. 18 of the Raymond H. Hammes Collection. Includes list of land applicants. This material is concerned with what is now Southern Illinois. Filmed by the Genealogical Society of Utah, 1988, 1 roll, FHL film 1543598.

■ **1807.** See ***Census of Indiana Territory for 1807* [Printed Book],** facsimile of the original manuscript, published by the Indiana Historical Society, 1980, 57 pages. In 1807, Indiana Territory included St. Clair and Randolph counties, now in Illinois. (Illinois Territory was formed in 1809). Includes name index. FHL book 977.2 X2c and FHL film #1033927. For access to a digital version of this title, see the online FHL catalog page. See **https://familysearch.org/search/catalog/270021.**

■ ***1810 Federal Census of Illinois Territory* [Printed Book],** an alphabetized name list, compiled by Accelerated Indexing Systems, North Salt Lake, UT, 1987, 27 pages. Includes only Randolph County, Illinois Territory, which then included the area of several modern counties of southern Illinois. (The only other Illinois county in 1810 was St. Clair, whose 1810 census schedules were lost). See FHL book 977.3 X28i.

■ **1810-1818.** See ***Illinois Census Returns, 1810-1818* [Printed Book],** edited by Margaret Cross Norton, originally published by the Trustees of the Illinois State Historical Library, Springfield, IL, 1935, as Collections of the Illinois State Historical Society,

vol. 24, (reprint, Genealogical Publishing Co., Inc., Baltimore, 1969), 329 pages. The volume is a printed extraction of the 1810 state census, 1818 state census, and an index of names. FHL book 977.3 B4i v. 24. Also on FHL film #897331. For a digitized version of this book, See
**http://search.ancestry.com/search/db.aspx?dbid=48327.**

■ **1810-1855.** See ***Name Index to Early Illinois Records*** **[Microfilm],** from the original card indexes located at the Illinois State Archives, Springfield, IL. This major work includes indexes to censuses of 1810 (federal); 1818 (Terr.); 1820, 1825, 1830, 1835, 1840, and 1845 (state); 1850 (federal); and 1855 (state); executive records to 1861; election returns of 1818-1847; House and Senate journals through 1830's; early laws to 1849; as part of the Perrin Collection at the State Archives. Filmed by the archives, 1975, 248 rolls. FHL film begins with film #1001592 (Aacer – Adams). For a complete list of roll numbers and contents of each roll, see the online FHL catalog page for this title. See
**https://familysearch.org/search/catalog/40879.**

✓ **NOTE:** The previous item, *Name Index to Early Illinois Records,* was microfilmed by the IL Archives on 248 rolls of 16mm film. This database has nearly one million original index cards. Well before the first statewide census indexes were created for the Internet by various providers, this card index from Illinois was unique, the largest census index for any state in the U.S., dating back to the 1930s. Like many other publications of the Illinois State Archives, this 1810-1855 index is a legacy of the person responsible, Margaret Cross Norton, the first state archivist of Illinois (who happened to like genealogists).

■ **1814-1816.** See ***Colonial and Territorial Research Collection of Illinois: Land Sales, Preemptions,*** **[Microfilm],** vol. 19 of the Raymond H. Hammes Collection. These records identify squatters who wanted to claim land in southern Illinois. They are listed in alphabetical order. Filmed by the Genealogical Society of Utah, 1988, 1 roll, FHL film #1543598.

■ **1814-1872.** See ***Original Patent Land Record, Randolph County, Illinois, 1814-1872*** **[Printed Book],** abstracted by Lola Frazer Crowder, 1991, 174 pages. As one of two original counties of Illinois, the federal land sales during the early period represent a large part of the early population. These name lists are county records relating to the original public land buyers in Randolph County. FHL book 977.392 R28c. See also ***Kaskaskia Land Warrants, Military Certificates, Randolph County, Illinois*** **[Printed Book],** by Peggy Lathrop Sapp of Springfield, Illinois, from film at the Illinois State Archives, "An Alphabetical Listing of Names, Recipients or their Heirs, found in the Miscellaneous Monthly Abstracts of Land. (Under the Acts of 1847-1852)." Includes four alphabetical indexes. See FHL book 977.392 R2s.

■ **1814-1925. See Public Domain Sales Land Tract Record Listing, 1814-1925 [Microfilm],** from the original computer print-out (29,931 pages) made in 1984 at the Illinois State Archives, Springfield, IL. Includes name of purchaser, type of sale, description of the land purchased (including section, township, range, and principal meridian), number of acres purchased, total purchase price, date of purchase, and volume and page of the original land record on which the transaction was entered. This project was originally called the Public Domain Computer Conversion Project. It indexes over 550,000 individual entries obtained from sales records of the U.S. General Land Office, Illinois officials, and the Illinois Central Railroad. Alphabetically arranged. Filmed by the IL State Archives, 1984, FHL fiche #6016848 (144 fiche). For the Ancestry.com digital version of this index, see
**http://search.ancestry.com/search/db.aspx?dbid=3780.**

■ ***1818 Illinois State Census Index*** **[Printed Index],** edited by Ronald Vern Jackson, et al, Accelerated Indexing, North Salt Lake, UT,1997, 93 pages. The name list was generated from the Illinois State Historical Society's originals. FHL book 977.3 X28i.

■ **1818-1848.** See ***Illinois Election Returns, 1818-1848*** **[Microfilm],** from a book edited by Theodore Calvin Pease, published by the Trustees of Illinois State Historical Library, vol. 18, Collections of the Illinois State Historical Library: Statistical Series, 1923. Filmed by the Genealogical Society of Utah, 1984, 1 roll, FHL book 977.3 B4i v.18 and FHL film #1035628. For access to a digital version of this book, see the online FHL catalog page. See
**https://familysearch.org/search/catalog/197977.**

■ ***1820 Illinois State Census*** **[Originals],** at the Illinois State Archives, Record Series 103.002, 2 vols., no microfilm. Each county return includes name of county and for each household name or head of household and numbers of free white males twenty-one years of age and older, other white inhabitants, slaves and servants, and free Negroes and mulattoes. Returns are included for 18 of 19 counties existing at that time: Alexander, Bond, Clark, Crawford, Franklin, Gallatin, Jackson, Jefferson, Johnson, Madison, Monroe, Pope, Randolph, St. Clair, Union, Washington, Wayne, and White counties. Only Edwards county is missing. (Indexed in *Name Index to Early Illinois Records, 1810-1855* by the Illinois State Archives).

■ ***1820 Illinois Census Returns*** **[Printed Book],** edited by Margaret Cross Norton, published Springfield, IL: Trustees of the Illinois State Historical Library, 1934, 466 pages, as part of Collections of the Illinois State Historical Library, Statistical Series, Vol. 3. From preface: "This book contains not only the 1820 state census schedules but also notes comparing all discrepancies between the names as written in the 1818 territorial, the 1820 state, and the 1820 federal censuses." Includes an index of names FHL book 977.3 B4i v. 26 and FHL film #6051147.

■ ***1820 Federal Census of Illinois*** **[Printed Book],** compiled by Lowell M. Volkel and James V. Gill, published by Heritage House, Danville, IL, 1966, 79 pages. FHL book 977.3 X2v.

■ **1820-1825.** See ***Residents of Early Randolph County, Illinois*** **[Printed Book],** compiled by Lucille Wittnenborn Wiechens, published 1989, 26 pages. Names are in alphabetical order. Includes names from the 1825 state census and names from 1820 land records. Includes short history of Illinois and Randolph County. FHL book 977.392 X2w.

■ ***1825 Illinois State Census*** **[Originals],** at the Illinois State Archives, Springfield, IL. (no microfilm). Each county return includes name of county and names or legal descriptions of legal subdivisions contained in county (e.g., townships, towns, villages). Under each of these categories entries for each household include name of head of household; number of free white males twenty-one years of age and older, including heads of families; number of free white males under twenty-one years of age, including heads of families; number of free white females, including heads of families; numbers of male and female servants and slaves, and free persons of color; and type (e.g., mill, distillery) and number of manufacturing establishments. Returns are included for 3 of 43 counties existing at that time: Edwards, Fulton, and Randolph. Indexed in *Name Index to Early Illinois Records, 1810-1855* by the Illinois State Archives, as well as indexed online at the Ancestry.com website (part of the combined 1825-1865 state census database).

■ ***1825 Illinois State Census Index*** **[Printed Book],** compiled by W. David Samuelsen, published by Accelerated Indexing Systems, North Salt Lake, 1985, 26 pages. FHL book 977.3 X2j.

■ **1830.** See ***Illinois 1830 (Federal) Census Index*** **[Printed Book],** edited by Ronald Vern Jackson, et al, published by Accelerated Indexing Systems, Bountiful, UT, 1976, 63 pages. FHL book 977.3 X2ja 1830. See also ***Index to the 1830 Federal Census*** **[Printed Book],** compiled by James V. Gill and Maryan R. Gill, published by Illiana Genealogical Pub. Co., Danville, IL, 1968, 4 vols., FHL book 977.3 X22g 1830.

■ ***1835 Illinois State Census Index*** **[Printed Book],** edited by W. David Samuelsen, et al, published by Accelerated Indexing Systems, Bountiful, UT, 1984, 58 pages. FHL book 977.3 X2j 1835.

■ **1839-1929.** See ***Chicago (Illinois) City Directories*** **[Microfilm],** from the originals published by various publishers. Filmed by Research Publications, Woodbridge, CT, 1980-1984, 96 microfiche and 64 microfilm rolls. The FHL has 1839, 1843-1905, 1907-1917, 1923, 1928-1929. The fiche starts with FHL fiche #6043786 (1839 Fergus' Directory of the City of Chicago) through fiche #6043808 (1860-61 D.B. Cook's Chicago City Directory); and the microfilm starts with FHL film #1376659 (1861-62 Halpin & Bailey's Chicago City Directory) through film #1759649 (1928/29 Polk's Chicago City Directory). For a complete list of fiche/roll numbers, see the online FHL catalog page for this title. See **https://familysearch.org/search/catalog/533804.**

■ ***1840 Illinois State Census*** **[Microfilm],** from the original records at the Illinois State Archives, Springfield, IL. Filmed by the Genealogical Society of Utah, 1976, 2 rolls, as follows:

- **1840 IL State Census:** Adams, Alexander, Bond, Boone, Brown, Carroll, Champaign, Clark, Coles, De Kalb, DeWitt, Edgar, Calhoun, Clay, Effingham, Franklin, Fulton, Hardin, Jo Daviess, LaSalle, Whiteside, Clinton, Cook, Jasper, and Stark County, Illinois, FHL Film #1004694.
- **1840 IL State Census:** Greene, Hamilton, Hancock, Henry, Iroquois, Jackson, Jefferson, Jersey, Johnson, Lawrence, Lee, Monroe, Scott, Shelby, St. Clair, Tazewell, Wabash, Warren, Washington, Wayne, White, Will, and Winnebago County, Illinois, FHL Film #1004695.

■ **1840.** See ***Illinois 1840 State Census Index* [Printed Book],** edited by W. David Samuelsen, et al, published by Accelerated Indexing Systems, Bountiful, UT, 1984, 294 pages. FHL book 977.3 X2j 1840.

■ **1840.** See ***Illinois 1840 Federal Census Index* [Printed Book],** edited by Ronald Vern Jackson, et al, published by Accelerated Indexing Systems, Bountiful, UT, 1977, 192 pages, FHL book 977.3 X2i 1840.

■ **1844-1901.** See ***Chicago City Directories* [Microfilm],** from originals published by various publishers. Includes directories for the years 1844, 1854-1855, 1859-1860, 1865, and 1869-1901. Filmed by W.C. Cox, Tucson, AZ, 1974, 16 rolls, beginning with FHL film #1000739 (Chicago Directories, 1844-1869). For a complete list of roll numbers and the contents of each roll, see the online FHL catalog page for this title:
**https://familysearch.org/search/catalog/308691.**

■ **1846-1898.** See ***Report of the Adjutant General of the State of Illinois* [Microfilm],** from the original published by Phillips Bros., Springfield, IL, 1900-1902, 9 volumes. Includes index. This is an alphabetical index of men and 9 vols. of rosters of officers and men in the Mexican War, Indian Wars, Civil War, and the Spanish-American War. Filmed by the Genealogical Society of Utah, 1974, 63 rolls, beginning with FHL film 1001124 (Index, Mexican War: A- Smith, J.). For a complete list of roll numbers and contents of each roll, see the online FHL catalog page for this title:
**https://familysearch.org/search/catalog/277178.**

■ ***1847-1860 Illinois (State) Directories* [Microfilm],** from originals published by various publishers. Filmed by Research Publications, Woodbridge, CT, 1980-1984, 41 microfiche, as follows:

- **1847** Illinois annual register, and Western business directory (3 fiche), FHL film #6043985.
- **1854-1855** Montague's Illinois and Missouri state directory (9 fiche), FHL film #6043986.
- **1855-1856** The Northern counties gazetteer and directory. The Chicago city directory, and business advertiser (8 fiche), FHL film #6043987.
film #6043988
- **1858-1859** Illinois state gazetteer and business directory... by George W. Hawes (7 fiche), FHL
- **1860** Illinois state business directory ... by J. C. W. Bailey & Co., FHL film #6043989.

■ **1853-1898.** See ***Children of Orphan Trains: From New York to Illinois and Beyond* [Printed Book],** compiled by Janet Coble and members of the Elgin Genealogical Society. Includes index. Includes name of child, place and date of birth, age, date of trip, family taking child, address, informant, and a reference to file if more information is available. By January 1853, the New York Juvenile Asylum opened a House of Reception to accommodate children who were orphaned, or had parents unable or unfit to care for them, or who were otherwise without homes. The Department of Charities determined that children would benefit from being sent to Illinois where they were apprenticed to farm families. Children between ages 7-14 were sent to Illinois from 1853 until the fall of 1898. The names and facts are extracted from records of the Asylum and their reports from the families or the children who were apprenticed. Published by the Illinois State Genealogical Society, 1994, 122 pages, FHL book 973 J3c.

■ ***1855 State Census of Illinois* [Microfilm],** from the original schedules at the Illinois State Archives, Springfield, IL. Missing are schedules from Carroll, Champaign, Franklin, Gallatin, Henry, Jefferson, Jo Davies, Lake, Stark, Will and Woodford counties. Included in *Name Index to Early Illinois Records, 1810-1855* by the Illinois State Archives; as well as online databases at both the Ancestry.com and FamilySearch.org websites. The 1855 state census schedules were microfilmed by the Genealogical Society of Utah, 1975, 15 rolls, as follows:

- Adams Co. - FHL film #976178
- Alexander - Clay counties, FHL film #976179.
- Clinton - Cook counties, FHL film #976180.
- Crawford - Effingham counties, FHL film #976181.
- Fayette - Hamilton counties, FHL film #976182.
- Hancock - Kane counties, FHL film #976183.
- Kankakee - LaSalle counties, FHL film #976184.
- Lawrence and Lee counties, FHL film #976185.
- Livingston - McHenry counties, FHL film, #976186.
- McLean - Massac counties, FHL film #976670.
- Menard - Ogle counties, FHL film #976671.
- Peoria - Putnam counties, FHL film #976672.
- Randolph - Sangamon counties, FHL film #976673.
- Schuyler - Wabash counties, FHL film #977062.
- Warren - Winnebago counties, FHL film #977063.

■ ***1861-1862 Illinois Military Census* [Microfilm],** from the original records at the office of Secretary of State, Springfield, IL. A list, by county, of able-bodied male citizens between the ages of eighteen and forty-five in pursuance of General Orders No. 99 of the War

Department and instructions of the Adjutant General of the State of Illinois. Includes Adams, Cook, Jo Daviess & Lake counties. FHL film #2209347.

■ **1861-1865.** See ***Report of the Adjutant General of the State of Illinois*, [Microfilm],** from the original published Springfield, IL, 1867, 8 vols. Contents: Vol. 1: 7th to 46th regiment; vol. 2: 47th to 157th regiment; vol. 3: 1st to 17th cavalry regiment, 29th United States colored infantry; 1st & 2nd regiments and independent batteries of artillery; also rosters of enlisted men numbered from the 7th to the 20th regiment; vol. 4: 21st to 47th regiments; vol. 5: 48th to 76th regiment; v. 6: 1861-1866; 77th to 117th regiment; vol. 7. 1861-1865; 118th to 156 infantry regiment; 1st to 3rd cavalry regiment; v. 8. 1861-1866; 4th to 17th cavalry regiment; 1st & 2nd regiments & independent batteries of artillery; colored troops; 1st army corps; recruits for regular army. The 1st to the 3rd vols. contain rosters of Civil War officers. The 3rd vol. also contains rosters of enlisted men which continues to the end of the 8th vol. Filmed for the FHL by the Library of Congress, 1989, 3 rolls, beginning with FHL film #1674241. For a complete list of roll numbers and contents of each roll, see the online FHL catalog page for this title:
**https://familysearch.org/search/catalog/379629.**

■ ***1862-1866 Internal Revenue Assessment Lists for Illinois* [Microfilm],** from the originals at the National Archives. Includes a locality index (filmed at the beginning of each roll of film) that references counties to districts and film roll numbers. Counties included in each district are as follows: District 1: Cook -- District 2: Boone, De Kalb, Kane, Lake, McHenry, Winnebago -- District 3: Carroll, Jo Daviess, Lee, Ogle, Stephenson, Whiteside -- District 4: Adams, Hancock, Henderson, Mercer, Rock Island, Warren -- District 5: Bureau, Henry, Knox, Marshall, Peoria, Putnam, Stark -- District 6: Du Page, Grundy, Kankakee, Kendall, La Salle, Will -- District 7: Champaign, Coles, Cumberland, Douglas, Edgar, Ford, Iroquois, Macon, Moultrie, Piatt, Vermilion -- District 8: De Witt, Livingston, Logan, McLean, Sangamon, Tazewell, Woodford -- District 9: Brown, Cass, Fulton, McDonough, Mason, Menard, Pike, Schuyler -- District 10: Bond, Calhoun, Christian, Greene, Jersey, Macoupin, Montgomery, Morgan, Scott, Shelby -- District 11: Clark, Clay, Crawford, Effingham, Fayette, Franklin, Hamilton, Jasper, Jefferson, Lawrence, Marion, Richland, Wayne -- District 12: Clinton, Madison, Monroe, Randolph, St. Clair, Washington -- District 13: Alexander, Edwards, Gallatin, Hardin, Johnson, Massac, Perry, Pope, Pulaski, Saline, Union, Wabash, White, Williamson. Filmed by the National Archives, series M764, 63 rolls, beginning with FHL film #1534562 (District 1, 1862-1863). For a complete list of roll numbers and contents of each roll, see the online FHL catalog page for this title. See
**https://familysearch.org/search/catalog/577851.**

■ ***1865 Illinois State Census* [Microfilm],** from the original records at the Illinois State Library, Springfield, IL. At the time of filming, the state library was missing the 1865 census schedules for Gallatin, Mason & Monroe counties. Only Elm Grove Township is included for Tazewell County. Included in *Name Index to Early Illinois Records, 1810-1855* by the Illinois State Archives; as well as online databases at both the Ancestry.com and FamilySearch.org websites. Filmed by the Genealogical Society of Utah, 1964, 1977, 25 rolls, as follows:

- Adams, Bureau, Edwards, Ford, and Effingham counties, FHL film #972746.
- Fayette, Franklin, Grundy, Henderson, and Fulton counties, FHL film #972747.
- Jo Daviess, Pulaski, Alexander, Bond, and Boone counties, - FHL film # 972748.
- Clinton, Champaign, Clark, Cumberland, and Christian counties, FHL film #972749.
- Crawford, Carroll, DeWitt, DeKalb, Douglas, DuPage, and Brown counties, FHL film #972750.
- Coles, Calhoun, Cass, Clay, and Greene counties, FHL film #972751.
- Edgar, Jasper, Pike, Hardin, and Jefferson counties, FHL film #972752.
- Jackson, Johnson, Henry, and Hancock counties, FHL film #972753.
- Hamilton, Iroquois, Kankakee, and Knox counties, FHL film #972754.
- Jersey County, FHL film #972755.
- Kane, Kendall, and Logan counties, FHL film #972756.
- Lake, Lawrence, Lee, and Livingston counties, FHL film #972757.
- McHenry, Montgomery, Macoupin, and Ogle counties, FHL film #1012404.
- Madison and Macon counties, FHL film #972758.
- Menard, Morgan, Pope, and Richland counties, FHL film #972759.
- Cook Co. (Chicago wards 1-12), FHL film #972760.
- Cook Co. (Chicago wards 12-16; other towns), FHL film #972761.
- Randolph, Saline, Mercer, McDonough, and McLean counties, FHL film #972762.
- Marshall, Peoria, Piatt, Perry, and Putnam counties, FHL film #972763.
- Rock Island Co., FHL film #972764.
- Sangamon, St. Clair, and Tazewell (Elm Grove Township only) counties, FHL film #972765.
- Vermilion, Will, and La Salle counties, FHL film #972766.

- Marion, Massac, Moultrie, Shelby, Stephenson, Schuyler, and Stark counties, FHL film #972767.
- Scott, Union, Wayne, White, Woodford, and Washington counties, FHL film #972768.
- Williamson, Winnebago, Wabash, and Warren counties, FHL film #972769.

■ ***1861-1865 Rosters of Illinois Regiments of the Civil War* [Microfilm],** from the original Report of the Adjutant General of the State of Illinois, published Springfield, IL, 1867, 8 vols. Contents: Vol. 1. 1865-1866, 7th to 46th regiment; v. 2. 1861-1866, 47th to 157th regiment; v. 3. 1861-1866; 1st to 17th cavalry regiment, 29th United States colored infantry; 1st & 2nd regiments and independent batteries of artillery; also rosters of enlisted men numbered from the 7th to the 20th regiment; v. 4. 1861-1865; 21st to 47th regiments; v. 5. 1861-1866; 48th to 76th regiment; v. 6. 1861-1866; 77th to 117th regiment; v. 7. 1861-1865; 118th to 156 infantry regiment; 1st to 3rd cavalry regiment; v. 8. 1861-1866; 4th to 17th cavalry regiment; 1st & 2nd regiments & independent batteries of artillery; colored troops; 1st army corps; recruits for regular army. The 1st to the 3rd vols. contain rosters of Civil War officers. The 3rd vol. also contains rosters of enlisted men which continues to the end of the 8th vol. Filmed for the FHL by the Library of Congress, 1989, 3 rolls, FHL film #1674241-1674243.

■ ***1871-1906 Indexes to Naturalization Records, Cook County, Illinois* [Microfilm],** from the original records at the Cook County Courthouse, Chicago, IL. Filmed by the Genealogical Society of Utah, 1980, 2 rolls, as follows:

- Naturalization index, A-L, 1871-1906, FHL film #1023967.
- Naturalization index, M-Z, 1871-1906, FHL film #1023968.

■ ***1847-1860 Illinois (State) Directories* [Microfilm],** from the originals published by various publishers. Filmed by Research Publications, Woodbridge, CT, 1980-1984, 41 microfiche, as follows:

- 1847 Illinois annual register, and Western business directory (3 fiches), FHL film #6043985.
- 1854-1855 Montague's Illinois and Missouri state directory (9 fiches), FHL film #6043986.
- 1855-1856 The Northern counties gazetteer and directory. The Chicago city directory, and business advertiser (8 fiches), FHL film #6043987.
- 1858-1859 Illinois state gazetteer and business directory... by George W. Hawes (7 fiches), FHL film #6043988
- 1860 Illinois state business directory ... by J. C. W. Bailey & Co., FHL film #6043989.

■ ***1869 Illinois Central Directory* [Microfilm],** from the original published 1869, filmed by the Genealogical Society of Utah, 1975, 1 roll, FHL film #969494.

■ **1871-1933.** See ***Indexes to Deaths in the City of Chicago During the Years 1871-1933: Showing Name, Address, and Date of Death* [Microfilm],** from original records at the Cook County Courthouse, Chicago, IL. These indexes are believed to be for burial permits, the actual deaths having occurred both in and outside the city of Chicago, often times out of state. Filmed by the Genealogical Society of Utah, 1980, 13 rolls, beginning with FHL film #1295943 (Deaths, A-Bou 1871-1933). For a complete list of roll numbers and contents of each rolls, see the online FHL catalog page for this title:
**https://familysearch.org/search/catalog/293534.**

■ **1871-1948.** See ***Chicago Delayed Birth Indexes, 1871-1948* [Microfilm],** from the originals at the Cook County Courthouse, Chicago, IL. Not in strict alpha order. Filmed by the Genealogical Society of Utah, 1981, 7 rolls, beginning with FHL film #378352 (Aabel – Crabb). For a complete list of roll numbers and contents of each roll, see the online FHL catalog page for this title. See
**https://familysearch.org/search/catalog/263696.**

# INDIANA
## Censuses & Substitutes, 1763-2015

Indiana Territory was created in 1800, taken from the Northwest Territory, with bounds virtually the same as Knox County, Northwest Territory of 1790. The early settlements of old Knox County were confined to two areas: most of the population was near Vincennes, on the Wabash River; or near Jeffersonville, on the Ohio River. By 1810, the population was within four counties: Clark, Dearborn, Knox, and Harrison – these four counties are included with the statewide censuses and substitutes in the bibliographies that follow.

The only census taken before statehood was the 1807 Indiana Territory census. After statehood in 1816, Indiana began taking state censuses at various intervals, but few of them have survived. Original census schedules for Blackford County (1857, 1871, 1877, 1883, 1889); Henry County (1919, 1931); Ripley County (1919); Starke County (1919); and Washington County (1901) can be found at the Indiana State Library in Indianapolis (none microfilmed, none digitized).

## Indiana State Digital Archives

This new service of the Indiana State Archives is a model project being developed on a multi-state basis, initiated and sponsored by the Library of Congress. The project is administered by the lead agency of the Washington State Digital Archives. The new Indiana State Digital Archives already has several searchable databases online, with about 3 million names indexed. The databases include the following:

- **Death Records:**
  - Social Security Death Index
- **Institution Records:**
  - Women's Prison 1873-1969
  - Boy's School 1867-1937
  - Girl's School 1873-1935
  - Prison North 1858-1897
  - Prison North 1897-1966
  - Prison South 1822-1897
  - Indiana Life Prisoners
  - Julia E. Work Training School
  - School for the Deaf Admission Register
  - Secretary of State Petitions
  - Soldiers and Sailors Childrens Home
  - Closed Nursing Schools (Database Pending)
- **Military Records:**
  - Book of Merit
  - Civil War
  - Early Military
  - Franklin County Auditor Military Service Verification – Civil War
  - Gold Star
  - Indiana Veterans Home
  - Mexican War Veterans
  - National Guard, 1898-1940
  - United Spanish War Veterans Membership Files
- **Miscellaneous Historical Records:**
  - Clark County Negro and Mulatto Register
  - Clark County Negro Register
  - Foster Children, 1892-1910
  - Franklin County Negro and Mulatto Register
  - Indiana Public Lands
  - Marion County Bar Association, 1822-1980
  - Marion County Court
  - Marion County Department of Public Safety
  - Marion County Wills
  - Orange County Department of Public Safety
  - Switzerland County Negro and Mulatto Register
  - Vigo County Negro and Mulatto Register
- **Naturalization Records.** Pending databases are in work for several Indiana counties.

**Search the Records.** The Indiana State Digital Archives home page starts with Search the Digital Archives. The search screen allows for 1) People Search, 2) Keyword Search, and 3) Detailed Search. For a People Search, choices are for Record Series (all or one), First Name, and/or Last Name. As an example, a search for the surname Dollarhide in "All Record Series" brought up three Record Series: Death Records (3 results); History Records (4 results); and Misc. Historical Records (17 results, mostly Military). The results list has the full name of the person, county name (or statewide) database, and whether an image is available. For the main Indiana State Digital Archives search screen, see **www.indianadigitalarchives.org.**

## Indiana State Archives Online Collection Indexes

These databases were prepared and indexed online at the Indiana State Archives site before the State Digital Archives project was begun. For now, these special searchable databases are still available at the archives site: **www.in.gov/icpr/2355.htm.** The database titles listed below are also listed and described in more detail (by date) within the bibliography that follows.

- **Cultural Records:**
  - Indian Lands Noted on the LaPorte-Winamac Land Office (Table)
- **Military Records:**
  - Indiana Soldier's and Sailor's Children's Home
- **Court Records:**
  - State Supreme Court Cases
  - Posey County Circuit Court Records
- **Police/Criminal Records:**
  - Index to Life Prisoner's Statements: State Prison at Michigan City
- **Land Records:**
  - Land Office
  - The Indianapolis Donation
  - Hoosier Homestead Awards Database
  - Internal Improvements Projects: Contracts for Canal Structures, 1930's-1950's
- **History of Government Records**
  - Indianapolis-Marion County Employees
  - Governor Oliver P. Morton Telegraph Books

## Online Databases at the Indiana State Library

These databases can be accessed at the Indiana State Library's webpage: **www.in.gov/library/databases.htm.** The following searchable databases are listed. Click on the title for more details:

- Howey Political Report 1994-2012
- Indiana Biography Index Published Before 1990
- Indiana Biography Index Published Since 1990
- Indiana Cemetery Locator Index
- Indiana Marriages 1993-2004

- Indiana Marriages Through 1850
- Indiana Memory
- Indiana World War II Servicemen
- Indianapolis Commercial Newspaper Death Listing Index
- Indianapolis Newspaper Index, 1848-1991 INSPIRE
- Logansport Newspaper Index, 1848-1855
- New Albany Newspaper Index, 1849-1889
- Online Family History Databases
- State Documents Checklist Database, 1990-2001
- USGS Topographic Quadrangle Map Database
- Vincennes Newspaper Index, 1804-1827
- VINE (Vital INformation Exchange)

## Indiana Databases Online at Ancestry.com

The Ancestry.com subscription website allows free access to all indexes, but to view any particular record requires a membership. Ancestry offers trial memberships and subscriptions for short periods and reduced rates. The following databases at the Ancestry.com website are unique to Indiana under the categories, Census & Voter Lists, Vital Records, Military, Immigrations, et al.

■ **1763-1784.** See ***French and British Land Grants in the Post Vincennes (Indiana) District, 1750-1784*** **[Online Database],** indexed at the Ancestry.com website. Source: Clifford Neal Smith's *French and British Land Grants in the Post Vincennes (Indiana) District, 1750-1784*, publ. 2004. Smith's four booklets were extracted from the American State Papers. Vincennes Post was established by the French in 1732. Although the title says 1750, the earliest record found in a global search in this database was for 1763, the same year the British took over Vincennes from the French. American forces, aided by the local French residents, captured Post Vincennes in 1779. The indexes to each of these four books include mostly French surnames. This database has nearly 3,000 records. See
**http://search.ancestry.com/search/db.aspx?dbid=49217.**

■ **1798-1999.** See ***Indiana, Wills and Probate Records, 1798-1999*** **[Online Database],** indexed at the Ancestry.com website. Source: Ancestry database, extractions from Indiana county, district, and probate courts. The contents of a probate file can vary from case to case, but certain details are found in most probates, most importantly, the names and residences of beneficiaries and their relationship to the decedent. An inventory of the estate assets can reveal personal details about the deceased's occupation and lifestyle. There may also be references to debts, deeds, and other documents related to the settling of the estate. This database has 455,287 records. See
**http://search.ancestry.com/search/db.aspx?dbid=9045.**

■ **1800-1941.** See ***Indiana, Marriage Index, 1800-1941*** **[Online Database],** indexed at the Ancestry.com website. Source: Jordan Dodd, editor, Liahona Research, from county records on microfilm at the Family History Library, Salt Lake City. Also cited is a WPA index done in 1938-1940. Information contained in these indexes includes: Spouses' names, Marriage date, Marriage county, and Source information. This database has 3,245,823 records. See
**http://search.ancestry.com/search/db.aspx?dbid=5059.**

■ **1800-2010.** See ***Web: Indiana and Michigan, Michiana Genealogical Cemetery Index, 1800-2010*** **[Online Database],** indexed at the Ancestry.com website. This database is also accessible at the South Bend Area Genealogical Society website. This database has 187,743 records. See
**http://search.ancestry.com/search/db.aspx?dbid=70492.**

■ **1802-1850.** See ***Indiana Marriages to 1850*** **[Online Database],** indexed at the Ancestry.com website. Source: Jordan Dodd, from county records on microfilm at the Family History Library, Salt Lake City. A single alpha list has both brides and grooms, date and place of marriage, and source. This database has 199,945 records. See
**http://search.ancestry.com/search/db.aspx?dbid=2087.**

■ **1802-1892.** See ***Indiana, Marriage Index, 1802-1892*** **[Online Database],** indexed at the Ancestry.com website. Jordan Dodd, a revised version of the 1802-1850 database. This database has 199,807 records. See
**http://search.ancestry.com/search/db.aspx?dbid=7852.**

■ **1806-1861.** See ***Web: Indiana, Marriage Index, 1806-1861*** **[Online Database],** indexed at the Ancestry.com website. This database is also accessible at the IN State Library website. This database has 317,373 records. See
**http://search.ancestry.com/search/db.aspx?dbid=9760.**

■ **1807-1890.** See ***Indiana, Compiled Census and Census Substitutes Index, 1790-1890*** **[Online Database],** indexed at the Ancestry.com website. Originally edited by Ronald Jackson, Accelerated

Indexing Systems, Salt Lake City, UT. This collection contains the following indexes: 1807 State (Terr.) Census Index; 1810 Wayne County Census Index; 1820 Federal Census Index; 1830 Federal Census Index; 1840 Federal Census Index; 1840 Pensioners List; 1850 Federal Census Index; 1860 Federal Census Index; 1870 Federal Census Index; 1890 Veterans Schedule. The description incorrectly states that this database includes the 1790 (Northwest Territory) federal census index. There was no 1790 census taken in the Northwest Territory. The added "1812 census" in the description is also unlikely. This database has 7,879 records. See
**http://search.ancestry.com/search/db.aspx?dbid=3546.**

■ **1812-2015.** See ***Web: Grant County, Indiana, Marion Public Library Death Index, 1812-2015*** **[Online Database],** indexed at the Ancestry.com website. This database is also accessible at the Marion Public Library website. This database has 570,815 records. See
**http://search.ancestry.com/search/db.aspx?dbid=9242.**

■ **1818-1993. See** ***Indiana, Select Marriages Index, 1748-1993*** **[Online Database],** indexed at the Ancestry.com website. Source: FamilySearch. Includes names of bride and groom, date and place of marriage, and possibly more information. **Note:** A global search for 1748 revealed one record (from Michigan). The earliest Indiana marriage was in 1818. This database has 3,938,237 records. See
**http://search.ancestry.com/search/db.aspx?dbid=60281.**

■ **1831-2008.** See ***Web: Indiana, Marion Public Library Marriage Index, 1831-2008*** **[Online Database],** indexed at the Ancestry.com website. This database is also accessible from the Marion Public Library website. Includes names of bride and groom, date and place of marriage, and possibly more information. This database has 170,642 records. See
**http://search.ancestry.com/search/db.aspx?dbid=70708.**

■ **1836-1921.** See ***Indiana, Selected Quaker Meeting Directories, 1836-1921*** **[Online Database],** indexed at the Ancestry.com website. Source: Friends Historical Library, Earlham College, Richmond, IN. The directories include names, and often street addresses, of meeting members. Additionally they can provide any posts (e.g., ministers, overseers, elders, trustees, clerks, etc.) members held in the meeting. Some directories also list committee members. Directories in this collection are from monthly and quarterly meetings at Indianapolis (Indianapolis, Marion Co.), Whitewater (Richmond, Wayne Co.), Walnut Ridge (Carthage, Rush Co.), and Knightstown (Knightstown, Henry Co.), as well as the yearly meeting for Indiana, 1889.This database has 14,836 records. See
**http://search.ancestry.com/search/db.aspx?dbid=8211.**

■ **1837-1970.** See ***Indiana, United Methodist Church Records, 1837-1970*** **[Online Database],** digitized and indexed at the Ancestry.com website. Source: DePauw University Archives, Greencastle, IN. This collection contains indexed images of United Methodist Church registers from Indiana. The registers may contain baptisms, marriages, burials, memberships, and lists of clergy. See the browse menu for a list of the churches included in this collection. This database has 434,135 records. See
**http://search.ancestry.com/search/db.aspx?dbid=60715.**

■ **1861-1865.** See ***Web: Indiana, Civil War Soldier Database Index, 1861-1865*** **[Online Database],** indexed at the Ancestry.com website. This database is also accessible at the IN State Digital Archives website. This database has 212,959 records. See
**http://search.ancestry.com/search/db.aspx?dbid=9762.**

■ **1880-1920.** See ***Indiana Births, 1880-1920*** **[Online Database],** indexed at the Ancestry.com website. Source: WPA index, 1938-1940. The WPA began to index vital records, county-by-county, for the entire state, but the agency was abolished before the project was completed. This database indexes births for thirty-one of the counties indexed by the WPA. Counties included in this database are: Adams, Allen, Boone, Cass, Clay, Davies, De Kalb, Harrison, Hendricks, Henry, Howard, Huntington, Jay, Johnson, Knox, Madison, Martin, Monroe, Morgan, Orange, Owen, Parke, Perry, Posey, Putnam, Spencer, Vanderburgh, Vigo, Warrick, and Washington Counties. This database has 674,773 records. See
**http://search.ancestry.com/search/db.aspx?dbid=4745.**

■ **1882-1920.** See ***Indiana Deaths, 1882-1920*** **[Online Database],** indexed at the Ancestry.com website. Source: WPA index, 1938-1940. The WPA began to index vital records, county-by-county, for the entire state, but the agency was abolished before the project was completed. Only sixty-seven of the ninety-two counties had their birth and death records (1882-1920) and marriages (generally 1850-1920) collected. This database has 793,965 records. See
**http://search.ancestry.com/search/db.aspx?dbid=7834.**

■ **1887-1890.** See ***Indianapolis, Indiana Directories, 1887-1890*** **[Online Database],** indexed at the Ancestry.com website. Source: R.L. Polk and Co Directories, 1887, 1888, 1889, and 1890, Indianapolis, IN. This database has 91,256 records. See **http://search.ancestry.com/search/db.aspx?dbid=4577.**

■ ***1890 Census Substitute*** **[Online Database],** indexed at the Ancestry.com website. This is nationwide collection of city directories for the time of the 1890 federal census (lost in a fire in Washington DC in 1921). A global search includes directories from several Indiana cities. See **http://search.ancestry.com/search/group/1890census.**

■ **1896.** See ***Indiana Spanish American War Records*** **[Online Database],** indexed at the Ancestry.com website. Source: *Record of Indiana Volunteers in the Spanish-American War,* by Gen. James K. Gore, publ. 1900. This database is a list of Indiana residents who answered the 1898 call by the President to serve in the Army for two years. It provides the volunteer's name and rank, as well as location of enlistment. Enlistment and discharge dates are also included. This database has 7,862 records. See **http://search.ancestry.com/search/db.aspx?dbid=4305.**

■ **1899-2011.** See ***Indiana, Death Certificates, 1899-2011*** **[Online Database],** digitized and indexed at the Ancestry.com website. Source: IN State Archives. State-level registration began for deaths in Indiana in January 1900. Prior to that, registration was done at the county level, with most counties beginning in 1882. This collection includes an index and images of Indiana death certificates for the years 1899–2011.
Death records can provide a wide variety of details, including the following: name of the decedent and place of death, gender, color or race, marital status, date of birth, age, occupation, birthplace, father's name and birthplace, mother's name and birthplace, name and address of informant, date filed, date of death, physician's statement and cause of death, length of residence, if in a hospital or institution, date and place of burial, name and address of undertaker, later records may include spouse's name. This database has 16,683,304 records. See **http://search.ancestry.com/search/db.aspx?dbid=60716.**

■ **1907-1940.** See ***Indiana, Birth Certificates, 1907-1940*** **[Online Database],** indexed at the Ancestry.com website. Source: IN State Archives. Information contained in the searchable index typically includes: Child's full name, Sex, Birth date, Birth place, Registration year, Full names of both parents, Birth certificate number, In addition, birth records will generally also contain the following information: Child: time of birth, hospital. Father: race, birthplace, age, occupation. Mother: race, birthplace, age, occupation, residence. Sometimes, birth records may also list the parents' length of residence in the community, length of pregnancy, marital status, number of other living children, number of other deceased children, or number of children born dead. This database has 7,077,520 records. See **http://search.ancestry.com/search/db.aspx?dbid=60871.**

■ **1914-1918.** See ***Indiana Gold Star Honor Roll, 1914-1918*** **[Online Database],** indexed at the Ancestry.com website. Source: *Indiana World War Records: Gold Star Honor Roll, A Record of Indiana Men and Women who died in the service of the United States and the Allied Nations in the World War, 1914-1918,* publ. 1921. This database contains information about 10,500 men and women from Indiana who died in World War I. The database includes, wherever possible, name, rank, birth date and place, parents' names, place living at time of entry into service, service record (abbreviated version), occupation, place and date of death, place of burial, cause of death, and other valuable information. This database has 3,370 records. See **http://search.ancestry.com/search/db.aspx?dbid=5182.**

■ **1939-1974.** See ***Wayne County, Indiana, Quaker Funeral Home Records, 1939-1974*** **[Online Database],** indexed at the Ancestry.com website. Source: Quaker Archives, Earlham College, Richmond, IN. This collection includes: death certificates, burial transits (permits to move a body from one location to another), obituary memorandums (forms filled out by family members with details to be used in obituaries), cemetery invoices, various invoices and receipts relating to the funeral. This database has 5,388 records. See **http://search.ancestry.com/search/db.aspx?dbid=2889.**

■ **1941-1946.** See ***Web: Indiana, WWII Servicemen Database Index, 1941-1946*** **[Online Database],** indexed at the Ancestry.com website. This database is also accessible at the IN State Library website. This database has 26,054 records. See **http://search.ancestry.com/search/db.aspx?dbid=9761.**

■ **1957-1960.** See ***Indiana, Passenger and Crew Manifests, 1957-1960*** **[Online Database],** indexed at

the Ancestry.com website. Source: National Archives microfilm series A3773 (**Indianapolis only**). Details may include the arrival date, ports of departure and arrival dates of departure and arrival, full name, age, gender, physical description, military rank (if any), occupation, birthplace, citizen of what country, and residence. This database has 84 pages. See
**http://search.ancestry.com/search/db.aspx?dbid=9113.**

■ **1958-2005.** See ***Indiana, Marriage Certificates, 1958-2005*** **[Online Database],** digitized and indexed at the Ancestry.com website. Source: IN State Archives. Each record may include: name, residence, spouse, marriage date and place, race/color, age, occupation, witnesses, father's name, and mother's name, This database has 8,081,574 records. See
**http://search.ancestry.com/search/db.aspx?dbid=61009.**

■ **1993-2015.** See ***Web: Indiana, County Marriage Indexes, 1993-2015*** **[Online Database],** indexed at the Ancestry.com website. This database is also accessible at the Indiana Supreme Court Public Lookup website. Includes name of bride and groom, date and place of marriage, and possibly more information. This database has 1,886,850 records. See
**http://search.ancestry.com/search/db.aspx?dbid=70802.**

---

## Indiana Databases Online at the FamilySearch.org Website

The following databases are available for free at the FamilySearch.org website. To see the current list, visit the Indiana Indexed Historical Records and Indiana Image Only Historical Records webpage. Both lists are updated periodically. See
**https://familysearch.org/search/collection/location/15.**

■ **1773-1933.** See ***Indiana Births and Christenings, 1773-1933*** **[Online Database],** indexed at the FamilySearch.org website. Name index to birth, baptism and christening records from microfilm at the Family History Library. This database has 35,760 records. See
**https://familysearch.org/search/collection/1674814.**

■ **1773-1933.** See ***Indiana, Select Births and Christenings, 1773-1933*** **[Online Database],** indexed at the Ancestry.com website. Name index to birth, baptism and christening records from microfilm at the Family History Library. This database has 103,702 records. See
**http://search.ancestry.com/search/db.aspx?dbid=60280.**

■ **1780-1992.** See ***Indiana Marriages, 1780-1992*** **[Online Database],** indexed at the FamilySearch.org website. Name index to marriage records from microfilm at the Family History Library.
This database has 1,008,158 records. See
**https://familysearch.org/search/collection/1674830.**

■ **1811-2007.** See ***Indiana Marriages, 1811-2007*** **[Online Database],** indexed at the FamilySearch.org website. Indexed in partnership with the Indiana Genealogical Society. The description/search screen incorrectly asks for "deceased person" but searching seems to work to find marriage records. Names of a person and spouse are consistent, as well as a date and place of marriage. Added names are usually identified as "mother" "father" or "other." There may be a license and a registration for the same couple. This collection includes marriage records from all Indiana counties except Howard, Johnson, and Montgomery. This database has 3,564,564 records. See
**https://familysearch.org/search/collection/1410397.**

■ **1828-1957.** See ***Indiana, Civil Marriages, 1828-1957*** **[Online Database],** indexed at the FamilySearch.org website. Source: FamilySearch extractions from Carroll and Pike counties, Indiana. This database has 10,571 records. See
**https://familysearch.org/search/collection/2469545.**

■ **1848-1992.** See ***Indiana Naturalization Records and Indexes, 1848-1992*** **[Online Database],** digitized and indexed at the FamilySearch.org website. Source: This collection contains naturalization records (images and indexes) from microfilm at the Regional NARA facility in Chicago. Includes records from South Bend, Hammond, Indianapolis, Fort Wayne, and Lafayette. Each record has the person's name, event year, and type of event (naturalization, birth, etc.). This database has 88,015 records. See
**https://familysearch.org/search/collection/2137708.**

■ **1861-2007.** See ***Indiana, Ripley County, Osgood, Greendale Cemetery Records, 1861-2007*** **[Online Database],** digitized at the FamilySearch.org website. This image only database includes burial records, cemetery plots, and lists of veterans. Browse the records, organized as follows: Cemetery Act 1882-1912 vol. 2, Cemetery records-miscellaneous 1950, 1972-2007, Death certificates, miscellaneous, permits 1899-1962 Southwest, Death certificates, miscellaneous, permits 1963-2006 Southwest, Decedents 1890-2007, Deeds 1914-1943, 1950-1986 vol. 1, Deeds 1987-1999 vol. 2, Deeds 2000-2005 vol.

3, Deeds 2005-2007 vol. 4, History, minutes 1880-1965 vol. 1, Interments 1879-1979 vol. 3, Interments 1880-2007, Ledgers 1938-1968 vol. 4, List of veterans 1861-2006, Plot maps no date, Section books 1880-1983 Northeast, Section books 1880-1983 Northwest, Section books 1880-1983 Southeast, and Section books 1880-1983 Southwest. This database has 3,977 images. See **https://familysearch.org/search/collection/1548494.**

■ **1882-1920.** See ***Indiana Death Index, 1882-1920*** **[Online Database],** indexed at the FamilySearch.org website. Source: IN State Board of Health. This is a WPA index, compiled in the late 1930s. This database has 793,965 records. See **https://familysearch.org/search/collection/1947977.**

■ **1945-1956.** See ***Indiana, Gary and East Chicago Crew Lists, 1945-1956*** **[Online Database],** indexed at the FamilySearch.org website. Source: National Archives microfilm series A3475. This collection contains crew lists of vessels arriving at East Chicago, Indiana, from April 12, 1945 to November 25, 1956, and at Gary, Indiana, on May 1, 1955, and on August 25, 1955. The records usually include name of the vessel, ports and dates of departure and arrival, and the following information about each crew member: full name, position in ship's company, age, gender, race, and nationality. This database has 16,011 records. See **https://familysearch.org/search/collection/2438215.**

■ **1984-2012.** See ***Indiana, Daviess County, Washington Times Herald Obituaries, 1984-2012*** **[Online Database],** indexed at the FamilySearch.org website. Index and images of obituary clippings from the Washington Times Herald bound in book form. Contains deaths from Daviess, Martin, Pike and Knox Counties and other areas. The collection was compiled by Kay Hedrick. Some years are missing. This database has 32,135 records. See **https://familysearch.org/search/collection/2300886.**

## Indiana Databases Online At Various Websites

■ **1700s-2000s.** See ***Indiana USGenWeb Archives*** **[Online Database].** The INGenWeb Archives site offers free genealogical databases with searchable statewide name lists and for all Indiana counties. Databases may include Bibles, Biographies, Cemeteries, Censuses, Court Records, Deaths, Deeds, Directories, Histories, Marriages, Military, Newspapers, Obituaries, Photos, Schools, Tax Lists, Wills, and more. See **http://usgwarchives.net/in/infiles.htm.**

■ **1700s-2000s.** See ***Linkpendium – Indiana: Family History & Genealogy, Census, Birth, Marriage, Death, Vital Records & More*** **[Online Databases].** Linkpendium is a genealogical portal site with links to state, county, town, and local databases. Currently listed are selected sites for Indiana statewide resources (639), Adams County (425), Allen County (800), Bartholomew County (389), Benton County (277), Blackford County (324), Boone County (391) and 86 more Indiana counties. See **www.linkpendium.com/in-genealogy.**

■ **1780s –2000s.** See ***Indiana Collections at World Vital Records*** **[Online Database],** over 900 databases can be searched at the "Search All Indiana Collections" search/browse screen at the World Vital Records website. Databases include censuses, directories, family histories, town histories, military rosters, college/school year books, and more. This is a subscription site, but all initial searches are free. A free search can be done for a name, place, year, or keyword. See **www.worldvitalrecords.com/contentview.aspx?&p=Indiana&fh=0.**

■ **1780s-1975.** See ***Military Records, Lawrence County, Indiana*** **[Online Database],** indexed at the USGenWeb site for Lawrence Co IN. See **www.ingenweb.org/inlawrence/military.htm.**

■ **1780s-1991.** See ***Soldiers and Veterans, Daviess County, Indiana*** **[Online Database],** an index to county residents who served in the military, from the Revolutionary War to Desert Storm. Compiled for the USGenWeb site for Daviess Co IN. See **www.ingenweb.org/indaviess/military.html.**

■ **1787.** See ***Enumeration of Males Currently Residing in the District of Poste Vincennes, 8 October 1787*** **[Online Database],** indexed at the Genealogy Trails website. See **http://genealogytrails.com/ind/knox/1787.html.**

■ **1804-1992.** See ***Indiana Newspaper Archives, 1804-1992*** **[Online Databases],** digitized and indexed newspapers at the GenealogyBank website, for Attica, Bloomington, Brookville, Corydon, Covington, Elkhart, Evansville, Fort Wayne, Indiana

Harbour, Indianapolis, Lawrenceburg, Logansport, Madison, New Albany, New Harmony, Richmond, Salem, South Bend, Terre Haute, Vevay, and Vincennes, Indiana. See www.genealogybank.com/explore/newspapers/all/usa/indiana.

■ ***1807 Indiana Territory Census, Dearborn County, Indiana* [Online Database].** Indiana Territory in 1807 had three counties in present Indiana and two counties in present Illinois. Knox, Clark, and Dearborn were the three Indiana counties. Dearborn County in 1807 included an area from Ft. Recovery, Ohio, southwest to Madison, Indiana. The area of old Dearborn today includes all or part of current Wayne, Franklin, Union, Fayette, Dearborn, Ohio, Rush, and Switzerland counties. This database was indexed at the USGenWeb site for Franklin Co IN. See www.ingenweb.org/infranklin/pages/census/1807main.html.

■ ***1807-1820 Land Entries, Martin County, Indiana* [Online Database],** indexed at the USGenWeb site for Martin Co IN. See http://files.usgwarchives.net/in/martin/1868/land/1868/land.txt.

■ **1811-1883.** See ***Early Land Entries, Orange County, Indiana* [Online Database],** indexed at the USGenWeb site for Orange Co IN. Separate databases for each township. See http://files.usgwarchives.net/in/orange/land.

■ ***1812 Sheriff Tax Sale, Franklin County, Indiana* [Online Database],** indexed at the USGenWeb site for Franklin Co IN. See www.ingenweb.org/infranklin/pages/census/1812sale.html.

■ ***1813 Tax List, Franklin County, Indiana* [Online Database],** indexed at the USGenWeb site for Franklin Co IN. See www.ingenweb.org/infranklin/pages/census/1813taxfc.html

■ ***1816 Indiana Territory Post Offices* [Online Database],** index of post office, postmaster, and place of birth of postmaster, at the USGenWeb site for Indiana. See http://files.usgwarchives.net/in/post-off.txt.

■ **1817-1900s.** See ***Biographies and Obituaries, Daviess County, Indiana* [Online Database],** indexed by the USGenWeb site for Daviess Co IN. See www.ingenweb.org/indaviess/bio.html.

■ **1819-1849.** See ***Index to Probates Before 1850, Owen County, Indiana* [Online Database],** indexed in groups at the Sweet Owen website. See www.sweetowen.net.

■ **1820s-1830s.** See ***Early Land Entries, Union County, Indiana* [Online Database],** indexed at the USGenWeb site for Union Co IN. See http://files.usgwarchives.net/in/union/land/land-rec.txt.

■ **1820-1835.** See ***Early Landowners, Decatur County, Indiana* [Online Database],** indexed at the Ye Olde Genealogie Shoppe website. See www.yogs.com/in/surnames/Decatur_Landowners.html.

■ **1820s-1850s.** See ***Original Land Entries, Ohio County, Indiana* [Online Database],** indexed at the USGenWeb site for Ohio Co IN. See http://files.usgwarchives.net/in/ohio/cemetery/land/1868/land-rec.txt.

■ **1820s-1850s.** See ***Original Land Entries, Morgan County, Indiana* [Online Database],** indexed at the USGenWeb site for Morgan Co IN. See http://files.usgwarchives.net/in/morgan/land.

■ **1820s-1850s.** See ***Original Land Entries, Scott County, Indiana* [Online Database],** indexed at the RootsWeb site for Scott Co IN. See www.rootsweb.ancestry.com/~inscott/ScottLand.html.

■ **1820s-1850s.** See ***Original Land Entries, Rush County, Indiana* [Online Database],** indexed at the USGenWeb site for Rush Co IN. See www.ingenweb.org/inrush/history1.html.

■ **1820s-1850s.** See ***Original Land Entries, Switzerland County, Indiana* [Online Database],** indexed at the USGenWeb site for Switzerland Co IN. http://files.usgwarchives.net/in/switz/land/land-rec.txt.

■ **1820s-1870s.** See ***Will Books, Orange County, Indiana* [Online Database],** indexed at the USGenWeb site for Orange Co IN. See http://files.usgwarchives.net/in/orange/wills.

■ ***1821 Tax List, Bartholomew County, Indiana* [Online Database],** indexed at the USGenWeb site for Bartholomew Co See http://files.usgwarchives.net/in/bartholomew/land/1821tax.txt.

■ ***1821 Settlers, Shelby County, Indiana* [Online Database],** indexed at the Shelby County website. See **www.shelbycountyindiana.org/historical_articles/history_earliest_settlers.htm.**

■ **1822-1876.** See ***History of Shelby County, Indiana* [Online Database],** full text and index located at the Shelby Co History website. See **www.shelbycountyindiana.org/historical_articles/history_1876.htm.**

■ ***1822-1940 Probate Index, Montgomery County, Indiana* [Online Database],** part of the Crawfordsville District Public Library Local History Database. See **www.cdpl.lib.in.us/lh/probate/probate.pdf.**

■ ***1825-1874 Guardian's Docket, Montgomery County, Indiana* [Online Database],** part of the Crawfordsville District Public Library Local History Database, see **http://history.cdpl.lib.in.us/guardian.html.**

■ ***1826-1839 Naturalization Records, Franklin County, Indiana* [Online Database],** indexed at the USGenWeb site for Franklin Co IN. See **www.ingenweb.org/infranklin/pages/tier2/Naturalize1.html.**

■ **1830s.** See ***Tract Book, Blackford County, Indiana* [Online Database],** indexed at the USGenWeb site for Blackford Co IN. See **http://files.usgwarchives.net/in/blackford/land/tract-bk.txt.**

■ **1830s-1840s.** See ***Early Land Entries, Randolph County, Indiana* [Online Database],** indexed at the USGenWeb site for Randolph Co IN. See **http://files.usgwarchives.net/in/randolph/land/land-rec.txt.**

■ **1830s-1930s.** See ***Saint Joseph County Graves Registration Project* [Online Database],** an index to all males buried in the county who served in the military and died before 1938. Indexed at the RootsWeb site for the South Bend Area Genealogical Society, Mishawaka-Penn-Harris Public Library, Mishawaka, IN. See **www.rootsweb.ancestry.com/~insbags/grave.htm.**

■ **1830-1971.** See ***Index to Saint Joseph County Wills, 1830-1971* [Online Database],** indexed at the RootsWeb site for the South Bend Area Genealogical Society, Mishawaka-Penn-Harris Public Library, Mishawaka, IN. See **www.rootsweb.ancestry.com/~insbags/wills.htm.**

■ **1833-1867.** See ***Original Land Owners, Marshall County, Indiana* [Online Database],** indexed at the RootsWeb site for Marshall Co IN. See **www.rootsweb.ancestry.com/~inmarsha/original.html.**

■ **1833-1860s.** See ***Original Land Owners, Miami County, Indiana* [Online Database],** indexed in groups at the USGenWeb site for Miami Co IN. See **http://files.usgwarchives.net/in/miami/land.**

■ **1834-1899, 1900-present.** See ***Vital Statistics From Local Newspapers, Montgomery County, Indiana* [Online Database],** part of the Crawfordsville District Public Library Local History Database. See **http://history.cdpl.lib.in.us/vitals.html.**

■ ***1834-1910 Newspaper Index, Cass County, Indiana* [Online Database],** indexed at the Genealogical Roots in Newspapers website. See **http://grins.freeservers.com/cass_co_,_in.htm.**

■ ***1835-1850s.* See *Original Land Owners, Kosciusko County, Indiana* [Online Database],** indexed at the USGenWeb site for Kosciusko Co IN. See **www.ingenweb.org/inkosciusko/OrigTract.htm.**

■ **1835-1923.** See ***Naturalizations Index, Kosciusko County, Indiana* [Online Database],** indexed at the USGenWeb site for Kosciusko Co IN. See **www.ingenweb.org/inkosciusko/naturalizations.html.**

■ ***1844-1920 Index to Early Wills, Kosciusko County, Indiana* [Online Database],** indexed at the USGenWeb site for Kosciusko Co IN. See **www.ingenweb.org/inkosciusko/willsndx.htm.**

■ **1840s-1930s.** See ***Naturalization Info Gleaned from Voter Registration Records, Marshall County, Indiana* [Online Database],** indexed at the RootsWeb site for Marshall Co IN. See **www.rootsweb.ancestry.com/~inmarsha/naturalization.html.**

■ ***1848 List of Voters, Tippecanoe County, Indiana* [Online Database],** indexed at the RootsWeb site for Tippecanoe Co IN. See **www.rootsweb.ancestry.com/~intcags/1848Voters.html.**

■ ***1849 Cholera Deaths, Tippecanoe County, Indiana* [Online Database],** indexed at the USGenWeb site for Tippecanoe Co IN. See **www.ingenweb.org/intippecanoe/chlradths.htm.**

■ ***1849 Delinquent Tax List, Vanderburgh County, Indiana* [Online Database],** indexed at the USGenWeb site for Vanderburgh Co IN. See **http://files.usgwarchives.net/in/vanderburgh/vitals/1849list.txt.**

■ **1850-2012.** See ***Local History Database, Evansville Newspapers, Evansville, Indiana* [Online Database].** An index to newspaper clippings by Charles Browning from about 537,000 index cards. Digitized online at the Evansville Local History website. See **http://local.evpl.org.**

■ ***1850s-1950s Will Index, Noble County, Indiana* [Online Database],** indexed at the RootsWeb site for Noble Co IN. See **www.rootsweb.ancestry.com/~ohnoble/wills1.htm.**

■ ***1853 Voter List, Marshall County, Indiana* [Online Database],** indexed at the RootsWeb site for Marshall Co IN. See **www.rootsweb.ancestry.com/~inmarsha/1853vote.html.**

■ ***1854-1929 Naturalizations, Marshall County, Indiana* [Online Database],** indexed at the RootsWeb site for Marshall Co IN. See **www.rootsweb.ancestry.com/~inmarsha/natrlz.html.**

■ **1863-1939.** See ***Carroll County, Indiana Plat Maps* [Online Database]**, indexed at the Carroll County Historical Museum website. Data in this file includes more than 16,000 names of land owners indicated on the published plat books and maps for Carroll County in 1863, 1869, 1874, 1882, 1897, 1919, and 1939. Names were taken from the county or township maps and are susceptible to error. In addition to owner name, records include township, section, and number of acres, if given. None of these are still in print but copies are in the Museum and some libraries. See **www.in.gov/library/2619.htm**.

■ **1914.** See ***Index of Names, History of Huntington County, Indiana* [Online Database]**, indexed at the RootsWeb site for Huntington Co IN. See **www.rootsweb.ancestry.com/~inhuntin/1914.htm.**

■ ***1914-1915 Directory and Gazetteer, Wabash City and County, Indiana* [Online Database]**, indexed at the Distant Cousin site. See **http://distantcousin.com/directories/in/wabash/1914/.**

■ ***1915 Directory, Jackson County, Indiana [*Online Database]**, indexed at the Jackson County History website. See **http://history.myjclibrary.org/books/toc.asp?book=1915directory.**

■ ***1916 Biographies, Jasper County, Indiana* [Online Database]**, indexed at the Lanewood.com site. See **www.lanewood.com/1916bioindex.htm**.

■ **1977-Current.** See ***Indiana Recent Newspaper Obituaries (1977-Current)* [Online Database],** digitized and indexed newspaper obituaries at the GenealogyBank website, including newspapers for Anderson, Aurora, Avon, Batesville, Bedford, Beech Grove, Bloomington, Bluffton, Booneville/Newburgh, Bremen, and 54 more Indiana cities. See **www.genealogybank.com/explore/obituaries/all/usa/indiana.**

---

## Indiana Periodical Articles
### Censuses & Substitute Name Lists in Genealogical Periodicals

PERSI (PERiodical Source Index) is a digitized database project of the Allen County Public Library (ACPL), Fort Wayne, IN. Since 1986, the PERSI extractors have indexed article titles, places, and surnames from over 11,000 genealogical & historical periodicals. The PERSI database is currently available online through the FindMyPast.com subscription website. The Genealogy Center of the ACPL in Fort Wayne IN holds all 11,000 periodicals and will make copies of any article by special request. To obtain an order form for requesting a printed copy of any article indexed in the PERSI database, see **http://genealogycenter.org/docs/default-source/resources/articlerequest.pdf?sfvrsn=2.**
**Indiana PERSI Search:** Using the FindMyPast.com website, the keywords "Indiana Tax" had 520 results. Early census substitutes include the following:

■ **"1787 Census, Post Vincennes, Knox County, Indiana" [Printed Article]**, in *Sycamore Leaves* (Wabash Valley Genealogical Society, Terra Haute, IN), Vol. 15, No. 4 (Jun 1985).

■ **"1802 Taxable Property, Knox County, Indiana" [Printed Article]**, in *Northwest Trail Tracer* (Northwest Territorial Genealogical Society, Vincennes, IN), Vol. 10, No. 2 (Jun 1989) through Vol. 10, No. 4 (Dec 1989).

■ **"1807 Landowners Unpaid Taxes, Clark County, Indiana" [Printed Article]**, in *Southern Indiana Genealogical Society Quarterly (*So. Indiana Gen. Soc., New Albany, IN), Vol. 7, No. 4 (Oct 1986).

■ **"1807 Census, Knox County, Indiana" [Printed Article]**, in *Sullivan County Historical Society Newsletter*, (Sullivan Co Hist. Soc., Sullivan, IN), Vol. 8, No. 3 (May 1981) through Vol. 8, No. 6 (Nov 1981).

■ **"1808 Tax Sale, Knox County, Indiana" [Printed Article]**, in *Northwest Trail Tracer* (Northwest Territorial Genealogical Society of Knox County, Indiana, Vincennes, IN), Vol. 6, No. 2 (Jun 1985).

■ **"1811 - Indiana's First Tax List" [Printed Article],** in *American Monthly Magazine*, Vol. 87, No. 5 (May 1953); and as "Taxpayers, 1811," in *Hoosier Genealogist*, Vol. 11, No. 3 (Jul 1971); and *Genealogist*, Vol. 10 (Feb 1972).

■ **"1816 Tax Levy, Harrison County, Indiana" [Printed Article]**, in *Hoosier Genealogist* (Indiana Historical Society, Indianapolis, IN), Vol. 1, No. 1 (Jan 1973).

■ **"1821 Tax List, Bartholomew County, Indiana" [Printed Article]**, in *Hoosier Journal of Ancestry* (Naomi Keith Sexton, Little York, IN), Vol. 5, No. 1 (Jan 1978).

■ **"1822 Poll Tax List, Lawrence County, Indiana" [Printed Article],** in *Seedling Patch* (Lawrence County Historical & Genealogical Society, Bedford, IN), Vol. 3 (1983).

■ **"1829 Taxpayers, Fayette County, Indiana" [Printed Article],** in *Hoosier Genealogist* (Indiana Historical Society, Indianapolis, IN), Vol. 11, No. 4 (Oct 1971).

■ **"1829 Assessment Rolls of Taxable Persons & Property, Marion County," Indiana [Printed Article]**, in *Hoosier Genealogist* (Indiana Historical Society, Indianapolis, IN), Vol. 20, No. 2 (Jun 1980).

■ **"1837 Assessment List of Taxable Property, Kosciusko County, Indiana" [Printed Article]**, in *Our Missing Links*, (Kosciusko County Historical Society, Warsaw, IN), Vol. 6, No. 1 (Spring 1982).

## Indiana Books & Microfilms at the Family History Library

The most important of Indiana's statewide census substitutes are cited below in chronological order. Each item includes a FHL book number or FHL film number, which can be used to search the FHL catalog for more details. To review an item, start at the FamilySearch catalog search page. See **https://familysearch.org/search/catalog/results.** Select "Search by Place" then "United States, Indiana" to see a list of catalog categories. Or, select "Call Number" then type an FHL book number; or select "Film/Fiche Number" to view a specific title.

■ ***1783-1815 Knox County, Indiana, Early Land Records and Court Indexes* [Printed Book]**, published by Genealogical Services and Publications, Chicago, IL, 1973, 2 vols. Contents: vol. 1: Locations entered at Vincennes, 1807-1813; Common Pleas, and county business, 1806-1810; estates; vol. 2: Lists of land donations; claims; militia donations; indexes. FHL book 977.239 R2 and R2k.

■ **1790s-1825.** See ***Indiana Marriages, Early to 1825: A Research Tool* [Printed Book]**, compiled, extracted & transcribed by Liahona Research, Inc.; edited by Jordan R. Dodd and Norman L. Moyes, published by Precision Indexing, Bountiful, UT, 1991, 345 pages. Lists names of brides and grooms in alphabetical order by surname, with name of spouse, date of marriage, and county where married. See FHL book 977.2 V22i.

■ ***1790-1829 Knox County, Indiana Deed Records* [Microfilm]**, from the original records at the Knox County Courthouse, Vincennes, IN. Original deeds recorded 1790 to 1813 were destroyed in a courthouse fire, but many of the earlier deeds were brought in and recorded again soon after the fire in 1814. Filmed by the Record Registry Corp., Indianapolis, 1936, 2 rolls, FHL film #7768 (General Index to deeds) and FHL film #7769 (Deed records).

■ **1800s.** See ***Index, Indiana Source Books* [Printed Index]**, compiled by Dorothy Riker, published by the Indiana Historical Society, Family History Section, 1983, 406 pages. Contains an index to marriages, wills and naturalizations which appeared in the *Hoosier Genealogist* (1961-1979) and which have been compiled into three volumes, including more than 115,000 names. FHL book 977.2 D29h index.

■ **1800s.** See ***Surname Index to Roster of Soldiers and Patriots of the American Revolution Buried in Indiana, Vols. I & II*** **[Typescript],** compiled by Jane E. Darlington, typed by Linda Lauer. Published by the Fort Wayne Public Library, 1976, 140 pages, FHL book 977.2 M2o v.1-2 index. For a link to a digital version, see the FHL catalog page for this title: **https://familysearch.org/search/catalog/957313.**

■ **1800s-1900s.** See ***Indiana Genealogy And Local History Sources Index*** **[Printed Book],** by Stuart Harter. Contains a list of nearly seven thousand sources of genealogy and local history for the State of Indiana, including books, booklets, periodical articles, newspaper articles, etc. dealing with virtually every type of record useful to genealogy and local history. Published by CompuGen Systems, Ft. Wayne, IN, 1985, 195 pages, FHL book 977.2 D27h.

■ **1800s-1900s.** See ***Indiana Genealogical Society Ancestor File*** **[Printed Book],** Vol. 1 compiled by Joan Morgan; Vol. 2 compiled by Karen Zach. Contains information compiled from 3x5 cards submitted by members of the society. Shows ancestor name and file number, birth place, spouse, Indiana county where settled, etc. Published by the society, Fort Wayne, IN, 1994-1997, 2 vols., 87 pages, FHL book 977.2 D22m v.1-2.

■ **1800s-1900s.** See ***Cemetery Locator File*** **[Microfilm],** from the originals compiled by the Indiana State Library, Indianapolis, IN. Consists of a card file alphabetically arranged by name of cemetery. Also indicates the county and township each cemetery is in. Filmed by the Genealogical Society of Utah, 1980, 4 rolls, beginning with FHL film #1292061 (Cemeteries A-Hi). For a complete list of roll numbers and contents of each roll, see the online FHL catalog page for this title: **https://familysearch.org/search/catalog/197640.**

■ **1800s-1900s.** See ***Cemetery Records of Indiana*** **[Typescript],** copied and typed by members of the LDS Church in Indiana. Contains inscriptions arranged alphabetically by surname, from various cemeteries in many counties and cities of Indiana. Contents: Vol. 1: Bartholomew, Hamilton, Knox, Marion, Morgan, Owen, Saint Joseph, Vigo, and Wells counties; Vol. 2: Allen, Marion, and Montgomery counties; Vol. 3: Decatur, Elkhart, Fulton, Johnson, Marion, and Miami counties; Vol. 4: Blackford, Delaware, Fayette, Hancock, Hendricks, Marion, Monroe, Morgan, Rush, and Shelby counties; Vol. 5: Blackford, Delaware, Henry, Howard, and Wabash counties; Vol. 6: Decatur, Delaware, Hendricks, Henry, Marion, Morgan, and Shelby counties. Published 1954, 6 vols., FHL book 977.2 V39c v.1-6.

■ **1800s-1900s.** See ***Index to Encyclopedia of American Quaker Genealogy*** **[Printed Book],** an index to the 600,000 names found in the six volumes by William Wade Hinshaw covering the records of the monthly Quaker meetings held in the states of Virginia, North Carolina, New Jersey, Pennsylvania, New York, Ohio, and Indiana. Many of Indiana's early Quaker communities were founded by people moving into the area from North Carolina meetings, and the Quaker monthly meeting records usually give details about the movement of members from one meeting to another. Quakers did not believe in civil recording of vital records, and any Quaker member of any Indiana meeting will have multiple mentions for birth, parents, marriage, death and burial. This comprehensive index shows the name, volume, and page where to look. Published by Genealogical Publishing Co., Baltimore, 1999, 1,155 pages, FHL book 973.D2he index.

■ **1800-1941.** See ***Indiana Vital Records Deaths Index, 1800 to 1941*** **[CD-ROM]**, published by Heritage Quest, Bountiful, UT, 2001. Includes 867,132 entries covering the period of 1800-1941, along with a few entries outside that range of years. Each entry gives details on surname, given name, sex, ethnicity, age, death month, death day, death year, county, book, page, and fiche. FHL CD No. 1188.

■ **1801-1818.** See ***Estray Book, Clark County, Indiana, 1801-1818*** **[Microfilm],** from the original at the Clark County Recorder's office, Jeffersonville, IN. Filmed by the Indiana Exchange, 1968, 1 roll, FHL film #549320.

■ **1801-1820.** See ***Indiana Territorial Pioneer Records, 1801-1820*** **[Printed Book],** compiled by Charles M. Franklin, published by Heritage House, 1983, 2 vols., 99 pages. Includes index. Contains miscellaneous records of election returns, military records, census returns, births, history, etc. Contents: v. 1. 1810-1815 -- v. 2. 1801-1820. FHL book 977.2 N4i vol. 1 & 2.

■ **1801-1877.** See ***Indiana Land Entries* [Printed Book]**, by Margaret R. Waters, originally published Indianapolis, 1948, reprinted by The Bookmark, Knightstown, IN, 1977, 2 vols. Lists names of persons who obtained (from the federal government) an original entry of land in Indiana. Contents: v. 1, Cincinnati District, 1801-1840; v. 2, Vincennes District, 1807-1877. FHL book 977.2 R2W. Also on microfilm, FHL film #6046718.

■ **1801-1899.** See ***The Hoosier Journal of Ancestry, Clark County Special* [Printed Book]**, published by the *Hoosier Journal*, Little York, IN, 1983-1992, 2 vols., includes indexes. Contains various records of genealogical value, including township histories, marriages, probate records, census records, land records, biographies, etc., gathered from many sources in Clark County. FHL book 977.2185 B2hj vol. 1 & 2.

■ ***1801-1901 Deed Records; Grantee/Grantor Index to Deeds, Clark County, Indiana* [Microfilm]**, from records located in the Clark County Recorder's Office, Jeffersonville, Indiana. Filmed by the Genealogical Society of Utah, 1985, 38 rolls, beginning with FHL film #1428648 (Grantor Index, A-R, 1801-1850). For a complete list of roll numbers and contents of each roll, see the online FHL catalog page for this title: See https://familysearch.org/search/catalog/622392.

■ **1801-1938.** See ***Clark County, Indiana, Index of Names of Persons and of Firms* [Microfilm],** from the original book compiled by the WPA of Indiana, 1938, 319 pages. Contains an index of the names of persons and firms contained in county histories, atlases, gazetteers, and miscellaneous publications. Filmed by the Genealogical Society of Utah, 1985, 1 roll, FHL film #1428705. For a link to a digital version, see the FHL catalog page for this title: **https://familysearch.org/search/catalog/622743.**

■ ***1802, 1809 Voters, Clark County, Indiana,* [Microfilm],** from a typescript located in the Jeffersonville Township Library, Jeffersonville, IN. Contains lists of voters compiled from the *National Genealogical Society Quarterly*, vol. 3, # 4, and from the *Hoosier Genealogist*, v. 2 (Mar/Apr 1961). Filmed by the Genealogical Society of Utah, 1985, 1 roll, FHL film #1428704.

■ ***1805-1830 Deed Records, Index to Deeds, 1805-1936, Dearborn County, Indiana,*** [Microfilm] from the original records at the Dearborn County courthouse, Lawrenceburg, Indiana. Filmed by the Indiana State Library, 1936, 5 rolls, beginning with FHL film #209865 (Deed index, A-B, 1805-1936). For a complete list of roll numbers and contents of each roll, see the online FHL catalog page for this title. See **https://familysearch.org/search/catalog/10794.**

■ **1806-1813.** See ***Knox County, Indiana Early Land Records, Court Indexes* [Printed Book],** by June B. Barekman and Roberta Lee Lent. Contents: Vol. 1: Locations entered at Vincennes, 1807-1813; Common Pleas, and county business, 1806-1810 estates; Vol. 2: lists of land donations; claims; militia donations; indexes. Includes index. Published by the Allen County Public Library, Ft. Wayne, IN, 1986, 2 vols., FHL book 977.239 R2b v.1-2.

■ ***1806-1833 Marriages, Dearborn County, Indiana* [Printed Book & Microfilm]**, compiled by Colleen Ridlen, published Beech Grove, IN, 1989, 44 pages. Contains an index to marriages in Dearborn County, giving names of brides and grooms, name of spouse, and date of marriage. FHL book 977.211 V22r, and FHL film #6088449.

■ ***1807 Indiana Territory Census* [Printed Book]**, facsimile of the original manuscript, published by the Indiana Historical Society, Indianapolis, 1980, 57 pages. Includes surname index. In 1807, Indiana Territory included Dearborn, Clark, and Knox counties, plus St. Clair and Randolph counties of Illinois. The 1807 Clark County census name list was missing, so the IHS added an 1807 voters list for Clark County, Indiana, and also for Kaskaskia (Randolph Co, IL). FHL book 977.2 X2c and FHL film #1033927. Another filming, FHL film #1428705.

■ **1807.** See ***Indiana 1807 Census Index* [Printed Index]**, compiled by Ronald Vern Jackson, et al, published by Accelerated Indexing Systems International, North Salt Lake, UT, 1986, 56 pages, FHL book 977.2 X22j.

■ **1807.** See ***Index to Clark County, Indiana Territory Census, 1807***, microfilm of typescript located in the Jeffersonville Township Library, Jeffersonville, Indiana. Filmed by the Genealogical Society of Utah, 1985, 1 roll, FHL film #1428704.

■ **1807-1832.** See ***Early Marriages in Indiana, Knox County, 1807-1832* [Printed Book],** by Kenneth Gene Lindsay, published by Kenma Pub., Evansville, IN, 1977, 60 pages, FHL book 977.239 V2L.

■ **1807-1840.** See ***Marriage Records of Knox County, Indiana, 1807-1840*** **[Printed Book],** copied from the originals by Mary R. Hibel and M. Joanne Coan. Contains an alphabetical listing by surname of men, and of women showing to whom they were married and date of marriage. Published by M.R. Hibel, Vincennes, IN, 1964, 134 pages, FHL book 977.239 V2h. For a link to a digital version, see the FHL catalog page for this title:
**https://familysearch.org/search/catalog/565857.**

■ **1807-1841.** See ***Tract Book, Lands Sold, Harrison County, Indiana, 1807-1841*** **[Microfilm],** from the original at the Harrison County Recorder's Office, Corydon, IN. Filmed by the Indiana Exchange, 1968, 1 roll, FHL film #549372.

■ **1807-1960.** See ***Marriage Records, Knox County, Indiana, 1807-1960*** **[Microfilm],** from the original Circuit Court marriage volumes located at the Knox County Courthouse in Vincennes, IN. Each volume indexed. Filmed by the Genealogical Society of Utah, 2009, 26 rolls, beginning with FHL film #1149418 (Marriages, 1807-1832). For a complete list of roll numbers and contents of each roll, see the online FHL catalog page for this title:
**https://familysearch.org/search/catalog/1780486.**

■ **1808-1817.** See **Estray Book, Harrison County, Indiana [Microfilm],** from the original at the Harrison County Recorder's Office, Corydon, IN Filmed by the Indiana Exchange, 1968, 1 roll, FHL film #549372.

■ **1809, 1812.** See ***Indiana Election Returns, 1809, 1812*** **[Printed Book],** compiled by John D. & Diane Stemmons. Published by Census Pub. LLC, Sandy, UT, 2004, 278 pages. FHL book 977.2 N4s.

■ **1808-1818.** See ***Jeffersonville Land Entries*** **[Printed Book],** compiled by Janet C. Cowen. Entries are arranged both alphabetically by surname and in numerical order. Contains an index to entries in the original land office records. Includes the counties of Bartholomew, Brown, Clark, Crawford, Decatur, Floyd, Harrison, Jackson, Jefferson, Jennings, Lawrence, Monroe, Orange, Ripley, Scott, Switzerland, and Washington counties. Published by J.C. Cowen, Indianapolis, 1984, 200 pages, FHL book 977.2 R2c.

■ ***1809-1886 Deed Records; Grantee-Grantor Index to Deeds, 1809-1888, Harrison County, Indiana*** **[Microfilm],** from the original records located at the Harrison County Courthouse, Corydon, Indiana. Filmed by the Genealogical Society of Utah, 1984, 28 rolls, beginning with FHL film #1404902 (Grantee Index, 1809-1863). For a complete list of roll numbers and contents of each roll, see the online FHL catalog page for this title:
**https://familysearch.org/search/catalog/470691.**

■ **1809-1923.** See ***Will Records, Harrison County, Indiana, 1809-1923*** **[Microfilm],** from the original records at the Harrison County Courthouse, Corydon, IN. Filmed by the Genealogical Society of Utah, 1984, 4 rolls, beginning with FHL film #1404686 (Will records 1809-1832). For a complete list of roll numbers and contents of each roll, see the online FHL catalog page for this title:
**https://familysearch.org/search/catalog/90532.**

■ **1810-1813**. See ***Early Records of Harrison County, Indiana*** **[Microfilm]**, microfilm of original manuscript compiled by Walter S. Beanblossom, published 1975. Includes index. Contains the 1810 census and the 1813 tax list of Harrison Co., Indiana. Filmed by the Genealogical Society of Utah, 1976, 1 roll, FHL film #928263.

■ **1810-1920.** See ***Records of Harrison County, Indiana, from Walter Beanblossom's Collection, and Reprints From the "Ancestral News"*** **[Printed Book]**, compiled by Sherry Healy for the Ancestral Trails Historical Society, Inc., Vine Grove, KY, published by McDowell Publications, Utica, KY, 150 pages; Includes surname index. Contains abstracts from 1810 census records, tax lists of 1812-1813, voter lists of 1818, mortality schedule for 1850, naturalizations of 1841-1846, and 1855-1920, citizenships for 1852, Indiana Legion (organization of companies with lists of officers and soldiers), short histories of townships, and first marriage records of Harrison County. FHL book 977.221 H2h.

■ **1810-1918.** See ***Probate Records, Harrison County, Indiana, 1810-1918*** **[Microfilm],** from the original Circuit Court records located at the Harrison County Courthouse, Corydon, IN. Includes surname indexes. Filmed by the Genealogical Society of Utah, 1984, 25 rolls, beginning with FHL film #1404691 (Index, 1810-1923). For a complete list of roll numbers and contents of each roll, see the online FHL catalog page for this title:
**https://familysearch.org/search/catalog/91332.**

■ **1815-1860.** See ***Knox County, Indiana, Divorce Records, 1815-1860*** **[Printed Book],** compiled by Brian Spangle. Contains an index to divorce records, arranged in alphabetical order by surname of plaintiff, giving name of spouse, year when filed, code to original record (circuit court order book, Knox County court files or common pleas order book), volume and page numbers, box and file numbers. Cases were filed between 1815 and 1860. Publisher info not given, published 1996, 14 pages, FHL book 977.239 V22s.

■ **1815-1817.** See ***Knox County, Indiana, Index to Deed Record, A, 1815-1817*** **[Typescript],** compiled by Roberta Lee Lent and June B. Barekman, 24 pages, FHL book 977.239 R2L. For a link to a digital version, see the FHL catalog page for this title: **https://familysearch.org/search/catalog/167578.**

■ **1816-1884.** See ***Mortality Records, Knox County, Indiana, 1816-1884*** **[Microfilm],** from the original manuscript prepared by the DAR, Francis Vigo Chapter, Vincennes, IN, 1946, 42 pages. Filmed by the Genealogical Society of Utah, 1970, 1 roll, FHL film #849926.

■ **1820s-1930s.** See ***Indiana Biographical Index*** **[Microfiche]**, compiled by Lyman Platt and Jimmy Parker, microfiche of original typescript published by Genealogical Indexing Associates, Salt Lake City, 1983. This is an updated name index to biographical sketches in virtually all published Indiana county histories, which began as a WPA project in 1938, and was continued by the Indiana Historical Society in 1979. Earlier version: ***Index to Persons and Firms***, which, along with all of the county histories referenced, can be found at the Indiana State Library in Indianapolis; the Allen County Public Library in Fort Wayne; or the Family History Library in Salt Lake City. Filmed by the Genealogical Society of Utah, 1984, 16 microfiche, FHL fiche #6331353.

■ **1821-1906.** See ***Marion County, Indiana Records Miscellanea*** **[Printed Book[,** compiled by Jane E. Darlington. Includes surname index. Contains abstracts of: naturalizations filed 1832-1903; naturalizations filed 1904-1906; delinquent tax returns for 1842; Probate Court record A, 1822-1832; land records 1821-1824; tract book 1821-1851; hack licenses 1865-1871. Published by the Indiana Historical Society, Family History Section, Indianapolis, 1986, FHL book 977.252 P4d.

■ **1822-1849.** See ***Marriages and Deaths From Indianapolis Newspapers*** **[Printed Book & CD-ROM],** compiled by Ron Darrah from information in three Indianapolis newspapers. Printed volume: 1822-1829; 2 CD volumes: 1830-1839 & 1840-1849. Also includes abstracts of divorce and probate notices. Published by the Genealogical Society of Marion County, Indiana, Indianapolis, 2001. FHL book 977.252/I1 B38d, FHL CD No. 6982 (1830-1839) and CD No. 6982 (1840-1849).

■ ***1823-1852 Ft. Wayne Land Office Entries*** **[Printed Index]**, transcribed from the original tract books at the Indiana State Archives, Indianapolis. Tract books transcribed by Barbara S. Wolfe; data compiled by Helen S. Morrison, published by the State Archives, 199?, 138 pages. Contains an alphabetical listing by surname prepared by the Indiana State Archives of individual names of persons who purchased land in the areas now covered by the counties of Adams, Allen, Blackford, Cass, Clinton, DeKalb, Delaware, Grant, Howard, Huntington, Jay, Kosciusko, Lagrange, Madison, Miami, Noble, Randolph, Steuben, Tipton, Wabash, Wells and Whitley. This index serves a computerized database of 73,250 records that can be accessed at the Indiana State Archives in Indianapolis. See FHL book 977.2 R22f.

■ **1824-1848.** See ***Indiana Tax Lists*** **[Printed Book]**, compiled by Jane E. Darlington, pub. 1990, 2 vols. Includes surname indexes. Arranged by county and townships, and lists name, poll, acres, section, township, and range. Contents: v. 1: Bartholomew Co., 1843, Dearborn Co., 1842, Fayette Co., 1842, Greene Co., 1843, Harrison Co., 1844, Marshall Co., 1843 (with Starke Co.), Morgan Co., 1840, Noble Co., 1847, Perry Co., 1835, and 1824-1826, 1828, 1829, 1832, 1836-1837, 1840-1843, 1845, Scott Co., 1839; v. 2: Posey Co., 1842, Putnam Co., 1845, Spencer Co., 1846, Tippecanoe Co., 1848, Switzerland Co., 1843, Vigo Co., 1824-1828, Whitley Co., 1841. FHL book 977.2 R4d v. 1 & 2.

■ **1835.** See ***Lockerbie's Assessment List of Indianapolis 1835*** **[Printed Book],** edited by Eliza G. Browning. Originally published as Volume IV, Number 7, 1909 of Indiana Historical Society. Published by the Genealogical Society of Marion County, Indiana, Indianapolis, IN, 2001, 100 pages, FHL book 977.252/I1 R4b.

■ **1848-1888.** See ***Indianapolis Newspaper Divorce Notices, 1848-1888*** **[Microfilm],** from the original index cards located at the Indiana State Library, Indianapolis. Contains a card index to divorce notices arranged alphabetically by surname, and giving date of divorce, and names of parties involved, page and column numbers, and reference to a newspaper. Filmed by the Genealogical Society of Utah, 1986, 1 roll, FHL film #1462568.

■ **1852-1865.** See ***Indiana Negro Registers*** **[Printed Book],** compiled by Coy D. Robbins. Includes surname index. The registers were compiled by the clerks of the circuit courts within the counties of Bartholomew, Floyd, Franklin, Gibson, Harrison, Hendricks, Jackson, Jefferson, Jennings, Knox, Martin, Ohio, Orange, Switzerland and Washington counties. If free negroes could provide written evidence of their manumission, they were entitled to have their names registered. Once registered, a free negro had legal status in the county. This was a protection against slave hunters from slave states (like Kentucky) raiding Indiana areas looking for escaped slaves. Published by Heritage Books, Bowie, MD, 1994, 185 pages, FHL book 977.2 F2r.

■ ***1858-1861 Indiana (State) Directories*** **[Microfilm],** from originals, filmed by Research Publications, Woodbridge, CT, 1980-1984, 22 fiche, as follows:

- **1858-1859** G. W. Hawes' Indiana State Gazetteer and Business Directory, (10 fiche) FHL film #6043990.
- **1860-1861** George W. Hawes' Indiana State Gazetteer and Business Directory (12 fiche), FHL film #6043991.

■ ***1857-1935 Richmond (Indiana) City Directories*** **[Microfilm],** from originals published by various publishers. The FHL has 1857, 1860-1861,1883-1891, 1893-1894, 1897-1898, 1901-1908, 1910, 1912, 1914, 1916, 1918, 1921-1931, 1933 & 1935. Filmed by Research Publications, Woodbridge, CT, 1980-1984, 1995, 3 fiche, 7 rolls, beginning with FHL fiche #6044389 (1857 directory), and FHL film #2156576 (1883-1884 directory). For a complete list of fiche/roll numbers and contents of each, see the online FHL catalog page for this title:
**https://familysearch.org/search/catalog/534213.**

■ ***1858-1935 Fort Wayne (Indiana) City Directories*** **[Microfilm],** from originals published by various publishers. The FHL has 1858-1862, 1864-1880, 1883-1912, and 1914-1935. Filmed by Research Publications, Woodbridge, CT, 1980-1984, 4 fiche & 31 rolls, beginning with FHL fiche #6043916 (2 fiche, 1858-1859 directory) and fiche #6043917 (2 fiche, 1860-1861 directory); and FHL roll #1376874 (1861-1862 directory). For a complete list of roll numbers and contents of each roll, see the online FHL catalog page for this title:
**https://familysearch.org/search/catalog/534762.**

■ **1861-1865.** See ***Index to Compiled Service Records of Volunteer Union Soldiers Who Served in Organizations from the State of Indiana*** **[Microfilm],** from the original records at the National Archives, Washington, DC. Filmed by the National Archives, series M540, 1964, 86 rolls, beginning with FHL film #881722 (A-Al), For a complete list of roll numbers and contents of each roll, see the online FHL catalog page for this title:
**https://familysearch.org/search/catalog/87183.**

■ **1861-1865.** See ***Indiana Substitutes Hired for Civil War*** **[Microfilm],** from the original index cards located at the Indiana State Library, Indianapolis, IN. Contains name of man hiring a substitute and the "see" reference to a service record card (with the name of the substitute). Filmed by the Genealogical Society of Utah, 1988, 1 roll, FHL film #1556876.

■ **1861-1940s.** See ***American Legion Record Book of Burials in Indiana*** **[Microfilm],** from the original record book located at the Morrison Reeves Library, Richmond, IN. Contains a list of cemeteries found in the record and an alphabetical list by surname of veterans of the Civil War, World War I, and World War II, and the cemetery in which each is buried. Filmed by the Genealogical Society of Utah, 1988, 1 roll, FHL film #1548951.

■ ***1862-1866 Internal Revenue Assessment Lists for Indiana*** **[Microfilm],** from original manuscripts located in the National Archives, Washington, DC. Lists are arranged alphabetically by surname of those being assessed for each period. Filmed by the National Archives, 1987, 42 rolls, beginning with FHL film #1491004 (District 1, division 9, special lists 1864, annual lists 1862-1864; and Divisions 9 and 11, monthly and special lists, Dec. 1862-Dec. 1866). For a complete list of roll numbers and contents for each roll, see the online FHL catalog page for this title:
**https://familysearch.org/search/catalog/636046.**

■ **1864-1970.** See ***Burial Records, Crown Hill Cemetery, Indianapolis, Indiana*** **[Microfilm],** from the original card index to burials, giving name of deceased and location of grave or crypt, and date of burial. Filmed by the Records Security Corp., Indianapolis, 1970, 23 rolls, beginning with FHL film #543343 (Burials A-Bartlein). For a complete list of roll numbers and contents of each roll, see the online FHL catalog page for this title:
**https://familysearch.org/search/catalog/340557.**

■ **1886-1894.** See ***Enrollment of the Late Soldiers, Their Widows and Orphans of the Late Armies of the United States, Residing in the State of Indiana for the year 1886-1894*** **[Microfilm],** from original records located at the Indiana State Library, Indianapolis. Contains an enrollment of persons in the War of 1812; the War with Mexico; the Civil War and of all wars of the United States with Indian tribes. Arranged by county and by each township within a county, alphabetically by surname. By enactment of

the General Assembly of the State of Indiana, each township assessor at the time of taking lists of property for taxation, was to list all persons who served in the United States armies, as well as their widows and orphans. Assessors were to return their listings to the County Clerks who in turn sent them to the Adjutant General for the State to be put on permanent file in his office. Filmed by the Genealogical Society of Utah, 1988-1990, 89 rolls, beginning with FHL film #1605057 (Adams, Bartholomew counties, 1886- ). For a complete list of roll numbers and the contents of each roll, see the online FHL catalog page for this title:
**https://familysearch.org/search/catalog/596163.**

■ **1889-1935.** See ***Muncie (Indiana) City Directories*** **[Microfilm],** from the original records published by various publishers. The FHL has 1889, 1897-1932, 1934-1935. Various directories include Delaware County towns of Gaston, Daleville, Albany, Cowan, Desoto, Eaton, Oakville, Royerton, Selma, Shideler, Wheeling, and Yorktown. Filmed by Research Publications, Woodbridge, CT, 1995, 10 rolls, beginning with FHL film #2156575 (Emerson's 1889 Muncie directory). For a complete list of roll numbers and contents of each roll, see the online FHL catalog page for this title:
**https://familysearch.org/search/catalog/982206.**

■ ***1914-1919 World War I Indiana Enrollment Cards*** **[Microfilm],** from the originals at the Indiana State Archives, Indianapolis, IN. Contains: statement-of-service cards, arranged in alphabetical order by surname, furnished primarily for historical and statistical purposes. Lists name, army serial number, race, residence, where inducted, date inducted, place of birth, age, organizations served in with dates of assignments and transfers, grades with date of appointment, engagements, wounds or other injuries received in action, service overseas, honorably discharged or demobilization date, percent disabled in view of occupation, and remarks. Filmed by the Genealogical Society of Utah, 1990, 35 rolls, beginning with Aarnink, Clifford F. – Baker, Ollie, FHL film #1674855. For a complete of roll numbers and contents of each roll, see the online FHL catalog page for this title:
**https://familysearch.org/search/catalog/625091.**

■ ***1917-1918 World War I Selective Service System Draft Registration Cards (Indiana)*** **[Microfilm],** from the originals at the National Archives Regional Branch in East Point, GA, part of series M1509. The draft cards are arranged alphabetically by state, then alphabetically by county or city draft board, and then alphabetically by surname of the registrants. 115 rolls cover the Indiana cards on microfilm, beginning with FHL film #1439777 (Adams County, A-Z, Allen County, A-F). For a complete list of roll numbers and contents of each roll, see the online FHL catalog page for this title:
**https://familysearch.org/search/catalog/746975.**

■ **1919-1970.** See ***Cemetery Records to 1970, Washington Park Cemetery, Indianapolis, Indiana*** **[Microfilm],** from the original records. Includes interments in the Garden Mausoleum, Mount Vernon Mausoleum and cemetery burials. Filmed by the Records Security Corp., Indianapolis, 1970, 6 rolls, beginning with FHL film #543440 (Garden Mausoleum, et al). For a complete list of roll numbers and contents of each roll, see the online FHL catalog page for this title:
**https://familysearch.org/search/catalog/340554.**

■ ***1942 World War II Draft Registration Cards (Indiana), United States Selective Service System,*** **[Microfilm]** of original records at the National Archives and Records Administration, Great Lakes Region, Chicago, Illinois. These cards represent older men, ages 45 to 65 on April 27, 1942, that were registered for the draft. They had birth dates between 28 April 1877 and 16 Feb 1897. The cards are arranged in alphabetical order by surname. Includes name, place of residence, age, place of birth, date of birth, race, weight, height, employer's name and address, name and address of person who would always know their address, color of eyes and hair. Filmed by the Genealogical Society of Utah, 2001, 174 rolls, beginning with FHL film #2240128 (Aabel, Hans - Alexander, Harley J.). For a complete list of roll numbers and contents of each roll, see the online FHL catalog page for this title:
**https://familysearch.org/search/catalog/1106813.**

■ **1963-1973.** See ***Hoosier Ancestors Index*** **[Microfilm],** compiled by Eloise R. Means and Pearl Brenton. Contains all newspaper columns and an index to all queries and responses published in the Hoosier Ancestors, a column written by Pearl Benton, and appearing in the Indianapolis Sunday Star between June 1963 and June 1973. The original copy is located at the Martinsville Public Library. Filmed by the Genealogical Society of Utah, 1987, 2 rolls, FHL #1502906 (Index, June 1963-Dec 1970 ; column, July 1967-Sep 1969), and FHL film #1502907 (Column, Sept 1969 – June 1973).

# MICHIGAN
## Censuses & Substitutes, 1700-2015

For a thorough review of Michigan's State Censuses, see "State Censuses of Michigan: A Tragedy of Lost Treasures," by LeRoy Barnett, an article in *Family Trails* (MI State Library), Vol. 6, No. 1 (Summer-Fall 1978). The following list of censuses taken in the area of Michigan covers the French colonial period, British colonial period, Michigan Territory period; and censuses taken by the state of Michigan. Name lists for all of the censuses were published as printed extracts/indexes, microfilm of originals, or online digitized versions. Refer to the full bibliographic entries for more details for each of the following:

■ **Michigan Censuses, 1710-1830,** ***Under the French, British and Americans,*** a book by Donna Valley Russell:

- **1710. French Colonial Census**. Detroit area.
- **1750. French Colonial Census.** Detroit area.
- **1762. French Colonial Census.** Detroit area.
- **1765. British Colonial Census.** Detroit area.
- **1768. British Colonial Census.** Detroit area.
- **1779. British Colonial Census.** Detroit area.
- **1780. British Colonial Census.** Fort St. Joseph.
- **1782. British Colonial Census.** Detroit, and south shore of Detroit River.
- **1792. British Colonial Census.** Petite Côte (south shore of Detroit River).
- **1796. British Colonial Census.** Detroit area.
- **1805-1806. Michigan Territorial Census.** Detroit area.

■ **State Censuses, 1827-1874.** Searchable databases online at the Seeking Michigan website:

- **1827. Michigan Territorial Census.** Surviving Name lists for Wayne (Detroit), Monroe (Lawrence Twp.), Chippewa, and Washtenaw counties only.
- **1834. Michigan Territorial Census.** Tallies only; names not included except in Crawford Co (now Wisconsin) and Lenawee County.
- **1837. Michigan State Census.** Tallies only; individual names not included except in Kalamazoo County.
- **1845. Michigan State Census**. Only males over 21 years by name, and females in age categories. Includes Eaton, Lenawee, Oakland, St. Clair, St. Joseph, Van Buren, and Washtenaw counties only.
- **1854. Michigan State Census**. Only males over 21 years by name, and females in age categories. Includes population, agricultural, and industrial schedules, for Eaton County only.
- **1864. Michigan State Census**. Only males over 21 years by name, and females in age categories. Includes population, agricultural, and industrial schedules, with name lists for Clinton, Eaton, Houghton, and Sanilac counties only.
- **1874. Michigan State Census.** Only males over 21 years by name, and females in age categories. Incudes population schedules for Branch, Eaton, Houghton, and Kalamazoo counties only.

■ **State Censuses, 1884-1894.** Searchable databases online at the Seeking Michigan website:

- **1884. Michigan State Census.** This detailed modern census lists the names of all members of a household, relationship to the head of house, age, sex, color, place of birth, parent's place of birth, occupation, and much more. Includes population, mortality, agricultural, industrial, or social statistics schedules in Allegan, Braga, Barry, Bay, Benzie, Emmet, Hillsdale, Ingham, Iosco, Isabella, Jackson, Kalamazoo, Kent, Keweenaw, Lake, Lapeer, Leelanau, Lenawee, Menominee, Midland, Montcalm, Muskegon, Newaygo, Ottawa, Roscommon, Sanilac, St. Clair, St. Joseph, Van Buren (Paw Paw Twp.), Washtenaw, Wayne (excluding Detroit), and Wexford counties.
- **1894. Michigan State Census.** (Available online at several websites). This detailed modern census lists the names of all members of a household, relationship to the head of house, age, sex, color, place of birth, parent's place of birth, occupation, and much more. Includes population, mortality, agricultural, industrial, or social statistics schedules in Allegan, Barry, Bay, Benzie, Dickinson, Emmet, Gratiot, Hillsdale, Ingham, Iosco, Isabella, Jackson, Kalamazoo, Kent, Keweenaw, Lapeer, Lenawee, Livingston, Menominee, Midland, Montcalm, Muskegon, Newaygo, Ottawa, Roscommon, Sanilac, St. Clair, St. Joseph, and Washtenaw counties.

■ **Michigan's Federal Censuses:** 1810 (fragments from Michillimackinac & Detroit only), 1820-1880 (extant); 1890 (lost); 1900-1940 (extant). The Michigan state copies of federal censuses for 1820, 1850, 1860, 1870 &1880 are unique. These state copies are identified in the FHL Books/Microfilm section.

## SEEKING MICHIGAN: Online Databases at the Archives of Michigan Website

The ***Seeking Michigan*** collection is an online service of the Archives of Michigan. It includes digitized databases and indexes, research guides, a blog, and educator resources. New material is added frequently, and there are a number of collections ranging from pre-statehood to the late 1960s. These include letters, diaries, photographs, postcards, and video. For the complete list of databases, see the "About" page: **http://seekingmichigan.org/about.** There are searchable databases of primary interest to genealogists, including the following:

■ **1820s-1950s.** See ***GLO Plat Maps (Archives of Michigan)* [Online Database],** digitized at the Seeking Michigan collection of the Archives of Michigan website. Poorly described at the website, this collection is potentially a powerful finding aid to the first land owners of Michigan. These GLO Plat Maps are from the first surveys done in Michigan, all based on the *Michigan Meridian*, first established in 1815. The first Government Land Office (GLO) was at Detroit, followed by those at Monroe, Genesee Township, Ionia, and Kalamazoo. You can browse through over 1,800 images, or use the Advanced Search option to search by county, township, date, and more. The best use of these GLO Plat Maps may be after you have an exact property description (Range/Township/Section) from an original entry of land or a deed record. See **http://seekingmichigan.contentdm.oclc.org/cdm/search/collection/p15147coll10.**

■ **1827-1874.** See ***Michigan State Census Records, 1827-1874* [Online Database],** digitized and indexed at the Seeking Michigan collection at the Archives of Michigan website. This collection consists of approximately 1,000 page images of Michigan state census population schedules. The information collected varies by year and location, but only male heads of households and males over the age of 21 were listed by name. Other household members may have been counted, but not named. This collection of state census records is incomplete because many of the documents have been lost over time. It contains records from the following counties and years: Branch (1857, 1874), Clinton (1864), Eaton (1845, 1854, 1864, 1874), Houghton (1864, 1874), Lenawee (1845), Kalamazoo (1874), St. Joseph (1845), Sanilac (1864), and Washtenaw (1827, 1845, 1854). To search for a name, go to the Advanced Search option. When the menu opens, the default collection is for "Death Records, 1897-1920" which needs to be unchecked, then check "State Census Records, 1827-1874." See **http://seekingmichigan.org/discover/state-census-1827-1874.**

■ **1861-1865.** See ***Michigan Civil War Service Records* [Online Database],** digitized and indexed at the Seeking Michigan collections of the Archives of Michigan website. These documents are from the Michigan Adjutant General. See **http://cdm16317.contentdm.oclc.org/cdm/search/collection/p4006coll15.**

■ **1861-1865.** See ***Michigan Civil War Photographs* [Online Database],** digitized and indexed at the Seeking Michigan collections of the Archives of Michigan website. See **http://cdm16317.contentdm.oclc.org/cdm/search/collection/p4006coll3.**

■ **1861-1865.** See ***Michigan Civil War Manuscripts* [Online Database],** digitized and indexed at the Seeking Michigan collections of the Archives of Michigan website. See **http://cdm16317.contentdm.oclc.org/cdm/search/collection/p129401coll15.**

■ **1880s-1990s.** See ***The Detroit News Indexes* [Online Database],** indexed at the Seeking Michigan collection at the Archives of Michigan website. This subject index of *The Detroit News* newspaper totals more than 1 million index cards. The tables are arranged alphabetically by subject and date approximately from the late 1800's to the late 1990's. An index card at Seeking Michigan indicates that there is a clipping file for those articles. Researchers may then request to look in the clippings file at the Archives of Michigan for the actual articles cited or visit a research institution that has the newspaper on microfilm. See **http://seekingmichigan.org/about/indexes.**

■ **1884-1894.** See ***Michigan State Census Records, 1884-1894* [Online Database],** digitized and indexed at the Seeking Michigan collection at the Archives of Michigan website. Both the 1884 and 1894 state censuses can be searched here, and a scanned image of the census page can be viewed and printed, as well as the indexed textual information. To search for a name, go to the Advanced Search option. When the menu opens, the default collection is for "Death Records, 1897-1920" which needs to be unchecked, then check "Michigan State Census Records, 1884-1894." This database has about 62,000 page images of Michigan state census population schedules. See **http://seekingmichigan.org/discover/state-census-1884-1894.**

■ **1897-1920.** See ***Michigan Death Records, 1897-1920* [Online Database],** digitized and indexed at the Seeking Michigan collections of the Archives of Michigan. A scanned image of a death certificate can be viewed and printed. See **http://cdm16317.contentdm.oclc.org/cdm/search/collection/p129401coll7.**

■ **1921-1952.** See ***Michigan Death Records, 1921-1952* [Online Database],** digitized and indexed at the Seeking Michigan collections at the Archives of Michigan website. This collection consists of over 1.6 million death records created between 1921 and 1952. Records created between 1921 and 1939 include an image of the death certificate. Records from 1940-1952 are index-only. To search for a name, go to the Advanced Search option. When the menu opens, the default collection is for "Death Records, 1897-1920" which needs to be unchecked, then check "Michigan Death Records, 1921-1952." See **http://seekingmichigan.org/discover/death-records-1921-1952.**

---

## Michigan Databases Online at Ancestry.com

The Ancestry.com subscription website allows free access to all indexes, but to view any particular record requires a membership. Ancestry offers trial memberships and subscriptions for short periods and reduced rates. The following databases at the Ancestry.com website are unique to Michigan under the categories, Census & Voter Lists, Vital Records, Military, Immigrations, et al.

■ **1784-1980.** See ***Michigan, Wills and Probate Records, 1784-1980* [Online Database],** indexed at the Ancestry.com website. An Ancestry database extracted from Michigan county, district, and probate courts. In most cases, probates mention the names and residences of beneficiaries and their relationship to the decedent. An inventory of the estate assets can reveal personal details about the deceased's occupation and lifestyle. There may also be references to debts, deeds, and other documents related to the settling of the estate. This database has 251,274 records. See **http://search.ancestry.com/search/db.aspx?dbid=8793.**

■ **1800-2010.** See ***Web: Indiana and Michigan, Michiana Genealogical Cemetery Index, 1800-2010* [Online Database],** indexed at the Ancestry.com website. This database is also accessible at the South Bend Area Genealogical Society website. This database has 187,743 records. See **http://search.ancestry.com/search/db.aspx?dbid=70492.**

■ **1820-1989.** See ***Wayne County, Michigan* [Online Databases],** indexed at the Ancestry.com website. Includes 1820-1965 Wyandotte, Wayne County, Michigan, Death Index; 1852-1853 Shove's business advertiser, and Detroit directory; 1853-1857 Johnston's Detroit city directory; 1863-1872 Clark & Co.'s city directory of Detroit; 1869 Holland's Detroit business directory; 1872-1873 Hubbell & Weeks' city directory of Detroit; 1872-1873 Detroit city directory 1873-1874 Weeks directory of Detroit; 1874-1875 Weeks directory of Detroit; 1875-1876 Weeks directory of Detroit; 1876-1877 Weeks directory of Detroit 1879 Detroit city directory; 1881-1908 Dau's Detroit blue book 1882 Detroit city directory; 1883 Detroit blue book; 1884 Detroit city directory; 1885 Detroit city directory; 1886 Detroit city and Wayne County directory; 1887 Detroit city directory; 1890 Detroit, Michigan Directory; 1893 Detroit city directory; 1894 Detroit city directory; 1895 Detroit city directory; 1897 Detroit pocket business directory 1905-1963 Detroit Border Crossings and Passenger and Crew Lists; 1941 Polk's Dearborn (Wayne County, Mich.) city directory; 1942 The new church register of the Grosse Pointe Woods Presbyterian Church; 1943 Polk's Dearborn (Wayne County, Mich.) city directory; 1946 Dearborn (Wayne County, Mich.) city directory; 1947 Detroit? Directory; 1948 Dearborn (Wayne County, Mich.) city directory; 1952 Directory of Negro businesses, professions and churches for Detroit and environs; and 1989 Directory, Vinewood Avenue Church of Christ. See **http://search.ancestry.com/Places/US/Michigan/Wayne/Default.aspx.**

■ **1807-1908.** See ***Michigan, Homestead and Cash Entry Patents, Pre-1908* [Online Database],** indexed at the Ancestry.com website. This database was originally digitized by the Bureau of Land Management as part of the General Land Office Automated Records Project, 1994. The 1807-1907 Card Files database (FHL microfilm) is not indexed by the name of the person purchasing land – this database is fully indexed by name, land office, and more. This database has 160,962 records. See **http://search.ancestry.com/search/db.aspx?dbid=2075.**

■ **1817-1850.** See ***Michigan Marriages to 1850* [Online Database],** indexed at the Ancestry.com website. Originally compiled by Liahona Research, edited by Jordan Dodd, from microfilm at the Family History Library in Salt Lake City. Each entry includes groom, bride, marriage date, county, and state. Every name is indexed so you can search for one name, or two names that are linked. This database has 13,881 records. See **http://search.ancestry.com/search/db.aspx?dbid=2092.**

■ **1827-1870.** See ***Michigan, Compiled Census and Census Substitutes Index, 1827-1870*** **[Online Database],** indexed at the Ancestry.com website. Source: Ronald Jackson, editor, Accelerated Indexing Systems, Salt Lake City, 1999. This collection contains the following indexes: 1827 Territorial Census Index; 1837 Kalamazoo County Index; 1840 Federal Census Index; 1840 Pensioners List; 1845 State Census Index; 1850 Federal Census Index; 1860 Federal Census Index; 1870 Federal Census Index; Early Census Index. This database has 299,144 records. See
**http://search.ancestry.com/search/db.aspx?dbid=3554.**

■ **1837-1903.** See ***Michigan, Index to Eastern District Naturalizations, 1837-1903*** **[Online Database],** indexed at the Ancestry.com website. Source: Book, same title, by Loretto Szucs, 1977. This database has 60 pages. See
**http://search.ancestry.com/search/db.aspx?dbid=6613.**

■ **1851-1875.** See ***Michigan Marriages, 1851-1875*** **[Online Database],** indexed at the Ancestry.com website. Originally compiled by Liahona Research, edited by Jordan Dodd, from microfilm at the Family History Library in Salt Lake City. This update adds records of Wayne County to those of Branch, Hillsdale, Jackson, and Kent counties. Includes the names of both bride and groom, the date of the marriage, and the place of the marriage. This database has 51,913 records. See
**http://search.ancestry.com/search/db.aspx?dbid=5299.**

■ **1855-1870.** See ***Marriages and Deaths Mentioned in the Lansing State Republican, 1855-1870*** **[Online Database],** indexed at the Ancestry.com website. Source: Book, same title, by Theodore G. Foster, publ. 1990. This database has 94 pages. See
**http://search.ancestry.com/search/db.aspx?dbid=20188.**

■ **1861-1865.** See ***Record of Service of Michigan Volunteers in the Civil War, 1861-1865*** **[Online Database],** indexed at the Ancestry.com website. Source: Book, same title, publ. Ihling Bros. & Everad, Kalamazoo, MI, 1903. This is a 46-vol. set of records for every regiment of Michigan, including rosters of all participants. This database has 7,479 pages. See
**http://search.ancestry.com/search/db.aspx?dbid=18555.**

■ **1861-1865.** See ***Alphabetical General Index to Public Library Sets of 85,271 Names of Michigan Soldiers and Sailors Individual Records*** **[Online Database],** indexed at the Ancestry.com website. Source: *Michigan Soldiers and Sailors Individual Records*, publ. by the MI Secretary of State, 1915. The GAR is referenced as the major proponent of this publication. This database has 1,081 pages. See
**http://search.ancestry.com/search/db.aspx?dbid=18556.**

■ **1867-1911.** See ***Michigan, Births and Christenings Index, 1867-1911*** **[Online Database],** indexed at the Ancestry.com website. FamilySearch extractions from county records on microfilm at the Family History Library. Each record may include: name, gender, race, birthplace, birth date, date of christening, place of christening, age at christening, death date, age at death father's name, age, birthplace, mother's name, age, birthplace, paternal grandparents, maternal grandparents, and FHL film number. This database has 916,602 records. See
**http://search.ancestry.com/search/db.aspx?dbid=2560.**

■ **1867-1950.** See ***Michigan, Death Records, 1867-1950*** **[Online Database],** indexed at the Ancestry.com website. Source: MI State Vital Records. This collection contains death registers (1867-1897) as well as certificates (1897-1941) from the state of Michigan. Records may include: name of the decedent and place of death, gender, color or race, marital status, date of birth, age, occupation, birthplace, father's name and birthplace, mother's name and birthplace, name and address of informant, date filed, date of death, physician's statement and cause of death, length of residence, if in a hospital or institution, date and place of burial, name and address of undertaker, later records may include spouse's name. This database has 8,380,545 records. See
**http://search.ancestry.com/search/db.aspx?dbid=60872.**

■ **1867-1952.** See ***Michigan, Marriage Records, 1867-1952*** **[Online Database],** indexed at the Ancestry.com website. Source: MI State Vital Statistics. This collection contains marriage registers (1868-1925) as well as licenses and certificates (1926-1952) from the state of Michigan. Records may include: name, residence, spouse, marriage date and place, race/color, age, occupation, witnesses, father's name, and mother's name. This database has 15,032,934 records. See
**http://search.ancestry.com/search/db.aspx?dbid=9093.**

■ **1867-1995.** See ***Michigan, Deaths and Burials Index, 1867-1995*** **[Online Database],** indexed at the Ancestry.com website. Source: FamilySearch extractions from county records on microfilm at the Family History Library. Each record may include:

name, gender, race, birth date, birthplace, occupation, residence, street address, marital status, spouse, date of death, age at death, place of death, place of burial, date of burial, cemetery name, father's name and birthplace, mother's name and birthplace, and FHL film number. This database has 1,335,443 records. See **http://search.ancestry.com/search/db.aspx?dbid=2549.**

■ ***1884 Census of the State of Michigan (2 Vol. Statistical Report)* [Online Database],** digitized and indexed at the Ancestry.com website. Source: Census of the State of Michigan, 1884, publ. 1886. The 1884 MI State Census population schedules were indexed at the Seeking Michigan website. This database has 1,337 pages. See
**http://search.ancestry.com/search/db.aspx?dbid=18557.**

■ **1887-1931.** See ***Michigan, Federal Naturalization Records, 1887-1931* [Online Database],** indexed at the Ancestry.com website. Source: National Archives microfilm. This database consists of naturalization records for Michigan from U.S. District Courts. Includes: Name, Birth Date, Birth Place, and Year. This database has 430,149 records. See
**http://search.ancestry.com/search/db.aspx?dbid=61201.**

■ **1890. See *Detroit, Michigan Directory, 1890* [Online Database],** indexed at the Ancestry.com website. Source: R. L. Polk's Detroit City Directory, 1890. This database has 99,799 records. See
**http://search.ancestry.com/search/db.aspx?dbid=4542.**

■ ***1890 Census Substitute* [Online Database],** indexed at the Ancestry.com website. This is nationwide collection of city directories for the time of the 1890 federal census (lost in a fire in Washington DC in 1921). A global search includes directories from several Michigan cities. See
**http://search.ancestry.com/search/group/1890census.**

■ **1894.** See ***Michigan, State Census, 1894* [Online Database],** indexed at the Ancestry.com website. This database contains information for Barry, Bay, Benzie, Dickinson, Emmet, Gratiot, Iosco, Ingham, Kalamazoo, and Keweenaw, MI. Includes the name of every member of the household, age, race, and birthplace. This version of the 1894 MI state census appears to be somewhat smaller than the *Seeking Michigan* set (combined 1884 & 1894 MI state census) at MI State Archive website. This database has 173,120 records. See
**http://search.ancestry.com/search/db.aspx?dbid=7307.**

■ ***1894 Census of the State of Michigan* (3-Vol. Statistical Report, w/list of Civil War Veterans Living in Michigan) [Online Database],** digitized and indexed at the Ancestry.com website. Source: *Census of the State of Michigan, 1894*, publ. by the state, 1896. Vol. 3 includes a list of the names of surviving Civil War soldiers living in Michigan in 1894. This database has 2,351 pages. See
**http://search.ancestry.com/search/db.aspx?dbid=18558.**

■ **1897-1920.** See ***Michigan, Death Records, 1897-1920* [Online Database],** indexed at the Ancestry.com website. Source: Michigan State Archives. The entire collection is arranged chronologically and alphabetically by county with the only exception being Wayne County, which follows Wexford. City of Detroit records, as part of Wayne County, are always at the end of each year. In total there are 83 counties. Each record includes: Given name, Surname, Death date, Place of death, and Physician who attended death. This database has 925,891 records. See
**http://search.ancestry.com/search/db.aspx?dbid=1561.**

■ **1897-1952.** See ***Michigan, Divorce Records, 1897-1952* [Online Database],** indexed at the Ancestry.com website. Source: MI State Vital Statistics. Divorce court summaries are in a ledger format by year. They typically asked: county and court of decree, names and ages of both parties, marriage date and place, number of children, who filed the complaint and the date of filing, date of the final action, alleged cause of divorce, whether the case was contested, whether case was granted, refused, or withdrawn, This database has 1,089,951 records. See
**http://search.ancestry.com/search/db.aspx?dbid=9092.**

■ **1898-1899.** See ***Michigan Volunteers of '98: A Complete Photographic Record of Michigan's Part in the Spanish-American War of 1898* [Online Database],** digitized and indexed at the Ancestry.com website. Source: Book, same title, publ. G.F. Sterling & Co. Detroit, 1898. After an introduction to the Spanish-American War, the book includes muster rolls for the 31st, 32nd, 33rd, 34th, and 35th Michigan Volunteers; and the Michigan Naval Reserves. This database has 99 pages. See
**http://search.ancestry.com/search/db.aspx?dbid=20058.**

■ **1903-1965.** See ***Michigan Passenger and Crew Lists, 1903-1965* [Online Database],** indexed at the Ancestry.com website. Source: National Archives

microfilm. This database contains the following Immigration and Naturalization Service (INS) records: Crew lists of vessels arriving at: Alpena, Michigan (May 27, 1948-November 22, 1956); Bay City, Michigan (August 17, 1948-September 19, 1965); Hancock, Michigan (July 7-17, 1952); Isle Royale, Michigan (1946-1948); Mackinac Island, Michigan (May 14, 1946-August 31, 1956); Marquette, Michigan (June 7, 1946-November 20, 1956); Menominee, Michigan (June 6, 1949-October 14, 1956); Rogers City, Michigan (April 7, 1948-December 7, 1956); Saginaw, Michigan (July 21, 1949-June 16, 1964); Saint Clair, Michigan (June 27, 1945-January 4, 1956); Sault Sainte Marie, Michigan (January 1, 1946-January 1, 1957); Manifests of alien arrivals and some returning U.S. citizens at: Algonac, Michigan (1926-1954); Marine City, Michigan (1923-1955); Port Huron, Michigan (1902-1952); Roberts Landing (1917-1955); Saint Clair, Michigan (1910-1955); and Sault Saint Marie, Michigan (1903-1955); This database has 377,263 records. See
**http://search.ancestry.com/search/db.aspx?dbid=1247.**

■ ***1904 Census of the State of Michigan*** **(2-Vol. Statistical Report) [Online Database],** digitized and indexed at the Ancestry.com website. Source: *Census of the State of Michigan, 1904*, publ. by the state, 1906. The population schedules for the MI 1904 state census were lost. This database has 1,647 pages. See
**http://search.ancestry.com/search/db.aspx?dbid=18559.**

■ **1971-1996.** See ***Michigan, Death Index, 1971-1996*** **[Online Database],** indexed at the Ancestry.com website. Source: MI State Vital Statistics. Each entry includes the full name of the decedent, gender, birth and death dates, the state, county and town of residence at time of death, and a link to order a copy of the original record. This database has 2,052,472 records. See
**http://search.ancestry.com/search/db.aspx?dbid=3171.**

## Michigan Databases Online at the FamilySearch.org Website

The following databases are available for free at the FamilySearch.org website. To see the current list, visit the Michigan Indexed Historical Records and Michigan Image Only Historical Records webpage. Both lists are updated periodically. See
**https://familysearch.org/search/collection/location/17.**

■ **1775-1995.** See ***Michigan Births and Christenings, 1775-1995*** **[Online Database],** indexed at the FamilySearch.org website. Name index to birth, baptism and christening records from microfilm at the Family History Library. This database has 1,612,291 records. See
**https://familysearch.org/search/collection/1675348.**

■ **1797-1973.** See ***Michigan Probate Records, 1797-1973*** **[Online Database],** an image only database digitized at the FamilySearch.org website. Source: FamilySearch extracts from Michigan county court records on microfilm at the Family History Library. Some county probate courts also include guardianship, naturalization, and/or military records. Browse the records, organized by county, then Volume, and Year range. This database has 4,723,861 records. See
**https://familysearch.org/search/collection/2013878.**

■ **1800-1995.** See **Michigan Deaths and Burials, 1800-1995 [Online Database],** indexed at the FamilySearch.org website. Name index to death and burial records from microfilm at the Family History Library. This database has 1,372,536 records. See
**https://familysearch.org/search/collection/1675357.**

■ **1820-1937.** See ***Michigan, County Marriages Index, 1820-1937*** **[Online Database],** indexed at the FamilySearch.org website. Source: FamilySearch extractions from county records on microfilm at the Family History Library. This collection includes some records from the following counties: Allegan, Alpena, Eaton, and Missaukee. This database has 9,052 records. See
**https://familysearch.org/search/collection/2473289.**

■ **1820-1940.** See **Michigan, County Marriages, 1820-1940 [Online Database],** indexed at the FamilySearch.org website. Source: FamilySearch extractions from county records on microfilm at the Family History Library. This collection includes records from most Michigan counties (except Alger, Alpena, Barry, Eaton, Gladwin, Kalkaska, Kent, Lenawee, Missaukee, Monroe, Montmorency, Oceana, Oscoda, Schoolcraft, and Shiawassee). This database has 1,030,574 records. See
**https://familysearch.org/search/collection/1810350.**

■ **1820-2006.** See ***Michigan Obituaries, 1820-2006*** **[Online Database],** indexed at the FamilySearch.org website. Source: FamilySearch extractions. Index and images of obituary collections organized by county or newspaper and then alphabetically. Extracted

information as well as newspaper clippings are represented. The originals are housed in several libraries and repositories throughout Michigan. This database has 517,228 records. See
**https://familysearch.org/search/collection/2215693.**

■ **1822-1995.** See ***Michigan Marriages, 1822-1995*** **[Online Database],** indexed at the FamilySearch.org website. Name index to marriage records from microfilm at the Family History Library. This database has 1,267,961 records. See
**https://familysearch.org/search/collection/1675359.**

■ **1834-1974.** See ***Michigan Civil Marriages, 1834-1974*** **[Online Database],** indexed at the FamilySearch.org website. FamilySearch extracts from Saginaw and Wayne counties, mostly from published transcripts. This database has 34,763 records. See
**https://familysearch.org/search/collection/2515912.**

■ **1865-1931.** See ***Michigan Church Marriages, 1865-1931*** **[Online Database],** indexed at the FamilySearch.org website. Source: FamilySearch extracts from church records from Lenawee, Manistee, Saginaw, Washtenaw, and Wayne counties This database has 817 pages. See
**https://familysearch.org/search/collection/2515887.**

■ **1867-1897.** See ***Michigan Deaths, 1867-1897*** **[Online Database],** indexed at the FamilySearch.org website. Source: MI State Vital Statistics. Name index and images of statewide death registrations. This database has 507,104 records. See
**https://familysearch.org/search/collection/1452402.**

■ **1867-1902.** See ***Michigan Births, 1867-1902*** **[Online Database],** indexed at the FamilySearch.org website. Source: MI State Vital Statistics. From statewide birth registrations. This database has 1,409,988 records. See
**https://familysearch.org/search/collection/1459684.**

■ **1868-1925.** See ***Michigan Marriages, 1868-1925*** **[Online Database],** indexed at the FamilySearch.org website. MI State Vital Statistics. Name index and images of marriages recorded in the State of Michigan between 1868 and 1925. In some instances, marriages were celebrated and recorded in a county different from the county where the marriage license was issued. This database has 1,533,863 records. See
**https://familysearch.org/search/collection/1452395.**

■ **1894.** See ***Michigan State Census, 1894*** **[Online Database],** indexed at the FamilySearch.org website. Source: MI State Archives. Name index of the Michigan state census taken in June 1894. Due to destroyed and missing records, in addition to a partial acquisition of records, this collection includes the following counties: Barry, Benzie, Bay, Dickinson, Emmet, Gratiot, Ingham, Iosco, Kalamazoo, Kent, Keweenaw, Lapeer, Leelanau, Menominee, Montcalm, and Washtenaw. This database has 381,961 records. See
**https://familysearch.org/search/collection/1825187.**

■ **1906-1954. See *Michigan, Detroit Manifests of Arrivals at the Port of Detroit, 1906-1954* [Online Database],** indexed at the FamilySearch.org website. Source: National Archives microfilm series M1478. This is an alphabetical card file manifest of individuals entering the United States through the Port of Detroit, 1906-1954. Includes a few records of persons entering at Port Huron, Sault St. Marie, and other Michigan ports. This database has 845,964 records. See
**https://familysearch.org/search/collection/1916040.**

■ **1907-1995.** See ***Michigan, Eastern District, Naturalization Index, 1907-1995*** **[Online Database],** an image only database digitized at the FamilySearch.org website. Source: National Archives microfilm series M1917. Images of Soundex cards to naturalization petitions. Browse through the images, organized by Soundex: A-000 (Adelle) to A-136 (Theresia Maria) – Z-630 (Jozef) to Z-663 (Boleslaw). This database has 577,690 records. See
**https://familysearch.org/search/collection/2110745.**

■ **1921-1952.** See ***Michigan Death Certificates, 1921-1952*** **[Online Database],** indexed at the FamilySearch.org website. Source: MI State Vital Statistics. This database has 1,681,256 records. See
**https://familysearch.org/search/collection/1968532.**

■ **1929-1966.** See ***Michigan, Crew Lists for Various Ports, 1929-1966*** **[Online Database],** indexed at the FamilySearch.org website. Source: National Archives microfilm. This collection contains crew lists from the following ports in Michigan with corresponding NARA publication number: Crew Lists of Vessels Arriving at Hancock, Isle Royale, Marquette, Menominee, and Sault Sainte Marie, Michigan, January 1946-January 1957 (A3432). Crew Lists of Vessels Arriving at Escanaba, Michigan, May 1946-

November 1956 (A3413). Crew Lists of Vessels Arriving at Algonac, Marine City, Marysville, and Roberts Landing, Michigan, May 1937-January 1957 (A3418). DeTour, Michigan, 1946-1956 (A3421). Alpena, Bay City, Mackinac Island, Rogers City, Saginaw, and Saint Clair, Michigan, June 1945-June 1966 (A3430). Port Huron, Michigan, October 1929-January 1957 (A3443). Grand Haven, Manistee, Muskegon, and South Haven, Michigan, May 1948-December 1956 (A3433). This database has 140,720 records. See
**https://familysearch.org/search/collection/2426314.**

■ **1957-1959.** See ***Michigan, South Haven Crew Lists, 1957-1959*** **[Online Database],** an image only database digitized at the FamilySearch.org website. Source: National Archives microfilm series A3812.
This collection contains Crew Lists of Vessels Arriving at South Haven, Michigan, May 1957-October 1959. The records usually include the name of the ship, the ports and dates of arrival and departure, and the following information about each person: name, citizenship, passport number, crew position, and where the crewman was shipped or engaged. This database has 61 records. See
**https://familysearch.org/search/collection/2443337.**

■ **1971-1996.** See ***Michigan Death Index, 1971-1996*** **[Online Database],** indexed at the FamilySearch.org website. Source: MI State Vital Statistics. An Ancestry database. This database has 2,052,472 records. See
**https://familysearch.org/search/collection/1949333.**

## Michigan Databases Online at Various Websites

■ **1700s-2000s.** See ***Michigan USGenWeb Archives*** **[Online Database].** The MIGenWeb Archives site offers free genealogical databases with searchable statewide name lists and for all Michigan counties. Databases may include Bibles, Biographies, Cemeteries, Censuses, Court Records, Deaths, Deeds, Directories, Histories, Marriages, Military, Newspapers, Obituaries, Photos, Schools, Tax Lists, Wills, and more. See
**http://usgwarchives.net/mi/mifiles.htm.**

■ **1700s-2000s.** See ***Linkpendium – Michigan: Family History & Genealogy, Census, Birth, Marriage, Death Vita Records & More*** **[Online Databases].** Linkpendium is a genealogical portal site with links to state, county, town, and local databases. Currently listed are selected sites for Michigan statewide resources (538), Independent Cities, Renamed Counties, Discontinued Counties (32), Alcona County (274), Alger County (146), Allegan County (552), Alpena County (552), Antrim County (527), Arenac County (159) and 80 more Michigan counties. See **www.linkpendium.com/mi-genealogy.**

■ **1817-1995.** See ***Indiana Newspaper Archives, 1817-1995*** **[Online Databases],** digitized and indexed newspapers at the GenealogyBank website, for Adrian, Ann Arbor, Bay City, Coldwater, Detroit, Flint, Grand Rapids, Jackson, Kalamazoo, Muskegon, Ontonagon, Saginaw, Sault Ste. Marie, St. James, and Ypsilanti, Michigan. See
**www.genealogybank.com/explore/newspapers/all/usa/michigan.**

■ **1820s-1950s.** See ***GLO Plat Maps (Michigan Department of Natural Resources)*** **[Online Database],** digitized maps at the MI Dept. of Natural Resources website. Select a county from the interactive map of Michigan, or click on a county link. A color map for one county appears, and blow-ups of the GLO Plat Maps are available. See
**www.michigan.gov/dnr/0,4570,7-153-10371_14793-31058--,00.html**

■ **1821-1929.** See ***Probate Index, Macomb County, Michigan*** **[Online Database],** indexed at the Mount Clemens Public Library website. See
**www.mtclib.org/search/probate.php.**

■ **1829-1990s.** See ***Surname Index, Van Buren Regional Genealogical Society*** **[Online Database],** includes a listing of where surnames can be found in the Local History Room at the Webster's Memorial Library in Decatur, MI. Indexed at the RootsWeb site for Van Buren Co MI. See
**www.rootsweb.ancestry.com/~mivanbur/vbrgsindex.htm.**

■ **1831-2015.** See ***Online Searchable Databases of the Western Michigan Genealogical Society*** **[Online Databases],** the WMGS of Grand Rapids, MI has one of the largest collection of online databases of any genealogical group in America. Included are the following:

- 1910-2015 West Michigan Newspapers
- 1903-1925 Kent County School Census
- 1831-1877 West Michigan Church Records
- 1954-2014 *Michigana (*Quarterly) Index
- 1880-2014 Home for Veterans
- 1917-1918 World War I soldiers
- 1978-1991 WMGS manuscripts

- WMGS Member's Genealogies
- 1894-1933 Monument Orders
- 1918-1926 Farm Bureau News
- 1860-1894 Michigan Censuses
- 1845-1939 Kent County Deaths
- 1903-1962 Latzek Funeral Home
- 1881 Chapman's History of Kent County
- 1905 Goss History of Grand Rapids
- Quigley files

The combined total is now over 2.6 million entries. For the database home page, see **http://data.wmgs.org.**

■ **1866-1940.** See ***Saginaw City Directories*** **[Online Database],** indexed at the Public Library of Saginaw website. See **http://dtsearch.saginawlibrary.org/index.asp.**

■ **1867-1883.** See ***Unrecorded Births of Newaygo County, Michigan, 1867-1883*** **[Online Database],** indexed at the MIGenWeb site, Newaygo Co MI. See **www.migenweb.org/newaygo/births.html.**

■ **1868-1887.** See **Births, Ontonagon County, Michigan, 1868-1887 [Online Database],** indexed at the USGenWeb site for Ontonagon Co MI. See **http://files.usgwarchives.net/mi/ontonagon/vitals/births/o53504.txt.**

■ **1867-1907.** See **Deaths, Ontonagon County, Michigan, 1867-1907 [Online Database],** indexed at the USGenWeb site for Ontonagon Co MI. See **http://files.usgwarchives.net/mi/ontonagon/vitals/deaths/o53505.txt.**

■ **1867-1920s.** See ***Birth Records, Otsego County, Michigan*** **[Online Database],** indexed at the RootsWeb site for Otsego Co MI. See **www.rootsweb.ancestry.com/~miotsego/BirthsIndex.htm.**

■ **1867-1960.** See ***Index to Birth Records, Ottawa County, Michigan*** **[Online Database],** indexed at the MIGenWeb site for Ottawa Co MI. See **http://ottawa.migenweb.net/births/index.html.**

■ **1867-1965.** See **Death Index, Muskegon County, Michigan [Online Database],** indexed at the Muskegon Co Clerk's website. See **www.co.muskegon.mi.us/clerk/websearch.cfm.**

■ **1867-1915.** See ***Birth Index, 1867-1915, Delta County, Michigan*** **[Online Database],** indexed at the Delta County Genealogical Society website. See **http://dcmigs.org/births/birth_index.htm.**

■ **1871-1893.** See **Michigan School Censuses [Online Database],** indexed at the Michigan Family History Network website. Intro: During the mid to late 1800's schools were taken care of by the township government. They produced censuses to keep track of the children attending. These records show up in various archives around the state for safe keeping. For the first search screen, see **www.mifamilyhistory.org/sch-census/default.aspx.**

■ **1873-1975.** See ***Probate Index, Delta County, Michigan, 1873-1975*** **[Online Database],** indexed at the Delta County Genealogical Society website. See **http://dcmigs.org/probate/index.htm.**

■ **1878-1879.** See ***Index to Tax Assessments, Georgetown Township, Ottawa County, Michigan*** **[Online Database],** indexed at the MIGenWeb site for Ottawa Co MI. See **http://ottawa.migenweb.net/twprecords/Georgetw/assess/index.html.**

**1879-1903.** See ***Index to Biographies, Hillsdale County, Michigan*** **[Online Database],** an index to biographies in the 1879, 1888, and 1903 histories of Hillsdale Co MI. Located at the MIGenWeb site. See **www.migenweb.org/hillsdale/bios.html.**

■ ***1881 Voters, Delta County, Michigan*** **[Online Database],** indexed at the Delta County Genealogical Society website. See **http://dcmigs.org/voters/1881.htm.**

■ **1881-1892.** See ***Memorial Report from the book, Michigan Pioneer and Historical Collection, Tuscola County, Michigan*** **[Online Database],** includes a list of deaths of the Tuscola County Pioneer Society for 1881-1892. Indexed at the USGenWeb site for Tuscola CO MI. See **http://files.usgwarchives.net/mi/tuscola/multiple/pioneers/p56001.txt.**

■ **1883.** See **List of Pensioners on the Roll, Michigan [Online Database],** indexed at the Michigan Family History Network website. See **www.mifamilyhistory.org/civilwar/1883Pension.**

■ **1883.** See ***Surname Index from the History of Upper Peninsula of Michigan*** **[Online Database],** indexed at the Delta County Genealogical Society website. *The History of Upper Peninsula of Michigan* was pub. by A.T. Andreas, Western Historical Co., Chicago, 1883. See **http://dcmigs.org/up_history.htm**

■ **1883-1886.** See ***Births From the Pioneer Tribune, Schoolcraft County, Michigan* [Online Database],** indexed at the MIGenWeb site for Schoolcraft Co MI. See **http://schoolcraft.migenweb.net/birth1.htm.**

■ **1883-1887.** See ***Marriage Records from Arenac County, Michigan, Book 1* [Online Database],** indexed at the RootsWeb site for Arenac Co MI. See **http://www.rootsweb.ancestry.com/~miarenac/people/civil_marriages_book_1.pdf.**

■ **1892.** See ***Index to Tax Assessments, Georgetown Township, Ottawa County, Michigan* [Online Database],** indexed at the MIGenWeb site for Ottawa Co MI. See **http://ottawa.migenweb.net/twprecords/Georgetw/assess/1892.html.**

■ **1894.** See ***Soldiers, Sailors and Marines, Volume III, Census of the State of Michigan 1894* [Online Database],** indexed at the Michigan Family History Network website. See **www.mifamilyhistory.org/civilwar/1894VetsCensus.**

■ **1894.** See ***An Illustrated City Directory of Hillsdale, Michigan* [Online Database],** digitized at the University of Michigan Digital Library site. See **http://quod.lib.umich.edu/cgi/t/text/text-idx?c=micounty;idno=2745648.0001.001.**

■ **1897-1914.** See ***Hospital Patient Records, Delta County, Michigan, 1897-1914* [Online Database],** indexed at the Delta County Genealogical Society website. See **http://dcmigs.org/hospital/a-b.htm.**

■ **1896-1935.** See ***City Directory Master Index, Mount Clemens, Michigan* [Online Database],** and index to the collection of city directories located at the Mount Clemens Public Library. Includes 1896-1897, 1899-1900, 1901-1902, 1903-1904, 1905-1906, 1911-1912, 19134-1914, 1915-1916, 1917-1918, 1919-1920, 1921-1922, 1923-1924, 1925-1926, 1927, 1929, 1930, 1932, and 1935. The indexes for the remaining directories, 1937-1966, are still in work. Indexed at the Mount Clemens Public Library website. See **www.mtclib.org/search/MCDirectory.php.**

■ **1898.** See ***Michigan Volunteers in the Spanish American War* [Online Database],** indexed at the Michigan Family History Network website. Select a county at this "Veterans by County" page. See **www.mifamilyhistory.org/spanam/sawcounty.aspx.**

■ ***1906 Patrons' Reference Directory of Gladwin County, Michigan* [Online Database],** indexed at the MIFamilyhistory.org website. See **www.mifamilyhistory.org/gladwin/Gladwin1906directory.htm.**

■ **1912.** See ***Biographies, Residents in 1912, Van Buren County, Michigan* [Online Database],** indexed at the RootsWeb site for Van Buren Co MI: **www.rootsweb.ancestry.com/~mivanbur/bioindex.htm.**

■ **1913.** See ***Index to History of Gratiot County, Michigan* [Online Database],** indexed at the Michigan Family History Network website. **www.mfhn.com/gratiot/tucker/index-1.html.**

■ **1977-Current.** See ***Michigan Recent Newspaper Obituaries (1977-Current)* [Online Database],** digitized and indexed newspaper obituaries at the GenealogyBank website, including newspapers for Adrian, Ann Arbor, Bad Axe, Baldwin, Big Rapids, Branson, and 78 more Michigan cities. See **www.genealogybank.com/explore/obituaries/all/usa/michigan.**

■ **1997-1998.** See ***Death Records, St. Joseph County, Michigan* [Online Database],** indexed at the RootsWeb site for St. Joseph Co MI. See **www.rootsweb.ancestry.com/~mistjose/death/maindeath.htm.**

## Michigan Periodical Articles
### Censuses & Substitute Name Lists in Genealogical Periodicals

PERSI (PERiodical Source Index) is a digitized database project of the Allen County Public Library (ACPL), Fort Wayne, IN. Since 1986, the PERSI extractors have indexed article titles, places, and surnames from over 11,000 genealogical & historical periodicals. The PERSI database is currently available online through the FindMyPast.com subscription website. The Genealogy Center of the ACPL in Fort Wayne IN holds all 11,000 periodicals and will make copies of any article by special request. To obtain an order form for requesting a printed copy of any article indexed in the PERSI database, see **http://genealogycenter.org/docs/default-source/resources/articlerequest.pdf?sfvrsn=2.**
**Michigan PERSI Search:** Using the FindMyPast.com website, the keywords "Michigan Tax" had 237 results. Early census articles include the following:

■ **1710-1810.** See **"State Censuses, 1710-1810" [Printed Article],** in *Family Trails* (MI State Library), Vol. 6, No. 1 (1978).

■ **1710.** See **"Census for du Detroit de Pontchartrain, 1710" [Printed Article],** in *Michigan's Habitant Heritage* (French Canadian Heritage Society of Michigan), Vol. 26, No. 4 (Oct 2005).

■ **1762.** See **"Census, 1752, Detroit" [Printed Article],** in *National Genealogical Society Quarterly* (NGS, Arlington, VA), Vol. 68, No. 1 (Mar 1980).

■ **1765.** See **"Census, 1765, Detroit" [Printed Article],** in *Detroit Society for Genealogical Research Magazine* (DSGR, Detroit), Vol. 43, No. 1 (Fall 1979).

■ **1796.** See **"Census, 1796, Detroit" [Printed Article],** in *National Genealogical Society Quarterly* (NGS, Arlington, VA), Vol. 69, No. 3 (Sep 1981).

■ **1810.** See **"Census, 1810, Detroit" [Printed Article],** In *Detroit Society for Genealogical Research Magazine* (DSGR, Detroit), Vol. 32, No. 1 (Fall 1968), and Vol. 34, No. 3 (Spring 1971).

■ **1820.** See **"Census, 1820, Detroit and Wayne County" [Printed Article],** in *Detroit Society for Genealogical Research Magazine* (DSGR, Detroit), Vol. 12, No. 5 (May 1949) through Vol. 14, No. 2 (Dec 1950).

■ **"1827 Michigan Territorial Census, Chippewa County" [Printed Article],** in *Sault Channels* (Sault St. Marie/District Branch, Ontario Genealogical Society), Vol. 12, No. 1 (Winter 1994).

■ **"1827 Michigan Territorial Census, Wayne County" [Printed Article],** in *Detroit Society for Genealogical Research Magazine*, Vol. 19, No. 2 (Winter 1955).

■ **"1837 Michigan State Census, Ionia County" [Printed Article],** in *Michigan Heritage* (Ethel W. Williams, Kalamazoo, MI), Vol. 1, No. 2 (Winter 1962) through Vol. 6, No. 2 (Winter 1964).

■ **"1845 Michigan State Census, Washtenaw County" [Printed Article],** in *Family History Capers*, (Gen. Soc. of Washtenaw Co, Ann Arbor, MI), beginning with Vol. 5, No. 2 (Oct 1981); and by townships in various issues through Vol. 11, No. 1 (Summer 1987).

■ **"1854 Michigan State Census, Emmet County"[Printed Article],** in *Detroit Society for Genealogical Research Magazine,* Vol. 52, No. 1 (Fall 1988) through Vol. 52, No. 2 (Winter 1989).

■ **"1884 Michigan State Census, Wayne County" [Printed Article],** in *Detroit Society for Genealogical Research Magazine,* abstracted by townships beginning with Vol. 44 (1981) and various issues through Vol. 64 (2001).

## Michigan Books & Microfilms at the Family History Library

The most important of Michigan's statewide census substitutes are cited below in chronological order. Each item includes a FHL book number or FHL film number, which can be used to search the FHL catalog for more details. To review an item, start at the FamilySearch catalog search page. See **https://familysearch.org/search/catalog/results.** Select "Search by Place" then "United States, Michigan" to see a list of catalog categories. Or, select "Call Number" then type an FHL book number; or select "Film/Fiche Number" to view a specific title.

■ **1700-1918.** See ***Deed Records, 1766-1918; Grantee-Grantor Index, 1700-1903, Wayne County, Michigan*** **[Microfilm],** from the original records at the Wayne County courthouse, Detroit, Michigan. Early deeds are written in French and English. Additional indexes are at front of some volumes. Filmed by the Genealogical Society of Utah, 1974, 210 rolls, beginning with FHL film #926443 (Grantee Index, A-D, 1700-1885). For a complete list of roll numbers and contents of each roll, see the online FHL catalog page for this title. See **https://familysearch.org/search/catalog/244568.**

■ **1701-1710.** See ***Cadillac's Village, or, Detroit Under Cadillac: With a List of Property Owners and a History of the Settlement, 1701-1710*** **[Printed Book],** compiled by Clarence Monroe Burton, publ. C.M. Burton, 1896, Detroit, 43 pages, FHL book 977.434 H2bc.

■ **1701-1710.** See ***First Land Owners of Wayne County, Michigan*** **[Printed Book],** compiled by E. Gray Williams and Ethel W. Williams, publ. E.G. Williams, 1964, 93 pages, FHL book 973.433 R2.

■ **1703-1869.** See ***Early Land Transfers, Detroit and Wayne County, Michigan, Michigan Works Progress Administration, Vital Records Project, Michigan State Library and DAR, Louisa St. Clair Chapter*** **[Microfilm],** from the original records (58 vols.) at the DAR Library, Washington, DC. Includes index. Filmed by the Genealogical Society of Utah, 1971, 13 rolls, beginning with FHL film #857329 (Master index to Records, vols. A, B, & C). For a complete list of roll numbers and contents of each roll, see the online FHL catalog page for this title. See **https://familysearch.org/search/catalog/241736.**

■ **1703-1973.** See ***Michigan Biography Index*** **[Microfilm],** from a book by Frances Loomis, part of County and Regional Histories of the Old Northwest. Series 5, Michigan; No. 9. Filmed by Research Publications, New Haven, CT, 1973, 4 rolls, beginning with FHL film #485331 (Aagaard – Azure). For a complete list of roll numbers and contents of each roll, visit the online FHL catalog page for this title. See **https://familysearch.org/search/catalog/17261.**

■ **1710-1830.** See ***Michigan Censuses, 1710-1830, Under the French, British and Americans*** **[Printed Book],** edited by Donna Valley Russell. Name lists included:

- **1710.** French Colonial Census. Detroit area.
- **1750.** French Colonial Census. Detroit area.
- **1762.** French Colonial Census. Detroit area.
- **1765.** British Colonial Census. Detroit area.
- **1768.** British Colonial Census. Detroit area.
- **1779.** British Colonial Census. Detroit area.
- **1780.** British Colonial Census. Fort St. Joseph.
- **1782.** British Colonial Census. Detroit, and south Shore of Detroit River.
- **1792.** British Colonial Census. Petite Côte (south Shore of Detroit River).
- **1796.** British Colonial Census. Detroit area.
- **1805-1806.** Michigan Territorial Census. Detroit.
- **1810.** Michigan Territory Federal Census. Detroit & Michillimackinac areas.
- **1820.** Michigan Territory Federal Census. Includes Oakland, Wayne, Michillimackinac, Brown (now Wisconsin), Crawford (now Wisconsin), Monroe, and Macomb counties.
- **1827.** Michigan Territorial Census. Surviving fragments for Wayne (Detroit), Monroe (Lawrence Twp.), Chippewa, and Washtenaw counties only.
- **1830.** Michigan Territory Federal Census. Includes Wayne, Monroe, Oakland, Lenawee, Macomb, St. Clair, Washtenaw, St. Joseph, Berrien, Cass, Van Buren, Michillimackinac, Brown (now Wisconsin), Crawford (now Wisconsin), Chippewa, and Iowa (later Wisconsin, now Iowa) counties.

Published by the Detroit Society for Genealogical Research, 1982, 291 pages. FHL book 977.4 X2r.

■ **1799, 1806, 1827 Detroit Censuses.** See ***Early Michigan Census Records*** **[Printed Book],** compiled by Ronald Vern Jackson, et al, published by Accelerated Indexing Systems, Bountiful, UT, 1976, 11 pages. Contains the early census records of Detroit, Wayne County, Michigan, 1799, 1806, 1827. FHL book 977.433 X2p.

■ **1807-1907.** See ***Card Files (Index to Land Entry Files of the Government Land Offices in Michigan)*** **[Microfilm],** from the original index cards at the Bureau of Land Management, Eastern States Office, Washington, DC. The card files serve as an index to the Tract Books, Plat Books, and Case Files relating to ten million public land sales in America. **Content:** Each card contains the following information: Certificate Number, District Land Office, Kind of entry (cash, credit, warrant, etc.), Name of Patentee (Buyer, Entryman, etc.), and county of origin, Land description, Number of acres, Date of patent, Volume, and Page where document can be located. Filmed by the Bureau of Land Management, Washington, DC, c1970, 160 rolls, including 4 rolls for Michigan, beginning with FHL film #1501558 (Twp 1 North to Twp 36 North; Twp 41 North to 43 North; Ranges 3 East – 6 East). For a complete list of roll numbers and contents of each roll, visit the online FHL catalog page for this title. See **https://familysearch.org/search/catalog/511740.**

■ **1809-1868.** See ***Marriage and Death Newspaper Notices, Wayne County, Michigan, 1809-1868: Newspaper Notices from Michigan at the Michigan Historical Collections, Bentley Historical Library, University of Michigan*** **[Printed Book],** abstracted by Marguerite N. Lambert; edited and indexed by James N. Jackson. Abstracted newspapers include: *Commercial Advertiser,* 1861-1865; *Detroit Courier,* 1828-1833; *Detroit Advertiser & Tribune,* 1862-1866; *Detroit Daily Advertiser,* 1833-1862; *Detroit Daily Post,* 1861-1867; *Detroit Daily Tribune,* 1857-1865; *Detroit Gazette,* 1817-1833; *Detroit Weekly Advertiser,* 1857; *Detroit Weekly Free Press,* 1862-1868; and *Michigan Essay,* 1809. Includes separate alphabetical listings for marriages and deaths. Publ. Detroit Society for Genealogical Research, Detroit, 1998, 144 pages, FHL book 977.433 V2L.

■ **1812-1848.** See ***Michigan's Early Military Forces: A Roster and History of Troops Activated Prior to the American Civil War*** **[Printed Book],** compiled by LeRoy Barnett, with histories by Roger Rosentreter. Includes surname index. Contains lists of soldiers for each war, arranged in alphabetical order by surname, and gives name, rank, military unit, service dates and remarks. Also contains brief histories of Michigan and its involvement in each war: pre-territorial militia, War of 1812, Black Hawk War, 1832, Toledo War, 1835, Patriot War, 1838-1839, Mexican War, 1846-1848. Publ. Wayne State University, Detroit, MI, 2003, 518 pages, FHL book 977.4 M2ba.

■ **1818-1903.** See ***Monroe County, Michigan: Marriage Records Index 1818-1903*** **[Printed Index],** by Lois Vidolich, publ. Genealogical Society of Monroe Co MI, 1995, 123 pages, FHL book 977.432 V22v.

■ **1818-1935.** See ***Macomb County, Michigan Deeds and Mortgages, 1818-1935; Indexes, 1818-1908*** **[Microfilm],** from the originals at the Macomb County Courthouse, Mt. Clemens, MI. Filmed by the Genealogical Society of Utah, 1975, 83 rolls, beginning with FHL film #979527 (Deed index, 1818-1845). For a complete list of roll numbers and contents of each roll, visit the online FHL catalog page for this title. See **https://familysearch.org/search/catalog/244435.**

■ **1819-1871.** See ***Marriage Index, 1819-1871, Macomb County, Michigan*** **[Printed Book],** by Karen L. Hemme Rogers and Nancy L. Hudson Burge. 4 Vols. Contents: Vol. 1: 1819-1852; Vol. 2: 1852-1861; Vol. 3: 1861-1867; and Vol. 4: 1868-1871. Publ. K.N. Mulberry Pub., 1992, 4 vols., FHL book 977.439 V223r v.1-4.

■ ***1820 Michigan Territory Federal Census (Federal Copy)*** **[Microfilm],** from originals at the National Archives, Washington, DC. This federal copy and the MI State Archives copy should be compared side-by-side to see if there are differences. Any handwritten copy of an original is prone to error, and this federal set was copied from the MI Territory copy, now located at the MI State Archives. This federal copy was filmed by the National Archives (as part of a combined set of 1820, 1830, & 1840), 1 roll, FHL film #506762 (Michigan 1820: Oakland, Wayne, Michillimackinac, Brown [now Wisconsin], Crawford [now Wisconsin], Monroe, and Macomb counties).

■ ***1820 Michigan Territory Federal Census (MI State Archives Copy)*** **[Microfilm],** from Michigan Territory's original manuscript copy, now located at the Archives of Michigan, Lansing, MI. This state archives copy and the federal copy should be compared side-by-side to see if there are differences. Any handwritten copy of an original is prone to error, and this MI Territory set was used to make a copy to be sent to Washington, DC (the federal copy). Contents: Oakland, Wayne, Michillimackinac, Brown (now Wisconsin), Crawford (now Wisconsin), Monroe, and Macomb counties. Filmed by the Genealogical Society of Utah, 1973, 1 roll, FHL film #927678.

■ **1820-1980.** See ***Name Index File, Monroe County, Michigan, 1820-1980*** **[Microfilm],** from the original card file index at the Monroe County Historical Commission, Monroe, MI. From intro: "This file contains references to miscellaneous information, including funeral home records, cemetery listings, church histories, census records, Civil War records, and death, birth and marriage records. The majority of sources can be found at the Monroe County Historical Commission Archives." Filmed by the Genealogical Society of Utah, 2006, 44 rolls, beginning with FHL film #1358112 (Abbey, Alvin – Auten, Caroline). For a complete list of roll numbers and contents of each roll, visit the online FHL catalog page for this title: **https://familysearch.org/search/catalog/1324774.**

■ **1820s-1980s.** See ***The Michigan Surname Index*** **[Printed Book],** compiled by the Michigan Genealogical Council, 1984-1989, 2 vols., FHL book 977.4 D22m v.1-2.

■ ***1827 Detroit, Michigan Territorial Census*** **[Microfilm],** from a typescript (location of original not noted), filmed by the Genealogical Society of Utah, 1976, 1 roll, FHL film #928180.

■ **1827.** See ***Michigan Territorial Census, Detroit, 1827*** **[Microfilm],** from a typescript compiled by B.F.H. Witherell, filmed by the Michigan State Library, 1960, 15 pages. Filmed by the Genealogical Society of Utah, 1973, FHL film 927477.

■ **1837-1935.** See ***Detroit (Michigan) City Directories*** **[Microfilm],** from the originals published by various publishers. This series includes city directories for 1837, 1845, 1846, 1850, and every year (or two-year span) thereafter through 1935. Filmed by Research Publications, Woodbridge, CT, 1980-1984, 46

microfiche, 72 rolls of microfilm, beginning with FHL fiche #6043862. For a complete list of fiche/roll numbers, visit the online FHL catalog page for this title. See
**https://familysearch.org/search/catalog/539682.**

■ **1838-1861.** See ***General Roster of the Militia of the State of Michigan, 1838-1861*** **[Microfilm],** from the originals at the Michigan Adjutant General's Office. Filmed by the Genealogical Society of Utah, 1973, 2 rolls, FHL film #915335 (Roster, 1838-1848) and FHL film #915336 (Roster, 1846-1861).

■ **1850 Michigan Federal Census (Original County Copies) [Microfilm],** from the manuscripts originally retained at county courthouses for all Michigan counties. Genealogists using the 1850 federal census for Michigan should be aware that there are two original sets of census records for these five counties: Barry, Eaton, Kent, Montcalm, and Washtenaw. Comparing a county copy with a federal copy side-by-side will reveal copious errors, e.g., misspelled names, omitted names, duplicated entries, different dates of birth, changing a male to a female, and a myriad of mistakes that can only be explained by the fact that the originals were large, cumbersome books difficult to hand copy from one page to another. These original county copies were microfilmed by the Genealogical Society of Utah, 1972, as follows:

- **Barry Co MI 1850**, original at the MI State Archives, FHL film #915278.
- **Eaton Co MI 1850**, original at the MI State Archives, FHL film #915300.
- **Kent Co MI 1850**, original at the Grand Rapids Public Library, FHL film #984116.
- **Montcalm Co MI 1850**, original at the MI State Archives, FHL film #915325.
- **Washtenaw Co MI 1850**, original at the Bentley Historical Library, Univ. of Michigan, FHL film #915278.

■ **1860 Michigan Federal Census (Original County Copies) [Microfilm],** from the manuscripts originally retained at county courthouses for all Michigan counties. Genealogists using the 1860 federal census for Michigan should be aware that there are two original sets of census records for these seven counties: Barry, Bay, Eaton, Clinton, Houghton, Kent, and Montcalm. Comparing a county copy with a federal copy side-by-side will reveal copious errors, e.g., misspelled names, omitted names, duplicated entries, different dates of birth, changing a male to a female, and a myriad of mistakes that can only be explained by the fact that the originals were large, cumbersome books difficult to hand copy from one page to another. These original county copies were microfilmed by the Genealogical Society of Utah, 1972, as follows:

- **Barry Co MI 1860**, original at the MI State Archives, FHL film #915279.
- **Bay Co MI 1860**, original at the MI State Archives, FHL film #915287.
- **Eaton Co MI 1860**, original at the MI State Archives, FHL film #915301.
- **Kent Co MI 1860**, original at the MI State Archives, FHL film #915275.
- **Clinton Co MI 1860**, original at the MI State Archives, FHL film #915296.
- **Houghton Co MI 1860**, original at the MI State Archives, FHL film #915275.
- **Montcalm Co MI 1860**, original at the MI State Archives, FHL film #915325.

■ **1870 Michigan Federal Census (Original County Copies) [Microfilm],** from the manuscripts originally retained at county courthouses for all Michigan counties. Genealogists using the 1870 federal census for Michigan should be aware that there are two original sets of census records for these thirteen counties: Barry, Bay, Benzie, Clinton, Eaton, Houghton, Kent, Keweenaw, Menominee, Montcalm, St. Joseph, Van Buren, and Washtenaw. Comparing a county copy with a federal copy side-by-side will reveal copious errors, e.g., misspelled names, omitted names, duplicated entries, different dates of birth, changing a male to a female, and a myriad of mistakes that can only be explained by the fact that the originals were large, cumbersome books difficult to hand copy from one page to another. These original county copies were microfilmed by the Genealogical Society of Utah, 1972, as follows:

- **Barry Co MI 1870**, originals at the MI State Archives, 2 rolls, FHL film #915280 (Towns of Woodland, Carlton, Irving, Yankee Springs, Rutland, Nashville, Castleton, Thornapple, Middleville, and Hastings); and FHL film #915283 (Towns of Assyria, Baltimore, Barry, Carlton, Nashville, Hastings, Hope, Irving, Johnstown, Maple Grove, Orangeville, Prairieville, Rutland, Thornapple, Middleville, Woodland, and Yankee Springs).
- **Bay Co MI 1870**, original at the MI State Archives, FHL film #915287.
- **Benzie Co MI 1870**, original at the MI State Archives, FHL film #915294.
- **Clinton Co MI 1870**, original at the MI State Archives, FHL film #915298.
- **Eaton Co MI 1870**, original at the MI State Archives, FHL film #915303.
- **Houghton Co MI 1870**, original at the MI State Archives, FHL film #915276.

- **Kent Co MI 1870**, original at the MI State Archives, FHL film #914117
- **Keweenaw Co MI 1870**, original at the MI State Archives, FHL film #915274.
- **Menominee Co MI 1870**, original at the MI State Archives, FHL film #915322.
- **Montcalm Co MI 1870**, original at the MI State Archives, FHL film #915325.
- **St. Joseph Co MI 1870**, original at the MI State Archives, FHL film #915334.
- **Van Buren Co MI 1870**, original at the MI State Archives, FHL film #915325.
- **Washtenaw Co MI 1870**, original at the Bentley Historical Library, Univ. of Michigan, FHL film #955813.

■ **1880 Michigan Federal Census (Original County "Short Forms") [Microfilm],** from the manuscripts originally retained at county courthouses for all Michigan counties. Genealogists using the 1880 federal census for Michigan should be aware that there was a name list prepared for each county's 1880 federal census schedules, a "Short Form" which was to remain in the courthouse for public inspection. The Short Forms were not in family order, but listed for all individuals, regardless of relationship, by the first letter of their surname. After 30 days, the county could do what they wanted with the Short Forms, and most were discarded. More of the Short Forms have survived for Michigan counties than for most states – they exist for these eleven counties: Barry, Eaton, Ionia, Kalamazoo, Kent, Keweenaw, Lapeer, Mecosta, Oceana, Ottawa, and Washtenaw. These original county copies were microfilmed by the Genealogical Society of Utah, 1972, as follows:

- **Barry Co MI 1880 Short Form**, original at the MI State Archives, FHL film #915282.
- **Eaton Co MI 1880 Sort Form**, original at the MI State Archives, FHL film #915304.
- **Ionia Co MI 1880 Short Form**, original at the MI State Archives, FHL film #915310.
- **Kalamazoo Co MI 1880 Short Form**, original at the MI State Archives, FHL film #915313.
- **Kent Co MI 1880 Short Form**, original at the MI State Archives, FHL film #984115.
- **Keweenaw Co MI 1880 Short Form**, original at the MI State Archives, FHL film #915274.
- **Lapeer Co MI 1880 Short Form**, original at the Lapeer County Clerk's Office, Lapeer, MI, FHL film #915317.
- **Mecosta Co MI 1880 Short Form**, original at the MI State Archives, FHL film #915321.
- **Oceana Co MI 1880 Short Form**, original at the MI State Archives, FHL film #915328.
- **Ottawa Co MI 1880 Short Form**, original at the Bentley Historical Library, Univ. of Michigan, FHL film #915330.
- **Washtenaw Co MI 1880 Short Form**, original at the Bentley Historical Library, Univ. of Michigan, FHL film #955815.

■ **1885-1927.** See ***Historical Register of Inhabitants, 1885-1927 (Soldiers' Home, Grand Rapids, MI)* [Microfilm],** from the originals at the MI State Archives, Lansing, MI. Includes index. Filmed by the Genealogical Society of Utah, 1972, 10 rolls, beginning with FHL film #925039 (Index). For a complete list of roll numbers and contents of each roll, visit the online FHL catalog page for this title. See **https://familysearch.org/search/catalog/85612.**

■ **1885-1934.** See ***Flint (Michigan) City Director*ies [Microfilm],** from various publishers. FHL has 1885, 1888-1889, 1892-1894, 1897-1899, 1903, 1905-1910, 1912-1932, and 1934. Filmed by Research publications, Woodbridge, CT, 1995, 17 rolls, beginning with FHL film #2156759 (1885 Flint City & Genesee Co Directory). For a complete list of roll numbers and contents of each roll, visit the online FHL catalog page for this title. See **https://familysearch.org/search/catalog/992054.**

■ **1889-1935.** See ***Kalamazoo (Michigan) City/County Directories* [Microfilm],** by various publishers. FHL has 1889, 1896, 1899, 1901-1902, 1904-1917, 1919, 1921-1922, 1924, 1926-1927, 1929, 1931, and 1934-1935. Filmed by Research Publications, Woodbridge, CT, 1980-1990, 12 rolls, beginning with FHL film #2156767 (1889 Directory, Kalamazoo and Kalamazoo County). For a complete list of roll numbers and contents of each roll, visit the online FHL catalog page for this title. See **https://familysearch.org/search/catalog/620530.**

■ ***1890 Residents oi Livingston County, Michigan* [Printed Book & Microfilm],** edited by Kennie L. King. Sources include pupil listings and censuses from local schools (1889-1891), the *1891 Portrait & Biographical Album - Ingham & Livingston Counties,* and the 1890 Union Veteran's & Widows of the Civil War. Names are listed alphabetically. From intro: "Contains transcriptions of marriage and death records from 1889 through 1891 and birth records from 1880 through 1891. Plus many other records." Publ. Livingston County Genealogical Society, Howell, MI, 2000, 990 pages, FHL book 977.436 V2r. Also on microfilm, FHL film #1145794.

■ **1897-1935.** See ***Ann Arbor (Michigan) City Directories* [Microfilm],** from various publishers. FHL has 1899, and 1901-1935. Filmed by Research

Publications, Woodbridge, CT, 1980-1990, 16 rolls, beginning with FHL film #2156751 (1899 Directory). For a complete list of roll numbers and contents of each roll, visit the online FHL catalog page for this title. See
**https://familysearch.org/search/catalog/554844.**

■ **1899-1935.** See **Battle Creek (Michigan) City Directories [Microfilm],** from various publishers. FHL has 1899-1916, 1918, 1921, 1922, 1924, 1926, 1927, 1929, 1931, 1933, and 1935. Filmed by Research Publications, Woodbridge, CT, 1980-1984, 10 rolls, beginning with FHL film #2156753 (1899-1900 Polk's Battle Creek City Directory), For a complete list of roll numbers and contents of each roll, visit the online FHL catalog page for this title. See
**https://familysearch.org/search/catalog/555523.**

■ **1903-1934.** See ***Holland (Michigan) City Directories*** **[Microfilm],** by various publishers. Filmed by Research Publications, Woodbridge, CT, 1995, 2 rolls, as follows:

- **1903-1904** Holland city directory, FHL film #2309181.
- **1906** Holland city directory, FHL film #2309181.
- **1908.** The Inter-state Directory Company's directory of Holland, Mich., and Ottawa County, FHL film #2309181.
- **1921** Polk's Holland City directory, FHL film #2309181.
- **1929** Polk's Holland, Michigan city directory, including Zeeland, FHL film #2309182.
- **1931** Polk's Holland, Michigan city directory, including Zeeland, FHL film #2309182.
- **1934** Polk's Holland, Ottawa County, Mich., city directory, 1934, including Zeeland, FHL film #2309182.

■ **1905-1932.** See ***Owosso (Michigan) City Directories*** **[Microfilm],** by various publishers. FHL has 1905-1906, 1907-1908, 1910-1911, 1913-1914, 1915-1916, 1917-1918, 1919-1920, 1921, 1924, 1926, 1928, 1930-1931, and 1932 Most directories include Owosso, Corunna, and Shiawassee county areas. Filmed by Research Publications, Woodbridge, CT, 4 rolls, beginning with FHL film #2309224 (1905-1906 Polk's Owosso and Corunna City Directory). For a complete list of roll numbers and contents of each roll, visit the online FHL catalog page for this title. See
**https://familysearch.org/search/catalog/1059486.**

■ **1905-1935.** See ***Hillsdale (Michigan) City Directories*** **[Microfilm],** from various publishers. FHL has 1905-1906, 1908-1909, 1911-1912, 1915, 1923, 1925, 1927, 1932, 1929, 1933, and 1935. Filmed by Research Publications, Woodbridge, CT, 1 roll, FHL film #2309180 (1905-1935 Hillsdale City and County Directories, Jonesville, Reading, and all other villages in Hillsdale County).

■ **1917-1918.** See ***World War I Card Index for Michigan*** **[Microfilm],** from the originals at the State Archives, Lansing, MI. Card files include names of the soldiers' parents and addresses. Filmed by the Genealogical Society of Utah, 1976, 37 rolls, beginning with FHL film #1001930 (A – Ath). For a complete list of roll numbers, visit the online FHL catalog page for this title. See
**https://familysearch.org/search/catalog/434638.**

■ **1917-1918.** See ***Deserters From Draft Index, 1917-1918*** **[Microfilm],** from the original records at the Michigan State Archives, Lansing, MI. Includes names of the organizations, soldiers, and addresses. Filmed by the Genealogical Society of Utah, 1991, 4 rolls, beginning with FHL film #1765776 (A-Colt). For a complete list of roll numbers and contents of each roll, visit the online FHL catalog page for this title. See
**https://familysearch.org/search/catalog/502894.**

■ ***1917-1919 Michigan Veterans Serving with Allied Forces: Census of World War I Veterans*** **[Microfilm],** from the original records at the Michigan State Archives in Lansing. The list is alphabetical by veteran's name. Michigan State Archives No.: MS78-92 v. 368-373. Filmed by the Genealogical Society of Utah, 1996, 5 rolls, as follows:

- WWI veterans (A-Cole), FHL film #2056789.
- WWI veterans (Cole-Kee), FHL film #2056790.
- WWI veterans (Kel-Pl), FHL film #2056791.
- WWI veterans (Po-Williams, F), FHL film #2056792.
- WWI veterans (Williams, G-Z), FHL film #2056793.

■ **1920-1935.** See ***Pontiac (Michigan) City Directories*** **[Microfilm],** from various publishers. FHL has 1920, 1922, 1923, 1925, 1927, 1928, 1929, 1930, 1931, and 1935. Filmed by Research Publications, Woodbridge, CT, 1984, 6 rolls, beginning with FHL film #2310333 (Polk's Pontiac Directory, 1920). For a complete list of roll numbers and contents of each roll, visit the online FHL catalog page for this title. See
**https://familysearch.org/search/catalog/1130597.**

■ **1924-1940.** See ***Applications for Admission to Veteran's Facility, 1924-1940*** **[Microfilm],** from the originals at the MI State Archives, Lansing, MI. The dates are based on the date of the application for admission to the Michigan Soldiers' Home – some admissions did not occur until well into the 1960s. These records contain correspondence relating to each individual, completed application forms for admission to the facility, and military discharge papers. They all provide a good deal of personal information about veterans seeking to live at the Michigan Soldiers' Home. Data from these records include military history, physical characteristics, and details about the immediate family. Filmed by the Genealogical Society of Utah, 2001, 53 rolls, beginning with FHL film #2217099 (Applications, 1924-1925). For a complete list of roll numbers and contents of each roll, visit the online FHL catalog page for this title. See **https://familysearch.org/search/catalog/1131989.**

■ **1933.** See ***Census Cards, Sanilac County, Michigan, 1933*** **[Microfilm],** from the original records at the Archives of Michigan, Lansing, MI. In 1933, the legislature passed Act 237 which was designed to provide assistance to the elderly. To implement this act it was deemed wiser to have enumerators canvass the county, rather than require each adult to come to the clerk's office to register. Accordingly, a house to house survey was undertaken to record everyone 21 years of age or older as of November 15, 1933. These are the 1933 census cards for Sanilac County. (Most other counties were lost). The census cards were filmed in alphabetical order according to the first letter of the last name. Each card includes name, sex, color, date, county, city or township, precinct, street, age, date of birth, place of birth, parents' names, spouse's name, employed by, occupation, length of unemployment, source of welfare aid, U.S. citizen, naturalization data, etc. Filmed by the Genealogical Society of Utah, 2002, 6 rolls, beginning with FHL film #2139708 (A-C). For a complete list of roll numbers and contents of each roll, visit the online FHL catalog page for this title. See **https://familysearch.org/search/catalog/1132766.**

■ **1942.** See ***Michigan Selective Service System Registration Cards [World War II]: Fourth Registration*** **[Microfilm],** from the original records at the National Archives, Washington, DC. These cards represent older men, ages 45 to 65 in April 1942, that were registered for the draft. They had birth dates between 28 Apr 1877 and 16 Feb 1892. Registration of deceased men may be located on the latter part of some microfilms. Includes name of individual, date and place of birth, address, age, telephone number, employer's name and address, name and address of person who would know where the individual can be located, signature, and physical description. Filmed by the Genealogical Society of Utah, 243 rolls, beginning with FHL film #1669945 (Aab, Casper – Agostin, Peter). For a complete list of roll numbers and contents of each roll, visit the online FHL catalog page for this title. See **https://familysearch.org/search/catalog/1447661.**

# MINNESOTA
## Censuses & Substitutes, 1830-2006

The area of present Minnesota east of the Mississippi River was included in the formation of the United States per the Treaty of Paris of 1783. The western area of Minnesota was part of la Louisiane Française, 1717-1762; part of Spanish Louisiana, 1762-1802; part of (Napoleon's) Louisiana, 1802-1803; and part of the Louisiana Purchase of 1803, when the rest of Minnesota became American territory.

**Early Census Jurisdictions.** At the time of the 1820 and 1830 federal censuses, Minnesota east of the Mississippi River was part of Michigan Territory. But, no census enumerators made the 700 mile trip from Detroit to see if there were any people living there. Missed was the fur trading post at Fond du Lac (now Duluth) established in 1817 by John Jacob Astor, and a busy community into the 1840s.

The area west of the Mississippi was part of the Unorganized Territory, 1820-1830, and was assumed to be uninhabited. Although ignored by the census takers, there were a good number of French-Canadians known to be living in the Pembina/Red River region in the 1820s and 1830s.

The first census that recorded people living in present Minnesota was the 1836 Wisconsin Territory Census, as part of St. Croix Co, WI Terr. In the 1840 federal census, present Minnesota was part of two territories, with a few people enumerated along the Mississippi River at Ft. Snelling and Wabasha as part of Clayton County, Iowa Territory. Although still part of unceded Indian lands, the fur trading posts on Lake Superior were enumerated as part of St. Croix County, Wisconsin Territory.

**Minnesota Territory Censuses.** Wisconsin became a state in May 1848, leaving the area between the St. Croix River and the Mississippi River without any government. The approximately 4,500 residents of the area immediately began petitioning Congress to become a territory, and in March 1849, Minnesota Territory was born. The area of the new territory spanned between the present Wisconsin border and the Missouri River.

The first MN Territory census was taken in June 1849, with two counties (St. Croix and La Pointe) inherited from Wisconsin Territory. By the end of 1849, the two were replaced with nine original Minnesota Territory counties: East of the Mississippi River: Benton, Ramsay, Washington, and Itasca counties; West of the Mississippi: Pembina, Mahkahta, Wahnahta, Dakotah, and Wabashaw counties.

The 1850 federal census taken for MN Territory survives complete for the nine original counties with a total population of about 6,100. The next territorial census was taken in 1853, and again in 1855; but both are very incomplete. Just prior to statehood, the U.S. federal government funded a special Minnesota Territory census in 1857. By 1860, Minnesota's population had gone from 4,500 people in nine counties to 172,000 people in sixty counties.

The surviving manuscripts for Minnesota's territorial censuses were microfilmed by the Minnesota Historical Society (MHS) in St. Paul. The 1857 special federal census was microfilmed by the National Archives. **Territorial Censuses Online:** The microfilms of the 1849, 1853, 1855, and 1857 censuses taken during the territorial period of Minnesota have all been digitized and indexed at the MHS website and at the Ancestry.com website.

**Minnesota State Censuses.** After statehood in 1858, Minnesota took state censuses for 1865, 1875, 1885, 1895, and 1905. All of these can be viewed at the Family History Library (FHL) in Salt Lake City. However, none of the Minnesota state censuses on microfilm can be borrowed on interlibrary loan through the FHL – they must be borrowed through the MHS. **State Censuses Online:** The MN State Censuses from 1865, 1875, 1885, 1895 and 1905 have all been digitized and indexed at the MHS website, as well as the Ancestry.com website and the FamilySearch.org website.

**Minnesota Federal Censuses (federal copies).** The 1850 federal census for Minnesota Territory is complete for all nine original counties, and the special 1857 federal census for Minnesota Territory is also complete (but with some strange anomalies). The state of Minnesota is complete for 1860-1880; lost for 1890 (like all states); and complete for 1900-1940. All federal censuses digitized and indexed online for all states are identified in *Chapter 5W - Nationwide* (Vol. 3, Ch. 5W).

**Minnesota Federal Census (state copies).** The MHS also holds the original 1850 and 1860 federal censuses for all Minnesota counties – the state copies. For these census years, researchers have two versions to compare: the federal copy and the state copy. The 1850 state copy was extracted and indexed in a book published by the MHS; the 1860 state copy has other schedules mixed in with the population schedules, and page numbers for the schedules do not always agree with those found on the federal set. The MHS has a microfilmed card index to their 1860 state copy.

## Resources at the Minnesota Historical Society

Online searching for resources at the MHS is enhanced by a special **People Finder** index. People Finder searches include materials of the State Archives of the Minnesota Historical Society. For any item associated with a person, use a direct or key word search. For an instruction page and link to the People Finder, see **http://sites.mnhs.org/library/search-help-people-finder-and-searchmnhsorg.**

**MHS People Finder - Types of Records**

- Birth records, 1900-1934; 1935-2002
- Death records, 1908-2002
- Territorial/State census records, 1849-1905
- Veteran's grave registrations
- World War I Bonus Records
- Objects, books and photos
- Collection inventories (Finding aids)
- And much more!

**MHS Search Tips & Guides Available**

- Video Tutorial on the new searches
- Search Help
- Family History Research Guide
- Birth Certificate Index FAQ
- Death Certificate Index FAQ
- State Census Index FAQ
- Veterans' Grave Index FAQ
- Library Video Tutorials

**MHS Library Catalog:** A search of the MHS library catalog is also useful to find titles of resources not obviously part of the collections. A separate search screen is at
**http://mnhs.mnpals.net/F?RN=590157597&func=file&file_name=basic.**

---

## Minnesota Databases Online at Ancestry.com

The Ancestry.com subscription website allows free access to all indexes, but to view any particular record requires a membership. Ancestry offers trial memberships and subscriptions for short periods and reduced rates. The following databases at the Ancestry.com website are unique to Minnesota under the categories, Census & Voter Lists, Vital Records, Military, Immigrations, et al.

■ **1800s-1925.** See ***Minnesota, Wills and Probate Records, 1801-1925*** **[Online Database],** indexed at the Ancestry.com website. Source: MN county, district, and probate courts. In most cases, probates reveal the names and residences of beneficiaries and their relationship to the decedent. An inventory of the estate assets can reveal personal details about the deceased's occupation and lifestyle. There may also be references to debts, deeds, and other documents related to the settling of the estate. This database has 689,918 records. See
**http://search.ancestry.com/search/db.aspx?dbid=9070.**

■ **1830-1850s.** See ***Minnesota Cemetery Inscription Index, Select Counties*** **[Online Database],** indexed at the Ancestry.com website. Source: book, same title, by John Dalby, publ. 2003. This is an index of cemeteries in Blue Earth, Carver, Dakota, Dodge, Goodhue, Hennepin, Le Sueur, McLeod, Olmsted, Rice, Scott, Sibley, Steele, and Waseca counties and also in the cities of St. Paul and Winnebago Minnesota; and Beloit, Illinois. This database has 338,304 records (and nearly 600,000 names). See
**http://search.ancestry.com/search/db.aspx?dbid=3775.**

■ **1830s-1907.** See ***Minnesota, Homestead and Cash Entry Patents, Pre-1908*** **[Online Database],** indexed at the Ancestry.com website. Source: BLM's GLO Automated Records Project. A patent is the first-title deed and the true beginning of private ownership of the land. The patent describes in legal terms the land to which the title is given. Information recorded in these records includes: Name, Land Office, Sequence Document number, Total acres, Signature, Canceled document, Issue date, Mineral rights reserved, Metes and bounds, Statutory reference, Multiple warrantee and patentee names, Act or treaty, Entry classification, and Land description (Section/Range/Township). This database has 160,634 records. See
**http://search.ancestry.com/search/db.aspx?dbid=2076.**

■ **1835-1890.** See ***Minnesota, Compiled Census and Census Substitute Index, 1835-1890*** **[Online Database],** indexed at the Ancestry.com website. Originally edited by Ronald Jackson, Accelerated Indexing Systems, Salt Lake City, UT. This collection contains the following indexes: 1835-39 Tax Lists Index; 1849 Territorial Census Index; 1850 Federal Census Index; 1860 Federal Census Index; 1870 Federal Census Index; 1880 Federal Census Index; and 1890 Veterans Schedule. This database has 337,169 records. See
**http://search.ancestry.com/search/db.aspx?dbid=3555.**

■ **1840-1980.** See ***Minnesota, Births and Christenings Index, 1840-1980*** **[Online Database],** indexed at the Ancestry.com website. Source: FamilySearch extractions from original and compiled records on microfilm at the Family History Library. Each record may list a Name, Gender, Race, Birthplace, Birth date, Christening date, Christening place, Age at christening, Father's name, Age, Birthplace, Mother's name, Age, Birthplace, Paternal grandparents, Maternal grandparents, and FHL film number. This database has 1,026,005 records. See
**http://search.ancestry.com/search/db.aspx?dbid=2550.**

■ **1849-1905.** See ***Minnesota, Territorial and State Censuses, 1849-1905*** **[Online Database],** indexed at the Ancestry.com website. Source: MN Hist. Soc., St. Paul, MN. This combined database of territorial and state censuses is also accessible at the MHS website. Each record may include: Name, Enumeration place, Age, Gender, Race, and Birthplace. **Contents, Territorial Censuses: 1849:** includes the counties of St. Croix and La Pointe inherited from Wisconsin Territory (from which nine original Minnesota counties were created by the end of 1849: Benton, Dakota, Itasca, Mankatah, Pembina, Ramsey, Wabashaw, Wahnahta, and Washington counties). **1853:** Dakota and Washington counties only. **1855:** surviving counties include Chisago, Doty, Superior, and Wright counties only. **1857:** Includes Anoka, Benton, Blue Earth, Brown, Buchanan, Carlton,

Carver, Cass, Chisago, Cottonwood, Crow Wing, Dakota, Dodge, Faribault, Fillmore, Freeborn, Goodhue, Hennepin, Houston, Isanti, Itasca, Jackson, Lake, Le Sueur, Mahnomen, Martin, McLeod, Meeker, Morrison, Mower, Murray, Nicollet, Nobles, Olmsted, Pembina, Pierce, Pine, Pipestone, Ramsey, Renville, Rice, Rock, Scott, Sherburne, Sibley, St. Louis, Stearns, Steele, Todd, Wabasha, Waseca, Washington, Winona, and Wright. **Note:** see the FHL Books & Microfilms entry for the microfilmed 1857 MN Census, with a note regarding falsified records (page 83). **Contents, State Censuses: 1865, 1875, 1885, 1895, & 1905:** Complete for all MN counties. Includes all members of a household, with names, ages, birthplaces, etc. In 1865, "Soldier in service on June 1, 1865" was included. The 1875 census gives the birthplaces of father and mother. The 1895 and 1905 censuses included the length of time an individual had lived in the state. This database has 5,710,993 records. See
**http://search.ancestry.com/search/db.aspx?dbid=1058.**

■ **1849-1950.** See ***Minnesota, Marriages Index, 1849-1950*** **[Online Database],** indexed at the Ancestry.com website. Source: FamilySearch extractions from original and compiled records on microfilm at the Family History Library. Each record may include: name, age, marital status, birth date, birthplace, race, place of marriage, date of marriage, father's name, mother's name, grandparent, spouse's name, birth date, birthplace, race, age, previous spouse, spouse's grandparent, previous spouse, and FHL film number. The starting year of 1849 probably came from titles of microfilm used to compile this database. But, searching the earliest records by year of marriage reveals hundreds of marriages between 1800 and 1849. This database has 778,376 records. See
**http://search.ancestry.com/search/db.aspx?dbid=2561.**

■ **1854-1957.** See ***Minnesota, Naturalization Records Index, 1854-1957*** **[Online Database],** indexed at the Ancestry.com website. Source: *Minnesota, Naturalization Records Index, 1854-1957,* edited by Conrad Peterzen. This is an index to the name of each person requesting citizenship and includes Spouses name, county of residence, microfilm reel reference, print volume, and page number. The index also includes records of people who were denied citizenship and those who never completed the process. The index contains 61 counties and roughly 865,000 records. See
**http://search.ancestry.com/search/db.aspx?dbid=3826.**

■ **1861-1865.** See ***Minnesota, Civil War Records, 1861-1865*** **[Online Database],** indexed at the Ancestry.com website. Source: *MN Civil War Muster Rolls,* MHS, St. Paul. This database has 107,586 records. See
**http://search.ancestry.com/search/db.aspx?dbid=1715.**

■ **1861-1865.** See ***Minnesota Civil War Soldiers*** **[Online Database],** indexed at the Ancestry.com website. Book, same title, by John Dalby, publ. 1999. This database has 26,088 records. See
**http://search.ancestry.com/search/db.aspx?dbid=3729.**

■ **1877-1948.** See ***Minnesota County History Name Index*** **[Online Database],** indexed at the Ancestry.com website. Source: John Dalby's *Minnesota County History Name Index*, publ. 1999. This database is a name index of eleven county histories and plat books for the area immediately south of St. Paul. Researchers will find the name of county resident, the book in which the person's name appears, and the page number. Where information is available, town of residence is also given. Dakota, Dodge, Goodhue, Le Sueur, Olmsted, Rice, Steele, and Winona counties are covered in this collection. This database has 216,812 records. See
**http://search.ancestry.com/search/db.aspx?dbid=3721.**

■ **1880-1920.** See ***Minnesota, Federal Naturalization Records, 1880-1920*** **[Online Database],** indexed at the Ancestry.com website. Source: National Archives microfilm, MN district and circuit court records. Records include petitions, declarations, and certificates. This database has 71,368 records. See
**http://search.ancestry.com/search/db.aspx?dbid=61202.**

■ **1889-1891.** See ***Minneapolis, Minnesota Directories, 1889-1891*** **[Online Database],** indexed at the Ancestry.com website. Source: Minneapolis Directory Co, 1889-1889, and 1890-1891. This database has 77,037 records. See
**http://search.ancestry.com/search/db.aspx?dbid=4561.**

■ **1889-1891.** See ***St. Paul, Minnesota City Directories, 1889-1891*** **[Online Database],** indexed at the Ancestry.com website. Source: R.L. Polk Directories, 1889-1890 and 1890-1891. This database has 71,443 records. See
**http://search.ancestry.com/search/db.aspx?dbid=4491.**

■ **1890-1963.** See ***U.S., Northern Pacific Railway Company Personnel Files, 1890-1963*** **[Online Database],** indexed at the Ancestry.com website. Source: MHS, St. Paul. This collection of personnel

files from the Northern Pacific Railway Company in Minnesota includes company correspondence, job history, salary and promotion documents, and leaves of absence, and more. This database has 167,628 records. See
**http://search.ancestry.com/search/db.aspx?dbid=2157.**

■ **1898-1899.** See ***Minnesota Volunteers in the Spanish American War and the Philippine Insurrection*** **[Online Database],** indexed at the Ancestry.com website. Source: Book, same title, by Franklin F. Holbrook, publ. 1923. There are a total of 9,846 records which each include the Name, Unit, Company, Rank, Age (if given), Birthplace (if given), Residence, and Page Number (from original book). The additional information in the book is a description of his military service. Index also includes Army, Navy and Marine personnel as well as Minnesotans who served in other state units. This database has 9,847 records. See
**http://search.ancestry.com/search/db.aspx?dbid=4816.**

■ **1898-1899.** See ***Minnesota, Spanish American War Muster Rolls and Casualty Lists, 1898-1899*** **[Online Database],** indexed at the Ancestry.com website. Source: Adjutant General's report at the MHS. This database includes muster-in and muster-out rolls for the four Minnesota regiments that served in the Spanish-American War: the 12th, 13th, 14th, and 15th regiments. Some field returns and casualty reports are also included. Details listed can include name, date, rank, place, residence, regiment, and death date where applicable, depending on the form. This database has 3,992 records. See
**http://search.ancestry.com/search/db.aspx?dbid=6070.**

■ **1900-1934.** See ***Web: Minnesota, Birth Index, 1900-1934*** **[Online Database],** indexed at the Ancestry.com website. Source: MN Birth Certificates Index, MHS). This database is also accessible at the MHS website. Each record includes the child's full name, father's full name, mother's maiden name, birth date, birth county, and state file number. Most of the records are linked to the People Finder at the MHS website. This database has 1,820,984 records. See
**http://search.ancestry.com/search/db.aspx?dbid=9196.**

■ **1900-1999.** See ***Web: Minnesota, Cemetery Index, 1900-1999*** **[Online Database],** indexed at the Ancestry.com website. This database is also accessible at the Iron Range Research Center website. This database has 15,567 records. See
**http://search.ancestry.com/search/db.aspx?dbid=9746.**

■ **1908-2002.** See ***Minnesota, Death Index, 1908-2002*** **[Online Database],** indexed at the Ancestry.com website. Source: MN Dept of Health. The index may include: Name of the deceased, City and county of death, Date of death, Birth date, Birthplace, Mother's maiden name, and State file number. This database has 2,931,700 records. See
**http://search.ancestry.com/search/db.aspx?dbid=7316.**

■ **1918.** See ***Web: Minnesota, Alien Registration Index, 1918*** **[Online Database],** indexed at the Ancestry.com website. This database is also accessible at the Iron Range Research Center website. This database has 111,827 records. See
**http://search.ancestry.com/search/db.aspx?dbid=70801.**

■ **1919.** See ***Web: Minnesota, Women in Industry, 1919*** **[Online Database],** indexed at the Ancestry.com website. This database is also accessable at the Iron Range Research Center website. This database has 41,684 records. See
**http://search.ancestry.com/search/db.aspx?dbid=70787.**

■ **1929-1956.** See ***Minnesota, Crew Lists, 1929-1956*** **[Online Database],** indexed at the Ancestry.com website. Source: National Archives microfilm: *Crew Lists of Vessels Arriving at Two Harbors, Minnesota, August 1929-October 1956.* And *Crew Lists of Vessels Arriving at Baudette, Grand Marais, International Falls, Ranier, and Warroad, Minnesota, 1946-1956.* Passengers are not included. This database has 12,671 records. See
**http://search.ancestry.com/search/db.aspx?dbid=8987.**

■ **1930-1988.** See ***Minnesota, Naturalization Card Index, 1930-1988*** **[Online Database],** indexed at the Ancestry.com website. Source: FamilySearch, from National Archives microfilm. The collection consists of two naturalization card indexes from the District Court of Minnesota 3rd division and 4th division. The index cards include: Certificate number, Name, Residence, Birth date, Admission date, Certificate date, Name of court, Place of court, Petition number, Alien registration number, and Signature of immigrant. This database has 71,367 records. See
**http://search.ancestry.com/search/db.aspx?dbid=60723.**

■ **1935-2002.** See **Minnesota Birth Index, 1935-2002 [Online Database],** indexed at the Ancestry.com website. Source: MN Dept of Health. Each record includes the child's full name, father's full name, mother's maiden name, birth date, birth county, and state file number. Most of the records are linked to an order form to obtain a copy of the original document. This database has 4,267,629 records. See **http://search.ancestry.com/search/db.aspx?dbid=8742.**

■ **1958-2001.** See ***Minnesota, Marriage Index, 1958-2001*** **[Online Database],** indexed at the Ancestry.com website. Source: MN Dept of Health. Information available in this database includes: Names of bride and groom, Ages of bride and groom, Birth dates of bride and groom (year of birth based on age at time of marriage), Marriage date, Marriage place, and State file number. This database has 2,712,387 records. See **http://search.ancestry.com/search/db.aspx?dbid=8721.**

■ **1970-1995.** See ***Minnesota, Divorce Index, 1970-1995*** **[Online Database],** indexed at the Ancestry.com website. Source: MN Dept of Health. Each record includes: Husband's name, Husband's age, Wife's name, Wife's age, Divorce date, and County where the divorce was filed. Searching the individual records (index cards) by date reveals hundreds of divorces that supposedly took place in the 1950s and 1960s, yet they were recorded with MN printouts dated in the 1970s, 1980s, and 1990s. (Trust the digitized MN Printout, not Ancestry's individual index record). This database has 734,109 records. See **http://search.ancestry.com/search/db.aspx?dbid=1081.**

## Minnesota Databases Online at the FamilySearch.org Website

The following databases are available for free at the FamilySearch.org website. To see the current list, visit the Minnesota Indexed Historical Records and Minnesota Image Only Historical Records webpage. Both lists are updated periodically. See **https://familysearch.org/search/collection/location/18.**

■ **1835-1990.** See ***Minnesota Deaths and Burials, 1835-1990*** **[Online Database],** indexed at the FamilySearch.org website. Source: FamilySearch extractions of death and burial records from microfilm at the Family History Library, Salt Lake City, UT. This database has 1,434,142 records. See **https://familysearch.org/search/collection/1680831.**

■ **1840-1980.** See ***Minnesota Births and Christenings, 1840-1980*** **[Online Database],** indexed at the FamilySearch.org website. Source: FamilySearch extractions of birth, baptism and christening records from microfilm at the Family History Library, Salt Lake City, UT. This database has 1,203,969 records. See **https://familysearch.org/search/collection/1680827.**

■ **1849-1950.** See ***Minnesota Marriages, 1849-1950*** **[Online Database],** indexed at the FamilySearch.org website. Source: FamilySearch extractions of marriage records from various collections at the Family History Library, Salt Lake City, UT. This database has 438,331 records. See **https://familysearch.org/search/collection/1680832.**

■ **1849-1985.** See ***Minnesota Will Records, 1849-1985*** **[Online Database],** indexed at the FamilySearch.org website. Source: court records at the MHS, St. Paul. This project was indexed in partnership with the Minnesota Historical Society. Name indexes of the Probate Court will books for the counties of the state and territory of Minnesota. Some testators who resided outside of Minnesota recorded their wills in these Probate Courts. Three Minnesota counties are not in this collection: Hennepin, Marshall, and St. Louis. This database has 189,458 records. See **https://familysearch.org/search/collection/1607922.**

■ **1850-2001.** See ***Minnesota, County Deaths, 1850-2001*** **[Online Database],** digitized at the FamilySearch.org website. Source: FamilySearch imaging from county records on microfilm at the Family History Library. This image only database includes digital images of birth records from various county courthouses. Browse the collection, organized by county, then by the county's death index books. This database has 367,790 records. See **https://familysearch.org/search/collection/2185953.**

■ **1857.** See ***Minnesota Territorial Census, 1857*** **[Online Database],** indexed at the FamilySearch.org website. Source: National Archives microfilm series T1175. This special federal census taken in Minnesota Territory in 1857 contains a listing of families (by Dwelling No. and Family No. in order of enumeration); names of each member of a family (starting with the assumed head of household, but with no relationships given) whose usual abode was in this household on 21 September 1857; each individual's age; sex; color, place of birth; whether a native voter or a naturalized voter; and occupation (of every male over 15 years of age). **Note:** In May 1857, the MN territorial legislature had created seven new "paper" counties in the southwestern part of present

Minnesota. The entire region was unceded Indian land and had no white population. In September 1857, the federal government mandated and funded a census to be taken in Minnesota Territory. That census included the seven paper counties (Cottonwood, Jackson, Martin, Murray, Nobles, Pipestone, and Rock) that had no population, but Democrats fabricated census schedules complete with names, ages, occupations, etc. Having previously stuffed ballot boxes with made-up names of voters, the census schedules were fraudulently created to cover their ballot fraud. For the history of this census fraud, see Robert J. Forrest, "Mythical Cities of Southwestern Minnesota," in *Minnesota History*, Vol. 14 (1933), pp243-52. This database has 156,888 records (including the fabricated records in seven counties). To view the fabricated names, use the View Images in this Collection and select one of the newly created counties. See **https://familysearch.org/search/collection/1503055.**

■ **1860-1949.** See ***Minnesota, County Marriages, 1860-1949*** **[Online Database],** indexed at the FamilySearch.org website. Source: FamilySearch extractions from county courthouse records from Anoka, Blue Earth, Brown, Carver, Cottonwood, Dodge, Faribault, Fillmore, Freeborn, Goodhue, Hennepin, and Kanabec counties, Minnesota. See the FamilySearch Wiki for this title for the years of coverage for each county. This database has 870,856 records. See **https://familysearch.org/search/collection/1803974.**

■ **1863-1983.** See ***Minnesota, County Birth Records, 1863-1983*** **[Online Database],** digitized at the FamilySearch.org website. Source: FamilySearch imaging from county records on microfilm at the Family History Library. This image only database includes digital images of birth records from various county courthouses. Some birth registers are for cities or townships. The year range varies by county. Browse the collection, organized by county, then by county's birth index books (for a range of years). This database has 150,669 records. See **https://familysearch.org/search/collection/1920099.**

■ **1865.** See ***Minnesota State Census, 1865*** **[Online Database],** indexed at the FamilySearch.org website. Source: MHS-State Archives, St. Paul. The 1865 census contains a listing of families (by Family No. in order of enumeration); names of each member of a family (starting with the assumed head of household, but with no relationships given) whose usual abode was in this household on 1 June 1865; whether male or female; the color of each person; whether any member of household was deaf, dumb, blind, or insane; and whether any male of the household was serving in the military on June 1, 1865. **Note:** Each family member is listed with surnames and given names, but since no ages are given for any member of a family, it is difficult to predict the family positions of a spouse or child, except by the order they are listed. This database has 246,591 records. See **https://familysearch.org/search/collection/1503054**.

■ **1865-2006.** See ***Minnesota, Clay and Steele County Obituaries, 1865-2006*** **[Online Database],** indexed at the FamilySearch.org website. Index and images of newspaper obituary files filmed by FamilySearch at the Clay County Historical Society and the Steele County Historical Society in Minnesota. This database has 29,797 records. See **https://familysearch.org/search/collection/2281907.**

■ **1866-1916.** See ***Minnesota Death Records, 1866-1916*** **[Online Database],** indexed at the FamilySearch.org website. Source: extractions from microfilmed records of the MN Dept of Health. This is a name index of municipal death records in St. Paul (Ramsey County) and Minneapolis (Hennepin County), Minnesota. The collection includes death registers, mortuary records, and death certificates. This database has 383,230 records. See **https://familysearch.org/search/collection/1858352.**

■ **1869-1940.** See ***Minnesota, Grand Army of the Republic Membership Records, 1869-1940*** **[Online Database],** indexed at the FamilySearch.org website. Source: MHS, St. Paul. This database includes membership records of the Minnesota Department Grand Army of the Republic, an organization of Union army and navy veterans of the Civil War. The collection consists of registers, lists, adjutant and quartermaster reports and descriptive books of local posts (chapters). Records include town of residence, military unit, date of enlistment, date of discharge, age and birthplace. This database has 164,338 records. See **https://familysearch.org/search/collection/2239221.**

■ **1872-1930.** See ***Minnesota, Itasca County Land Records, 1872-1930*** **[Online Database],** digitized at the FamilySearch.org website. Source: Itasca County Recorder, Grand Rapids, MN. Land records, including grantee and grantor indexes. Browse the images, organized by record type, date range, and volume. This database has 7,328 records. See **https://familysearch.org/search/collection/2030516.**

■ **1872-1947.** See ***Minnesota, Clay County Land and Property Records, 1872-1947* [Online Database],** digitized at the FamilySearch.org website. Images of records from the courthouse in Moorhead, Minnesota. The land records include grantor indexes, grantee indexes, deeds, abstract books, and other books. Some indexes go beyond the year 1947. Browse the records, organized by Record Type, Year Range, and Volume. This database has 31,590 records. See **https://familysearch.org/search/collection/1762576.**

■ **1875.** See ***Minnesota State Census, 1875* [Online Database],** indexed at the FamilySearch.org website. Source: MHS-State Archives, St. Paul. The 1875 census contains a listing of families (by Family No. in order of enumeration); names of each member of a family (starting with the assumed head of household, but with no relationships given) whose usual abode was in this household on 1 June 1875; the individual's age; sex, color, nativity (state or country); and nativity of a person's father and mother. This database has 612,847 records. See **https://familysearch.org/search/collection/1503053.**

■ **1876-2006.** See ***Minnesota, Stevens County Genealogical Society Records, 1876-2006* [Online Database],** digitized at the FamilySearch.org website. Images of records housed at the Morris Public Library in Donnelly, MN. The records include a marriage card index, obituary index, and obituaries. This database has 63,363 records. See **https://familysearch.org/search/collection/1419635.**

■ **1885.** See ***Minnesota State Census, 1885* [Online Database],** indexed at the FamilySearch.org website. Source: MHS-State Archives, St. Paul. The 1885 census contains a listing of families (by Family No. in order of enumeration); names of each member of a family (starting with the assumed head of household, but with no relationships given) whose usual abode was in this household on 1 June 1885; the individual's age; sex, color, nativity (state or country); whether father of foreign birth; whether mother of foreign birth, and whether a person "served as a soldier in the federal army during the Rebellion." This database has 1,133,198 records. See **https://familysearch.org/search/collection/1503044.**

■ **1892-1930.** See ***Minnesota, Roseau County Land Records, 1892-1930* [Online Database],** digitized at the FamilySearch.org website. Images of deeds, mortgages, bonds, probate records, homesteads, quit claims, U.S. Patent records, and Misc. Records from the courthouse in Roseau, MN. Browse the records, organized by Record Type, Date Range, and Volume. This database has 109,958 records. See **https://familysearch.org/search/collection/2019834.**

■ **1895.** See ***Minnesota State Census, 1895* [Online Database],** indexed at the FamilySearch.org website. Source: MHS-State Archives, St. Paul. The 1895 census contains a listing of families (by Family No. in order of enumeration); names of each member of a family (starting with the assumed head of household, but with no relationships given) whose usual abode was in this household on 1 June 1895; the individual's age; sex, color, nativity (state or country); for males over 21: length of residence in MN in years and months, and residence in the enumeration district in year and months; regular occupation; number of months employed at regular occupation; whether a soldier or sailor in the War of the Rebellion; father of foreign birth (yes or no); and mother of foreign birth (yes or no). This database has 1,570,739 records. See **https://familysearch.org/search/collection/1503031.**

■ **1905.** See ***Minnesota State Census, 1905* [Online Database],** indexed at the FamilySearch.org website. Source: MHS-State Archives, St. Paul. The 1905 census contains a listing of families (by Family No. in order of enumeration); names of each member of a family (starting with the assumed head of household, but with no relationships given) whose usual abode was in this household on 1 June 1905; the individual's sex; age; color, nativity (state or country); nativity of father; nativity of mother; length of residence in MN in years and months, and residence in the enumeration district in year and months; regular occupation; Army Service (Sold. or Sail.); and Wars (Civil War, Spanish War). This database has 1,973,884 records. See **https://familysearch.org/search/collection/1503056.**

■ **1908-2002.** See ***Minnesota Death Index, 1908-2002* [Online Database],** indexed at the FamilySearch.org website. Source: MN Dept of Health (indexed by Ancestry). The index may include: Name of the deceased, City and county of death, Date of death, Birth date, Birthplace, Mother's maiden name, and State file number. This database has 2,931,700 records. See **https://familysearch.org/search/collection/1937234.**

■ **1909-1962.** See ***Minnesota, Clay County, School Census Records, 1909-1962* [Online Database],** digitized at the FamilySearch.org website. Images of school census records arranged by district number.

The records include the pupil's name, age, and name of a parent or guardian. This database has 14,457 records. See
**https://familysearch.org/search/collection/1760963.**

■ **1910-1923.** See ***Minnesota, Baudette, Warroad, and International Falls Passenger Lists, 1910-1923*** **[Online Database],** indexed at the FamilySearch.org website. Source: National Archives microfilm series A3490. The records usually include the person's name, gender, age, marital status, citizenship, race, place of last permanent residence, and destination, how long they intend to remain in the U.S or become a U.S. citizen. This database has 793 records. See
**https://familysearch.org/search/collection/2443340.**

■ **1917-1919.** See ***Minnesota, YMCA World War I Service Cards, 1917-1919*** **[Online Database],** digitized at the FamilySearch.org website. Source: Univ. of Minnesota, Kautz Family YMCA Archive, Minneapolis, MN. Images of approximately 27,600 index cards with the names of individuals who served with the YMCA during WWI. Cards are arranged alphabetically by surname and include age, home address, and occupation. This database has 27,364 records. See
**https://familysearch.org/search/collection/2513098.**

■ **1930-1988.** See ***Minnesota Naturalization Card Index, 1930-1988*** **[Online Database],** indexed at the FamilySearch.org website. Source: National Archives microfilm of two card indexes from the District Court 3rd Division and 4th Division (Minnesota). The index cards include the following information: Certificate number, Name, Residence, Birth date, Admission date, Certificate date, Name of court, Place of court, Petition number, and Alien registration number. This database has 71,367 records. See
**https://familysearch.org/search/collection/2120721.**

■ **1935-2002.** See ***Minnesota Birth Index, 1935-2002*** **[Online Database],** indexed at the FamilySearch.org website. Source: MN Dept of Health. Each record includes the child's full name, father's full name, mother's maiden name, birth date, birth county, and state file number. Most of the records are linked to an order form to obtain copy of the original document. This database has 4,267,620 records. See
**https://familysearch.org/search/collection/1949334.**

■ **1958-2001.** See ***Minnesota Marriage Index, 1958-2001*** **[Online Database],** indexed at the FamilySearch.org website. Source: MN Dept of Health (indexed by Ancestry). The index may contain any of the following information: Name of bride and groom, Birthplace and estimated year of birth for bride and groom, Ages, Parents' names, Previous spouses, Marriage place and date, and Race. This database has 2,414,040 records. See
**https://familysearch.org/search/collection/1949335.**

■ **1970-1995.** See ***Minnesota Divorce Index, 1970-1995*** **[Online Database],** indexed at the FamilySearch.org website. Source: MN Dept of Health (indexed by Ancestry). The index lists the following information: Name of husband, Name of wife, Docket number, Divorce date, Divorce place, and Reference number (page, volume, entry number). This database has 366,350 records. See
**https://familysearch.org/search/collection/1967743.**

## Minnesota Databases Online at Various Websites

■ **1830s-1900s.** See ***Minnesota USGenWeb Archives*** **[Online Database].** The MNGenWeb Archives site offers free genealogical databases with searchable statewide name lists and for all Minnesota counties. Databases may include Bibles, Biographies, Cemeteries, Censuses, Court Records, Deaths, Deeds, Directories, Histories, Marriages, Military, Newspapers, Obituaries, Photos, Schools, Tax Lists, Wills, and more. See
**http://usgwarchives.net/mn/mnfiles.htm.**

■ **1830s-1900s.** See ***Linkpendium – Minnesota: Family History & Genealogy, Census, Birth, Marriage, Death Vita Records & More*** **[Online Databases].** Linkpendium is a genealogical portal site with links to state, county, town, and local databases. Currently listed are selected sites for Minnesota statewide resources (434), Independent Cities, Renamed Counties, Discontinued Counties (29), Aitkin County (140), Anoka County (211), Becker County (207), Beltrami County (158), Benton County (171), Blue Earth County (352) and 81 more Minnesota counties. See
**www.linkpendium.com/mn-genealogy.**

■ **1830s-1900s Minnesota Original Land Owners.** See the ***Family Maps*** series for Minnesota counties, maps of all original land patents, compiled by Greg Boyd and published by Arphax Publishing Co., Norman, OK. These privately-produced computer-generated maps show the first property owners for an entire county, produced as a book of maps, each map laid out on the federal township grid, and includes indexes to help you locate a person, place-name, or cemetery. Additional maps are added for each county to show roads, waterways, railroads, selected city centers, and cemeteries within a county. At this writing, *Family Maps* books have been published for the following Minnesota counties: Carlton, Douglas, Hennepin, Houston, Hubbard, Kandiyohi, Lac qui Parle, Marshall, Martin, McLeod, Mille Lacs, Murray, Norman, Otter Tail, Pennington, Pope, Red Lake, Roseau, Swift, Todd, Wadena, Washington, and Winona County, Minnesota. Visit the publisher's information and ordering website for more details and updated county coverage. See **www.arphax.com/.** Arphax's entire *Family Maps* series is also available as a subscription service online. See **www.historygeo.com.**

■ **1841-1855.** ***Early Settlers of Washington County, Minnesota*** **[Online Database],** indexed at the RootsWeb site for Washington Co MN. See **www.rootsweb.ancestry.com/~mnwashin/settlers.htm.**

■ *1849 Minnesota Territorial Census* **[Online Database],** indexed at the Park Genealogical Books website. The originals are located at the State Archives at the MN Hist. Soc. The names are listed by precincts within St. Croix County and La Pointe County (the two counties inherited from Wisconsin Territory, but reorganized a few months later into the nine original counties of Minnesota Territory). See **www.parkbooks.com/Html/res_18~1.html.**

■ **1849-1923.** See ***Minnesota Newspaper Archives, 1849-1923*** **[Online Databases],** digitized and indexed newspapers at the GenealogyBank website, for Duluth, Minneapolis, Red Wing,. Saint Anthony, and St. Paul. Minnesota. See **www.genealogybank.com/explore/newspapers/all/usa/minnesota.**

■ **1857-1930.** See ***Dakota County, Minnesota Census Combined Index, 1857, 1865, 1860, 1865, 1900, 1920, and 1930 Censuses*** **[Online Database],** a combined index available at the Dakota County Historical Society website. See **www.dakotahistory.org/genelogy-research.**

■ *1890 Census Substitute* **[Online Database],** indexed at the Ancestry.com website. This is nationwide collection of city directories for the time of the 1890 federal census (lost in a fire in Washington DC in 1921). A global search includes directories from several Minnesota cities. See **http://search.ancestry.com/search/group/1890census.**

■ **1986-Current.** See ***Minnesota Recent Newspaper Obituaries (1986-Current)*** **[Online Database],** digitized and indexed newspaper obituaries at the GenealogyBank website, including newspapers for Albany, Albert Lea, Apple Valley, Austin, Blooming Prairie, Ellendale, Brooklyn Center, Brooklyn Park, Burnsville, and 60 more Minnesota cities. See **www.genealogybank.com/explore/obituaries/all/usa/minnesota.**

---

## Minnesota Periodical Articles
### Censuses & Substitute Name Lists in Genealogical Periodicals

PERSI (PERiodical Source Index) is a digitized database project of the Allen County Public Library (ACPL), Fort Wayne, IN. Since 1986, the PERSI extractors have indexed article titles, places, and surnames from over 11,000 genealogical & historical periodicals. The PERSI database is currently available online through the FindMyPast.com subscription website. The Genealogy Center of the ACPL in Fort Wayne IN holds all 11,000 periodicals and will make copies of any article by special request. To obtain an order form for requesting a printed copy of any article indexed in the PERSI database, see **http://genealogycenter.org/docs/default-source/resources/articlerequest.pdf?sfvrsn=2.**
**Minnesota PERSI Search:** Using the FindMyPast.com website, the keywords "Minnesota state census" had 57 results. A sampling of articles for the territorial/state census years 1849-1905 included the following:

■ **"1849 Territorial Census of Minnesota" [Printed Article],** in *Minnesota Genealogist*, Vol. 11, No. 3 (Sep 1980); and *Minnesota Genealogical Journal*, Vol. 17 (Mar 1997).

■ **"1853 List of Inhabitants, Stillwater" [Printed Article],** in *Minnesota Genealogical Journal*, Vol. 9 (Mar 1993).

■ **1855.** See **"Census, 1855, Winona Prairie" [Printed Article],** in *Minnesota Genealogical Journal*, Vol. 26 (Sep 2001);

■ **1855.** See **"Census, 1855" [Printed Article],** in *Minnesota Genealogical Journal,* Vol. 8 (Sep 1992).

■ **"1865 Minnesota State Census, Carlton County" [Printed Article],** in *Genealogical Society of Carlton County Quarterly,* Vol. 12, No. 1 (Oct 1989).

■ **"1865 Minnesota State Census, Clay County" [Printed Article],** in *Northland Newsletter*, Vol. 1, No. 3 (Jul 1969).

■ **"1865 Minnesota State Census, Civil War Soldiers & Officers" [Printed Article],** in *La Crosse Area Genealogical Quarterly,* Vol. 21, No. 1 (Feb 1999).

■ **"1875 Minnesota State Census, Lincoln County" [Printed Article],** in *Prairieland Pioneer*, Vol. 9, No. 2 (Summer 1992) through Vol. 10, No. 4 (Winter 1993).

■ **"1875 Minnesota State Census, Lyon County" [Printed Article],** abstracts by townships, in *Prairieland Pioneer,* Vol. 3, No. 3 (Spring 1987), and various issues through Vol. 9, No. 4 (Summer 1993).

■ **"1885 Minnesota State Census, Lyon County" [Printed Article],** in *Prairieland Pioneer*, Vol. 4, No. 2 (Winter 1988).

■ **"1885 Minnesota State Census, McLeod County" [Printed Article],** in *Prairieland Pioneer*, Vol. 1, No. 2 (Nov 1984).

■ **"1885 Minnesota State Census, Lake Sarah Township, Murray County" [Printed Article],** in *Prairieland Pioneer*, Vol. 4, No. 3 (Spring 1988).

■ **"1885 Minnesota State Census, Surnames in Girard Township, Otter Tail County" [Printed Article],** in *Otter Tail County Genealogical Society Newsletter,* Vol. 19, No. 1 (Mar 2001).

■ **"1895 Minnesota State Census, Menahga, Becker County" [Printed Article],** in *Heart O'Lakes Genealogical Newsletter,* Vol. 16, No. 1 (Mar 1993) and Vol. 16, No. 2 (Jun 1993).

■ **"1905 Minnesota State Census, Chippewa County, by Townships" [Printed Article],** in *Chippewa County Clippings*, Vol. 1, No. 1 (Sep 1994) through various issues to Vol. 6, No. 4 (Dec 1999).

■ **"1905 Minnesota State Census, Tyler, Lincoln County" [Printed Article],** in *Prairieland Pioneer*, Vol. 3, No. 1 (Fall 1986) and Vol. 3, No. 2 (Winter 1986).

■ **"1905 Minnesota State Census, Lyon County" [Printed Article],** in *Prairieland Pioneer*, Vol. 1, No. 2 (Nov 1984) through Vol. 4, No. 2 (Winter 1988).

## Minnesota Books & Microfilms at the Family History Library

The most important of Minnesota's statewide censuses and substitutes are cited below in chronological order. Each item includes a FHL book number or FHL film number, which can be used to search the FHL catalog for more details. To review an item, start at the FamilySearch catalog search page: **https://familysearch.org/search/catalog/results.** Select "Search by Place" then "United States, Minnesota" to see a list of catalog categories. Or, select "Call Number" then type an FHL book number; or select "Film/Fiche Number" to view a specific title.

■ **1836.** See **"1836 Wisconsin Territorial Census" [Microfilm],** from an article in *Collections of the Wisconsin State Historical Society,* v. 13, p. 247-270. People living between the St. Croix and Mississippi Rivers (now Minnesota) were enumerated as part of St. Croix County, Wisconsin Territory. Filmed by the Genealogical Society of Utah, 1980, 1 roll, FHL film #1293922.

■ **1836.** See ***The First Census of the Original Counties of Dubuque and Demoine (Iowa) Taken in July, 1836* [Microfilm],** from the book edited by Benjamin F. Shambaugh, originally published by the Historical Department of Iowa, Des Moines, IA, 1897-1898, 93 pages. Contents: pt. 1. Dubuque County, pt. 2. Demoine County. From the original manuscript returns preserved in the office of the Secretary of State of Wisconsin. Census taken in accordance with the act of Congress erecting the territory of Wisconsin (of which these two counties at the time formed a part) comprising the present states of Iowa, Minnesota and part of North and South Dakota. Filmed by the Genealogical Society of Utah, 1978, 1 roll, FHL film #1022202.

■ **1840 Federal Census of Clayton County, Iowa Territory and St. Croix County, Wisconsin Territory (now Minnesota),** indexed in ***Minnesota 1840 Census Index* [Printed Index],** another impossible title by Ronald Vern Jackson, publ. Accelerated Indexing Systems, Bountiful, UT, 1981, 57 pages. FHL book 977.6 X22m.

■ **1840s-1907.** See ***Card Files (Index to Land Entry Files of the Government Land Offices in Minnesota)*** **[Microfilm],** from the original index cards at the Bureau of Land Management, Eastern States Office, Washington, DC. The card files serve as an index to the Tract Books, Plat Books, and Case Files relating to ten million public land sales in America. **Content:** Each card contains the following information: Certificate Number, District Land Office, Kind of entry (cash, credit, warrant, etc.), Name of Patentee (Buyer, Entryman, etc.), and county of origin, Land description, Number of acres, Date of patent, Volume, and Page where document can be located. Filmed by the Bureau of Land Management, Washington, DC, c1970, 160 rolls, including 1 roll for Minnesota, FHL film #1501676 (Townships 3N, 20N, 25N-42N, 49N, 90N, 101N, 9, 16, 27, 36, 41, 45 Ranges 20W-32W, 34W, 21-23, 26, 31). For a complete list of roll numbers and contents of each roll, visit the online FHL catalog page for this title. See **https://familysearch.org/search/catalog/511740.** This microfilm collection was digitized as ***Land Records: AL, AR, FL, LA, MI, MN, OH, WI, 1790-1907*** **[CD-ROM]**, by Broderbund, 1996, FHL CD No. 9 pt. 255.

■ ***1849 Census of Minnesota Territory*** **[Printed Abstract],** a typescript located at the Minnesota Historical Society, St. Paul, MN. FHL book 977.6 A1 No. 3 and FHL film #908224. Indexed in ***Minnesota 1849 Census Index*** **[Printed Book],** edited by Ronald Vern Jackson, et al, published by Accelerated Indexing Systems, Bountiful, UT, 1981, 34 pages. FHL book 977.6 X22m 1849.

■ **1850.** See ***Minnesota Territorial Census, 1850*** **[Printed Book],** edited by Patricia C Harpole and Mary D Nagle. This is a complete extract and index to the Minnesota Secretary of State's copy of the 1850 federal census. Publ. MHS, St. Paul, MN, 1972, 115 pages, FHL book 977.6 X2ph 1850.

■ **1853 Minnesota State Census (Fragments).** See ***Mendota Township, Dakota County Assessment Record and Census of Families, 1853*** **[Printed Book],** compiled by Mary Bakeman, publ. MHS, St. Paul, 1995. MHS call no CS42 M553 no. 13; and ***List of Inhabitants in the Town of Stillwater, 1853*** **[Printed Book],** by Mary Bakeman, publ. MHS, St. Paul, 1993. MHS call no. CS42 M553 no.9;

■ **1855 Minnesota Territory Census [Original Manuscript]** at the Minnesota Historical Society, St. Paul, MN. Fragments only, not on microfilm, but a digital version is included with Ancestry's ***Minnesota, Territorial and State Censuses, 1849-1905*** **[Online Database].** See also, ***Minnesota Population Census Schedule for Chisago, Doty, and Superior Counties, Manuscript 1855*** **[Printed Book],** State Archives Notebooks (Barcode 192489-10). See also a few printed abstracts from what appears to be names from the 1855 census: ***Census of Winona Prairie and Town Proper, 1855*** **[Printed Book],** compiled by Mary Bakeman, publ. MHS, St. Paul, 2001. MHS call no CS42 M553 no. 26; which may be the same as **"Census, 1855, Winona Prairie" [Printed Article],** in *Minnesota Genealogical Journal,* Vol. 26 (Sep 2001); and ***The Lost "1855" Census*** **[Printed Book],** by Mary Bakeman, publ. MHS, St. Paul, 1992. MHS call no. CS42 M553 no.8; which may be the same as **"Census, 1855" [Printed Article],** in *Minnesota Genealogical Journal*, Vol. 8 (Sep 1992).

■ ***1857 Minnesota Territory (Federal) Census*** **[Microfilm],** from the original records located at the National Archives, Central Plains Region. Filmed by the National Archives, 1973, series T1175, 8 rolls, available from the FHL as follows:

- Counties of Anoka – Dodge, FHL film #944283.
- Counties of Fairbault – Freeborn, FHL film #944284.
- Counties of Goodhue – Hennepin, FHL film #944285.
- Counties of Houston – Murray, FHL film #944286.
- Counties of Nicollet – Pipestone, FHL film #944287.
- Counties of Ramsey – Sibley, FHL film #944288.
- Counties of Stearns – Waseca, FHL film #944289.
- Counties of Washington – Wright, FHL film #944290.

✓ **NOTE:** the 1857 federal census of Minnesota Territory included seven counties (Cottonwood, Jackson, Martin, Murray, Nobles, Pipestone, and Rock) that had no population, but Democrats fabricated census schedules complete with names, ages, occupations, etc. Having stuffed ballot boxes with made-up names of voters, the census schedules were fraudulently created to cover their ballot fraud. For the history of this census fraud, see Robert J. Forrest, **"Mythical Cities of Southwestern Minnesota" [Printed Article],** in *Minnesota History*, Vol. 14 (1933), pp243-52.

■ ***1860 Federal Census, Minnesota (Federal Copy)*** [Microfilm], from the original records at the National Archives, Washington, DC. Filmed twice by the

National Archives, 1950, 1967, 13 rolls, beginning with FHL film #803567 (2nd filming, Anoka, Becker, Benton, Blue Earth, Brown, Buchanan, Carver, Crow Wing, Morrison, Cass, and Itasca Counties). For a complete list of roll numbers and contents of each roll, see the online FHL catalog page for this title. See **https://familysearch.org/search/catalog/705415.**

■ **1860.** See ***Index to the 1860 Federal Census Schedules for Minnesota (State Copy)*** **[Microfilm],** from the original card index at the State Archives at the Minnesota Historical Society, St. Paul, MN. From FHL catalog: "Cards are arranged by surname in a single alphabetical sequence without respect to residential location. Discrepancies may occur (pagination, name spellings, order of county subdivisions, etc.) because the index was compiled from the original state copy of the 1860 federal census, not the microfilm (federal) copy." The 1860 census card index was filmed by the MHS, 31 rolls. Available from the FHL in Salt Lake City, beginning with FHL film #1373881 (Aakers, Anna - Bacon, William). Interlibrary loan of the microfilm is available from the Minnesota Historical Society only. For more information, including roll contents, see Dennis E. Meissner, ***Guide to the use of the 1860 Minnesota Population Census Schedules and Index,*** publ. MHS, 1978; FHL book 977.6 A1 no. 28).

■ ***1862-1866 Internal Revenue Assessment Lists for Minnesota*** **[Microfilm],** from the originals at the National Archives, Washington, DC, series M0774. The first roll indicates location of county name lists, 3 rolls, beginning with FHL film #1602225 (District 1, division 1-6, Annual, monthly lists Jan-Dec 1866).

■ ***1865 Minnesota State Census*** **[Microfilm],** from the original manuscripts. Filmed by the Minnesota State Library and Records Service, 1969, 3 rolls, available at the Family History Library as follows:

- 1865 Counties of Blue Earth, Brown, Carlton, Lake, St. Louis, Carver, Cass, Chisago, Clay, Crow Wing, Dakota, Dodge, Faribault, Fillmore, Freeborn, and Goodhue, FHL film #565714.
- 1865 Counties of Hennepin, Houston, Insanti, Kanabec, Le Suer, McLeod, Mahnomen, Martin, Meeker, Morrison, Mower, Nicollet, Olmsted, Pine, Ramsey, Rice, FHL film #565715.
- 1865 Counties of Scott, Sherburne, Sibley, Stearns, Steele, Todd, Wabasha, Waseca, Washington, Watonwan, Winona, Wright - FHL film #565716.

The 1865 microfilm is available on interlibrary loan only from the Minnesota Historical Society in St. Paul. As a guide, refer to ***Inventory to a Microfilm Edition of the Minnesota State Population Census Schedules, 1865,*** published 1977 by the society, 25 pages. This inventory includes four aids: a county index, an introduction, a roll list, and a roll contents list. FHL book 977.6 X23i 1865.

■ **1866.** See ***Minnesota Adjutant General's Report of 1866*** **[Printed Book],** by the Adjutant General's Office, 1866, reprinted by Park Genealogical Books, Roseville, MN, 1997, 464 pages. Gives soldier's name, age, birthplace, rank, regiment, company, date and place mustered in, date and place mustered out, and other information. Arranged in alphabetical order by soldier's name. FHL book 977.6 M2ma.

■ ***1873 Minnesota State Business Directory: Alphabetic List of Business Firms, Proprietors and Artisans, State and County Officers—With Town and County Locations*** **[Printed Book],** compiled by Antona Hawkins Richardson, reprint by Paduan Press, St. Paul, MN, 2001, FHL book 977.6 E4.

■ **1873-1961.** See ***Obituary Index Card File, ca. 1873-1961*** **[Microfilm],** from the original card file at the Prairieland Genealogical Society, Southwest State University, Marshall, MN. Abstracts of obituaries for people from southwest Minnesota. Filmed by the Genealogical Society of Utah, 2003, 7 rolls, beginning with FHL film #2367279 (A to Butler, Alice). For a complete list of roll numbers and contents of each roll, see the online FHL catalog page for this title. See **https://familysearch.org/search/catalog/1197864.**

■ ***1875 Minnesota State Census*** **[Microfilm],** from the original manuscripts (all MN counties). Filmed by the State Library and Records Service, 1969, 16 rolls,. Available at the FHL in Salt Lake City, beginning with FHL film #565717 (Counties of Aitkin, Anoka, Becker, Benton, Blue Earth, and Brown). Film available on interlibrary loan only from the Minnesota Historical Society in St. Paul. As a guide, refer to ***Inventory to a Microfilm Edition of the Minnesota State Population Census Schedules, 1875,*** published 1977 by the society, 39 pages. This inventory includes four aids: a county index, an introduction, a roll list, and a roll contents list. FHL book 977.6 X23i 1875.

■ ***1885 Minnesota State Census*** **[Microfilm],** from the originals (all MN counties). Filmed by the State Library and Records Service, St. Paul, MN, 1969, 28 rolls. Available at the FHL beginning with FHL film #56733 (Counties of Aitkin, Carlton, Kanabec, Hubbard, Cass, Anoka, Becker, Beltrami, Cook, Lake, Pipestone, and Benton). Film available on interlibrary loan only from the Minnesota Historical Society in St. Paul. As a guide, refer to ***Inventory to a Microfilm Edition of the Minnesota State Population Census Schedules, 1885,*** published 1977 by the society, 54 pages. This inventory includes four aids: a county index, an introduction, a roll list, and a roll contents list. FHL book 977.6 X23i 1885 And FHL film #6101555.

■ ***1895 Minnesota State Census*** **[Microfilm],** from the originals (all MN counties). Filmed by the State Library and Records Service, St. Paul, MN, 59 rolls. Available at the FHL beginning with FHL film #565761 (Counties of Aitkin, Anoka, Becker (thru township of Green Valley). Film available on interlibrary loan only from the Minnesota Historical Society in St. Paul. As a guide, refer to ***Inventory to a Microfilm Edition of the Minnesota State Population Census Schedules, 1895,*** published 1977 by the society, 71 pages. This inventory includes a county index, and a roll contents list. FHL book 977.6 X23i 1895.

■ ***1905 Minnesota State Census*** **[Microfilm],** from the originals (all MN counties). Filmed by the State Library and Records Service, St. Paul, MN, 58 rolls. Available at the FHL in Salt Lake City, beginning with FHL film #928767 (Aitkin, Anoka, Becker Counties). Film available on interlibrary loan only from the Minnesota Historical Society in St. Paul. As a guide, refer to ***Inventory to a Microfilm Edition of the Minnesota State Population Census Schedules, 1905,*** published 1977 by the society, 79 pages. FHL book 977.6 X23i 1905 and FHL film #6003117.

■ **1905-1960.** See ***Pines, Mines and Lakes: The Story of Itasca County, Minnesota*** **[Printed Book],** by James E. Rottsolk, published by the Itasca County Historical Society, 1960, 155 pages. Includes a transcription of the 1905 state census for the county and a list of 50-year residents living in 1958. FHL book 977.678 H2r.

■ **1908 History.** See ***Minnesota in Three Centuries, 1655 – 1908*** **[Printed Book],** by Lucius Frederick Hubbard, et al, published New York, 1908, 4 vols., FHL book 977.6 H2mi. Indexed in ***An Every-Name Index to Minnesota in Three Centuries*** **[Printed Index],** compiled by Rod & Marie Nordberg for the Southern California Genealogical Society, 1990, 17 pages, FHL book 977.6 H2mi index.

# OHIO
## Censuses & Substitutes, 1786-2013

There has never been a state-sponsored census taken in Ohio, at least not one using the name "census." An enumeration was authorized in the State Constitution of 1802, which provided for a listing of white males over the age of 21 to be taken every four years. They became known as *Quadrennial Enumerations*. In addition, there were a series of tax lists from each of the Ohio counties that became known as *Duplicate Tax Lists*. Together, these name lists have become the primary census substitutes for all of Ohio:

**OH Quadrennial Enumerations.** The first of these enumerations was taken in 1803, and continued every four years until they officially ended in 1911. Tax assessors from each county were in charge of the quadrennial enumerations, and they were often taken simultaneously with lists of property owners subject to taxes. But the quadrennial enumeration lists were separate from tax assessment lists – they were compiled specifically for determining the number of males of voting age and reapportioning the state legislature every four years. Of the more than 1,800 county-wide Quadrennial Enumerations taken between 1803 and 1911, less than 100 lists have survived.

**OH Duplicate Tax Lists.** During the first half of the 19th century, numerous tax lists were taken at the county level in Ohio. The lists were gathered and maintained by county tax assessors, with a copy sent to the state auditor's office. Some of the original county tax lists have survived, but most of the surviving name lists today are the state auditor's originals (duplicates). It is the duplicate tax lists that are more common census substitutes with microfilm copies available for virtually all counties of Ohio.

**OH Federal Censuses.** The earliest census taken in the Northwest Territory was for 1800, and the first federal census taken in the state of Ohio was for 1810. Both censuses were lost for most areas. The exception was for Washington County, where Rufus Putnam's Ohio Company of Associates kept good records beginning in 1788, and saved copies of the earliest censuses. Putnam's papers are located today at the Campus

Museum of Marietta College, Marietta, Ohio. The federal censuses, 1820 through 1940 are complete for all counties of Ohio, with the exception of the 1890, lost in a fire in Washington, DC in 1921 (like all states).

## Online Resources at Ohio State Websites

**Ohio History Connection.** The Ohio History Center in Columbus houses the largest collection of materials of interest to genealogists in the state of Ohio. The building is also the headquarters for the Ohio History Connection (formerly the Ohio Historical Society, renamed in 2014), which, among other state functions, serves as the State Archives of Ohio. To view a list of topics at the Ohio History Connection website, see **www.ohiohistory.org.**

**Ohio Memory.** Along with the State Library of Ohio, also located in Columbus, the Ohio History Connection hosts some online databases that have proved very useful to genealogical researchers. Ohio Memory contains over 500,000 items in a variety of materials including

- Manuscripts (letters, diaries, etc.)
- Photographs
- Maps
- Archaeological and historical objects
- Newspapers
- Video
- Government records

To view the long list of Ohio Memory collections, see **www.ohiohistoryhost.org/ohiomemory/collections.**

**Ohio Network of American History Research Centers.** This regional archives system was organized by the Ohio History Connection in 1970. Currently, the ONAHR is composed of four state universities and Ohio's two largest historical societies. The network preserves and makes available all forms of documentation from local governments. For more information about each of the six centers, see

1. **University of Akron Libraries**, Archival Services, Akron, OH. Coverage includes Ashland, Coshocton, Holmes, Portage, Richland, Stark, Summit, Tuscarawas, and Wayne counties, Ohio. See **www.uakron.edu/libraries/archives/collections/local-government-records.dot.**

2. **University of Cincinnati Libraries**, Archives & Rare Books Department. Coverage includes Adams, Brown, Butler, Clermont, Clinton, Hamilton, and Warren counties. See **www.libraries.uc.edu/arb/collections/local-government.html.**

3. **Ohio History Connection,** Archives & Library, Columbus. Coverage includes the entire state. See **http://catalog.ohiohistory.org/Presto/home/home.aspx.**

4. **Western Reserve Historical Society Library,** Cleveland, OH. Coverage includes Ashtabula, Cuyahoga, Geauga, Lake, Lorain, and Medina counties. See **www.wrhs.org/research/library.**

5. **Paul Laurence Dunbar Library, Special Collections and Archives, Wright State University,** Dayton, OH. Coverage includes Auglaize, Champaign, Clark, Darke, Greene, Logan, Mercer, Miami, Montgomery, Preble, and Shelby Counties. See **www.libraries.wright.edu/special/localgovernment.**

6. **Youngstown Historical Center of Industry and Labor, Archives & Library, Youngstown State University,** Youngstown, OH. **http://web.ysu.edu/contentm/modules/display_dynamic.php?menu_id=338&params=MjksMjY1LA==.**

## Ohio Databases Online at Ancestry.com

The Ancestry.com subscription website allows free access to all indexes, but to view any particular record requires a membership. Ancestry offers trial memberships and subscriptions for short periods and reduced rates. The following databases at the Ancestry.com website are unique to Ohio under the categories, Census & Voter Lists, Vital Records, Military, Immigrations, et al.

■ **1787-1929.** See **The *Official Roster of the Soldiers of the American Revolution Buried in the State of Ohio* [Online Database],** indexed at the Ancestry.com website. Source: Ancestry cites the Adjutant General's report, 1929 (But, this 3-vol. set contains hundreds of pages regarding DAR projects in Ohio, leading one to assume that the DAR had something to do with the production of this book). This database has 1,336 pages. See **http://search.ancestry.com/search/db.aspx?dbid=20105.**

■ **1787-1973.** See ***Ohio, Births and Christenings Index, 1774-1973*** **[Online Database],** indexed at the Ancestry.com website. Source: FamilySearch extractions from original and compiled records. A number of records have birthdates in the 1770s in Ohio counties that did not exist until after 1805. Each record may include: name, gender, race, birthplace, birth date, date of christening, place of christening, age at christening, father's name, age, birthplace, mother's name, age, birthplace, and FHL film number. This database has 13,086,969 records. See
**http://search.ancestry.com/search/db.aspx?dbid=2541.**

■ **1788-1855.** See ***Abstract of Probate Records, Washington County, Ohio*** **[Online Database],** indexed at the Ancestry.com website. Source: Bernice Graham's *Abstract of Probate Records, Washington County, Ohio,* publ. 1995. When it was created in 1788, Washington County covered nearly half of the present state of Ohio. This volume contains abstracts of wills, estates, and guardian records of Washington County from 1789 to 1855 – the earliest on record. Some 4,000 early Washington residents are identified in all. See
**http://search.ancestry.com/search/db.aspx?dbid=49011.**

■ **1789-1898.** See ***Ohio Marriages, 1789-1898*** **[Online Database],** indexed at the Ancestry.com website. Source: Marjorie Smith's *Ohio Marriages. Extracted from The Old Northwest Genealogical Quarterly*. Publ. 1986. The records include: name, spouse, marriage place (county, sometimes a church), and marriage date. Some records may also include details on the officiant, race, and emancipation. This database has 10,511 records. See
**http://search.ancestry.com/search/db.aspx?dbid=3717.**

■ **1789-1998.** See ***Ohio, Wills and Probate Records, 1786-1998*** **[Online Database],** digitized and indexed at the Ancestry.com website. Source: Extracts from OH county, district, and probate courts (from 85 of Ohio's 88 counties). Some dates are based on the date a will was signed, rather than the date a will was probated. It appears that the first probates begin in 1789. In most cases, probates include the names and residences of beneficiaries and their relationship to the decedent. An inventory of the estate assets can reveal personal details about the deceased's occupation and lifestyle. There may also be references to debts, deeds, and other documents related to the settling of the estate. This database has 1,372,985 records. See
**http://search.ancestry.com/search/db.aspx?dbid=8801.**

■ **1790-1890.** See ***Ohio, Compiled Census and Census Substitutes Index, 1790-1890*** **[Online Database],** indexed at the Ancestry.com website. Source: Accelerated Indexing Systems, Salt Lake City, 1999. This collection contains the following indexes: 1790 Northwest Territory Federal Census (Substitute) Index; 1800 Federal Census Index (Washington County); 1810 Washington County Census Index; 1820 Federal Census Index; 1830 Federal Census Index; 1840 Federal Census Index; 1840 Pensioners List; 1850 Federal Census Index; 1860 Federal Census Index; 1870 Federal Census Index; Early Census Index; 1890 Veterans Schedule. This database has 472,914 records. See
**http://search.ancestry.com/search/db.aspx?dbid=3567.**

■ **1796-1908.** See ***Ohio, Homestead and Cash Entry Patents, Pre-1908*** **[Online Database],** indexed at the Ancestry.com website. Source: BLM General Land Office Automated Records Project, 1996. A land patent is a document recording the passing of a land title from the government, or other proprietor, to the patentee/grantee. This is the first-title deed and the true beginning of private ownership of the land. The patent describes in legal terms the land to which the title is given. Information recorded in these records includes: Name, Land Office, Sequence, Document number, Total acres, Signature, Canceled document, Issue date, Mineral rights reserved, Metes and bounds Statutory reference, Multiple warrantee and patentee names, Act or treaty, Entry classification, and Land description. This database has 97,934 records. See
**http://search.ancestry.com/search/db.aspx?dbid=2077.**

■ **1796-2004.** See ***Diocese of Toledo, Ohio, Catholic Parish Records, 1796-2004*** **[Online Database],** indexed at the Ancestry.com website. Source: FamilySearch extractions from the microfilmed images of register books from parishes in northwestern Ohio. Entries were extracted from register books for births, confirmations, marriages, deaths, and burials, organized by county, then by community, and finally by parish within each community. Some records are available for the following Ohio counties: Allen, Crawford, Defiance, Erie, Fulton, Hancock, Henry , Huron, Lucas, Ottawa, Paulding, Putnam, Richland, Sandusky, Seneca, Van Wert, Williams, Wood, and Wyandot. This database has 102,728 records. See
**http://search.ancestry.com/search/db.aspx?dbid=60099.**

■ **1797-1951.** See ***Jefferson County, Ohio, Court Records, 1797-1951* [Online Database],** indexed at the Ancestry.com website. Source: FamilySearch extractions from microfilm at the Family History Library, Salt Lake City, UT. Includes Probate Records, 1797-1947; Birth Records, 1797-1947; Marriage Records, 1867-1947; and Death Records, 1867-1947. This database has 1,009,365 records. See **http://search.ancestry.com/search/db.aspx?dbid=60100.**

■ **1800-1850.** See ***Ohio, Tax Records, 1800-1850* [Online Database],** indexed at the Ancestry.com website. Source: County auditor's tax voucher books, digitized from microfilm at the Family History Library and indexed by FamilySearch indexers. The records include an index and images of taxation records as recorded with the County Auditor of each county. The records in this collection cover the years 1800 to 1850. However, the majority are from the years 1816 through 1838. Entries are recorded in voucher books, one person per page. Included are the following Ohio counties: Ashtabula, Belmont, Carroll, Columbiana, Guernsey, Harrison, Jackson, Jefferson, Monroe, Trumbull, and Washington counties. This database has 1,101,150 records. See **http://search.ancestry.com/search/db.aspx?dbid=60104.**

■ **1800-1977.** See ***Ohio, County Naturalization Records, 1800-1977* [Online Database],** indexed at the Ancestry.com website. Source: FamilySearch extractions from county records on microfilm at the Family History Library in Salt Lake City, UT. Includes declarations, petitions, and certificates. This database has 385,282 records. See **http://search.ancestry.com/search/db.aspx?dbid=60096.**

■ **1803.** See ***Washington County, Ohio, US Territorial Census Population Schedules, 1803* [Online Database],** indexed at the Ancestry.com website. Source: National Archives microfilm series M1804. This database was part of the original records of the Ohio Company of Associates, and was more likely a Quadrennial Enumeration than a census. Listed are males over 21 years of age. This database has 1,242 records. See **http://search.ancestry.com/search/db.aspx?dbid=2208.**

■ **1803-1900.** See ***Ohio, Marriages, 1803-1900* [Online Database],** indexed at the Ancestry.com website. Source: Liahona Research extractions from county records on microfilm at the Family History Library, Salt Lake City. Each record provides the names of both bride and groom, along with the marriage date. Records from the following counties may be found in this database: Allen, Ashland, Athens, Auglaize, Belmont, Columbiana, Coshocton, Clark, Crawford, Darke, Defiance, Fairfield, Franklin, Gallia, Hancock, Henry, Highland, Hocking, Holmes, Huron, Paulding, Jackson, Lawrence, Mahoning, Muskingum, Ottawa, Preble, Putnam, Richland, Ross, Sandusky, Scioto, Seneca, Shelby, and Wayne Counties. This database has 429,836 records. See **http://search.ancestry.com/search/db.aspx?dbid=5194.**

■ **1809-1917.** See ***Stark County, Ohio, Court Records, 1809-1917* [Online Database],** indexed at the Ancestry.com website. Source: FamilySearch extractions from microfilm at the Family History Library in Salt Lake City, UT. The original records are from the Court of Common Pleas, now located at the Stark County Records Center, Canton, OH. The records include Land Records and Naturalization Witnesses and Depositions. This database has 255,616 records. See **http://search.ancestry.com/search/db.aspx?dbid=60102.**

■ **1810-2013.** See ***Ohio, Rutherford B. Hayes Presidential Center Obituary Index, 1810s-2013* [Online Database],** indexed at the Ancestry.com website. This data collection is an index to newspapers obituaries and local government records, such as probate case files, funeral home records, society membership records, biographical files, brief references in history books, etc. Information extracted from these documents generally includes: Name of deceased, Death Date, Place of Death (City, State), Age at Death, Birth Date, Parents' Names, Marriage Date, Spouse Name, Newspaper Source (Title, Date, Page, Column), Newspaper Location, Newspaper Repository Location, Other Source (Title, Data, Location Description), and Notes. This database has 2,532,564 records. See **http://search.ancestry.com/search/db.aspx?dbid=1671.**

■ **1811-2012.** See ***Web: Ohio, MOLO Obituary Index, 1811-2012* [Online Database],** indexed at the Ancestry.com website. Source: data gathered from several contributing libraries of the Mid Ohio Library Organization. This database is also accessible at the Northeast Ohio Regional Library website. This database has 405,566 records. See **http://search.ancestry.com/search/db.aspx?dbid=70643.**

■ **1819-1869.** See ***Cuyahoga County, Ohio, Tax Lists, 1819-1869* [Online Database],** indexed at the Ancestry.com website. Source: Ancestry's World

Archives Project contributors. The tax lists in this database begin in 1819, followed by a break in the records until 1823. The database includes records listing both individuals and corporate entities, such as real estate taxes levied in Cleveland and other municipalities; enumerations for assessment of both real and personal property; levies for improvements such as bridges, roads, and schools; delinquent tax lists; lists of physicians and lawyers subject to levies; fish surveys; and other items. This database has 576,973 records. See
**http://search.ancestry.com/search/db.aspx?dbid=2100.**

■ **1834.** See ***The Cincinnati directory for the year 1834*** **[Online Database],** indexed at the Ancestry.com website. Source: 1991 reprint by E. Deming. This database has 289 pages. See
**http://search.ancestry.com/search/db.aspx?dbid=21299.**

■ **1837-1838.** See **Cleveland, Ohio Directory, 1837-1838 [Online Database],** indexed at the Ancestry.com website. Source: *First Directory of Cleveland and Ohio City, 1837-38,* publ. Cleveland Directory Company, 1837. This database has 1,410 records. See
**http://search.ancestry.com/search/db.aspx?dbid=4228.**

■ **1850-2013.** See **Web: Dayton, Ohio, Obituary Index, 1850-2013 [Online Database],** indexed at the Ancestry.com website. This database is also accessible at the Dayton Metro Library website. This database has 523,226 records. See
**http://search.ancestry.com/search/db.aspx?dbid=70466.**

■ **1861-1865.** See ***Official Roster of the Soldiers of the State of Ohio in the War of the Rebellion, 1861-1865, Vols. 1-12*** **[Online Database],** indexed at the Ancestry.com website. Source: *Official Roster..* pub.1886-1895. This database has 2,792 pages. See
**http://search.ancestry.com/search/db.aspx?dbid=31412.**

■ **1880.** See ***The Cleveland directory, for the year ending June, 1880*** **[Online Database],** indexed at the Ancestry.com website. Source: Cleveland Directory Co, publ. 1879. This database has 717 pages. See
**http://search.ancestry.com/search/db.aspx?dbid=25775.**

■ **1880-1950.** See ***Cuyahoga County, Ohio, County Records 1880-1950*** **[Online Database],** digitized at the Ancestry.com website. Source: FamilySearch images from microfilm at the Family History Library. This image only database consists of the following types of records from the Cuyahoga County Courthouse in Cleveland: Birth affidavits (1860-1908); Delayed birth registrations and corrections (1873-1908); and Voter Registration/List of Electors (1890-1900). Browse the images, organized by Record Type, Date Range, and Volume. This database has 36,089 records. See
**http://search.ancestry.com/search/db.aspx?dbid=60098.**

■ **1888-1892.** See ***Dayton, Ohio Directories, 1888-1892*** **[Online Database],** indexed at the Ancestry.com website. Source: Williams and Co Dayton City directories for 1888, 1890, 1891, and 1892. This database has 59,449 records. See
**http://search.ancestry.com/search/db.aspx?dbid=4701.**

■ **1888-1946.** See ***Ohio, Naturalization Petition and Record Books, 1888-1946*** **[Online Database],** indexed at the Ancestry.com website. Source: National Archives microfilm series M1995. This database contains an index to naturalization records created in the United States District Court, Cleveland, including certificates of arrival, Declarations of Intention, Petitions for Naturalization, and other documents. This database has 395,871 records. See
**http://search.ancestry.com/search/db.aspx?dbid=2363.**

■ **1889-1891.** See ***Toledo, Ohio Directories, 1889-1891*** **[Online Database],** indexed at the Ancestry.com website. Source: R.L. Polk Toledo Directories, 1889-1891. This database has 74,207 records. See
**http://search.ancestry.com/search/db.aspx?dbid=4536.**

■ ***1890 Census Substitute*** **[Online Database],** indexed at the Ancestry.com website. This is nationwide collection of city directories for the time of the 1890 federal census (lost in a fire in Washington DC in 1921). A global search includes directories from several Ohio cities. See
**http://search.ancestry.com/search/group/1890census.**

■ **1890-1894.** See ***Springfield, Ohio Directories, 1890-94*** **[Online Database],** indexed at the Ancestry.com website. Source: Williams and Co Springfield City directories for 1890, 1892, and 1893. This database has 51,468 records. See
**http://search.ancestry.com/search/db.aspx?dbid=4856.**

■ **1890-2002.** See ***Stark County, Ohio, Coroner's Records, 1890-2002*** **[Online Database],** digitized at the Ancestry.com website. Source: FamilySearch digital versions of microfilmed images of the Stark County Coroner's records. This database consists of

images of Coroner's Inquest books, reports, and case files from the courthouse in Canton, Ohio. The following types of deaths were reported to the county coroner: Accidental deaths, Homicidal deaths, Occupational deaths, Sudden deaths (deaths of infants and young children, or deaths of individuals in any jail, confinement, or custody, Suicidal deaths, Therapeutic deaths (deaths which occurred during a medical procedure such as surgery), Any death where there is a doubt, question, or suspicion, and Deaths under any other special circumstances. Browse the images by type of record and range of years. This database has 56,154 records. See
**http://search.ancestry.com/search/db.aspx?dbid=60101.**

■ **1898-1899.** See ***Ohio Soldiers in the War with Spain, 1898-1899*** **[Online Database],** indexed at the Ancestry.com website. Source: Adjutant General's report: *The Official Roster of Ohio Soldiers in the War with Spain, 1898-99,* publ. 1916. This database has 15,587 records. See
**http://search.ancestry.com/search/db.aspx?dbid=5306.**

■ **1908-2007.** See ***Ohio, Deaths, 1908-1932, 1938-2007*** **[Online Database],** indexed at the Ancestry.com website. Source: OH Vital Statistics Unit. Extracted from a death certificate, each record may include: Name of the deceased, Place of residence, Death place, Death date, Age at time of death, Birth date, Race, Educational level, Father's name, and Mother's maiden name. This database has 8,266,980 records. See
**http://search.ancestry.com/search/db.aspx?dbid=5763.**

■ **1908-1964.** See ***Ohio, Birth Index, 1908-1964*** **[Online Database],** indexed at the Ancestry.com website. Source: OH Vital Statistics Unit. Extracted from a birth certificate, each record includes: name, birth date, place of birth, and state file number. This database has 8,222,080 records. See
**http://search.ancestry.com/search/db.aspx?dbid=3146.**

■ **1917-1918.** See ***Ohio Soldiers in WWI, 1917-1918*** **[Online Database],** digitized and indexed at the Ancestry.com website. Source: *The Official Roster of Ohio Soldiers, Sailors, and Marines in the World War, 1917-18,* publ. 1926. Each record may include the soldier's name, age, birthplace, address, branch of service and enlistment date, military rank and discharge status, brief history of military career, and date and cause of death if occurred during enlistment. This database has 248,539 records. See
**http://search.ancestry.com/search/db.aspx?dbid=7895.**

■ **1929-1958.** See ***Ohio, Crew List Arrivals, 1929-1958*** **[Online Database],** indexed at the Ancestry.com website. Source: National Archives microfilm series A3482. This database is an index to crew lists of vessels that arrived at Toledo, Ohio. Most of the crew members were U.S. and Canadian citizens. This database has 269,658 records. See
**http://search.ancestry.com/search/db.aspx?dbid=2139.**

■ **1952-1963.** See ***Ohio, Passenger and Crew Lists, 1952-1963*** **[Online Database],** indexed at the Ancestry.com website. Source: National Archives microfilm series A3559, A3822, A3838, and A3976. These passenger and crew lists from both ships and aircraft were recorded on a variety of forms that were then turned over to the Immigration and Naturalization Service. Details include the name of the vessel and arrival date, ports of departure and arrival (as well as future destinations on a ship's itinerary), dates of departure and arrival, shipmaster, full name, age, gender, physical description, military rank (if any), occupation, birthplace, citizen of what country, and residence. This database has 2,297 records. See
**http://search.ancestry.com/search/db.aspx?dbid=9126.**

■ **1962-2007.** See ***Ohio Divorce Index, 1962-1963, 1967-1971, 1973-2007*** **[Online Database],** indexed at the Ancestry.com website. Source: OH Vital Statistic Unit. Extracted from filed divorce papers, each record includes: name of person, year of birth, spouse's name, to whom decree was granted, county of decree, and date of divorce decree. This database has 3,850,954 records. See
**http://search.ancestry.com/search/db.aspx?dbid=2026.**

■ **1970-2007.** See ***Ohio Marriage Index, 1970, 1972-2007*** **[Online Database],** indexed at the Ancestry.com website. Source: OH Vital Statistic Unit. Extracted from a marriage return, each record includes: name of bride/groom, birth year of each, county of residence, county where license was issued, and date of marriage. This database has 6,777,875 records. See
**http://search.ancestry.com/search/db.aspx?dbid=2025.**

## Ohio Databases Online at the FamilySearch.org Website

The following databases are available for free at the FamilySearch.org website. To see the current list, visit the Ohio Indexed Historical Records and Ohio Image Only Historical Records webpage. Both lists are updated periodically. See
**https://familysearch.org/search/collection/location/43.**

■ **1789-1996.** See ***Ohio Probate Records, 1789-1996*** **[Online Database],** digitized at the FamilySearch.org website. Source: FamilySearch extractions from county courthouse records in all Ohio counties. This image only database includes Administrative dockets, Estate records, Guardianships, Journals, Wills, and Misc. files. In most cases, the files include the Name of the testator or deceased, Names of heirs, such as spouse, children, other relatives, or friends, Name of the executor, administrator, or guardian, Names of witnesses, Residence of the testator, and Document and recording dates. Browse the images, organized by Volume Title and Year. This database has 6,997,828 records. See
**https://familysearch.org/search/collection/1992421.**

■ **1789-2013.** See ***Ohio, County Marriages, 1789-2013*** **[Online Database],** indexed at the FamilySearch.org website. Source: FamilySearch extractions from microfilm of county records at the Family History Library. The records consist of: Licenses, Certificates, Declarations, Affidavits, Loose documents, Abstracts, and Licenses to perform marriages. The records are generally arranged by: County, volume and date, License number, and Page number. This database has 4,709,144 records. See
**https://familysearch.org/search/collection/1614804.**

■ **1791-1994.** See ***Ohio, Hamilton County Records, 1791-1994*** **[Online Database],** digitized at the FamilySearch.org website. Source: Court records from the County Recorder and the Probate Court in Cincinnati, Ohio. This image only database includes categories of Land records, Military records, Naturalization records, Probate records, and Vital records. Browse through the images, organized by category, then by Record Type, Volume, and Year Range. This database has 1,566,282 records. See
**https://familysearch.org/search/collection/2141016.**

■ **1793-1930.** See ***Ohio, Washington County Court Records, 1810-1930*** **[Online Database],** digitized at the FamilySearch.org website. Source: Records of the Court of Common Pleas, Washington Co OH, located at the county courthouse in Marietta, OH. This image only database includes records from the Chancery court, Circuit court, Court of common pleas, District court, Justice of the Peace, and Supreme court. (The records include an *Index to Court of Common Plea, 1793-1828*; followed by one for 1795-1877; both books digitized, but the earlier dates were missed in the title of this database). Browse the images, organized by Record Type, Volume, and Year Range. This database has 91,369 records. See
**https://familysearch.org/search/collection/2363038.**

■ **1795-2010.** See **Ohio, *Trumbull County Records, 1795-2010*** **[Online Database],** digitized at the FamilySearch.org website. Source: microfilmed records from the Trumbull Co OH courthouse. This image only database includes cemetery records, Common pleas court records, Misc. court records, Land and property records, Naturalization records, Probate records, Tax records, and Vital records. Browse through the images, organized by Record Type, Date Range, and Volume. **Note:** Perhaps the best census substitutes for Trumbull Co OH are the annual Tax Appraisement lists. They are part of this major database, beginning in 1811 and every year thereafter through 1931. This database has 800,274 records. See
**https://familysearch.org/search/collection/2065327.**

■ **1797-1947.** See ***Ohio, Jefferson County Court Records, 1797-1947*** **[Online Database],** digitized at the FamilySearch.org website. Source: Jefferson County Courthouse, Steubenville, OH. This image only database includes the categories of Census, County Court records, Hospital records, Land and property records, Naturalization records, Pensions, Probate records, and Vital records. Browse the images, organized by category, then Record Type, Volume, and Year Range. **Note. 1)** This database has a full digital index in work, a cooperative effort of FamilySearch and the Jefferson County Chapter, Ohio Genealogical Society. **2)** The only item under the category "census" is a digital capture of the 1880 federal census (Short Form) for Steubenville Township & Mingo Village. This database has 1,010,889 records. See
**https://familysearch.org/search/collection/1935519.**

■ **1800-1850.** See ***Ohio Tax Records, 1800-1850*** **[Online Database],** digitized and indexed at the FamilySearch.org website. This project was indexed

in partnership with the Ohio Genealogical Society. This database includes Images and name index of tax registers as recorded with the County Auditor of each county. Includes the following Ohio counties: Ashtabula, Belmont, Carroll, Columbiana, Guernsey, Harrison, Jackson, Jefferson, Monroe, Trumbull and Washington. The majority of the tax records in this collection are for the years 1816 through 1838. This database has 1,101,150 records. See
**https://familysearch.org/search/collection/1473259.**

■ **1800-1942.** See ***Ohio, Marriages, 1800-1942*** **[Online Database],** indexed at the FamilySearch.org website. Source: FamilySearch extractions from microfilm of county records at the Family History Library. This database has 3,567 records. See
**https://familysearch.org/search/collection/2367319.**

■ **1800-1958.** See **Ohio Marriages, 1800-1958 [Online Database],** indexed at the FamilySearch.org website. Name index to marriage records from microfilm at the Family History Library. This database has 2,198,000 records. See
**https://familysearch.org/search/collection/1681001.**

■ **1800-1977.** See ***Ohio, County Naturalization Records, 1800-1977*** **[Online Database],** indexed at the FamilySearch.org website. Source: FamilySearch extractions from microfilm of county records at the Family History Library. Information found in this collection may include: Full name of petitioner, Name of court, Date of emigration, Place of residence, Occupation, Date and place of birth, Date of declaration, Date of marriage, Spouse's full name (usually a woman's maiden name is given), Spouse's date and place of birth, Names of children and their places of birth, Name of judge, and Names of witnesses. This database has 385,282 records. See
**https://familysearch.org/search/collection/1987615.**

■ **1809-1917.** See ***Ohio, Stark County Court Records, 1809-1917*** **[Online Database],** digitized at the FamilySearch.org website. Source: Court of Common Pleas, County Recorder Center, Canton, OH. This image only database includes Appearance dockets, Common Pleas records, General Indexes, and Journals. Browse the images, organized by Record Type, Date Range, and Volume. This database has 252,043 records. See
**https://familysearch.org/search/collection/1878534.**

■ **1813-1932.** See ***Ohio, Cuyahoga County Probate Files, 1813-1932*** **[Online Database],** digitized at the FamilySearch.org website. Source: Cuyahoga County Archives, Cleveland, OH. This image only database includes Administrative dockets, Estate records, Guardianships, Journals, Wills, and Misc. files. In most cases, the files include the Name of the testator or deceased, Names of heirs, such as spouse, children, other relatives, or friends, Name of the executor, administrator, or guardian, Names of witnesses, Residence of the testator, and Document and recording dates. Browse the images, organized by Volume Title and Year. This database has 2,622,673 records. See
**https://familysearch.org/search/collection/1837736.**

■ **1821-1962.** See ***Ohio Births and Christenings, 1821-1962*** **[Online Database],** indexed at the FamilySearch.org website. Name index to birth, baptism and christening records from microfilm at the Family History Library. This database has 2,548,575 records. See
**https://familysearch.org/search/collection/1680845.**

■ **1824-2001.** See ***Ohio, Cleveland Cemetery Interment Records, 1824-2001*** **[Online Database],** indexed at the FamilySearch.org website. Cemetery interment records throughout Cleveland in Cuyahoga County. Index provided by the East Cuyahoga County Genealogical Society. This database has 346,248 records. See
**https://familysearch.org/search/collection/1884183.**

■ **1840-1941.** See ***Ohio, Summit County, Veteran Burial Cards, 1700-1941*** **[Online Database],** digitized and indexed at the FamilySearch.org website. Source: Burial and grave registration cards at the Summit County Library, Akron, OH. **Note:** The 1700 date is impossible. This database has 5,535 records. See
**https://familysearch.org/search/collection/1879059.**

■ **1840-2001.** See ***Ohio, County Death Records, 1840-2001*** **[Online Database],** digitized and indexed at the FamilySearch.org website. Source: FamilySearch extractions from microfilm of county records at the Family History Library. Index and images of death records from county courthouses Most of the records in this collection are death registers created before statewide death certificates in 1908. Each record may include the name of the person who died, date of death, and place of death. Later records have much more information. This database has 2,155,570 records. See
**https://familysearch.org/search/collection/2128172.**

■ **1841-2003. See *Ohio, County Births, 1841-2003* [Online Database],** indexed at the FamilySearch.org website. Source: FamilySearch extractions from microfilm of county records at the Family History Library. Each record may include: Date birth was recorded, Full name of child, Child's birth date, Place of birth, including city, country and state, Child's gender and race, Parents' names, including mother's maiden name, Parents' place of residence, and Name of the person reporting the birth,. Later records may also list the following: Parents' birth dates and places, Parents' age, Parents' occupation, and Name of attending physician or midwife. This database has 4,049,847 records. See
**https://familysearch.org/search/collection/1932106.**

■ **1850-1900.** See ***Ohio, Montgomery County, Probate Estate Files, 1850-1900* [Online Database],** digitized at the FamilySearch.org website. Source: Montgomery Co Records Center & Archives, Dayton, OH. This image only database includes Assignment case files, Civil case files, and Probate estate files. Browse the images, organized by Record Type, Date Range, and Volume. This database has 216,991 records. See
**https://familysearch.org/search/collection/1916172.**

■ **1852-1991.** See ***Ohio, Southern District Naturalization Index, 1852-1991* [Online Database],** indexed at the FamilySearch.org website. Source: National Archives, U.S. District Court Records, card index on microfilm. The index cards include the following: Name of immigrant, Declaration number, Declaration volume number, Declaration date, Petition number, Petition volume number, and Petition date. This database has 83,982 records. See
**https://familysearch.org/search/collection/2110749.**

■ **1854-1997.** See ***Ohio Deaths and Burials, 1854-1997* [Online Database],** indexed at the FamilySearch.org website. Source: FamilySearch extractions from microfilm of county records at the Family History Library. This database has 544,082 records. See
**https://familysearch.org/search/collection/1681000.**

■ **1855-1967.** See ***Ohio, Northern District, Eastern Division, Naturalization Index, 1855-1967* [Online Database],** digitized at the FamilySearch.org website. Source: National Archives microfilm series M1893. This image only database is from microfilmed index cards for naturalizations petitions, U.S. district courts of Ohio. Browse through the images, organized by surnames in alphabetical order. This database has 196,148 records. See
**https://familysearch.org/search/collection/2110746.**

■ **1860-1970.** See ***Ohio, Geauga County Records, 1860-1970* [Online Database],** digitized at the FamilySearch.org website. Source: Geauga Co Archives & Records Center, Chardon, OH. This image only database includes images of marriages, naturalizations, probates, and deeds. Browse the images, organized by Record Type, Date Range, and Volume. Included are digitized card indexes for Declarations, 1862-1959; Naturalizations, 1862-1959; and Petitions, 1880-1959. This database has 24,059 records. See
**https://familysearch.org/search/collection/2134457.**

■ **1860-2004.** See ***Ohio, Crawford County Obituaries, 1860-2004* [Online Database],** indexed at the FamilySearch.org website. Source: Obituary file from the Crawford County Genealogical Society in Galion, Ohio. This database has 29,278 records. See
**https://familysearch.org/search/collection/1384728.**

■ **1880-1950.** See ***Ohio, Cuyahoga County Records, 1880-1950* [Online Database],** digitized at the FamilySearch.org website. Source: Cleveland Div. of Vital Statistics. This image only database includes birth affidavits, delayed births and corrections; and voter registrations from the Cuyahoga County Courthouse in Cleveland. Browse through the images, organized by Record Type, Date Range, and Volume. This database has 36,089 records. See
**https://familysearch.org/search/collection/1908531.**

■ **1888-1919.** See ***Ohio Soldiers Home Records, 1888-1919* [Online Database],** digitized at the FamilySearch.org website. Source: OH History Connection. This image only database is for the images of the admission records of veterans, those admitted into the Ohio Soldiers Home. Browse through the images, organized by Admission Number, beginning with 1-500, 1888-1889. This database has 5,426 records. See
**https://familysearch.org/search/collection/2139859.**

■ **1890-2002. See *Ohio, Stark County Coroner's Records, 1890-2002* [Online Database],** indexed at the FamilySearch.org website. Source: Coroner records, now located at the Stark County Records Center, Canton, OH. This image only database

includes coroner's inquest books, reports, and case files. Browse through the records, organized by Record Type, Date Range, and Volume. This database has 57,294 records. See
**https://familysearch.org/search/collection/1922540.**

■ **1908-1932.** See ***Ohio Death Index, 1908-1932, 1938-1944, and 1958-2007*** **[Online Database],** indexed at the FamilySearch.org website. Source: OH Vital Statistic Unit (database indexed by Ancestry.com). Information found in this collection may include: Age at Death, Estimated Birth Year, Date of Death, Certificate Number or page number, Name of Deceased, Name of Father, Name of Mother, Name of Spouse, Place of Death, Sex, and Page Number. This database has 7,601,864 records. See
**https://familysearch.org/search/collection/1949341.**

■ **1908-1953.** See ***Ohio Deaths, 1908-1953*** **[Online Database],** digitized and indexed at the FamilySearch.org website. Source: FamilySearch images from microfilm of county records (death certificates or registers) at the Family History Library. Death entries include the following information: Name of deceased, Date and place of death including city, county and state, Residence of deceased; sometimes, a former residence, Gender and age of deceased in years, months, and days, Date and place of birth, Marital status, race and occupation of deceased, Spouse's name, if married, Father's name and birthplace, Mother's maiden name and birthplace, Cause of death, Name of informant, often a son, daughter or other family member, How long at current residence or length of time in United States, Occupation, and Burial information. This database has 3,544,429 records. See
**https://familysearch.org/search/collection/1307272.**

■ **1952-1974.** See ***Ohio, Passenger and Crew Lists arriving at Ashtabula and Conneaut, 1952-1974*** **[Online Database],** indexed at the FamilySearch.org website. Source: National Archives microfilm series A3405. Contains lists of immigrants, ship passengers, arrivals at seaports, passenger lists, and crew lists. This database has 79,671 records. See
**https://familysearch.org/search/collection/2421787.**

## Ohio Databases Online at Various Websites

■ **1790s-1900s.** See ***Ohio USGenWeb Archives*** **[Online Database].** The OHGenWeb Archives site offers free genealogical databases with searchable statewide name lists and for all Ohio counties. Databases may include Bibles, Biographies, Cemeteries, Censuses, Court Records, Deaths, Deeds, Directories, Histories, Marriages, Military, Newspapers, Obituaries, Photos, Schools, Tax Lists, Wills, and more. See
**http://usgwarchives.net/oh/ohfiles.htm.**

■ **1790s-1900s.** See ***Linkpendium – Ohio: Family History & Genealogy, Census, Birth, Marriage, Death Vita Records & More*** **[Online Databases].** Linkpendium is a genealogical portal site with links to state, county, town, and local databases. Currently listed are selected sites for Ohio statewide resources (689), Adams County (369), Allen County (828), Ashland County (546), Ashtabula County (763), Athens County (628), Auglaize County (404) and 82 more Ohio counties. See
**www.linkpendium.com/oh-genealogy.**

■ **1795-1991.** See ***Ohio Newspaper Archives, 1795-1991*** **[Online Databases],** digitized and indexed newspapers at the GenealogyBank website, for Akron, Cadiz, Canton, Chillicothe, Cincinnati, Cleveland, Clinton, Columbus, Dayton, Elyria, Lancaster, Lebanon, Marietta, New Richmond, Painesville, Ravenna, Sandusky, St. Clairsville, Steubenville, Toledo, Urbana, Warren, Williamsburg, Wooster, and Xenia. See
**www.genealogybank.com/explore/newspapers/all/usa/ohio**

■ **1819-1941.** See ***City Directories Collection at the Public Library of Cincinnati and Hamilton County*** **[Online Database],** Directories for cities and counties in Ohio and Kentucky, featuring volumes published as early as 1819. Most of the directories in this collection are located in the Genealogy and Local History and Information and Reference departments at Main Library. All directories in the collection are full-text searchable and can be downloaded for offline viewing and searching. Ohio Directories: Cincinnati, Hamilton, Cleveland, Hamilton County, Columbus, Huron County, Dayton, and Norwood. Kentucky Directories: Covington and Newport. To access a complete list of the years for each city, see
**http://digital.cincinnatilibrary.org/cdm/landingpage/collection/p16998coll5.**

■ **1830s-1900s Ohio Original Land Owners.** See the ***Family Maps*** series for Ohio counties, maps of original land patents, compiled by Greg Boyd and published by Arphax Publishing Co., Norman, OK. These privately-produced computer-generated maps show the first property owners for an entire county, produced as a book of maps, each map laid out on the federal township grid, and includes indexes to help you locate a person, place-name, or cemetery. Additional maps are added for each county to show roads, waterways, railroads, selected city centers, and cemeteries within a county. At this writing, *Family Maps* books have been published for the following Ohio counties: Allen, Auglaize, Coshocton, Ohio, Darke, Guernsey, Hancock, Jackson, Monroe, Noble, Putnam, Sandusky, Seneca, Van Wert, and Wyandot County, Ohio. Visit the publisher's information and ordering website for more details and updated county coverage. See **www.arphax.com/.** Arphax's entire *Family Maps* series is also available as a subscription service online. See **www.historygeo.com.**

■ **1832-1900s.** See ***Ohio's Digitized Newspapers* [Online Database],** digitized and indexed at the Ohio Memory website. The Ohio History Connection has digitized over 315,000 pages of Ohio newspapers through its participation in the National Digital Newspaper Program. This content is freely-available at Chronicling America. Partnerships between the Ohio History Connection and local institutions have made additional titles freely-available on Ohio Memory. These Ohio Memory titles comprise over 265,000 pages of content. To see the list of Newspaper title, city, county, region, and time period, see the special Ohio Memory webpage. See **www.ohiohistoryhost.org/ohiomemory/newspapers.** **Note:** to use the Library of Congress' Chronicling America digitized newspapers index for any state, see **http://chroniclingamerica.loc.gov.**

■ **1985-Current.** See ***Ohio Recent Newspaper Obituaries (1985-Current)* [Online Database],** digitized and indexed newspaper obituaries at the GenealogyBank website, including newspapers for Ada, Akron, Amherst, Ashtabula, Athens, Avon/Avon Park, Bay Village, Beachwood, Beavercreek, Bellbrook/Sugarcreek, and 90 more Ohio cities. See **www.genealogybank.com/explore/obituaries/all/usa/ohio.**

## Ohio Books & Microfilms at the Family History Library

The most important of Ohio's statewide censuses and substitutes are cited below in chronological order. Each item includes a FHL book number or FHL film number, which can be used to search the FHL catalog for more details. To review an item, start at the FamilySearch catalog search page: **https://familysearch.org/search/catalog/results.** Select "Search by Place" then "United States, Ohio" to see a list of catalog categories. Or, select "Call Number" then type an FHL book number; or select "Film/Fiche Number" to view a specific title.

■ ***1787-1840 Ohio* [CD-ROM],** part of the Family Tree Maker Archives, Land and Tax Records, published by Broderbund, 1999. Contents: Early Ohio Settlers: Purchasers of Land in Southeastern Ohio, 1800-1840 (Marietta Land Office), compiled by Ellen T. Berry and David A. Berry; Early Ohio Settlers: Purchasers of Land in Southeastern Ohio, 1800-1840 (Cincinnati Land Office), compiled by Ellen T. Berry and David A. Berry; Early Ohio Settlers: Purchasers of Land in East and East Central Ohio, compiled by Ellen Thomas Berry and David A. Berry; First Ownership of Ohio Lands, by Albion Morris Dyer; and Early Ohio Tax Records, by Esther Weygandt Powell. FHL CD No. 9, pt. 651.

■ **1787-1871.** See ***Virginia Military District Lands of Ohio; Indexes* [Microfilm].** from the index and original records at the State Auditor's Office in Columbus, Ohio (1958). The Index to entrymen gives name of soldier or heirs, entry/survey number, warrant number of soldier's claim, book and page number wherein found, and acreage. Indexes are included in Survey books v. A [1], B, B3, C, E, F; and in most Entry books. The following information comes from the State Auditor's Office from a directory and from a booklet, *Ohio Lands: A Short History*, copyrighted in 1991. "The Virginia Military District (VMD) lands lie north of the Ohio River and between the Scioto and Little Miami Rivers. It covers all the present-day counties of Adams, Brown, Clermont, Clinton, Fayette, Highland, Madison, and Union counties; and parts of Champaign, Clark, Delaware, Franklin, Greene, Hamilton, Hardin, Logan, Marion, Pickaway, Pike, Ross, Scioto, and Warren counties. The VMD lands were given by the State of Virginia as a reward to her Revolutionary War soldiers or their heirs. The rectangular survey system was not used in the VMD as used elsewhere in Ohio. To claim a warrant issued to a soldier, the soldier or his heirs sent the warrant to the Principal Surveyor of the Virginia District of Ohio. He in turn gave it to the Deputy Surveyor who gave a general description of the entry and then made a survey based on physical features such as certain trees, etc. The warrant then was sent to the U.S. Government and a U.S. Patent was made out. The first survey was made in 1787 and the first U.S. Patent was issued in 1796. In 1830 and 1852 the VMD warrants could be exchanged for land scrip and used to buy any public land open for sale. Virginia in 1852 ceded to the U.S. government any land not yet granted in the VMD. This land was given to Ohio in 1871 and they gave it to Ohio State University. The University sold these lands into the 1940s." Filmed by the Genealogical Society of Utah, 1995, 1958, 33 rolls, beginning with FHL film #2022655 (Index to entrymen: A – Coalier).

■ **1787-1900.** See ***The Ohio Surname Index*** **[Microfilm],** from a card index compiled by the Ohio Society of the Daughters of the American Revolution, under the supervision of Miss Alice Boardman, now located at the Ohio History Connection, Columbus, OH. Arranged alphabetically by surname. Some cards are out of order. Indexes individuals mentioned in various county histories and historical magazines. Film at FHL: 64 rolls, beginning with FHL film #398201 (Aarents, William - Alkire, Ruan). For a complete list of roll numbers and contents of each roll, see the online FHL catalog page for this title. See **https://familysearch.org/search/catalog/86323.**

■ **1787-1986.** See ***Ohio Source Records: From the Ohio Genealogical Quarterly*** **[Printed Book],** excerpted and reprinted from The Ohio Genealogical Quarterly, publ. Genealogical Publishing Co., Baltimore, 1986. with added publisher's note, contents, index, and textual notes. Contains abstracts of probate records, marriages, cemetery inscriptions, histories, family histories, tax lists, military records, etc. FHL book 977.1 D28o.

■ **1788-1817.** See ***Ohio Early Census Index*** **[Printed Book],** edited by Ronald Vern Jackson, Accelerated Indexing Systems, Salt Lake City, 1974, 2 vols. Contents: vol. 1: Cincinnati, 1798, 1799, 1817; vol. 2: Others, 1788, 1789, 1796, 1798, 1799. FHL book 977.1 X22jr. See also ***Early Ohio Census Records,*** 2nd edition, 3rd printing, published by Accelerated Indexing, Bountiful, UT, 1974, which adds censuses for 1800 Northwest Territory and Ohio 1803 and 1810 (Washington County only). FHL book 977.1 X2p.

■ **1788-1820.** See ***Ohio Marriages Recorded in County Courts Through 1820: An Index*** **[Printed Book],** compiled by Jean Nathan, et al, published by the Ohio Genealogical Society, Mansfield, OH, 1966, 1,167 pages. FHL book 977.1 V22o.

■ **1790.** See ***Territorial Census Index Substitute, Ohio, 1790*** **[Printed Book],** edited by Sue Powell Morgan, published by Genealogical Services, West Jordan, UT, 1998, 274 pages. Includes name, town, county, record type, date and page number. FHL book 977.1 X22m 1790.

**Note:** The Northwest Territory was left out of the 1790 census. This book purports that census substitutes exist, but there is no catalog information confirming the record types used.

■ **1798-1817.** See ***Census for Cincinnati, Ohio, 1817, and Hamilton County, Ohio, Voters' Lists 1798 and 1799*** **[Printed Book],** compiled by Marie Paula Dickoré, Publ. Historical and Philosophical Society of Ohio, 1960, 98 pages, FHL book 977.1 A1 no. 115. For access to a digital version of this book, see the online FHL catalog page. See **https://familysearch.org/search/catalog/70068.**

■ **1800-1803.** See ***Second Census of the United States, 1800, Population Schedules, Washington County, Territory Northwest of the River Ohio; and Population Census, 1803, Washington County, Ohio*** **[Microfilm],** from the originals at the National Archives, Washington, DC. Arranged in alphabetical order by township. These two name lists were part of the original papers of Rufus Putnam's Ohio Company, who kept a copy of the first (1800) federal census taken in Washington County, Ohio. The 1803 list was the first Quadrennial Enumeration for Washington Co OH, and lists the name of all free males over the age of 21. The area of 1800-1803 Washington County includes the modern counties of Washington, Meigs, Gallia, Lawrence, and Athens counties, Ohio. Special microfilm publication by the National Archives, 1994, series M1804, 1 roll, FHL film #2155491.

■ **1800.** See ***Northwest Territory, Washington County, Ohio 1800 Census Index: Taken Before Ohio's Statehood*** **[Printed Book],** by Fay Maxwell, publ. OH Genealogy Center, Austin, MN, 1973, 16 pages, FHL book 977.1 A1 no. 437.

■ **1800-1819.** See ***Indexes: Census 1800, 1803, 1810; Death Notices, 1811-1830; Lives of Early Settlers - Hildreth; Account Book, 1818-1819; Supreme Court, Washington Co., 1810; Henderson-Tomlinson Journal and Papers; Nahum Ward Letters*** **[Microfilm],** from an typescript at the Campus Museum, Marrietta College, Marrietta, OH. Filmed by the Genealogical Society of Utah, 1973, 1 roll, FHL film #940916.

■ *1801-1814 Tax Records of Ohio* **[Microfilm],** from the original records at the Ohio History Connection, Columbus, OH. Filmed by the Genealogical Society of Utah, 1967, 14 rolls, as follows:

- **1801. Land entries** of the lands of non-residents situated between the Scioto & Little Miami Rivers commonly known by the name of the Virginia Army Lands (Virginia Military District ), vol. 1, 1801, FHL film #522837.
- **1806-1807**. **Tax record**, vol. 2, 1806 (Adams, Athens, Franklin, Highland, Muskingum, Ross, Scioto counties), Tax record, vol. 3, 1806 (Belmont, Fairfield, Jefferson counties); Tax record, vol. 4, 1806 (Butler, Champaign, Clermont, Greene, Montgomery counties); Tax record, vol. 5, 1806 (Hamilton and Warren counties); Tax record, vol. 6, 1806 (Trumbull, Columbiana, Gallia counties; Tax record, vol. 7, 1807 (Adams, Champaign, Clermont, Green, Highland, Ross, Scioto counties), FHL film #522838.
- **1807. Tax record,** vol. 8, 1807 (Belmont, Columbiana, Jefferson counties; Tax record, vol. 9, 1807 (non- resident sixth district resident Geauga and Trumbull counties; Tax duplicates, vol. 10, 1807 (Franklin, Fairfield, Muskingum counties); Tax duplicate, vol. 11, 1807 (Butler, Warren, Hamilton, Montgomery counties), FHL film #522839.
- **1808. Tax duplicates**, vol. 12, 1808 (Fairfield and Washington counties); Tax record, vol. 13, 1808 (non residents fifth district residents Belmont, Columbiana, Jefferson counties; Tax record, vol. 14, 1808 (Adams, Greene, Hamilton, Montgomery counties), FHL film #522840.
- **1808. Tax record**, vol. 15, 1808 (Geauga, Muskingum, Trumbull counties); Tax record, vol. 16, 1808 (Athens, Franklin, Gallia, Highland counties; Tax record, vol. 17, 1808 (non residents fourth and sixth district), FHL film #522841.
- **1809. Tax Duplicate** of land tax, vol. 18, (A - N various counties) - FHL film #522842.
- **1811. Tax Duplicate** of land tax, vol. 19, (Adams – Hamilton), FHL film #522843.
- **1811. Duplicate** of land tax, vol. 20, (Jefferson – Warren) - FHL film #522844.
- **1812. Tax Duplicate** of land tax, vol. 21, (Adams – Hamilton), FHL film #514124.
- **1812. Tax Duplicate** of land tax, vol. 22, (Jefferson – Warren), FHL film #514125.
- **1813. Tax Duplicate** of land tax, vol. 23, (Adams – Hamilton), FHL film #514126.
- **1813 Tax Duplicate** of land tax, vol. 24, (Jefferson – Warren), FHL film #514127.
- **1814. Tax Duplicate** of land tax, vol. 25, (Adams – Franklin), FHL film #514128.
- **1814. Tax Duplicate** of land tax, vol. 26-27, (Gallia – Warren), FHL film #514129.

■ **1801-1824.** See ***Early Ohio Tax Records*** **[Printed Book],** abstracts compiled by Esther Weygant Powell, Ohio State Auditor, 1971, 459 pages. FHL book 977.1 R4op. See also ***The Index to Early Ohio Tax Records*** **[Printed Book],** compiled by Carol Willsey Bell, and friends of Esther Weygandt Powell in cooperation with the Ohio Genealogical Society, published Akron, OH, 1973, 173 pages. FHL book 977.1 R4op, and FHL film #1033949.

■ **1801-1824.** See ***Ohio's Virginia Military Tract: Index of 1801 Tax List*** **[Printed Book],** compiled by Fay Maxwell, published by the Ohio Genealogy Center, 1991, 19 pages. From title page: "Index of the Virginia Militiamen who served in the revolution. The tract is located west of Ohio's Scioto River." Includes Hardin County 1821 & 1833 tax record, and Marion County 1824 tax record. FHL book 977.1 R4m.

■ ***1802 Census of Clermont County: the Northwest Territory of the United States of America*** **[Printed Book],** compiled and published by the Brown County Genealogical Society, Georgetown, OH, 1988, 9 pages. FHL book 977.1 A1 no. 323 and FHL film #6088560.

■ **1803-1827, 1831 and 1847.** See ***Male Enumeration Lists of Adams County, Ohio*** **[Printed Book],** by the Adams County Genealogical Society, West Union, OH, 2 vols., 1995. From FHL catalog: "These records may include some names from Brown County until Brown County was formed in 1819." Includes index. Contents: v. 1. 1803-1827 -- v. 2. 1831 and 1847. Library has v. 1-2 bound together. FHL book 977.186 X2m and FHL film #2055364.

■ **1804.** See ***Resident Proprietors of the Connecticut Western Reserve, 1804: An Ohio Tax List of 1804*** [Printed Book], compiled by Nellie M. Raber, published R.D. Craig, Cincinnati, 1963, 26 pages. FHL book 977.1 A1 no. 30 and FHL film #896888. Another filming, FHL film #928353.

■ ***1807 Census of Butler County, Ohio*** **[Printed Book],** edited by Willard Heiss and R. Thomas Mayhill, published by Eastern Indiana Publishing Co., Knightstown, IN, 1968,. 23 pages. FHL book 977.1 A1 No. 137 and FHL film #1036243.

■ **1810.** See ***Third census of the United States, 1810, Population Schedules, Washington County, Ohio*** **[Microfilm],** Includes townships of Adams, Belpre,

Fearing, Grand View, Marietta, Newport, Roxburg, Salem, Warren, Waterford, Wesley, and Worcester. Lists name of head of the family and age brackets of other members of the family. Arranged in alphabetical order by township. Special microfilm publication by the National Archives, 1994, series M1803, 1 roll, FHL film #2155490.

■ ***Ohio 1810 Tax Duplicate Arranged in a State-wide Alphabetical List of Names of Taxpayers: With an Index of Names of Original Entries*** **[Printed Book],** compiled by Gerald M. Petty, published by the author, Columbus, OH, 1976, 221 pages. Includes index. FHL book 977.1 R4p and FHL film #982373.

■ ***1810 Tax Records of Various Ohio Counties*** **[Microfilm],** from the original records at the Ohio History Connection, Columbus, Ohio. Name lists are organized alphabetically by county. Filmed by the Genealogical Society of Utah, 1967, 3 rolls, as follows:

- Counties A - Gal, FHL film #534818.
- Counties Gea – P, FHL film #534819.
- Counties R – W, FHL film #534820.

■ **1812.** See ***The 1812 Census of Ohio: A Statewide Index of Taxpayers*** **[Printed Book],** publ. T.L.C Genealogy, Miami Beach, FL, 1992, 221 pages. This is an alphabetical list of all resident land owners in Ohio., taken from county tax lists. See FHL book 977.1 R2co.

■ ***1816-1838 Tax Duplicates, Adams County, Ohio*** **[Microfilm],** from the original records now at the Ohio History Connection, Columbus, OH. Filmed by the Genealogical Society of Utah, 1967-1968, 5 rolls, as follows:

- Tax Duplicates,1816-1823, FHL film #514130.
- Tax Duplicates, 1824-1829, FHL film #514131.
- Tax Duplicates, 1830-1832, FHL film #514132.
- Tax Duplicates, 1833-1836, FHL film #514133.
- Tax Duplicates,1837-1838, FHL film #514134.

■ ***1816-1838 Duplicate Tax Records of Ashtabula County, Ohio*** **[Microfilm],** from the original records now at the Ohio History Connection, Columbus, Ohio. These records include resident and non-resident owners, delinquent tax properties, and personal property. From 1816-1825 arranged by first letter of surname and beginning in 1826 arranged by township then first letter of surname. Filmed by the Genealogical Society of Utah, 1967, 9 rolls, as follows:

- Tax Duplicates,1816-1822, FHL film #514136.
- Tax Duplicates,1823-1824, FHL film #514137.
- Tax Duplicates,1825-1826, FHL film #528364.
- Tax Duplicates,1827-1828, FHL film #528365.
- Tax Duplicates,1829-1830, FHL film #514138.
- Tax Duplicates,1831-1832, FHL film #514139.
- Tax Duplicates,1833-1834, FHL film #514140.
- Tax Duplicates,1835-1836, FHL film #514141.
- Tax Duplicates,1837-1838, FHL film #514142.

■ ***1816-1838 Tax Duplicates, Athens County, Ohio*** **[Microfilm],** from the original records at the Ohio History Connection, Columbus, Ohio. Filmed by the Genealogical Society of Utah, 1967-68, 4 rolls, as follows:

- Tax Duplicates, 1816-1826, FHL film #514143.
- Tax Duplicates, 1827-1830, FHL film #514144.
- Tax Duplicates, 1831-1834, FHL film #514145.
- Tax Duplicates, 1835-1838, FHL film #514146.

■ ***1816-1838 Tax Duplicates, Belmont County, Ohio*** **[Microfilm],** from the original records at the Ohio History Connection, Columbus, Ohio. These records are duplicates that were made for the state auditors office. Filmed by the Genealogical Society of Utah, 1966, 10 rolls, as follows:

- Tax Duplicates, 1816-1823, FHL film #514147.
- Tax Duplicates, 1824-1826, FHL film #514148.
- Tax Duplicates, 1827-1828, FHL film #514149.
- Tax Duplicates, 1829-1830, FHL film #514150.
- Tax Duplicates, 1831, FHL film #830277.
- Tax Duplicates, 1832, FHL film #864973.
- Tax Duplicates, 1833, FHL film #864974.
- Tax Duplicates, 1834-1835, FHL film #864975.
- Tax Duplicates, 1836-1837, FHL film #864976.
- Tax Duplicates, 1838, FHL film #167679.

■ ***1816-1838 Tax Duplicates of Clinton County, Ohio*** **[Microfilm],** from the originals at the Ohio History Connection, Columbus, Ohio. Filmed by the Genealogical Society of Utah, 1967-1968, 4 rolls, as follows:

- Tax Duplicates, 1816-1823, FHL film #476484.
- Tax Duplicates, 1824-1828, FHL film #476485.
- Tax Duplicates, 1829-1833, FHL film #476486.
- Tax Duplicates, 1834-1838, FHL film #476487.

■ ***1816-1838 Tax Duplicates of Hamilton County, Ohio*** **[Microfilm],** from the originals at the Ohio History Connection, Columbus, Ohio. Filmed by the Genealogical Society of Utah, 1967-1968, 13 rolls, as follows:

- Tax Duplicates, 1816-1817, FHL film #559350.
- Tax Duplicates, 1818-1823, FHL film #506585.
- Tax Duplicates, 1824-1826, FHL film #506586.
- Tax Duplicates, 1827, FHL film #506587.
- Tax Duplicates, 1828, FHL film #506588.
- Tax Duplicates, 1829, FHL film #506589.
- Tax Duplicates, 1830, FHL film #506590.
- Tax Duplicates, 1833, FHL film #506591.

- Tax Duplicates, 1834, FHL film #506592.
- Tax Duplicates, 1835, FHL film #506593.
- Tax Duplicates, 1836, FHL film #506594.
- Tax Duplicates, 1837, FHL film #506595.
- Tax Duplicates, 1838, FHL film #506596.

■ **1820.** See ***Hamilton County, Ohio, 1820 Tax List*** **[Microfilm],** from a manuscript filmed by Wright State University, 1987, 1 roll, FHL film # 1562221.

■ **1825.** See **Index of the Ohio 1825 Tax Duplicates [Printed Book],** compiled by Gerald M. Petty, published by the author, Columbus, OH, 1981, 189 pages. FHL book 977.1 R42p and FHL film #1597666.

■ **1827.** See ***Genealogical Records in Belmont County, Ohio*** **[Printed Book],** compiled and published by the Belmont County Chapter of the Ohio Genealogical Society, 10 vols., including local genealogy, cemeteries, newspapers, church records, vital records, and the 1827 enumeration of males over 21 years of age. FHL book 977.193 D29o, vol. 1-10.

■ ***1832-1850 Duplicate Tax Records, Allen County, Ohio*** **[Microfilm],** from the original records now at the Center for Archival Collections, Bowling Green State University, Bowling Green, Ohio, and the Ohio Historical Society, Columbus. Includes surname indexes. Contains records of tax assessments of real estate, with description of property. Some volumes have indexes. Volume numbers for some volumes are those assigned by the Ohio Historical Society for filing purposes. Filmed by the Genealogical Society of Utah, 1967, 1974, 9 rolls, as follows:

- Tax Duplicates, no dates, FHL film #954812.
- Tax Duplicates, 1832-1833, 1832-1838, 1836-1839, FHL film #954813.
- Tax Duplicates, 1832-1838, FHL film #514135.
- Tax Duplicates, 1840, FHL film #954814.
- Tax Duplicates, 1841-1843, FHL film #954815.
- Tax Duplicates, 1844, FHL film #954816.
- Tax Duplicates, 1845-1846, FHL film #954817.
- Tax Duplicates, 1846-1848, FHL film #954818.
- Tax Duplicates, 1850, FHL film #954819.

■ ***1833-1994 Governor's Deeds Card Index*** **[Microfilm],** from the original records at the Ohio History Connection, Columbus, Ohio, filmed by the Genealogical Society of Utah, 1995, as follows:

- A – Downing, FHL film #2022287.
- Dubois - Millirams (includes some Mills), FHL film #2022288.
- Millisor – Solomon, FHL film #2022289.
- Whalen – Z, FHL film #2022290.

■ **1835.** See ***Index of the Ohio 1835 Tax Duplicate*** **[Printed Book],** compiled by Gerald M. Petty, published by Petty's Press, Columbus, OH, 1987, 320 pages. Includes information of name, county, township, town or village, type of tax record, and page. FHL book 977.1 R42pg.

■ **1846-1880.** See ***Ashland County, Ohio Research Aid*** **[Printed Book],** compiled and published by the Ashland County Chapter of the Ohio Genealogical Society, Ashland, Ohio, 1984, 10 vols. Includes deeds records, maps, tax and chattel lists, cemetery inscriptions, and biographical sketches. FHL book 977.129 R2a vol. 1-10.

■ **1851-1900.** See ***Ohio (Marriages) 1851-1900,*** **[CD-ROM],** part of the Family Tree Maker Family Archives, Marriage Index No. 236, published by Broderbund, 1998. Lists approximately 272,000 individuals who were married in Ohio between 1851 and 1900. FHL CD-ROM no. 9 pt. 236.

■ ***1851-1907 Quadrennial Enumerations, Auglaize County, Ohio*** **[Microfilm],** from the original records at the Archives and Special Collections, Paul L. Dunbar Library, Wright State University, Dayton, Ohio. These records are enumerations of all the male inhabitants above the age of 21 years. Filmed by Wright State Univ., 1979, 2 rolls. FHL film #1763576-1763577.

■ **1853-1861.** See ***Ohio (State) Directories*** **[Microfiche],** from the originals published by various publishers, filmed by Research Publications, Woodbridge, CT, 1980-1984, 41 microfiche, as follows:

- **1853-1854** W. W. Reilly & Co.'s Ohio State business directory by Morgan & Overend (11 fiche) FHL film #6044295.
- **1857** Williams' Ohio State register and business mirror, by C. S. Williams (5 fiche), FHL film #6044296.
- **1859-1860** George W. Hawes' Ohio State gazetteer and business directory by George W. Hawes (11 fiche), FHL film #6044297.
- **1860-1861** Geo. W. Hawes' Ohio State gazetteer, and business Directory, by George W. Hawes (14 fiche), FHL film #6044298.

■ **1861-1940.** See ***Cincinnati (Ohio) City Directories*** **[Microfilm],** from the originals, mostly by Williams & Co., Cincinnati. Collection contains directories for a complete annual run, 1861-1940. Filmed by Research Publications, Woodbridge, CT, 1980-1984,

64 rolls, beginning with FHL film #1376706 ( 1861 Williams' Cincinnati Directory). For a complete list of roll numbers and contents of each roll, see the online FHL catalog page for this title. See **https://familysearch.org/search/catalog/536579.**

■ **1895-1916.** See ***Ohio University Lands, 1895-1916* [Microfilm],** from the original records at the Ohio History Connection, Columbus, OH. Includes typescript cards referencing deeds and certificates for land sales. These records are related to the remaining public lands in Ohio never sold to individuals. In 1871, the lands were granted to the state of Ohio, who gave them to Ohio State University. The cards record the sale of lands obtained from the areas of the old Ohio Company Purchase (mostly in Athens Co OH), and the Virginia Military District (lands between the Scioto and Little Miami Rivers, see the 1787-1871 VMD description, page 95). Information on the cards includes the name of the purchaser, date of purchase, acreage and description of land; location in deed books, and certificate numbers. Filmed by the Genealogical Society of Utah, 1995, 4 rolls, as follows:

- Ohio University Land, conveyed 1895-1916 in Athens County, Township 8-9 Range 14, FHL film #2022654.
- Ohio University lands, conveyed in Athens County, Township 9 Range 14, FHL film #2022655.
- Virginia Military District, lands conveyed by Ohio State University 1890-1918, FHL film #2022655.
- Deeds, v. 1-6 1884-1916, FHL film #196146.
- Deeds, v. 7 1914-1916, FHL film #196147.

■ **1900-1925.** See ***Trumbull County, Ohio Marriage Record Index, 1900-1925* [Printed Book],** edited by Barbara Houser Layfield, publ. Trumbull Co Chapter, OH Genealogical Society, 2006, 413 pages, FHL book 977.138 V22L.

■ ***1907 Quadrennial Enumeration, Clinton County, Ohio* [Microfilm],** from the original records now located at the Special Collections Department, Blegen Library, University of Cincinnati, Cincinnati, Ohio. Includes townships of Adams, Chester, Clark, Green, Jefferson, Liberty, Marion, Richland, Union, Vernon, Washington, Wayne, and Wilson. Contains an enumeration of all male residents over the age of twenty one taken during the listing of property for taxation. Filmed by the Genealogical Society of Utah, 1983, 1 roll, FHL film #973424.

# WISCONSIN
## Censuses & Substitutes, 1685-2013

**French Era.** In 1671, a Jesuit mission was established at La Baie des Puants (now Green Bay). In 1685, French fur traders established a trading post at Prairie du Chien. During the entire French Era, any other French civilians in the Wisconsin region were single voyageurs engaged in fur trading with the Indians.

**British Era.** Near the end of the French and Indian War, British forces took control of the military fort at Green Bay and the fur trading post at Prairie du Chien. At the 1763 Treaty of Paris ending the war, the French were asked to leave North America. The French military left immediately, but the French voyageurs had lost their ties to France and remained. The few French settlements in the Great Lakes region accepted British rule without protest. In 1764, the first British fur trading settlement was established at Green Bay (planted with families from Quebéc).

**British Prairie du Chien.** By 1764, The British saw the strategic importance of the former French settlement at Prairie du Chien and established a military garrison there. The British then consolidated all of their fur trading enterprises at Prairie du Chien, with trappers, traders, and Indians coming together with furs collected in the Upper Mississippi region.

The British Army also used Prairie du Chien as their mustering point with their Indian allies during the Revolutionary War. The town became an attractive refuge to French-Canadian traders, as well as American Loyalists fleeing the war zones. Unlike the British-held former French settlements of Kaskaskia and Vincennes, Prairie du Chien was never lost by the British during the war. After the war, the British refused to cede their post at Prairie du Chien, continuing their fur trading operations there for another thirty years.

**Early American Census Jurisdictions:** Wisconsin was part of the area of the Old Northwest ceded by Britain to the U.S. in the Treaty of Paris in 1783. Between 1783 and 1820, nearly the entire white residential population lived in the villages of Green Bay and Prairie du Chien.

**1790.** Wisconsin was part of the Northwest Territory, which had no census taken. Prairie du Chien was under British occupation during and after the Revolutionary War, and not vacated by the British Army until after the War of 1812. Green Bay was still under control of British fur trading companies.

**1800.** Wisconsin was part of Indiana Territory, entirely within unceded Indian lands; but any possible population lists were lost for all of Indiana.

**1810.** Wisconsin was part of St. Clair County, Illinois Territory, whose 1810 schedule was also lost. By 1816, the entire area of present Wisconsin was brought under the protection of the Americans for the first time with the building of Fort Howard at Green Bay and Fort Crawford at Prairie du Chien.

**1820.** Nearly all whites lived near Fort Howard/Green Bay, Brown County, Michigan Territory; or near Fort Crawford/Prairie du Chien, Crawford County, Michigan Territory. The two counties had a population of 1,444 people. The 1820 census name lists have survived.

**1830.** Present Wisconsin was contained in Brown, Crawford, and Iowa counties, Michigan Territory. The WI areas had a population of 3,635 people. The census name lists survive for 1830 as well. The start of migrations into Wisconsin began in the early 1830s, with the main entry points at the Lake Michigan ports of Green Bay, Milwaukee, Racine, and Kenosha. Between 1832 and 1834, the first public land surveys were completed and land sales commenced at the first three federal GLOs at Green Bay, Milwaukie, and Mineral Point. In 1835, the US Army began building the *Military Ridge Road*, connecting Fort Howard with Fort Crawford via Fond du Lac, Fort Winnebago, Madison, and Dodgeville. The population surged as a result.

**Wisconsin Territory Censuses:** Wisconsin became a territory in 1836, taken from Michigan Territory. The original territorial bounds included the area of present Wisconsin plus the areas west to the Missouri River. In 1838, after the creation of Iowa Territory, Wisconsin's western line ended at the Mississippi River. The area between the St. Croix and Mississippi River was lost in May 1848 when Wisconsin became a state with the same bounds as today. Wisconsin's territorial censuses were taken in the years 1836, 1838, 1842, 1846 and 1847. A few counties are missing from the 1846 territorial census, but the others are fairly complete. The WI territorial censuses are all head of household censuses. All surviving originals, 1836-1847, are located today at the WI Historical Society in Madison. **WI Territorial Censuses Online:** Ancestry's Compiled Census & Census Substitutes database includes indexes to the 1836 through 1846 WI Territorial Censuses.

**Wisconsin State Censuses:** The state constitution of 1848 mandated state censuses every ten years for the purpose of apportionment of the state legislature. Accordingly, Wisconsin conducted state sponsored censuses for the years 1855, 1865, 1875, 1885, 1895, and 1905. Of these, the 1865 state census has only a handful of counties extant, while the others are mostly complete. All of the censuses 1855-1895 are head of household censuses, and they vary in content with added information, e.g., no. of males and females, no. of persons of foreign birth, deaf, dumb, blind, insane, etc. In the 1885 and 1895 state censuses, a special added list was prepared, giving the names of living war veterans. The only Wisconsin census to list the names of all family members was the 1905 state census. As the culmination of all Wisconsin territory and state censuses, it is in every way a detailed and useful genealogical tool, showing relationships, parent's birthplace, etc. An every-name index to the 1905 state census was prepared by the State Historical Society, a card index organized by county. **WI State Censuses Online:** all of the surviving state censuses taken in Wisconsin have been digitized and indexed online (1855-1905 at FamilySearch.org; 1855 (index only), 1895 & 1905 at Ancestry.com).

**Wisconsin Federal Censuses (federal copies), 1840-1940:** The only federal census taken under the name Wisconsin Territory was in 1840, with all 22 counties extant and 30,945 people. After statehood in 1848, the 1850 through 1940 federal censuses for Wisconsin are complete for all counties (with the exception of the 1890, lost for all states).

**Wisconsin Federal Censuses (state copies), 1850-1870:** Adding to the superb array of territorial and state censuses available, Wisconsin also has the original state copies of its 1850, 1860, and 1870 federal censuses. These original schedules have not been microfilmed, but the Historical Society has prepared every-name indexes to each of their state copies.

## Online Resources at the Wisconsin Historical Society (WHS)

The Library-Archives Division of the WHS is the home of the Genealogy and History Collection, one of the largest and most comprehensive family history library collections in the world. Online databases include vital records, biographies, cemeteries, censuses, histories, immigration records, land records, maps, military records, naturalizations, newspapers, obituaries, and probate records. The WHS databases for Civil War records, Vital Records, and the Wisconsin Name Index are outstanding genealogical tools. View the WHS resources available online, see **www.wisconsinhistory.org/Content.aspx?dsNav=N:1133.**

---

## Wisconsin Databases Online at Ancestry.com

The Ancestry.com subscription website allows free access to all indexes, but to view any particular record requires a membership. Ancestry offers trial memberships and subscriptions for short periods and reduced rates. The following databases at the Ancestry.com website are unique to Wisconsin under the categories, Census & Voter Lists, Vital Records, Military, Immigrations, et al.

■ **1685-1850.** See ***Prairie du Chien: French, British, American*** **[Online Database],** digitized and indexed at the Ancestry.com website. Source: book, same title, by Peter Lawrence Scanlan, publ. 1937. The names of the French explorers, traders, and settlers in and around Prairie du Chien are given for the 80 years of French rule, plus the main players of the British era, 1763-1814; and the American possessors thereafter. This database has 267 pages. See **http://search.ancestry.com/search/db.aspx?dbid=27459.**

■ **1800-1987.** See ***Wisconsin, Wills and Probate Records, 1800-1987*** **[Online Database],** digitized and indexed at the Ancestry.com website. Source: Ancestry extracts from original records at district, county, and probate courts of Wisconsin. Searchable database fields include the Probate Place, Place of Death, and Item Description (estate, will, petition, etc.). View a digitized original document, which may add substantial details about the deceased personal and real property, names of witnesses, heirs, and more. This database has 210,019 records. See **http://search.ancestry.com/search/db.aspx?dbid=9088.**

■ **1801-1928.** See ***Wisconsin, Births and Christenings Index, 1801-1928*** **[Online Database],** indexed at the Ancestry.com website. Source: FamilySearch extractions from original and compiled records on microfilm at the Family History Library, Salt Lake City, UT. Each record may include: name, gender, race, birthplace, birth date, christening place, christening date, father's name, age, birthplace; mother's name, age, birthplace; paternal grandparents, maternal grandparents, and FHL film number. This database has 4,138,236 records. See **http://search.ancestry.com/search/db.aspx?dbid=2544.**

■ **1820-1890.** See ***Wisconsin, Compiled Census and Census Substitutes Index, 1820-1890*** **[Online Database],** indexed at the Ancestry.com website. Originally compiled by Accelerated Indexing Systems, Salt Lake City, acquired by Ancestry in 1999. This collection contains the following indexes: 1820 Federal Census Index; 1821-29 Early Census Index; 1830 Federal Census Index; 1836 State Census Index; 1837 State Census Index; 1838 State Census Index; 1840 Federal Census Index; 1840 Pensioners List; 1842 State Census Index; 1846 State Census Index; 1850 Federal Census Index; 1855 State Census Index; 1860 Federal Census Index; 1890 Veterans Schedule. This database has 182,605 records. See **http://search.ancestry.com/search/db.aspx?dbid=3581**

■ **1820-1907.** See ***Wisconsin, Birth Index, 1820-1907*** **[Online Database],** indexed at the Ancestry.com website. Source: Pre-1907 Vital Records Collection, WI Historical Society. The records have a link to the Wisconsin Historical Society website, where a copy of the original record can be ordered. This database has 1,065,005 records. See **http://search.ancestry.com/search/db.aspx?dbid=4750.**

■ **1820-1907.** See ***Wisconsin, Marriage Index, 1820-1907*** **[Online Database],** indexed at the Ancestry.com website. Source: Pre-1907 Vital Records Collection, WI Historical Society. Wisconsin is one of the few states to have a wide-spread index of records prior to establishment of a state vital records office. The records have a link to the WHS website, where a copy of the original record can be ordered. This database has 1,368,708 records. See **http://search.ancestry.com/search/db.aspx?dbid=4997.**

■ **1820-1907.** See ***Wisconsin, Deaths, 1820-1907*** **[Online Database],** indexed at the Ancestry.com website. Source: Pre-1907 Vital Records Collection, WI Historical Society. The records have a link to the

Wisconsin Historical Society website, where a copy of the original death record can be ordered. This database has 439,245 records. See
**http://search.ancestry.com/search/db.aspx?dbid=4984.**

■ **1832-1907.** See ***Wisconsin, Homestead and Cash Entry Patents, Pre-1908*** **[Online Database],** indexed at the Ancestry.com website. Source: BLM General Land Office Automated Records Project. This database is the Wisconsin portion of the GLO patents issued by the federal government within the public domain of the United States. The patent was the first-title deed and the true beginning of private ownership of the land. The deeds recorded in these records includes: Name, Land Office, Sequence, Document number, Total acres, Signature, Canceled document, Issue date, Mineral rights reserved, Metes and bounds, Statutory reference, Multiple warrantee and patentee names, Act or treaty, Entry classification, and Land description (usually Section, Range, Township). This database has 187,635 records. See
**http://search.ancestry.com/search/db.aspx?dbid=2079.**

■ **1835-1900.** See ***Wisconsin Marriages, 1835-1900*** **[Online Database],** indexed at the Ancestry.com website. Source: Jordan Dodd, compiler, Liahona Research, from Grant County, Jackson County, and Monroe County, WI records on microfilm at the Family History Library, Salt Lake City, UT. This database has 27,383 records. See
**http://search.ancestry.com/search/db.aspx?dbid=5230.**

■ **1836.** See ***The First Census of the Original Counties of Dubuque and Demoine (Iowa) Taken in July, 1836*** **[Online Database],** indexed at the Ancestry.com website. Source: book, same title, edited by Benjamin F. Shambaugh, originally published by the Historical Department of Iowa, Des Moines, IA, 1897-1898, 93 pages. Contents: pt. 1. Dubuque County, pt. 2. Demoine County. From the original manuscript returns preserved in the office of the Secretary of State of Wisconsin. Census taken in accordance with the act of Congress erecting the territory of Wisconsin (of which these two counties at the time formed a part) comprising the present states of Wisconsin, Iowa, Minnesota and part of North and South Dakota. This database has 90 pages. See
**http://search.ancestry.com/search/db.aspx?dbid=23732.**

■ **1840-1970.** See ***Web: Oshkosh Area, Wisconsin, Naturalizations Index, 1840-1970*** **[Online Database],** indexed at the Ancestry.com website. This database is also accessible at the University of Wisconsin Oshkosh Archives and Area Research Center website. Each record may include a name, case type, date, place, archives, title, court, role (immigrant, returning citizen, etc.), call no. and location data. This database has 54,394 records. See
**http://search.ancestry.com/search/db.aspx?dbid=70824.**

■ **1848-1977.** See ***Web: Oshkosh Area, Wisconsin, Court Records Index, 1848-1977*** **[Online Database],** indexed at the Ancestry.com website. This database is also accessible at the University of Wisconsin Oshkosh Archives and Area Research Center website. Each record may include a name, case type, date, place, archives, title, court, role (immigrant, returning citizen, etc.), call no and location data. This database has 43,624 records. See
**http://search.ancestry.com/search/db.aspx?dbid=70823.**

■ **1848-1992.** See ***Wisconsin, Federal Naturalization Records, 1848-1992*** **[Online Database],** indexed at the Ancestry.com website. Source: Microfilm of Naturalization Records from U.S. District Courts, originals at the National Archives, Chicago, IL. These records are searchable by Name, Birth Date, Birth Place, and Immigration Year. Additional information in the original records may include: Place of Residence, Occupation, Date of Departure, Place of Departure, Place of Arrival, Spouse's Name, Birth Date, and Residence, Number of Children, Each child's Name, Birth Date, Birth Place, and Residence. This database has 331,780 records. See
**http://search.ancestry.com/search/db.aspx?dbid=61213.**

■ **1853-2012.** See ***Web: Outagamie County, Wisconsin, Appleton Public Library Obituary Index, 1853-2012*** **[Online Database],** indexed at the Ancestry.com website. This database is also accessible at the Appleton Public Library website. Each record may include: Name, Birth Date, Birth Place, Death Date, Burial Place, Cemetery, Date of Obituary, Place of Obituary, Title of Newspaper, Spouse's name, Notes, and the URL link to the database at the Appleton Public Library. This database has 128,147 records. See
**http://search.ancestry.com/search/db.aspx?dbid=9254.**

■ **1857-2013.** See ***Web: Milwaukee, Wisconsin, Catholic Archdiocese Burial Index, 1857-2013*** **[Online Database],** indexed at the Ancestry.com website. This database is also accessible at the Catholic Archdiocese of Milwaukee website. Each record may include: Name, Birth Date, Age at death,

Burial date, Name of Cemetery, and Location of Cemetery. This database has 15,900 records. See
**http://search.ancestry.com/search/db.aspx?dbid=70645.**

■ **1861-1865.** See ***Roster of Wisconsin Volunteers, War of the Rebellion, 1861-1865*** **[Online Database],** digitized and indexed at the Ancestry.com website. Source: Book, same title, publ. Madison, WI, 1886. This database has 1,834 records. See
**http://search.ancestry.com/search/db.aspx?dbid=29993.**

■ **1889-1890.** See ***Milwaukee, Wisconsin Directory, 1889-1890*** **[Online Database],** indexed at the Ancestry.com website. Source: Wright's 1889 and 1890 *Milwaukee Directory*. This database has 147,772 records. See
**http://search.ancestry.com/search/db.aspx?dbid=4749.**

■ ***1890 Census Substitute*** **[Online Database],** indexed at the Ancestry.com website. This is nationwide collection of city directories for the time of the 1890 federal census (lost in a fire in Washington DC in 1921). A global search includes directories from several Wisconsin cities. Too see an alpha list of all U.S. cities included, go to the *View all collections included in this search* tab. See
**http://search.ancestry.com/search/group/1890census.**

■ **1890-1892.** See ***Racine, Wisconsin Directories, 1890, 1892*** **[Online Database],** indexed at the Ancestry.com website. Source: Curtis & Co directories for 1890 and 1892. This database has 21,231 records. See
**http://search.ancestry.com/search/db.aspx?dbid=5201.**

■ **1895-1905.** See ***Wisconsin, State Censuses, 1895 and 1905*** **[Online Database],** indexed at the Ancestry.com website. Source: WHS, Madison. This database contains an index to the 1895 and 1905 Wisconsin state censuses. Both censuses cover all counties that existed at the time. This is basically all modern counties with the exceptions of Rusk (not included in the 1895 census because it was not created until 1905) and Menominee (not included in either year since it wasn't created until 1961). Information listed includes: Name of individual, and Place of enumeration. For the 1905 census the following information is also listed: Date of enumeration, Relationship to head of household, Race, Gender, Age, Marital status, Birthplace, Additional information about an individual, such as their occupation, may be available on the actual census record. This database has 2,690,489 records. See
**http://search.ancestry.com/search/db.aspx?dbid=1055.**

■ **1900-2001.** See ***New Holstein, Calumet, Wisconsin, Obituary Records, 1900-2001*** **[Online Database],** indexed at the Ancestry.com website. Source: FamilySearch image only database. The collection consists of an obituary card file from the New Holstein Public Library. The obituaries came from the *New Holstein Report*.. Browse through the images, organized in alphabetical order. Each index card may contain: Name of deceased, including maiden name of married women, Date and Place of Birth, Date and Place of Death, Date and Place of Burial, Marriage Date, Name of spouse, Death date of spouse, Nickname of the deceased, and Names of survivors, This database has 10,139 records. See
**http://search.ancestry.com/search/db.aspx?dbid=60373.**

■ **1917-1918.** See ***Wisconsin's Gold Star List: Soldiers, Sailors, Marines, and Nurses from the Badger State Who Died in the Federal Service During the World War*** **[Online Database],** indexed at the Ancestry.com website. Source: book, same title, compiled by John Goadby Gregory, publ. WHS, 1925. This database has 221 pages. See
**http://search.ancestry.com/search/db.aspx?dbid=27947.**

■ **1922-1963.** See ***Wisconsin, Passenger and Crew Lists, 1922-1963*** **[Online Database],** indexed at the Ancestry.com website. Source: National Archives microfilm series A3399. The index includes given name, surname, age, gender, ethnicity, nationality, destination, arrival date, port of arrival, port of departure, ship or airline name, microfilm roll and page number. This database has 324,017 records. See
**http://search.ancestry.com/search/db.aspx?dbid=2138.**

■ **1925-1969.** See ***Wisconsin Crew Lists, 1925-1969*** **[Online Database],** indexed at the Ancestry.com website. Source: National Archives microfilm series A3397, M2044, and M2045. This database is an index to crew lists (and a few passenger lists) of vessels (as well as a few aircraft) that arrived at various Wisconsin ports, departed from a Canadian or other foreign port. The index includes the following ports and years: **Green Bay** (1925-1969) (missing 1960, 1961, 1967); **Manitowoc** (1925-1956); **Ashland** (1955-1956); **Kenosha** (1937-1940); **Marinette** (1929-1940); **Sheboygan** (1929-1956); **Sturgeon Bay** (1946-1952); and **Washburn** (1925-1928). Each record may include: Given name and surname of crew member, Age, Gender, Ethnicity or nationality, Last Residence, Birth date, Birthplace, Port of departure, Port of arrival, Date of arrival, and Name of vessel. This database has 37,770 records. See
**http://search.ancestry.com/search/db.aspx?dbid=1005.**

■ **1959-1997.** See ***Wisconsin Death Index, 1959-1997*** **[Online Database],** indexed at the Ancestry.com website. Source: WI Dept of Health. Each record may include: Name of deceased, Death date, Death place (city and/or county), Race, Gender, Age at time of death, Residence county, and Birth date. This database has 1,629,536 records. See **http://search.ancestry.com/search/db.aspx?dbid=8790.**

■ **1965-1984.** See ***Wisconsin Divorce Index, 1965-1984*** **[Online Database],** indexed at the Ancestry.com website. Source: WI Dept of Health. Each record includes: Names of husband and wife, Ages of husband and wife, Divorce date, and Divorce county . This database has 231,594 records. See **http://search.ancestry.com/search/db.aspx?dbid=1244.**

■ **1973-1997.** See ***Wisconsin, Marriage Index, 1973-1997*** **[Online Database],** indexed at the Ancestry.com website. Source: WI Dept of Health. Each record may include: groom's name, groom's age, groom's residence (county and/or state), bride's name, bride's age, bride's residence (county and/or state), marriage date, marriage county, and marriage certificate number. This database has 1,897,933 records. See **http://search.ancestry.com/search/db.aspx?dbid=8744.**

---

## Wisconsin Databases Online at the FamilySearch.org Website

The following databases are available for free at the FamilySearch.org website. To see the current list, visit the Wisconsin Indexed Historical Records and Wisconsin Image Only Historical Records webpage. Both lists are updated periodically. See **https://familysearch.org/search/collection/location/59.**

■ **1820-1907.** See ***Wisconsin Birth Index, 1820-1907*** **[Online Database],** indexed at the FamilySearch.org website. Source: WI Dept of Health. Each record includes a name, date of birth, place of birth, and film numbers and record numbers. This database has 985,659 records. See **https://familysearch.org/search/collection/1946789.**

■ **1820-1907.** See ***Wisconsin Death Index, 1820-1907*** **[Online Database],** indexed at the FamilySearch.org website. Source: WI Dept of Health. Each record includes a name, date of death, place of death, and page number. This database has 435,208 records. See **https://familysearch.org/search/collection/1940759.**

■ **1820-1992.** See ***Wisconsin, County Naturalization Records, 1807-1992*** **[Online Database],** digitized at the FamilySearch.org website. Images only database, from FamilySearch imaging of naturalization records at Wisconsin county courthouses. The starting date of 1807 (in the title) is probably in error and was changed to the time of the earliest counties of Wisconsin before territorial status (say 1820). The records usually include the following information: Full name, Current residence, Birth date and place of birth, Date Naturalized, Name of court, Age when naturalized, Spouse's name, married, Names of children, Arrival date and port of entry, and Certificate number. Browse through the records, organized by county, then by Record Type, Year Range, and Volume No. This database has 1,135,393 records. See **https://familysearch.org/search/collection/2046887.**

■ **1825-1980.** See ***Wisconsin, Outagamie County Records, 1825-1980*** **[Online Database],** indexed at the FamilySearch.org website. Source: Outagamie County Register of Deeds, Appleton, WI. This is a image only database of land and probate records. Browse through the records, organized by Land and Property records or Probate records, then Record Type, Volume, and Year Range. This database has 70,159 records. See **https://familysearch.org/search/collection/1463639.**

■ **1826-1926.** See ***Wisconsin Births and Christenings, 1826-1926*** **[Online Database],** indexed at the FamilySearch.org website. Source: FamilySearch extractions from county records on microfilm at the Family History Library, Salt Lake City, UT. Each record includes a name, gender, date of birth, place of birth, race, father's name and birthplace, Mother's name and birthplace and FHL film number. This database has 1,440,965 records. See **https://familysearch.org/search/collection/1708703.**

■ **1835-1968.** See ***Wisconsin Deaths and Burials, 1835-1968*** **[Online Database],** indexed at the FamilySearch.org website. Source: FamilySearch extractions. This database is a name index to death and burial records from microfilm at the Family History Library, Salt Lake City, UT. This database has 34,943 records. See **https://familysearch.org/search/collection/1708699.**

■ **1836-1911.** See ***Wisconsin, County Marriages, 1836-1911*** **[Online Database],** indexed at the FamilySearch.org website. Source: WI Historical Society. Each record may include: Name of the groom, Name of the bride, Names of the officiator and witnesses, Names of the parents or guardians of the bride and groom, Date of the marriage, Race and Birthplaces of the bride and groom, Residences of the bride and groom, and Occupation of the groom. This database has 755,345 records. See **https://familysearch.org/search/collection/1803973.**

■ **1836-1930.** See ***Wisconsin Marriages, 1836-1930*** **[Online Database],** indexed at the FamilySearch.org website. Source: FamilySearch extractions. This database is a name index to marriage records from microfilm at the Family History Library, Salt Lake City, UT. This database has 197,702 records. See **https://familysearch.org/search/collection/1708704.**

■ **1848-1948.** See ***Wisconsin Probate Estate Files, 1848-1948*** **[Online Database],** digitized at the FamilySearch.org website. Source: WI Historical Society. This image only database includes probate estate case file from Barron County (1910-1930), Bayfield County (1874-1919), Door County (1862-1938), Dunn County (1858-1940), Fond du Lac County (1848-1948), Green County (1848-1885), Jackson County (1897-1935), La Crosse County (1877-1935), Pepin County (1900-1935), Shawano County (1861-1933), and Trempealeau County (1900-1920). Browse through the records, organized by County, then Case File Number and Year Range. This database has 1,399,485 records. See **https://familysearch.org/search/collection/1874190.**

■ **1848-1980.** See ***Wisconsin, Fond du Lac Public Library Records, 1848-1980*** **[Online Database],** digitized at the FamilySearch.org website. This image only database includes images of three separate card index files: 1) Calvary Cemetery, 1900-1980; 2) Marriage Applications, 1899-1930; and 3) Divorces, 1848-1950.. Browse through the records, organized by category, then alphabetically by surname. This database has 22,198 records. See **https://familysearch.org/search/collection/1391196.**

■ **1848-1990.** See ***Wisconsin, Milwaukee Naturalization Index, 1848-1990*** **[Online Database],** digitized and indexed at the FamilySearch.org website. Source: National Archives publication ID #6948573. This database reproduces the card index to naturalizations produced by the District Court of the Eastern District of Wisconsin (Milwaukee). The index cards include the following information: Certificate number, Full name of citizen, Residence, Birth date, Admission date, Certificate date, Name and place of court, Petition and Alien registration number. This database has 76,412 records. See **https://familysearch.org/search/collection/2138589.**

■ **1848-1991.** See ***Wisconsin, Milwaukee Petitions for Naturalization, 1848-1991*** **[Online Database],** digitized at the FamilySearch.org website. Source: National Archives publication ID #7267811. This image only database includes the petitions for naturalizations produced by the District Court of the Eastern District of Wisconsin (Milwaukee). Browse through the records, organized by volume and date range. This database has 176,312 records. See **https://familysearch.org/search/collection/2174939.**

■ **1850-2007.** See ***Wisconsin, Shawano and Oconto Counties, Indexes and Records, 1850-2007*** **[Online Database],** digitized at the FamilySearch.org website. Source: This image only database has images of original records now located at the Shawano Wisconsin Family History Center. The collection includes a partial obituary index, original obituaries, 1928-2005; land plat books, 1905-; and an index to the 1910 US Census for Shawano County. A few records originated in Oconto County, the parent county of Shawano. Browse through the records, organized by Record Type, Volume, and Year Range. This database has 27,614 records. See **https://familysearch.org/search/collection/1930024.**

■ **1855.** See ***Wisconsin State Census, 1855*** **[Online Database],** digitized and indexed at the FamilySearch.org website. Source: WI Historical Society. Includes name index and images of the population schedules for 1855, a head of household census listing, including: Name of head of family, Number of white males and white females in each household, Number of colored males and colored females in each household, Number of individuals who are deaf and dumb, blind, or insane, and the Number of individuals who are foreign born. The database is searchable by a first name, last name, or residence. This database has 133,164 records. See **https://familysearch.org/search/collection/1443825.**

■ **1865.** See ***Wisconsin State Census, 1865*** **[Online Database],** digitized and indexed at the FamilySearch.org website. Source: WI Historical Society. The original state copies of the 1865 state census were purposely destroyed. This database is for six counties only – county copies transferred to the WI Historical Society (Dunn, Green, Jackson, Kewaunee, Ozaukee, and Sheboygan County, WI). Includes name

index and images of the population schedules for 1865, a head of household listing, including: Name of head of family, Number of white males and white females in each household, Number of black males and black females in each household, and the Number of individuals who are foreign born. This database has 21,162 records. Source: See
**https://familysearch.org/search/collection/2058670/.**

■ **1867-1907.** See ***Wisconsin, Death Records, 1867-1907*** **[Online Database],** indexed at the FamilySearch.org website. Source: WI Historical Society. A database extracted from death registers, including: Full name of deceased, Maiden name (if deceased is a married woman), Color, Sex, Race, Occupation, Age, Name of father, Birthplace of father, Name of mother, Birthplace of mother, Birthplace of deceased, Name of spouse, Birth date of deceased, Marital status of deceased, Death date, Residence of deceased, Cause of death, Place of death, duration of disease, Was deceased a soldier or in the service of the United States, Burial place, Name of undertaker, Date of certificate, Number of burial permit, Place of burial permit, and Other remarks. This database has 432,959 records. See
**https://familysearch.org/search/collection/1803975.**

■ **1875.** See ***Wisconsin State Census, 1875*** **[Online Database],** indexed at the FamilySearch.org website. Source: WI Historical Society. Includes name index and images of the population schedules for 1875, a head of household listing, including: Name of head of family, Number of white males and white females in each household, Number of black males and black females in each household, and the Number of individuals who are foreign born. This database has 296,899 records. See
**https://familysearch.org/search/collection/1443778.**

■ **1885.** See ***Wisconsin State Census, 1885*** **[Online Database],** indexed at the FamilySearch.org website. Source: WI Historical Society. Includes name index and images of the population schedules for 1885, a head of household listing, including: Name of head of family, Number of white males and white females in each household, Number of colored males and colored females in each household, and the Number of individuals in the family whose Nativity was U.S., Great Britain, Ireland, France, British America, Scandinavian, Holland, or All Other Countries. A separate schedule includes the name of a Civil War veteran, with military rank, military regiment, and place of military service. This database has 407,138 records. See
**https://familysearch.org/search/collection/1443713.**

■ **1887-1945.** See ***Wisconsin, Dane County Naturalization Records, 1887-1945*** **[Online Database],** digitized at the FamilySearch.org website. Image only database of naturalization records from Dane County, Wisconsin. The records include declarations (1887-1915), petitions (1906-1945), photographs (1841-1955), depositions (1910-1929) and certificate stubs (1907-1926). Browse through the records, organized by Record Type, Year Range, and Volume No. This database has 34,494 records. See
**https://familysearch.org/search/collection/1384564.**

■ **1895.** See ***Wisconsin State Census, 1895*** **[Online Database],** indexed at the FamilySearch.org website. Source: WI Historical Society. Includes name index and images of the population schedules for 1895, a head of household listing, including: Name of head of family, Number of white males and white females in each household, Number of colored males and colored females in each household, and the Number of individuals in the family whose Nativity was U.S., Great Britain, Ireland, France, British America, Scandinavian, Holland, or All Other Countries. A separate schedule includes the name of a Civil War veteran, with military rank, military regiment, and place of military service. This database has 494,911 records. See
**https://familysearch.org/search/collection/1443712.**

■ **1900-2001.** See ***Wisconsin, Calumet County, New Holstein Public Library Records, 1900-2001*** **[Online Database],** digitized at the FamilySearch.org website. The collection consists of an obituary card file from the New Holstein Public Library. The obituaries came from the *New Holstein Report*.. Browse through the images, organized in alphabetical order. Each index card may contain: Name of deceased, including maiden name of married women, Date and Place of Birth, Date and Place of Death, Date and Place of Burial, Marriage Date, Name of spouse, Death date of spouse, Nickname of the deceased, and Names of survivors, This database has 10,139 records. See
**https://familysearch.org/search/collection/1391206.**

■ **1905.** See ***Wisconsin State Census, 1905*** **[Online Database],** indexed at the FamilySearch.org website. Source: WI Historical Society. Facts found in Wisconsin State Censuses for the year 1905 are: Town and county in which census was taken, Name of each

person in family, Relationship to head of household, Age, gender and birth place, Parents' names and their birthplace, Race, and marital status of each person, Occupation, Home owner or renter, Whether living on a farm or in a house. This database has 2,228,391 records. See
**https://familysearch.org/search/collection/1443899.**

■ **1922-1958.** See ***Minnesota, Duluth and Wisconsin, Superior Crew Lists, 1922-1958*** **[Online Database],** digitized and indexed at the FamilySearch.org website. Source: National Archives microfilm series A3452. Each record is indexed with a name, event type, event date, event place, gender, and name of ship. The digitized original document may have more details. This database has 186,334 records. See
**https://familysearch.org/search/collection/2140606.**

■ **1922-1963.** See ***Wisconsin, Milwaukee Passenger and Crew Lists, 1922-1963*** **[Online Database],** indexed at the FamilySearch.org website. Source: National Archives microfilm series A3399. Each record may contain: Port and date of departure, Port and date of entry, Name of ship, Country of citizenship, Name of passenger, including maiden name of women, Names of persons accompanying passenger, Age, gender, marital status and occupation of passenger, Date and place of birth of passenger, Address of last permanent residence, Name and address of friend or relative at last address, Final destination, Name and address of friend or relative in U.S., Physical description and distinguishing marks, Who paid for the passage, and the Purpose of visit. This database has 62,820 records. See
**https://familysearch.org/search/collection/2421844.**

■ **1925-1956.** See ***Wisconsin, Crew Lists of Ship Arrivals, 1925-1956*** **[Online Database],** indexed at the FamilySearch.org website. Source: National Archives microfilm series M2044. Images of crew lists for ship arrivals at **Ashland,** 1955-1956; **Kenosha,** 1937-1940; **Marinette,** 1929-1940; **Sheboygan,** 1929-1956; **Sturgeon Bay**, 1946-1952; and **Washburn**, 1925-1928. Crew lists may contain any of the following: Port and date of departure, Port and date of entry, Name of ship, Country of citizenship, Name of passenger, including maiden name of women, Names of persons accompanying passenger, Age, gender, marital status and occupation of passenger, Date and place of birth of passenger, Address of last permanent residence, Name and address of friend or relative at last address, Final destination, Name and address of friend or relative in U.S., Physical description and distinguishing marks, Who paid for passage, and Purpose of visit. This database has 3,993 records. See
**https://familysearch.org/search/collection/2299361.**

■ **1925-1956.** See ***Wisconsin, Crew Lists of Vessels Arriving at Manitowoc, 1925-1956*** **[Online Database],** digitized and indexed at the FamilySearch.org website. Source: National Archives microfilm series M2045. This database has 3,937 records. See
**https://familysearch.org/search/collection/2299401.**

■ **1959-1967.** See ***Wisconsin Death Index, 1959-1997*** **[Online Database],** indexed at the FamilySearch.org website. Source: WI Dept of Health. The index includes: Name of Deceased, Sex, Age at death, Date and place of death, Name of Father, Name of Mother, Name of Spouse, Certificate number/Page number, and FHL film number. This database has 1,629,093 records. See
**https://familysearch.org/search/collection/1947978.**

■ **1965-1984.** See ***Wisconsin Divorce Index, 1965-1984*** **[Online Database],** digitized and indexed at the FamilySearch.org website. Source: WI Dept of Health. The index includes: Name of husband, Name of wife, Docket number, Divorce date, Divorce place, and Reference number (page, volume, entry number). This database has 231,499 records. See
**https://familysearch.org/search/collection/1967741.**

■ **1973-1997.** See ***Wisconsin Marriage Index, 1973-1997*** **[Online Database],** indexed at the FamilySearch.org website. Source: WI Dept of Health. The index may include the following information: Name of bride and groom, Marriage date and place, Name of spouse (May only list surname) Reference ID-Page/Volume/Entry/Certificate Number. This database has 948,961 records. See
**https://familysearch.org/search/collection/1946794.**

## Wisconsin Databases Online at Various Websites

■ **1800s-1900s.** See ***Wisconsin USGenWeb Archives*** **[Online Database].** The WIGenWeb Archives site offers free genealogical databases with searchable statewide name lists and for all Wisconsin counties. Databases may include Bibles, Biographies, Cemeteries, Censuses, Court Records, Deaths, Deeds, Directories, Histories, Marriages, Military, Newspapers, Obituaries, Photos, Schools, Tax Lists, Wills, and more. See
**http://usgwarchives.net/wi/wifiles.htm.**

■ **1800s-1900s.** See ***Linkpendium – Wisconsin: Family History & Genealogy, Census, Birth, Marriage, Death Vita Records & More* [Online Databases].** Linkpendium is a genealogical portal site with links to state, county, town, and local databases. Currently listed are selected sites for Wisconsin statewide resources (451), Renamed/Discontinued Counties (4), Adams County (188), Ashland County (188), Barron County (211), Bayfield County (176), Brown County (450) and 67 more Wisconsin counties. See **www.linkpendium.com/wi-genealogy.**

■ **1800s-1900s Wisconsin Original Land Owners.** See the ***Family Maps*** series for Wisconsin counties, maps of original land patents, compiled by Greg Boyd and published by Arphax Publishing Co., Norman, OK. These privately-produced computer-generated maps show the first property owners for an entire county, produced as a book of maps, each map laid out on the federal township grid, and includes indexes to help you locate a person, place-name, or cemetery. Additional maps are added for each county to show roads, waterways, railroads, selected city centers, and cemeteries within a county. At this writing, *Family Maps* books have been published for the following Wisconsin counties:. Barron, Bayfield, Buffalo, Chippewa, Clark, Crawford, Dane, Dodge, Dunn, Eau Claire, Fond du Lac, Green, Iowa, Jackson, Langlade, Lincoln, Monroe, Oneida, Pepin, Pierce, Portage, Price, Racine, Rock, Rusk, Sawyer, Sheboygan, St. Croix, Taylor, Vernon, Vilas, Washburn, Washington, Waushara counties, Wisconsin. Visit the publisher's information and ordering website for more details and updated county coverage. See **www.arphax.com/.** Arphax's entire *Family Maps* series is also available as a subscription service online. See **www.historygeo.com.**

■ **1807-1907.** See ***Land Patents, Brown County, Wisconsin* [Online Database],** index to the patents issued to private purchasers of land at the first General Land Office in Wisconsin at Green Bay, Brown County. The first land patent took place in 1807, when Green Bay was still part of Michillimackinac County, Michigan Territory. Brown County was created by MI Terr. in 1818. The index gives the name of the land purchaser, no. of acres, and land description (Section, Township, Range). Indexed at the USGenWeb archives website for Brown Co WI. See **www.usgwarchives.net/wi/brown/old/brland.htm.**

■ **1818-1907.** See ***Land Patents, Crawford County, Wisconsin* [Online Database],** index to the patents issued to private purchasers of land in Crawford County, Wisconsin. Crawford County was created by Michigan Territory in 1818, and was an original county of Wisconsin Territory in 1836. The index gives the name of the land purchaser, no. of acres, and land description (Section, Township, Range). Indexed in alpha groups at the USGenWeb archives website for Crawford Co WI. See **http://files.usgwarchives.net/wi/crawford/land.**

■ ***1830 Census Index, Michigan Territory, Iowa County (now Wisconsin)* [Online Database],** indexed at the USGenWeb Archives website. See **http://files.usgwarchives.net/wi/territory/census/1830/cens1830.txt.**

■ **1833-1992.** See ***Wisconsin Newspaper Archives, 1833-1992* [Online Databases],** digitized and indexed newspapers at the GenealogyBank website, for Appleton, Beloit, Chilton, Fond du Lac, Fort Atkinson, Fox Lake, Galesville, Grafton, Gratiot, Green Bay, Janesville, La Crosse, Lancaster, Madison, Mauston, Milwaukee, Monroe, New Lisbon, Oshkosh, Racine, Sheboygan, and Waukesha, WI. See **www.genealogybank.com/explore/newspapers/all/usa/wisconsin.**

■ ***1836 Wisconsin Territory Census* [Online Database],** extracted and indexed at the WIGenWeb Archives website. See **http://files.usgwarchives.net/wi/territory/census/1836/1836cens.txt.**

■ **1874.** See ***Green Bay and Fort Howard Directory. Containing Historical Information of Their Early Settlement and Growth; Their Present Standing; Schools, Churches, Societies, etc. Also Business Directory of Principle Dealers. Street Directory, Ward Boundaries, etc., publ. Reid and Miller, 1874* [Online Database],** digitized and indexed at the Univ. of Wisconsin Digital Collection website. See **http://digicoll.library.wisc.edu/cgi-bin/WI/WI-idx?id=WI.NLHGBayDir1874.**

■ **1876-1907.** See ***Vital Records Index, Crawford County, Wisconsin* [Online Database],** an index to births, marriages, and deaths. Indexed at the USGenWeb Archives website for Crawford Co WI. For the parent directory, see **http://files.usgwarchives.net/wi/crawford/vitals.**

■ *1895 Wisconsin State Census – Veterans Home* **[Online Database],** index to the residents of the King Veterans Home, Town of Farmington, Waupaca County, Wisconsin, as part of the 1895 state census. Indexed at the WIClarkCountyHistory.org website: **www.wiclarkcountyhistory.org/clark/facts/1895_KingVets.htm.**

■ **1913.** See ***Biographical Index: History of Brown County, Wisconsin: Past and Present, Vol. II, 1913*** **[Online Database],** indexed at the USGenWeb Archives website for Brown Co WI. See **http://files.usgwarchives.net/wi/brown/bios/1913ndex.txt**

■ **1989-Current.** See ***Wisconsin Recent Newspaper Obituaries (1989-Current)*** **[Online Database],** digitized and indexed newspaper obituaries at the GenealogyBank website, including newspapers for Ashland, Baraboo, Bay View, Bayside, Beaver Dam, Beloit, Brookfield, Cambridge, Deerfield, Cedarburg, Chippewa Falls, Columbus, Cottage Grove, DeForest, Dousman, Edgerton, Fort Atkinson, Franklin, Germantown, Greenfield, Hartford, Hartland, Hayward, Kenosha, La Crosse, Lake Mills, Lodi, Madison, Mauston, McFarland, Menomonie, Milton, Milwaukee, Minocqua, Mukwonago, Muskego, New Berlin, Oconomowoc, Oneida, Park Falls, Phillips, Portage, Poynette, Reedsburg, Rhinelander, Rice Lake, Ripon, Sauk City, Spooner, Sun Prairie, Superior, Washburn, Waterloo, Waukesha, Waunakee, Wauwatosa, and West Bend, WI. See **www.genealogybank.com/explore/obituaries/all/usa/wisconsin.**

## Wisconsin Books & Microfilms at the Family History Library

The most important of Wisconsin's statewide censuses and substitutes are cited below in chronological order. Each item includes a FHL book number or FHL film number, which can be used to search the FHL catalog for more details. To review an item, start at the FamilySearch catalog search page: **https://familysearch.org/search/catalog/results.** Select "Search by Place" then "United States, Wisconsin" to see a list of catalog categories. Or, select "Call Number" then type an FHL book number; or select "Film/Fiche Number" to view a specific title.

■ **1816-1866.** See ***Index to Crawford County Marriages*** **[Printed Book],** compiled by Carol Higgins, publ. Lower Wisconsin River Genealogical & Historical Research Center, Wauzeka, WI, 1994, 96 pages, FHL book 975.574 V22h.

■ ***1820 Michigan Territory Federal Census (MI State Archives Copy)*** **[Microfilm],** from Michigan Territory's original manuscript copy, now located at the Archives of Michigan, Lansing, MI. This state archives copy and the national archives copy should be compared side-by-side to see if there are differences. This MI Territory set was used to make a copy to be sent to Washington, DC (the federal copy). Contents: Oakland, Wayne, Michillimackinac, Brown (now Wisconsin), Crawford (now Wisconsin), Monroe, and Macomb counties. Filmed by the Genealogical Society of Utah, 1973, 1 roll, FHL film #927678.

■ ***1820-1830 Michigan Territory Federal Census (Federal Copy)*** **[Microfilm],** from originals at the National Archives, Washington, DC. In 1820, Crawford and Brown counties (now Wisconsin) were part of Michigan Territory. In 1830, Crawford, Brown, and Iowa counties (now Wisconsin) were part of Michigan Territory. These federal copies were filmed by the National Archives (as part of a combined set of 1820, 1830, & 1840), as follows:

- **1820 MI Territory:** Oakland, Wayne, Michillimackinac, Brown (now Wisconsin), Crawford (now Wisconsin), Monroe, and Macomb counties, FHL film #506762.
- **1830 MI Territory:** Wayne, Monroe, Oakland, Lenawee, Macomb, St. Clair, Washtenaw, St. Joseph, Berrien, Cass, Van Buren, Michillimackinac, Brown (now Wisconsin), Crawford (now Wisconsin), Chippewa, and Iowa (now Wisconsin) counties, FHL film #363348.

■ **1820-1839.** See ***Brown County, Wisconsin, Deeds, 1820-1839*** **[Microfilm],** from the original records at the WI Historical Society, Madison, WI. Includes general deeds, tax deeds, quit claim deeds, warranty deeds, and any grantor/grantee indexes within certain volumes. Filmed by the Genealogical Society of Utah, 2003, 45 rolls, beginning with FHL film #2367060 (Deed Records, Vol. A, Nov 1820-Jan 1826). For a complete list of roll numbers and contents of each roll, see the online FHL catalog page for this title. See **https://familysearch.org/search/catalog/1137284.**

■ **1824-1910.** See ***Probate Index, Brown County, Wisconsin*** **[Microfilm],** from the original records at the WI Historical Society, Madison, WI. Although the index covers probate and guardianship matters, it is mostly an index to court records. Adoptions have been blanked out before filming. Filmed by the Genealogical Society of Utah, 1991, 1 roll, FHL film # 1753115.

■ **1830-1850.** See ***Iowa County (Wisconsin) Heritage* [Printed Book & Microfilm],** abstracts of censuses from the 1830 Michigan Territory census; the 1836, 1838, 1840, 1842, and 1847 Wisconsin Territory censuses; and the Wisconsin federal census of 1850. Published in 4 vols., 1967. FHL book 977.5 B4f vol. 1-4. (Vols. 1 & 2 relate to Iowa County, WI; Vol. 3 relates to Grant Co., WI; & Vol. 4 relates to Jo Daviess County, IL). From introduction: "When organized as a county, under the territorial government of Michigan, in 1829, Iowa county contained within its jurisdiction the present counties of Dane, Green, Grant, LaFayette, and a part of Rock, thus embracing almost one-half of Wisconsin which lies south of the Wisconsin River." Filmed by the Genealogical Society of Utah, 1987, FHL film #1320510.

■ ***1836 Wisconsin Territorial Census* [Microfilm & Printed Index],** from the original records at the WI Historical Society, Madison, WI. This is a head of households census similar in format to the 1830 federal census. Originals filmed by the Genealogical Society of Utah, 1980, 1 roll, FHL film #1293919. The name list was published in *Collections of the Wisconsin State Historical Society,* vol. 13, (1895), p. 247-270; reprinted as **"The Territorial Census For 1836,"** by Reuben Gold Thwaites, editor. The article was also filmed by the Genealogical Society of Utah, 1980, 1 roll, FHL film #1293922. Indexed in ***Wisconsin 1836 Census Index***, edited by Ronald Vern Jackson and Gary Ronald Teeples, published by Accelerated Indexing, Bountiful, UT, 1976, 24 pages. FHL book 977.5 X2 1836.

■ ***1838 Wisconsin Territorial Census* [Microfilm & Printed Index],** from the original records at the WI Historical Society, Madison, WI. Head of household census similar in format to the 1836 territorial census. Originals filmed by the Genealogical Society of Utah, 1980, 1 roll, FHL film #1293919. Indexed in ***Wisconsin 1838 Census Index***, edited by Ronald Vern Jackson, et al, Accelerated Indexing Systems, Bountiful, UT, 1984, 27 pages. FHL book 977.5 X22j 1838.

■ **1840.** See ***Minnesota 1840 Census Index* [Printed Index],** edited by Ronald Vern Jackson, publ. Accelerated Indexing Systems, Bountiful, UT, 1981, 57 pages. FHL book 977.6 X22m. **Note:** This is really an index to the 1840 population in the parts of two territories that later became part of Minnesota: 1) Fort Snelling and Wabasha in Clayton County, Iowa Territory, both communities on the west side of the Mississippi River; and 2), the people living in the area between the St. Croix and Mississippi Rivers, part of St. Croix County, Wisconsin Territory in 1840. A few people at the fur trading posts on Lake Superior may have been included in the St. Croix County enumeration as well.

■ ***1842 Wisconsin Territorial Census* [Microfilm & Printed Index],** from the original records at the WI Historical Society, Madison, WI. This is a head of households census similar in content to the 1838 territorial census. Filmed by the Genealogical Society of Utah, 1980, 1 roll, FHL film #1293919. Indexed in ***Wisconsin 1842 Census Index***, edited by Ronald Vern Jackson, et al, published by Accelerated Indexing Systems, Bountiful, UT, 1984, 110 pages. FHL book 977.5 X22j 1842.

■ ***1846 Wisconsin Territorial Census* [Microfilm],** from the original records at the WI Historical Society, Madison, WI. Includes name of head of family; number of males and females by color, those of foreign birth, deaf, dumb, blind, or insane. Incomplete schedules for the counties of Crawford and Fond du lac; and Grand Rapids in Portage County. No schedules at all for Chippewa, LaPointe, or Richland counties. Filmed by the Genealogical Society of Utah, 1980, 1 roll, FHL film #1293920.

■ ***1847 Wisconsin Territorial Census* [Microfilm],** from the original records at the WI Historical Society, Madison, WI. This was a head of households census with a format similar to the 1846 territorial census, complete for all counties except Sheboygan county is missing. Filmed by the Genealogical Society of Utah, 1980, 2 rolls, as follows:

- **1847 WI territorial census**, Brown to Sheboygan Co. (Sheboygan missing), FHL film #1293921.
- **1847 WI territorial census**, Walworth to Winnebago Co., FHL film #1293922.

■ ***1850 Wisconsin Federal Census (Federal Copy)* [Microfilm],** from the original records at the National Archives, Washington, DC. The census schedules include the names of all members of a family, age, sex, and place of birth. Since Wisconsin has the state copies of the same federal census schedules, a comparison can made between the federal and state copies. This federal set was filmed by the National Archives, 1964, 16 rolls, beginning with FHL film #34508 (Adams, Brown, Calumet, Chippewa, and Columbia Counties). For a complete list of roll

numbers and contents of each roll, see the online FHL catalog for this title. See
**https://familysearch.org/search/catalog/745188.**

■ **1850.** See ***Index to 1850 Federal Census of Wisconsin (State Copy)*** **[Microfilm],** from the original card index at the WI Historical Society, Madison, WI. The index is to the state copy, and volumes and page numbers given in the census index do not always match the federal copy of the census. The alphabetized list of names is for the entire state, regardless of county of residence. Filmed by the University of Wisconsin Film Laboratory, 1971, 36 rolls, beginning with FHL film #933599 (Aaby – Autthouse). For a complete list of roll numbers and contents of each roll, see the online FHL catalog page for this title. See
**https://familysearch.org/search/catalog/283885.**

■ ***1855 Wisconsin State Census*** **[Microfilm],** from the original records at the WI Historical Society, Madison, WI. This is a head of households census similar in format to the 1847 census layout. Complete for all counties except Kewaunee County, which is missing. Filmed by the Genealogical Society of Utah, 1979, 4 rolls, as follows:

- **1855 WI state census**, Adams - Dane, Douglas, Dunn counties, vols. 1-3, FHL film #1032686.
- **1855 WI state census**, Dodge, Fond du Lac - LaPointe counties, vols. 4-9, FHL film #1032687.
- **1855 WI state census**, Manitowoc - Rock counties, vols. 10-14, FHL film #1032688.
- **1855 WI state census**, St. Croix – Winnebago counties, vols. 15-18, FHL film #1032689.

■ **1855.** See ***Wisconsin 1855 Census Index*** **[Printed Index],** edited by Ronald Vern Jackson, et al, published by Accelerated Indexing, Bountiful, UT, 1984, 417 pages. FHL book 977.5 X22w 1855.

■ ***1857-1859 Wisconsin (State) Directories*** **[Microfiche],** from the originals published by various publishers. Filmed by Research Publications, Woodbridge, CT, 1980-1984, 17 microfiche, as follows:

- **1857-1858**, The Wisconsin State directory, by Smith, Du Moulin & Co. (7 fiche), FHL fiche #6044651.
- **1858,** Strickland's North-Western almanac and business directory by Strickland & Co. (2 fiche), FHL fiche #6044652.
- **1858-1859**, The Wisconsin State directory by Strickland & Co. (8 fiche), FHL fiche #6044653.

■ ***1860 Wisconsin Federal Census (Federal Copy)*** **[Microfilm],** from the original records at the National Archives, Washington, DC. The 1860 census was filmed twice. The second filming is listed first and is usually easier to read. Filmed by the National Archives, 1962, 1968, 49 rolls, beginning with FHL film #805399 (2nd filming, Adams and Bad Ax Counties). For a complete list of roll numbers and contents of each roll, see the online FHL catalog page for this title. See
**https://familysearch.org/search/catalog/708785.**

■ **1860.** See ***Index to the 1860 Federal Census of Wisconsin*** **(State Copy) [Microfilm],** from the original index cards at the WI Historical Society, Madison, WI. The index is to the state copy, and volumes and page numbers given in the index do not always match the federal copy of the census. The alphabetized list of names is for the entire state, regardless of county of residence. Filmed by the University of Wisconsin Film Laboratory, 1971, 95 rolls, beginning with FHL film #933635 (Aaby – Ambrosch). For a complete list of roll numbers and contents of each roll, see the online FHL catalog page for this title. See
**https://familysearch.org/search/catalog/283919.**

■ **1861-1865.** See ***Index to Compiled Service Records of Volunteer Union Soldiers Who Served in Organizations From the State of Wisconsin*** **[Microfilm],** from the original records at the National Archives, Washington, DC. Filmed by the National Archives, 1964, series M0559, 33 rolls, beginning with FHL film #882486 (Index, A-Bak, 1861-1865). For a complete list of roll numbers and contents of each roll, see the online FHL catalog page for this title. See
**https://familysearch.org/search/catalog/317099.**

■ ***1865 Wisconsin State Census*** **[Printed Index & Microfilm].** The state's original set was destroyed, but there are duplicate copies that exist for six counties, Dunn, Green, Jackson, Kewaunee, Ozaukee, Sheboygan. A transcription and index was compiled by Barry Christopher Noonan, published by the author, Madison, WI, 1993, 353 pages. Copy at the State Historical Society library, call no. F580 N66 1993. The original manuscripts of the six surviving counties are available on microfilm, as follows:

- **1865 WI State Census**, Dunn County, microfilm of original records now located at the Stout Area Research Center at Menomonie, WI. Head of households census. Filmed by the Genealogical Society of Utah, 1981, 1 roll, FHL film #1298908.

- **1865 WI State Census**, Green County, WI, microfilm of original records at the WI Historical Society, Madison, WI. Head of households census. Filmed by the Genealogical Society of Utah, 1981, 1 roll, FHL film #1306084.
- **1865 WI State Census**, Jackson County, WI, microfilm of original records at the WI Historical Society, Madison, WI. Head of households census. Filmed by the Genealogical Society of Utah, 1981, 1 roll, FHL film #1306084.
- **1865 WI State Census**, Kewaunee County, WI, microfilm of originals at the WI Historical Society, Madison, WI. Head of households census. Filmed by the WI Historical Society, 2003, 1 roll, FHL film #2311106.
- **1865 WI State Census**, Ozaukee County, WI, microfilm of originals at the WI Historical Society, Madison, WI. Head of households census. Filmed by the WI Historical Society, 2003, 1 roll, FHL film #2311107.
- **1865 WI State Census**, Sheboygan County, WI, microfilm of original records at the Sheboygan County courthouse, Sheboygan, WI. Heads of household census. Filmed by the Genealogical Society of Utah, 1983, 1 roll, FHL film #1392915. See also ***Copy of the Sheboygan County Census, 1865, State of Wisconsin: Enumeration of the Inhabitants in Sheboygan County***, copied by the Sheboygan County Genealogical Society, Sheboygan Falls, WI, 1985, 123 pages. FHL book 977.569 X2c.

■ ***1870 Wisconsin Federal Census (Federal Copy)*** **[Microfilm],** from the original records at the National Archives, Washington, DC. The 1870 census was filmed twice. Filmed by the National Archives, 1962, 1968, 60 rolls, beginning with FHL film #553202 (Adams, Ashland, Barron, Bayfield, and Brown Counties). For a complete list of roll numbers and contents of each roll, see the online FHL catalog page for this title. See **https://familysearch.org/search/catalog/698928**.

■ **1870.** See ***Index to the 1870 Federal Census of Wisconsin (State Copy)*** **[Microfilm],** from the original card index at the WI Historical Society, Madison, WI. The index is to the state copy, and volumes and page numbers given do not always match the federal copy of the census. The alphabetized list of names is for the entire state, regardless of county of residence. Filmed by the University of Wisconsin Film Laboratory, 1971, 135 rolls, beginning with FHL film #933730 (Aaby – Allen, Myron). For a complete list of roll numbers and contents of each roll, see the online FHL catalog page for this title. See **https://familysearch.org/search/catalog/284025.**

■ ***1875 Wisconsin State Census*** **[Microfilm],** from the original records at the WI Historical Society, Madison, WI. Head of household census similar to the 1855 state census format. Filmed by the Genealogical Society of Utah, 1979, 6 rolls, as follows:

- **1875 WI State Census**, Adams - Calumet (part) counties, vol. 1, FHL film #1032689.
- **1875 WI State Census**, Calumet (cont.) – Eau Claire counties, vol. 1-3, FHL film #1032690.
- **1875 WI State Census**, Fond du Lac- Juneau counties, vol. 4-5, FHL film #1032691.
- **1875 WI State Census**, Kenosha- Milwaukee counties, vol. 6-, FHL film #1032692.
- **1875 WI State Census**, Monroe- Sheboygan counties, vol. 8-10, FHL film #1032693.
- **1875 WI State Census**, Sheboygan – Wood counties, vol. 10-12, FHL film #1032694.

■ **1880.** See ***Wisconsin Soldiers and Sailors Reunion: Containing the Post Office Address, Occupation and Name of Every Wisconsin Soldier and Sailor Now Living ... Also the Name of Every Wisconsin Soldier Who Perished in the War ... Also, a Complete Roster of Wisconsin's Armed Military Organizations*** **[Microfiche],** contributed by J. A. Kellogg, et al, original published Fond du Lac, WI by Star Steam Job and Book Printing House, 1880, 309 pages. Reprinted by University Publications of America, Bethesda, MD, 1993, filmed by the Genealogical Society of Utah, 4 microfiche, FHL film #6118307.

■ ***1885 Wisconsin State Census*** **[Microfilm],** from the original records at the WI Historical Society, Madison, WI. Head of households census, schedules complete for all Wisconsin counties. Also includes county by county "Enumeration of Soldiers and Sailors of the Late War" (Civil War). Filmed by the Genealogical Society of Utah, 1979, 10 rolls, as follows:

- **1885 WI State Census**, Adams – Clark counties, FHL film #1032695.
- **1885 WI State Census**, Columbia – Dunn counties, FHL film #1032696.
- **1885 WI State Census**, Dunn – Green Lake counties, FHL film #1032697.
- **1885 WI State Census**, Iowa – Lincoln counties, FHL film #1032698.
- **1885WI State Census**, Manitowoc, Marathon, Marinette, Marquette, Monroe, Milwaukee County, & Milwaukee City, wards . FHL film #1032699.
- **1885 WI State Census**, Milwaukee City, wards 4-13; Oconto – Portage counties, FHL film #1032700.
- **1885 WI State Census**, Portage, Price, Pepin, Pierce, Racine, Richland, Rock, St. Croix, and Sauk counties, FHL film #1032701.

- **1885 WI State Census**, Sauk – Walworth counties, FHL film #1032702.
- **1885 WI State Census**, Waukesha - Wood counties; and Enumeration of Soldiers & Sailors, Adams - Dunn counties, FHL film #1032703.
- **1885 WI State Census**, Enumeration of Soldiers & Sailors, Eau Claire - Wood counties, FHL film #1032704.

■ **1885.** See ***Tabular Statements of the Census Enumeration, and the Agricultural, Mineral and Manufacturing Interests of the State: Also Alphabetical List of the Soldiers and Sailors of the Late War Residing in the State, June 20, 1885*** **[Printed Book & Microfilm],** an official report published for the Wisconsin Secretary of State by Democrat Printing Company, State Printers, Madison, WI, 1886, 791 pages. FHL book 977.5 X2w and FHL film #962237.

■ ***1895 Wisconsin State Census*** **[Microfilm],** from the original records at the WI Historical Society, Madison, WI. Head of households census, complete for all Wisconsin counties. Also includes, "Enumeration of Soldiers and Sailors," a separate name list of living veterans for each county. Filmed by the Genealogical Society of Utah, 1979, 12 rolls, as follows:

- **1895 WI State Census**, Adams – Columbia counties, FHL film #1032705.
- **1895 WI State Census**, Columbia – Dunn counties, FHL film #1032706.
- **1895 WI State Census**, Dunn – Green Lake counties, FHL film #1032707.
- **1895 WI State Census**, Iowa – La Crosse counties, FHL film #1032708.
- **1895 WI State Census**, Lafayette – Monroe counties, FHL film #1032709.
- **1895 WI State Census**, Milwaukee County, Milwaukee City, wards 1-9, FHL film #1032710.
- **1895 WI State Census**, Milwaukee City, wards 10-18, Milwaukee County, FHL film #1032711.
- **1895 WI State Census**, Milwaukee County & Oconto - Racine counties, FHL Film #1032712.
- **1895 WI State Census**, Racine – Taylor counties, FHL film #1032713.
- **1895 WI State Census**, Taylor – Waupaca counties, FHL film #1032714.
- **1895 WI State Census**, Waushara – Wood counties; and Enumeration of Soldiers & sailors, Adams – Jefferson counties, FHL film #1032715.
- **1895 WI State Census**, Enumeration of Soldiers & sailors, Jefferson – Wood counties, FHL film #1032716.

■ ***1895 Wisconsin Soldiers in Soldier Homes*** **[Printed Book],** compiled by Bev Hetzel, published by the author, West Bend, WI, 19[--], 24 pages. Names, with annotations, are in alphabetical order. The list was taken from a 1895 census report & from a two-volume set on the Civil War. FHL book 977.5 M2he.

■ ***1905 Wisconsin State Census*** **[Microfilm],** from the original records at the WI Historical Society, Madison, WI. Contents: Name of each individual; relationship to head of household; color/race; sex; age at last birthday; marital status; place of birth, by state or country; place of birth of parents; occupation, if 14 years or older; number of months unemployed; and whether a home or farm was owned outright, mortgaged, or rented. The 1905 WI state census schedules are complete for 71 of Wisconsin's 72 modern counties. (Menominee Indian Reservation became co-extensive with a new Menominee County in 1959). Filmed by the WI Historical Society, 1952, 36 rolls, as follows:

- **1905 WI State Census**, Adams, Ashland, Barron counties, FHL film #1020439.
- **1905 WI State Census**, Bayfield and Brown counties, FHL film #1020440.
- **1905 WI State Census**, Buffalo, Burnett, Calumet counties, FHL film #1020441.
- **1905 WI State Census**, Chippewa and Clark counties, FHL film #1020442.
- **1905 WI State Census**, Columbia and Crawford counties, FHL film #1020443.
- **1905 WI State Census**, Dane County, FHL film #1020444.
- **1905 WI State Census**, Dodge and Door counties, FHL film #1020445.
- **1905 WI State Census**, Douglas and Dunn counties, FHL film #1020446.
- **1905 WI State Census**, Eau Claire and Florence counties, FHL film #1020447.
- **1905 WI State Census**, Fond du Lac and Forest counties, FHL film #1020448.
- **1905 WI State Census**, Grant and Green counties, FHL film #1020449.
- **1905 WI State Census**, Green Lake, Iowa Iron, & Jackson counties, FHL film #1020450.
- **1905 WI State Census**, Jefferson and Juneau counties, FHL film #1020451.
- **1905 WI State Census**, Kenosha, Kewaunee, La Crosse counties, FHL film #1020452.
- **1905 WI State Census**, Lafayette, Langlade, Lincoln counties, FHL film #1020453.
- **1905 WI State Census**, Manitowoc County, FHL film #1020454 .
- **1905 WI State Census**, Marathon County, FHL film #1020455.
- **1905 WI State Census**, Marinette, Marquette, Monroe counties, FHL film #1020978.
- **1905 WI State Census**, Milwaukee County; and city of Milwaukee, Ward 1, FHL film #1020991.

- **1905 WI State Census**, city of Milwaukee, wards 2-8, FHL film #1020992.
- **1905 WI State Census**, city of Milwaukee, wards 8-11, FHL film #1020993.
- **1905 WI State Census**, city of Milwaukee, wards 11-14, FHL film #1020994.
- **1905 WI State Census**, city of Milwaukee, wards 15-19, FHL film#1020995.
- **1905 WI State Census**, city of Milwaukee wards, 19-23, FHL film #1020996.
- **1905 WI State Census**, Oconto, Oneida, Outagamie counties, FHL film #1020979.
- **1905 WI State Census**, Ozaukee, Pepin, Pierce, Polk counties, FHL film #1020980.
- **1905 WI State Census**, Portage and Price counties, FHL film #1020981.
- **1905 WI State Census**, Racine and Richland counties, FHL film #1020982.
- **1905 WI State Census**, Rock and Rusk counties, FHL film #1020983.
- **1905 WI State Census**, St. Croix, Sauk, Sawyer counties, FHL film #1020984.
- **1905 WI State Census**, Shawano and Sheboygan counties, FHL film #1020985.
- **1905 WI State Census**, Taylor, Trempealeau, Vernon, Vilas counties, FHL film #1020986.
- **1905 WI State Census**, Walworth, Washburn, Washington counties, FHL film #1020987.
- **1905 WI State Census**, Waukesha and Waupaca counties, FHL film #1020988.
- **1905 WI State Census**, Waushara and Winnebago counties, FHL film #1020989.
- **1905 WI State Census**, Wood County, FHL film #1020990.

■ ***1905 Wisconsin State Census Index*** **[Microfilm],** from the original card indexes (by county) at the WI Historical Society, Madison, WI. Surname, first name indexes in alphabetical order for each county. All county-wide indexes filmed by the Genealogical Society of Utah, 1978-1985, 444 rolls. 71 counties, No. of rolls, and FHL film numbers, as follows:

- **1905 WI State Census Index,** Adams County, 2 rolls: FHL film #1266809-1266816.
- **1905 WI State Census Index,** Ashland County, 5 rolls: FHL film #1379406-1379410.
- **1905 WI State Census Index,** Barron County, 6 rolls: FHL film #1275513-1275518.
- **1905 WI State Census Index,** Bayfield County, 3 rolls, FHL film #1275792-1275794.
- **1905 WI State Census Index,** Brown County, 10 rolls, FHL film #1308729-1308738.
- **1905 WI State Census Index,** Buffalo County, 4 rolls, FHL film #1205863-1205864; and 1205884-1205885.
- **1905 WI State Census Index,** Burnett County, 2 rolls, FHL film #1266822-1266823.
- **1905 WI State Census Index,** Calumet County, 4 rolls, FHL film #1205801-1205804.
- **1905 WI State Census Index,** Chippewa County, 6 rolls FHL film #1308739-1308744.
- **1905 WI State Census Index,** Clark County, 6 rolls, FHL film #1308912-1308915; and 1308930-1308931.
- **1905 WI State Census Index,** Columbia County, 6 rolls, FHL film #1266834-1266836; and 1266853-1266855.
- **1905 WI State Census Index,** Crawford County, 3 rolls, FHL film #1266817-1266819.
- **1905 WI State Census Index,** Dane County, 14 rolls, FHL film #1205164-1205177.
- **1905 WI State Census Index,** Dodge County, 9 rolls, FHL film #1266825-1266833.
- **1905 WI State Census Index,** Door County, 4 rolls, FHL film #1292223-1292226.
- **1905 WI State Census Index,** Douglas County, 8 rolls, FHL film #1292204-1292211.
- **1905 WI State Census Index,** Dunn County,5 rolls, FHL film #1308703-1308707.
- **1905 WI State Census Index,** Eau Claire County, 7 rolls, FHL film #1308716-1308722.
- **1905 WI State Census Index,** Florence County, 1 roll, FHL film #1292411.
- **1905 WI State Census Index,** Fond du Lac County, 10 rolls, FHL film #1275547-1275553; 1275657-1275658; and 1275721.
- **1905 WI State Census Index,** Forest County, 1 roll, FHL film #1266875.
- **1905 WI State Census Index,** Grant County, 8 rolls, FHL film #1292236, 1292258-1292261; 1292313-1292314; and 1292316.
- **1905 WI State Census Index,** Green County, 5 rolls, FHL film #1266655-1266659.
- **1905 WI State Census Index,** Green Lake County, 3 rolls, FHL film #1275544-1275546.
- **1905 WI State Census Index,** Iowa County, 4 rolls, FHL film #1275509-1275512.
- **1905 WI State Census Index,** Iron County, 1 roll, FHL film #1266824.
- **1905 WI State Census Index,** Jackson County, 4 rolls, FHL film #1205885-1205888.
- **1905 WI State Census Index,** Jefferson County, 7 rolls, FHL film #1205789-1205795.
- **1905 WI State Census Index,** Juneau County, 5 rolls, FHL film #1292531-1292535.
- **1905 WI State Census Index,** Kenosha County, 6 rolls, FHL film #1275787-1275792.
- **1905 WI State Census Index,** Kewaunee County, 4 rolls, FHL film #1292212- 1292215.
- **1905 WI State Census Index,** La Crosse County, 8 rolls, FHL film #1308708-1308715.
- **1905 WI State Census Index,** Lafayette County, 4 rolls, FHL film #1275795-1275796; and 1275826-1275827.
- **1905 WI State Census Index,** Langlade County, 3 rolls, FHL film #1292227-1292229.
- **1905 WI State Census Index,** Lincoln County, 4 rolls, FHL film #1292230-1292233.

- **1905 WI State Census Index,** Manitowoc County, 7 rolls, FHL film #1275931-1275935; and 1275979-1275980.
- **1905 WI State Census Index,** Marathon County, 10 rolls, FHL film #1275518- 1275522; 1275531-1275532; and 1275541-1275543.
- **1905 WI State Census Index,** Marinette County, 7 rolls, FHL film #1205854-1205860.
- **1905 WI State Census Index,** Marquette County, 2 rolls, FHL film #1266957-1266958.
- **1905 WI State Census Index,** Milwaukee County, 69 rolls, FHL film #1378977-1378979; 1381572-1381580; 1379186-1379193; 1379227-1379229; 1379237; 1379239; 1381616- 1379336; and 1379372-1379374.
- **1905 WI State Census Index,** Monroe County, 7 rolls, FHL film #1266803-1266809.
- **1905 WI State Census Index,** Oconto County, 5 rolls, FHL film #1205796-1205800.
- **1905 WI State Census Index,** Oneida County, 2 rolls, FHL film #1292218-1292219.
- **1905 WI State Census Index,** Outagamie County, 10 rolls, FHL film #1292521-1292530.
- **1905 WI State Census Index,** Ozaukee County, 4 rolls, FHL film #1205860-1205863.
- **1905 WI State Census Index,** Pepin County, 2 rolls, FHL film #1292216-1292217.
- **1905 WI State Census Index,** Pierce County, 5 rolls, FHL film #1292536; 1292514-1292517.
- **1905 WI State Census Index,** Polk County, 4 rolls, FHL film #1205999-1206000; and 1266802- 1266803.
- **1905 WI State Census Index,** Portage County, 6 rolls, FHL film #1308723-1308728.
- **1905 WI State Census Index,** Price County, 3 rolls, FHL film #1292220-1292222.
- **1905 WI State Census Index,** Racine County, 10 rolls, FHL film #1275980; 1266902-1266904; and 1266951-1266956
- **1905 WI State Census Index,** Richland County, 4 rolls, FHL film #1292234-1292235; and 1292250-1292251.
- **1905 WI State Census Index,** Rock County, 10 rolls, FHL film #1292317; and 1292382-1292390.
- **1905 WI State Census Index,** Rusk County, 2 rolls, FHL film #1266859-1266860.
- **1905 WI State Census Index,** Sauk County, 6 rolls, FHL film #1266876-1266881.
- **1905 WI State Census Index,** Sawyer County, 1 roll, FHL film #1266821
- **1905 WI State Census Index,** Shawano County, 7 rolls, FHL film #1275721-1275722; and 1275783-1275787.
- **1905 WI State Census Index,** Sheboygan County, 11rolls, FHL film #1308691-1308694; and 1308696-1308702.
- **1905 WI State Census Index,** St. Croix County, 6 rolls, FHL film #1292518-1292520; and 1308575-1308577.
- **1905 WI State Census Index,** Taylor County, 2 rolls, FHL film #1266856-1266857.
- **1905 WI State Census Index,** Trempealeau County, 5 rolls, FHL film # 1276463-1276465; and 1308910-1308911.
- **1905 WI State Census Index,** Vernon County, 6 rolls, FHL film #1292252-1292257.
- **1905 WI State Census Index,** Vilas County, 1 roll, FHL film #1266858
- **1905 WI State Census Index,** Walworth County, 6 rolls, FHL film #1276457-1276462.
- **1905 WI State Census Index,** Washburn County, 1 roll, FHL film #1266820.
- **1905 WI State Census Index,** Washington County, 5 rolls, FHL film #1205888-1205892.
- **1905 WI State Census Index,** Waukesha County, 7 rolls, FHL film #1308844-1308849; and 1276456.
- **1905 WI State Census Index,** Waupaca County, 7 rolls, FHL film #1266959-1266964; and 1266654.
- **1905 WI State Census Index,** Waushara County, 4 rolls, FHL film #1292407-1292410.
- **1905 WI State Census Index,** Winnebago County, 12 rolls, FHL film #1275827-1275828; 1275891-275899; and 1275930.
- **1905 WI State Census Index,** Wood County, 6 rolls, FHL film #1266660-1266661; 1002396; and 1266945-1266947.

# Chapter 2C

# The Central Plains

## Iowa, Kansas, Missouri, Nebraska, North Dakota & South Dakota

### Historical Timeline for the Central Plains

The six states of The Central Plains all have their American origins as part of the Louisiana Purchase. Here is a timeline of historical events for the region of the Louisiana Purchase, with an emphasis on changing jurisdictions:

**1673. Illinois Country.** French explorers Louis Jolliet and Jacques Marquette left their base at Sault Ste. Marie, and made their way to the Illinois River, which they descended to become the first Europeans to see the Mississippi River. They visited present Wisconsin, Illinois, Iowa, Missouri, and Arkansas – an area they described as the *Illinois Country*. They claimed everything they saw for France.

**1682. Louisiana.** French explorer René-Robert Cavelier (Sieur de LaSalle) erected a cross near the confluence of the Mississippi River and the Gulf of Mexico, after floating down river from the Illinois Country. He claimed the entire Mississippi Basin for Louis XIV of France, for whom Louisiana was named.

**1682-1720. Louisiana.** During this period, the jurisdiction of Louisiana ran from the Gulf of Mexico to the junction of the Arkansas River with the Mississippi River. The French administered Arkansas Post, Natchez, Baton Rouge, New Orleans, Mobile, and Biloxi as part of Louisiana. Fort Louis de la Louisiane (now Mobile), was the capital of Louisiana, 1702-1720.

**1720-1762. Upper and Lower Louisiana.** By 1720, The Illinois Country was separated from Quebéc and added to Louisiana. The original Louisiana area became known as *Lower Louisiana*. The capital of Lower Louisiana was at New Orleans, 1720-1762. *Upper Louisiana* extended from the Highlands (Terra Haute) on the Wabash River down the Ohio and Mississippi Valleys to the Arkansas River. The fur trading settlements of Upper Louisiana included Vincennes (now Indiana), Prairie du Chien (now Wisconsin); Cahokia, Kaskaskia, Chartres, Saint Philippe, and Prairie du Rocher (now Illinois); Ste. Genevieve (now Missouri), and Fort de Chavagnial on the Missouri River (now Kansas).

**1738. Dakota Country.** French explorer Pierre Gaultier de la Vérendrye visited Mandan villages near the Missouri River. This was the first known white expedition into what is now North Dakota.

**1763. Treaty of Paris.** This was the end of the French and Indian war. (In Europe it was called the "Seven Years War.") At the 1763 treaty, the French surrendered all their claims in North America. Spain acquired the former French areas west of the Mississippi, renamed *Spanish Louisiana*. Great Britain gained all of Québec, which they immediately renamed the *Province of Canada*. Britain also gained control of the rest of North America east of the Mississippi River. They named their entire area *British North America*.

**1764. St. Louis** was founded by French trader Pierre Laclede Liguest. Although part of Spanish Louisiana, St. Louis operated under French civilian control until it was occupied by Spanish soldiers in 1770.

**1783. Treaty of Paris.** As the official end of the Revolutionary War, the 1783 treaty recognized the United States as an independent republic, with borders from the Atlantic Ocean to the Mississippi River. The treaty also reaffirmed the claims of Britain to present-day Canada; and Spain's claim to lands west of the Mississippi River.

**1792. Dakota Country.** French-Canadian trader Jacques D'Englise opened trade on the Missouri River between Mandan villages and his Spanish employers located at St. Louis.

**1797. Dakota Country.** North West Company fur trader Jean Baptiste Chaboillez of the Red River Settlement (present Manitoba), established a trading post at Pembina (present North Dakota).

**1800. Louisiana.** Napoleon acquired title of Louisiana from Spain. At the Third Treaty of San Ildefonso, the Spanish acknowledged that it was too costly to explore the country and could not see the rewards being worth the investment. Spain retroceded Louisiana to France in exchange for the Grand Duchy of Tuscany (now part of Italy).

**1803. Louisiana Purchase.** The United States purchased Louisiana from France. Sent by President Jefferson to attempt the purchase of New Orleans, the American negotiators (James Madison and Robert Livingston) were surprised when Napoleon offered the entire tract to them. The Louisiana Purchase was officially described as the "drainage of the Mississippi and Missouri River basins." Adding the area doubled the size of the United States.

**1804.** On a expedition ordered by President Thomas Jefferson, Captains Meriwether Lewis and William Clark's Corps of Discovery left St. Louis in search of a passage to the Pacific Ocean. Based on bad information from his spies, the Spanish governor of New Mexico dispatched soldiers from Santa Fe to the Arkansas River to intercept the party and arrest them. But, the Lewis and Clark party had taken a more northern route, following the Missouri River. On July 2, 1804, at a campsite on the Missouri River between present Kansas City and Leavenworth, Lewis and Clark's journals noted the remains of old Fort Cavagnial, abandoned by the French in 1764.

**1804-1805**. In 1804, Congress divided the Louisiana Purchase into two jurisdictions: **Louisiana District** and **Orleans Territory**. The latter had north and south bounds the same as the present state of Louisiana, but did not include land east of the Mississippi River, and its northwestern corner extended on an indefinite line west into Spanish Tejas. For a year, Louisiana District was attached to Indiana Territory for judicial administration, but became Louisiana Territory with its own Governor on July 4, 1805.

**1805. 1st Pike Expedition.** U.S. Army Lieutenant Zebulon Pike led a small party of soldiers to investigate the Mississippi River above St. Louis. He was given specific orders to find the source of the Mississippi, and while doing so, to note "...any rivers, prairies, islands, mines, quarries, timber, and any Indian villages and settlements encountered."

**1805. Louisiana Territory** in 1805 had five original subdivisions: St. Louis District, St. Charles District, Ste. Genevieve District, Cape Girardeau District and New Madrid District. The unpopulated area north of these original districts was referred to as Upper Louisiana, and included all lands north to the U.S./British border and west to the Continental Divide.

**1806-1807. 2nd Pike Expedition.** Zebulon Pike, now a Captain, was again sent out, this time to explore and locate the source of the Red River in Lower Louisiana. Pike followed the Arkansas River through present southwest Kansas into Colorado and on to the Rocky Mountains, where Pike's Peak was later named for him. On his return, he skirted south in search of the headwaters of the Red River, putting him in an area claimed by the Spanish. Pike and his men were arrested by Spanish soldiers, taken to Santa Fe, but treated well and escorted back to the U.S. a short time later. Pike's journals were confiscated by the Spanish military and never returned to the U.S. until the 1900s. But, from memory, Pike wrote a book about his travels in 1810 that was a best seller in both America and Europe. In addition to the first English language observations of the Spanish culture in North America, Pike's descriptions of the Rocky Mountains became the inspiration for a whole generation of "mountain men."

**1812.** June 4th. **Louisiana Territory** was renamed **Missouri Territory**. This was to avoid any confusion after Orleans Territory became the State of Louisiana on April 30, 1812. The General Assembly of the Territory of Missouri met in St. Louis in October, and converted the first five original districts into counties: Cape Girardeau, New Madrid, St. Charles, St. Louis, and Ste. Genevieve. A year later, the territorial legislature created Arkansas County from lands ceded by the Osage Indians.

**1818. Anglo-American Convention.** The 49th parallel was agreed to as the boundary between the U.S. and the British territory of Rupert's Land. In the treaty, the United States acquired part of the Red River drainage in present Minnesota and North Dakota, and ceded part of the Missouri River drainage in present North Dakota and Montana.

**1819. Arkansas Territory** was created, reducing the size of Missouri Territory. The original area included all of present-day Arkansas and most of Oklahoma.

**1819. Nebraska Country.** Fort Atkinson was established, the first U.S. Army Post west of the Missouri River.

**1820.** The *Missouri Compromise* in Congress allowed Missouri to enter the Union as a slave state and Maine as a free state, thus keeping the balance of slave and free states equal in Congress. The Act dictated that the remaining area of Missouri Territory north of Latitude 36° 30' was to be free of slavery (that area included present Kansas, Nebraska, Iowa, Minnesota, North Dakota, South Dakota, Wyoming, and Montana).

**1821.** Aug 10th. **Missouri** was admitted as a state with St. Louis as the capital. After Missouri became a state, the remaining part of old Missouri Territory was officially described as *Unorganized Territory*.

**1821.** Sept. **Santa Fe Trail.** William Becknell, a Missouri trader, was the first American to follow the route that was to become known as the Santa Fe Trail, beginning at the Missouri River near present Independence, MO. His profitable success in trading with the newly independent Mexicans of Santa Fe was well publicized. Over the next few months, dozens of wagon trains were organized to transport and sell products to a new market.

**1822.** The Rocky Mountain Fur Company was formed by General William Ashley. He placed an ad in a St. Louis newspaper to recruit able-bodied men for his new fur-trading enterprise. There was no shortage of willing young men. Ashley did not build a chain of forts to manage his fur trading operation. Instead, he sent his men out alone and made arrangements to meet them all at a central place a year later. When Ashley finally reached his men each year, it was cause for celebration – a wild party they called "the rendezvous." In 1826, William Ashley retired a wealthy man and sold the Rocky Mountain Fur Company to his employees.

**1826. Missouri.** The state capital was moved from St. Louis to Jefferson City.

**1827. Independence, Missouri.** The frontier town of Independence was founded in 1827, the farthest point westward on the Missouri River where steamboats could travel at that time. Independence immediately became a supply point, staging area, and primary starting point for the growing number of trappers and traders using the Santa Fe Trail.

**1829 Sublette's Trace/Oregon Trail.** Before 1829, access to the Platte River Trail from Independence, Missouri, was via the Missouri River to the mouth of the Platte River in present Nebraska. But steamboat traffic ended at Independence and travel up river at that time required human-powered keel boats. The overland route of the Santa Fe Trail now started at Independence as well, heading west several miles into present Kansas, then southwest towards Santa Fe. A few miles into the Santa Fe Trail in present Kansas, at a point later called the Oregon Trail Junction, fur trader William Sublette blazed a cut-off from the Santa Fe Trail, turning northwest and connecting with the Platte River in present Nebraska. The new route across present northeast Kansas was more direct than the river route, and later became the first leg of the Oregon Trail.

**1832.** After dredging projects near the mouth of the Kansas River, steamboat traffic continued up the Missouri River. In 1832, the steamboat *Yellowstone* began the first of its annual fur-trading voyages up the Missouri River, reaching Fort Union (present North Dakota/Montana line).

**1833.** June 1st. **Black Hawk Cession.** After the Black Hawk War of 1832, the Sauk and Fox tribe of present-day Iowa was forced to cede land on the west side of the Mississippi River to the United States. The cession opened a large area of the Ioway Country for legal white settlement for the first time.

**1836. Wisconsin Territory** was created, taken from Michigan Territory. Its area extended from its present Lake Michigan border to the Missouri River.

**1838. Iowa Territory** was created, encompassing all lands north of the state of Missouri between the Mississippi and Missouri Rivers.

**1841.** The Western Emigration Society, a group of about 70 settlers bound for California and the Oregon Country set off on the Oregon Trail, beginning at

Independence, Missouri. This was the first organized wagon train to head for California and Oregon. It is usually called the "Bartleson-Bidwell party" named for the two leaders. John Bartleson led about half of the group to Oregon's Willamette Valley. John Bidwell took the other half to California's Sacramento Valley.

**1842. Nebraska Country.** The word "Nebraska" first began to appear in publications in 1842 after John C. Fremont explored the Platte Valley and Nebraska areas.

**1843.** May. **Oregon Trail.** A wagon train with over 120 wagons, a large herd of livestock, and 1,000 pioneers left Elm Grove, MO and headed out on the Oregon Trail. The largest wagon train to date, it became the model for the thousands of wagon trains that followed. For an online list of the members of the 1843 Wagon Train, see the OR RootsWeb site:
**http://freepages.history.rootsweb.ancestry.com/~mransom/pioneers.html**

**1846.** Dec 28th. **Iowa** became the 29th state in the Union. Iowa City was the state capital.

**1849. California Gold Rush.** With the discovery of gold in California, the Missouri towns of St. Louis, Independence, Westport, and St. Joseph became points of departure for emigrants bound for California, making Missouri the "Gateway to the West."

**1854.** May 30th. **Kansas-Nebraska Act** passed the U.S. Congress. The territories of Kansas and of Nebraska were established. The act also allowed residents of the two territories to decide for themselves whether or not to allow slavery within their borders. The Act served to repeal the Missouri Compromise of 1820 which had prohibited slavery north of latitude 36°30′. Separated on their present common boundary, Nebraska Territory and Kansas Territory both extended from the Missouri River to the Continental Divide. Nebraska Territory included parts of present North Dakota, South Dakota, Montana, and Wyoming. Kansas Territory included present Kansas and parts of present Colorado.

**1854-1861. Bleeding Kansas.** When Kansas Territory was officially opened to settlement in 1854, pro-slavery settlers from neighboring Missouri rushed to the new territory. But, abolitionist Free-Staters from New England marshalled their forces and sent settlers to Kansas Territory as well. The area was to become the scene of violence and chaos in its early days as the Pro-Slave and Anti-Slave forces battled, and became known as *Bleeding Kansas*.

✓ **NOTE: Territorial Kansas Timeline, 1854-1861,** is a webpage sponsored by the Kansas Historical Society. The Timeline gives a year-by-year look at the events and battles of *Bleeding Kansas*, when the fight for statehood was between Free-Staters and Pro-Slavery advocates. See
**www.territorialkansasonline.org/~imlskto/cgi-bin/index.php?SCREEN=timeline**

**1858-1861. Minnesota and Unorganized Dakota.** When Minnesota was admitted as a state in 1858 with its present boundaries, Dakota was orphaned. The area from the western Minnesota line to the Missouri River was enumerated in the 1860 federal census as *Unorganized Dakota*. This was not an official jurisdiction, but one invented by the Census Office to gather census data for the Red River/Pembina settlements, plus a series of outposts along the Missouri River.

**1860.** Apr. **Pony Express.** The 1,900-mile Pony Express route ran from St. Joseph, Missouri, to Sacramento, California. In competition with the Butterfield Overland Stage company, which held the U.S. Mail contract until the start of the Civil War, the Pony Express riders made the northern journey from St. Joseph to Sacramento in 10 days time. The Butterfield stages took a southern route from Memphis through Arkansas, Texas, and New Mexico, and into Los Angeles, then to Sacramento in an average of 25 days time. Still, the Pony Express could never gain the mail contract and stayed in business only until June 1861.

**1861.** Jan. **Kansas** was admitted to the Union as the 34th state, with the same boundaries as today. Topeka was named the state capital. Under the provisions of the 1854 Kansas-Nebraska Act, Kansas Territory submitted four proposed state constitutions to Congress. The second, and most controversial constitution is referred to historically as the "Lecompton Constitution of 1857" and would have admitted Kansas as a slave state. The proposed state constitution was submitted to Congress for approval in 1858 and became part of the intense national debate on the slavery issue. The Lecompton Constitution was a main subject of the famous Abraham Lincoln vs Stephen Douglas debates held in Illinois in 1858. Congress rejected the Lecompton Constitution, and

Kansas Territory did not become a state until a new territorial legislature was elected; and after the fourth (Wyandotte) state constitution was submitted to Congress in 1859. But Kansas still had to wait for the secession of several southern states before it had enough votes in Congress in favor of statehood.

**1861**. Mar. **Dakota Territory** was created by Congress. The original area included all of present North Dakota, South Dakota, and the parts of present Montana and Wyoming east of the Continental Divide. Yankton was the first territorial capital, replaced by Bismarck in 1863.

**1867.** Mar. **Nebraska** joined the Union as the 37th state, with Omaha as the capital until a year later, when Lincoln was chosen.

**1889.** Nov. **South Dakota** and **North Dakota** both admitted as states with the same boundaries as today. Although Dakota Territory had petitioned Congress to be a single state, that would have caused two Democratic senators to be added, which would have upset the balance in Congress. By splitting Dakota Territory into two states, two Republican senators and two Democratic senators were added to Congress, maintaining the balance of power.

**1918. Iowa.** Governor Harding issued a proclamation which forbid the use of any language but English in public gatherings of two or more people. This was nicknamed the "Babel Proclamation."

**1941. South Dakota.** The Mt. Rushmore monument was finished.

**1946. Missouri.** Winston Churchill, former Prime Minister of Great Britain, delivered his famous "Iron Curtain" speech at Fulton's Westminster College.

**1961. North Dakota.** Roger Maris from Fargo broke Babe Ruth's single season home run record.

**1965 St. Louis, Missouri**. The Gateway Arch (Jefferson National Expansion Memorial) designed by Eero Saarinen was completed. Located on the original settlement site of St. Louis, it symbolized the role of St. Louis in the development of the western frontier.

**1996. Kansas.** Bob Dole, from Russell, Kansas, ran for President of the United States. He lost.

# IOWA
## Censuses & Substitutes, 1835-2011

After the Black Hawk Cession of 1833, the Ioway Country was opened for white settlement. The area was still part of the Unorganized Territory. In 1836, the area of present Iowa was included in Wisconsin Territory. In 1838, Iowa Territory was created with an area between the Mississippi and Missouri rivers to the northern boundary of the U.S. And, in 1846, Iowa became a state with the same boundaries as today. **Territorial Censuses** include Iowa areas taken by Wisconsin Territory in 1836, and Iowa Territory in 1838, 1844 and 1846. A total of 21 **State Censuses** have survived in various completeness, including 15 heads of households only censuses, 1847-1897; and 6 every-name censuses for 1856, 1885, 1895, 1905, 1915, and 1925. Many of the original state census schedules were microfilmed by the Genealogical Society of Utah in 1977-1978. All of these (plus ten state census years not cataloged at the FHL) were scanned and indexed at the Ancestry.com website in 2007. (The source of the ten was the State Historical Society of Iowa, probably acquired after the GSU filming). A number of county-wide indexes to IA State Censuses were published as articles in various periodicals and added to this review. **Iowa State Censuses Online.** Ancestry.com has a very complete combined collection of IA State Censuses, 1836-1925; plus repeated separate databases for 1885, 1895, and 1905; as well as an earlier Census & Substitutes Index, 1838-1870. FamilySearch.org has separate databases for the 1885, 1895, 1905, 1915, and 1925 IA state censuses. For the period 1836-1849, this review includes a selection of online state census databases found at various Iowa county web sites..

### Resources at the State Historical Society of Iowa

The State Historical Society of Iowa (SHSI) has two major facilities in Iowa, both with public reading rooms friendly to amateur genealogists:

■ **SHSI – State of Iowa Historical Building, Des Moines, Iowa.** This facility houses a State Historical Museum, Library, and Archives.

■ **SHSI – Centennial Building, Iowa City, Iowa.** This facility houses a State Historical Society Library and Archives, with a unique archival collection of historical materials, photographs, and manuscripts not repeated at the Des Moines facility. In addition, the Iowa City facility holds the same microfilm collection as the Des Moines facility.

## SHSI Special Collections

The following is a brief description of the collections found at both facilities of the SHSI:

- **Books, Periodicals, and Photo Collections.**
- **Newspapers.** all of Iowa's 99 counties are represented in the Des Moines and Iowa City newspaper collections, spanning the period from 1836 to the present.
- **County Government Records.** Includes marriage, birth and death records, naturalization papers and land deeds. Microfilm copies of many of these county records are available in the libraries' reading rooms.
- **Birth, Marriage, and Death Records**. In 1880, legislation was enacted creating the Department of Public Health and requiring births, deaths and marriages to be recorded at both the county and state levels.
- **Census Materials.** Both reading rooms offer the microfilmed federal census records for Iowa from 1840 through 1940 as well as Iowa state census records for 1856, 1885, 1895, 1905, 1915 and 1925 and special census records for 1838, 1844, 1846-1847, 1849, and 1851-1854. Mortality, agricultural, industrial, and social census records are available for selected years. Federal records for some states other than Iowa are also held. The SHSI has partnered with both Ancestry.com and FamilySearch.org to post the indexes and images to the 1885, 1895, 1905, 1915, and 1925 Iowa State Censuses

To review the collections in more detail, see **https://iowaculture.gov/history/research/collections**.

## Iowa Research Guides

There are some valuable aids to genealogical research in Iowa. Each of the published Iowa guides shown below should be considered for further reading:

■ **1833-1940s.** See ***A Reference Guide to the DAR Volumes*** **[Printed Book],** an alphabetical listing by county of Iowa cemetery, marriage, death and probate records produced by the DAR and the WPA which are housed at the State Historical Society of Iowa, Iowa City, Iowa. This guidebook leads a researcher to the wealth of indexed materials for all Iowa counties. FHL book 977.7 V22in.

■ **1833-1900s.** See ***Guide to Public Records of Iowa Counties*** **[Printed Book],** by John P. Dolan, Jr. and Lisa Lacher, published by Connie Wimer, Des Moines, IA, 1988, 980 pages, FHL book 977.7 D27d.

■ **1833-2004.** See ***Iowa Name Lists: Published and Online Censuses & Substitutes, 1833-2004*** **[Printed Book],** by William Dollarhide, publ. Family Roots Publishing Co, Orting, WA, 2014, 105 pages. After the release of the two-volume set, *Census Substitutes & State Census Records* in 2008, a series of statewide guides began, beginning with Alabama, and continued through Michigan (as of 2016). The *Iowa Name Lists* book includes a National Name Lists chapter, and U.S. maps, 1763-1940. The Iowa book was the basis for the Iowa chapter of this book. Available from the publisher. See **www.familyrootspublishing.com.**

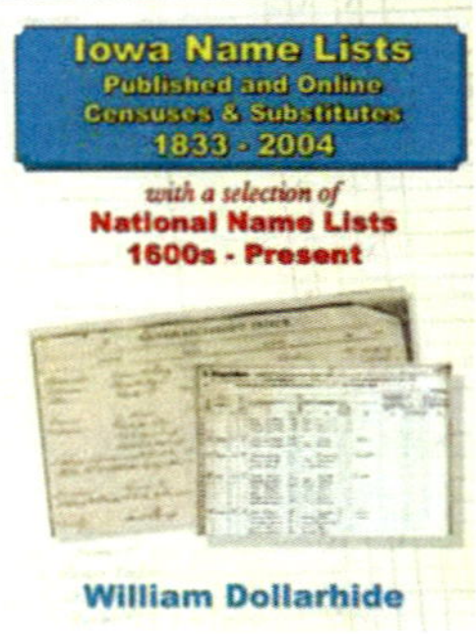


■ **1836-1880.** See ***Census of Iowa for 1880, And the Same Compared With the Findings of Each of the Other States: And Also With all Former Enumerations of the Territory Now Embraced Within the Limits of the State of Iowa, With Other Historical and Statistical Data*** **[Microfiche],** by John A. T. Hull, Secretary of State, printed by order of the General Assembly. Original published by F.M. Mills, Des Moines, 1883, 744 pages. This is an invaluable listing of Iowa territorial, state, and federal censuses, 1836-1880. It contains historical and statistical data about the state of Iowa and its counties, but does not enumerate the population by name or household. Population totals from various enumerations of each county, as well as totals for towns and villages are given. Filmed by the Genealogical Society of Utah, 1997, 10 microfiche, FHL fiche #6126432. Also filmed by W.C. Cox Co., Tucson, AZ, 1974, FHL film #1000024.

■ **1836-Current.** See ***County Records: Select A County to View Available Records*** **[Online Database**], a search box at the County Records webpage of the SHSI website. Records may include court records, naturalizations, probates, church, cemetery, family, historical records, original entries of land, deeds, mortgages, old age assistance records, homesteads, vital records, tax lists, and more. See **https://iowaculture.gov/history/research/collections/county-records.**

■ **1865.** See ***Iowa State Gazetteer*** **[Printed Book],** by James T. Hair, a very thorough listing and description of Iowa places at the time of the end of the Civil War. Published by Bailey & Hair, Chicago, 1865, 722 pages, FHL book 977.7 E4. Also on microfilm, FHL film #982200 & FHL film #1024846.

■ **1941 WPA Survey.** See ***Guide to Public Vital Statistics Records in Iowa*** **[Printed Book],** prepared by the Iowa Historical Records Survey, Division of Community Service Programs, Work Projects Administration, published 1941, Des Moines, IA, 113 pages, FHL book 977.7 V2h. For access to a digital version of this book, see the online FHL catalog page for this title. See
**https://familysearch.org/search/catalog/171080.**

---

## Iowa Databases Online at Ancestry.com

The Ancestry.com subscription website allows free access to all indexes, but to view any particular record requires a membership. Ancestry offers trial memberships and subscriptions for short periods and reduced rates. The following databases at the Ancestry.com website are unique to Iowa under the categories, Census & Voter Lists, Vital Records, Military, Immigrations, et al.

■ **1835-1990.** See ***Iowa, Births and Christenings Index, 1800-1999*** **[Online Database],** indexed at the Ancestry.com website. Source: FamilySearch extractions. There are many dates of birth in this database that precede the first white settlement of Iowa in 1833. Most records have at least the name, birth date and birth place. This database has 4,602,600 records. See
**http://search.ancestry.com/search/db.aspx?dbid=2547.**

■ **1835-1996.** See ***Iowa, Select Marriages Index, 1758-1996*** **[Online Database],** indexed at the Ancestry.com website. Source: FamilySearch extractions. The 1758 beginning date in the title relates to Rhode Island, not Iowa. A global search for Iowa gave the first marriage as 1835. All records have at least a name of bride and groom, date and place of marriage. This database has 5,026,461 records. See
**http://search.ancestry.com/search/db.aspx?dbid=60284.**

■ **1836.** See ***The First Census of the Original Counties of Dubuque and Demoine (Iowa) Taken in July, 1836*** **[Online Database],** indexed at the Ancestry.com website. Source: book, same title, edited by Benjamin F. Shambaugh, originally published by the Historical Department of Iowa, Des Moines, IA, 1897-1898, 93 pages. Contents: pt. 1. Dubuque County, pt. 2. Demoine County. From the original manuscript returns preserved in the office of the Secretary of State of Wisconsin. Census taken in accordance with the act of Congress creating the territory of Wisconsin (of which these two counties at the time formed a part) comprising the present states of Wisconsin, Iowa, Minnesota and part of North and South Dakota. This database has 90 pages. See
**http://search.ancestry.com/search/db.aspx?dbid=23732.**

■ **1836-1850.** See ***Iowa Marriages to 1850*** **[Online Database],** indexed at the Ancestry.com website. Source: Printed Index, same title, compiled by Jordan Dodd, publ. Precision Indexing, 2000. Each record includes a name of person, spouse of person, date of marriage, and place of marriage. This database has 21,236 records. See
**http://search.ancestry.com/search/db.aspx?dbid=2088.**

■ **1836-1925.** See ***Iowa, State Census Collection, 1836-1925*** **[Online Database]**, digitized and indexed at the Ancestry.com website in 2007, from microfilm of the mostly complete, every-name state censuses for 1856, 1885, 1895, 1905, 1915, 1925; as well as various special state censuses from 1836-1897 (and a few added federal censuses), all obtained from the microfilm collection of the State Historical Society of Iowa. This database has 9,549,935 records. See
**http://search.ancestry.com/search/db.aspx?dbid=1084**
Below is a list of all the years and counties included in this database:

- **1836:** Des Moines & Dubuque. See separate database.
- **1838:** Van Buren
- **1844:** Keokuk
- **1846:** Louisa, Polk & Wapello
- **1847:** Clinton, Louisa, Scott, Wapello, Davis, Marion & Van Buren
- **1849:** Benton, Boone, Clinton, Jackson, Louisa, Madison, Poweshiek, Scott, Van Buren & Washington
- **1850:** Van Buren (✓)
- **1851:** Cedar, Clinton, Decatur, Guthrie, Iowa, Jackson, Johnson, Madison, Mahaska, Page, Pottawattamie, Scott & Washington
- **1852:** Appanoose, Black Hawk, Boone, Bremer, Buchanan, Butler, Cass, Cedar, Clarke, Clayton, Clinton, Davis, Des Moines, Fayette, Fremont, Guthrie, Henry, Iowa, Jackson, Jasper, Jefferson, Johnson, Jones, Keokuk, Lee, Linn, Louisa, Mahaska, Marshall, Mills, Monroe, Muscatine, Polk,

Pottawattamie, Poweshiek, Scott, Tama, Taylor, Van Buren, Wapello, Warren & Washington

- **1853:** Warren (Allen, Greenfield, Lynn, and Richland townships)
- **1854:** Adair, Allamakee, Benton, Black Hawk, Boone, Bremer, Chickasaw, Clarke, Clayton, Clinton, Crawford, Dallas, Decatur, Des Moines, Dubuque, Fayette, Fremont, Hardin, Harrison, Henry, Jackson, Jasper, Jefferson, Johnson, Jones, Keokuk, Lee, Linn, Louisa, Madison, Mahaska, Marion, Marshall, Monona, Montgomery, Muscatine, Page, Polk, Pottawattamie, Poweshiek, Ringgold, Scott, Shelby, Story, Tama, Taylor, Union, Wapello, Washington, Wayne & Webster
- **1856:** All counties that were organized at the time except Warren (80 total)
- **1859:** Black Hawk, Buchanan, Carroll, Montgomery, Palo Alto, Plymouth, Pocahontas, Sac, Scott, Union, & Washington
- **1860**: Calhoun, Carroll, Cerro, Gordo, Clay, Crawford, Dickinson, Emmet, Fayette, Greene, Hancock, Humboldt, Iowa, Kossuth, Mitchell, Monona, Palo Alto, Plymouth, Sac, Shelby, Van Buren (✓), Webster, Winnebago, Woodbury, Worth & Wright
- **1870**: Van Buren (✓)
- **1881**: Cerro Gordo (Mason City)
- **1885:** All counties (99 total). See separate 1885 database.
- **1888:** Kossuth (Algona), Polk (North Des Moines) & Montgomery (Villisca)
- **1889:** Cherokee (Cherokee) & Emmet (Emmetsburg)
- **1891:** Clay (Spencer)
- **1892:** Carroll (Carroll), Emmet (Estherville), Greene (Jefferson), Tama (Tama) & Wright (Eagle Grove)
- **1893:** Davis (Bloomfield), Franklin (Hampton) & Story (Ames and Nevada)
- **1895**: Adair, Adams, Allamakee, Appanoose, Audubon, Benton, Buchanan, Hardin, Henry, Jones, Lee, Mills, Page, Polk, Pottawattamie, Washington, Wayne, Webster, Winnebago, Winneshiek, Woodbury, Worth & Wright. See separate 1895 database
- **1896:** Fayette (Oelwein)
- **1897:** Chickasaw (New Hampton)
- **1905:** All counties (99 total). See separate 1905 database..
- **1915:** All counties (99 total)
- **1925:** All counties (99 total)

**✓1836-1925 NOTE:** The above listing of Iowa State Census years and counties came from the Ancestry.com website. In 2007, Ancestry digitized each census name list from microfilm of the originals at the State Historical Society of Iowa (SHSI) in Des Moines. Ancestry's 2007 list shows ten more census years for Iowa than were microfilmed by the Genealogical Society of Utah in 1977 (per the FHL catalog). Ancestry's list also includes entries for 1850, 1860, and 1870, which are federal census years, not Iowa state census years.

Van Buren County was the only Iowa county listed for 1850 and 1870, and the 1850, 1860 and 1870 Van Buren County censuses are each limited to a one-page typescript, with a few families listed for Link Township, Van Buren County. They have the look of a typewritten extract done in the 1920s.

The 1860 censuses listed for the remaining counties are all very brief extracts, all on the 1860 federal census forms, usually one page per township; but poorly microfilmed. After state-of-the-art digitizing, they still have dark, unreadable top headings. By comparison, the federal set of the 1860 federal censuses has enhanced images, with clear, readable text. Placing two versions of the same page side-by-side, and comparing the 1860 SHSI census pages with Ancestry's online federal set, confirms that the SHSI pages are state copies of the federal census. (See the list of counties at the FHL Microfilms section under 1860 IA Federal Census-State Copy, page 136).

■ **1836-1997.** See ***Iowa, Wills and Probate Records, 1758(sic)-1997*** **[Online Database],** indexed at the Ancestry.com website. Source: Ancestry's extractions from the original records of Iowa county, district, and probate courts, in all Iowa counties. The contents of a probate file can vary from case to case, but certain details are found in most probates, most importantly, the names and residences of beneficiaries and their relationship to the decedent. An inventory of the estate assets can reveal personal details about the deceased's occupation and lifestyle. There may also be references to debts, deeds, and other documents related to the settling of the estate. This database has 593,870 records. See
**http://search.ancestry.com/search/db.aspx?dbid=9064.**

■ **1836-1999.** See ***Iowa, Cemetery Records, 1662-1999*** **[Online Database],** indexed at the Ancestry.com website. Source: WPA Graves Registration Project, ca1938. The starting date of 1662 in the title is from an incorrect date from Pleasant Hill Cemetery, an historic Amish cemetery in Johnson County, Iowa (platted ca1837). There are many more dates of death in this database that precede the first white settlement of Iowa in 1833, which must be attributed to unreadable tombstone inscriptions or copying errors. All records include at least a name, date, and place of burial. This database has 685,016 records. See
**http://search.ancestry.com/search/db.aspx?dbid=4711.**

■ **1836-2011.** See ***Web: Iowa Gravestones Index*** **[Online Database],** digitized and indexed at the Ancestry.com website. This database is also accessible at the **IowaGravestones** website, a project of the IAGenWeb Archives. The database has photographic images of grave stones from cemeteries all over Iowa. Includes a searchable index to inscriptions (names, keywords, etc.) from the tombstones and names of cemeteries. This database has 698,890 records. See
**http://search.ancestry.com/search/db.aspx?dbid=70558.**

■ **1838-1870.** See ***Iowa Census, 1838-1870*** **[Online Database],** indexed at the Ancestry.com website. Source: indexes originally compiled by Accelerated Indexing Systems, Salt Lake City, UT, acquired by Ancestry in 1999. This collection contains the following indexes: 1838 Territorial Census; 1840 Federal Census Index; 1840 Pensioners List; 1841-1849 Tax Lists; 1850 Federal Census Index; 1851 State Census Index; 1852 State Census Index; 1860 Federal Census Index; 1870 Federal Census Index.
This database has 48,152 records. See
**http://search.ancestry.com/search/db.aspx?dbid=3547.**

■ **1850.** See ***Iowa, Pottawattamie County, Annotated Record of US Census, 1850*** **[Online Database],** indexed at the Ancestry.com website. Source: Printed index, same title, compilers: Susan Easton Black, Harvey Bischoff Black, Sarah Allen, and Rebecca Allen. This database has 7,814 records. See
**http://search.ancestry.com/search/db.aspx?dbid=3208.**

■ **1850-1990.** See ***Iowa, Deaths and Burials, 1850-1990*** **[Online Database],** indexed at the Ancestry.com website. Source: FamilySearch extractions. Most records include at least a name, date of death, and place of death. This database has 703,870 records. See
**http://search.ancestry.com/search/db.aspx?dbid=60283.**

■ **1851-1900.** See ***Iowa, Select Marriages, 1851-1900*** **[Online Database],** indexed at the Ancestry.com website. Source: Liahona Research, edited by Jordan Dodd, from county records on microfilm at the Family History Library, Salt Lake City, UT. Includes marriages from Adair, Appanoose, Boone, Dallas, Greene, Guthrie, Hamilton, Johnson, Lee, Louisa, Lucas, Marion, Monroe, Muscatine, Plymouth, Polk, Scott, Warren, Webster, Woodbury, and Worth counties. This database has 197,647 records. See
**http://search.ancestry.com/search/db.aspx?dbid=4460.**

■ **1856-1937.** See ***Iowa, Federal Naturalization Records, 1856-1937*** **[Online Database],** indexed at the Ancestry.com website. Source: National Archives microfilm of Naturalization Indexes, Petitions, and Declarations from U.S. District Courts in Iowa. Searchable fields include: Name, Birth Date, Birth Place, and Immigration Year. Additional information that may be provided in the original records includes: Place of Residence; Occupation; Date of Departure; Place of Departure; Place of Arrival; Spouse's Name, Birth Date, and Residence; Number of Children, Each child's Name, Birth Date, Birth Place, and Residence. This database has 26,820 records. See
**http://search.ancestry.com/search/db.aspx?dbid=61198.**

■ **1861-1935.** See ***Iowa Civil War Soldier Burial Records*** **[Online Database],** indexed at the Ancestry.com website. Source: Book, same title, compiled by Susie Martin-Rott. This database is a listing of service men (and a few women) with Civil War service who died and were buried in the state, or who enlisted from the state of Iowa and are buried elsewhere. This database has 18,825 records. See
**http://search.ancestry.com/search/db.aspx?dbid=3854.**

■ **1866-1995 Iowa Directories.** See ***U.S. City Directories, 1822-1995*** **[Online Database],** indexed at the Ancestry.com website. This is Ancestry's 1.5 billion name index to city directory name lists from all over the U.S., including these Iowa cities: Ames, Boone, Burlington, Cedar Falls, Charles City, Clarinda, Clear Lake, Clinton, Council Bluffs, Creston, Davenport, Des Moines, Dougherty, Dubuque, Fort Dodge, Fort Madison, Grinnell, Iowa City, Keokuk, Marshalltown, Mason City, Muscatine, Nevada, Newton, Oelwein, Osceola, Ottumwa, Shenandoah, Sioux City, Spirit Lake, and Waterloo.
Go to *Browse This Collection* to see the available directories by state, city, and year. This database has 1,560,264,731 records. See
**http://search.ancestry.com/search/db.aspx?dbid=2469.**

■ **1867-1970.** See ***Iowa, Consecutive Registers of Convicts, 1867-1970*** **[Online Database],** indexed at the Ancestry.com website. Source: SHSI, Des Moines. This database includes convict registers from three Iowa state penitentiaries: the Iowa State Penitentiary at Fort Madison, established in 1839; the Anamosa State Penitentiary in Anamosa; and the Iowa State Reformatory for Women in Rockwell City. The registers varied somewhat through the years, but they typically list prisoner's name, sentencing and admission dates, sentence, crime, county, term of

court (in earlier records), judge, age, physical description, nativity, nationality, whether temperate/intemperate, education, religion, number of former incarcerations, and disposition. This database has 93,470 records. See
**http://search.ancestry.com/search/db.aspx?dbid=60384.**

■ **1878.** See ***Iowa Biographical Dictionary, 1878*** **[Online Database],** indexed at the Ancestry.com website. Source: part of *U.S. Biographical Dictionary*, publ. Chicago, 1878. This database has 746 pages. See
**http://search.ancestry.com/search/db.aspx?dbid=7722.**

■ **1880-1937.** See ***Iowa, Marriage Records, 1880-1937*** **[Online Database],** indexed at the Ancestry.com website. Source: IA Dept of Health originals on microfilm at the SHSI, Des Moines. Statewide registration of marriages began 1 July 1880 in Iowa. The marriage statistics are either from certificates, or entries from registers. Details include: groom's name, bride's name, bride and groom's current ages, or age at next birthday, marriage application date, marriage date, marriage county, places of residence for both parties, occupations, how many marriages for each party, places of birth for the bride and groom, color and nationality, parents' names for the bride and groom (including mother's maiden name), location of the marriage, name of the officiant, and names of witnesses. Some records may also include affidavits attesting to the age of the bride or groom, with permission from a guardian to marry. This database has 6,573,841 records. See
**http://search.ancestry.com/search/db.aspx?dbid=8823.**

■ **1885.** See ***Iowa Soldiers, Sailors, and Marines, 1885*** **[Online Database],** indexed at the Ancestry.com website. Source: Official report of the Adjutant General of Iowa, publ. 1886. This database contains a list of ex-soldiers, sailors, and marines who were living in Iowa in 1885. These individuals were supposed to have served in the War of 1812, the Mexican War, or the Civil War. Information found in this list includes name of soldier, sailor, or marine; rank; company; regiment; battery or vessel in which they served, and residence in 1885. This database has 781 pages. See
**http://search.ancestry.com/search/db.aspx?dbid=7715.**
See also ***List of Ex-soldiers, Sailors and Marines Living in Iowa*** **[Online Database**], another digitized version of the 1886 report. See
**http://search.ancestry.com/search/db.aspx?dbid=28266.**

■ **1885.** See ***Iowa State Census, 1885*** **[Online Database]**, digitized and indexed at the Ancestry.com website. Source: Microfilm at the ISHSI and FHL, noted for each county at Ancestry's title description page. This database contains information from the 1885 Iowa State Census for the counties of Adair, Audubon, Adams, Buena Vista, Carroll, Calhoun, Cass, Cherokee, Clarke, Clay, Crawford, Decatur, Dickinson, Emmet, Fremont, Hamilton, Hancock, Humboldt, Ida, Kossuth, Lyon, Madison, Mills, Montgomery, O'Brien, Osceola, Page, Palo Alto, Plymouth, Pocahontas, Ringgold, Sac, Sioux, Taylor, Union, Van Buren, Winnebago, Woodbury, and Wright. includes the names of every member of the household, their sex, ages, birthplaces, location (town, county, state), marital status, and much more. This database has 411,324 records. See
**http://search.ancestry.com/search/db.aspx?dbid=6812.**

■ **1889-1891.** See ***Des Moines, Iowa Directory, 1889-1891*** **[Online Database],** indexed at the Ancestry.com website. Source: Des Moines City Directory, 1889-1890; and 1891. This database has 53,347 records.
**http://search.ancestry.com/search/db.aspx?dbid=4547**

■ ***1890 Census Substitute*** **[Online Database],** indexed at the Ancestry.com website. This is Ancestry's collection of city directories (and other name lists) from all over the U.S. for the time of the lost 1890 federal census. Included are several Iowa databases, such as 1888-1892 city directories for several Iowa cities, and the 1885 and 1895 Iowa State Census). Go to *View All Collections Included in this Search* for a complete list of databases, alphabetically by place (county, city, state, etc.), and year. See
**http://search.ancestry.com/search/group/1890census#databases.**

■ **1895.** See **Iowa State Census, 1895 [Online Database]**, digitized and indexed at the Ancestry.com website. Source: Microfilm at the ISHSI and FHL, noted for each county at Ancestry's title description page. This database contains information from the 1895 Iowa State Census for all counties. Includes the name of every member of the household, sex, age, birthplace (town and county). This database has 1,934,349 records. See
**http://search.ancestry.com/search/db.aspx?dbid=7321.**

■ **1902.** See ***Men of Iowa: A Collection of Portraits of Representative Men in Business, Professional and Official Life in the Great State of Iowa*** **[Online Database],** indexed at the Ancestry.com website. Source: Book, same title, publ. Des Moines, 1902. This database has 429 pages. See
**http://search.ancestry.com/search/db.aspx?dbid=25893.**

■ **1905.** See ***Iowa State Census, 1905*** **[Online Database],** indexed at the Ancestry.com website. Source: SHSI database digitized by FamilySearch. This database contains information from the 1905 Iowa State Census for all counties. The records include: County, township and city of residence, Mailing address, Name, Sex, Can read and write, Color, Age, Birthplace, Birthplace of parents, Owner of home or farm, value of property and amount of incumbrance, If naturalized, Number of years in the US and in Iowa, Marital Status, Number of months in school and what type of school, Number of months unemployed, Occupation, and Details of military service. This database has 1,445,414 records. See **http://search.ancestry.com/search/db.aspx?dbid=60725.**

■ **1912-1913.** See ***R.L. Polk & Co.'s Des Moines City and Valley Junction directory for the year commencing December 1, 1912*** **[Online Database],** indexed at the FamilySearch.org website. This database has 1,628 records. See **http://search.ancestry.com/search/db.aspx?dbid=25266.**

■ **1947-1954.** See ***Iowa, World War II Bonus Case Files, 1947-1954*** **[Online Database],** indexed at the Ancestry.com website. Source: SHSI, Des Moines. In May 1947, the Iowa Legislature approved bonus payments of up to $500 for men and women who served on active duty in the U.S. armed forces between 16 September 1940 and 2 September 1945. To qualify, applicants had to be legal residents of Iowa for at least the six months prior to their service. This database contains applications for those payments. Along with name, birth date and place, place of residence for six months prior to enlistment or induction, and address where a check could be sent, forms may provide a wide variety of details related to the applicant's service: This database has 240,951 records. See **http://search.ancestry.com/search/db.aspx?dbid=8825.**

■ **1992-2008.** See ***Iowa, Divorce Index, 1992-2008*** **[Online Database],** indexed at the Ancestry.com website. Source: IA Bureau of Vital Records, Des Moines. Each record includes at least: Husband's name, Wife's name, Divorce date, and Divorce county. This database has 128,979 records. See **http://search.ancestry.com/search/db.aspx?dbid=61022.**

## Iowa Databases Online at the FamilySearch.org Website

The following databases are available for free at the FamilySearch.org website. To see the current list, visit the Iowa Indexed Historical Records and Iowa Image Only Historical Records webpage. Both lists are updated periodically. See **https://familysearch.org/search/collection/location/51.**

■ **1835-1998.** See ***Iowa, Armed Forces Grave Registrations, ca. 1835-1998*** **[Online Database],** digitized and indexed at the FamilySearch.org website. Index and images of grave registrations from the Soldiers Relief Commission (Polk County, Iowa). The grave registrations contain information on United States military veterans buried in Iowa, ranging from Revolutionary War veterans (ca. 1835) to 1998. These records were acquired from the Iowa State Historical Society in Des Moines. The collection is arranged alphabetically. This database has 147,078 records. See **https://familysearch.org/search/collection/2515886.**

■ **1836-1950.** See ***Iowa Births and Christenings, 1830-1950*** **[Online Database],** indexed at the FamilySearch.org website. Source: International Genealogy Index (IGI), and Vital Record Index Collections. Each record includes at least a name, date of birth, and place of birth. The 1830 starting date is impossible for Iowa. This database has 608,259 records. See **https://familysearch.org/search/collection/1674820.**

■ **1836-1992.** See ***Iowa Marriages, 1809-1992*** **[Online Database],** indexed at the FamilySearch.org website. Source: International Genealogy Index (IGI), and Vital Record Index Collections. Each record includes at least a name of bride and groom, date and place of marriage. The 1809 starting date is impossible for Iowa. This database has 1,261,966 records. See **https://familysearch.org/search/collection/1674842.**

■ **1837-1989.** See ***Iowa, Church and Civil Marriages, 1837-1989*** **[Online Database],** indexed at the FamilySearch.org website. Source: FamilySearch extractions from multiple archives. The index may include any of the following: Name of the groom, Name of the bride, often including the maiden name, Name of the officiator, Names of the parents or guardians of the bride and groom, Date of the marriage, Place of marriage, Birthplaces of the bride and groom, Residences of the bride and groom, and Ages. This database has 12,747 records. See **https://familysearch.org/search/collection/2366605.**

■ **1838-1934.** See ***Iowa, County Marriages, 1838-1934*** **[Online Database],** indexed at the FamilySearch.org website. Source: FamilySearch extractions from original records at county

courthouses for all counties of Iowa. The following information is usually included: Name of the groom, Name of the bride, often including the maiden name, Name of the officiator, Names of the parents or guardians of the bride and groom, Date of the marriage, Place of marriage, Birthplaces of the bride and groom, Residences of the bride and groom, Ages, Marital status or number of marriage, Occupation, Race, and Witnesses. This database has 2,271,641 records. See
**https://familysearch.org/search/collection/1805551.**

■ **1850-1954.** See ***Iowa, Poweshiek County Probate, School, and Court Records, 1850-1954*** **[Online Database],** digitized at the FamilySearch.org website. This is an image only database of various records recorded by the county clerk of Poweshiek Co IA, now located at the State Historical Society of Iowa at Des Moines. Browse through the images, organized by Volume Title, and Year Range. This database has 169,128 records. See
**https://familysearch.org/search/collection/2211980.**

■ **1850-1880.** See ***Iowa Non-Population Census Schedules, 1850-1880*** **[Online Database],** digitized at the FamilySearch.org website. Source: National Archives microfilm series T1156. This is an image only database of non-population census schedules for Iowa compiled by the United States Bureau of Census, including Industry, Social Statistics, and Agriculture schedules. Browse through the records, organized by Type of Schedule and Year, then by County. This database has 23,397 images. See
**https://familysearch.org/search/collection/2274801.**

■ **1850-1990.** See ***Iowa Deaths and Burials, 1850-1990*** **[Online Database],** indexed at the FamilySearch.org website. Source: International Genealogy Index (IGI), and Vital Record Index Collections. Each record has at least a name, date of death, and place of death. This database has 398,883 records. See
**https://familysearch.org/search/collection/1674841.**

■ **1851-1928.** See ***Iowa, Fayette County Probate Records, 1851-1928*** **[Online Database],** digitized at the FamilySearch.org website. This is an image only database of Probate Case Files at the Fayette County Courthouse, West Union, IA. Browse through the images, organized by Record Type, Volume, and Year Range. This database has 230,855 images. See
**https://familysearch.org/search/collection/1978346.**

■ **1855-1934.** See ***Iowa, Poweshiek County Land Records, 1855-1934*** **[Online Database],** digitized at the FamilySearch.org website. This is an image only database of deeds recorded by county officials of Poweshiek Co IA, now located at the State Historical Society of Iowa at Des Moines. Browse through the images, organized by Record Type, Volume, and Year Range. This database has 16,268 images. See
**https://familysearch.org/search/collection/2235530.**

■ **1861-1949.** See ***Iowa, Grand Army of the Republic Membership Records, 1861-1949*** **[Online Database],** digitized and indexed at the FamilySearch.org website. Source: SHSI, Des Moines. Index and images of the Department of Iowa Grand Army of the Republic membership records. The records are arranged by county and then by posts within each county. They include veteran's name, residence, occupation, date and place of birth, date and place of death, cemetery where buried, war record, dates of enlistment and discharge, names of parents, spouse, children (if given), and sources of information.
This database has 86,762 records. See
**https://familysearch.org/search/collection/2351982.**

■ **1880-1935.** See ***Iowa, County Births, 1880-1935*** **[Online Database],** indexed at the FamilySearch.org website. Source: FamilySearch extractions from original records at county courthouses for all counties of Iowa. The index contains the following information: Name of child, Birth date, Birthplace, Parent's names, Film number, Digital folder number, and Image number. This database has 2,282,689 records. See
**https://familysearch.org/search/collection/1821206.**

■ **1880-1992.** See ***Iowa, County Death Records, 1880-1992*** **[Online Database],** indexed at the FamilySearch.org website. Source: FamilySearch extractions from original records at county courthouses for all counties of Iowa. Each record may include any of the following: Name of the deceased, Date of birth, Place of birth, Marital status, Gender, Race, Age at death, Occupation, Date of death, Time of death, Place of death, Address of the deceased, Parents' names, Places of birth of the parents, Date of burial, Place of burial, Cause of death, and Name and address of the informant. This database has 543,429 records. See
**https://familysearch.org/search/collection/2110820.**

■ **1885.** See ***Iowa State Census, 1885*** **[Online Database],** indexed at the FamilySearch.org website. The IA 1885 census includes: Name of every person who resided in the family, Address, Age at birthday in

1884, Marital status, Sex, Race, Place of birth (if in Iowa, the county of birth, if not state or country), Parentage (if native or foreign) of father and mother, Whether subject to military duty, Whether entitled to vote, If an alien, whether or not have taken out naturalization papers, Whether literate or not, Any disabilities, and Occupation. This database has 1,737,228 records. See
**https://familysearch.org/search/collection/1803643.**

■ **1895.** See ***Iowa State Census, 1895*** **[Online Database],** indexed at the FamilySearch.org website. The 1895 IA census includes: Name of every person who resided in the family, Age range (18 or over, 5-18 years, under 5 years), Marital status, Gender, Race, Place of birth (if in Iowa, the county of birth; if not in Iowa, state or country), Religious belief, Whether subject to military duty, Whether entitled to vote, If a foreigner, whether or not naturalized, Births or deaths in 1894, Whether literate or not (by age category, under or over 10 years old), Children over 6 and under 17 not attending any school in 1894, Any disabilities, Occupation, If a soldier in the Civil War, the company, regiment, state, arm of service, and rank If a soldier in the Mexican war, the regiment and state. This database has 2,110,508 records. See
**https://familysearch.org/search/collection/1803957.**

■ **1905.** See ***Iowa State Census, 1905*** **[Online Database],** indexed at the FamilySearch.org website. The 1905 IA census includes: County, township and city of residence, Mailing address, Name, Sex, Can read and write, Color, Age, Birthplace, Birthplace of parents, Owner of home or farm, value of property and amount of incumbrance, If naturalized, Number of years in the US and in Iowa, Marital Status, Number of months in school and what type of school, Number of months unemployed, Occupation, Details of military service, and a Signature, This database has 2,171,126 records. See
**https://familysearch.org/search/collection/2126961.**

■ **1914-1924.** See ***Iowa, Polk County Probate Records, 1914-1924*** **[Online Database],** digitized at the FamilySearch.org website. This is an image only database of Probate Case Files of Polk County, IA now located at the State Historical Society of Iowa in Des Moines. Browse through the images, organized by Record Type, Volume, and Year Range. This database has 157,848 images. See
**https://familysearch.org/search/collection/2138591.**

■ **1915.** See ***Iowa State Census, 1915*** **[Online Database],** indexed at the FamilySearch.org website. The 1915 IA census includes: County, township and city of residence, Mailing address, Name, Sex, Can read and write, Color, Age, Birthplace, Birthplace of parents, Owner of home or farm, value of property and amount of encumbrance, If naturalized, Number of years in the US and in Iowa, Marital status, Number of months in school and what type of school, Number of months unemployed, Occupation, Details of military service, and a Signature. This database has 2,483,506 records. See
**https://familysearch.org/search/collection/2240483.**

■ **1925.** See ***Iowa State Census, 1925*** **[Online Database],** indexed at the FamilySearch.org website. Complete contents of the IA 1925 State Census: 1. PLACE OF ABODE: Street, Avenue, Boulevard or Road; House Number. 2. NAME: of each Person whose Place of Abode on Jan 1, 1925 was in this Family. Enter Surnames First, Then Given Name and middle Initial, If any. Include Every Person Living on Jan 1, 1925. Omit Children born since Jan 1, 1925. 3. RELATION: Relationship of this Person to the Head of the Family. 4. PERSONAL DESCRIPTION: A. Sex, B. Color of Race, C. Age at Last Birthday, D. Single, Married, Widowed or Divorced. 5. TENURE: A. Home owned or Rented. B. If Owned, Free or Mortgaged, C. Value of this Home, D. Amount of Mortgage Debt Against this Home Jan 1, 1925, E. If rented, Amount of rent paid Monthly, F. If Owned Amount of all Insurance Carried on this House. 6. CITIZENSHIP: A. If Foreign Born are You Naturalized, B. No. Years In U.S., C. No. Years In Iowa. 7. EDUCATION and LITERACY: 1. High School Attended (Check Proper Space A,B, C, or D): A. Rural, B. Grade, C. High School, D. College or University, 2. HIGHEST GRADE REACHED: A. RURAL - State Highest Reader Completed as 1st, 2nd, 3rd, 4th. B. GRADE in GRAMMAR - State Highest Grade completed (Grades 1 to 8 Incl.). C. HIGH SCHOOL - State Highest Grade Completed (Grades 9 to 12 Incl.). D. COLLEGE or UNIVERSITY - State No. Years Attended. 3. How Many Months of School attended in Year 1924. 4. Whether able to Read, 5. Whether able to Write. 8. NATIVITY: Place of Birth of each Person enumerated and Name, Place of Birth, Age and Place of Marriage of Parents. (If Place is in U. S. give State or Territory, if outside of U. S. give Country). Person enumerated: A. Place of Birth. FATHER,. B. Name of Father, C. Place of Birth, D. Age last Birthday. MOTHER, E. Full Maiden Name of Mother, F. Place of Birth,

G. Age last Birthday. Parents of Person enumerated, H. Place of Marriage. 9. MILITARY SERVICE: A. Which War They Served In (Civil War, Spanish-American, World War), B. Branch of Service in Which They Served. C. What State Enlisted or Drafted From. 10. OCCUPATION: A. Are you engaged in Agricultural Pursuits, B. Are you engaged in Professional Services, C. Are you engaged in domestic and Personal Services, D. Are you engaged in Trade and Transportation, E. Are you engaged in Manufacturing and Mechanical work, F. Are you a Laborer unclassified. G. No. months in 1924 unemployed because of illness from communicable diseases only. H. Amt. of salary or income loss because of illness from communicable diseases, I. No. months in 1924 unemployed on account of labor conditions. 11. CHURCH AFFILIATION: What Church are You Affiliated With. This database has 2,756,529 records. See **https://familysearch.org/search/collection/2224537.**

✓ **1925 NOTE:** The 1925 IA State Census was the only American census (territorial, state or federal), that asked the Name of Father and Full Maiden Name of Mother, with their Place of Birth, Age, and Place of Marriage for every person enumerated. (See 8. NATIVITY).

## Iowa Databases Online At Various Websites

■ **1833-1900s Iowa Original Land Owners.** See the ***Family Maps*** series for Iowa counties, maps of all original land patents, compiled by Greg Boyd, publ. Arphax Publishing Co., Norman, OK. These privately-produced computer-generated maps show the first property owners for an entire county, produced as a book of maps, each map laid out on the federal township grid, and includes indexes to help you locate a person, place-name, or cemetery. Additional maps are added for each county to show roads, waterways, railroads, selected city centers, and cemeteries within a county. At this writing, *Family Maps* books have been published for the following Iowa counties: Benton, Black Hawk, Cedar, Clayton, Decatur, Dubuque, Fayette, Henry, Iowa, Jasper, Jefferson, Johnson, Jones, Keokuk, Linn, Madison, Mahaska, Page, Poweshiek, Ringgold, Story, Union, Warren, Washington, Wayne, and Winneshiek counties. Visit the publisher's information and ordering website for more details and updated county coverage. See **www.arphax.com.** Arphax's entire *Family Maps* series is also available as a subscription service online. See **www.historygeo.com.**

■ **1833-2000s.** See ***Iowa US GenWeb Archives*** **[Online Databases],** name lists are available for all Iowa counties. Typical county records include Bibles, Biographies, Cemeteries, Censuses, Court, Death, Deeds, Directories, Histories, Marriages, Military, Newspapers, Obituaries, Photos, Schools, Tax Lists, Wills, and more. The Special Projects include:

- Iowa Family Group Sheet Project
- Iowa Genealogy Boards
- Iowa Gravestone Photo Project
- Iowa History Project
- Iowa in the Civil War
- Iowa in the Great War
- Iowa in World War II
- Iowa Old Press
- Iowa State Census Project
- Orphan Train Riders to Iowa
- Iowa WPA Graves Registration Survey

Links to all Iowa counties and projects are located at the USGenWeb home page for Iowa. See **http://iagenweb.org/.**

■ **1833-2000s.** See ***Linkpendium – Iowa: Family History & Genealogy, Census, Birth, Marriage, Death, Vital Records & More*** **[Online Databases].** Linkpendium is a genealogical portal site with links to state, county, town, and local databases. Currently listed are selected sites for Iowa statewide resources (465), Renamed/Discontinued Counties (10), Adair County (257) Adams County (285), Allamakee County (780), Appanoose County (421), Audubon County (285), Benton County (848), Black Hawk County (492) and 92 more Iowa counties. See **www.linkpendium.com/ia-genealogy.**

■ **1836 Wisconsin Territorial Census, Des Moines County (now Iowa) [Online Database]**, indexed at the USGenWeb site for Des Moines Co IA. See **http://iagenweb.org/muscatine/1836census/desmoines1836.htm.**

■ **1837-1976.** See ***Iowa Newspaper Archives*** **[Online Databases],** digitized and indexed newspapers at the GenealogyBank website, for Anamosa, Burlington, Corning, Council Bluffs, Davenport, Denison, Des Moines, Dubuque, Eddyville, Independence, Iowa City, Jefferson, La Porte City, and Sioux City. See **www.genealogybank.com/explore/newspapers/all/usa/iowa.**

■ **1838 Census, Henry County, Iowa [Online Database]**, indexed at USGenWeb site for Henry Co IA. See http://iagenweb.org/henry/census/1838henry.htm.

■ **1838 Grand Jurors, Slaughter County, Wisconsin Territory [Online Database]**, indexed at the USGenWeb for Washington Co IA. See http://files.usgwarchives.net/ia/washington/history/1838gj.txt. **NOTE:** Slaughter County was formed by Wisconsin Territory in January 1838, and the area was included in the new Iowa Territory created in July 1838. Slaughter was renamed Washington a year later.

■ **1838-1845 Original Land Entries, Clinton County, Iowa [Online Database]**, indexed at the USGenWeb site for Clinton Co IA. See http://iagenweb.org/clinton/places/land/original_land_entries.htm.

■ **1838-1865.** See **1838 Census, Clayton County, Wisconsin Territory and 1865 Gazetteer, Clayton County, Iowa [Online Database]**, indexed at the Sharyl's Cabin site. See http://sharylscabin.com/Clayton/directory/gazetteer_p126.htm#census.

■ **1839-1841 Jurors, Johnson County, Iowa [Online Database]**, indexed at the USGenWeb site for Johnson Co IA. See http://iagenweb.org/johnson/JCdistrictCourtJurors.htm.

■ **1839-1841 Jurors, Washington County, Iowa [Online Database]**, indexed at the USGenWeb site for Washington Co IA. See http://files.usgwarchives.net/ia/washington/history/jurors.txt.

■ **1840s-1850s.** See **Settlement of Ringgold County, Iowa [Online Database]**, text at the USGenWeb site for Ringgold Co IA. See http://iagenweb.org/ringgold/history/misc/hist-beforestatehood-settlement.html.

■ **1840s-1860s**. See **Stories of Early Fayette County History [Online Database]**, published at the USGenWeb site for Fayette Co IA. See http://files.usgwarchives.net/ia/fayette/history/stories.txt

■ **1840s-1860s**. See **Original Land Owners, Warren County, Iowa [Online Database]**, published at the USGenWeb site for Warren Co IA. See http://iagenweb.org/warren/land/land_dg.html.

■ **1840s-1970s.** See **Military Information & Links, Madison County, Iowa [Online Database],** includes info for veterans who lived in Madison Co IA. See http://iagenweb.org/madison/military/military_index.html.

■ **1842.** See **First Tax Assessment Roll of 1842, Delaware County, Iowa [Online Database]**, indexed at the USGenWeb site for Delaware Co IA. See http://iagenweb.org/delaware/taxes/1842-1stax.htm.

■ **1844-1886 Indentured Children, Des Moines County, Iowa [Online Database]**, indexed at the USGenWeb site for Des Moines Co IA. See http://files.usgwarchives.net/ia/desmoines/court/indent.txt.

■ **1845-1851 County Probate Book A, Marion County, Iowa [Online Database]**. Originally indexed at the USGenWeb site for Marion Co IA. For an archived database, see http://web.archive.org/web/20110824101021/http://iagenweb.org/marion/ProbateBkA.htm.

■ **1845-1900s.** See **Index to Monroe County, Iowa Will Books A, B, and C [Online Database]**, indexed a the USGenWeb site for Monroe Co IA. See http://iagenweb.org/monroe/Wills/wills.html.

■ **1845-1995.** See **Index, Pioneer History, Calhoun County, Iowa [Online Database],** indexed at the USGenWeb site for Calhoun Co IA. See http://iagenweb.org/calhoun/records/histories/pioneer/index.php.

■ **1846 Iowa Territorial Census Index, Polk County, Iowa Territory [Online Database].** This name index came from a typescript created in 1940 as a WPA project, now available online at the USGenWeb site for Polk Co IA. See http://iagenweb.org/polk/census/1846_polk_county_census_index_te.htm.

■ **1846 Iowa Territorial Census, Wapello County, Iowa [Online Database],** indexed at the USGenWeb site for Wapello Co IA. See http://files.usgwarchives.net/ia/wapello/census/1846.txt.

■ **1846 Directory, Davenport, Iowa [Online Database]**, indexed at the Celtic Cousins website. See www.celticcousins.net/scott/1846dir.htm.

■ **1846-1850s. Wills and Probates, Polk County, Iowa [Online Database]**. Includes Will Book 1 and Probate Book A. This webpage gives the address for the Clerk of the Court of Polk County, the availability

of indexes to the probate records, 1847- present, and the fee for copies. Originally indexed at the USGenWeb site for Polk Co IA. For an archived version, see
http://web.archive.org/web/20120109115055/http://iagenweb.org/polk/Wills%20and%20Probates/wills_and_probates.htm.

■ **1846-1860. Early Pioneers of Warren County, Iowa [Online Database]**, indexed at the USGenWeb site for Warren Co IA. See
http://files.usgwarchives.net/ia/warren/history/pioneers.txt.

■ **1846-1865 Probate Index, Jasper County, Iowa [Online Database]**, indexed at the USGenWeb site for Jasper Co IA. See
http://iagenweb.org/jasper/probate/.

■ **1847 Iowa State Census, Wapello County, Iowa [Online Database]**, indexed at the USGenWeb site for Wapello Co IA. See
http://files.usgwarchives.net/ia/wapello/census/1847.txt.

■ **1847 Non-Resident Tax List, Louisa County, Iowa [Online Database]**, indexed at the RootsWeb site for Louisa Co IA. See
www.rootsweb.ancestry.com/~ialcgs/nrltx47.htm.

■ **1847-1851. See Military Land Warrants, Jefferson County, Iowa [Online Database]**, indexed at the USGenWeb site for Jefferson Co IA. See
http://iagenweb.org/jefferson/Land_Records/Military_Land_grants.html.

■ **1848 Delinquent Taxes, Louisa County, Iowa [Online Database]**, indexed at the RootsWeb site for Louisa Co IA. See
www.rootsweb.ancestry.com/~ialcgs/ldtx48.htm.

■ **1848-1849 Personal Tax Lists, Louisa County, Iowa [Online Database]**, indexed at the RootsWeb site for Louisa Co IA. See
www.rootsweb.ancestry.com/~ialcgs/perstx48-49.htm.

■ **1849 Iowa State Census, Clinton County, Iowa [Online Database]**, indexed at the USGenWeb site for Clinton Co IA. See
http://files.usgwarchives.net/ia/clinton/census/1849cen.txt.

■ **1849 Iowa State Census, Van Buren County, Iowa [Online Database]**, indexed in alpha groups at the USGenWeb site for Van Buren Co IA. See
http://iavanburen.org/1849vbc_census.html.

■ **1849 Tax List, Warren County, Iowa [Online Database],** an index to the "First Tax List of Warren County, Iowa, August, 20, 1849," originally indexed at the USGenWeb site for Warren Co IA. For an archived version, see
http://web.archive.org/web/20120606000009/http://iagenweb.org/warren/tax_lists/1849taxlist.html.

■ **1849-1850 Poll Tax List, Jasper County, Iowa [Online Database]**, indexed at the USGenWeb for Jasper Co IA. See
http://iagenweb.org/jasper/resources/polltax1849.htm.

■ **1849-1853 First Land Entries, Fremont County, Iowa [Online Database]**, listed at the USGenWeb site for Fremont Co IA. See
http://iagenweb.org/fremont/deeds/landent1.htm.

■ **1849-1853 Earliest Land Entries, Tama County, Iowa [Online Database]**, listed at the USGenWeb site for Tama Co IA. See
http://files.usgwarchives.net/ia/tama/deeds/tama-lnd.txt.

■ **1849-1925. See Iowa State Censuses, Madison County, Iowa [Online Database]**, includes 1849, 1851, 1852, 1854, 1856, 1859, 1873, 1885, 1895, 1905, 1915, and 1925 state censuses, indexed at the USGenWeb site for Madison Co IA. See
http://iagenweb.org/census/madison/.

■ **1992-Current.** See ***Iowa Recent Newspaper Obituaries* [Online Database],** digitized and indexed newspaper obituaries at the GenealogyBank website, including newspapers for Adel, Algona, Ames, Atlantic, Bettendorf, Boone, Burlington, Cedar Rapids, Centerville, Charles City, Clarinda, Clinton, Council Bluffs, Creston, Davenport, Decorah, Denison, Dubuque, Forest City, Fort Madison, Glenwood, Hamburg, Kalona, Keokuk, Knoxville, Logan, Lone Tree, Mason City, Muscatine, Nevada, New Hampton, Newton, Osage, Osceola, Oskaloosa, Ottumwa, Pella, Perry, Red Oak, Riverside, Shenandoah, Sioux City, Story City, and Waterloo, Iowa. See
www.genealogybank.com/explore/obituaries/all/usa/iowa.

## Iowa Periodical Articles

### Censuses & Substitute Name Lists in Genealogical Periodicals

PERSI (PERiodical Source Index) is a digitized database project of the Allen County Public Library (ACPL), Fort Wayne, IN. Since 1986, the PERSI extractors have indexed article titles, places, and surnames from over 11,000 genealogical & historical periodicals. The PERSI database is currently available online through the **FindMyPast.com** subscription website. The Genealogy Center of the ACPL in Fort Wayne IN holds all 11,000 periodicals and will make copies of any article by special request. To obtain an order form for requesting a printed copy of any article indexed in the PERSI database, see **http://genealogycenter.org/docs/default-source/resources/articlerequest.pdf?sfvrsn=2.**

**Iowa PERSI Search:** Using the FindMyPast.com website, the keywords "Iowa State Census" had 96 results. A sampling of Iowa state census articles available is shown below. Any of the names lists that were later posted online are also noted:

■ **1838.** See **"The Census of 1838" [Printed Article]**, by Marie Haefner, in *The Palimpsest* (State Historical Society of Iowa, Iowa City, IA), Vol. 19 (May 1938), pp 185-192.

■ **"1847 Iowa State Census, Davis County, Iowa" [Printed Article & Online Database],** in *The American Genealogist*, Vol. 42, No. 4 (Oct 1966); and in *Hawkeye Heritage*, Vol. 11, No. 1 (Jan 1976). This name list was also indexed online at the USGenWeb site for Davis Co IA. See **http://iagenweb.org/davis/census_1847.htm.**

■ **"1847 Iowa State Census, Van Buren County" [Printed Article & Online Database]**, in *Hawkeye Heritage*, Vol. 1, No. 1 (Winter 1966); and in *Van Buren Iowa Quill*, beginning with Vol. 2, No. 1 (Winter 1967). This name list was also indexed at the USGenWeb site for Van Buren Co IA. See **http://iavanburen.org/1847index.htm.**

■ **"1849 Iowa State Census, Boone County" [Printed Article]**, name list in *Hawkeye Heritage*, Vol. 1, No. 2 (Spring 1966).

■ **"1856 Iowa State Census, Adair County, Iowa" [Printed Article & Online Database]**, name list published serially in the *Adair County Anquestors,* beginning with Vol. 9, No. 1 (Dec 1996).

■ **"1856 Iowa State Census, Clarke County, Iowa" [Printed Article]**, name list in *Clarke County Roots & Branches*, beginning with Vol. 5, No. 4 (Dec 1996).

■ **"1856 Iowa State Census, Davis County, Iowa" [Printed Article]**, name list in *Davis County Genealogical Society Newsletter*, beginning with Vol. 5, No. 3 (Fall 1987).

■ **"1856 Iowa State Census, Franklin County, Iowa" [Printed Article]**, name list in the *Franklin Record*, beginning with the April 1988 issue; and in *Hawkeye Heritage*, Vol. 22, No. 3 (1987).

■ **"1856 Iowa State Census, Greene County, Iowa" [Printed Article & Online Database]**, name list in *Greene Gleanings*, beginning with the February 1993 issue. This name list was also indexed online at the USGenWeb site for Greene Co IA. See **http://iagenweb.org/census/textdisplay.php?file=/census/greene/1856-IA-greene-jefferson.txt.**

■ **"1856 Iowa State Census, Hardin County, Iowa" [Printed Article]**, name list in *Hawkeye Heritage,* Vol. 3, No. 3 (Jul 1968). This name list was indexed online at the USGenWeb site for Hardin Co IA. See **http://iagenweb.org/hardin/56census/56census.html.**

■ **"1856 Iowa State Census, Jones County, Iowa" [Printed Article],** in *News 'N' Notes*, beginning with Vol. 3, No. 1 (Jan 1992).

■ **"1856 Iowa State Census, Kossuth County" [Printed Article]**, name list in *Hawkeye Heritage*, Vol. 3, No. 1 (Jan 1968).

■ **"1867 Iowa State Census (Statistics), Newton, Jasper County, Iowa" [Printed Article]**, in *Jasper County Gleaner*, Vol. 8, No. 1 (Jan 1986).

■ **"1875 Iowa State Census, Webster County" [Printed Article]**, name list in *Webster County Genie Gleaners*, Vol. 12, No. 3 (Jul 2000).

■ **"1885 Iowa State Census, Wapello County, Iowa" [Printed Article]**, in *Southern Genealogists Exchange Quarterly*, Vol. 22, No. 100 (Winter 1981).

■ **"1895 Iowa State Census, Webster County, Iowa" [Printed Article, Printed Book & Microfilm],** name list in *Webster County Genie Gleaners*, beginning with Vol. 2, No. 3 (Oct 1990). Complete name list published in 6 vols. by the Iowa Genealogical Society, 1991. FHL has bound 6 vols. into 3 vols., FHL book 977.751 X2w vol. 1-3 and FHL film #2055294.

## Iowa Books & Microfilms at the Family History Library

Iowa's state censuses and most important census substitutes are cited below in chronological order. Each item includes a FHL book number or FHL film number, which can be used to search the FHL catalog for more details. To review an item, start at the FamilySearch catalog search page. See **https://familysearch.org/search/catalog/results.** Select "Search by Place" then "United States, Iowa" to see a list of catalog categories. Or, select "Call Number" then type an FHL book number; or select "Film/Fiche Number" to view a specific title.
**NOTE:** any microfilm versions of the 1836-1925 IA state censuses are noted below. They are all indexed online as part of Ancestry's online database, ***Iowa, State Census Collection, 1836-1925.*** The IA State Censuses for 1885, 1895, 1905, and 1925 are also digitized and indexed at the FamilySearch.org website.

■ **1833–1850.** See ***Iowa Marriages, Early to 1850: A Research Tool*** **[Printed Book]**, compiled and published by Liahona Research, Orem, UT, 1990, 373 pages, FHL book 977.7 V22i.

■ **1833–1900s.** See ***Family Record Collection*** **[Microfilm],** from originals at the Iowa State Historical Society, Des Moines, IA. Filmed by the Genealogical Society of Utah, 1978, 6 rolls, beginning with FHL film #1023616 (Albrock – Blanchard). For a complete list of roll numbers and contents of each roll, see the online FHL catalog page for the title: **https://familysearch.org/search/catalog/331202.**

■ **1833-1900s.** See **Biographical Data Collection [Microfilm],** from originals at the Iowa State Historical Society, Des Moines, IA. Filmed by the Genealogical Society of Utah, 1978, 6 rolls, beginning with FHL film #1023885 (Adams – Curtiss). For a complete list of roll numbers and contents of each roll, see the online FHL catalog page for this title. See **https://familysearch.org/search/catalog/409051**.

■ **1833-1900s**. See ***Iowa Biography Index*** **[Printed Book]**, an index to county histories, biographical records, town, county, church, fraternal, governmental, vital, state, etc. covering all 99 counties in the State of Iowa available from the State of Iowa Lending and Research Library, Menlo, IA, 1986, 167 pages, FHL book 977.7 D22. For access to a digital version of this book, see the online FHL catalog page for this title: **https://familysearch.org/search/catalog/583062.**

■ **1836.** See ***The First Census of the Original Counties of Dubuque and Demoine (Iowa) Taken in July, 1836*** **[Microfilm]**, edited by Benjamin F. Shambaugh, microfilm of original published by the Historical Department of Iowa, Des Moines, 1897-1898. 2 parts in 1 vol., 93 pages. Contents: part 1: Dubuque County; part 2: Demoine County. From the original manuscript returns preserved in the office of the Secretary of State of Wisconsin. The census was taken in accordance with the act of Congress erecting the territory of Wisconsin (of which these two counties at the time formed a part) comprising the present states of Wisconsin, Iowa, Minnesota and part of North and South Dakota. Includes names of heads of households with number of males and females by age brackets. Filmed by the Genealogical Society of Utah, 1978, 1 roll, FHL film #1022202, another filming, #989450.

■ **1836.** See ***Iowa 1836 Territorial Census Index*** **[Printed Book]**, edited by Ronald Vern Jackson, et al, published by Accelerated Indexing Systems, Bountiful, UT, 1976, 35 pages. FHL book 977.7 X22j. **Note:** This is actually for the 1836 Wisconsin Territorial Census that included Iowa areas. Iowa Territory was created in 1838.

■ **1838.** See ***Iowa 1838 Territorial Census Index*** **[Printed Book]**, edited by Ronald Vern Jackson, et al, published by Accelerated Indexing Systems, Bountiful, UT, 1984. FHL book 977.7 X22ji 1838.

■ **1841-1849.** See ***Iowa Census Records, 1841-1849*** **[Printed Index]**, edited by Ronald Vern Jackson, et al. The actual years are not noted, but it is probable that the Iowa territorial and state censuses of 1844, 1846, 1847, and 1849 are included in this combined index. Published by Accelerated Indexing Systems, Salt Lake City, UT, 1979, 1981, FHL book 977.7 X22i.

■ ***1846 Census of Louisa, Polk, and Wapello Counties, Iowa*** **[Microfilm],** from the originals at the SHSI, Des Moines. This filming includes a 4-page typescript of the Polk County census that was done by the Iowa Writers Project of the Works Progress Administration in 1940. Filmed by the Genealogical Society of Utah, 1978, 1 roll, FHL film #1022202.

✓ **1846 NOTE:** The last of three territorial censuses for Iowa Territory was dated Sept 16, 1846, and was for all of the 18 counties of Iowa Territory at that time. But apparently, only the three counties of Louisa, Polk, and Wapello are extant. The results of this census gave Iowa the evidence that it had met the minimum population requirement for statehood, which was granted on Dec 29, 1846. The peopling of Iowa began on June 1, 1833, and at statehood, 13 years later, Iowa's population was over 96,000.

■ **1846 Directory.** See ***A Glimpse of Iowa in 1846*** **[Microfiche]**, from the original 1846 directory by John B. Newhall; published by Thurston and Tizzard, 2 fiche, FHL fiche #6043998.

■ **1847.** See ***Census of Clinton, Davis, Louisa, Marion, Scott, Van Buren, and Wapello counties, Iowa, 1847*** **[Microfilm],** from the surviving originals of the 1847 Iowa State Census at the SHSI, Des Moines. Includes a 9-page typescript of the Davis County census transcribed by Joe and Madeline Huff in 1975 and an 8-page photocopy of a typescript of the Louisa County census transcribed by Madeline Huff in 1974. Names heads of households and total numbers in the family. Filmed by the Genealogical Society of Utah, 1978, 1 roll, FHL film #1022202.

✓ **1847 NOTE:** The Iowa Constitution of 1846 provided that within one year after its ratification and within every subsequent term of two years, an enumeration of all the white inhabitants of the state should be made. In accordance with this provision an act was passed by the First General Assembly, and approved January 20, 1847, requiring the assessors to take an enumeration of white inhabitants on or before the first day of August, 1847. In the census of 1847, thirty-two counties in all were included. The total population was 116,454. (Excerpted from the introduction to the online index to Van Buren County's 1847 Iowa State Census). See **http://iavanburen.org/1847index.htm.**

■ **1849.** See ***Census of Benton, Boone, Clinton, Jackson, Louisa, Madison, Poweshiek, Scott, Van Buren and Washington counties, Iowa, 1849*** **[Microfilm]**, from the typescript copies of the surviving 1849 Iowa State Census population schedules at the SHSI, Des Moines. Heads of households only. Includes photocopies of typescript material transcribed by Madeline and Joe Huff, Lida Lisle Greene, Mary A. Fullbright, and Robert Fisher. The typescript of Washington County was filmed with the Madison County record. See FHL film #1022202.

■ **1850.** See ***Iowa, 1850 Federal Census: Population Schedules (Federal Copy)*** **[Microfilm]**, from the originals at the National Archives, Washington, DC. The census schedules include the names of all members of a family, age, sex, and place of birth. Since the SHSI has the original state copies of the same federal census schedules, a comparison can be made for possible copying errors (very common). Filmed by the National Archives, 1964, 8 rolls, beginning with FHL film #7791 (Allamakee, Appanoose, Benton, Black Hawk, Boone, Buchanan, Cedar, Clarke, Clayton, Clinton, Dallas, and Davis Counties). For a complete list of roll numbers and contents of each roll, see the online FHL catalog page for this title. See **https://familysearch.org/search/catalog/744479.**

■ **1850.** See ***Federal Census of Iowa for 1850 (State Copy)*** **[Microfilm]**, from the Iowa Secretary of State's originals now at the SHSI, Des Moines. This state original set was used to make a copy to be sent to the Census Office in Washington, DC. Filmed by the Genealogical Society of Utah, 1977, 7 rolls, beginning with FHL film #1021283 (Allamakee, Appanoose, Benton, Buchanan, Black Hawk, Clayton, Cedar, Clinton, Clarke, Des Moines, & Lucas counties). For a complete list of roll numbers and contents of each roll, see the online FHL catalog page for this title. See **https://familysearch.org/search/catalog/280372.**

■ **1851.** See ***Census of Cedar, Clinton, Decatur, Guthrie, Iowa, Jackson, Jasper, Jefferson, Johnson, Madison, Mahaska, Page, Pottawattamie, Poweshiek, Scott, and Washington Counties, Iowa, 1851*** **[Microfilm]**, from the extant population schedules of the 1851 IA State Census at the SHSI, Des Moines. Filmed by the Genealogical Society of Utah, 1978, FHL film #1022203.

■ **1851-1859.** See ***Iowa Census Records, 1851-1859*** **[Printed Index]**, edited by Ronald Vern Jackson, et al. Actual years not noted, but the index probably includes the Iowa state censuses of 1851, 1852, 1853, 1854, 1856, and 1859. Published by Accelerated Indexing Systems, North Salt Lake, UT, 1981, FHL book 977.7 X2i 1851-1859.

■ ***1852 Census of Various Counties in Iowa*** **[Microfilm]**, from the extant population schedules of the 1852 IA State Census at the SHSI, Des Moines. Heads of households census for 42 Iowa counties. Filmed by the Genealogical Society of Utah, 1978, 2 rolls, as follows:

- Appanoose - Lucas Counties, FHL film #1022204.
- Madison - Wayne counties, FHL film #1022205.

■ **1852.** See ***Iowa 1852*** **[Printed Index]**, edited by Ronald Vern Jackson, published by Accelerated Indexing Systems, 1988, 610 pages. FHL book 977.7 X22io.

■ ***1854 Census of Various Counties in Iowa*** **[Microfilm]**, from the originals of extant population schedules at the State Historical Society of Iowa, Des Moines, Iowa. Heads of households for 51 Iowa counties. Filmed by the Genealogical Society of Utah, 1978, 3 rolls, as follows:

- Adams - Lee Counties, FHL film #1022206.
- Linn - Winneshiek Counties, FHL film #1022207.
- Duplicate film of Page, Polk, Pottawattamie, and Poweshiek Counties, FHL film #1022210.

■ ***1855-1935 City Directories, Davenport, Iowa*** **[Microfiche/Microfilm],** from originals published by various publishers. Filmed by Research Publications, Woodbridge, CT, 1980-1984, 16 microfiche and 21 microfilm rolls, beginning with FHL fiche #6043849 (1855-1856 Davenport city directory, 3 fiche). For a complete list of fiche and roll numbers, and the contents of each, see the online FHL catalog page for this title. See **https://familysearch.org/search/catalog/536168.**

■ ***1856 State Census of Iowa*** **[Microfilm]**, from the extant population schedules at the SHSI, Des Moines. The first modern state census for Iowa, the 1856 identifies all members of family listed by name, age, nativity, occupation, length of time in Iowa, etc., plus agriculture, domestic and general manufactures. Includes all Iowa counties of 1856 except Warren County. Filmed by the Genealogical Society of Utah, 1977, 26 rolls, beginning with FHL film #1021290 (Adair-Audubon counties). For a complete list of roll numbers and the contents of each roll, see the online FHL catalog page for this title. See **https://familysearch.org/search/catalog/409022.**

■ ***1856-1897 City Directories, Dubuque, Iowa*** **[Microfilm],** from originals published by Hardie & Scharle, Dubuque, IA. Filmed by the Genealogical Society of Utah, 1976, 1978, 5 rolls, as follows:

- **1861**, **1856-1859**, **1867**, **1874-1876, 1884-1887** Dubuque directories, FHL film #985427.
- **1888-1889** Dubuque directories, FHL film #985428.
- **1863**, **1870-1871**, **1873-1874**, **1883-1885** Dubuque directories, FHL film #1024142.
- **1880-1881**, **1894-1897** Dubuque directories, FHL film #1024143.
- **1858**, **1884-1885** Dubuque directories, FHL film #1024843.

■ ***1856-1899 City Directories, Davenport, Scott County, Iowa*** **[Microfilm],** from the originals published by H.N. Stone, Davenport, IA. Filmed by the Genealogical Society of Utah, 1976, 1978, 8 rolls, as follows:

- **1856-1863**, 1866-1870 directories, FHL film #989491.
- **1873-1878**, 1880-1881 directories, FHL film #989492.
- **1876** directory, FHL film #1024842.
- **1882-1888**, directories, FHL film #989493.
- **1890-1891**, 1894-1895 directories, FHL film #989494.
- **1896-1899** directories, FHL #989495.
- **1874-1875**, **1885-1886**, **1894-1897** directories, FHL film #1024141.
- **1892-1893** directories, FHL film #1024843.

■ ***1857-1900 City Directories, Iowa City, Johnson County, Iowa*** **[Microfilm],** from originals published by A.G. Tucker, Iowa City, IA. Filmed by the Genealogical Society of Utah, 1976, 1978, 2 rolls, as follows:

- **1857**, **1868**, **1875**, **1878**, **1891-1894** & **1897-1900**, FHL film #989476.
- **1857**, FHL film #1024845.

■ **1859-1912.** See ***Iowa City Assessor's Book, 1859-1912*** **[Microfilm],** from originals at the Iowa State Historical Society, Des Moines, IA. Filmed by the Genealogical Society of Utah, 1990, 6 rolls, beginning with FHL film #1728635 (Iowa City Assessor's book, 1858-1860). For a complete list of rolls and contents of each, see the online FHL catalog page for this title: **https://familysearch.org/search/catalog/551040.**

■ **1860.** See ***Iowa, 1860 Federal Census: Population Schedules*** **(Federal Copy) [Microfilm],** from the originals at the National Archives. Since the SHSI has original state copies of the same federal census schedules (fragments of 30 counties only), a comparison can made for possible copying errors (very common). Filmed twice by the National Archives, 1950, 1957, 43 rolls, beginning with FHL film #803310 (2nd filming: Adair, Adams, and Allamakee Counties). For a complete list of roll numbers and contents of each roll, see the online FHL catalog page for this title. See **https://familysearch.org/search/catalog/704803.**

■ **1860.** See ***Iowa, 1860 Federal Census (State Copy)*** **[Microfilm],** from the Iowa Secretary of State's originals at the SHSI, Des Moines. FHL title: ***1860 Federal Census for Cherokee, Pocahontas, O'Brien, Clay, Dickinson, Emmett, Shelby, Audubon, Buena Vista, Sioux, Plymouth, Palo Alto, Woodbury,***

***Wright, Sac, Monona, Ida, Webster, Humboldt, Kossuth, Calhoun, Greene, Carroll, Crawford, Mitchell, Worth, Cerro Gordo, Hancock and Winnebago Counties, Iowa.*** The state's original set (for all Iowa counties) was used to make a copy to be sent to the Census Office in Washington, DC. These surviving state copies of 30 counties are all fragments, usually one page per county only. Since the federal copy is complete for all Iowa counties, this original state copy set was obviously decimated by time and neglect. Filmed by the Genealogical Society of Utah, 1977, 1 roll, FHL film #1021283. See the 1860 note at the 1836-1925 IA State Census item under Ancestry's Online Databases (p. 124).

■ **1861-1865.** See ***Iowa Colonels and Regiments: Being a History of Iowa Regiments in the War of the Rebellion and Containing a Description of the Battles in Which They Have Fought*** **[Printed Book]**, by Addison A. Stuart, published by Mills, Des Moines, IA, 1865, 656 pages, FHL book 977.7 M2s.

■ **1861-1865**. See ***Grand Army of the Republic Records, Iowa Posts: Indexes to Veterans; Post Membership Records*** **[Microfilm],** from the originals at the State Historical Society of Iowa, Des Moines, IA. Contains indexes made by members of the Daughters of the American Revolution chapters in Iowa, giving names of soldiers, birth dates and places, death dates (if available) and cemeteries where buried, and the G.A.R. posts which veterans belonged to, as well as their membership records. The membership records are arranged by county and then by posts within each county. They include veteran's name, residence, occupation, date and place of birth, date and place of death, cemetery where buried, war record, dates of enlistment and discharge, names of parents, spouse, children (if given), and sources of information. Filmed by the Genealogical Society of Utah, 1978, 1987, 69 rolls, beginning with FHL film #1487370 (Surname Index to Veterans and their GAR Posts – Aaker, Drengman Oleson – Boyce, William H.). For a complete list of roll numbers and contents of each roll, see the online FHL catalog page. See **https://familysearch.org/search/catalog/155392.**

■ **1861-1865.** See ***Index to Compiled Service Records of Volunteer Union Soldiers Who Served in Organizations from the State of Iowa*** **[Microfilm]**, from the originals at the National Archives, Washington, DC. Filmed by the National Archives, 1964, 29 rolls, FHL film #881808 (Index, A-Bam 1861-1865). For a complete list of roll numbers and contents of each roll, see the online FHL catalog page for this title. See **https://familysearch.org/search/catalog/315985.**

■ **1861-1866.** See ***Roster and Records of Iowa Soldiers in the War of the Rebellion: Together with Historical Sketches of Volunteer Organizations, 1861-1865*** **[Printed Book],** prepared by the Iowa Adjutant General's office, published by authority of the General Assembly, Des Moines, IA: E. H. English, 1908-1911, 6 vols., FHL book 977.7 M2i. To view a digital version, see the online FHL online catalog page for this title. See **https://familysearch.org/search/catalog/27.**

■ **1861-1866.** See ***Index to Iowa Soldiers*** **[Typescript],** an index to *Roster and Records of Iowa Soldiers in the War of Rebellion*, by the Iowa Adjutant General. Contents: vol. 1: A-C, vol. 2: D-G, vol. 3: H-K, vol. 4: L-Mc, vol. 5: N-R, vol. 6: S-T, vol. 7: U-Z., compiled by the Idaho State Historical Society, Boise, ID, 1979, FHL book 977.7 M21 Index, v.1-7.

■ **1861-1865.** See ***Iowa Soldiers Residing in Kansas*** **[Printed Book]**, compiled by Keo-Mah Genealogical Society. From intro: "This publication was copied from a small booklet housed at the Nelson Pioneer Farm in Oskaloosa, Iowa. It evidently was a publication of a magazine called *The Western Veteran,* printed after the Civil War, in Topeka, Kansas. Its purpose was to keep veterans updated as to the whereabouts of their friends and comrades. Therefore, the original booklet was organized by regiments, and contains an alphabetical listing by surname of veterans of the Civil War, giving name and rank, company, regiment and Kansas town of residence." Published by the Iowa Genealogical Society, Des Moines, IA, 1996, 80 pages, FHL book 977.7 M2io.

■ **1862-1910.** See ***Persons Subject to Military Duty, ca. 1862-1910*** **[Microfilm],** from original records of the Iowa Adjutant General's Office, located at the Iowa State Historical Society, Des Moines, IA. Names are organized by county. Filmed by the Genealogical Society of Utah, 1978, 94 rolls, beginning with FHL film #1024847 (Adair co). For a complete list of roll numbers and contents of each roll, see the online FHL catalog page for this title. See **https://familysearch.org/search/catalog/388617.**

■ **1866-1935 City Directories, Des Moines, Polk County, Iowa [Microfilm],** from originals published by various publishers. Filmed by Research Publications, Woodbridge, CT, 1980-1984. FHL has 41 rolls, as follows:

- **1866, 1869, 1871, 1873, & 1874** Des Moines city directory, FHL film #1376808.

- **1876, 1877**, & **1881** Des Moines city directory, FHL film #1376809.
- **1882** (2) & **1884** Des Moines city directories, FHL film #1376810.
- **1886** & **1888** Des Moines city directory, FHL film #1376811.
- **1889** & **1890** Des Moines City Directory, FHL film #1376812.
- **1892** & **1893** Des Moines city and Polk county directory, FHL film #1376813.
- **1894** & **1895** Des Moines, Valley Junction and Polk county directory, FHL film #1376814.
- **1896** & **1897** Des Moines, Valley Junction and Polk county directory, FHL film #1376815.
- **1898** & **1899** Des Moines city, Valley Junction and Polk county directory, FHL film #1376816.
- **1900** & **1901** Des Moines city, Valley Junction and Polk county directory, FHL film #1376817.
- **1902** & **1903** Des Moines city, Valley Junction and Polk county directory, FHL film #1844278.
- **1904** & **1905** Des Moines city, Valley Junction and Polk county directory, FHL film #1844279.
- **1906** Des Moines city, Valley Junction and Polk county directory, FHL film #1844280.
- **1907** Des Moines city, Valley Junction and Polk county directory, FHL film #1844281.
- **1908** Des Moines city and Valley Junction directory, FHL film #1844282.
- **1909** Des Moines city and Valley Junction directory, FHL film #1844283.
- **1910** Des Moines city and Valley Junction directory, FHL film #1844284.
- **1911** Des Moines city and Valley Junction directory, FHL film #1844285.
- **1912** Des Moines city and Valley Junction directory, FHL film #1844286.
- **1913** Des Moines city and Valley Junction directory, FHL film #1844287.
- **1914** Des Moines city and Valley Junction directory, FHL film #1844288.
- **1915** Des Moines city and Valley Junction directory, FHL film #1844289.
- **1916** Des Moines city and Valley Junction directory, FHL film #1844290.
- **1917** Des Moines city and Valley Junction directory, FHL film #1844291.
- **1919** Des Moines city and Valley Junction directory, FHL film #1844292.
- **1920** Des Moines city and Valley Junction directory, FHL film #1844293.
- **1921** Des Moines city and Valley Junction directory, FHL film #1844294.
- **1922** Des Moines city and Valley Junction directory, FHL film #1844295.
- **1923** Des Moines city and Valley Junction directory, FHL film #1844296.
- **1924** Des Moines and Valley Junction directory, FHL film #1844297.
- **1925** Des Moines and Valley Junction directory, FHL film #1844298.
- **1926** Des Moines and Valley Junction directory, FHL film #1844299.
- **1927** Des Moines and Valley Junction directory, FHL film #1844300.
- **1928** Des Moines city directory, including Valley Junction, FHL film #1844301.
- **1929** Des Moines city directory, including Valley Junction, FHL film #1844302.
- **1930** Des Moines city directory, including Valley Junction, FHL film #1844303.
- **1931** Des Moines city directory, including Valley Junction, FHL film #1844304.
- **1932** Des Moines city directory, including Valley Junction, FHL #1844305.
- **1933** Des Moines city directory, including Valley Junction, FHL film #1844306.
- **1934** Des Moines city directory, including Valley Junction, FHL film #1844307.
- **1935** Des Moines city directory, including Valley Junction, FHL film #1844308.

■ **1875 Biographies.** As part of ***A. T. Andreas' Illustrated Historical Atlas of the State of Iowa, 1875*** **[Microfilm]**, from the book by A. T. Andreas, published by Lakeside Press, Chicago, 1875. This is the standard history of Iowa, and includes biographical sketches of Iowa's earliest settlers and statistics from the 1875 state census of Iowa, fully indexed. Filmed by the Genealogical Society of Utah, 1975, 1 roll, FHL film #980875; 3 additional filmings: #908275, #966235, and #981935.

■ ***1880 Federal Census (Short Form), Floyd County, Iowa*** **[Microfilm]**, from the county's original volumes of the 1880 name list, located at the Floyd County Courthouse in Charles City, Iowa. This was a name list prepared from the county's 1880 federal census schedules, a "Short Form" which was to remain in the courthouse for public inspection. The Short Forms were not in family order, but listed for all individuals, regardless of relationship, by the first letter of their surname. After 30 days, the county could do what they wanted with the Short Forms, and most were discarded. This is one of only two county lists that survived for Iowa. Includes name, color, age, and sex. Filmed by the Genealogical Society of Utah, 1987, 1 roll, FHL film #1481693.

■ ***1880 Federal Census (Short Form), Hardin County, Iowa*** **[Microfilm]**, from the county's original volumes of the 1880 name list, located at the Hardin County Courthouse in Eldora, Iowa. This was a name list prepared for the county's 1880 federal census schedules, a "Short Form" which was to remain in the courthouse for public inspection. The Short Forms were not in family order, but listed for all individuals, regardless of relationship, by the first letter of their surname. After 30 days, the county could do what they wanted with the Short Forms, and most were discarded. This is one of only two county lists that survived for Iowa. Includes name, color, age, and sex. Filmed by the Genealogical Society of Utah, 1988, 2 rolls, FHL film #1547838 (Ackley, Etna, Iowa Falls, Hardin, Alden, Ellis Buckeye, Jackson, Clay, and Eldora (A-T); and FHL film #1547839 (Eldora (T-Z), Pleasant, Sherman, Tipton, Concord, Grant, Providence, and Union).

■ ***1884-1935 City Directories, Sioux City, Woodbury County, Iowa* [Microfilm]**, from the originals published by various publishers, filmed by Research Publications, 1980-1995. FHL has 20 rolls, as follows:

- **1884**, **1887**, **1888** & **1889** Sioux City directory, FHL film #2156595.
- **1890**, **1891** & **1892** Sioux City directory, FHL film #2156596.
- **1893**, **1894** & **1895** Sioux City directory, FHL film #2156597.
- **1896**, **1897**, **1898**, **1899** & **1900** Sioux City directory, FHL film #2156598.
- **1899** Sioux City and Woodbury County directories, FHL film #2258312.
- **1901**, **1902** & **1903** Sioux city directory, FHL film #1844203.
- **1904**, **1906** & **1907** Sioux City directory, FHL film #1844204.
- **1908**, **1909** & **1910** Sioux City directory, FHL film #1844205.
- **1911** & **1912** Sioux City directory, FHL film #1844206.
- **1913** & **1914** Sioux City directory, FHL film #1844207.
- **1915** & **1916** Sioux City directory, FHL film #1844208.
- **1917** & **1918** Sioux City directory, FHL film #1844209.
- **1919** & **1920** Sioux City directory, FHL film #1844210.
- **1921** & **1922** Sioux City directory, FHL film #1844211.
- **1923** & **1924** Sioux City directory, FHL film #1844212.
- **1925** & **1926** Sioux City directory, FHL film #1844213.
- **1927** & **1928** Sioux City directory, FHL film #1844214.
- **1929** & **1930** Sioux City directory, FHL film #1844215.
- **1931** & **1932** Sioux City directory, FHL film #1844216.
- **1933**, **1934** & **1935** Sioux City directory, FHL film #1844217.

■ ***1885 Iowa State Census* [Microfilm]**, from the originals at the State Historical Society of Iowa, Des Moines, IA. Some townships are missing, but every county is represented with census schedules of the population. The census schedules provide detailed information for all members of a family, relationship to head of house, an exact property location, whether a street address in a town or an indication of a Range-Township-Section of a farm; age, birthplace by county for a person born in Iowa, or the state/country of birth; nativity of parents, whether first papers filed for aliens; occupation, and military information. Filmed by the Genealogical Society of Utah, 1977, 95 rolls, beginning with FHL film #1021316 (Adair County). For a complete list of roll numbers and contents of each roll, see the online FHL catalog page for this title: **https://familysearch.org/search/catalog/388625.**

■ **1885-1926**. See ***Polk County, Iowa, Newspapers, Des Moines Capital, Index: 1885-1926* [Printed Book]**, compiled by Ankeny Genealogical Society. 3 volumes contain alphabetical listings by surname of persons, events (births, deaths, marriages, marriage licenses, miscellaneous data, divorces, and killed in action in war), date of the event and publication date of the newspaper. Published by the Iowa Genealogical Society, Des Moines, IA, 1996-1997, 3 vols., FHL book 977.758/D1 B32po v.1-3.

■ **1889-1935 City Directories, Council Bluffs, Pottawattamie County, Iowa [Microfilm]**, from originals by various publishers. Filmed by Research Publications, Woodbridge, CT, c1990. FHL has 11 rolls, as follows:

- **1889**, **1892**, **1893** & **1894** Council Bluffs city directory, FHL film #2156587.
- **1895**, **1897**, **1899**, **1900** & **1901** Council Bluffs City directory, FHL film #2156588.
- **1902**, **1904** & **1906** Council Bluffs city directory, FHL film #2308796.
- **1907**, **1908** & **1909** Council Bluffs directory, FHL film #2308797.
- **1910**, **1911** & **1912** Council Bluffs city directory, FHL film #2308798.
- **1913**, **1914** & **1915** Council Bluffs city directory, FHL film #2308799.
- **1916**, **1917** & **1918** Council Bluffs city directory, FHL film #2308800.
- **1919**, **1921, 1922** & **1924** Council Bluffs city directory, FHL film #2308801.
- **1925**, **1926**, **1927** & **1928** Council Bluffs city directory, FHL film #2308802.
- **1929**, **1930**, **1931** & **1932** Council Bluffs city directory, FHL film #2308803.
- **1933**, **1934** & **1935** Council Bluffs city directory, FH film #2308804.

■ **1892 Farm Directory.** See ***Farmers of Iowa: A List of Farmers of Each County With Post Office*** **[Microfilm]**, from the original book published 1892 (publisher not noted). Filmed by the Genealogical Society of Utah, 1978, FHL film #1024846.

■ **1895 Iowa State Census [Microfilm]**, from originals at the State Historical Society of Iowa, Des Moines, Iowa. Complete for all counties. The census schedules provide detailed information about persons, similar to the 1885 but adding special questions for military service in the Civil War and the Spanish American War, including the exact company and regiment of service. Also, the 1895 asks for a person's "Religious Belief." Filmed by the Genealogical Society of Utah, 1977. 121 rolls, beginning with FHL film #1021706 (Adair County). For a complete list of roll numbers and contents of each roll, see the online FHL catalog page for this title. See **https://familysearch.org/search/catalog/388621.**

■ **1897-1904.** See ***Iowa City Register of Voters, 1897-1904*** **[Microfilm],** from originals at the State Historical Society of Iowa, Des Moines, IA. Filmed by the Genealogical Society of Utah, 1990, 4 rolls, beginning with FHL film #1728631 (Register of voters, ward 1, 1897-1903). For a complete list of roll numbers and contents of each, see the online FHL catalog page for this title. See **https://familysearch.org/search/catalog/551006.**

■ **1899 History.** See ***Biographies and Portraits of the Progressive Men of Iowa: Leaders in Business, Politics and the Professions; Together With an Original and Authentic History of the State*** **[Printed Book],** by B.F. Gue and Benjamin Franklin Shambaugh, published by Conaway and Shaw, Des Moines, IA, 1899, 2 vols., FHL book 977.7 D3b. For access to a digital version of this book, see the online FHL catalog page for this title. See **https://familysearch.org/search/catalog/166616.**

■ ***1901-1919 Iowa State Directories*** **[Microfilm]**, from originals published by various publishers. Filmed by Research Publications, Inc., Woodbridge, CT, 1980-1984, 9 rolls at FHL, as follows:

- **1901-1902** Polk's Iowa state gazetteer and business directory, FHL film #1759801.
- **1903-1904** Polk's Iowa state gazetteer and business directory, FHL film #1759802.
- **1905-1906** Polk's Iowa state gazetteer and business directory, FHL film #1759803.
- **1908-1909** Polk's Iowa state gazetteer and business directory, FHL film #1759804.
- **1910-1911** Polk's Iowa state gazetteer and business directory, FHL film #1759805.
- **1912-1913** Polk's Iowa state gazetteer and business directory, FHL film #1759806.
- **1914-1915** Polk's Iowa state gazetteer and business directory, FHL film #1759807.
- **1916-1917** Polk's Iowa state gazetteer and business directory, FHL film #1759807.
- **1918-1919** Polk's Iowa state gazetteer and business directory, FHL film #1759808.

■ ***1901-1935 City Directories, Waterloo, Black Hawk County, Iowa*** **[Microfilm],** from originals in various libraries and societies. Filmed by Research Publications, Woodbridge, CT, c1980, 5 rolls at FHL, as follows:

- **1901**, **1904**, **1906** & **1908** Waterloo city directories, FHL film #2308832.
- **1909**, **1910** & **1912** Waterloo city directories, FHL film #2308833.
- **1921**, **1922** & **1924** Waterloo and Black Hawk County directory, FHL film #2308834.
- **1925**, **1927**, **1928** & **1930** (start) Waterloo and Black Hawk County directories, FHL film #2308835.
- **1930** (end), **1931**, **1933** & **1935** Waterloo and Black Hawk County directories, FHL film #2308836.

■ **1903 History.** See ***History of Iowa From the Earliest Time to the Beginning of the Twentieth Century*** **[Printed Book],** by Benjamin F. Gue, Contents: Vol. 1: Pioneer period; Vol. 2: Civil War; Vol. 3: from 1866 to 1903; Vol. 4: Iowa biography. Published by Century History Co., New York, NY, 4 vols., includes index. FHL book 977.7H2g. To access a digital version of this book (4 vols.), see the online FHL catalog page for this title. See **https://familysearch.org/search/catalog/166700.**

■ ***1903-1935 City Directories, Cedar Rapids, Linn County, Iowa*** **[Microfilm],** from the originals by various publishers. Filmed by Research Publications, Woodbridge, CT. ca1980. FHL has 8 rolls, as follows:

- **1903**, **1904**, **1906** & **1907** Cedar Rapids city directory, FHL film #2308784.
- **1910**, **1911** & **1912** Cedar Rapids city directory, FHL film #2308785.
- **1917**, **1921** Cedar Rapids city directory, FHL film #2308786.
- **1922** & **1923** Cedar Rapids city directory, FHL film #2308787.
- **1924** & **1925** Cedar Rapids city Directory, FHL film #2308788.
- **1926** & **1928** Cedar Rapids city directory, FHL film #2308789.
- **1929**, **1931** & **1932** Cedar Rapids city directory, FHL film #2308790.

- **1933**, **1934** & **1935** Cedar Rapids city directory, FHL film #2308791.

■ ***1905 Iowa State Census Schedules*** **[Microfilm]**, from the original records located at the State Historical Society of Iowa, Des Moines, Iowa. Includes name of each member of a family, age, nativity, time in US, time in Iowa, nativity of parents, and extensive military information, including branch of service, company, regiment, and war. Filmed by the Genealogical Society of Utah, 1985, 453 rolls, beginning with FHL film #1430251 (Adair County). For a complete list of roll numbers and contents of each roll, see the online FHL catalog page for this title. See **https://familysearch.org/search/catalog/486033.**

■ ***1905 Iowa State Census Register*** **[Microfilm]**, from the originals at the State Historical Society of Iowa, Des Moines. Taken from the full census schedules, the *Census Register* is a series of cards, organized by township within each county, showing a page number, surname, first name, post office, township, and town or city. The Register provides a quicker look-up of names in the full census schedules. Filmed by the Genealogical Society of Utah, 1978, 45 rolls, beginning with FHL film #1026366 (Adair and Adams counties). For a complete list of roll numbers and contents of each roll, see the online FHL catalog page for this title. See **https://familysearch.org/search/catalog/411798.**

■ ***1915 Iowa State Census*** **[Microfilm]**, from the extant census records located at the State Historical Society of Iowa, Des Moines, Iowa. The 1915 census name lists were prepared on cards, and organized alphabetically within each county. Cards that were illegible or that contained only a first name appear at the beginning of each county under the heading "miscellaneous." There are a number of duplicate filmings of various counties included in the set. The 1915 census gives a name for each member of a family, relationship to head, age, occupation, total earnings, birthplace, if foreign born, if naturalized, years in Iowa and U.S., marital status, etc. Filmed by the Genealogical Society of Utah, 1985-1986, 1989, 583 rolls, beginning with FHL film #1379445 (Adair County, Abbott, A. – Fredricks, J.). For a complete list of roll numbers and contents of each roll, see the online FHL catalog for this item. See **https://familysearch.org/search/catalog/539259.**

■ ***1925 Iowa State Census*** **[Microfilm],** from original records at the State Historical Society of Iowa, Des Moines, IA. In addition to a person's name, age, marital status, and nativity, this census recorded the full names of each person's parents – the only census ever taken by any state to give a *Father's Name* and *Mother's Maiden Name* for every person listed. Then, incredibly, the 1925 Iowa state census adds the age of both parents, their place of marriage, and where each were born. (Iowa researchers have discovered that when a parent's age is missing, it usually means that parent was deceased). The 1925 also gives religion, details about military service, and more. This was the most comprehensive and final state census taken by the state of Iowa. Filmed by the State Historical Society of Iowa, 1976, 434 rolls, beginning with FHL film #1429191 (Adair County). For a complete list of roll numbers and contents of each roll, see the online FHL catalog page. See **https://familysearch.org/search/catalog/501121.**

■ ***1925 Iowa State Census Index (for Selected Cities)*** **[Microfilm],** for residents of selected cities, from the original records at the State Historical Society of Iowa, Des Moines, Iowa. Arranged by city, then alphabetically by surname. Index lists name, address, book/line (from schedules), county of residence, for the following cities:

- **Boone** (Boone Co.),
- **Cedar Falls** (Black Hawk Co.),
- **Centerville** (Appanoose Co.),
- **Cedar Rapids** (Linn Co.),
- **Clinton** (Clinton Co.),
- **Council Bluffs** (Pottawattamie Co.),
- **Dubuque** (Dubuque Co.),
- **Ottumwa** (Wapello Co.),
- **Sioux City** (Woodbury Co.),
- **Waterloo** (Black Hawk Co.),
- **Davenport** (Scott Co.)
- **Des Moines** (Polk Co.).

Filmed by the State Historical Society of Iowa, Des Moines, IA, 1980, 29 rolls, beginning with FHL film #1430705 (Boone, Cedar Falls, Centerville, & Cedar Rapids, pt. 1). For a complete list of roll number and contents of each roll, see the online FHL catalog page for this item. See **https://familysearch.org/search/catalog/494967.**

# KANSAS
## Censuses & Substitutes, 1854-2009

Kansas Territory was created in May 1854 as part of the unique *Kansas-Nebraska Act*, landmark legislation that allowed the two territories to choose whether they would be a slave state or a free state upon statehood. When Kansas Territory was officially opened to settlement in 1854, pro-slavery settlers from neighboring Missouri rushed to the new territory. But, abolitionist Free-Staters from New England sent settlers to Kansas Territory as well.

**KS Territorial Censuses.** In 1855, Kansas Territory began taking annual censuses, mainly as a means of counting voters and to determine their political views on the slavery issue. In fact, some of these censuses were separated by voters who were "Free State," "Pro-Slavery," or "Doubtful." Territorial censuses were taken in 1855, 1856, 1857, 1858, and 1859. Limited to the names of voters and heads of households, a territorial census served the same purpose as a local election. The KS territorial censuses must be viewed within the historical background of a divided territory, in which thousands of non-residents invaded the area to vote. Over half of the voters were not registered in Kansas. One community census total was shown to have 20 registered voters out of the 600 who voted. But any census name list that survives is worthwhile, because it identifies actual people by name, whether locals or invaders. From 1855-1861, Kansas Territory included a substantial portion of present-day Colorado, and the first censuses taken in that area were those taken by Kansas Territory.

**KS State censuses.** After statehood in 1861, Kansas began taking state censuses as a means of apportioning the seats in the Kansas legislature. The first state census was taken in 1865, followed by 1875, 1885, 1895, 1905, 1915, and the last one in 1925. All surviving territorial and state census originals are located today at the Kansas Historical Society in Topeka. They are all on microfilm, and in cooperation with Ancestry.com, digitized and indexed online. The online KHS "Kansas Names Index' database includes the KS 1895 State Census. Over the years, many periodicals published by genealogical societies in Kansas have printed extracts and indexes to censuses for one or more counties.

## Online Resources of the Kansas Historical Society

The Kansas Historical Society (KHS) website has more historical-genealogical resources available as online databases and indexes than any other state archives website in the U.S. They include the selected KHS databases described below. Other KHS databases are shown as part of the Ancestry.com collections.

■ **Kansas Memory.** This digital archives preserves photographs, documents, and maps important to Kansas history. Use the Search Box to look for a keyword; or Browse by Kansas County (by clicking on a map); or use the Category Browser. See **www.kansasmemory.org.**

■ **Kansas Names Index.** This index searches within all of the combined biographical databases listed below. See **www.kshs.org/p/people/15899.**

- 1895 Kansas State Census
- Affidavits of Alien Enemies and Alien Females, 1917-1918
- Biographical sketches, obituaries, to the early 1900s
- License Application Files of Medical Doctors, 1901-2001
- A Day In My Community
- Fraternal Order Death Notices
- History of the State of Kansas by Andreas, 1883
- Index to Journal of the Kansas Medical Society
- Biographical clippings files
- Kansas Marriage Index, 1854-1861
- Kansas Physicians and Midwives
- Kansas State Soldiers' Home Admissions and Military History of Members
- Index to admissions to the Fort Dodge Soldier's Home from about 1890-1957.
- Knights & Ladies of Security Deaths (see Ancestry)
- Pioneer Women (Lilla Day Monroe Collection)
- The Purple Pinnacle: the Top 40 Athletes in Kansas State History by David Smale, 1998.
- Taps index to death notices of the members of the United Spanish War Veterans group
- Topeka State Hospital Cemetery
- Who Was Who in America (People with Kansas Connections)
- Other Kansas research websites

■ **Kansas Places Index.** This index searches within all of the databases listed below. See **www.kshs.org/p/places-in-kansas/11306.**

- **Post Offices.** The database can be searched by date, town or county to find every known Kansas post office with its dates of operation.
- **Little Known or Extinct Towns of Kansas ("Dead Towns").** Information about approximately 4,500 Kansas towns from the territorial period to ca.1940.

- **Townships in Kansas.** In Kansas, townships are a government entity larger than a town or city, but smaller than a county.
- **Counties.** Brief histories of current and former Kansas counties with a map showing their location and links to additional resources.
- **Cemeteries in Kansas, 1906.** A list of Kansas cemeteries, published in 1906, that gives the county location, but not the names of the people buried there.

■ **Territorial Kansas Online, 1854-1861.** This is a virtual repository for territorial Kansas history. TOPICS: Territorial Politics & Government; Border Warfare; Immigration & Early Settlement; Personalities; and National Debate About Kansas. RESOURCES: Timeline, Annals of Kansas, Lesson Plans, Bibliography, Historic Sites, FAQs, and Related Links. See
**www.territorialkansasonline.org/~imlskto/cgi-bin/index.php?SCREEN=location.**

■ **Kansas Censuses, 1855-1940.** Microfilm of all KS territorial, state, and federal censuses are available at the KHS from 1855 through 1930. The 1940 federal census is available online only. Guides and Indexes for selected years are also available. The Kansas Territorial and State Census records are available online from Ancestry free to Kansans by verifying their driver's license. For the 1855-1940 Kansas Censuses webpage, see
**www.kshs.org/p/kansas-censuses-1855-1930/10961.**

■ **Kansas Military Index.** This index searches (by surname, given name) within all of the databases listed under the categories of Civil War, Spanish-American War, World War I, World War II, Post-World War II Conflicts, and Links to Guides not included in the military index. See
**www.kshs.org/p/kansas-military-index/15797.**

■ **Kansas Newspaper Database (Microfilm and Electronic).** The KHS has a comprehensive collection of newspapers for the state. This is the search screen, where a city, word in title, county, state, or date range can be used to search the database. Visit the site for information about interlibrary loan of newspapers on microfilm or purchase of microfilm See
**www.kshs.org/p/kansas-newspaper-database-microfilm-and-electronic/11528.**

**Kansas Newspapers Online:**

- **Chronicling America.** Historic American Newspapers by the Library of Congress. For the links to Kansas newspapers, see
**http://chroniclingamerica.loc.gov/newspapers/#Kansas.**
- **Kansas Digital Newspapers Program.** This program seeks to digitize and make available on the Internet digital editions of historic Kansas newspapers. See
**www.kshs.org/p/kansas-digital-newspaper-program/16126.**

■ **County Records on Microfilm.** The Kansas Historical Society has thousands of reels of microfilm of Kansas county and city government records. Most of this film came to the society in cooperation with the Genealogical Society of Utah. Visit this site for the list of 105 Kansas counties, and the types of records available for each. See
**www.kshs.org/p/county-records-on-microfilm/11121.**

■ **State Archives Catalogs and Guides.** Use this webpage to access each of the following. See
**www.kshs.org/p/catalogs-and-guides/13858.**

**Online Catalogs.** Includes Archives Catalog - manuscripts and government records, ATLAS online catalog used since 1994; shared with other Topeka libraries, Menninger Archives & World Cat.

**Genealogy Guides.** Includes Kansas Names Index, Kansas Military Index, Kansas Places Index, County records on microfilm, Kansas Censuses, Kansas directories, Vital Records in Kansas, Government Records for Genealogical Research, and Links for other genealogy sites.

**Guides to Online Collections.** Includes Kansas Memory, Territorial Kansas Online, 1854-1861, Civil War on the Western Border, Kansas Historical Collections (Transactions), Kansas Historical Quarterly, Kansas History magazine, and Kansas state agency publications.

**Guides to KSHS Collections.** Includes Subject guides, Architectural & engineering drawings, Audio-visual Material, Books and magazines, Online index to Kansas periodicals, 1978-1981; 2002-2009, State Officials and their records, Manuscripts, Maps, Photographs, Preservation & restoration of collections, Federal publications, and State publications.

## Kansas Databases Online at Ancestry.com

The Ancestry.com subscription website allows free access to all indexes, but to view any particular record requires a membership. Ancestry offers trial memberships and subscriptions for short periods and reduced rates. The following statewide databases at the Ancestry.com website are unique to Kansas under the categories, Census & Voter Lists, Vital Records, Military, Immigrations, et al. See
**http://search.ancestry.com/Places/US/Kansas/Default.aspx.**

■ **1854.** See ***Kansas Election List, 1854* [Online Database],** indexed at the Ancestry.com website. Original data: U.S. House of Representatives, Special Committee. *Report of the Special Committee Appointed to Investigate the Troubles in Kansas; With Views of the Minority of Said Committee.* House of Representatives, Report Number 200, 34th Congress, 1st Session. Washington: Cornelius Wendell, printer, 1856. Ancestry used the book extracted from the report, edited by Debra Graden, 1999. This database has 3,240 records. See
**http://search.ancestry.com/search/db.aspx?dbid=4099.**

■ **1854-1856.** See ***Kansas Voter Registration Lists, 1854-1856* [Online Database],** indexed at the Ancestry.com website. Source: Book, same title, edited by Debra Graden, publ. 1999. With the passage of the Kansas-Nebraska Act of 1854, Kansas became a territory. However, with the issue of slavery still undecided in the Union, this new territory became "bleeding Kansas," as pro- and anti-slavery factions sought local control. This database is a transcription of voter registration lists compiled between 1854 and 1856. It provides the resident's name along with city, district, and precinct or township where they were registered to vote. Page numbers are included. This database has 16,051 records. See
**http://search.ancestry.com/search/db.aspx?dbid=3961.**

■ **1854-1873.** See ***Kansas Marriage Index, 1854-1873* [Online Database],** indexed at the Ancestry.com website. Source: database, same title, compiled by Linda Carpenter, publ. 1998. See the *About* description for the counties included. This database has 21,805 records. See
**http://search.ancestry.com/search/db.aspx?dbid=3444.**

■ **1854-1879.** See ***Kansas Settlers, 1854-1879* [Online Database],** indexed at the Ancestry.com website. Source: Charles Gleed's *Kansas Memorial, A Report of the Old Settlers' Meeting Held at Bismark Grove, Kansas, September 15th and 16th, 1879.* This database has 3,263 records. See
**http://search.ancestry.com/search/db.aspx?dbid=4132.**

■ **1854-1981.** See ***Kansas, Cemetery Records, 1812-1981* [Online Database],** digitized and indexed at the Ancestry.com website. This database is a compilation of cemetery records held at the KHS and scanned onsite. (1812 impossible for Kansas).They include the following titles:

- Jackson County Cemeteries
- Miscellaneous Cemetery Records
- Index to Six Cemeteries of Southeast Kansas
- Civil War Soldiers Buried in Kansas
- Cherokee County Cemeteries Vol. 1
- Cherokee County Cemeteries Vol. 2
- Cherokee County Cemeteries Index
- Big Springs Cemetery, Douglas County
- Belle Springs Brethren Cemetery, Dickinson County
- Church of God in Christ Cemetery Records, Montezuma
- Vital Records, Graham County
- McPherson City Cemetery Records Index
- St. Patrick's Cemetery, Vine Creek
- Wabaunsee County Cemetery
- Vital Records, Stafford County

Some records may provide little more than a name, while others may include some of the following details: burial plot number, birth date, death date, age family relationships (in particular, young children may have parents listed), military rank and unit, descriptions of a marker or cemetery, and cemetery location. This database has 33,123 records. See
**http://search.ancestry.com/search/db.aspx?dbid=5951.**

■ **1854-2009.** See ***Kansas, Vital Record Abstracts, 1854-2009* [Online Database],** indexed at the Ancestry.com website. Source: extractions from archival records by the KHS, Topeka. Each record may include: Name, Age, Birth date and place, Marriage date and place, Death date and place, Spouse name, Spouse age and birth place, and Parents' names. This database has 30,293 records. See
**http://search.ancestry.com/search/db.aspx?dbid=2551.**

■ **1855.** See ***Kansas Territorial Census, 1855* [Online Database**], indexed at the Ancestry.com website. Source: book, same title, edited by Debra Graden, publ. 1999. The name list was taken from the Special Committee's report, indexed at the Ancestry.com website. This database has 3,008 records. See
**http://search.ancestry.com/search/db.aspx?dbid=4056.**

■ **1855-1890.** See ***Kansas, Compiled Census Index, 1850-1890* [Online Database],** indexed at the Ancestry.com website. Source: Accelerated Indexing Systems, Salt Lake City, ca1999. This collection contains the following indexes: 1850 Federal Census Index (has no Kansas people); 1855 Territorial Census Index; 1856 State Census Index; 1857 State Census Index; 1858 State Census Index; 1859 State Census Index; 1860 Federal Census Index; 1870 Federal Census Index; and 1890 Veterans Schedule. This database has 103,882 records. See
**http://search.ancestry.com/search/db.aspx?dbid=3548.**

■ **1855-1911.** See ***Kansas, County Marriages, 1855-1911* [Online Database],** indexed at the Ancestry.com website. Source: FamilySearch extractions from county records on microfilm at the

Family History Library, Salt Lake City, UT. This database has 151,823 records. See
http://search.ancestry.com/search/db.aspx?dbid=60292.

■ **1855-1925.** See ***Kansas State Census Collection, 1855-1925*** **[Online Database],** digitized and indexed at the Ancestry.com website. Source: Microfilm at the KHS, Topeka. This combined database includes the KS Territorial Censuses for 1855, 1856, 1857, 1858, and 1859 (they are often referred to as "Voter Lists" because their main purpose was to determine the number of people who were "Free State," "Pro-Slavery," or "Doubtful"). The KS State Censuses began in 1865, followed by 1875, 1885, 1895, 1905, 1915, and 1925. This is a searchable database, by name, date, keyword, etc., but the database can also be searched using the Browse. This collection is organized by year, county, and township. The database has 8,238,557 records. See
http://search.ancestry.com/search/db.aspx?dbid=1088.

■ **1859.** See ***Leavenworth, Kansas Voter Registration, 1859*** **[Online Database],** indexed at the Ancestry.com website. Source: book, same title, edited by Debra Graden, publ. 1998. This database has 2,953 records. See
http://search.ancestry.com/search/db.aspx?dbid=3489.

■ **1859-1935.** See ***Kansas, Atchison, Topeka and Santa Fe Railway Prior Service Records, 1859-1935*** **[Online Database],** indexed at the Ancestry.com website. Source: AT&SF company records, now at the KHS, Topeka. Prior service refers to employment with the railroad before 29 August 1935, when the Railroad Retirement Board took control of most railway employee pensions. Cards vary in the details they list. Some may include only a name and a department, while others may record a birth date, retirement date, years of service, and other details. This database has 95,958 records. See
http://search.ancestry.com/search/db.aspx?dbid=2122.

■ **1861-1865.** See ***Kansas Civil War Soldiers*** **[Online Database],** indexed at the Ancestry.com website. Source: database compiled by Debra Graden, 1999; extracted from *Kansas Adjutant General Roll, Civil War Soldiers, 1861-1865*. This database provides the soldier's name, rank, residence, enlistment date, and muster date. This database has 20,644 records. See
http://search.ancestry.com/search/db.aspx?dbid=3916.

■ **1862-1868.** See ***Kansas, Civil War Enlistment Papers, 1862, 1863, 1868*** **[Online Database],** indexed at the Ancestry.com website. Source: Enlistment Records of Volunteer Regiments and Batteries, KHS, Topeka. A two-page form for each recruit includes a name, birthplace, age, occupation, enlistment date, unit, and a physical description. This database has 4,707 records. See
http://search.ancestry.com/search/db.aspx?dbid=1766.

■ **1865-1984.** See ***Kansas, Federal Naturalization Records, 1865-1984*** **[Online Database],** digitized and indexed at the Ancestry.com website. Source: National Archives microfilm, records of District Courts; and records of U.S. Attorneys and Marshals. Includes petitions, intentions, and declarations. Searchable fields: Name, Birth Date, Birth Place, and Immigration Year. Additional information that may be provided in the original records includes: Place of Residence, Occupation, Date of Departure, Place of Departure, Place of Arrival, Spouse's Name, Birth Date, and Residence, Number of Children, Each child's Name, Birth Date, Birth Place, and Residence. This database has 31,595 records. See
http://search.ancestry.com/search/db.aspx?dbid=61199.

■ **1866-1931.** See ***Kansas, Grand Army of the Republic Bound Post Records, 1866-1931*** **[Online Database],** indexed at the Ancestry.com website. Source: KHS, Topeka. These bound post records were those retained by each post of the GAR. After the last GAR member in Kansas died in the 1950s, the GAR was disbanded, and these medical rolls and descriptive rolls were transferred to the KHS. Each record may include: Name, Age, Birthplace, Residence, Occupation, Service history, Unit(s), Rank, Discharge details, Engagements, Wounds, Date joined the GAR, and Date and place of death. This database has 29,019 records. See
http://search.ancestry.com/search/db.aspx?dbid=2580.

■ **1873-1969.** See ***Web: Kansas, Fraternal Order Death Index, 1873-1969*** **[Online Database],** indexed at the Ancestry.com website. This database is also accessible at the KHS website as ***Fraternal Order Death Notices.*** Fraternal orders included and dates of coverage are: AOUW = Ancient Order of United Workmen, 1879-1908; KP = Knights of Pythias, 1877-1918; IOOF = Independent Order of Odd Fellows, 1873-1970; Rebekah = Rebekah Assembly of the IOOF, 1891-1953. Each record has a name, place of residence, date of death, and the codename of fraternal order/lodge No. This database has 53,132 records. See
http://search.ancestry.com/search/db.aspx?dbid=70657.

■ **1880-1940.** See ***Kansas, Grand Army of the Republic Post Reports, 1880-1940*** **[Online Database],** indexed at the Ancestry.com website. Source: KHS, Topeka. This collection consists of quarterly muster rolls sent to the state department from 500 local posts. The Grand Army of the Republic (GAR) was a veteran's organization for Union soldiers after the Civil War. The records include: Name, Age, Birthplace, Residence, Occupation, and Military service. This database has 563,516 records. See
**http://search.ancestry.com/search/db.aspx?dbid=1700.**

■ **1885-1911.** See ***Kansas, Births and Christenings Index, 1885-1911*** **[Online Database],** indexed at the Ancestry.com website. Source: FamilySearch extractions from records on microfilm at the Family History Library, Salt Lake City, UT. Each record may include: Name, Gender, Race, Birthplace, Birth date, Christening date, Christening place, Age at christening, Father's name, age, birthplace; Mother's name, age, birthplace; Paternal grandparents, Maternal grandparents, and FHL film number. This database has 51,418 records. See
**http://search.ancestry.com/search/db.aspx?dbid=2567.**

■ **1885-1930.** See ***Kansas, Deaths and Burials, Index, 1885-1930*** **[Online Database],** indexed at the Ancestry.com website. Source: FamilySearch extractions from microfilm of records at the Family History Library, Salt Lake City, UT. Each record may include: Name, Birth date, Birthplace, Age, Occupation, Race, Gender, Residence, Marital status, Spouse, Street address, Date of death, Place of death, Date of burial, Place of burial, Cemetery, Father's name and birthplace, Mother's name and birthplace, and FHL film number. This database has 32,781 records. See
**http://search.ancestry.com/search/db.aspx?dbid=2570.**

■ **1889.** See ***Kansas, Enrollment of Civil War Veterans, 1889*** **[Online Database],** indexed at the Ancestry.com website. Source: Report of the KS Adjutant General: *Enrollment of Ex-Soldiers and Sailors, their Widows and Orphans,* publ. 1889, 69 vols., original at the KHS, Topeka. Various Acts from the 1860s to 1880s authorized pensions for Union veterans. Since most of Civil War veterans were former members of state militia units, it was the responsibility of each state's adjutant general to gather the applications for pensions from individuals. This database of the Kansas enrollments is essential. The application forms were used by veterans, widows, or orphans to state their qualification based on the service records. Each index record has the applicant's name, rank at discharge, state of service, and place of KS residence. The image of each enrollment record reveals a very detailed questionnaire that includes a name of a widow (if applicable) and any orphaned children of a deceased veteran. This database has 50,977 records. See
**http://search.ancestry.com/search/db.aspx?dbid=2956.**

■ ***1890 Census Substitute*** **[Online Database],** indexed at the Ancestry.com website. This is Ancestry's collection of city directories (and other name lists) from all over the U.S. for the time of the lost 1890 federal census. Included are several Kansas databases. Go to *View All Collections Included in this Search* for a complete list of databases, alphabetically by place (county, city, state, etc.), and year. See
**http://search.ancestry.com/search/group/1890census.**

■ **1902-1930.** See ***Web: Kansas, Security Benefit Association, Death Index, 1902-1930*** **[Online Database],** indexed at the Ancestry.com website. This database is also accessible at the KHS website as ***Knights and Ladies of Security/Security Benefit Association.*** The index was compiled from monthly newsletters published by the K & L of Security Assoc., wherein death benefits paid out to members were noted. This database has 10,209 records. See
**http://search.ancestry.com/search/db.aspx?dbid=70658.**

■ **1914-1919.** See ***Kansas, Camp Funston Military Records, 1914-1919*** **[Online Database],** indexed at the Ancestry.com website. Source: Military History Collection, KHS, Topeka. Camp Funston was established at Fort Riley in Kansas as a World War I training center for recruits from Arizona, Colorado, Kansas, Missouri, Nebraska, New Mexico, and South Dakota. This collection includes personnel records from the 89th Division, 353rd Infantry, and the 314th Engineers. Each record may include: Name, Enlistment date, Next of kin, Home address, Education level, Occupation, Rank and serial number, Posts held, Promotions, and Record of injuries. This database has 49,580 records. See
**http://search.ancestry.com/search/db.aspx?dbid=2396.**

■ **1917-1919.** See ***Kansas, World War I Veteran Collection, 1917-1919*** **[Online Database],** indexed at the Ancestry.com website. Source: KHS, Topeka. This is an image only database of newspaper clippings, photos, service records, letters from family and friends, biographical sketches, and other

documents related to Kansas veterans who served in World War I. Materials are filed by the veteran's name, and the files vary widely in content. Browse through the images, organized in alpha groups of about 500-600 pages each. This database has about 25,000 pages. See
**http://search.ancestry.com/search/db.aspx?dbid=2021.**

■ **1919-1961.** See ***Kansas, City and County Census Records, 1919-1961* [Online Database],** digitized and indexed at the Ancestry.com website. Source: KS Board of Agriculture Population Schedules on microfilm at the KHS, Topeka. This is one of the largest non-federal census databases ever done, an exclusive indexing project of the Ancestry World Archives Project. this little-know collection of city and county censuses is separate from the Kansas state censuses or local federal censuses. They were done in two parts: 1) Population schedules, with name(s) in a household; and 2) Agricultural Schedules, with name and address of a head of household, and details about crops and Ag products. Only the population schedules were microfilmed. The original Ag schedules date back to the 1870s, and are available to the public, but only in person at the KHS reading room in Topeka. From 1919 through 1952, the population schedules include a name of a head of household, street address, and the number of persons living at that address. From 1953 through 1961, the schedules listed all members of a family, their ages, and the address. This searchable database is indexed for all city lists, but not all of the county lists. It is possible to browse through the images, organized by year, city, and county. This database has 16,144,107 records. See
**http://search.ancestry.com/search/db.aspx?dbid=2270.**

■ **1930.** *See* ***Kansas, Enrollment of WWI Veterans, 1930* [Online Database],** indexed at the Ancestry.com website. Source: Report of the KS Adjutant General: *Enrollment of World War One Veterans or Their Widows and Orphans,* publ. 1930, on 30 rolls of microfilm at the KHS, Topeka. This database contains forms used to enroll eligible Kansans for World War I veterans' benefits. Forms were to be filled out by anyone who had served in any branch of service during World War I or by a widow or child under sixteen whose deceased husband or father had served. The forms asked for the following details: Name, Branch of service, Address, Widow's name (if applicable), Names and addresses of orphan children under 16, Rank at discharge, Whether wounded or injured (in service) or deceased, and American Legion post if a member. This database has 34,377 records. See
**http://search.ancestry.com/search/db.aspx?dbid=2955.**

■ **1940-1946.** See **Web: Kansas, WWII Selective Service Index, 1940-1946 [Online Database],** indexed at the Ancestry.com website. This database is also assessable at the KHS website as ***World War II Selective Service Records, 1940-1946.*** Each record includes: Name, Entry date, Entry place, Military branch, and Service number. This database has 28,398 records. See
**http://search.ancestry.com/search/db.aspx?dbid=70795.**

---

## Kansas Databases Online at FamilySearch.org

The following databases are available for free at the FamilySearch.org website. To see the current list, visit the Kansas Indexed Historical Records and Kansas Image Only Historical Records webpage. Both lists are updated periodically. See
**https://familysearch.org/search/collection/location/35.**

■ **1854-1936.** See ***Kansas Births and Christenings, 1818-1936* [Online Database],** indexed at the FamilySearch.org website. Source: FamilySearch extractions from birth, baptism, and christening records on microfilm at the Family History Library, Salt Lake City, UT. The starting date of 1818 is impossible. The index contains the following information: Name of child, Birth date, Birthplace, Parent's names, FHL film number, Digital folder number, and Image number. This database has 49,926 records. See
**https://familysearch.org/search/collection/1674839.**

■ **1855-1911.** See ***Kansas County Marriages, 1855-1911* [Online Database],** indexed at the FamilySearch.org website. Source: FamilySearch extractions from marriage registers and records made by county clerks in Kansas. Includes the following counties: Allen, Anderson, Bourbon, Brown, Chase, Chautauqua, Cherokee, Clay, Coffey, Crawford, Doniphan, Douglas, Elk, Franklin, Geary, Greenwood, Harvey, Jackson, Jefferson, Johnson, Labette, Linn, Marshall, McPherson, Miami, Montgomery, Morris, Nemaha, Neosho, Osage, Pottawatomie, Riley, Saline, Sedgwick, Wabaunsee, Washington, Wilson, and Woodson. This database has 392,355 records. See
**https://familysearch.org/search/collection/1851040.**

■ **1885-1930.** See ***Kansas Deaths and Burials, 1885-1930* [Online Database],** indexed at the FamilySearch.org website. Source: FamilySearch extractions from death and burial records on microfilm at the Family History Library, Salt Lake City, UT. The index may include any of the following: Name of the deceased, Date of birth, Place of birth, Marital status, Date of death, Place of death, Parents' names, Name of spouse, Date of burial, and Place of burial. This database has 31,747 records. See **https://familysearch.org/search/collection/1674844**.

■ **1854-1935.** See **Kansas Marriages, 1840-1935 [Online Database],** indexed at the FamilySearch.org website. Source: FamilySearch extractions from marriage records on microfilm at the Family History Library, Salt Lake City, UT. The starting date of 1840 is possible, but unlikely (a recorded marriage between Kansa Indians?). The following is usually included in the index: Name of the groom, Name of the bride, often including the maiden name, Date of the marriage, Place of marriage, and Residences of the bride and groom. This database has 87,932 records. **https://familysearch.org/search/collection/1674845.**

■ **1854-1911.** See **Kansas, Marriages, 1811-1911 [Online Database],** indexed at the FamilySearch.org website. Source: FamilySearch extractions from KHS microfilm of county records. The starting date of 1811 is impossible. The following is usually included in the index: Name of the groom, Name of the bride, often including the maiden name, Date of the marriage, Place of marriage, and Residences of the bride and groom. This database has 185,068 records. See **https://familysearch.org/search/collection/2381595.**

✓ **NOTE:** A Coverage Table at the Wiki for KS Births, KS Marriages, and KS Deaths shows the places and time periods of the original records in the collection. The table indicates how many records the collection has from each Kansas county. At the FamilySearch description for each database, click on "Learn More" to access the Wiki page.

---

## Kansas Databases Online At Various Websites

■ **1854.** See ***List of Settlers, Miami County, Kansas, 1854* [Online Database],** indexed at the USGenWeb site for Miami Co KS. See **www.ksgenweb.com/miami/library/1854Settlers.html**.

■ **1854-1981.** See ***Kansas Newspaper Archives* [Online Database],** digitized and indexed newspapers at the GenealogyBank website for the following cities: Atchison, Baxter Springs, Cedar Vale, Centropolis, Cherokee, Coffeyville, Emporia, Fort Riley, Fort Scott, Hutchinson, Kansas City, Lawrence, Leavenworth, Minneola, Nicodemus, Olathe, Parsons, Peru, Pittsburg, Salina, Sedan, Shawnee, Topeka, Valley Falls, Weir City, Wichita, and Winfield. See **www.genealogybank.com/explore/newspapers/all/usa/kansas.**

■ **1854-2000s.** See ***Digital Library of the KSGenWeb* [Online Databases].** The KSGenWeb is affiliated with the USGenWeb system One of their webpages is the Digital Library of the KSGenWeb. Their Statewide Files & Projects include the following:

- Troubles in Kansas
- "A Standard History of Kansas and Kansans"
- 1917-1918 Civilian Draft Registration Cards
- Old Settlers' Tales
- Criminal X-Ray, October 1915
- The Kansas State Guard 1917-1919
- Alumni News Section of the Graduate Magazine of the University of Kansas
- Letters, Memoirs & Family Stories of our Kansas Ancestors
- 1912 Cyclopedia of Kansas
- The Fighting Twentieth
- 1883 List of Pensioners on the Roll
- Department of the Kansas G.A.R.
- World War II Honor List of Dead and Missing of the State of Kansas
- 1878 County Maps
- Kansas Migrations
- KSGenWeb Digital Library Military Events Page
- Kansas Decennial Census Forms and Agricultural Schedule 2's

This webpage also serves as the access to the Kansas County USGenWeb sites, where name lists are available for all Kansas counties. Typical county records include Bibles, Biographies, Cemeteries, Censuses, Court, Death, Deeds, Directories, Histories, Marriages, Military, Newspapers, Obituaries, Photos, Schools, Tax Lists, Wills, and more. For the Table of Contents page of the Digital Library of the KSGenWeb. See **www.ksgenweb.org/archives**.

■ **1854-2000s.** See **Kansas Collections at World Vital Records [Online Database]**, over 250 databases can be searched at the "Search All Kansas

Collections" search/browse screen at the World Vital Records website. Databases include censuses, directories, family histories, town histories, military rosters, college/school year books, and more. This is a subscription site, but all initial searches are free. A free search can be done for a name, place, year, or keyword. See
**www.worldvitalrecords.com/contentsearch.aspx?p=ks&rt=census.**

■ **1854-2000s.** See ***Linkpendium – Kansas: Family History & Genealogy, Census, Birth, Marriage, Death, Vital Records & More*** **[Online Databases].** Linkpendium is a genealogical portal site with links to state, county, town, and local databases. Currently listed are selected sites for Kansas statewide resources (480), Renamed/Discontinued Counties (40), Allen County (435) Anderson County (387), Atchison County (745), Barber County (392), Barton County (542), Bourbon County (381), Butler County (456) and 98 more Kansas counties. See
**www.linkpendium.com/ks-genealogy.**

■ **1855-1865.** See **History of Bourbon County, Kansas to the Close of 1865 [Online Database]**, digitized and indexed at the USGenWeb site for Bourbon Co KS. See
**www.ksgenweb.com/archives/bourbon/history/1894.**

■ **1855-1870s.** See **Index to The Early Settlements of Atchison County [Online Database]**, indexed at the USGenWeb site for Atchison Co KS. See
**www.ksgenweb.com/atchison/EarlySettlers.html.**

■ **1855-1900s.** See **Naturalization Papers, Washington County, Kansas [Online Database],** indexed at the USGenWeb site for Washington Co KS. See
**www.ksgenweb.com/washingt/naturali.htm.**

■ **1855-1926.** See **Vital Records, Woodson County, Kansas [Online Database]**, includes births and deaths, indexed in alpha groups at the USGenWeb site for Woodson Co KS. See
**www.ksgenweb.com/archives/woodson/vital.**

■ **1855-1956. See Postmasters of Franklin County [Online Database]**, listed at the Franklin CountyKansas.net website. See
**www.franklincountykansas.net/fcgs/v2n1/postmast.htm.**

■ **1855-2001 Probate Records, Coffee County, Kansas [Online Database],** indexed alphabetically by surname groups, case no., party's last name, first name, date of filing, and type of case. Available at the KScourts.org site. For archived database, see
**http://web.archive.org/web/20061020164654/http://www.kscourts.org/dstcts/4coprrec.htm.**

■ **1867-1900s Kansas Original Land Owners.** See the ***Family Maps*** series for Kansas counties, maps of all original land patents, compiled by Greg Boyd, publ. Arphax Publishing Co., Norman, OK. At this writing, *Family Maps* books have been published for Ford County and Meade County. See
**www.arphax.com.**

■ **1984-Current.** See ***Kansas Recent Newspaper Obituaries*** **[Online Database],** digitized and indexed newspaper obituaries at the GenealogyBank website, including newspapers for Abilene, Augusta, Chanute, Columbus, Derby, Dodge City, El Dorado, Emporia, Garden City, Girard, Greensburg, Hays, Hutchinson, Kansas City, Lansing, Lawrence, Leavenworth, Liberal, Manhattan, McPherson, Newton, Olathe, Ottawa, Parsons, Pittsburg, Prairie Village, Pratt, Salina, St. John, Topeka, Wellington, and Wichita, Kansas. See
**www.genealogybank.com/explore/obituaries/all/usa/kansas.**

## Kansas Periodical Articles
### Censuses & Substitute Name Lists in Genealogical Periodicals

PERSI (PERiodical Source Index) is a digitized database project of the Allen County Public Library (ACPL), Fort Wayne, IN. Since 1986, the PERSI extractors have indexed article titles, places, and surnames from over 11,000 genealogical & historical periodicals. The PERSI database is currently available online through the **FindMyPast.com** subscription website. The Genealogy Center of the ACPL in Fort Wayne IN holds all 11,000 periodicals and will make copies of any article by special request. To obtain an order form for requesting a printed copy of any article indexed in the PERSI database, see
**http://genealogycenter.org/docs/default-source/resources/articlerequest.pdf?sfvrsn=2.**

**Kansas PERSI Search:** Using the FindMyPast.com website, the keywords "Kansas State Census" had 89 results. "Territorial Census" had 28 results. A sampling of Kansas census articles available is shown below:

■ **"1855 Kansas Territorial Census" [Printed Article],** name index serialized in *Kansas Records and Reviews*, beginning with Vol. 1, (Apr 1994); and in *Bluestem Root Diggers Genealogical Quarterly* (Fox Valley Genealogical Society, Eureka, KS), starting with Vol. 6, No. 3 (Jul 1996).

■ **"1856 Kansas Territorial Census, Geary County" [Printed Article]**, name list in *Kansas Kin* (Riley County Genealogical Society, Manhattan, KS), Vol. 18, No. 1 (Feb 1980).

■ **"1856 Kansas Territorial Census, Pottawatomie County" [Printed Article[**, name list in *Kansas Kin* (Riley County Genealogical Society, Manhattan, KS) Vol. 18, No. 1 (Feb 1980).

■ **"1856 Kansas Territorial Census, Riley County" [Printed Article]**, name list in *Kansas Kin* (Riley County Genealogical Society, Manhattan, KS), Vol. 18, No. 1 (Feb 1980).

■ **"1857 Kansas Territorial Census, Bourbon" County [Printed Article]**, name list in *Relatively Seeking* (Columbus, KS), Vol. 9, No. 1 (Spring 1988).

■ **"1857 Kansas Territorial Census, Calhoun County" [Printed Article]**, name list in *Topeka Genealogical Society Quarterly*, Vol. 3, No. 1 (Jan 1973).

■ **"1857 Kansas Territorial Census, Davis County (now Geary County)" [Printed Article]**, name list in *Kansas Kin* (Riley County Genealogical Society, Manhattan, KS), Vol. 17, No. 2 (May 1979).

■ **1857 Kansas Territorial Census, Douglas County [Printed Article]**, name list in *Pioneer*, Vol. 6, No. 1 (Summer 1982).

■ **"1857 Kansas Territorial Census, Jefferson County"[Printed Article]**, name list in *Yesteryears* (Wilson County Historical Society, Fredonia, KS) Vol. 5, No. 2 (Oct 1984).

■ **"1857 Kansas Territorial Census, Marshall County" [Printed Article]**, name list in *Kansas Kin* (Riley County Genealogical Society, Manhattan, KS), Vol. 17, No. 2 (May 1979).

■ **"1857 Kansas Territorial Census, McGee County" [Printed Article]**, name list in *Relatively Seeking* (Columbus, KS), Vol. 9, No. 1 (Spring 1988).

■ **"1857 Kansas Territorial Census, Nemaha County" [Printed Article]**, name list in *Nemaha County Genealogical Society Newsletter* (Seneca, KS), Vol. 2, No. 3 (Feb 1995). An online version of this name list was indexed at the USGenWeb site for Nemaha Co KS. See **http://files.usgwarchives.net/ks/nemaha/census/1857cens.txt.**

■ **"1857 Kansas Territorial Census, Neosho County" [Printed Article]**, name list in *Relatively Seeking* (Columbus, KS), Vol. 9, No. 1 (Spring 1988).

■ **"1857 Kansas Territorial Census, Pottawatomie County" [Printed Article]**, name list in *Kansas Kin* (Riley County Genealogical Society, Manhattan, KS), Vol. 17, No. 2 (May 1979).

■ **"1858 Kansas Territorial Census, Marshall County" [Printed Article]**, name list in *Kansas Kin* (Riley County Genealogical Society, Manhattan, KS), Vol. 20, No. 3 (Aug 1982).

■ **"1859 Kansas Territorial Census, Pottawatomie County" [Printed Article]**, name list in *Kansas Kin* (Riley County Genealogical Society, Manhattan, KS), Vol. 18, No. 4 (Nov 1980).

■ **"1859 Kansas Territorial Census, Shawnee County" [Printed Article]**, name list in *Hedge Post*, Vol. 25, No. 3 (Dec 1999).

■ **"1859 Kansas Territorial Census, Wabaunsee County" [Printed Article]**, in *Kansas Kin* (Riley County Genealogical Society, Manhattan, KS), Vol. 19, No. 2 (May 1981).

■ **"1859 Kansas Territorial Census, Washington County" [Printed Article]**, name list in *Kansas Kin* (Riley County Genealogical Society, Manhattan, KS), Vol. 18, No. 3 (Aug 1980).

■ **"1859 Kansas Territorial Census, Wyandot County" [Printed Article]**, see "Members of Wyandot families, 1859," in *Kansas State Historical Society Collections*, Vol. 15 (1919).

■ **"1865 Kansas State Census, Bourbon County" [Printed Article]**, name list in *Four States Genealogist* (Galena, KS), Vol. 2, No. 2 (Jan 1970).

■ **"1865 Kansas State Census, Butler County" [Printed Article]**, extract and index in *Midwest Genealogical Register* (Wichita, KS), Vol. 19, No. 3 (Oct 1984).

■ **"1865 Kansas State Census, Franklin County" [Printed Article]**, surname index in *Franklin County Kansas Genealogical Society Quarterly* (Ottawa, KS), Vol. 3, No. 2 (Feb 1995).

■ **"1875 Kansas State Census, Barton County" [Printed Article]**, name list in *Barton County Genealogical Society Quarterly* (Great Bend, KS), beginning with Vol. 10, No. 2 (Spring 1990).

■ **"1875 Kansas State Census, Franklin County" [Printed Article]**, surname index in *Franklin County Kansas Genealogical Society Quarterly* (Ottawa, KS), Vol. 3, No. 3 (Aug 1995).

■ **"1885 Kansas State Census, Butler County" [Printed Article]**, name list published serially in *Midwest Genealogical Register* (Wichita, KS), beginning with Vol. 18, No. 2 (Jul 1983).

■ **"1885 Kansas State Census, Cherokee County" [Printed Article],** complete name index published in *Relatively Seeking* (Columbus, KS), Vol. 11, No. 1 (Spring 2000).

■ **"1885 Kansas State Census, Franklin County" [Printed Article]**, name lists by townships, in *Franklin County Kansas Genealogical Society Quarterly* (Ottawa, KS), beginning with Vol. 7, No. 1 (1999).

■ **"1895 Kansas State Census, Cherokee County" [Printed Article]**, name list in *Prospectors, Diggers, and Doers*, beginning with Vol. 5 (1983).

■ **"1895 Kansas State Census, Barton County" [Printed Article]**, name list in *Barton County Genealogical Society Quarterly (Great Bend, KS)*, beginning with Vol. 2, No. 2 (1982).

■ **"1895 Kansas State Census, Morton County" [Printed Article]**, in *Genealogical Council of Kansas Newsletter* (Topeka, KS), beginning with Vol. 21, No. 1 (Jul 1995).

■ **"1895 Kansas State Census, Sedgwick County" [Printed Article]**, see "Residents age 21+ years, 1895," in *Midwest Genealogical Register* (Wichita, KS), Vol. 6, No. 1 (Jun 1971).

■ **1905 Kansas State Census, Wilson County [Printed Article]**, index of names in *Heritage Genealogical Society Quarterly*, Vol. 16, No. 2 (Sep 1986) through Vol. 17, No. 1 (Jul 1987).

## Kansas Books & Microfilms at the Family History Library (and Kansas Historical Society)

Kansas territorial and state censuses, and statewide census substitutes are cited below in chronological order. Each item includes a FHL book number or FHL film number, which can be used to search the FHL catalog for more details. To review an item, start at the FamilySearch catalog search page. See **https://familysearch.org/search/catalog/results.** Select "Search by Place" then "United States, Kansas" to see a list of catalog categories. Or, select "Call Number" then type an FHL book number; or select "Film/Fiche Number" to view a specific title.
**Note:** Several of the KS state census schedules and indexes on microfilm are located only at the KHS in Topeka. Included here with the FHL films, they are listed by date and include their KHS call nos.

■ **1854-1856.** See ***Report of the Special Committee Appointed to Investigate the Troubles in Kansas, With the Views of the Minority of Said Committee* [Digitized Book]**, original published Washington, DC, C. Wendell, Printer, 1856, 1,206 pages. Digitized by the Genealogical Society of Utah, 2013, from original copy at the Allen County Public Library, Ft. Wayne, IN. To view the digital images, see the online FHL catalog page for this title:
**https://familysearch.org/search/catalog/2115850.**

■ **1854-1856.** See ***An Index to the Report of the Special Committee Appointed to Investigate the Troubles in Kansas, 1856* [Printed Book & Microfilm]**, compiled by Robert A. Hodge, published by the author, Fredericksburg, Virginia, 1984, 2 vols. 396 pages. The Kansas-Nebraska Act of 1854 provided for the organization of the Kansas Territory in preparation for statehood. This act required the citizens of the territory to vote on the issue of slavery. Due to disagreement as to what constituted authorized voters, the House of Representatives of the U.S. Congress appointed a special committee to investigate the issue. The bulk of the report consisted of testimonies, lists of names from the census records, poll books and voting registers. This is an index to that report. Contents: Vol. 1: A-L. Vol. 2: M-Z. FHL book 978.1 X3h, v.1 & 2, also on 6 microfiche, FHL fiche #6111324.

■ **1854-1856.** See ***Kansas Pioneers of 1855: That Came by Way of New England Emigrant Aid Company* [Printed Book]**, extracted by Debra F. Graden. In 1856 the U.S. House of Representatives ordered a special committee to investigate the pro-slave vs free-state troubles in Kansas. One purpose of the hearings was to determine whether the Massachusetts Emigrant Aid Society hired men to come to Kansas solely to manipulate the voting. This extract contains excerpts from testimony given by some of the settlers whose emigration to Kansas was sponsored by the New England Emigrant Aid Society. Also includes lists of all who emigrated to Kansas under the Emigrant Aid Society's sponsorship during early 1855. Published by the author, Leavenworth, KS, 1997, 72 pages, FHL book 978.1 W2g.

■ **1854-1856.** See ***The Conquest of Kansas: by Missouri and her Allies; a History of the Troubles in Kansas, from the Passage of the Organic Act Until the Close of July, 1856*** **[Digitized book]**, by William Phillips, published Boston: Phillips, Sampson and Co., 1856, 414 pages. This is a history written during the era of *Bleeding Kansas*, and is a rather one-sided view of the events taking place there. Written by a Boston editor, obviously on the Free-Stater side of things, he offers no apologies for his viewpoints. The book is listed here because many of the names of the players involved in the conflict are mentioned. See the FHL catalog page to access the digital images of this book. **https://familysearch.org/search/catalog/2115851.**

■ **1854-1861.** See ***Death Notices from Kansas Territorial Newspapers, 1854-1861*** **[Printed Book]**, compiled by Alberta Pantle, originally published in the Kansas Historical Quarterly, reprinted by the Jefferson Co Genealogical Society, Oskaloosa, KS, ca1985, FHL book 978.1 V4p. For a digital version of this title, see the online FHL catalog page. See **https://familysearch.org/search/catalog/360360.**

■ **1854-1880s**. See ***Pioneers of the Bluestem Prairie, Full Name Index*** **[Printed Book]**, compiled and published by the Riley County Genealogical Society, Manhattan, KS, 2005, 212 pages, FHL book 978.1 D3pi index.

■ **1854-1900s**. See ***Cemetery Records of Kansas*** **[Printed Books],** compiled by members of the Kansas Mission (LDS), published by the Family History Library, Salt Lake City, 1966 – , 18 vols., includes the names of persons buried, name of cemetery, and name of county, as follows: Vol. 1: Cemeteries in Allen, Chase, Dickinson, Geary, Gove, Gray, Harvey, Montgomery, Pottawatomie, Reno, Riley, Sedgwick, and Sumner counties. Vol. 2: Hamilton, Harvey, Meade, Montgomery, Neosho, Rice, Riley, Saline, and Stafford counties. Vol. 3: Pottawatomie, and Sedgwick counties. Vol. 4: Butler, Finney, Grant, Kearney, Logan, Saline, Stanton, Pottawatomie, and Riley counties. Vol. 5: Allen, Dickinson, Geary, Harvey, Labette, Lyon, Montgomery, Neosho, and Sedgwick counties. Vol. 6: Butler, Harvey, Montgomery, Pottawatomie, Riley, Saline, and Sedgwick counties. Vol. 7: Butler, Clay, Montgomery, Marshal, Harvey, Seward, Sumner, Wabaunsee, Geary, Pottawatomie, and Riley counties. Vol. 8: Pottawatomie county. Vol. 9: Butler, Hamilton, Marshall, Montgomery, Pottawatomie, and Riley counties. Vol. 11: Clay, Cowley, Finney, Franklin, Grant, Greeley, Harvey, Haskell, Lincoln, Marshall, Montgomery, Morton, Pottawatomie, Saline, Sedgwick, Seward and Wichita counties. Vol. 11: Cowley, Edwards, Ford, Gray, Hodgeman, Edwards, Ford, Gray, and Hodgeman counties. Vol. 12: McPherson, Marshall, Montgomery, Reno, Sedgwick, Seward, Sumner, and Thomas counties. Vol. 13: Gove, Jewell, Montgomery, Ottawa, Saline, Scott, Sedgwick, Seward, Wallace, and Wichita counties. Vol. 14: Butler, Coffey, Greeley, Greenwood, Kingman, Republic, Sherman, Sumner, and Wallace counties. Vol. 15: Butler, Coffey, Greenwood, Kingman, Sedgwick, and Sumner counties. Vol. 16: Butler, Greenwood, Harvey, Jewell, Kingman, Ottawa, Sedgwick, and Sumner counties. Vol. 17: Cloud and Ottawa counties. Vol. 18: Butler, Crawford, Ellis, Jefferson, Jewell, Marion, Norton, Republic, Rooks, Russell, and Stafford counties. See FHL book 978.1 V22 v.1-18. Names of cemeteries/counties for all 18 volumes were indexed in ***Cemetery Records of Kansas, Combined Table of Contents***, compiled by James Davis Moore, published by Genidex, Santa Margarita, CA, 1967, 10 pages, FHL book 978.1 V22 index.

■ **1854-1917.** See ***Roll of Attorneys of the State of Kansas: Arranged (First) by Counties, and (Second) Alphabetically Regardless of Counties, Also a Register of the Supreme Court and Court Officers from 1854 to date, etc.*** **[Digitized Book]**, by D. A. Valentine, original published by the state printer, Topeka, KS, 1917, 65 pages. To view the digital images of the entire book, see the FHL catalog page for this title:
**https://familysearch.org/search/catalog/2013775.**

■ **1854-2001.** ***Kansas Biographical Index: Town, Community & Organization Histories: More Than 35,000 Citations From 258 Volumes of Kansas Town, Community and Organization Histories***, **[Printed Book]**, compiled by Patricia Douglass Smith and Stanley Clifford Smith, published by the authors, Garden City, KS, 2001, 1st Edition, 328 pages. 2nd Edition: "69,000 Citations From 183 Volumes." Index lists name of person, county or community name, and source, and page number in original source. FHL book 978.1 D32sp (1st ed.) and 978.1 D32sm (2nd ed.).

■ *1855 Kansas Territorial Census* **[Microfilm],** from the originals at the KHS, Topeka. The 1855 census, called by the governor, lists the inhabitants of Kansas Territory by election districts. There is a map at the beginning of the microfilm showing the location of the election districts. KHS film #K-1 shows election districts, filmed in the following order: 1-4; 7-8; 5-6; 9-13; 15; 14; and 16-17. Reel KS-1 contains a name index to the entire state. Filmed by the society, 1951. FHL's copy is film #570188.

■ *1856, 1857, and 1858 Kansas Territorial Censuses* **[Microfilm]**, from the original records at the KHS, Topeka. The 1856, 1857, and 1858 census name lists were filmed together on one roll (KHS reel no. K-1). Contents: **1856:** 4th district, Kansas Territory (includes part of Douglas, Johnson and Franklin counties). District No. 4 was divided by "Free State," "Pro-Slavery," or "Doubtful." **1857:** Counties of Allen (part of 18th district), 4th district (copy of 1856 list), Anderson, Atchison (3rd district), Bourbon, Dorn, McGee, Brown, Calhoun, Davis, Doniphan, Douglas, Jefferson, Johnson, Leavenworth, Linn, Lykins, Marshall, Nemaha, Pottawatomie, and Riley. Also the census of Shawnees, native or adopted. **1858:** Johnson and Marshall counties only. These census records represent only a partial listing of voters. Filmed by the Kansas Historical Society, 1972, 1 roll, FHL film #1405337. For descriptions/call nos. of the 1855, 1856, 1857, 1858, and 1859 Kansas territorial censuses, visit the Kansas Historical Society webpage: **www.kshs.org/p/kansas-territorial-censuses-1855-1859/10960.**

■ **1856-1858.** See ***Kansas 1856-1858*** **[Printed Index]**, edited by Ronald Vern Jackson, et al, published by Accelerated Indexing Systems, North Salt Lake, UT, 1987, 318 pages. FHL book 978.1 X2k 1856-1858.

■ *1859 Kansas Territorial Census* **[Microfilm],** from the original records at the KHS, Topeka. The census lists voters by county, giving names of voters, dates of settlement, heads of families not voters, number of minors, number of colored persons, total, and remarks (often gives occupation). Filmed by the KSHS, 1972, reel No. K-1, FHL film #1654575.

■ *1860 Kansas Territory Federal Census (Federal Copy)* **[Microfilm]**, from the original records at the National Archives, Washington, DC. Since the KHS has the original territorial copy of the same federal census schedules, a comparison can be made for possible copying errors (very common). Filmed twice by the National Archives, 1960, 1967, 9 rolls, beginning with FHL film #803346 (2nd filming, Allen, Anderson, Atchison, Bourbon, and Breckenridge counties). For a complete list of roll numbers and contents of each roll, see the online FHL catalog page for this title: See **https://familysearch.org/search/catalog/704817.**

■ *1860 Kansas Territory Federal Census (Territory's Original Copy) and WPA Index* **[Microfilm],** from the original records at the KHS, Topeka. (No copy at FHL). This census manuscript is the original territorial set of the 1860 federal census, filmed separately from the federal copy. It is also fairly complete, taken six months prior to statehood, and includes the area around Denver City, now Colorado. This Kansas original set was used to make a copy to be sent to the Census Office in Washington, DC. Filmed by the KHS, 4 reels. In addition to the four reels of census schedules, a handwritten, eleven volume name index to the 1860 Kansas Territory Census was compiled by the WPA in the late 1930s and the index was microfilmed by the KHS on 33 reels. This index may differ from any printed or online index to the 1860 federal census schedules taken from the federal copy. For information, indexes, and the microfilm of the 1860 federal census schedules, see **www.kshs.org/genealogists/census/kansas/census1860ks.htm.**

■ **1860**. See ***Kansas Territorial Settlers of 1860 who were born in Tennessee, Virginia, North Carolina and South Carolina: A Compilation With Historical Annotations and Editorial Comment*** **[Printed Book]**, by Clara Hamlett Robertson, published by Genealogical Publishing Co., Inc. Baltimore, 1976, 187 pages. Taken from the WPA index of the eleven-volume hand-written census books in the Kansas Historical Society archives together with maps of Kansas and eastern Colorado showing the area included in Kansas Territory, 1854-1860. FHL book 978.1 H2ro.

■ **1860-1930.** See ***Kansas Orphan Train Riders – These We Know*** **[Printed Book]**, by Robert A. Hodge, first compiled in 1996 for the annual Kansas

Orphan Train Reunion Group, Great Bend, Kansas. From 1860-1930, an estimated 5,000+ orphans and abandoned children were gathered from New York and brought to Kansas. This book contains three annual reports for the years 1996, 1997, and 1998, each with documented accounts of confirmed train arrivals arranged in geographical, then chronological order, and adds orphan train riders from sources other than the newspaper reports of their arrivals in Kansas. Published by the author, Emporia, KS, 1996-1998, 160+ pages, FHL book 978.1 J3h.

■ **1861-1865.** See ***Index to Compiled Service Records of Volunteer Union Soldiers Who Served in Organizations From the State of Kansas*** **[Microfilm]**, from the originals of the Adjutant General's Office, now at the National Archives, Washington, DC. Indexed by surname of soldier. Filmed by the National Archives, Washington, DC, 1964, FHL has 10 rolls, as follows:

- A-Br, FHL film #881837.
- Bu-C, FHL film #881838.
- D-F, FHL film #881839.
- G-Hom, FHL film #881840.
- Hon-Le, FHL film #881841.
- Lg-Mi, FHL film #881842.
- Mo-Ral, FHL film #881843.
- Ram-Sk, FHL film #881844.
- Sl-U, FHL film #881845.
- V-Z, FHL film #881846.

■ ***1862-1866 Internal Revenue Lists for Kansas*** **[Microfilm]**, from the originals at the National Archives, Central Plains Region, Kansas City, MO. Filmed by the National Archives, 1985, 3 rolls, as follows:

- Annual lists 1863-1864; Monthly lists Sept. 1862-Dec. 1864; and Special lists Aug.-Dec. 1864, FHL film #1578484.
- Annual lists 1865; Monthly lists 1865; Special lists 1865, FHL film #1578485.
- Annual lists 1866; Monthly lists 1866, FHL film #1578486.

■ ***1865 Kansas State Census*** **[Microfilm]**, from the originals at the KHS, Topeka. The 1865 census lists all members of a household by name, including age, sex, race or color, and state or country of birth. Filmed by the KHS, 1951, 8 rolls, (FHL set has 9 rolls) as follows:

- Allen, Anderson, and Atchison Counties, KHS reel K-1, FHL film #570189.
- Bourbon, Brown, Butler, Chase, Clay and Coffey Counties, KHS reel K-2; FHL film #570190.
- Davies, Dickinson, Doniphan and Douglas Counties, KSHS reel K-3; FHL film #570191 (excludes Douglas).
- Douglas County, FHL film #570192.
- Franklin, Greenwood, Jackson, Jefferson, and Johnson Counties, KHS reel K-4; FHL film #570193.
- Leavenworth County, KHS reel K-5; FHL film #570194.
- Linn, Lyon, Marion, Marshall, Miami and Morris Counties, KHS reel K-6; FHL film #570195.
- Nemaha, Neosho, Osage, Ottawa, Pottawatomie, Riley, Saline, Shawnee, Wabaunsee, Woodson, and Wyandotte Counties, KHS reel K-7; FHL film #570196.
- Social Statistics (no names listed), KSHS reel K-8; FHL film #570197.

For indexes and KHS call nos. of the KS 1865 state census schedules, see **www.kshs.org/genealogists/census/kansas/census1865ks.htm#microfilm.**

■ ***1865 Kansas State Census Index*** **[Microfilm]**, available at the KHS, Topeka. (No copy at FHL). The KHS microfilmed index circulates through interlibrary loan. Filmed by the KHS, 37 rolls, beginning with KS-1, No Name - Babcock, Eli). For indexes and microfilm of the KS 1865 state census schedules, see **www.kshs.org/genealogists/census/kansas/census1865ks.htm#microfilm.**

■ ***1868-1935 City Directories, Topeka, Kansas*** **[Microfilm]**, from originals of various publishers. Includes directories for 1868-1869, 1870-1871, 1871, 1872-1873, 1876-1877, 1878-1879, 1880, 1902, 1906, 1907, 1909, 1910, 1912, 1916, 1921, 1924, 1925, 1926, 1927-1928, 1929-1930, 1931, 1933, and 1935. Filmed by Research Publications, Woodbridge, CT, 1980-1984, 6 rolls, beginning with FHL film #1377556 (1868-1880 Topeka directories). For a complete list of roll numbers and contents of each roll, see the online FHL catalog page: **https://familysearch.org/search/catalog/546282.**

■ ***1875 Kansas State Census*** **[Microfilm],** from originals at the KHS, Topeka. (No copy at FHL). The 1875 census lists all members of household by name, including age, sex, race or color, state or country of birth, and where from to Kansas (state or country). Filmed by the KHS, 21 rolls, 1951, beginning with KHS reel 1875 K-1 (Allen, Anderson, Atchison and Barber Counties). For the indexes and microfilm of the KS 1875 state census schedules, see **www.kshs.org/p/kansas-1875-state-census/10946.**

The FHL set contains 23 rolls, beginning with FHL film #570198 (Allen – Barber counties). For a complete list of roll numbers and the contents of each roll, see the online FHL catalog page for this title. See **https://familysearch.org/search/catalog/188296.**

■ **1875 Kansas State Census Index [Microfilm]**, available at the KHS, Topeka. (No copy at FHL). The KSHS microfilm index circulates through interlibrary loan. List the year and reel number when placing an interlibrary loan request. Filmed by the KHS, 157 rolls, beginning with reel #KS-1 (Child – Alexander, E. M.). For indexes and microfilm of the KS 1875 state census schedules, see **www.kshs.org/p/kansas-1875-state-census/10946.**

■ ***1880 Kansas Federal Census (Short Form), Brown County, Kansas* [Microfilm]**, from the original records at the Brown County Courthouse in Hiawatha, Kansas. FHL title: ***List of Persons in Brown County, Kansas***. This is the county's original copy of the 1880 federal census, often called the "Short Form." The name lists are divided by township and arranged within each township in alphabetical order by the first letter of a surname. The abbreviated list gives a name, color, sex and age only. Filmed by the Genealogical Society of Utah, 1993, 1 roll, FHL film #1871055.

■ ***1880 Kansas Post Offices: Originally Published in Edwin Green's Leavenworth City Directory* [Digitized Book]**, extracted by Debra F. Graden, ca2000, 29 pages. To view a digital version of this book, visit the online FHL catalog page: **https://familysearch.org/search/catalog/1531089.**

■ **1883.** See ***History of the State of Kansas: Containing a Full Account of its Growth From an Uninhabited Territory to a Wealthy and Important State, of its Early Settlement, A Supplementary History and Description of its Counties, Cities, Towns and Villages, Their Advantages, Industries and Commerce, to Which Are Added Biographical Sketches and Portraits of Prominent Men and Early Settlers* [Printed Book & Microfilm]**, by A. T. Andreas, original published Chicago, 1883, reprint published by Walsworth Pub. Co., Marceline, MO, 1976, 2 vols., Includes index. FHL book 978.1 H2hi 1976 and FHL film #982248.

■ ***1885 Kansas State Census* [Microfilm]**, from the originals at the KHS, Topeka. The 1885 census lists all members of a household by name, including age, sex, race or color, and state or country of birth. Also listed: where from to Kansas (state or country) and military record (condition of discharge, state of enlistment, letter or name of company or command, number of regiment or other organization to which attached, arm of the service, and name of military prison if confined in one). Filmed by the society, 1969-1970, 146 rolls beginning with KHS reel K-1 (Allen Co. – Humboldt city and twp.; Iola Twp.). For indexes and microfilm of the KS 1885 state census schedules, see
**www.kshs.org/p/kansas-1885-state-census/10948#microfilm.**
The FHL set contains of 151 rolls, beginning with FHL film #975699 (Allen Co. - Humboldt city and twp.; Iola Twp.). For a complete list of roll numbers and contents of each roll, see the online FHL catalog page for this title:
**https://familysearch.org/search/catalog/292166.**

■ ***1885 Kansas State Census Index (City of Topeka)* [Microfilm]**, available at the KHS, Topeka. (No copy at FHL). The KSHS microfilm index circulates through interlibrary loan. List the year and reel number when placing an interlibrary loan request. Filmed by the KSHS, 7 rolls, beginning with reel #KS-1 (Abarr, Mary - Collisi, Wm.). For the indexes and microfilm of the KS 1885 state census schedules, see
**www.kshs.org/p/kansas-1885-state-census/10948#microfilm.**

■ ***1886-1935 City Directories, Wichita, Kansas* [Microfilm]**, from the originals by various publishers, Includes directories for 1886, 1887, 1888, 1892, 1894, 1898-1899, 1900, 1903-1904, 1904-1905, 1906, 1907, 1908, 1909, 1910, 1911, 1912, 1913, 1914, 1915, 1916, 1917, 1918, 1919, 1920, 1922, 1923, 1924, 1925, 1926, 1927, 1928, 1929, 1930, 1931, 1932, 1934, and 1935. Filmed by Research Publications, Woodbridge, CT, ca1995, 16 rolls, beginning with FHL film #2258174 (1866 Directory of Wichita). For a complete list of roll numbers and contents of each roll, see the online FHL catalog for this title:
**https://familysearch.org/search/catalog/1025593.**

■ ***1895 Kansas State Census* [Microfilm]**, from the originals at the KHS, Topeka. The 1895 census lists all members of the household by name, including age, sex, race or color, and state or country of birth. Also listed: where from to Kansas (state or country) and military record (condition of discharge, state of enlistment, letter or name of company or command, number of regiment or other organization to which

attached, arm of the service, and name of military prison if confined in one). Filmed by the society, 1953-1958, KHS set contains 169 rolls, beginning with #1895-K-1 (Allen County, townships, A-Z) For the Indexes and Microfilm of the KS 1895 state census schedules, see
**www.kshs.org/p/kansas-1895-state-census/10951.**
The FHL set contains 202 rolls, beginning with FHL film #570221 (Allen County, townships, C-S). For a complete list of roll numbers and contents of each roll, see the online FHL catalog page for this title:
**https://familysearch.org/search/catalog/188308.**

■ ***1895 Kansas State Census Index*** **[Microfilm & Online Database]**, available at the KHS, Topeka. (No copy at FHL). Includes indexes for Clay and Ness counties and the cities of Topeka and Fort Scott, and Soldier and Topeka townships in Shawnee county. This microfilm circulates through interlibrary loan from KSHS:

- 1895 Index - Clay & Ness Counties (KS-1-7).
- 1895 Index - City of Fort Scott (KS-8-11).
- 1895 Index - City of Topeka, Topeka Township & Soldier Township, all in Shawnee County

**Online Index:** A searchable index is located at the KHS website. Search by Surname, Soundex, First name, City/township, and/or County. See **www.kshs.org/p/kansas-1895-state-census/10951.**

■ ***1902-1928 City Directories, Lawrence, Kansas*** **[Microfilm],** from the originals by various publishers. Includes directories for 1902-1903, 1905, 1907, 1909, 1911, 1913-1914, 1915, 1917, 1919, 1925-1926, and 1927-1928. Filmed by Research Publications, Woodbridge, CT, ca1995, 2 rolls, FHL film #2308854 (1902-1914 Lawrence directories) and FHL film #2308855 (1915-1928 Lawrence directories).

■ ***1902-1935 City Directories, Salina, Kansas*** **[Microfilm]**, from the originals by various publishers. Includes directories for 1902-1903, 1904-1905, 1907-1908, 1909, 1911, 1913, 1915, 1917, 1919, 1921, 1923, 1925, 1927, 1929, 1931, 1933, and 1935. Filmed by Research Publications, Woodbridge, CT, ca1995, 4 rolls, beginning with FHL film #2310452 (Salina & Saline Co Directory). For a complete list of roll numbers and the contents of each roll, see the online FHL catalog page for this title. See **https://familysearch.org/search/catalog/1051402.**

■ ***1904-1935 City Directories, Hutchinson, Kansas*** **[Microfilm]**, from the originals by various publishers. Includes directories for 1904, 1906, 1907, 1909, 1910, 1912, 1913, 1915, 1917, 1919, 1923, 1924, 1933, and 1935. Filmed by Research Publications, Woodbridge, CT, ca1995. 4 rolls, beginning with FHL film #308844 (1904 Hutchinson City Directory). For a complete list of roll numbers and the contents of each roll, see the online FHL catalog page for this title. See **https://familysearch.org/search/catalog/1050888.**

■ ***1904-1934 City Directories, Kansas City (Kansas)*** **[Microfilm]**, from the originals by various publishers. Includes directories for 1904, 1909, 1912, 1924-1925, 1925, 1927, 1929, 1930, 1932, and 1934. Filmed by Research Publications, Woodbridge, CT, ca1995, 4 rolls, beginning with FHL film #2308850 (1904, 1909, 1912 Kansas City, KS directories). For a complete list of roll numbers and the contents of each roll, see the online FHL catalog page for this title: **https://familysearch.org/search/catalog/1050979.**

■ ***1905 Kansas State Census*** **[Microfilm]**, from the originals at the KHS, Topeka. (No copy at FHL). The 1905 census lists all members of household by name, including age, sex, race or color, and state or country of birth. Also listed: where from to Kansas (state or country) and military record (condition of discharge, state of enlistment, letter or name of company or command, number of regiment or other organization to which attached, arm of the service, and name of military prison if confined in one). Filmed by the society, 181 rolls, beginning with #1905-K-1 (Allen County cities of Bassett, Elsmore, Gas City, Humboldt & Iola, pt. 1). For the Indexes and microfilm of KS 1905 state census schedules, see **www.kshs.org/p/kansas-1905-state-census/10953.**

■ ***1905 Kansas State Census Index*** **[Microfilm]**, (For residents of selected cities), from the originals at the KHS, Topeka. (No copy at FHL). Arranged by city, then alphabetically by surname. Index lists full name, county of residence, and page on the census schedules where the person was shown. Index for the following cities:

- **Ft. Scott** (Bourbon Co.), KS-1-4.
- **Pittsburg** (Crawford Co.), KS-41-45.
- **Lawrence** (Douglas Co.), KS-29-33.
- **Ottawa** (Franklin Co.), KS-39-41.
- **Leavenworth** (Leavenworth Co.), KS-33-39.
- **Hutchinson** (Reno Co.), KS-4-7.
- **Salina** (Salina Co.), KS-45-47.
- **Topeka** (city), **Topeka Township**, and **Soldier Township** (Shawnee Co.), KS-48-60.
- **Wichita** (Sedgwick Co.), KS-60-69.
- **Kansas City**, **Argentine** and **Rosedale** (Wyandotte Co.), KS-7-29.

This microfilm circulates through interlibrary loan from KHS. When ordering, list the year and reel number when placing an interlibrary loan request loan request (e.g., "1905-KS-7"). For the Indexes and microfilm of KS 1905 state census schedules, see **www.kshs.org/p/kansas-1905-state-census/10953.**

■ ***1915 Kansas State Census*** **[Microfilm]**, from the originals at the KHS, Topeka. (No copy at FHL). The 1915 census lists all members of household by name, including age, sex, race or color, and state or country of birth. Also listed: where from to Kansas (state or country) and military record (condition of discharge, state of enlistment, letter or name of company or command, number of regiment or other organization to which attached, arm of the service, and name of military prison if confined in one). Filmed by the society, 271 rolls, beginning with #1915-K-1 (Allen County cities of Bassett, Carlyle, Elsmore, Gas City, Geneva, Humboldt & Iola, pt. 1). For the indexes and microfilm of the KS 1915 state census schedules, see **www.kshs.org/p/kansas-1915-state-census/10955.**

■ ***1915 Kansas State Census Index*** **[Microfilm]**, (For residents of selected cities), from the originals at the KHS, Topeka. (No copy at FHL). This microfilm circulates through interlibrary loan from KHS. List the year and reel number when placing an interlibrary loan request.

- **Fort Scott** (Bourbon County), 1915-KS-69, KS-1, and KS-2
- **Pittsburg** (Crawford County), 1915-KS-36-40.
- **Leavenworth** (Leavenworth County), 1915-KS-30-36.
- **Topeka Township** (excludes city of Topeka), and **Soldier Township** (Shawnee County), 1915-KS-41- 42.
- **Wichita** (Sedgwick County), 1915 - KS-42-57.
- **Kansas City** & **Rosedale** (Wyandotte County), 1915-KS-3-30.

For the indexes and microfilm of the KS 1915 state census schedules, see **www.kshs.org/p/kansas-1915-state-census/10955.**

■ **1917-1918**. See ***Kansas, World War I Selective Service System Draft Registration Cards, 1917-1918*** **[Microfilm]**, from the originals at the National Archives, East Point, GA. The draft cards are arranged alphabetically by county or city, then by the surname of the registrants. Filmed by the National Archives, 1987-1988, 71 rolls, beginning with FHL film #1643420 (KS Allen Co A-Z, Anderson Co A-G). For a complete list of roll numbers and contents of each roll, see the online FHL catalog page for this title: **https://familysearch.org/search/catalog/746978.**

■ ***1918 Registration Affidavits of Aliens (Kansas)*** **[Microfilm]**, from the originals at the National Archives Branch in Kansas City, Missouri. Alphabetical name lists are by county. Filmed by the Genealogical Society of Utah, 1991, 20 rolls, beginning with FHL film #1769240 (Registration affidavits of alien enemy 1918, Allen County-Atchison County). For a complete list of roll numbers and contents of each roll, see the online FHL catalog page for this title: **https://familysearch.org/search/catalog/663093.**

■ **1918.** See ***Registration of Axis Aliens in Kansas: January, 1918 through June, 1918*** **[Printed Book]**, indexed and published by Kansas Statistical Publications Company, Overland Park, KS, 1992, 76 pages. All males not naturalized who were subjects of the German Empire, Alsace-Lorraine in France, and Schleswig-Holstein in Denmark were required to register with the Department of Justice. A number of their spouses were also listed. See FHL book 978.1 P4r. To access a digital version of this book, see the online FHL catalog for this title. See **https://familysearch.org/search/catalog/640820.**

■ ***1925 Kansas State Census*** **[Microfilm]**, from the originals at the KHS, Topeka. (No copy at FHL). The 1925 census lists all members of household by name, including age, sex, race or color, marital status, state or country of birth, and relationship to head of household. Also listed: where from to Kansas (state or country), military record (condition of discharge, state of enlistment, letter or name of company or command, number of regiment or other organization to which attached, arm of the service, and name of military prison if confined in one), and citizenship (year of immigration to the U.S. and year of naturalization if naturalized). Filmed by the society, 177 rolls, beginning with KHS reel #1925-K-1 (Allen County: Bassett, Elsmore, Gas City, Humboldt, Iola, LaHarpe, Mildred, Moran, Carlyle & Cottage Grove Twp.). Locate film numbers for all 271 reels at the KSHS website. For the indexes and microfilm of the KS 1925 state census schedules, see **www.kshs.org/p/kansas-1925-state-census/10957.**

■ ***1925 Kansas State Census Index, Shawnee County*** **[Microfilm]**, from the originals at the KHS, Topeka. (No copy at FHL). This microfilm circulates through interlibrary loan from KSHS. List the year and reel number when placing an interlibrary loan request.

- **Topeka Township** (excluding city of Topeka) & **Soldier Township** (Shawnee County), 1925-K-57, K - 1, & K – 2.

For the indexes and microfilm of the KS 1925 state census schedules, see **www.kshs.org/p/kansas-1925-state-census/10957.**

# MISSOURI
## Censuses & Substitutes, 1752-2014

**French Colonial Era, 1682-1763:** The only settlement in the present Missouri area of French Louisiana was at Ste. Genevieve, established as a fur trading post in 1750. A few land records from the French era are located today at the Ste. Genevieve County Courthouse. And, a 1752 French tax list for Ste. Genevieve is at the MO State Archives.

**Spanish Colonial Era, 1763-1800:** At the 1763 Treaty of Paris ending the French and Indian War, France officially transferred title of Louisiana west of the Mississippi to Spain, and Louisiana east of the Mississippi to Britain. In 1764, French traders established the settlement at St. Louis. The existing French Louisiana settlements were occupied by the Spanish military between 1766 (New Orleans) and 1770 (St. Louis). For the next 30 years, the Spanish presence in Louisiana consisted of one governor at New Orleans, and about 30 soldiers, billeted at New Orleans, Baton Rouge, and St. Louis. Within the period 1770-1800, a few name lists of civilian residents exist for St. Louis, Ste. Genevieve, New Madrid, and Cape Girardeau, The Spanish government finally gave up on Louisiana in 1800, trading the tract to Napoleon for land in Europe. The civilian population (of European stock) in the area of Missouri at the end of the Spanish era was about 2,500 people. Most of them spoke French as their first language.

**American Jurisdictions:** The United States purchased Louisiana from France in 1803. The following year, Congress created two jurisdictions in the area, Orleans Territory, which was nearly the same as the present-day state of Louisiana; and Louisiana District, the rest of the tract. In 1805, Louisiana District became Louisiana Territory, with the seat of government at St. Louis. When the state of Louisiana was admitted to the Union in 1812, the original Louisiana Territory was renamed Missouri Territory. The first General Assembly of the Territory of Missouri met in October 1812, and designated the first five districts as counties: Cape Girardeau, New Madrid, St. Charles, St. Louis, and Ste. Genevieve. In 1813, Arkansas County was created from lands ceded by the Osage Indians.

**MO Territorial Censuses:** Several censuses were taken for Missouri Territory, 1812-1819, and the surviving name lists are for Arkansas County in 1814 (now at the AR History Commission), St. Charles County in 1817 and 1819, and Cape Girardeau and Ste. Genevieve in 1818. The 1820 federal census taken for Missouri Territory was lost.

**MO State Censuses:** The *Missouri Compromise of 1820* was landmark legislation allowing Missouri to become a slave state and Maine to become a free state. Maine was admitted in March 1820, Missouri in August 1821.

The state of Missouri took several state censuses, but few have survived. An inventory of county repositories at the Missouri State Archives reveals a few county copies of state censuses survive for 1844, 1845, 1846, 1852, 1856, 1864, 1868, and 1876. The most complete surviving census was for 1876, with 28 county name lists (out of 114 counties).

**MO Censuses Online.** The 1844-1881 MO State Census Collection at Ancestry.com includes some years which were actually tax lists, rather than censuses, all derived from the MO State Archives collection. The 1732-1933 MO Territorial and State Censuses database at FamilySearch.org starts with an Illinois census, not Missouri; but adds several county name lists not at the MO State Archives.

**MO Census Substitutes:** More common than censuses are the countywide tax lists from the 1820s to the 1890s, which exist for all 114 Missouri counties (and the independent city of St. Louis). Most of the county tax lists have been indexed in books, microfilm, or articles in periodicals. Unpublished extant tax lists can be found using the Missouri State Archives' Local Records Inventory Database, where a search can made for every county of Missouri for original county records, including censuses; tax lists; birth, marriage, and death records; and miscellaneous court records residing in local repositories.

### Resources at the Missouri State Archives

The genealogy-friendly Missouri State Archives in Jefferson City features Missouri's history under French and Spanish colonial rule, as an American territory, and during early statehood. For a list of the

record types available, see
**www.sos.mo.gov/archives/resources/resources.**

- Census Records 1752-1940
  - Territorial Censuses, 1752-1818; and Tax Lists, 1814-1821
  - State Censuses, 1840-1876; and Tax Lists (years vary by county)
  - Special Censuses, 1857-2004
  - Federal Censuses, 1830-1940
- County and Municipal Records
- Judicial Records
- Land Records
- Legislative records
- Manuscripts
- Military records of Missourians from the War of 1812 through World War I, including more than 9 million pages related to the Civil War
- Penitentiary Records
- Photographs and Digital Collections
- Resources for Family & Community History
- State agency records
- State government publications

**Searchable Online Databases.** Visit the Missouri State Archives website for access to each of following searchable databases. Some of these databases are also accessible at the Ancestry.com or the various websites. See
**www.sos.mo.gov/archives/resources/resources.**

- Archives' Online Catalog
- Birth & Death Records Database, pre-1910
- Civil War Provost Marshal Index Database
- Coroner's Inquest Database
- County and Municipal Records on Microfilm
- Digital Collections
- Finding Aids
- Land Records Database
- Local Records Inventory Database
- Missouri Death Certificates, 1910 – 1965
- Missouri Digital Heritage
- Missouri Judicial Records
- Missouri State Penitentiary Database
- Missouri Supreme Court Historical Database
- Naturalization Records Database
- Soldiers' Records: War of 1812 - World War I
- St. Louis Circuit Court Historical Records Project
- St. Louis Probate Court Digitization Project (now a part of Missouri Judicial Records)

## Missouri Databases Online at Ancestry.com

The Ancestry.com subscription website allows free access to all indexes, but to view any particular record requires a membership. Ancestry offers trial memberships and subscriptions for short periods and reduced rates. The following statewide databases at the Ancestry.com website are unique to Missouri under the categories of Census & Voter Lists, Vital Records, Military, Immigrations, et al. See
**http://search.ancestry.com/Places/US/Missouri/Default.aspx.**

■ **1763-1800.** The ***Spanish Regime in Missouri: A Collection of Papers and Documents Relating to Upper Louisiana, Principally within the Present Limits of Missouri During the Dominion of Spain, From the Archives of the Indies at Seville, etc.*** **[Online Database],** digitized and indexed at the Ancestry.com website. Source: Book, same title, publ. 1909. Included are censuses taken between 1770 and 1800 by the Spanish in Louisiana (including Cape Girardeau, St. Louis, Ste. Genevieve, and New Madrid). This database has 913 pages. See
**http://search.ancestry.com/search/db.aspx?dbid=28134.**

■ **1766-1850. See** ***Missouri Marriages to 1850*** **[Online Database],** indexed at the Ancestry.com website. Source: Jordan Dodd, compiler, from extractions of county marriage records on microfilm at the Family History Library, Salt Lake City, UT. Each record includes: Name, Spouse's name, Marriage date, and Marriage county. This database has 126,161 records. See
**http://search.ancestry.com/search/db.aspx?dbid=2094.**

■ **1766-1983.** See ***Missouri Marriages, 1766-1983*** **[Online Database],** indexed at the Ancestry.com website. Source: *Hunting for Bears* extractions from county records on microfilm at the Family History Library, Salt Lake City, UT. Each record includes: Name, Spouse's name, Location, and State. This database has 116,795 records. See
**http://search.ancestry.com/search/db.aspx?dbid=7843.**

■ **1766-1988.** See ***Missouri, Wills and Probate Records, 1766-1988*** **[Online Database],** digitized and indexed at the Ancestry.com website. Source: Ancestry extractions from original records in Missouri county, district, and probate courts. The contents of a probate file can vary from case to case, but certain details are found in most probates, most importantly, the names and residences of beneficiaries and their relationship to the decedent. An inventory of the estate assets can reveal personal details about the deceased's occupation and lifestyle. There may also be references to debts, deeds, and other documents related to the settling of the estate. It is possible to browse the images in the database, organized by county, then

Record Type, and Date Range. Most counties include index books to court records, probates, wills, etc. This database has 496,224 records. See
**http://search.ancestry.com/search/db.aspx?dbid=9071.**

■ **1766-2010.** See ***Web: St. Louis, Missouri, Burial Index, Archdiocese of St. Louis, 1700-2010*** **[Online Database],** indexed at the Ancestry.com website. Source: Archdiocese of Saint Louis: Cemeteries. This database is also accessible at the Archdiocese of St. Louis website. Each record includes: Name, Gender, Death date, Burial date, Burial place, Age, and Birth date. This database has 270,792 records. See
**http://search.ancestry.com/search/db.aspx?dbid=70379.**

■ **1790s-1840.** See ***Missouri Marriages Before 1840*** **[Online Database],** digitized and indexed at the Ancestry.com website. Source: Book, same title, by Susan Ormesher, publ. 1998. See pages iii and iv for a list of counties included in this compilation of published marriages. This database has 321 pages. See
**http://search.ancestry.com/search/db.aspx?dbid=48333.**

■ **1800s-1900s.** See ***Missouri, Bible Records, 1600-1963*** **[Online Database],** indexed at the Ancestry.com website. Source: Elizabeth Prather Ellsberry's *Bible Records of Missouri*, Vol. 1, publ. 1963. The database is the first volume in a series of Bible records that includes such information as births, marriages, probate information, and deaths of individuals who settled in Missouri. Some dates noted in the Bible records may precede Missouri settlement. This database has 8,699 records. See
**http://search.ancestry.com/search/db.aspx?dbid=5401.**

■ **1804-1876.** See ***St. Louis, Missouri Marriages, 1804-1876*** **[Online Database],** indexed at the Ancestry.com website. Source: St. Louis Marriage Index, 1804-1876, publ. 1999. Each record includes: Name, Spouse's name, Marriage date, and Vol./Page of the book. This database has 153,816 records. See
**http://search.ancestry.com/search/db.aspx?dbid=5413.**

■ **1805-2002.** See ***Missouri Still Birth & Miscellaneous Records, 1805-2002*** **[Online Database],** digitized at the Ancestry.com website. Source: Various county records on microfilm at the MO State Archives. This is an image only database. Examples of types of miscellaneous records presented here include: Still birth records, School censuses, Board of Education minute books, Receipts, and Probate records. This database is not indexed and is not searchable by name or date. Browse through the records, organized by county. This database has 214,105 images. See
**http://search.ancestry.com/search/db.aspx?dbid=1226.**

■ **1805-2002.** See ***Missouri, Marriage Records, 1805-2002*** **[Online Database],** digitized and indexed at the Ancestry.com website. Source: MO State Archives. Each record may include: Groom's name, Groom's race, Groom's birth date or age, Groom's parents' names, Bride's name, Bride's race, Bride's birth date or age, Bride's parents' names, Marriage place, and Marriage date. More information may be available at the digitized document. This database has 5,968,946 records. See
**http://search.ancestry.com/search/db.aspx?dbid=1171.**

■ **1826-2014.** See ***Web: Jackson County, Missouri, Marriage Records, 1826-2014*** **[Online Database],** indexed at the Ancestry.com website. This database is also accessible at the JacksonGov.org website. Each record includes: Name, Registration date, Marriage date, Marriage place, Spouse, and License number. This database has 1,408,681 records. See
**http://search.ancestry.com/search/db.aspx?dbid=60383.**

■ **1827-1860.** See ***Jackson County, Missouri, Marriage Index, 1827-1860*** **[Online Database],** indexed at the Ancestry.com website. Source: Elizabeth Prather Ellsberry's *Jackson County, Missouri Marriage Records, 1827-1860*, publ. 1965. Each record includes: Name, Gender, Marriage date, Marriage place, and Spouse. This database has 3,831 records. See
**http://search.ancestry.com/search/db.aspx?dbid=5471.**

■ **1830-1870.** See ***Missouri, Compiled Census and Census Substitutes Index, 1830-1870*** **[Online Database],** indexed at the Ancestry.com website. Source: Accelerated Indexing Systems, Salt Lake City, UT. This collection contains the following indexes: 1830 Federal Census Index; 1830-39 Census Index; 1840 Federal Census Index; 1840 Pensioners List; 1850 Federal Census Index; 1850 Slave Schedules; 1860 Federal Census Index; 1860 Slave Schedules; 1870 Federal Census Index; Early Census Index. This database has 52,451 records. See
**http://search.ancestry.com/search/db.aspx?dbid=3557.**

■ **1834-1910.** See ***Missouri, Death Records, 1834-1910*** **[Online Database],** digitized and indexed at the Ancestry.com website. Source: County death registers at the MO State Archives. Each record includes: Name, Death date, Birth date, County, Race/Ethnicity,

Age, Mother's name, Father's name. The images may have more information. This database has 752,904 records. See
**http://search.ancestry.com/search/db.aspx?dbid=1172.**

■ **1840-1985.** See ***Missouri, Jackson County Marriage Records, 1840-1985*** **[Online Database],** digitized and indexed at the Ancestry.com website. Source: Jackson Co Clerk's office, Kansas City, MO. Each record includes: Name, Gender, Marriage place, Record place, Spouse, Certificate number, and a link to an image of a marriage certificate. This database has 1,391,340 records. See
**http://search.ancestry.com/search/db.aspx?dbid=8700.**

■ **1844-1881.** See ***Missouri, State Census Collection, 1844-1881*** **[Online Database],** digitized and indexed at the Ancestry.com website. Source: MO State Archives. This database contains the images and index to the surviving state census records located at the MO State Archives. The following is a list of the counties and years covered in this database.

- **1844:** Callaway
- **1856:** Audrain
- **1857-1858:** St. Louis
- **1868-1869:** Cape Girardeau, Franklin
- **1873:** Cole (Jefferson City)
- **1876:** Atchison, Benton, Butler, Callaway, Cape Girardeau, Carroll, Cass, Christian, Daviess, Franklin, Gasconade, Greene, Holt, Howard, Madison, McDonald, Moniteau, Montgomery, Osage, Perry, Phelps, Reynolds, Ripley, St Francois, Stone, Texas, Webster, Worth
- **1880:** Cass (Big Creek, Pleasant Hill, City of Pleasant Hill). This is an 1880 federal census "short form.'
- **1881:** Reynolds (these records are actually land list assessment records)

Information contained in this index includes: Name, Gender, County of enumeration, Marital status, Race, Age, Birth location (1857 only). Additional information about an individual may be found by viewing the corresponding image. The 1876 census recorded ages in categories according to race, gender, and age-span. Sections were also available to indicate whether a person was deaf and dumb, blind, or insane. In addition, information regarding people's live stock and agricultural products was recorded. This database has 315,589 records. See
**http://search.ancestry.com/search/db.aspx?dbid=1024.**

■ **1847-1910.** See ***Missouri, Birth Records, 1847-1910*** **[Online Database],** digitized and indexed at the Ancestry.com website. Source: County birth registers at the MO State Archives. Each record includes: Name, Gender, Race/Ethnicity, Birth date, Birth place, Father, and Mother. The images may have more information. This database has 1,967,346 records. See
**http://search.ancestry.com/search/db.aspx?dbid=1170.**

■ **1848-190.** See ***Missouri, Western District Naturalization Index, 1848-1990*** **[Online Database],** indexed at the Ancestry.com website. Source: National Archives microfilm, records of U.S. District courts of Missouri, Kansas, and Oklahoma. This is a digitized card index to naturalization records. Each record may include: Given name and surname, Naturalization date, Birth date or age, Nationality, and reference to page/vol. no. This database has 127,004 records. See
**http://search.ancestry.com/search/db.aspx?dbid=2494.**

■ **1850-1902.** See ***St. Louis City Death Records, 1850-1902*** **[Online Database],** indexed at the Ancestry.com website. Source: *Index to Death Records in the City of St. Louis, 1850-1902*, publ. 1999. This index covers all deaths recorded in the Death Registry Books for St. Louis during the period August 1850 through December 1902. There are some gaps in the records. This database has 368,300 records. See
**http://search.ancestry.com/search/db.aspx?dbid=5696.**

■ **1851-1900.** See ***Missouri Marriages, 1851-1900*** **[Online Database],** indexed at the Ancestry.com website. Source: Jordan Dodd, compiler, from extractions of county marriage records on microfilm at the Family History Library, Salt Lake City, UT. Each record includes: Name, Spouse's name, Marriage date, and Marriage county. This database has 116,919 records. See
**http://search.ancestry.com/search/db.aspx?dbid=4474.**

■ **1856-1942.** See ***Missouri, Federal Naturalization Records, 1856-1942*** **[Online Database],** indexed at the Ancestry.com website. Source: National Archives microfilm of Naturalization Indexes, Petitions, and Declarations from U.S. District Courts in Missouri Searchable fields include: Name, Birth Date, Birth Place, and Immigration Year. Additional information that may be provided in the original records includes: Place of Residence; Occupation; Date of Departure; Place of Departure; Place of Arrival; Spouse's Name, Birth Date, and Residence; Number of Children, Each child's Name, Birth Date, Birth Place, and Residence. This database has 72,971 records. See
**http://search.ancestry.com/search/db.aspx?dbid=61203.**

■ **1856-1970.** See ***Missouri, United Methodist Church Records, 1856-1970*** **[Online Database],** digitized and indexed at the Ancestry.com website. Source: MO United Methodist Commission on Archives and History, Fayette, MO. This collection contains indexed images of United Methodist Church registers from Missouri. The registers may contain baptisms, marriages, burials, memberships, and lists of clergy. Browse through the church registers, organized by the churches located at Armstrong, Berger, Bethel, Brighton, Conway, Crandall, Edgerton, Ferguson, Goodman, Miami, Missouri Valley, Moundville, Richwoods, Rocheport, Rockville, Salem, St. Joseph, St. Louis, Summersville, Swans Prairie, Vanduser, Vinta Park, and Woodlandville, Missouri. This database has 77,792 records. See
**http://search.ancestry.com/search/db.aspx?dbid=60969.**

■ **1861.** See ***Adjutant General's Report of Missouri State Militia for 1861*** **[Online Database],** indexed at the Ancestry.com website. Source: Report, publ. 1962. This database has 16 pages. See
**http://search.ancestry.com/search/db.aspx?dbid=29985.**

■ **1861-1865.** See ***Missouri Confederate Death Records*** **[Online Database],** indexed at the Ancestry.com website. Source: database, same title, compiled by Kenneth Weant, publ. 1999, from a list originally published in the *St. Louis Republic,* 1895. Each record includes: Soldier's name, County of residence, Location and/or cause of death, and Death Date. This database has 2,002 records. See
**http://search.ancestry.com/search/db.aspx?dbid=3697.**

■ **1861-1865.** See ***Missouri Confederate Volunteers*** **[Online Database],** indexed at the Ancestry.com website. Source: database, same title, compiled by Debra Graden, publ. 1999, taken from *History of the First and Second Missouri Confederate Brigades, 1861-1865,* publ. 1879. Each record includes: Name, Unit, Residence, and Occupation. This database has 1,629 records. See
**http://search.ancestry.com/search/db.aspx?dbid=3736.**

■ **1867-1933.** See ***Missouri, Quaker Records Index, 1867-1933*** **[Online Database],** indexed at the Ancestry.com website. Source: Missouri Monthly Meetings: Fairfield, Kansas City, Jackson County, and Jasper County, Missouri. This database contains records of Quaker Meetings for the late 19th and early 20th centuries. The data includes records of marriages, deaths, births and other events for those living in the western portion of the state. This database has 2,604 records. See
**http://search.ancestry.com/search/db.aspx?dbid=4998.**

■ **1873-1976.** See ***Missouri, Deaths and Burials Index, 1873-1976*** **[Online Database],** indexed at the Ancestry.com website. Source: FamilySearch extractions from records on microfilm at the Family History Library, Salt Lake City, UT. Each record may include: Name, Birth date, Birth place, Age, Occupation, Race, Marital status, Gender, Residence, Street address, Date of death, Place of death, Date of burial, Place of burial, Cemetery, Father's name and birthplace, Mother's name and birthplace, Spouse's name, and FHL film number. This database has 36,148 records. See
**http://search.ancestry.com/search/db.aspx?dbid=2569.**

■ **1878.** See ***Missouri Biographical Dictionary*** **[Online Database],** digitized and indexed at the Ancestry.com website. Source: Book, same title, publ. 1878. This database has 1,103 pages. See
**http://search.ancestry.com/search/db.aspx?dbid=7980.**

■ **1880-2009.** See ***Web: St. Louis, Missouri, St. Louis Post-Dispatch Obituary Index, 1880-2009*** **[Online Database],** indexed at the Ancestry.com website. This database is also accessible at the St. Louis Public Library website. Ancestry's index includes: Name, Death date, Publication date, Notes, and a link to the Obituary Search webpage of the St. Louis Public Library. This database has 516,250 records. See
**http://search.ancestry.com/search/db.aspx?dbid=70465.**

■ **1880-2011.** See ***Web: Missouri, St. Louis Public Library Obituary Index, 1880-2011*** **[Online Database],** indexed at the Ancestry.com website. This database is also accessible at the St. Louis Public Library website. Ancestry's index includes: Name, Death date, Publication date, Notes, and a link to the *Obituary Search* webpage of the St. Louis Public Library. This database has 1,083,256 records. See
**http://search.ancestry.com/search/db.aspx?dbid=9197.**

■ ***1890 Census Substitute*** **[Online Database],** indexed at the Ancestry.com website. This is Ancestry's collection of city directories (and other name lists) from all over the U.S. for the time of the lost 1890 federal census. Included are city directories for Kansas City, St. Joseph, and St. Louis, Missouri. Go to *View All Collections Included in this Search* for

a complete list of databases, alphabetically by place (county, city, state), and year. See
**http://search.ancestry.com/search/group/1890census.**

■ **1899.** See ***Encyclopedia of the History of St. Louis: A Compendium of History and Biography for Ready Reference*** **[Online Database],** digitized and indexed at the Ancestry.com website. Source: Book, same title, 4 vols., publ. New York, 1899. This database has 2,901 pages. See
**http://search.ancestry.com/search/db.aspx?dbid=23727.**

■ **1901.** See ***Missouri History Encyclopedia, 1901*** **[Online Database],** digitized and indexed at the Ancestry.com website. Source: Book, same title, 6 vols., publ. 1901.
This database has 4,060 pages. See
**http://search.ancestry.com/search/db.aspx?dbid=8553.**

■ **1908.** See ***A history of Missouri: From the Earliest Explorations and Settlements Until the Admission of the State into the Union*** **[Online Database],** digitized and indexed at the Ancestry.com website. Source: Book, same title, publ. 1908. This database has 1,231 pages. See
**http://search.ancestry.com/search/db.aspx?dbid=22578.**

■ **1910-1962.** See ***Web: Missouri, Death Certificates, 1910-1962*** **[Online Database],** indexed at the Ancestry.com website. This database is also accessible at the MO State Archives Digital Heritage website. Ancestry's index has a Name, Date of Death, Death place, and Certificate number only. At any record, go to the MO State Archives site to view the death certificate image for full details. This database has 2,413,021 records. See
**http://search.ancestry.com/search/db.aspx?dbid=60382.**

■ **1916.** See ***Missouri National Guard, the Mexican Border, 1916*** **[Online Database],** indexed at the Ancestry.com website. Source: Reports of the Adjutant General of Missouri, publ. 1915-1916. Each record includes: Name, Rank, Company, Regiment, Page No., and Place organized. This database has 6,274 records. See
**http://search.ancestry.com/search/db.aspx?dbid=4028.**

■ **1916.** See ***The service of the Missouri National Guard on the Mexican border, under the President's order of June 18, 1916: With a Roster*** **[Online Database],** digitized and indexed at the Ancestry.com website. Source: Report of the Adjutant General, publ. 1919. This database has 589 images. See
**http://search.ancestry.com/search/db.aspx?dbid=25642.**

■ **1921-1924.** See ***Report of the Adjutant General of Missouri, January 10, 1921 - December 31, 1924*** **[Online Database],** digitized and indexed at the Ancestry.com website. Source: Report of the Adjutant General, publ. 1925. Index and images of rosters. This database has 171 pages. See
**http://search.ancestry.com/search/db.aspx?dbid=27186.**

■ **1958-1963.** See ***Missouri, Passenger Lists, 1958-1963*** **[Online Database],** digitized and indexed at the Ancestry.com website. Source: National Archives microfilm series A4194 (St. Louis) and A3511 (Kansas City), *Passenger & Crew Manifests of Airplanes Arriving at St. Louis and Kansas City, Missouri.* Each record includes: Name, Nationality, Age, Birth date, Birth place, Arrival date, Arrival Port, Airline, and Flight number. This database has 1,127 pages. See
**http://search.ancestry.com/search/db.aspx?dbid=9114.**

■ **2002-2010.** See ***Web: Jackson County, Missouri, Marriage Index, 2002-2010*** **[Online Database],** indexed at the Ancestry.com website. This database is also accessible at the JacksonGov.org website. Each record includes: Name, Spouse, Marriage date, and Marriage place. This database has 90,973 records. See
**http://search.ancestry.com/search/db.aspx?dbid=70488.**

---

## Missouri Databases Online at FamilySearch.org

The following databases are available for free at the FamilySearch.org website. To see the current list, visit the Missouri Indexed Historical Records and Missouri Image Only Historical Records webpage. Both lists are updated periodically. See
**https://familysearch.org/search/collection/location/38.**

■ **1752-1933.** See ***Missouri State and Territorial Census Records, 1732-1933*** **[Online Database],** digitized and indexed at the FamilySearch.org website. Source: MO State Archives (MSA) & FHL microfilm. The part of this collection from the MSA includes a copy of a French language census identified as "All Counties – 1732 Illinois Country," which has no Missouri locations. The earliest censuses for any Missouri areas begin with a 1752 French census of Ste. Genevieve, followed by a 1791 Spanish census of St. Louis; and a 1797 Spanish census of New Madrid. American censuses begin with the 1818 MO Territorial census of Cape Girardeau and Ste. Genevieve. The MO State Archives set incorporates

transferred county originals of territorial, state, or federal censuses, all from surviving county copies of the census records. Any of the county originals of federal census years should be compared with the federal copies on microfilm. This collection adds county tax lists and federal censuses from FHL county microfilm. From both MSA and FHL sources, the collection includes census images for the following counties (years): **Adair,** Novinger (1906); **Atchison** (1876); **Barton,** Liberal (1908); **Benton** (1876); **Boone,** Centralia (1909); **Butler** (1876), **Callaway** (1850 federal, 1852, 1864, 1868, 1876); **Cape Girardeau** (1818, 1868), **Carroll** (1876); **Cass** (1876, 1880 federal); **Cass,** Belton (1911, 1927); **Christian** (1876); **Clinton,** Lathrop (1930 federal); **Daviess,** Gallatin (1915); **DeKalb,** Maysville (1931); **Franklin** (1868, 1876); **Gasconade** (1844); **Greene** (1844, 1852, 1876); **Greene**, Republic (1916); **Holt** (1876); **Howard** (1876); **Iron** (1876); **Jackson**, Grandview (1929); **Jackson,** Independence City (1887); **Jackson**, Sugar Creek (1922); **Jasper**, Carthage (1933); **Lincoln**, Elsberry (1906); **Madison** (1876); **McDonald** (1876); **Moniteau** (1876); **Montgomery** (1876); **New Madrid** (1797 Spanish, 1840 federal); **New Madrid,** Lilbourn (1930 federal); **Newton** (1840 federal); **Osage** (1876); **Perry** (1876, 1840 federal); **Pettis** (1840 federal); **Phelps** (1876); **Pike** (1840 federal); **Polk** (1840 federal); **Polk,** Humansville (1911); **Pulaski** (1840 federal); **Pulaski,** Richland (1920 federal); **Ralls** (1840 federal); **Randolph** (1840 federal); **Randolph**, Higbee (1931); **Ray** (1840 federal); **Reynolds** (1876); **Ripley** (1876); **Rives** (1840 federal); **Saline** (1840 federal); **Scott** (1876); **Scott**, Illmo (1914); **Scott,** Oran (1931); **Shelby** (1840 federal); **St. Charles** (1868, 1876); **Ste. Genevieve** (1752 French, 1818, 1844); **St. Francois** (1876, 1840 federal); **St. Louis** (1791 Spanish); **Stoddard** (1840 federal); **Stone** (1876); **Taney** (1840 federal); **Van Buren** (1840 federal); **Warren** (1840 federal); **Washington** (1840 federal); **Wayne** (1840 federal); and **Webster** (1876). This database has 109,803 records. See
**https://familysearch.org/search/collection/2075262.**
**Note:** The FamilySearch list of counties and census years shown above does not agree with a list at the MO State Archives website. To see a table of extant MO territorial censuses, visit the MO State Archives Digital Heritage webpage. See
**www.sos.mo.gov/records/archives/census/pages/territorial.**

■ **1766-1920.** See ***Missouri Marriages, 1750-1920* [Online Database],** indexed at the FamilySearch.org website. FamilySearch extractions from records on microfilm at the Family History Library, Salt Lake City, UT. Each record includes: Name, Spouse's name, Marriage date, and Marriage place. This database has 473,531 records. See
**https://familysearch.org/search/collection/1680838.**

■ **1800-1991.** See ***Missouri, County Marriage, Naturalization, and Court Records, 1800-1991* [Online Database],** digitized and indexed at the FamilySearch.org website. Index and digital images of microfilmed marriage records from Missouri counties including recorded marriages, marriage applications, licenses, and certificates. This collection includes records from the microfilm collections of FamilySearch and of the Missouri State Archives in Jefferson City, Missouri. Each record includes: Name, Event type, Event date, Gender, Spouse's name, Spouse's gender, and page number. This database has 573,023 records. See
**https://familysearch.org/search/collection/2060668.**

■ **1800s-1998.** See ***Missouri Probate Records, 1750-1998* [Online Database],** digitized at the FamilySearch.org website. Source: FHL microfilm. This image only database is a collection of probate records created by county courts including wills and records of estates. A starting date of 1750 is unlikely (for a probate document) - most of the records in this collection fall between 1840 and 1930, but the content and years of the court records varies by county. In a few instances, if the court heard other cases in addition to probate, such as civil disputes or even some criminal matters, the records are mixed in with the probate records. Browse through the images, organized by county, then vol. title (wills, probates, settlements, indexes, etc.), then by date range. This database includes all Missouri counties except Andrew and Cole, noted below. This database has 6,142,790 records. See
**https://familysearch.org/search/collection/2399107.**
See also ***Missouri, Andrew and Cole County Probate Records, 1826-1945* [Online Database],** digitized at the FamilySearch.org website. Source: MO State Archives. The original probate records from these two counties were scanned by the MSA. This database has 160,690 records. See
**https://familysearch.org/search/collection/2060218.**
**Note:** Browsing the records reveals that court records of Clinton County, Missouri are also included in this database. It appears that this Clinton set includes circuit court, probate court, and other records not included in the Clinton set digitized as part of the Missouri Probate Records database.

■ **1820-1874.** See ***Missouri, Civil Marriages, 1820-1874* [Online Database],** digitized and indexed at the FamilySearch.org website. Source: FamilySearch extractions from county records on microfilm at the

Family History Library, Salt Lake City, UT. Currently, the index to selected marriage transcripts are from the counties of Greene, Jackson, Nodaway, and Pike counties, Missouri. Each record includes: Name, Event type, Event place, Gender, Spouse's name, and Spouse's gender. This database has 4,883 records. See
**https://familysearch.org/search/collection/2521615.**

■ **1820-1927.** See ***Missouri, Cole County Circuit Court Case Files, 1820-1927*** **[Online Database],** digitized at the FamilySearch.org website. Source: MO State Archives. This is an image only database of circuit court case files, primarily regarding disputed estates and divorces. Browse through the images, organized by case file number, then date range. This database has 185,934 records. See
**https://familysearch.org/search/collection/2076858.**

■ **1827-1945.** See ***Missouri Births and Christenings, 1827-1935*** **[Online Database],** indexed at the FamilySearch.org website. Source: FamilySearch extractions from records on microfilm at the Family History Library, Salt Lake City, UT. Each record includes: Name, Gender, Event type, Event date, Event place, Father's name, and Mother's name. This database has 66,660 records. See
**https://familysearch.org/search/collection/1680833.**

■ **1861-1865.** See ***Missouri, Civil War Service Records of Union Soldiers, 1861-1865*** **[Online Database],** indexed at the FamilySearch.org website (with a link to the images at the Fold3 website). Source: National Archives microfilm series M405. The records include a jacket-envelope for each soldier, labeled with his name, his rank, and the unit in which he served. The jacket-envelope typically contains card abstracts of entries relating to the soldier as found in original muster rolls, returns, rosters, payrolls, appointment books, hospital registers, prison registers and rolls, parole rolls, inspection reports; and the originals of any papers relating solely to the particular soldier. This database has 2,099,748 records. See
**https://familysearch.org/search/collection/1932408.**

■ **1861-1865.** See ***Missouri, Civil War Service Records of Confederate Soldiers, 1861-1865*** **[Online Database],** indexed at the FamilySearch.org website (with a link to the images at the Fold3 website). Source: National Archives microfilm series M322. The records include a jacket-envelope for each soldier, labeled with his name, his rank, and the unit in which he served. The jacket-envelope typically contains card abstracts of entries relating to the soldier as found in original muster rolls, returns, rosters, payrolls, appointment books, hospital registers, Union prison registers and rolls, parole rolls, inspection reports; and the originals of any papers relating solely to the particular soldier. This database has 348,259 records. See
**https://familysearch.org/search/collection/1932374.**

■ **1865-1872.** See ***Missouri, Freedmen's Bureau Field Office Records, 1865-1872*** **[Online Database],** digitized at the FamilySearch.org website. Source: National Archives microfilm series M1908. This is an image only database. The Bureau of Refugees, Freedmen, and Abandoned Lands (often called the Freedmen's Bureau) was created in 1865 at the end of the American Civil War to supervise relief efforts including education, health care, food and clothing, refugee camps, legalization of marriages, employment, labor contracts, and securing back pay, bounty payments and pensions. These records include letters and endorsements sent and received, account books, applications for rations, applications for relief, court records, labor contracts, registers of bounty claimants, registers of complaints, registers of contracts, registers of disbursements, registers of freedmen issued rations, registers of patients, reports, rosters of officers and employees, special and general orders and circulars received, special orders and circulars issued, records relating to claims, court trials, property restoration, and homesteads. Browse through the images, organized by 1) A descriptive pamphlet. 2) List of book records. And 3) Office of the disbursing officer (correspondence). This database has 24,504 records. See
**https://familysearch.org/search/collection/2333775.**

■ **1867-1976.** See ***Missouri Deaths and Burials, 1867-1976*** **[Online Database],** indexed at the FamilySearch.org website. Source: FamilySearch extractions from records on microfilm at the Family History Library, Salt Lake City, UT. Each record includes: Name, Gender, Death date, Death place, Age, Birth date, Birthplace, Occupation, Race, and Marital status. This database has 58,813 records. See
**https://familysearch.org/search/collection/1680837.**

■ **1883-1927.** See ***Missouri, County Naturalization Records, 1883-1927*** **[Online Database],** digitized at the FamilySearch.org website. Source: Clinton County Courthouse, Plattsburg, MO. This is an image only database, currently with Intentions, Petitions, and Naturalization records from Clinton Co MO only. Browse through the records, organized by county, then Record type, Year range, and Vol. No.
This database has 898 records. See
**https://familysearch.org/search/collection/1880587.**

■ **1883-1930.** See ***Missouri Deaths, 1883-1930*** **[Online Database],** digitized at the FamilySearch.org website. Source: MSA, Jefferson City. This is an image only database. Currently, the database has the images of county death registers for Andrew, Audrain, Buchanan, Cape Girardeau, Clinton, Cole, Howard, Jefferson, Macon, Marion, Monroe, Morgan, Scotland, Texas, and Warren County, Missouri. Browse through the images, organized by county, then Year range. This database has 13,734 images. See **https://familysearch.org/search/collection/2448947.**

■ **1897-1950.** See ***Missouri, Confederate Pension Applications and Soldiers Home Applications*** **[Online Database],** digitized at the FamilySearch.org website. Source: MO State Archives. These records are digital images of Confederate pension files and applications for admission to the Confederate soldiers' home. The pensions are for Confederate veterans who were living in Missouri, although they may have enlisted from another state. The Confederate Soldiers' Home in Higginsville, Missouri, was open for infirm and dependent former Confederate soldiers and sailors, their wives, widows, and orphans. Browse through the images, organized by Pension Applications (Approved or Disapproved), then in alpha groups, A to Z; and by Soldiers Home Applications (Approved or Disapproved), A to Z. This database has 27,874 records. See **https://familysearch.org/search/collection/1865475.**

■ **1900-1941.** See ***Missouri, Pre-WWII Adjutant General Enlistment Contracts, 1900-1941*** **[Online Database],** digitized at the FamilySearch.org website. This collection includes records from the Missouri State Archives and from FamilySearch. This is an image only database, with digital images of enlistment papers and extracts from a soldier's service record for members of the Missouri National Guard. Includes records from all counties in Missouri. There are details about a person's birth, residence, physical exam results, and multiple pages of information concerning a person's enlistment. Browse through the images, organized in 450 alpha groups of about 1,300 names each, Aarant, Herald-Abbott, William to Zieba, Michael-Zytowski, Knighten T. This database has 607,070 records. See **https://familysearch.org/search/collection/2576872.**

■ **1928-1956.** See ***Missouri, Jackson County Voter Registration Records, 1928-1956*** **[Online Database],** digitized at the FamilySearch.org website. Source: Midwest Missouri Genealogy Center, Independence, MO. This image only database is a collection is digital images of voter registration books from Jackson County, Missouri. The information in the registers includes the voter's name, address, birthplace, race (color), term of residence, township and voting precinct. Browse through the images, organized by Blue Township, Brooking Township, Fort Osage Township, Sni-A-Bar Township, or Washington Township, then by Precinct Number, and Date Range. This database has 61,961 records. See **https://familysearch.org/search/collection/1992425.**

■ **1941-1946.** See ***Missouri, Reports of Separation Notices, 1941-1946*** **[Online Database],** indexed at the FamilySearch.org website. Index and images of World War II Reports of Separation, 1941-1946. The records are located at the Missouri State Archives in Jefferson City. This database has 316,539 records. See **https://familysearch.org/search/collection/2392705.**

## Missouri Databases Online At Various Websites

■ **1765-1840.** See ***Church of Ste. Genevieve Vital Records, 1765-1840*** **[Online Database],** indexed at the USGenWeb Archives site for Ste. Genevieve Co MO. See **http://files.usgwarchives.net/mo/stegenevieve/vital/stegenvi.txt.**

■ **1790s-1803.** See ***St. Louis Co, MO – Land Survey Decrees Before 1803*** **[Online Database**], indexed at the USGenWeb site for St. Louis Co MO. See **http://files.usgwarchives.net/mo/stlouis/land/1803land.txt.**

■ ***1796 Census of New Madrid District*** **[Online Database],** a Spanish census taken for New Madrid, indexed at the RootsWeb, New Madrid Co MO. See **www.rootsweb.ancestry.com/~monewmad/sec2.html.**

■ **1800s-1900s Missouri Original Land Owners.** See the ***Family Maps*** series for Missouri counties, maps of all original land patents, compiled by Greg Boyd, publ. Arphax Publishing Co., Norman, OK. These privately-produced computer-generated maps show the first property owners for an entire county, produced as a book of maps, each map laid out on the federal township grid, and includes indexes to help you locate a person, place-name, or cemetery. Additional maps are added for each county to show roads, waterways, railroads, selected city centers, and cemeteries within a county. At this writing, *Family Maps* books have been published for Audrain, Barry, Bates, Benton, Boone, Callaway, Camden, Carter, Cass, Clark, Clay, Clinton, Crawford, Dade, Dallas, Daviess, Dent, Douglas, Franklin, Gasconade, Gentry, Harrison, Henry, Howell, Jackson, Jasper, Jefferson,

Johnson, Knox, Linn, Macon, Madison, Miller, Monroe, Montgomery, Newton, Oregon, Ozark, Pettis, Phelps, Polk, Pulaski, Randolph, Scotland, Shelby, St. Clair, St. Francois, Ste. Genevieve, Sullivan, Taney, Texas, Washington, Wayne, and Wright County, Missouri. See **www.arphax.com/.**

■ **1800s-1900s.** See **Biography Index, St. Louis County, Missouri [Online Database],** indexed at the GenealogyTrails.com website. See **http://genealogytrails.com/mo/stlouis/biographies.htm.**

■ **1800s-2000s.** See ***Missouri GenWeb Archives* [Online Database].** The MOGenWeb site offers free genealogical databases with searchable statewide name lists and for all Missouri counties. Databases may include Bibles, Biographies, Cemeteries, Censuses, Court Records, Deaths, Deeds, Directories, Histories, Marriages, Military, Newspapers, Obituaries, Photos, Schools, Tax Lists, Wills, and more. See **http://usgwarchives.net/mo/mofiles.htm.**

■ **1800s-2000s.** See ***Linkpendium – Missouri: Family History & Genealogy, Census, Birth, Marriage, Death, Vital Records & More* [Online Databases].** Linkpendium is a genealogical portal site with links to state, county, town, and local databases. Currently listed are selected sites for Missouri statewide resources (622), Renamed/Discontinued Counties (10), Adair County (315) Andrew County (457), Atchison County (252), Audrain County (395), Barry County (303), Barton County (372), Bates County (358) and 107 more Missouri counties. See **www.linkpendium.com/mo-genealogy.**

■ **1802-1900.** See ***St. Louis Probate Court Digitization Project, 1802-1900* [Online Database],** digitized and indexed at the Missouri Digital Archives website. This database has been incorporated into the Missouri Judicial Records section at the MO State Archives website. For the search screen, see **https://s1.sos.mo.gov/records/archives/archivesdb/JudicialRecords.**

■ **1808-1940.** See ***Missouri Newspaper Archives* [Online Database],** digitized and indexed newspapers at the GenealogyBank website for the following cities: Hannibal, Kansas City, Sedalia, St. Louis, and Washington, Missouri. See **www.genealogybank.com/explore/newspapers/all/usa/missouri.**

■ **1821-1835.** See ***Baptisms, Church of the Immaculate Conception, New Madrid County, Missouri*** [Online Database], The church was formerly St. Johns. Baptisms indexed at the RootsWeb site for New Madrid Co MO. See **www.rootsweb.ancestry.com/~monewmad/nm-baptisms/nm-baptisms.htm.**

■ **1833-1900.** See ***Greene County Archives Material: Searchable* [Online Database],** separate indexes to Greene County Divorces, Springfield MO Land Sales Records, Plat Records, and Naturalization Records, all at the home page of the RootsWeb site for Green Co MO. See **www.rootsweb.ancestry.com/~mogreene/test.html.**

■ **1843.** See ***Residents of New Madrid City, 1843* [Online Database],** indexed at the RootsWeb site for New Madrid Co MO. See **www.rootsweb.ancestry.com/~monewmad/nm-papers/nm-1845.htm.**

■ **1988-Current.** See ***Missouri Recent Newspaper Obituaries* [Online Database],** digitized and indexed newspaper obituaries at the GenealogyBank website, including newspapers for Ashland, Aurora, Bellefontaine-Neighbors, Belton, Bethany, Blue Springs, Boonville, Bowling Green, Brookfield, Byrnes Mill, California, Camdenton, Carthage, Chesterfield, Chillicothe, Farmington, Festus, Florissant-BlackJack, Fredericktown, Fulton, Grandview, Greenfield-Miller, Hannibal, Harrisonville, Hazelwood, Independence-Blue Springs- Grain Valley, Jefferson City, Joplin, Kansas City, Kirksville, Kirkwood, Lake Ozark, Laurie, Lebanon, Lee's Summit, Macon, Maryville, Mexico, Moberly, Monett, Neosho, Noel-Lanagan, O'Fallon, Oakville, Overland, Park Hills, Raytown, Rolla, Sedalia, Seymour, St. Charles, St. James, St. Joseph, St. Louis, St. Peters, St. Robert, Town and Country, Warrenton, Waynesville, & Wentzville. See **www.genealogybank.com/explore/obituaries/all/usa/missouri**

## Missouri Books & Microfilms at the Family History Library

Missouri's microfilmed territorial and state censuses at the county level and major census substitutes are cited below in chronological order. Each item includes a FHL book number or FHL film number, which can be used to search the FHL catalog for more details. To review an item, start at the FamilySearch catalog search page. See **https://familysearch.org/search/catalog/results.** Select "Search by Place" then "United States, Missouri" to see a list of catalog categories. Or, select "Call Number" then type an FHL book number; or select "Film/Fiche Number" to view a specific title.

■ **1766-1800.** See ***Index to French and Spanish Land Grants, Recorded in Registers of Land Titles in Missouri: Books A, B, C, D, E*** **[Printed Book],** copied from an index prepared by the staff at the Missouri State Archives by Betty Harvey Williams, Warrensburg, MO, 1977, 25 pages, FHL book 977.8 R22if.

■ **1766-1839.** See ***Missouri Genealogical Records & Abstracts*** **[Printed Book],** by Sherida K. Eddlemon; surname index by Marlene Towle, published by Heritage Books, Bowie, MD, 1990, 7 vols. Includes records from over 40 Missouri counties: marriage records, Spanish censuses, tax lists, estrays, cemetery listings, slave bills of sale, land records including French and Spanish land grants, military records, mortality schedules, court records, marriage records, etc. Contents: vol. 1: 1766-1839; vol. 2: 1752-1839; vol. 3: 1787-1839; vol. 4: 1741-1839; vol. 5: 1755-1839; vol. 6: 1621-1839; vol. 7: 1535-1839. FHL book 977.8 R4e, v.1-7.

■ **1781-1797.** See ***Anglo-Americans in Spanish Archives: Lists of Anglo-American Settlers in the Spanish Colonies of America; A Finding Aid*** **[Printed Book],** by Lawrence H. Feldman, published by Genealogical Publishing Co., Inc., Baltimore, 1991, 349 pages. From source materials available in Spanish archives, the author has abstracted from original census documents genealogical data about individuals and families who settled in Spanish lands within the present-day states of Florida, Alabama, Mississippi, Louisiana, and Missouri in the US and parts of Central America. Includes bibliographical references and an index of personal names. FHL book 973 X2fe.

■ **1817-1819.** See ***Enumeration of the County of St. Charles, Missouri Territory for the years 1817 and 1819: With Some Selected Marriage and Cemetery Records And a Full Surname Index*** **[Printed Book],** transcribed by Melvin B. Goe, Sr., published by McDowell Publications, Utica, KY, 1980, 63 pages. FHL book 977.839 X2g.

■ ***1818-1883 Missouri pioneers, New Madrid County*** **[Printed Book],** compiled by Audrey L. Woodruff, published by Boyd Publications, Milledgeville, GA, 1995, 32 pages. From 1812 to 1830, New Madrid County covered an area of 23 modern Missouri counties. Includes abstracts of administrative [probate] records, Book A, 1832-1846, the 1860 mortality schedule for New Madrid County, an 1818 list of delinquent taxes for part of New Madrid County, and an 1883 list of military pensioners. Book A includes early wills and administrative bonds for intestate estates. Includes index of surnames. FHL book 977.8985 P2w.

■ **1819-1826.** See **Missouri Taxpayers, 1819-1826 [Printed Book],** compiled by Lois Stanley, George F. Wilson, and Maryhelen Wilson, published by the Southern Historical Press, Greenville, SC, 1990, 133 pages. Extracted from county tax lists in Missouri, the names are in alphabetical order by county. Includes about 14,000 names. FHL book 977.8 R4s.

■ **1819-1900.** See ***Ten Thousand Missouri Taxpayers*** **[Printed Book],** compiled by Sherida K. Eddlemon, published by Heritage Books, Bowie, MD, 1996, 239 pages. FHL book 977.8 R48k.

■ **1819-1931.** See ***Missouri Ancestors*** **[Printed Book],** a compilation of various county records, published by Stan and Jackie Parks, Burkburnett, TX, 1980, 9 vols. Contents: vol. 1: Crawford County, index to probate records 1851-1920 and Pleasant Hill Baptist Cemetery records, compiled by Rosalea Hopper; vol. 2: Washington County deed book "A" 1821-1834 and Horine Cemetery, Richwoods, Missouri, Masonic Cemetery, Blackwell, Missouri; vol. 3: Jefferson County 1930 election poll book, DeSoto, Missouri, and Jefferson County cemeteries; vol. 4: General election poll book, DeSoto, Missouri 1928, and Jefferson County cemeteries; vol. 5: Potosi City Cemetery, Potosi, Missouri; vol. 6: Jefferson County original land entries; vol. 7: Wayne County cemeteries; vol. 8: Madison County deed books "A" & "B," 1819-1830; and vol. 9: Jefferson County 1931 election poll book, DeSoto, Missouri, and Herculaneum Cemetery. FHL book 977.862 P22h.

■ ***1824-1831 Tax Books, St. Louis County, Missouri*** **[Microfilm],** from the original records, filmed by the St. Louis Microfilm Dept., 1964, FHL film #1005418.

■ **1833-1843.** See ***Greene County, Missouri Tax Assessors' List, 1833, 1834, 1835 & 1843*** **[Printed Book],** compiled by members of the Ozarks Genealogical Society, Springfield, MO, published by the society, 1988, 151 pages. During this period, Greene County comprised what is now all of the counties of: Barry, Barton, Christian, Dade, Greene, Jasper, Lawrence, McDonald, Newton, Stone and Webster, and portions of Cedar, Dallas, Douglas, Laclede, Polk, Taney, Vernon and Wright. FHL book 977.878 R4g.

■ *1836 Tax List of St. Charles County, Missouri* **[Printed Book],** photocopies of original records at the county courthouse in St. Charles, MO. Compiled by the St. Charles County Genealogical Society, published by the society, 1996, 40 pages. FHL book 977.839 R4e 1836.

■ *1837 Tax List of St. Charles County, Missouri* **[Printed Book],** photocopies of original records at the county courthouse in St. Charles, MO. Compiled by the St. Charles County Genealogical Society, published by the society, 1998, 50 pages. FHL book 977.839 R4s 1837. See also ***Non-Resident Tax Lists, St. Charles Co., MO, 1836-1845***, FHL book 977.839 R4n.

■ *1844 Missouri State Census, Callaway County, Missouri* **[Microfilm],** from the original records at the Callaway County courthouse, Fulton, MO. Filmed (with 1876 census) by the Genealogical Society of Utah, 1976, 2 rolls, FHL film #1006456.

■ **"1846 Missouri State Census, St. Joseph, Buchanan County" [Printed Article],** name list in *Northwest Missouri Genealogical Society Journal,* Vol. 16, No. 1 (Apr 1996).

■ *1852 Missouri State Census, St. Charles County, Missouri* **[Printed Book],** extracted from originals at the St. Charles city clerk's office and the county clerk's office, by Mary Ethel Buschmeyer, Eunice Webbink, and Vera Haeussermann, published by Lineage Press, Bridgeton, MO, 1985, 63 pages. FHL book 977.839 X2st.

■ *1818-1950 Tax Lists, City of St. Louis, Missouri* **[Microfilm],** of original records, as follows:

- 1818, 1820, 1822-1827, 1829, 1831-1835, 1837-1838 Tax Records, FHL film #980602.
- 1838, 1840, 1843, 1844 Tax records, FHL film #980603.
- 1844-1846 Tax records, FHL film #980604.
- 1846-1849 Tax records, FHL film #980605.
- 1849-1850 Tax records, FHL film #980606.
- 1850-1852 Tax records, FHL film #981624.
- 1852-1853, 1863, 1849 Tax records, FHL film #981625.
- 1828-1829, 1836-1837, 1843 Tax records, FHL film #981626.
- 1844, 1847-1848, 1850, 1898 Index to securities and contracts, 1900 Office plats; abstract of certified, special tax bills; and 1944 real estate tax book, FHL film #981627.
- 1824-1827, 1829, 1831 Tax records, FHL film #981628.
- 1859-1862 Collector's account; City revenue 1851-1870; and Record of real estate sales 1859, FHL film #981656.
- 1849-1851 Collector's account; Real estate assessments and collections 1860-1863; Personal property and poll tax 1862-1866, FHL film #981657.
- 1853 Account books of collection of taxes, real & personal property, Comptrollers Office, FHL film #981642.
- 1853-1904 Index card to special tax books, FHL #1001239, #1001238, and #1001240.
- 1864-1865 Individual Tax Bills Paid to St. Louis Assessor, FHL film #1005420.
- 1864-1866 Merchant, Real Estate, and Personal Tax Bills, Carondelet. FHL film # 981656.
- 1867-1869 Special Tax,; and 1863-1864 Delinquent tax claims, FHL film #981654.
- 1869-1881 St. Louis Comptrollers Office, 72 rolls, beginning with FHL film # 981637.
- 1861-1922 Special tax bills, FHL film #981653.

■ *1862-1866 Internal Revenue Assessment Lists for the State of Missouri* **[Microfilm],** from the originals at the National Archives, Washington, DC. Names are in alphabetical order by first letters of surnames only. Names are grouped by the divisions of each tax district. Typically, each roll of film contains several divisions. Filmed by the National Archives, series M0776, 1984, 22 rolls, District 1 (St. Louis), beginning with FHL film #1695299 (District 1, St. Louis Co, 1862). For a complete list of roll numbers and contents of each roll, see the online FHL catalog page for this title. See **https://familysearch.org/search/catalog/479008.**

■ *1864 Missouri State Census, Gasconade County, Missouri* **[Printed Book],** photocopies of original documents at the Gasconade County courthouse, Hermann, MO, reproduced and indexed by Robert E. Parkin, published by Genealogical Research and Productions, 1980, 64 pages. FHL book 977.861 X2e and FHL film #6075652.

■ *1868 Missouri State Census, Cape Girardeau County, Missouri* **[Microfilm],** from the original records at the Cape Girardeau County courthouse, Jackson, Missouri. Filmed (with 1876 census) by the Genealogical Society of Utah, 1976, 1 roll, FHL film #1006668.

■ *1868 Missouri State Census, St. Charles County, Missouri* **[Printed Book],** transcribed from originals at the County Clerk of St. Charles County by Carrol Geerling, published by Lineage Press, Bridgeton, MO, 1988, 212 pages. FHL book 977.839 X2g.

■ ***1869 Census of Carondelet (now part of St. Louis, Missouri)*** **[Microfilm],** from the originals by Carondelet city assessor, Filmed by the City of St. Louis, 1963, FHL film #981654.

■ **1875-1885.** See ***Howell County, Missouri, Personal Property Tax Books, 1875 & 1885 and West Plains, Missouri, School Records, 1884-1887*** **[Printed Book],** compiled by Jacqueline Hogan Williams and Betty Harvey Williams, published by the authors, Warrensburg, MO, 1973, 61 pages. Includes index. FHL book 977.885 R4w.

■ ***1876 Missouri State Census, Benton County, Missouri*** **[Microfilm],** from the original records at the Benton County courthouse, Warsaw, MO. Filmed by the Genealogical Society of Utah, 1973, 1 roll, FHL film #945728. Indexed in ***1876 Benton County, Missouri State Census*** **[Printed Index],** compiled by Jacqueline Hogan Williams and Betty Harvey Williams, published by the authors, Warrensburg, MO, 1969, 119 pages, FHL book 977.849 X2p.

■ ***1876 Missouri State Census, Butler County, Missouri*** **[Printed Book],** photocopies of original documents at the Butler County Courthouse, Poplar Bluff, MO, compiled by Thelma S. McManus and Robert E. Parkin, published by Genealogical Research & Publications, 1981, 80 pages. Includes index. FHL book 977.893 X2e. See also **"1876 Missouri State Census Index, Butler County" [Printed Article],** in *Area Footprints*, Vol. 10, No. 3-4

■ ***1876 Missouri State Census, Callaway County, Missouri*** **[Microfilm],** from the original records at the Callaway County courthouse, Fulton, MO. Filmed (with 1844 census) by the Genealogical Society of Utah, 1976, 2 rolls, FHL film #1006456.

■ ***1876 Missouri State Census, Cape Girardeau County, Missouri*** **[Microfilm],** from the originals at the Cape Girardeau County courthouse, Jackson, Missouri. Filmed (with 1868 census) by the Genealogical Society of Utah, 1976, 2 rolls, FHL film #100666-1000667.

■ ***1876 Missouri State Census of Christian County*** **[Microfilm],** from the original records at the Christian County courthouse, Ozark, MO. Filmed by the Genealogical Society of Utah, 1973, 1 roll, FHL film #931909.

■ **1876.** See ***An Index to 1876 Census of Greene County, Missouri*** **[Printed Book],** compiled by the Greene County Archives and Records Center, Springfield, MO, 1992, 202 pages. FHL book 977.878 X22es.

■ ***1876 Missouri State Census, Holt County, Missouri*** **[Microfilm],** from the original records in the Holt County courthouse, Oregon, Missouri. Arranged by township and range numbers. Filmed by the Genealogical Society of Utah, 1976, 1 roll, FHL film #1005363.

■ ***1876 Missouri State Census, Howard County, Missouri*** **[Microfilm],** from the originals at the County Clerk's office, Fayette, Missouri. Filmed by the Genealogical Society of Utah, 1974, 1 roll, FHL film #963407.

■ ***1876 Census of the County of Iron, State of Missouri*** **[Printed Book],** from originals at the Iron County Courthouse, Ironton, MO. Information transcribed by Millie and Edward Preissle, published by the authors, Houston, MO, 198?, 194 pages. Includes index. FHL book 977.8883 X2c and FHL film #1320670.

■ ***1876 Missouri State Census, McDonald County, Missouri*** **[Microfilm],** from the original records at the Recorder of Deeds, McDonald County courthouse, Pineville, MO. Filmed by the Genealogical Society of Utah, 1984, 1 roll, FHL film #930080. Another filming, #1016634. See also **"1876 Missouri State Census, McDonald County" [Printed Article],** in *Newton County Roots*, Vol. 4, No. 3 (Sep 1992).

■ ***1876 Missouri State Census, Moniteau County, Missouri, by Township*** **[Microfilm],** from the original manuscript at a private residence in California, Missouri. Filmed by the Missouri State Archives, 1983, 1 roll FHL film #1759291.

■ ***1876 Census, Montgomery County, Missouri*** **[Printed Book],** extracted and published by Mid-Missouri Genealogical Society, Jefferson City, Missouri, 1996, 191 pages. Includes index. FHL book 977.8382 X2c.

■ **1876.** See ***County of Perry, State of Missouri, 1876*** **[Printed Book],** compiled by Bill Bow for the Perry County Historical Society, Perryville, Missouri, 1989,

56 pages. Includes 1876 census; and some 1875-1876 articles from the Weekly Perryville Union. FHL book 977.8694 X2c.

■ ***1876 Missouri State Census, Phelps County, Missouri* [Printed Book],** from originals at the Phelps County Clerk's office, Rolla, MO. Copy transcribed by John E.C. Simmons, published by the author, St. John, MO, 1987, 3 pages, 238 columns. FHL book 977.8594 X2s. See also, **"1876 Missouri State Census, Phelps County" [Printed Article],** in *Phelps County Genealogical Society Quarterly*, Vol. 4, No. 2 (Apr 1988) through Vol. 5, No. 3 (Jul 1989).

■ ***1876 Missouri State Census, Reynolds County* [Microfilm],** from originals at the County Clerk's office, Centerville, Missouri. Filmed by the Genealogical Society of Utah, 1977, as *Census Record, 1876*, FHL film #1016081.

■ ***1876 Missouri State Census of St. Charles County, Missouri* [Printed Book],** transcribed and indexed by Carrol Geerling, published by Lineage Press, Bridgeton, MO, 1988, 333 pages.

■ ***1876 Missouri State Census, St. Francois County, Missouri* [Microfilm],** from the original records at the St. Francois County Clerk's office, Farmington, Missouri. filmed by the Genealogical Society of Utah, 1976, 1 roll, FHL film #1006662.

■ ***1876 Census, County of Texas, State of Missouri: Books One and Two* [Printed Book],** transcribed by Edward and Millie Preissle, published by Texas County Missouri Genealogical Society, Houston, MO, 1983, 180 pages. Includes surname index. Includes Boone, Carroll, Current, Date, Jackson, Lynch, Ozark, Ribidoux, Sherrill, and Upton townships. Parts of Clinton, Morris, Pierce, and Piney townships are also included. FHL book 977.884 X2c; FHL film #1597827; and microfiche # 6005969.

■ ***1890 Real Estate Tax Book Index, St. Charles County, Missouri* [Printed Book],** compiled by Colleen Heitmann Schaeper, published by St. Charles County Genealogical Society, St. Charles, MO, 1999, 50 pages. FHL book 977.839 R42s 1890. See also ***1890 School Tax Book Index, St. Charles County, Missouri* [Printed Book],** compiled by Maryalee Roellig, published by St. Charles County Genealogical Society, St. Charles, Missouri, 1999, 73 pages, FHL book 977.839 R42r.

■ **1887-1901.** See ***Buchanan County, Missouri Taxpayers List* [Printed Book],** compiled by Debra Graden, published by Grey Ink, Leavenworth, KS, 2001, 4 vols. Compiled from portions of the Hoye city directories. Contains names, townships, and post offices of taxpayers. Contents: Vol. 1: Taxpayers from St. Joseph, Missouri, 1887-1890; Vol. 2: Taxpayers from Buchanan County, Missouri (excluding St. Joseph, Missouri), 1902-1906; Vol. 3: Taxpayers from Buchanan County, Missouri (excluding St. Joseph, Missouri) 1891-1895 [and] 1896-1901, FHL book 977.8132 R4g, vol. 1-4.

■ **1921 History.** See ***Centennial History of Missouri (The Center State): One Hundred Years in the Union, 1820-1921* [Printed Book],** by Walter Barlow Stevens, published by S.J. Clarke Pub. Co., St. Louis, 1921, 7 vols., FHL book 977.8 H2s. Biographies in Vols. 3 and 6, which were indexed in ***Biographical Index to the Centennial History of Missouri,*** compiled and published by Mrs. Leister E. Presley, Searcy, AR, 19??, 21 pages. FHL book 977.8 H2s index. See also ***Biographical Index to the Centennial History of Missouri: Volumes III, IV, V, and VI,*** by Elizabeth B. Langley, Billings, Missouri, 1968, 22 pages. FHL book 977.8 H2s index.

# NEBRASKA
## Censuses & Substitutes, 1854-2000

As part of the Louisiana Purchase of 1803, the area of Nebraska became part of Louisiana Territory in 1805; renamed Missouri Territory in 1812.

- In 1819, the U.S. Army established Fort Atkinson on the west side of the Missouri River (now the town of Fort Calhoun in Washington Co NE).

- In 1820, Major Stephen Long explored the Platte and South Platte river routes of present Nebraska and Colorado. His official report referred to the central plains as the "Great American Desert" and had the effect of diverting interest in the area for several years. Long's report ignored the fact that over one million bison depended on the Nebraska Country for survival, and that the prairie had an abundance of fertile soil. Eighty years later, the Ogallala Aquifer, the largest aquifer in the world, began irrigating the "Great American Desert," including the entire state of Nebraska.

- After Missouri became a state in 1821, the remaining portion of the Louisiana Purchase area was designated as "Unorganized Territory." The entire region was inhabited exclusively by American Indian tribes, except for a few left-over French-Canadian voyageurs roaming the rivers.

- In 1832, the first steamboats were able to travel up the Missouri River from Independence, MO, to the fur trading posts as far north as Fort Union, at the present North Dakota/Montana line.

- In 1846, the Utah-bound Mormons sent work parties ahead of their wagon trains to plant crops in Nebraska a year before the main body of immigrants passed through. This was when Nebraska was first discovered to be a great place to grow things.

- The 1849 onset of the California Gold Rush is when Nebraska was discovered as the best way to get there. A natural wagon route across the entire length of present Nebraska was the Platte River Trail (aka Mormon Trail, Oregon Trail, or Immigrant Trail).

- By 1852, over 250,000 people had passed through Nebraska en route to California. Few stopped for any length of time, because the area was not legally open for settlement yet.

- Nebraska Territory was created in 1854 as part of the *Kansas-Nebraska Act*, landmark legislation relating to free versus slave states prior to the Civil War. The Act authorized the first land surveys west of the Missouri River, opening both territories for settlement. Both Kansas and Nebraska were expected to vote on the slavery issue, and both territories immediately began taking annual censuses to determine their numbers of qualified voters.

- In 1854, a large portion of eastern Nebraska Territory was surveyed for public land sales. The first GLOs were established at Brownsville, Dakota City, Nebraska City, and Omaha City. After the first year of land sales, about 4,500 people had settled in Nebraska Territory.

**NE Territory Censuses.** The first Nebraska Territory censuses were taken in 1854, 1855, and 1856. They were heads of households name lists covering the eastern half of present-day Nebraska. The first three census years are mostly complete for all counties in place at the time. The fourth (and last) territorial census was taken in 1865, but only two full county name lists survive today. The originals of all surviving territorial census schedules are located at the Nebraska State Historical Society (NSHS) in Lincoln.

**NE State Censuses, 1869-1884.** After statehood in 1867, the Nebraska legislature passed a law that called for annual censuses, including lists of births and deaths to be gathered by the county tax assessors. It is not known how diligent the counties were in complying with the law, and only a few of the county census name lists have survived. The NSHS has some original annual name lists for 1869-1870, 1874-1879, and 1882-1884, but for just a few counties.

**NE State Census, 1885.** The Nebraska state census law was repealed in 1885. In that year, the Federal Government offered any state or territory an option for an assisted state census, providing federal money to help defray the cost. Nebraska was one of only five states or territories that took up the offer. An 1885 state census of Nebraska was completed using a similar format as the 1880 federal census. The 1885 proved to be the last state census in Nebraska, and stands complete for all counties in place in 1885, except for one missing county (Chase). Nebraska's original state copy of their 1885 census was lost – but as part of the deal with the Federal Government, a transcription copy had been made and sent to Washington, DC. That copy was microfilmed by the National Archives.

**NE Censuses Online:** The NE Territorial censuses for 1854, 1855, and 1856 are indexed in Ancestry's Compiled Census Index database. Full extractions of the NE 1854, 1855, and 1856 Terr. censuses are at the USGenWeb site for Nebraska. One county (Lancaster) of the 1865 NE Territory Census was digitized and indexed at Ancestry's NE State Census collection. Two more 1865 counties (Otoe & Cuming) have full extractions at the USGenWeb site for Nebraska. The NE State Censuses, 1870-1884 are online at Ancestry.com (1 or 2 counties only for each census year). Both Ancestry.com and FamilySearch.org have the 1885 NE State Census, the only NE State Census that is mostly complete.

**NE Federal Censuses.** The 1860 federal census taken in Nebraska Territory included mining camps in present-day Colorado (Boulder, Altoona, and a few other northeastern Colorado towns). They were added at the end of the enumeration lists for Nebraska towns, identified on the census schedules as *Unorganized West of 101° 30'*. The 1870-1940 federal censuses for Nebraska are complete for all counties (with the exception of the 1890, lost for all states). The 1950 federal census will open to the public in 2022.

## Online Resources at the Nebraska State Historical Society

The NSHS presence on the Internet includes both online archives collections and online indexes. In addition to the Nebraska Virtual Exhibits, searchable databases include the following. See **http://nebraskahistory.org/databases/more_databases.htm.**

- Atlases / Plat Books Name Index
- BLOG - Search the Nebraska State Historical Society blog for recent posts.
- Cemetery Registry
- City / County Directories
- Civil War Veterans
- Gazetteer Index, 1890 and 1911
- Hastings Regional Center Cemetery, 1889-1959
- Wyuka Cemetery Burials, (Lincoln, NE), 1877-1881
- Norfolk Regional Center Cemetery Records, 1888-1954
- U.S. General Land Office Tract Books - Search homestead applications, proofs, & final certificates
- Land Entry Files - Nebraska: Name Index to Cancelled, Rejected, and Relinquished Files (National Archives website)
- Nebraska - Our Towns (University of Nebraska database)
- Newspaper Project - over 200,000 names indexed from Nebraska newspapers. ( NEGenWeb website)
- Newspapers on Microfilm. Indexed by town and newspaper name - PDF
- Orphan Train riders
- Prison Records, 1870-1990
- Sherard's Nebraska Place Names
- Telephone Directories
- WWI Draft Registration Cards: 1917-1918, Nebraska Over 276,000 records, arranged by county

---

## Nebraska Databases Online at Ancestry.com

The Ancestry.com subscription website allows free access to all indexes, but to view any particular record requires a membership. Ancestry offers trial memberships and subscriptions for short periods and reduced rates. The following databases at the Ancestry.com website are unique statewide Nebraska databases under the categories of Census & Voter Lists, Vital Records, Military, Immigrations, and Wills & Probates. To review the complete list of statewide databases, and several countywide databases, see **http://search.ancestry.com/Places/US/Nebraska/Default.aspx.**

■ **1854-1860.** See ***Nebraska, Compiled Census Index, 1854-1870*** **[Online Database],** indexed at the Ancestry.com website. Source: Accelerated Indexing Systems databases, acquired by Ancestry in 1999. The 1854, 1855, and 1856 NE Territorial Census name lists were indexed in separate databases by A.I.S. This collection also includes the A.I.S. index to the 1860 NE Territory Federal Census. The cited 1870 NE Federal Censuses could not be confirmed. Any search for an 1869, 1870, or 1871 date could not be found, and brought up an 1860 date instead. Each index record includes: Name, State, County (1854 was by District), Township, Year, Page, and Database title. This database has 8,303 records. See **http://search.ancestry.com/search/db.aspx?dbid=3559.**

■ **1854-1881.** See ***Douglas County, Nebraska Marriages, 1854-1881*** **[Online Database],** indexed at the Ancestry.com website. Source: Book, same title, by Greater Omaha Genealogical Society and Friends, publ. 2002, GPC, Baltimore. This database has the scanned images from the text of the book, with OCR index. This database has about 50,000 records. See **http://search.ancestry.com/search/db.aspx?dbid=49043.**

■ **1854-1989.** See ***Nebraska, Wills and Probate Records, 1806-1989*** **[Online Database],** digitized and indexed at the Ancestry.com website. Source: Ancestry extractions from Nebraska county, district, and probate courts. Bound and loose papers may include Letters of Administration, Inventories, Distribution and Accounting, Bonds, and Guardianships. (Note: the 1806 date in the title was a mis-interpretation of one date appearing in the digitized images). See the Browse Collection box for the list of counties included in this database. The index to each record includes: Name, Probate date, Probate place, Inferred death year, Inferred death place, and Item description/type of record. The digitized image may have much more detail about the deceased and heirs, etc. This database has 2,699 records. See **http://search.ancestry.com/search/db.aspx?dbid=9073.**

■ **1856-1898.** See ***Nebraska, Marriage Index, 1856-1898*** **[Online Database],** indexed at the Ancestry.com website. Source: Liahona Research extractions from microfilmed records at the Family History Library, Salt Lake City, UT. This database has marriage records from Adams, Buffalo, Cuming, Dodge, Sarpy, and Washington County, Nebraska only. Each record includes: Name, Spouse's name,

Marriage date and place, and source information. This database has 9,214 records. See
**http://search.ancestry.com/search/db.aspx?dbid=7871.**

■ **1860-1885.** See ***Nebraska, State Census Collection, 1860-1885*** **[Online Database],** digitized and indexed at the Ancestry.com website. Source: 1860-1884, NSHS, Lincoln; 1885, National Archives microfilm series M352. This database includes an index and images of an 1860 Federal Census (1 county); an 1865 NE Territorial Census (1 county); countywide NE State Censuses for 1870, 1874-1879; 1880, and 1881-1884; and the statewide 1885 NE State Census – for the following years and counties:

- **1860** Federal: Lancaster Co only
- **1865** NE Territorial: Lancaster Co only
- **1870** NE State: Cass and Lancaster Co only
- **1874** NE State: Lancaster Co only
- **1875** NE State: Lancaster Co only
- **1876** NE State: Cass Co only
- **1877** NE State: Cass Co and Lancaster Co only
- **1878** NE State: Cass Co, Lancaster Co, and Saunders Co only
- **1879** NE State: Cass Co and Lancaster Co only
- **1880** NE State: Cass Co and Lancaster Co only
- **1881** NE State: Cass Co only
- **1882** NE State: Cass Co only
- **1883** NE State: Cass Co only
- **1884** NE State: Cass Co only
- **1885** NE State: All counties that existed at the time, except for Chase Co (Blaine Co was created in 1885, but not organized in time to make it into this census).

The census schedules usually include: Name, Race, Gender, Age, Birthplace, Location (town, county, state), Enumeration district number, Date the census was taken, and the Census page number. Additional information may be found on the actual census image. This database has 851,345 records. See
**http://search.ancestry.com/search/db.aspx?dbid=1668.**
NOTE: The one 1860 federal census digitized as part of this series was from Lancaster Co NE. This original set was used to make the copy that was sent to Washington, DC - the one later microfilmed by the National Archives. Therefore, it would be possible to compare the two digitized versions and look for copying errors. Also, note that both Cass and Lancaster Cos NE have state census name lists for 1870 and 1880.These can be compared with the 1870 and 1880 federal censuses for such things as name spellings, places of birth, and other persons living within a family, etc.

■ **1861-1865.** See ***Roster of Nebraska Volunteers from 1861 to 1869*** **[Online Database],** digitized and indexed at the Ancestry.com website. Source: book, same title, by Edgar S. Dudley, from documents at the Nebraska Adjutant General's office, publ. 1888. This database has the scanned images from the text of the book, with an OCR name index for searching. This database has 237 pages. See
**http://search.ancestry.com/search/db.aspx?dbid=29983.**

■ **1861-1869.** See ***Nebraska Volunteers, 1861-1869*** **[Online Database],** indexed at the Ancestry.com website. This is an index to the book, *Roster of Nebraska Volunteers from 1861 to 1869*, publ. 1888. The index includes: Given name, Surname, Company, Regiment or Battalion, Rank, and Residence. This database has 5,169 records. See
**http://search.ancestry.com/search/db.aspx?dbid=3734.**

■ **1885.** See ***Nebraska, State Census, 1885*** **[Online Database],** indexed at the Ancestry.com website. Source: National Archives microfilm series M352. This is an every-name index to the NE 1885 State Census (no images), separate from Ancestry's 1860-1885 collection. For each person listed, the index includes: Name, Age, Birth year, Birth place, Race, Census date, Census location, Enumerator, Film roll, and Page. This database has 737,606 records. See
**http://search.ancestry.com/search/db.aspx?dbid=6585.**

■ ***1890 Census Substitutes (Nebraska Locations)*** **[Online Database],** indexed at the Ancestry.com website. This is Ancestry's collection of city directories (and other name lists) from all over the U.S. for the time of the lost 1890 federal census. Included are city directories for Adams Co NE; Beatrice, NE; Buffalo Co NE; Fremont, NE; Kearney, NE; McCook, NE; Omaha, NE; and the full 1885 NE State Census. Go to *View All Collections Included in this Search* for an alpha list of databases, by place (county, city, state), and year(s). See
**http://search.ancestry.com/search/group/1890census.**

■ **1890-1957.** See ***Nebraska, Federal Naturalization Records, 1890-1957*** **[Online Database],** digitized and indexed at the Ancestry.com website. Source: National Archives microfilm (NE Declarations & NE Petitions). Includes index and images of Declarations of Intentions, Petitions for Naturalization, and Naturalization Certificates. The index includes: Name, Gender, Petition age, Record type, Birth date, Birth place, Petition date, Petition place, Spouse, and Petition no. This database has 32,628 records. See
**http://search.ancestry.com/search/db.aspx?dbid=61205.**

■ **1891.** See ***Nebraska Resident Military Roster on June 1, 1891*** **[Online Database],** indexed at the Ancestry.com website. Source: *Roster of Soldiers, Sailors, and Marines of the War of 1812, the Mexican*

*War, and the War of the Rebellion, Residing in Nebraska on June 1, 1891,* Nebraska Secretary of State, publ. 1892 The index includes: Given name, Surname, Rank, Company, City (Nebraska residence), State (of military service). This database has 14,972 records. See
**http://search.ancestry.com/search/db.aspx?dbid=4755.**

■ **1895.** See ***Roster of Soldiers, Sailors, and Marines of the War of 1812, the Mexican War, and the War of the Rebellion, Residing in Nebraska* [Online Database]**, indexed at the Ancestry.com website. Source: Newspaper reproduction of the 1892 report, publ. York, NE: Nebraska Newspaper Union, 1895. This database has the scanned images from the text of the newspaper reproduction, with an OCR name index for searching. This database has 551 pages. See
**http://search.ancestry.com/search/db.aspx?dbid=23886.**

■ **1958-1965.** See ***Omaha, Nebraska, Passenger and Crew Manifests of Airplanes, 1958-1965* [Online Database],** digitized and indexed at the FamilySearch.org website. Source: National Archives microfilm series A3541. This is a set of handwritten index cards, almost totally unreadable. The index for each record needs to be trusted, because the image can not be read for verification or added information. Each index record includes: Name, Nationality, Age, Birth date, Birth place, Arrival date, Arrival place, and Airline. This database has about 400 images. See
**http://search.ancestry.com/search/db.aspx?dbid=60979.**

## Nebraska Databases Online at FamilySearch.org

The following databases are available for free at the FamilySearch.org website. To see the current list, visit the Nebraska Indexed Historical Records and Nebraska Image Only Historical Records webpage. Both lists are updated periodically. See
**https://familysearch.org/search/collection/location/40.**

■ **1861-1865.** See ***Nebraska Civil War Service Records of Union Soldiers, 1861-1865* [Online Database],** indexed at the FamilySearch.org website. Source: National Archives microfilm series M1787. Union service records of soldiers who served in organizations from the Territory of Nebraska. The records include a jacket-envelope for each soldier, labeled with his name, his rank, and the unit in which he served. The jacket-envelope typically contains card abstracts of entries relating to the soldier as found in original muster rolls, returns, rosters, payrolls, appointment books, hospital registers, prison registers and rolls, parole rolls, inspection reports; and the originals of any papers relating solely to the particular soldier. Each index record includes: Name, Event type, Event year, Age, and Military unit. This database has 74,800 records. See
**https://familysearch.org/search/collection/1932417.**

■ **1855-1995.** See ***Nebraska Marriages, 1855-1995* [Online Database],** indexed at the FamilySearch.org website. Source: NSHS, Lincoln, NE. Each index record includes: Name, Birth place, Residence, Marriage date, Marriage place, and Spouse. Each record includes a link to the images of these marriage records available at the NSHS website. This database has 193,370 records. See
**https://familysearch.org/search/collection/1708654.**

■ **1885.** See ***Nebraska State Census, 1885* [Online Database],** digitized and indexed at the FamilySearch.org website. Source: National Archives microfilm series M352. This Nebraska 1885 state census set was copied from the state's original set (now lost) and sent to Washington, DC. Although a state census, not a federal census, the 1885 enumeration was prompted by the Federal Government, who offered to provide the paper forms (identical to the 1880 federal census), and to help pay for the canvasing. This Federal copy includes all Nebraska counties that existed at the time, except Chase Co NE is missing. Of the five NE counties created in 1885 (Blaine, Dawes, Logan, Rock, and Sheridan Co NE), any that were organized by 1 June 1885 were included. Each index record includes: Name, Birth year, Parents (names of father and mother, if relationship was given on the census page), Spouse (if married), Children (names of any sons & daughters included in a family group), Other (names of other people living in a family), and Residence. At each record, the full image of an 1885 census page is accessible, adding considerable information, e.g., occupation, birth place of each person and birth place of the parents of each person. This database has 747,367 records. See
**https://familysearch.org/search/collection/1810728.**

■ **1890-1908.** See ***Nebraska, Broken Bow Homestead Records, 1890-1908* [Online Database],** indexed at the FamilySearch.org website. Source: National Archive microfilm series M1915. This database consists of 1,824 Homestead Land Entry Case Files of the Broken Bow (Nebraska) Land Office. The records are unbound documents that include final certificates, applications with land descriptions, affidavits showing proof of citizenship, Register and Receiver receipts, notices and final proofs, and testimonies of witnesses.

The files were arranged chronologically and assigned a final certificate number. The index record includes: Name Event date, Certificate number, State, Township, Range, and Section. At each record there is a link to the images, located at the Fold3 website. Generally, the case files can be very mundane; but once in a while, the records explode. For example, if a person applying for a homestead were not born in the U.S. a proof of citizenship was required, either a petition/declaration of intention to become a citizen, or an actual naturalization certificate. In some cases, original documents can be found in the case files, because the applicant brought the original document to the land office for proof, but never got it back. The index does not indicate the quantity or quality of documents in the case files, so the accessible images are a godsend to review what may be stored there. This "treasure chest" database has 39,373 records. See **https://familysearch.org/search/collection/1840496.**

## Nebraska Databases Online At Various Websites

■ **1854-1869.** See ***Census Records of Nebraska* [Online Database].** Extant lists for 1854, 1855, 1856, 1865 (Territorial), and 1869 were extracted and published in *Nebraska & Midwest Genealogical Records* (N&MGR), a publication of the Nebraska Genealogical Society, 1922-1944. The USGenWeb site for Nebraska has put all of the census articles from the N&MGR online. See
**www.usgennet.org/usa/ne/topic/resources/OLLibrary/Journals/NMGR/censindx.html.**
Contents: The 1854, 1855, and 1856 territorial censuses are fairly complete for all counties. The 1865 territorial has name lists for Cuming and Otoe counties only; and the 1869 state census has lists for Butler and Stanton counties only. Direct links to the name lists by Year, N&MGR Vol. No. & Issue No. are organized as follows:

- **1854** NE Territorial: District 1 (includes Pawnee & Richardson Co, and parts of current Gage, Johnson, Nemaha Co)
- **1854** NE Territorial: District 2 (primarily Nemaha & Otoe counties)
- **1854** NE Territorial: District 3 (Cass Co)
- **1854** NE Territorial: District 4 (Douglas & Sarpy Co)
- **1854** NE Territorial: District 5 (Dodge Co plus).
- **1854** NE Territorial: District 6 (Burt & Washington Co)
- **1855** NE Territorial: Cass Co.
- **1855** NE Territorial: Dodge Co.
- **1855** NE Territorial: Douglas Co.
- **1855** NE Territorial: Nemaha Co.
- **1855** NE Territorial: Otoe Co.
- **1855** NE Territorial: Pawnee Co.
- **1855** NE Territorial: Richardson Co.
- **1855** NE Territorial: Washington Co.
- **1856** NE Territorial: Burt Co.
- **1856** NE Territorial: Cass Co.
- **1856** NE Territorial: Clay Co (area that is now Lancaster & Gage Co)
- **1856** NE Territorial: Colfax Co (see Platte Co)
- **1856** NE Territorial: Cuming Co
- **1856** NE Territorial: Dakota Co (includes Dixon Co)
- **1856** NE Territorial: Dixon Co (see Dakota Co)
- **1856** NE Territorial: Dodge Co
- **1856** NE Territorial: Douglas Co (Southern district – now Sarpy Co)
- **1856** NE Territorial: Douglas Co (Northern District)
- **1856** NE Territorial: Gage Co (see Clay Co)
- **1856** NE Territorial: Johnson Co (see Nemaha Co)
- **1856** NE Territorial: Lancaster Co
- **1856** NE Territorial: Lancaster Co (also see Clay Co)
- **1856** NE Territorial: Nemaha Co
- **1856** NE Territorial: Otoe Co
- **1856** NE Territorial: Pawnee Co
- **1856** NE Territorial: Platte Co
- **1856** NE Territorial: Richardson Co
- **1856** NE Territorial: Sarpy Co (see Douglas Co, Southern District)
- **1856** NE Territorial: Washington Co
- **1865** NE Territorial: Cuming Co
- **1865** NE Territorial: Otoe Co
- **1869** NE State: Butler Co
- **1869** NE State: Stanton Co

■ **1854-1900s Nebraska Original Land Owners.** See the ***Family Maps*** series for Nebraska counties, maps of all original land patents, compiled by Greg Boyd, publ. Arphax Publishing Co., Norman, OK. These privately-produced computer-generated maps show the first property owners for an entire county, produced as a book of maps, each map laid out on the federal township grid, and includes indexes to help you locate a person, place-name, or cemetery. Additional maps are added for each county to show roads, waterways, railroads, selected city centers, and cemeteries within a county. At this writing, *Family Maps* books have been published for Blaine, Garden, Garfield, Grant, Hooker, Logan, Loup, McPherson, Scotts Bluff, Sioux, and Thomas County, Nebraska. See **www.arphax.com.**

■ **1854-1900s.** See ***Nebraska GenWeb Archives* [Online Database].** The NEGenWeb site offers free genealogical databases with searchable statewide name lists and for all Nebraska counties. Databases may include Bibles, Biographies, Cemeteries, Censuses, Court Records, Deaths, Deeds, Directories, Histories, Marriages, Military, Newspapers, Obituaries, Photos, Schools, Tax Lists, Wills, and more. See **http://usgwarchives.net/ne/nefiles.htm.**

■ **1854-1857.** See ***Pioneers, Douglas County, Nebraska, 1854-1857*** **[Online Database],** indexed at the Genealogy Trails website. See **http://genealogytrails.com/neb/douglas/pioneers_1854-57.htm.**

■ **1854-1900s.** See **Biographies - Douglas County, Nebraska [Online Database],** indexed at the Genealogy Trails website. See **http://genealogytrails.com/neb/douglas/bios_index.htm.**

■ **1854-1900s.** See ***Database Search: Lincoln Lancaster County Genealogical Society*** **[Online Database],** search all databases, including Cemetery, Marriage, Mortuary, Probate, Newspaper, Naturalization records, and more. Indexed at the LLCGS.net website. See **www.llcgs.net/searchhome.php.**

■ **1854-1983.** See ***Nebraska Newspaper Archives*** **[Online Database],** digitized and indexed newspapers at the GenealogyBank website for Bloomington, Lincoln, Nebraska City, and Omaha, Nebraska. See **www.genealogybank.com/explore/newspapers/all/usa/nebraska.**

■ **1854-2000.** See ***Linkpendium – Nebraska: Family History & Genealogy, Census, Birth, Marriage, Death, Vital Records & More*** **[Online Databases].** Linkpendium is a genealogical portal site with links to state, county, town, and local databases. Currently listed are selected sites for Nebraska statewide resources (398), Renamed/Discontinued Counties (9), Adams County (602) Antelope County (329), Arthur County (82), Banner County (92), Blaine County (96), Boone County (270), Box Butte County (147) and 86 more Nebraska counties. See **www.linkpendium.com/ne-genealogy.**

■ ***1878-1927 School Census Records, Lancaster County, Nebraska*** **[Online Database],** indexed at the sites.google.com webpage for Lancaster Co NE. See **https://sites.google.com/site/lancastercountyne/school-census-records.**

■ **1883.** See ***Federal Pensioners, 1 January 1883*** **[Online Database],** indexed at the USGenWeb site for Nebraska. The statewide lists are broken into four alpha groups, and there is one list for each Nebraska county. See **www.usgwarchives.net/ne/state/military/penstabl.htm.**

■ ***1890-1891 Nebraska State Gazetteer, Business Directory and Farmer List, Lancaster County, Nebraska*** **[Online Database],** indexed at the USGenWeb site for Lancaster Co NE. See **www.usgennet.org/usa/ne/topic/resources/NSHS/1890Gaz/lancfarm.htm.**

■ ***1893 Roster of Nebraska Veterans – Nebraska Enlistees*** **[Online Database],** indexed at the USGenWeb site for Nebraska. The list includes the Name, Rank, Unit, 1893 Residence, and State of enlistment. See **www.usgennet.org/usa/ne/county/holt/1893/nebraska.html.**

■ **1940.** See ***Who's Who in Nebraska – 1940*** **[Online Database],** index to biographies published by the Nebraska Press Association, Lincoln, NE. The biographies are organized by county. Search the county list, which includes some historical background on each county, and then a list of Who's Who for that county. Indexed at the USGenWeb site for Nebraska. See **www.usgennet.org/usa/ne/topic/resources/OLLibrary/who1940/whowho40.html.**

■ ***1950 Tomahawk Yearbook, University of Omaha*** **[Online Database],** the complete book was digitized at the RootsWeb site for Douglas Co NE. See **www.rootsweb.ancestry.com/~nedougla/html/uom1950/UOM50-1.htm.**

■ ***1951 Tomahawk Yearbook, University of Omaha*** **[Online Database],** the complete book was digitized at the RootsWeb site for Douglas Co NE. See **www.rootsweb.ancestry.com/~nedougla/html/uom1951/.**

■ ***1957 Tomahawk Yearbook, University of Omaha*** **[Online Database],** the complete book was digitized at the Univ. of Omaha website. See **www.e-yearbook.com/sp/eybb?school=72560&year=1957.**

■ **1996-Current.** See ***Nebraska Recent Newspaper Obituaries*** **[Online Database],** digitized and indexed newspaper obituaries at the GenealogyBank website, including newspapers for Ashland, Beatrice, Bellevue, Broken Bow, Chadron, Columbus, David City, Fremont, Gering, Grand Island, Gretna, Hemingford, Kearney, Lexington, Lincoln, Nebraska City, North Platte, Omaha, Papillion, Plattsmouth, Ralston, Schuyler, Scottsbluff, Syracuse, Wahoo, Waverly, and York, Nebraska. See **www.genealogybank.com/explore/obituaries/all/usa/nebraska.**

## Nebraska Periodical Articles
### Censuses & Substitute Name Lists in Genealogical Periodicals

PERSI (PERiodical Source Index) is a digitized database project of the Allen County Public Library (ACPL), Fort Wayne, IN. Since 1986, the PERSI extractors have indexed article titles, places, and surnames from over 11,000 genealogical & historical periodicals. The PERSI database is currently available online through the **FindMyPast.com** subscription website. The Genealogy Center of the ACPL in Fort Wayne IN holds all 11,000 periodicals and will make copies of any article by special request. To obtain an order form for requesting a printed copy of any article indexed in the PERSI database, see **http://genealogycenter.org/docs/default-source/resources/articlerequest.pdf?sfvrsn=2.**

**Nebraska PERSI Search:** Using the FindMyPast.com website, the keywords "Nebraska Tax" had 128 results. "Census" had 392 results. Examples of Nebraska articles available are shown below:

■ **"1854 Nebraska Territory Census" [Printed Article],** in *Roots and Leaves* (Eastern Nebraska Genealogical Society, Fremont, NE), Jan 1978 issue.

■ **"1854 Nebraska Territory Census, Nemaha County" [Printed Article],** in *Genealogist's Post* (R. T. Williams, Miami, FL), Vol. 4, No. 11 (Nov 1967) through Vol. 5, No. 2 (Feb 1968).

■ **"1855 Nebraska Territory Census, Dodge County" [Printed Article],** *in Roots and Leaves*, (Eastern Nebraska Genealogical Society, Fremont, NE), Vol. 17, No. 3 (Fall 1994).

■ **"1855 Nebraska State Census, Washington County" [Printed Article],** in *Roots and Leaves*, (Eastern Nebraska Genealogical Society, Fremont, NE), Vol. 3, No. 3 (Fall 1980).

■ **"1856 Nebraska Territory Census, Burt County" [Printed Article],** name list in *Roots and Leaves*, (Eastern Nebraska Genealogical Society, Fremont, NE), Vol. 3, No. 3 (Fall 1980).

■ **"1856 Nebraska Territory Census, Dodge County" [Printed Article],** name list in *Roots and Leaves*, (Eastern Nebraska Genealogical Society, Fremont, NE), Vol. 17, No. 4 (Winter 1994).

■ **"1856 Nebraska Territory Census, Pawnee County" [Printed Article],** name list in *Genealogist's Post*, (R. T. Williams, Miami, FL), Vol. 4, No. 6 (Jun 1967).

■ **"1856 Nebraska Territory Census, Sarpy County" [Printed Article],** name list in *Remains to be Found*, (Greater Omaha Genealogical Society), March 1986 issue.

■ **"1856 Nebraska Territory Census, Washington County" [Printed Article],** name list in *Roots and Leaves,* (Eastern Nebraska Genealogical Society, Fremont, NE), Vol. 4, No. 1 (Spring 1981).

■ **"1859 Nebraska Territory Census, Saunders County, Salt Creek" [Printed Article],** name list in *Nebraska Ancestree,* (Nebraska State Genealogical Society, Lincoln, NE), Vol. 2, No. 1 (Summer 1979).

■ **"1865 Nebraska Territory Census, Cuming County" [Printed Article],** name list and annotations in Roots and Leaves, (Eastern Nebraska Genealogical Society, Fremont, NE), Vol. 3, No. 1 (Spring 1980).

■ **"1872 Tax List, Antelope County, Nebraska" [Printed Article],** in *Nebraska Ancestree*, (Nebraska State Genealogical Society, Lincoln, NE),Vol. 9, No. 3 (Winter 1987), and Vol. 11, No. 1 (Summer 1988).

■ **"1875-1877 Tax Receipts, Dawson County, Nebraska" [Printed Article],** in *Dawson County Genealogical Newsletter,* (Dawson Co Genealogical Society, Cozad, NE), Vol. 12, No. 2 (Summer 1998) and Vol. 12, No. 3 (Fall 1998).

■ **"1879 Tax Assessors Book, Center Township, Buffalo County, Nebraska" [Printed Article],** in *Buffalo Chips,* (Fort Kearney Genealogical Society, Kearney, NE), Vol. 14, No. 1 (Spring 1991).

■ **"1881 Tax Assessors Book of Personal and Real Estate, Buffalo County, Nebraska" [Printed Article],** in *Buffalo Chips*, (Fort Kearney Genealogical Society, Kearney, NE), Vol. 17, No. 2-3 (Summer 1994).

■ **"1881 Personal Tax List, Greeley County, Nebraska"** [Printed Article], in *Nebraska Ancestree*, (Nebraska State Genealogical Society, Lincoln, NE),Vol. 11, No. 1 (Summer 1988).

■ **"1882 Personal Property Tax List, Shelton Precinct, Buffalo County, Nebraska" [Printed Article],** in *Buffalo Chips*, (Fort Kearney Genealogical Society, Kearney, NE), Vol.. 8, No. 1 (Winter 1985) and Vol. 8, No. 2-4 (Spring 1985).

■ **"1882-1885 Poll Tax, Dawson County, Nebraska" [Printed Article],** in *Nebraska Ancestree*, (Nebraska State Genealogical Society, Lincoln, NE),Vol. 20, No. 1 (Summer 1987) and Vol. 20, No. 2 (Fall 1997).

■ **"1888 Tax List, Fillmore County, Nebraska" [Printed Article],** in *Nebraska Ancestree*, (Nebraska State Genealogical Society, Lincoln, NE),Vol. 7, No. 2 (Fall 1984).

■ **"1889 Tax List, Personal Property, Brown County, Nebraska, (by Precinct)" [Printed Article],** in *Nebraska Ancestree*, (Nebraska State Genealogical Society, Lincoln, NE),Vol. 5, No. 2 (Fall 1982) through Vol. 8, No. 2 (Fall 1984), and Vol. 23, No. 3 (Spring 2001).

## Nebraska Books & Microfilms at the Family History Library

Nebraska's microfilmed territorial and state censuses and major census substitutes are cited below in chronological order. Each item includes a FHL book number or FHL film number, which can be used to search the FHL catalog for more details. To review an item, start at the FamilySearch catalog search page. See **https://familysearch.org/search/catalog/results.** Select "Search by Place" then "United States, Nebraska" to see a list of catalog categories. Or, select "Call Number" then type an FHL book number; or select "Film/Fiche Number" to view a specific title.

■ ***1854, 1855, 1856 Nebraska Territory Censuses* [Printed Index & Microfilm],** extracted by E. Evelyn Cox, published by the author, Ellensburg, WA, 1977. FHL book 978.2 X2p 1854-1856, and FHL film #1036024, and microfiche #6051283.

■ ***1854, 1855, 1856 Nebraska Territorial Census Index* [Printed Index],** edited by Ronald Vern Jackson, publ. Accelerated Indexing Systems, Salt Lake City, UT, 1980, 57 pages, FHL book 978.2 X2jrv 1854-56.

■ **1854-1996.** See ***Nebraska Newspaper Abstracts* [Printed Book],** compiled and publ. Nebraska State Genealogical Society, Alliance, NE, 1984-1996. Contains abstracts arranged in alphabetical order by surname, giving name of person, type of event (birth, marriage, death, obituary, divorce, etc.), date of publication, newspaper name, contents of event, page, town and county.10 Vols., See FHL book 978.2 B32n v. 1-10.

■ **1855-1870.** See ***Douglas County, Nebraska, Naturalization Records, 1855-1870* [Microfilm],** from the originals at NSHS, Lincoln, NE. Filmed by the Genealogical Society of Utah, 1999, 1 roll, FHL film #2168455.

■ **1855-1940.** See ***Irish and Scotch-Irish Who Made a Declaration of Intention to Naturalize From Cass, Douglas, Lancaster, Nemaha, Otoe, Richardson, Sarpy and York Counties in Nebraska, 1855-1940* [Printed Book],** compiled by Ellen M. and Raymond D. DeVries, publ. 1997, Lincoln, NE, 152 pages, FHL book 978.22 P4d.

■ **1861-1865.** See ***Index to Compiled Service Records of Volunteer Union Soldiers Who Served in Organizations from the Territory of Nebraska* [Microfilm],** from the originals at the National Archives, Washington, DC. Filmed by the National Archives, 1964, 2 rolls, FHL film #821905 (Surnames A-La); and FHL film #821906 (Surnames Le-Z).

■ **1866-1909.** See ***An Index to the Early Marriage Records of Lancaster County, Nebraska: 1866-1909* [Printed Book],** compiled and publ. Lincoln-Lancaster County Genealogical Society, 1987, 3 vols. Vol. 1: Books 1-13; Vol. 2: Books 14-26; Vol. 3: Books 27-31. See FHL book 978.2293 V22i 1866-1906 v.1-3.

■ ***1866-1921 Omaha and Douglas County Directories* [Microfilm],** from the originals at various libraries and societies, filmed by Research Publications, Woodbridge, CT, 1980-1984, 25 rolls, beginning with FHL film #1377220 (1866 Collins' Omaha Directory). For a complete list of roll numbers and contents of each roll, see the online FHL catalog page for this title. See **https://familysearch.org/search/catalog/545787.**

■ **1873-1900.** See ***Sittler Index of Surnames: For Which Information has been Abstracted from the (Lincoln) Nebraska State Journal*** **[Printed Book],** by Melvin Sittler, publ. Lincoln-Lancaster County Genealogical Society, 1983-1993, 5 vols: Vol. 1: 1873-1899, A-D; Vol. 2: 1873-1899, E-K; Vol. 3: 1873-1899, L-R; Vol. 4: 1873-1899, S-Z; and Vol. 4: 1900. See FHL book 978.2293 D22sl v. 1-5.

■ ***1876 Tax List, Dodge County, Nebraska*** **[Printed Book],** compiled and published by the Eastern Nebraska Genealogical Society, Fremont, NE, 2000, 26 pages. Includes surname index. Contains name of property owner, taxation number, description of property, amount of tax liability. Includes Dodge County tax books, nos. 6, 8 and 10. FHL book 978.2235 R4d.

■ **1876-1885.** See ***1876 Nebraska State Census, Sarpy County, with Mortality Schedule; and 1885 State Census*** **[Printed Book],** compiled and published by the Eastern Nebraska Genealogical Society, Fremont, NE, 1989, 63 pages. Contains an abstract of the 1885 and 1876 Sarpy County census, arranged in alphabetical order by surname, showing name of head of household, names of other persons in the household, ages, places of birth, other information, township where living, and frame number on microfilm of original census. See FHL book 978.2256 X22s.

■ **1882 History.** See ***History of the State of Nebraska: Containing a Full Account of its Early Settlements; Also an Extended Description of its Counties, Cities, Towns and Villages. and Biographical Sketches*** **[Printed Book & Microfilm],** by A. T. Andreas, published by Western Historical Co., Chicago, 1882, 2 vols., 1,506 pages. This is the standard history of Nebraska. In the "Military History" section are complete rosters of those persons serving in Nebraska units during the Civil War and Indian campaigns on the Plains, 1861-1869. These rosters list names, dates of service, Nebraska residence, and remarks about their service. Contents: Part 1: Early history of Nebraska to Dundy County; Part 2: Fillmore County to York County. FHL book 978.2 H2h and FHL film #1000178. See also, ***Index to History of the State of Nebraska: Published in Chicago by the Western Historical Company, A.T. Andreas, Proprietor, 1882, and Commonly Known as Andreas' History of Nebraska*** **[Microfilm],** compiled by Raymond E. Dale, originally published by the Nebraska State Historical Society, 1963, 500 pages. Filmed by the Genealogical Society of Utah, FHL film #1689292.

■ **1883-1935 Lincoln (Nebraska) City Directories [Microfilm],** from the original records located in various libraries and societies, filmed by Research Publications, Inc., Woodbridge, CT, 199?, 15 rolls, beginning with FHL film #2156801 (1883-1884 Wolfe's Lincoln city directory). For a complete list of roll numbers and contents of each roll, see the online FHL catalog page for this title. See **https://familysearch.org/search/catalog/993193.**

■ **1884-1897.** See **Lancaster County Probate Records, 1884-1897 [Printed Index & Microfilm],** compiled by Ellen DeVries, publ. Lincoln-Lancaster Co Genealogical Society, 2000, 99 pages, FHL book 978.2293 P22d. Also on microfilm, FHL film #1440468.

■ **1885.** See ***Schedules of the Nebraska State Census of 1885*** **[Microfilm],** from the originals located at the Central Plains National Archives Branch, Kansas City, MO. This 1885 state census was taken on the same forms used for the 1880 federal census. However, first names were rarely shown, but given as initials only, followed by the surname. The Federal Government proposed this census to all states and territories with an offer to help financially. Nebraska was one of five states and territories that took up the offer. But this was a state census, not a federal census. The feds also provided the printed forms, and asked that a copy of the enumeration be kept in Nebraska, another sent to Washington, DC. The state copy was lost. This is the federal copy, which is missing Chase county only. Filmed by the National Archives, 1961, 56 rolls, beginning with FHL film #499529 (Adams County, vol. 1). For a complete list of roll numbers and contents of each roll, see the online FHL catalog page for this title. See **https://familysearch.org/search/catalog/181869.**

■ ***1885 Lincoln County, Nebraska State Census*** **[Printed Book],** transcribed and published by Gloria Pressnall, aided by members of the North Platte Genealogical Society, 1987, 150 pages. Includes index and reprints of 1885 maps of North Platte and Lincoln County. FHL book 978.282 X2p. Also on 3 microfiche, FHL film #6050983.

■ ***1885 Washington County, Nebraska State Census*** **[Printed Book],** compiled and published by the Eastern Nebraska Genealogical Society, Fremont, NE, 1989, 97 pages. Contains an abstract of the Washington County, Nebraska 1885 census arranged in alphabetical order by surname. FHL book 978.2245 X28w.

✓ **NOTE: 1886-1891 Directories.** The Nebraska State Historical Society (NSHS) has an 1886 and an *1890-91 Nebraska Gazetteer and Business Directory* that lists farmers and businessmen by towns and counties. Both provide name, occupation, post office address, and county of residence. The 1886 Gazetteer is indexed, the 1890-1891 Gazetteer is online at the USGenWeb site for Nebraska (see Various Websites section, p. 177).The NSHS has Nebraska gazetteers for other years that list businessmen, but not farmers, by towns and counties only. These were published irregularly between 1879-1917. Microfilm copies of the gazetteers are available through interlibrary loan. None of these directories are available at the FHL in Salt Lake City. For information about borrowing materials on microfilm from the NSHS, visit their Web site relating to interlibrary loans at: **www.nebraskahistory.org/lib-arch/services/refrence/loans.htm.**

■ ***1886 Douglas County, Nebraska Voter Registration List*** **[Printed Book],** published by the Greater Omaha Genealogical Society, 1981, 84 pages. Includes index. FHL book 978.2254 N4d.

■ ***1887 Abstract of Tax List, Box Butte County, Nebraska*** **[Printed Book],** compiled by Janella Guthrie, published by the Northwest Genealogical Society, Alliance, NE, 1980, 49 pages.

■ ***1889-1906 Scotts Bluff County, Nebraska, Index of Head of Family Names, Personal Property Assessment; Incomplete: Castle Rock Precinct, Ford Precinct, Gering Precinct, Highland Precinct, Kiowa Precinct, Mitchell Precinct, Rose Precinct, Robidoux Precinct, Tabor Precinct, and Winter Creek Precinct*** **[Printed Book],** compiled and published by the Rebecca Winters Genealogical Society, Scottsbluff, NE, 1 vol., 1998, FHL book 978.298 R4.

■ ***1892-1896 Poll & Personal Taxes, Buffalo County, Nebraska*** **[Printed Book],** typed by Wilma Holderness Burgland; printed by Lynnda Wohleb Shaffer, published by the Fort Kearny Genealogical Society, Fort Kearny, NE, 1985, 141 pages. From introduction: "In this book, you will find the names of the heads of the household that were levied a personal or poll tax during 1892-96 in Buffalo County, Nebraska. We have not indicated whether the tax was for personal or poll in this index. We felt it more important to just get the list of the names of people living in the area." See FHL book 978.245 R4p.

■ **1903-1904.** See ***Index to Selected Information From Lincoln Evening News*** **[Printed Book],** by Teresa Sullivan, et al. Contains an alphabetical listing by surname of persons in notices of birth, death, marriage, divorce and other, and pension published in the *Evening News*. Gives full name, place of event or residence, type of event, date of publication, newspaper page and column number. Publ. Lincoln-Lancaster Co Genealogical Society, 2002, 220 pages, FHL book 978.2293/L1B32L 1903-1904.

■ ***1906-1916 York City/County Directories*** **[Microfilm],** from the original records located in various libraries and societies, filmed by Primary Source Microfilm, Woodbridge, CT, 199?, 1 roll, containing R.L. Polk & Co.'s York City directory, including a list of taxpayers in York County, 1906-1907; FHL film #2310390 Item 1; R.L. Polk & Co.'s York City directory, 1908, and list of taxpayers in York County, FHL film #2310390 Item 2; R.L. Polk & Co.'s York City directory, 1911 FHL film #2310390 Item 3 ; R.L. Polk & Co.'s York City directory, 1913-1914, FHL film #310390 Item 4; and R.. Polk & Co.'s York City directory, 1915-1916 and taxpayers in York County, FHL film #10390, Item 5.

■ ***1976 Bicentennial Album of Pawnee County: Containing Plats of the Precincts, Directory, Pictures, Histories, Cattle Brands, etc.*** **[Printed Book],** compiled by Brand Irons Pictorial County Albums, McPherson, KS, 1976, 406 pages. Includes biographical sketches of many Pawnee County families. FHL book 978.2284 H2b.

## DAKOTA COUNTRY
### Censuses & Substitutes before ND / SD Statehood

The French-Canadian trading posts known as the Red River Settlements were mainly in what is now Manitoba. There were a number of Métis traders who followed the Red River south into the Dakota Country to establish trade with the Indians. In 1797, Jean Baptiste Chaboillez, working for the North West Company, established a trading post at Pembina (present North Dakota). Soon after, a Hudson's Bay Company trading post was established near Pembina as well. The Pembina settlements were not American territory until the Anglo-American Convention of 1818, when the U.S. and Britain agreed on the 49th parallel as the international boundary.

**Manitoba Censuses, 1832-1870.** There are several extant censuses available at the Provincial Archives of Manitoba relating to the Red River Settlements. The people identified therein may be some of those who traveled back and forth into the Dakota Country.

**American Censuses, 1836-1857**. The first American census taken in the Dakota Country was the 1836 Wisconsin Territory census, which included the Pembina settlements on the Red River (2 miles south of the Canadian border). In the 1850 federal census, the Dakota Country areas east of the Missouri River were part of Pembina County, Minnesota Territory. The same area was included in the 1857 MN Territory Census.

**Dakota Country, 1858-1861:** When Minnesota became a state in 1858, a part of the Dakota Country was orphaned, and remained without jurisdiction for three years. The area from the Minnesota line to the Missouri River was enumerated as *Unorganized Dakota* in the 1860 federal census, while Dakota areas west of the Missouri River were part of Nebraska Territory.

**Dakota Territory, 1861-1884:** Dakota Territory was created in 1861. The original area included all of present North Dakota, South Dakota, and the parts of present Montana and Wyoming east of the Continental Divide. Yankton was the first territorial capital, replaced by Bismarck in 1863. The territory took only one territorial census, a special enumeration taken in 1885 with federal assistance. The original manuscripts for the 1885 Dakota Territory census schedules were divided, the northern counties now kept at the State Historical Society of North Dakota in Bismarck; the southern counties at the South Dakota State Historical Society in Pierre.

**Censuses Online:** Both the North Dakota portion and South Dakota portion of the 1885 Dakota Territory census are available online. Because the original census was divided, the databases (images and indexes) are shown under their respective states.

## Censuses and Substitutes for the Dakota Country, 1832-1885

■ **1832-1870 Red River Censuses.** See ***Red River Settlement and Province of Manitoba: A Typed Card Index to the Nominal Census Returns, 1832-1870*** **[Microfilm],** from records at the Provincial Archives of Manitoba, Winnipeg, Canada. The early censuses were taken by the Hudson's Bay Company, which had taken over the North West Company in 1821. The Red River Settlements were located in the Red and Assiniboine Rivers area of Manitoba. Early French trappers, traders, and settlers were known to move up and down the Red River between present Manitoba and North Dakota. They were the founders of the Pembina settlements in present North Dakota. This is a combined index to the nominal (head of household) census returns for 1832, 1833, 1838, 1840, 1843, 1846-47, 1849, 1856 (incomplete) and every-name 1870, for the Lower Settlement, Grant Town and Indian villages. Filmed by the Genealogical Society of Utah, 1985, 3 rolls, beginning with FHL film #1420272. See also ***Surname Index to the 1870 Census of Manitoba and Red River*** **[Printed Book],** compiled by Eric Jonasson, publ. Wheatfield Press, Winnipeg, 1981, 27 pages, FHL book 971.27 X22j 1870.

✓ **NOTE:** The 1870 Manitoba/Red River census names all members of a family, relationship to head, age, sex, occupation, religion, whether Métis (French & Indian blood), or other race; and identifies the full name of a father and full maiden name of a mother for each person. It is one of the most detailed censuses ever done in North America.

■ **1836 Wisconsin Territory Census.** See ***The First Census of the Original Counties of Dubuque and Demoine (Iowa) Taken in July, 1836*** **[Microfilm],** from a book edited by Benjamin F. Shambaugh, published by the Historical Department of Iowa, 1897-1898, 93 pages. Includes Pembina settlements in present-day North Dakota. Names were extracted from the original manuscript returns preserved in the office of the Secretary of State of Wisconsin. The census taken in accordance with the act of Congress erecting the territory of Wisconsin (of which these two counties at the time formed a part) comprising the present states of Iowa, Minnesota and part of North Dakota and South Dakota. Filmed by the Genealogical Society of Utah, 1978, 1 roll, FHL film #1022202. Another filming, #989450.

■ **1838 Iowa Territory Census,** see ***Iowa 1838 Territorial Census Index*** **[Printed Index],** edited by Ronald Vern Jackson, et al, publ. Accelerated Indexing Systems, Bountiful, UT, 1984, FHL book 977.7 X22ji 1838. Includes the Pembina settlements in present-day North Dakota. See also Marie Haefner, **"The Census of 1838,"** in *The Palimpsest* (IA State Hist. Soc., Des Moines), Vol. 19 (May 1938) pp 185-192.

■ **1840 Federal Census, Iowa Territory.** In 1840, Iowa Territory included lands between the Mississippi and Missouri Rivers, from its present boundary with Missouri to the western part of present Minnesota, and

North and South Dakota. An extract was done as ***The 1840 Iowa Census*** **[Printed Book],** compiled by Rowene Obert, Helen Blumhagen, Wilma Adkins, published Salt Lake City, UT 1968. Includes index. Includes the 18 original counties and several precincts which comprised the entire area of Iowa Territory. FHL book 977.7 X2p 1840 and FHL film #844885.

■ **1850 Federal Census, Minnesota Territory.** See ***Dakota Census Index; 1850 Pembina District,*** **[Printed Index]** edited by Ronald Vern Jackson, published by Accelerated Indexing Systems, Bountiful, UT, 1982, 61 pages. The names from Pembina County were extracted from the state copy of the Minnesota Territory 1850 census, located at the Minnesota State Historical Society in St. Paul. FHL book 978 X22d 1850. See also ***Minnesota Territorial Census, 1850*** **[Printed Book],** edited by Patricia C. Harpole and Mary D. Nagle, published by the Minnesota Historical Society, 1972, 115 pages. FHL book 977.6 X2ph 1850. The federal copy of the ***1850 MN Territory Census*** schedules can be found on FHL film #14834.

■ ***1857 Federal Census, Minnesota Territory*** **[Microfilm],** from the original records located at the National Archives, Central Plains Region, Kansas City, MO. Filmed by the National Archives, 1973, series T1175, 8 rolls, available from the FHL, including Pembina County (present North Dakota) on FHL film #944287.

■ ***1857 Federal Census Abstracts, Minnesota Territory*** **[Printed Book],** county-wide abstracts by Mary Bakeman, published by the Minnesota Historical Society, 1994-2003 for all counties, including 1857 Pembina County, MHS call no. CS42 .M553 no. 21-23.

■ **1860.** See ***Unorganized Dakota, 1860 Federal Census: Population Schedules*** **[Microfilm],** from the originals at the National Archives, Washington, DC. The name *Unorganized Dakota* was used only by the U.S. Census Office to describe the area. The main population centers of Unorganized Dakota were the communities of Sioux Falls, Yankton Agency, and the Pembina settlements on the Red River, with about 4,800 people total. For convenience, this 1860 federal census enumerated a few inhabitants of the western frontier, even though the outposts were actually part of Nebraska Territory. Ft. Union, on the Missouri River; and Ft. Alexander on the Yellowstone River, were both included with Unorganized Dakota. Ft. Alexander was located in present-day Rosebud County, Montana; while Ft. Union was located almost exactly on the present-day North Dakota/Montana line. Other outposts enumerated in the Unorganized Dakota census were the Missouri River outposts at Ft. Clark, Ft. William, and Ft. Stevenson; as well as the Orphan's Village on the Red River; and the Old Trading House on the Niobrara River. The 1860 census was filmed twice. The second filming is easier to read, with one census page per frame, compared to the first filming, which had two census pages per frame. Filmed by the National Archives, 1950, 1967, 2 rolls, FHL film #14889 (1st filming: Dakota, entire territory); and FHL film #803094 (2nd filming: Dakota, entire territory). See also ***Dakota Territory 1860*** **[Printed Book],** edited by Ronald Vern Jackson, publ. Accelerated Indexing Systems, North Salt Lake, UT, 55 pages, FHL book 978 X22. See also, ***United States Census, 1860*** **[Online Database],** digitized and indexed at the FamilySearch.org website, for all states and territories, including "Unorganized Dakota."

■ ***1860 Federal Census Images (Unorganized Dakota)*** **[Online Database],** digitized 1860 census pages, organized Post Office, town, or area descriptions, such as "between Red River and Big Sioux." The images are the actual census forms, where the County of and State are replaced with "Unorganized Dakota" See **www.usgwarchives.net/sd/census/1860images.html.**

■ **1860.** See ***Dakota Territory 1860 Census – Interactive Search*** **[Online Database].** Type a couple letters of a surname to search the entire database. See **www.rootsweb.ancestry.com/cgi-bin/sdcensus/sd1860cen.pl.**

■ **"1861 Dakota Inhabitants, A-D,"** in *Wy-Mon-Dak Messenger* (Tri-State Genealogical Society, Belle Fourche, SD), (Summer 1989).

■ **"1861 Dakota Inhabitants, D-M,"** in *Wy-Mon-Dak Messenger,* (Tri-State Genealogical Society, Belle Fourche, SD), (Fall 1989).

■ **"1861 Dakota Inhabitants, M-Z,"** in *Wy-Mon-Dak Messenger* (Tri-State Genealogical Society, Belle Fourche, SD), (Winter 1990).

■ **1861-1865.** See ***Index to Compiled Service Records of Volunteer Union soldiers Who Served in Organizations From the Territory of Dakota*** **[Microfilm],** from the original records at the National Archives, Washington, DC, series M0536, 1 roll, NARA film #M536-1, FHL film #881616.

■ **1861-1889.** See **History of Dakota Territory [Online Database],** digitized and indexed at the Ancestry.com website. Source: Book, same title, by George W. Kingsbury, 2 Vols., publ. 1915. This book includes a good read about the battle between the Republicans and the Democrats in Congress, and the split of Dakota Territory into North and South Dakota. This database has 5,248 records. See **http://search.ancestry.com/search/db.aspx?dbid=25507.**

■ **1870 and 1880 Federal Census, Dakota Territory [Online Databases],** identified in the Federal Censuses and National Name Lists chapter. See Vol. 3 – Western States & National Name Lists.

■ **"1882 Tax List, Burleigh County, Dakota Territory" [Printed Article],** in *Bismarck-Mandan Historical and Genealogical Society Quarterly,* (Bismarck, ND), (Vol. 10, No. 1 (Mar 1981) through Vol. 12, No. 4 (Dec 1983); and Vol. 14, No. 4 (Dec 1985) through Vol. 15, No. 3 (Sep 1986).

■ **1883 Directory.** See ***The Leading Business Men of Dakota Cities: Accompanying the Map of Dakota Territory, Name and Address*** **[Microfilm],** from the original published by Warner & Foote, Minneapolis, MN, 1883, 105 pages. Filmed for the FHL by the Library of Congress, 1984, 1 roll, FHL film #1464014.

■ **1883.** See ***Pensioners on the Roll as of January 1, 1883 (Living in Dakota Territory)*** **[Printed Book],** an extraction from the U.S. Pension Bureau's publication for all states, compiled and publ. Park Genealogical Books, Roseville, MN, 26 pages, FHL book 976 M2pr.

# NORTH DAKOTA
## Censuses & Substitutes, 1861-2015

In November 1889, both North Dakota and South Dakota were admitted as states with the same boundaries as today. Although Dakota Territory had petitioned Congress to be a single state, that would have caused two Democratic senators to be added, which would have upset the balance in Congress. By splitting Dakota Territory into two states, two Republican senators and two Democratic senators were added to Congress, maintaining the balance of power.

After admission to the Union, the state of North Dakota conducted three state censuses, in 1905, 1915 and 1925. Only a statistical summary of the 1905 state census survives, but the full census schedules for the 1915 and 1925 censuses are extant. The original state censuses are located at the State Historical Society of North Dakota in Bismarck. There are no complete printed indexes, but both censuses were microfilmed by the SHSND and are available on inter-library loan. Copies of the microfilm can be also used at the Family History Library in Salt Lake City, but as part of the agreement to acquire the film, they are not allowed to circulate on interlibrary loan through the FHL. The North Dakota censuses begin with the Dakota Territory census of 1885, which was later divided into northern and southern counties. The original manuscripts for the 1885 census for the North Dakota counties are located at the State Historical Society of North Dakota in Bismarck.

**Censuses Online:** The North Dakota portion of the 1885 Dakota Territory census was indexed online at the ND State Univ. website; and indexed as well at the Ancestry.com website. The 1915 and 1925 North Dakota Sate Censuses are digitized and indexed online at both Ancestry.com and FamilySearrch.org.

---

## Online Resources at North Dakota State Websites

■ **1861-1900s.** ***North Dakota Biography Index*** **[Online Database],** indexed at the ND State Univ. website. This database is an ongoing project of the NDSU Institute for Regional Studies to provide access to biographical sketches found in a wide variety of North Dakota publications. It currently contains some 250,000 names to published biographical sketches of North Dakotans found in over 800 publications. Additional names continue to be added on a regular basis. Consult the Institute's **information page** for the scope and content of the records and for ordering copies. See **https://library.ndsu.edu/db/biography.**

■ **1873-1952.** See **North Dakota Naturalization Records Index [Online Database],** indexed at the ND State University website. The North Dakota Naturalization Records index was compiled at the State Historical Society of North Dakota, where all original county naturalization records are preserved and have been microfilmed. In cooperation with the NDSU Institute for Regional Studies, the index is made available as a searchable database. The database contains over 212,000 names, giving the county where the declaration of intention (1st papers) was filed and the naturalization occurred (2nd papers), the date of both events, and from what country the person emigrated. Consult the State Historical Society of

North Dakota's Naturalization Records' information sheet regarding the history of the naturalization laws, types of records and how to use them. See **www.history.nd.gov/archives/datanaturalization.html**. You may also consult the Institute for Regional Studies' information page for the scope and content of the records, and access to the database. See **https://library.ndsu.edu/ndsuarchives/north-dakota-naturalization-records-database.**

■ **1881-2015.** See ***Public Death Index* [Online Database],** indexed at the ND Dept of Health website. The search criteria includes Last name, First name, Date of death, County of death, which can ordered by name, birth date, death date, or county. The records of the previous 12 months from the date of search are not available. Searching is a bit restrictive, because a name, date of death, and county of death is required. No global searching. Still, North Dakota has an enlightened policy about death records open to the public. See **https://apps.nd.gov/doh/certificates/deathCertSearch.htm.**

■ **1885.** See **Dakota Territory 1885 Census [Online Database],** indexed at the ND State Univ. website. The NDSU Institute for Regional Studies headed a statewide cooperative project to index the entire original Dakota Territory 1885 Census schedules for the counties that today form North Dakota. The database contains over 151,500 names. Each entry includes: name, age, nativity, occupation, county of residence, and exact location of the entry in the census schedule. Consult the Institute's information page for the scope and content of the records, ordering copies, and access to the database. See **https://library.ndsu.edu/ndsuarchives/dakota-territory-1885-census-database**.

■ **1890-1940.** See **Index to Oral History Collection [Online Database],** a PDF list of oral history interviews, located at the State Historical Society of North Dakota website. The collection has over 1,000 tapes created from 1974-1977, covering personal history from 1890-1940. This 50-page PDF list of the people involved in the interviews also explains how to access them. See **http://history.nd.gov/archives/ORALHIST.pdf.**

## North Dakota Databases Online at Ancestry.com

The Ancestry.com subscription website allows free access to all indexes, but to view any particular record requires a membership. Ancestry offers trial memberships and subscriptions for short periods and reduced rates. The following databases at the Ancestry.com website are unique statewide North Dakota databases under the categories of Census & Voter Lists, Vital Records, Military, Immigrations, and Wills & Probates. To review the complete list of statewide databases, and several countywide databases, see **http://search.ancestry.com/Places/US/North-Dakota/Default.aspx.**

■ **1870-1890.** See ***North Dakota, Compiled Census Index, 1870-1890* [Online Database],** indexed at the Ancestry.com website. Source: Accelerated Indexing Systems databases acquired by Ancestry in 1999. This collection contains the following indexes: 1870 Federal Census Index; 1885 ND State Census Index; 1890 Veterans Schedules. This database has 5,833 records. See **http://search.ancestry.com/search/db.aspx?dbid=3565.**

■ **1873-1944.** See **Web: Cass County, North Dakota, Marriage License Index, 1873-1944 [Online Database],** indexed at the Ancestry.com website. This database is also accessible at the North Dakota State University Archives website. Each index record includes: Name, Gender, Marriage date, Marriage place, Spouse, and License no. This database has 29,886 records. See **http://search.ancestry.com/search/db.aspx?dbid=70839.**

■ **1876-1950.** See ***Web: Cass County, North Dakota, Probate Index, 1876-1950* [Online Database],** indexed at the Ancestry.com website. This database is also accessible at the North Dakota State University Archives website. Each index record includes: Name, Death date, Death place, and Case number. This database has 6,183 records. See **http://search.ancestry.com/search/db.aspx?dbid=70842.**

■ **1885-1925.** See ***North Dakota, Territorial and State Censuses, 1885, 1915, 1925* [Online Database],** digitized and indexed at the Ancestry.com website. Source: ND State University Archives, Fargo, ND. This database contains an index and images of the North Dakota state censuses 1885, 1915 and 1925. The 1885 ND State Census is actually a portion of the Dakota Territory Census, taken before North Dakota became a state in 1889. The South Dakota portion is not included here. Also, schedules have survived for fifty of the fifty-six counties that existed in the northern half of Dakota Territory. All fifty counties are now indexed and contained in this database. The missing county schedules include Boreham, DeSmet, Flannery, Hettinger, Sheridan and Stevens County, ND. Information that may be available in this index includes: Place of enumeration (locality, county, and state), Enumeration date, Name (which may include a nickname or maiden name), Gender, Race, and Age. This database has 1,423,483 **http://search.ancestry.com/search/db.aspx?dbid=1078.**

■ ***1890 Census Substitutes (North Dakota Locations)*** **[Online Database],** indexed at the Ancestry.com website. This is Ancestry's collection of city directories (and other name lists) from all over the U.S. for the time of the lost 1890 federal census. Included are city directories for Grand Forks, ND, 1889-1892. Go to *View All Collections Included in this Search* for an alpha list of databases, by place (county, city, state), and year(s). See **http://search.ancestry.com/search/group/1890census.**

■ **1903-1944.** See ***North Dakota and Washington, Chinese Passenger Arrivals and Disposition, 1903-1944*** **[Online Database],** indexed at the Ancestry.com website. Source: National Archives microfilm, same title. Contained in this database are passenger arrival and disposition lists for Chinese immigrants between the years 1903 and 1944. The primary port of entry was Seattle, Washington; however, some additional entry ports, listed below, are also included in these records. Information that can be found includes surname, vessel name, arrival date, class or citizenship status, and whether the individual was admitted or denied. Ports of entry in these records: Seattle Washington, 1903–1944; Vancouver, British Columbia, Canada, 1911–1916 (in transit to U.S.); Sumas, Washington, 1903–1909; and Portal, North Dakota, 1903–1910. This database has 61,051 records. See **http://search.ancestry.com/search/db.aspx?dbid=2033.**

■ **1903-1997.** See ***Web: North Dakota, Select Funeral Home Indexes, 1903-1997*** **[Online Database],** indexed at the Ancestry.com website. This database is also accessible at the Red River Valley Genealogy Society website. Each index record includes: Name, Birth date, Death age, Funeral Home/Location, and Vol. no. This database has 29,420 records. See **http://search.ancestry.com/search/db.aspx?dbid=70788.**

■ **1917-1918.** See ***Roster of the Men and Women Who Served in the Army or Naval Service (including the Marine Corps) of the United States or its Allies From the State of North Dakota in the World War, 1917-1918, Vols. 1-4*** **[Online Database],** indexed at the Ancestry.com website. Source: Book, same title, publ. 1931, Bismarck Tribune Co. This database has the scanned images from the text of the 4-vol. book, with an OCR name index for searching. This database has 1,803 pages. See **http://search.ancestry.com/search/db.aspx?dbid=31404.**

■ **1917-1918.** See ***North Dakota Military Men, 1917-1918*** **[Online Database],** indexed at the Ancestry.com website. Source: *Roster of the Men and Women,* publ. 1931. This database is a collection of military records for men who served in the war from North Dakota. Originally compiled in 1931, it provides the names for men who served in the army, navy, and marines. In addition to providing the individual's name, it reveals city of residence, unit of service, birth date or age, and other helpful facts. It also contains the location and date of enlistment and discharge information. The names of over 32,000 men are included in the collection. This database has 26,753 records. See **http://search.ancestry.com/search/db.aspx?dbid=4569.**

■ **1958.** See ***Fargo, North Dakota, Passenger Lists, 1958*** **[Online Database],** indexed at the Ancestry.com website. Source: National Archives microfilm, same title. These passenger and crew lists from aircrafts were recorded on a variety of forms that were then turned over to the Immigration and Naturalization Service. Details requested on the forms varied, but they typically include the name of the vessel and arrival date, ports of departure and arrival, dates of departure and arrival, full name, age, gender, physical description, military rank (if any), occupation, birthplace, citizen of what country, and residence. This database has 280 records. See **http://search.ancestry.com/search/db.aspx?dbid=9270.**

## North Dakota Databases Online at FamilySearch.org

The following databases are available for free at the FamilySearch.org website. To see the current list, visit the North Dakota Indexed Historical Records and North Dakota Image Only Historical Records webpage. Both lists are updated periodically. See **https://familysearch.org/search/collection/location/40.**

■ **1861-1865.** See ***Dakota Territory Civil War Service Records of Union Soldiers, 1861-1865*** **[Online Database],** indexed at the FamilySearch.org website. Source: National Archives microfilm series M1960. This database consists of Union service records of soldiers who served in the 1st Battalion Dakota Cavalry from the Territory of Dakota. The records include a jacket-envelope for each soldier, labeled with his name, his rank, and the unit in which he served. The jacket-envelope typically contains card abstracts of entries relating to the soldier as found in original muster rolls, returns, rosters, payrolls, appointment books, hospital registers, prison registers and rolls, parole rolls, inspection reports; and the originals of any papers relating solely to the particular soldier. This database has 4,693 records. See **https://familysearch.org/search/collection/1932393.**

■ **1910-1952.** See ***North Dakota Manifests of Immigrant Arrivals, 1910-1952* [Online Database],** indexed at the FamilySearch.org website. Source: National Archives microfilm series A3479 & A3560. This collection contains Arrival Manifests of Immigrants Arriving in Ambrose, Antler, Carbury, Fortuna, Noonan, Northgate, Portal, Saint John, Sherwood, and Westhope, North Dakota, 1910-1952. The records may include full name, age, gender, marital status, citizenship, last permanent residence, birthplace, and final destination. This database has 5,740 records. See **https://familysearch.org/search/collection/2443935.**

■ **1915.** See ***North Dakota Census, 1915* [Online Database],** digitized and indexed at the FamilySearch.org website. Source: State Historical Society of North Dakota, Bismarck. The index record includes: Name Birth, Parents, Spouse, Children, Other (names living in the household), and Residence. More details can be viewed on the digitized census page. This database has 619,486 records. See **https://familysearch.org/search/collection/2346284**.

■ **1925.** See ***North Dakota Census, 1925* [Online Database],** indexed at the FamilySearch.org website. Source: State Historical Society of North Dakota, Bismarck. The index record includes: Name Birth, Parents, Spouse, Children, Other (names living in the household), and Residence. More details can be viewed on the digitized census page. This database has 678,504 records. See **https://familysearch.org/search/collection/2351024.**

## North Dakota Databases Online At Various Websites

■ **1861-1862.** See ***Gazetteer of Pioneers and Others in North Dakota Previous to 1862* [Online Database],** extracted from "Collection of the State Historical Society," Vol. 1, 1906. Alpha list and annotations at the Genealogy Trails website. See **http://genealogytrails.com/ndak/earlysettlers.html.**

■ **1861-1900s North Dakota Original Land Owners.** See the ***Family Maps*** series for North Dakota counties, maps of all original land patents, compiled by Greg Boyd, publ. Arphax Publishing Co., Norman, OK. These privately-produced computer-generated maps show the first property owners for an entire county, produced as a book of maps, each map laid out on the federal township grid, and includes indexes to help you locate a person, place-name, or cemetery. Additional maps are added for each county to show roads, waterways, railroads, selected city centers, and cemeteries within a county. At this writing, *Family Maps* books have been published for Barnes County, North Dakota, Kidder County, North Dakota. See **www.arphax.com.**

■ **1861-1900s.** See ***Original Land Owners, Burleigh County, North Dakota* [Online Database],** index of the BLM Landowner records by surname, at the USGenWeb Archives site for Burleigh Co ND. See **www.usgwarchives.net/nd/burleigh/burlland.html**.

■ **1861-1900s.** See ***North Dakota GenWeb Archives* [Online Database].** The NDGenWeb site offers free genealogical databases with searchable statewide name lists and for all North Dakota counties. Databases may include Bibles, Biographies, Cemeteries, Censuses, Court Records, Deaths, Deeds, Directories, Histories, Marriages, Military, Newspapers, Obituaries, Photos, Schools, Tax Lists, Wills, and more. See **http://usgwarchives.net/nd/ndfiles.htm.**

■ **1865-1931.** See ***North Dakota Newspaper Archives* [Online Database],** digitized and indexed newspapers at the GenealogyBank website for Bismarck, Fargo, Fort Rice, Grand Forks, Mandan, Michigan, and Tower City. See **www.genealogybank.com/explore/newspapers/all/usa/north-dakota.**

■ **1865-2000.** See ***Linkpendium – North Dakota: Family History & Genealogy, Census, Birth, Marriage, Death, Vital Records & More* [Online Databases].** Linkpendium is a genealogical portal site with links to state, county, town, and local databases. Currently listed are selected sites for North Dakota statewide resources (304), Renamed/Discontinued Counties (19), Adams County (97), Barnes County (182), Benson County (124), Billings County (97),

Bottineau County (132), Bowman County (101), and 47 more North Dakota counties. See
www.linkpendium.com/nd-genealogy.

■ **1873-1900.** See ***Early History-Pioneers of Burleigh County, North Dakota*** **[Online Database],** indexed at the Genealogy Trails website. See
http://genealogytrails.com/ndak/burleigh/history.html#pioneers.

■ **1987-Current.** See ***North Dakota Recent Newspaper Obituaries*** **[Online Database],** digitized and indexed newspaper obituaries at the GenealogyBank website, including newspapers for Beulah, Bismarck, Center, Devils Lake, Garrison, Grand Forks, Hankinson, Hazen, McClusky, New Town, Parshall, Turtle Lake, Underwood, Valley City, Velva, Wahpeton, Washburn, and Williston. See
www.genealogybank.com/explore/obituaries/all/usa/north-dakota.

## North Dakota PERSI Search

Using the **FindMyPast.com** website, the keywords "North Dakota Census" had 236 results. Examples of North Dakota articles available are shown below:

■ **"1915 North Dakota State Census, Bottineau County, Blaine Twp." [Printed Article],** in *North Central North Dakota Genealogical Record,* (Mouse River Loop Genealogical Society, Minot, ND), No. 84 (Sep 2000).

■ **"1915 North Dakota State Census, Burke County" [Printed Article],** in *North Central North Dakota Genealogical Record,* (Mouse River Loop Genealogical Society, Minot, ND), Vol. 1, (Nov 1983).

■ **"1915 North Dakota State Census, Mountrail County" [Printed Article],** in *North Central North Dakota Genealogical Record,* (Mouse River Loop Genealogical Society, Minot, ND), No. 82, (Mar 2000); and Mar 2001.

## North Dakota Books & Microfilms at the Family History Library

North Dakota's microfilmed statewide censuses and substitutes are cited below in chronological order. Each item includes a FHL book number or FHL film number, which can be used to search the FHL catalog for more details. To review an item, start at the FamilySearch catalog search page. See **https://familysearch.org/search/catalog/results.** Select "Search by Place" then "United States, North Dakota" to see a list of catalog categories. Or, select "Call Number" then type an FHL book number; or select "Film/Fiche Number" to view a specific title.

■ **1885 Territorial Census, Dakota Territory (North Dakota Counties) [Microfilm],** from the original records located at the State Historical Society of North Dakota, Bismarck. Filmed by the SHSNC, 12 rolls, available on interlibrary loan. (Film not available at the FHL). 50 of the 56 northern counties that existed in 1885 are extant. For information about the Interlibrary Loan service at the SHSND, see
http://history.nd.gov/archives/genealogy.html.

■ **1885.** See **"Dakota Territorial Census of 1885: From the Original Records on File at Bismarck, N.D. [Printed Article],** in *North Dakota Historical Quarterly,* Vol. 4 (1913), pages 338-448. Information includes name, sex, age, relationship to head of family, occupation, birthplace, father's birth-place, and mother's birthplace. Census returns for the North Dakota counties of Allred, Bowman, Buford, Dunn, McIntosh, McKenzie, Mercer, Mountraille, Oliver, Renville, Stanton, Towner, Villard, Wallace, Ward, Wells and Wynn. FHL book 978.4 B5h. See also ***1885 Census Index*** **[Printed Index],** edited by Ronald Vern Jackson, publ. Accelerated Indexing Systems, Bountiful, UT, 1982, 61 pages, extracted from the ND Historical Quarterly article (17 counties only). FHL book 978.4 X22j 1885.

■ ***1885 Dakota Territory Census (North Dakota Counties)*** **[Printed Books],** published indexes by county. This project was a division of work between the North Dakota Institute for Regional Studies, North Dakota State University, Fargo, ND, and the Bismarck-Mandan Historical and Genealogical Society, Bismarck, ND. These countywide indexes were used to input the electronic database now online. The individual books produced are all available at the FHL in Salt Lake City:

- Barnes County, by NDIRS, FHL book 978.432 X22s and FHL film #2055549.
- Benson County, by B-MHGS, FHL book 978.439 X22b, and FHL film #1425174.
- Billings County, by B-MHGS, FHL book 978.494 X22b.
- Burleigh County, by B-MHGS, FHL book 978.494 X22b and FHL film #2055286.
- Cass County, by NDIRS, FHL book 978.432 X22s.
- Dickey County, by B-MHGS, FHL book 978.454 X22b.

- Emmons County, by B-MHGS, FHL book 978.447 X22b.
- Fargo (city), by NDIRS, FHL book 978.413/F1 X22s.
- Griggs County (with Steele Co.), by NDIRS, FHL book 978.433 X22s.
- Kidder County, by B-MHGS, FHL book 978.457 X22b.
- La Moure County, by B-MHGS, FHL book 978.453 X22b.
- Logan County, by B-MHGS, FHL book 978.456 X22b.
- McLean County, by B-MHGS, FHL book 978.475 X22b.
- Morton County, by B-MHGS, FHL book 978.485 X22b.
- Nelson County (with Ramsey Co.), by NDIRS, FHL book 978.435 X22b.
- Ramsey County (with Nelson Co.), by NDIRS, FHL book 978.435 X22b.
- Richland County, by NDIRS, FHL book 978.412 X22s.
- Rolette County, by B-MHGS, FHL book 978.4592 X22b.
- Stark County, by B-MHGS, FHL book 978.4844 X22b.
- Steele County (with Griggs Co.), by NDIRS, FHL book 978.433.X22s.
- Traill County, by NDIRS, FHL book 978.414 X22b.

**Note:** more counties were added to this project and the culmination was the online database accessible at the ND St. Univ. website. See **Online Databases at North Dakota State Websites** (p. 185).

✓ **1890-1924 NOTE:** The ***Declaration of Intention to become a U.S. Citizen*** ("1st Papers") gave an immigrant legal status in the U.S. as an alien. In most cases, the immigrant went on with the naturalization process, filing a ***Petition***, a formal request to become a naturalization citizen, and finally, receiving a ***Naturalization Certificate***, proving one's citizenship. But, with only the 1st Papers on file, an alien could legally stay in the U.S. indefinitely (unless they got in trouble with the law). The naturalization process could be initiated at any court of record in the U.S. (municipal, county, state, or federal). The following Declarations listed below are from the U.S. Circuit Courts held at Fargo, Devil's Lake, Grand Forks, Bismarck, and Minot, ND.

■ **1890-1924.** *See* ***Declarations of Intention, 1890-1924*** **[Microfilm],** from the originals at the U.S. Circuit Court, Fargo, ND. Filmed by the Genealogical Society of Utah, 1991, 2 rolls, FHL film #1737977 & #1737978.

■ **1891-1906.** See ***Declarations of Intention, 1891-1906*** **[Microfilm],** from the originals at the U.S. Circuit Court, Devil's Lake, ND. Filmed by the Genealogical Society of Utah, 1991, 1 roll, FHL film #1737978.

■ **1891-1910.** See ***North Dakota Pioneers From the Banat*** **[Printed Book],** by John M. Michels, publ. Univ. of Mary Press, Bismarck, ND, 1992, 44 pages. The Banat was a district in southeastern Austria-Hungary and was settled by Germans; later the area came under administration of the Hungarians. The Banat Germans immigrated from 1891 to 1910 when the Balkan wars restricted travel. These Germans settled in Stark and Hettinger counties, North Dakota. Includes a list of immigrants with their village of origin in the Banat. Also includes a list of Banat village names with German, Hungarian, and current names. The North Dakota township maps give names of homesteaders. Includes a discussion of farm houses in the Banat and North Dakota. See FHL book 978.48 W 2m.

■ **1892-1909.** See ***Declarations of Intention, 1892-1909*** **[Microfilm],** from the originals at the U.S. Circuit Court, Grand Forks, ND. Filmed by the Genealogical Society of Utah, 1991, 1 roll, FHL film #137977.

■ **1892-1917.** See ***Declarations of Intention, 1892-1917*** **[Microfilm],** from the originals at the U.S. Circuit Court, Bismarck, ND. Filmed by the Genealogical Society of Utah, 1991, 2 rolls, FHL film #137978 & #173979.

■ **1906-1916.** See ***Declarations of Intention, 1906-1916*** **[Microfilm],** from the originals at the U.S. Circuit Court, Minot, ND. Filmed by the Genealogical Society of Utah, 1991, 2 rolls, FHL film #1737976 & 1737977.

■ **1906-1924.** See ***Naturalization Records, 1906-1924*** **[Microfilm],** from the originals at the U.S. Circuit Court, Fargo, ND. Includes Declarations, Petitions, and Certificates. Filmed by the Genealogical Society of Utah, 1991, 1 rolls, FHL film #173977.

■ **1907-1948.** See ***Index to over 2,000 Obituaries From Various Minot Area Newspapers, 1907-1948*** **[Printed Book],** compiled and publ. Mouse River Loop Genealogical Society, Minot, ND, 1994, 43 pages. The newspapers indexed were the *Minot Daily News, Berthold Tribune, Carpio Free Press, Democrat-Minot, Donnybrook Courier, Douglas Herald, Griggs County Sentinel, Kenmare News, Kenmare Journal, Oakes Times, Ryder Journal, Sawyer Telegraph, Stanley Run, Washburn Leader, White Earth Record, Mohall Tribune*, and *Ward County Independent*. See FHL book 978.463 V42m.

■ **1914.** See ***Northwestern Gazetteer, Minnesota, North and South Dakota and Montana Gazetteer and Business Directory*** **[Microfilm],** from the original publ. R. L. Polk Co, 1914. Filmed by the Genealogical Society of Utah, 1986, 2 rolls, FHL film #1321220 & #131221.

■ ***1915 North Dakota State Census Schedules*** **[Microfilm],** from the original records at the State Historical Society of North Dakota, Bismarck. Filmed by the society, 1975. FHL has 25 rolls, no circulation to family history centers. Contents:

- Adams County, FHL film #1731408.
- Benson County, FHL film #1731409.
- Bottineau, Bowman, & Burke counties, FHL film #1731410.
- Burleigh & Cass (part), FHL film #1731411.
- Cass (part) & Cavalier (part), FHL film #1731412.
- Cavalier (part), Dickey, & Divide (part), FHL film #1731413.
- Divide (part), Dunn & Emmons counties, FHL film #1731414.
- Foster, Golden Valley counties; & Grand Forks City (part), FHL film #1731415.
- Grand Forks City (part), Griggs County, Hettinger County (part), FHL film #1731416.
- Hettinger (part), Kidder & La Moure counties, FHL film #1731417.
- Logan, McHenry counties, & McIntosh (school dist. #1), FHL film #1731418.
- McIntosh (school dist. #2), McKenzie & McLean county (part), FHL film #1731419.
- McLean County (part), Mercer & Morton County (part), FHL film #1731420.
- Morton County (part) & Mountrail County (part), FHL film #1731421.
- Mountrail County (part), Nelson & Oliver County, FHL film #1731422.
- Pembina, Pierce, & Ramsey County (part), FHL film #1731423.
- Ramsey County (part), Ransom & Renville County (part), FHL film #1731424.
- Renville County (part), Richland & Rolette County (part), FHL film #1731425.
- Rolette County (part), Sargent & Sheridan counties, FHL film #1731426.
- Sioux, Slope, & Stark counties, FHL film #1731427.
- Steele & Stutsman County (part), FHL film #1731428.
- Stutsman County (part), Towner, & Traill County (part), FHL film #1731429.
- Traill County (part), Walsh & Ward County (part), FHL film #1731430.
- Ward County (H-W) Wells County (part), FHL film #1731431.
- Wells County (part), & Williams County, FHL film #1731432.

**Note:** For information about the Interlibrary Loan service at the SHSND, see **http://history.nd.gov/archives/genealogy.html.**

■ **1917-1918.** See ***North Dakota, World War I Selective Service System Draft Registration Cards, 1917-1918*** **[Microfilm],** from the original records at the National Archives branch at East Point, Georgia. The draft cards are arranged alphabetically by state, then alphabetically by county or city, and then alphabetically by surname of registrants. Filmed by the National Archives, 1987-1988, 30 rolls, beginning with FHL film #1819402 (Adams Co., A-Z; Barnes Co., A-S). For a complete list of roll numbers and contents of each roll, see the online FHL catalog page for this title. See **https://familysearch.org/search/catalog/746993.**

■ **1917-1918.** See ***Roster of the Men and Women Who Served in the Army or Naval Service Including the Marine Corps, or the United States or its Allies From the State of North Dakota in the World War, 1917-1918*** **[Printed Book & Microfilm],** prepared and published under the direction of Brigadier General G. Angus Fraser, Legislative Assembly of North Dakota, printed by Bismarck Tribune Co., Bismarck, ND, 1931, 4 vols. Contents: vol. 1: Asberg to Flagg; vol. 2: Flagg to Lark; vol. 3: Larkee to Rice; and vol. 4: Rich to Zygmond. FHL book 978.4 M23a v. 1-4, and FHL film #982257 (vols. 1-2) and #982258 (vols. 3-4).

■ ***1925 North Dakota State Census Schedules*** **[Microfilm],** from the original records filmed by the State Historical Society of North Dakota, Bismarck, ND. FHL has 16 rolls, no circulation to family history centers. Contents:

- Adams, Barnes, Benson, Billings counties, FHL film #1731393.
- Bottineau, Bowman, Burke, Burleigh counties, FHL film #1731394 (another copy, FHL film #1433999).
- Bismarck (city), Cass County & Fargo (city), FHL film #1731395.
- Fargo (city), Cass, Cavalier, Dickey & Divide counties, FHL film #1731396.
- Divide, Dunn, Eddy, Emmons, Foster & Golden Valley counties, FHL film #1731397.
- Grand Forks, Grant & Griggs counties, FHL film #1731398.
- Hettinger, Kidder, La Moure, Logan & McHenry counties, FHL film #1731399.
- McHenry, McIntosh, McKenzie & McLean counties, FHL film #1731400.
- Mercer, Morton, Mountrail & Nelson counties, FHL film #1731401.
- Oliver, Pembina, Pierce & Ramsey counties, FHL film #1731402.
- Ransom, Renville, Richland & Rolette counties, FHL film #1731403.

- Sargent, Sheridan, Sioux, Slope, Stark & Steele counties, FHL film #1731404.
- Stutsman, Towner & Traill counties, FHL film #1731405.
- Walsh & Ward counties, FHL film #1731406.
- Wells & Williams counties, Fort Berthold (McLean County) & Devil's Lake Sioux Reservation. Includes list of townships with population in each county, FHL film #1731407.

**Note:** For information about the Interlibrary Loan service at the SHSND, see **http://history.nd.gov/archives/genealogy.html.**

■ **1942.** See ***North Dakota, World War II 4th Draft Registrations Cards, 1942*** **[Microfilm & Digital Images],** from the originals at the National Personnel Records Center, St. Louis, MO. These cards represent older men, ages 45 to 65 in April 1942, that were registered for the draft. They had birth dates between 28 Apr 1877 and 16 Feb 1892. Includes name of individual, date and place of birth, address, age, telephone number, employer's name and address, name and address of person who would know where the individual can be located, signature, and physical description. Film located at the FHL was digitized in 2015. Access the images by the DGS numbers, beginning with DG #101549908. For a complete list of DGS numbers and contents of each, see the online FHL catalog page for this title. See **https://familysearch.org/search/catalog/2624775.**

# SOUTH DAKOTA
## Censuses & Substitutes, 1861-2014

For information about the area of South Dakota before statehood, see the Dakota Country (page 181). Censuses for the South Dakota area began with the Dakota Territory census of 1885, which was later divided by northern and southern counties. The originals for the southern portion are located today at the South Dakota State Historical Society (SDSHS) in Pierre, SD.

**SD State Censuses:** After statehood in 1889, South Dakota began taking state censuses as a means of apportionment of their state legislature. The first one was for 1895, taken with a page format with names of persons listed without relationships, ages in categories, and nationalities. Unfortunately, only six counties for the SD 1895 State Census have survived. Subsequent state censuses taken every ten years, 1905 through 1945, are virtually complete for all counties, the originals located today at the SDSHS. The 1905, 1915, 1925, 1935, and 1945 censuses were all tabulations compiled on 3 x 5 index cards, one card per person, giving a full name and detailed personal information for each. The ingenious South Dakotans made use of college and high school students to take their censuses, using sortable index cards for each person enumerated. The cards were then arranged in alphabetical order by surname for the entire state, which is how the censuses are still organized and stored today at the SDSHS archives.

The digitized card index database allows for a global search within the state, and is very convenient for finding an individual, regardless of name, age, or place of residence. But, using the digitized index cards to recreate a family grouping is rather daunting. Since the card sequence numbers are not part of the search criteria, one can not recreate the original order the cards were prepared house to house. A search for one name needs to be followed by a search for people at the same street address, or perhaps common keywords, but, there is no proof of relationship possible, because the individual cards do not indicate a name of a parent, or the names of any children.

In spite of the family grouping limitation, the South Dakota state censuses all have details about a person rarely found in other state censuses, e.g., for 1915, 1925, and 1935, the SD index cards ask for the maiden name of a wife, a census question found only in South Dakota.

**Censuses Online:**

- **Ancestry.com:** Digitized and Indexed 1885 Dakota Territory Census (southern counties); and digitized and Indexed 1895 SD State Census (partial); and indexed only 1905, 1915, 1925, 1935 & 1945 SD State Census.
- **FamilySearch.org:** Digitized and Indexed SD State Censuses: 1905, 1915, 1925, 1935 & 1945.
- **SDSHS Website:** Indexed SD State Census: 1905 only.

---

### Online Resources at the South Dakota State Historical Society

**South Dakota Digital Archives.** This online collection includes Photos, Manuscripts, Government Documents, Land Survey Field Notes, and more. Searchable databases of interest to genealogists include the following.

■ **South Dakota State Surname Search Form.** The South Dakota State Archives Surname Research Form allows a search through a database of birth, marriage,

death, and other notices printed in South Dakota newspapers. This database is not complete and currently only recent newspapers are being added. The majority of newspaper surname entries are from 2000 to present, but some earlier entries were included as well. See
**http://history.sd.gov/forms/surname/SurnameArchive.aspx.**

■ **1905 State Census Index.** The images and index to the 1905 census cards are at the FamilySearch.org website. The 1905 SD State Census was also indexed at the Ancestry.com website. This is another database, indexed by the SDSHS and can be used to compare the results. See
**http://history.sd.gov/archives/Data/1905census/1905Search.aspx.**

■ **Cemetery Record Search**. This searchable database includes records that were cataloged as part of the WPA Cemetery Project (pre-1940s) plus any cemetery updates that SDSHS has received. It is not a complete listing of all the burials in South Dakota.
See **https://apps.sd.gov/dt58cemetery.**

■ **South Dakota State Newspapers Search Form.** Use this form to search for SD state newspapers. You can search using as many or as few criteria as you want. Be sure that a field is blank if you do not want to enter it as a search criteria. To see a listing of all newspapers, just leave all of the fields blank. By only specifying a year you will see all the reports pertaining to that particular year. See
**http://history.sd.gov/forms/NewspaperArchive.aspx.**

■ **Biographical File Index** is an alphabetical listing of offline files on individuals kept by the SD Archives. Search for a surname by a letter of the alphabet. See
**http://history.sd.gov/Archives/Data/Biofile/default.aspx.**

■ **Gold Star Volume: American Legion Auxiliary South Dakota World War I.** This is an index of 549 South Dakotans who lost their lives in World War I. Auxiliary members created the volume from 1929-1931. See
**http://history.sd.gov//archives/Data/goldstar/default.aspx.**

■ **Naturalization Records Index: First Papers.** See the **information page** for details. To start a search, see
**http://history.sd.gov/Archives/Data/naturalization/FirstPapersSearch.aspx.**

■ **South Dakota Farmer's Alliance**. This searchable index includes over 17,500 names of South Dakotans who were dues paying members of the South Dakota Farmer's Alliance from 1890 to 1894. The Farmers Alliance was an organized agrarian economic movement amongst U.S. farmers. Information found in the index includes: Last Name, First Name, Post Office Address, County, Organization Name and Number, and the year dues were paid. See
**http://history.sd.gov/Archives/farmers/Search.aspx.**

■ **General Federation of Women's Clubs Pioneer Daughters Collection.** This collection came from a statewide GFWC effort to collect and preserve the stories of female pioneers in South Dakota. Arranged by county, married name, and maiden name, this collection of nearly 6,000 stories is the largest body of women's histories in the State Archives. At the main information page, select County List, Married Name, Maiden name, or Request a File. See
**http://history.sd.gov/Archives/Data/gfwc/default.aspx.**

■ **Other Online Indexes.** Visit the Genealogists page to access more searchable databases, such as the Fourth SD Infantry 1917, the 1870 Agricultural Census, the Library of Congress Digitized Newspapers Database, the 1885 Civil War Veterans Census, SD G.A.R. Annual Journal Deaths, American Indian Research, SD Sons of American Revolution, Spanish American War Roster, SD Brand Book Index, 1898-99, and SD Legislator Historical Listing. See
**http://history.sd.gov/Archives/genealogists.aspx.**

## South Dakota Databases Online at Ancestry.com

The Ancestry.com subscription website allows free access to all indexes, but to view any particular record requires a membership. Ancestry offers trial memberships and subscriptions for short periods and reduced rates. The following databases at the Ancestry.com website are unique statewide South Dakota databases under the categories of Census & Voter Lists, Vital Records, Military, Immigrations, and Wills & Probates. To review the complete list of statewide databases, and several countywide databases, see
**http://search.ancestry.com/Places/US/South-Dakota/Default.aspx.**

■ **1862-2008. See Web: South Dakota, Cemetery Index, 1831-2008 [Online Database],** indexed at the Ancestry.com website. This database is also accessible at the SDSHS Digital Archives website. This was an indexing project of the WPA for pre-1940s burials, and added to by the SDSHS. The date

of 1831 was for a Bon Homme County burial (Bon Homme County was created in 1862, it is unlikely that a cemetery was there much before then). Each record includes: Name, Death date, Burial place (city, county, state), and Cemetery. This database has 251,619 records. See
**http://search.ancestry.com/search/db.aspx?dbid=9253.**

■ **1878-1928.** See ***North Dakota and South Dakota, Wills and Probate Records, 1878-1928*** **[Online Database],** digitized and indexed at the Ancestry.com website. Source: North Dakota and South Dakota County, District, and Probate Courts. The contents of a probate file can vary from case to case, but usually includes names and residences of beneficiaries and their relationship to the decedent. An inventory of the estate assets can reveal personal details about the deceased's occupation and lifestyle. There may also be references to debts, deeds, and other documents related to the settling of the estate. This database has 5,121 records. See
**http://search.ancestry.com/search/db.aspx?dbid=9081.**

■ **1879-1955.** See ***South Dakota, Death Index, 1879-1955*** **[Online Database],** digitized and indexed at the Ancestry.com website. Source: SD Dept of Health, from state registrations, 1905-1955; and from county registrations from 1879 (Dakota Territory). This is an index and images of death certificates (state registrations) and death registers (county registrations). The index contains the following information: Death certificate number, Name of deceased, County or county code, and Date of death. Ancestry's webpage for this title has the list of counties and their code numbers. This database has 322,632 records. See
**http://search.ancestry.com/search/db.aspx?dbid=8659.**

■ **1879-1970.** See **South Dakota, School Records, 1879-1970 [Online Database],** indexed at the Ancestry.com website. Source: FamilySearch. This an image only database, mostly School census and attendance records, with name of parent or guardian, males of school age, females of school, and their ages. Browse through the records, organized by county, then school districts. The **FamilySearch version of this database** has a name index, and is a later (and larger) version. This database has 200,731 records. See
**http://search.ancestry.com/search/db.aspx?dbid=60158.**

■ **1879-1971. See Web: Rapid City, South Dakota, Mortuary Indexes, 1879-1971** [Online Database], indexed at the Ancestry.com website. This database is also accessible at the Rapid City Society for Genealogical Research website. Each record includes: Name, Birth year, Death date, Age at death, Burial Place, Cemetery, and Mortuary. This database has 16,222 records. See
**http://search.ancestry.com/search/db.aspx?dbid=9752.**

■ ***1885 Dakota Territory Census (Southern Counties)*** **[Online Database],** digitized and indexed at the Ancestry.com website. Source: SDSHS, state archives microfilm collection. This database is an index and images of the 20 surviving southern counties of the 1885 Dakota Territory census. Index entries include name, race, age, and birthplace for each individual enumerated on the census. More information is shown on the census page image. The following counties are represented in this database: Beadle, Edmunds, Hand, Hyde, Marshall, Roberts, Stanley, Butte, Fall River, Hanson, Lake, McPherson, Sanborn, Turner, Charles Mix, Faulk, Hutchinson, Lincoln, Moody, and Spink counties. This database has 76,472 records. See
**http://search.ancestry.com/search/db.aspx?dbid=6247.**

■ **1895.** See ***South Dakota, State Census, 1895*** **[Online Database],** digitized and indexed at the Ancestry.com website. Source: SDSHS, state archives microfilm collection. This database is an index with images of the first official state census in 1895. Of the 66 current counties of South Dakota, only six counties survived for this census year: Beadle, Brule, Campbell, Charles Mix, Pratt (now Jones), and Presho (now Lyman). On some of the printed census schedules, some enumerators took leave of the rules and listed people and facts differently, but the information is generally readable and understandable. This database has 21,007 records. See
**http://search.ancestry.com/search/db.aspx?dbid=6120.**

■ **1904-1928.** See ***South Dakota, Federal Naturalization Records, 1904-1928*** **[Online Database],** digitized and indexed at the Ancestry.com website. Source: National Archives records of District Courts. Includes images and index to Declarations of Intention, Petitions, and Oath of Allegiance-Naturalization Records. The index to petitions includes: Name, Age, Record type, Birth date, Birth place, Arrival date, Arrival place, Petition date, and Petition place. Index to naturalizations are similar. **Note:** During this period of the naturalization process, the form for the Oath of Allegiance and Naturalization Record gives a detailed history of the person from date, place of arrival in America, the place from where

departed, and the name of the steamship; then the date and place of filing of an Intention to Become A Citizen; and listing all places of residences since; and then the place/court where the final Naturalization Record was recorded. This database has 2,453 records. See
**http://search.ancestry.com/search/db.aspx?dbid=61209.**

■ **1905.** See ***South Dakota, State Census, 1905*** **[Online Database],** indexed at the Ancestry.com website. Source: FamilySearch index (no images), extracted from the FHL microfilm of the originals at the SDSHS, Pierre, SD. The original 1905 census cards are complete for all counties in place at that time. Each index record includes: Name, Gender, Race, Marital Status, Age, Birth date, Birth place, Years in state, Arrival year in state (estimated), Residence place, Years in U.S., Arrival year in U.S. (estimated), Father's birthplace, Mother's birthplace, and FHL film number. This database has 472,575 records. See
**http://search.ancestry.com/search/db.aspx?dbid=60159.**

■ **Pre-1905 & 1905-1915.** See ***South Dakota, Birth Index, 1856-1915*** **[Online Database],** indexed at the FamilySearch.org website. Source: SD Dept of Health, Pierre, SD. The recording of vital records began in South Dakota in 1905. Shortly after the commencement of this system people born before 1905 were allowed to create records of their births. This database contains all the records that were filed for births from 1905 to 1915 and includes delayed birth records. The earliest delayed birth date recorded is for 1856 (a date that precedes South Dakota or Dakota Territory) and was probably a delayed birth record filed in South Dakota, but for a birth that occurred somewhere else. Each record includes: Birth date, Sex, Mother's maiden name, Father's name, and Place of birth. This database has 828,907 records. See
**http://search.ancestry.com/search/db.aspx?dbid=6996.**

■ **1905-2013.** See ***South Dakota, Marriages, 1905-2013*** **[Online Database],** indexed at the Ancestry.com website. This index was compiled from two sources. The first is from actual marriage certificates (covering 1905-49), and the second is from marriage certificates indexes created by the South Dakota Department of Health (covering 1905-14 and 1950-2013). From the actual marriage certificates, information that may be provided in this database includes certificate number, registration number, marriage county, marriage date, and names of husband and wife, along with their genders, residences, and ages. From the certificates index, information that may be found in this database includes certificate number, date of marriage entry into the index, marriage place, marriage date, and names of husband and wife, along with their ages and residences. This database has 1,366,522 records. See
**http://search.ancestry.com/search/db.aspx?dbid=8561.**

■ **1915.** See ***South Dakota, State Census, 1915*** **[Online Database],** indexed at the Ancestry.com website. Source: FamilySearch index (no images), extracted from the FHL microfilm of the originals at the SDSHS, Pierre, SD. The original 1915 census cards are complete for all counties in place at that time. Each record includes: Name, Age, Birth year, Gender, Race, Birth place, Nationality, Marital status, Religion, Father's birth place, Mother's birth place, FHL film number, Sheet number, and Residence in 1915. This database has 613,769 records. See
**http://search.ancestry.com/search/db.aspx?dbid=60160.**

■ **1925.** See ***South Dakota, State Census, 1925*** **[Online Database],** indexed at the Ancestry.com website. Source: FamilySearch index (no images), extracted from the FHL microfilm of the originals at the SDSHS, Pierre, SD. The original 1925 census cards are complete for all counties in place at that time. Each index record includes: Name, Age, Gender, Race, Birth year, Birth place, Ethnicity, Marital status, Marriage date, Spouse (females only, w/maiden names), Religion, Father's birth place, Mother's birth place, FHL film number, and Sheet number. This database has 705,319 records. See
**http://search.ancestry.com/search/db.aspx?dbid=60161.**

■ **1935.** See ***South Dakota, State Census, 1935*** **[Online Database],** indexed at the Ancestry.com website. Source: FamilySearch index (no images), extracted from the FHL microfilm of the originals at the SDSHS, Pierre, SD. The original 1935 census cards are complete for all counties in place at that time. Each index record includes: Name, Age, Birth year, Race, Gender, Birth place, Marital status, Event place, Post office, Naturalized (y/n), Father's birth place, Mother's birth place, and FHL film number. This database has 673,322 records. See
**http://search.ancestry.com/search/db.aspx?dbid=60162.**

■ **1945.** See ***South Dakota, State Census, 1945*** **[Online Database],** indexed at the Ancestry.com website. Source: FamilySearch index (no images), extracted from the FHL microfilm of the originals at the SDSHS, Pierre, SD. The original 1945 census

cards are complete for all counties in place at that time. Each index record includes: Name, Gender, Race, Birth year, Birth place, Event year (1945), Event place (residence), Post office, Age, Marriage date, Years in U.S., Arrival date, Mother's birth place, Naturalized (y/n), and FHL film number. This database has 570,085 records. See
**http://search.ancestry.com/search/db.aspx?dbid=60163.**

■ **1958-1961.** See ***Sioux Falls, South Dakota, Passenger Manifests of Airplanes, 1958-1961*** **[Online Database],** digitized and indexed at the Ancestry.com website. Source: National Archives microfilm series A4072. This database includes an index and images of passenger manifests. Each index record includes: Name, Birth date, Birth place, Departure date, Departure place, Nationality, and Airline. The image record may add information, including a place of residence, and a date a visa was issued. This database has 149 records. See
**http://search.ancestry.com/search/db.aspx?dbid=60613.**

■ **1968-2012.** See ***Web: Rapid City, South Dakota, Obituary Index, 1968-2012*** **[Online Database],** indexed at the FamilySearch.org website. This database is also accessible at the Rapid City Society for Genealogical Research website. Each record includes: Name, Birth year, Age, Death date, Death place, Cemetery, and Obituary date. There are a number of obituaries for surrounding areas, including Wyoming. This database has 124,313 records. See
**http://search.ancestry.com/search/db.aspx?dbid=9754.**

## South Dakota Databases Online at FamilySearch.org

The following databases are available for free at the FamilySearch.org website. To see the current list, visit the South Dakota Indexed Historical Records and South Dakota Image Only Historical Records webpage. Both lists are updated periodically. See
**https://familysearch.org/search/collection/location/45.**

■ **1861-1865. See Dakota Territory Civil War Service Records of Union Soldiers, 1861-1865 [Online Database],** indexed at the FamilySearch.org website. Source: National Archives microfilm series M1960. Includes Union service records of soldiers who served in the 1st Battalion Dakota Cavalry from the Territory of Dakota. The records include a jacket-envelope for each soldier, labeled with his name, his rank, and the unit in which he served. The jacket-envelope typically contains card abstracts of entries relating to the soldier as found in original muster rolls, returns, rosters, payrolls, appointment books, hospital registers, prison registers and rolls, parole rolls, inspection reports; and the originals of any papers relating solely to one soldier. This database has 4,693 records. See
**https://familysearch.org/search/collection/1932393.**

■ **1861-1941.** See **South Dakota, Grand Army of the Republic Membership Records, 1861-1941 [Online Database],** indexed at the FamilySearch.org website. Source: SDSHS, Pierre, SD. Images of G.A.R post records from the Dakota and South Dakota Departments. The collection includes membership rosters, attendance registration books of various encampments (some include Women's Relief Corps.), post descriptive books, member deaths, adjutant reports, muster rolls, lists of officers, applications to form a post, reunion rosters, etc. The descriptive books are arranged by post name and number. Most records include item number, name, post name and number. The descriptive books may list name, age, state of birth, residence in South Dakota, occupation, date-rank-company-regiment of service and final discharge, cause of discharge, when mustered into G.A.R., status, and date of death. This database has 75,635 records. See
**https://familysearch.org/search/collection/2239227.**

■ **1865-1972.** See ***South Dakota, County Naturalization Records, 1865-1972*** **[Online Database],** indexed at the FamilySearch.org website. Source: County Circuit and District court naturalization records from county courthouses in South Dakota. Coverage dates vary by county. The records were acquired from the South Dakota State Historical Society. Includes Declarations, Petitions, and Naturalization Records. This an image only database. Browse through the records, organized by county, then Record Type, Year Range, and Volume Number. This database has 124,277 records. See
**https://familysearch.org/search/collection/2078640.**

■ **1873-1935.** See ***South Dakota, Minnehaha County, Probate Case Records, 1873-1935*** **[Online Database],** indexed at the FamilySearch.org website. Source: SDSHS, Pierre, SD. Minnehaha County (Sioux Falls) is South Dakota's largest county, created by Dakota Territory in 1862. This is an image only database. Browse through the records, organized by Record Type (Probate Case Files), then Box and File Number, and Year Range. Many of the images begin with an typed index to the names of people in a probate case. This database has 71,073 records. See
**https://familysearch.org/search/collection/1392773.**

■ **1879-1970.** See **South Dakota, School Records, 1879-1970 [Online Database],** digitized and indexed at the FamilySearch.org website. Source: SDSHS, Pierre, SD. This database includes an index and images of School records, including teacher's term reports, school census and attendance records. The records are generally arranged by county, year and school district number. Each index record includes: Name, Event type, Event place, Gender, Age, and Birth year (estimated). This database has 2,740,436 records. See
**https://familysearch.org/search/collection/1389778.**

■ **1880-1937.** See **South Dakota, Pennington County Probate Case Files, 1880-1937 [Online Database],** indexed at the FamilySearch.org website. Source: SDSHS, Pierre, SD. Pennington County (Rapid City) is South Dakota's second largest (after Minnehaha), created by Dakota Territory in 1875. This is an image only database. Browse through the records, organized by Case File Number and Year Range. This database has 69,017 records. See
**https://familysearch.org/search/collection/1389957.**

■ **Pre-1905-2014.** See **South Dakota, Department of Health, Index to Births 1843-1914 and Marriages 1950-2014 [Online Database],** indexed at the FamilySearch.org website. Source: SD Dept of Health, Pierre, SD. The recording of statewide vital records began in South Dakota in 1905. **Births:** This database contains all the records that were filed for births from 1905 to 1914 and births that occurred before 1905, filed as delayed birth records. (The starting 1843 date was probably for a delayed birth record filed in South Dakota, but for a birth that occurred somewhere else). Each birth index record includes: Birth date, Sex, Mother's maiden name, Father's name, and Place of birth. **Marriages:** From the actual marriage certificates, information includes Certificate number, Registration number, Marriage county, Marriage date, and Names of husband and wife, and their Gender, Residence, and age. From the marriage registers, this database includes Certificate number, Date of marriage entry into the index, Marriage place, Marriage date, and Names of husband and wife, their Age, and Residences. This database has 693,053 records. See
**https://familysearch.org/search/collection/2549807.**

■ **1905.** See ***South Dakota State Census, 1905* [Online Database],** digitized and indexed at the FamilySearch.org website. Source: SDSHS, state archives microfilm collection. This database is an index and images to the 1905 census cards, filed in alphabetical order for the entire state. Each index record includes: Name Age, Birth year (estimated), Gender, Race, Birthplace, Marital Status, Years in state, Arrival year in state (estimated), Event place (South Dakota), Years in the U.S. (Estimated), Father's birthplace, Mother's birthplace. View the image of the card to add information, such as Occupation, Post Office, Named township, and property description (Section, Township, and Range). This database has 472,575 records. See
**https://familysearch.org/search/collection/1477737.**

■ **1915.** See **South Dakota State Census, 1915 [Online Database],** indexed at the FamilySearch.org website. Source: SDSHS, state archives microfilm collection. This database is an index and images to the 1915 census cards, filed in alphabetical order for the entire state. Each index record includes: Name, Age, Birth year (estimated), Gender, Race, Birthplace, Nationality, Marital Status, Marriage year, Spouse's maiden name, Event place (South Dakota), Years in state, Arrival year in the U.S. (estimated), Naturalized (y/n), Father's birthplace, Mother's birthplace, and Sheet (card) number. View the image of the card to add information, such as Occupation, Post Office, Owner of home or farm (y/n), Extent of Education, Graduate of (name of school), Military service: (Civil War, Mexican, or Spanish), and Naturalized? (y/n), This database has 613,769 records. See
**https://familysearch.org/search/collection/1476041.**

✓ **1915-1935 NOTE (SD State Censuses):** re the census card question, *Maiden Name of Wife*, some cards indicate a first and last name, other cards indicate a surname only. Although the question was obviously designed for a married man to answer, some cards give a maiden name for a married woman. In such cases, it may be possible to find the husband's card and confirm the marriage link. Without the husband's first name, the index search might be concentrated on the surname, then a look at each card with that surname for the place of residence, or a card number in close sequence, (If your search is for a husband in 1915 named Johnson, you will have only 8,326 cards to browse. Good luck).

■ **1925.** See **South Dakota State Census, 1925 [Online Database],** indexed at the FamilySearch.org website. Source: SDSHS, state archives microfilm collection. This database is an index and images to the 1925 census cards, filed in alphabetical order for the entire state. Each index record includes: Name, Age, Birth year (estimated), Gender, Race, Birthplace, Ethnicity, Marital status, Marriage year, Spouse's maiden name, Event place (South Dakota), Naturalized (y/n), Religion, Father's birthplace, Mother's birthplace, and Sheet (card) Number. View the image of the card to add information, such as Occupation,

Post Office, Town or Township, Owner of house or farm (y/n), Extent of Education, Graduate of (name of school), Military service (Civil war, Spanish war, World war, State, Company, Regiment, Division). This database has 705,319 records. See **https://familysearch.org/search/collection/1476077.**

■ **1935.** See **South Dakota State Census, 1935 [Online Database],** indexed at the FamilySearch.org website. Source: SDSHS, state archives microfilm collection. This database is an index and images to the 1935 census cards, filed in alphabetical order for the entire state. Each index record includes: Name, Age, Birth year (estimated), Gender, Race, Birthplace, Marital Status, Marriage date, Spouse's (maiden) name, Event place, Post Office, Naturalized? (y/n), Father's birthplace, Mother's birthplace, and Sheet (card) number. View the image of the card to add information, such as Occupation, Town or Township, Ward, Owner of house or farm (y/n), Extent of Education, Graduate of (name of school), Military service (Civil war, Spanish war, World war, State, Company, Regiment, Division). This database has 673,322 records. See **https://familysearch.org/search/collection/1614831**.

■ **1945.** See **South Dakota State Census, 1945 [Online Database],** indexed at the FamilySearch.org website. Source: SDSHS, state archives microfilm collection. This database is an index and images to the 1935 census cards, filed in alphabetical order for the entire state. Each index record includes: Name, Event type (census), Even year (1945), Event place, Post Office, Gender, Age, Marital status, Race, Birthplace, marriage date, Birth year (estimated), Mother's birthplace. View the image of the card to add information, such as Town or Township, Ward, Owner of house or farm? (y/n), Father's birthplace, Extent of Education, Graduate of (name of school), Military service (Civil war, Spanish war, World war, State, Company, Regiment, Division), and more. This database has 570,085 records. See **https://familysearch.org/search/collection/1747589.**

## North Dakota Databases Online At Various Websites

■ **1859-1995.** See ***South Dakota Land Patents Database* [Online Database],** indexed by county, then surnames in alpha groups. This database was extracted from data provided by the Bureau of Land Management. It includes every homestead, mining and timber claim, as well as cash sales and Indian allotments. Not included are parcels still owned by the U. S. Government, including the Bureau of Indian Affairs, the Forest Service, and the National Park System. Indexed at the USGenWeb site for South Dakota. See **www.usgwarchives.net/sd/land/sdland.htm.**

■ **1861-1900s South Dakota Original Land Owners.** See the ***Family Maps*** series for South Dakota counties, maps of all original land patents, compiled by Greg Boyd, publ. Arphax Publishing Co., Norman, OK. These privately-produced computer-generated maps show the first property owners for an entire county, produced as a book of maps, each map laid out on the federal township grid. At this writing, *Family Maps* books have been published for Clark County, South Dakota, and Davison County, South Dakota. See **www.arphax.com/.**

■ **1861-1900s.** See ***South Dakota GenWeb Archives* [Online Database].** The SDGenWeb site offers free genealogical databases with searchable statewide resources and a link to all county files. The following categories are accessible at the Welcome Page, see **http://usgwarchives.net/sd/sdfiles.htm.**

- **County Files:** A listing of files arranged and organized primarily by county
- **Search the Archives:** A search engine for all the SDGENWEB Archives files.
- **State Files:** A listing of files from state, regional, ethnic, and other non-county sources.

■ **1861-2002.** See ***South Dakota Newspaper Archives* [Online Database],** digitized and indexed newspapers at the GenealogyBank website for Aberdeen, Artesian, Deadwood, Eureka, Fort Randall, Miner, Pierre, Sioux Falls, Vermillion, and Yankton, South Dakota. See **www.genealogybank.com/explore/newspapers/all/usa/south-dakota.**

■ **1865-2000.** See ***Linkpendium – South Dakota: Family History & Genealogy, Census, Birth, Marriage, Death, Vital Records & More* [Online Databases].** Linkpendium is a genealogical portal site with links to state, county, town, and local databases. Currently listed are selected sites for South Dakota statewide resources (313), Renamed/Discontinued Counties (26), Aurora County (138), Beadle County (253), Bennett County (71), Bon Homme County (272), Brookings County (299), Brown County (333), and 59 more South Dakota counties. See **www.linkpendium.com/sd-genealogy.**

■ **1897-1929.** See ***Order of The Easter Star, South Dakota Deceased Member 1897-1929* [Online Database],** indexed at the RootsWeb site for South Dakota. See **www.rootsweb.ancestry.com/~sddaviso/OESMemoriam 1897_1929.htm.**

■ **1899 History.** See ***History of Minnehaha County* [Online Database],** includes the full text of *History of Minnehaha County, South Dakota*, by Dan R. Bailey, publ. 1899. An added index to biographies is also available. Digitized and indexed at the USGenWeb Archives site for Minnehaha Co SD. See **http://usgwarchives.net/sd/minnehaha/bailey.htm.**

■ **1999-Current.** See ***South Dakota Recent Newspaper Obituaries* [Online Database],** digitized and indexed newspaper obituaries at the GenealogyBank website, including newspapers for Aberdeen, Belle Fourche, Brookings, Hot Springs, Madison, Pierre, Rapid City, Spearfish, and Sturgis, South Dakota. See **www.genealogybank.com/explore/obituaries/all/usa/south-dakota.**

## South Dakota Books & Microfilms at the Family History Library

South Dakota's microfilmed statewide censuses and substitutes are cited below in chronological order. Each item includes a FHL book number or FHL film number, which can be used to search the FHL catalog for more details. To review an item, start at the FamilySearch catalog search page. See **https://familysearch.org/search/catalog/results.** Select "Search by Place" then "United States, South Dakota" to see a list of catalog categories. Or, select "Call Number" then type an FHL book number; or select "Film/Fiche Number" to view a specific title.

■ ***1885 Dakota Territory Census* [Microfilm],** from the original records (for southern Dakota Territory counties) at the SDSHS, Pierre, SD. Most of the 1895 Census has been lost or destroyed. The only known county schedules are for Beadle, Brule, Charles Mix, Edmunds, Fall River, Faulk, Hand, Hanson, Hutchinson, Hyde, Lake, Lincoln, Marshall, McPherson, Moody, Roberts, Sanborn, Spink, Stanley, and Turner counties. Filmed by the SDSHS in 1971, 2 rolls at the FHL, as follows:

- Beadle, Butte, Charles Mix, Edmunds, Fall River, Faulk, Hand, Hanson, Hutchinson and Hyde Counties, FHL film #1405268.
- Lake, Lincoln, Marshall, McPherson, Moody, Roberts, Sanborn, Spink, Stanley and Turner Counties, FHL film #1405269.

The above surviving schedules were indexed in ***South Dakota 1885 Census Index* [Printed Index],** compiled by Ronald Vern Jackson, Scott D. Rosenkilde, and W. David Samuelsen, published by Accelerated Indexing Systems, 1984, 296 pages. FHL book 978.3 X22j.

■ **1889-1989.** See ***South Dakota Historical Collections Cumulative Index: Lasting Legacy Project* [Printed Book],** compiled by Suzanne Julin, publ. 1989, SDSHS Press, 469 pages, FHL book 978.3 H2sh index.

■ **1889-1990.** See ***Pioneer Certificates, Sioux Valley Genealogical Society (Sioux Falls, South Dakota)* [Microfilm],** from the original records of the society. Some records include: pioneer certificate applications, application letters, genealogy charts, memo letters, certificates of pioneer, marriage, baptism and death, biographical, naturalization and deed records, marriage licenses, personal notes and checks. Filmed by the Genealogical Society of Utah, 1990, 20 rolls, beginning with FHL film #1710503 (Index, A-Berreth). For a complete list of roll numbers and contents of each roll, see the online FHL catalog page for this title. See **https://familysearch.org/search/catalog/441686.**

■ ***1890 Federal Census, Population Schedules, Jefferson Township, Union County, South Dakota* [Microfilm],** from the original records at the National Archives, Washington, DC. Most of the 1890 population schedules were so badly damaged by fire in the Commerce Department Building in January 1921 that they were disposed of. Only a few schedules are extant. Included on the microfilm are all surviving census pages from Jefferson Township, Union County, South Dakota on FHL film # 926499.

■ ***1895 South Dakota State Census* [Microfilm],** from the originals located at the SDSHS, Pierre, SD, filmed by the society, 1971, 1 roll. FHL title: *Partial South Dakota 1895 Census Population Schedules.* Most of the 1895 schedules were destroyed. Surviving counties: Beadle, Brule, Pratt, Presho, Campbell and Charles Mix counties. See FHL film #1405183.

■ **1897.** See ***Memorial and Biographical Record (South Dakota): an Illustrated Compendium of Biography Containing a Compendium of Local Biography.* [Printed Book & Digital Version),** publ. Chicago: G.A. Ogle & Co., 1897, 680 pages, FHL book 978.3 D3mb. For a digital version of this book, see the online FHL catalog page for this title. See **https://familysearch.org/search/catalog/27906.**

■ *1905 South Dakota State Census* **[Microfilm],** from the original records at the SDSHS, Pierre, SD. Consists of cards containing statistical data for all individuals enumerated in the state. The cards are arranged alphabetically by surname. The last name on each roll is repeated as the first name on the next roll. Information given includes the individual's name, address, age, sex, color, nationality, occupation, ability to read and write, whether blind, deaf and dumb, idiotic or insane, place of birth, years in South Dakota, years in United States, birthplace of father and birthplace of mother. Filmed by the Genealogical Society of Utah, 2002, 125 rolls, beginning with FHL film #2139869 (Aaberg, Albert – Aldous, William). For a complete list of roll numbers and contents of each roll, see the online FHL catalog page. See **https://familysearch.org/search/catalog/1116537.**

■ *1915 South Dakota State Census* **[Microfilm],** from the original records at the SDHS. Pierre, SD. Consists of cards containing statistical data for all individuals enumerated in the state. The cards are arranged in alphabetical order. The cards for the last name on each roll are filmed again at the beginning of the next roll. Each person's card includes: county; post office where person received mail; township name; if in a city, city name; ward; age; occupation; owner or renter of residence; place of birth; ancestry; years living in SD; years living in US; birthplace of father and birthplace of mother; extent of education and whether a graduate; military service, including wars fought, state of service, company, regiment; marital status; maiden name of wife; year married; church affiliation; sex; ethnicity (color); and marital status; whether the person could read and write; whether blind, deaf, idiotic, or insane; naturalized, if foreign born; and the name of the enumerator. Filmed by the Genealogical Society of Utah, 2002, 182 rolls, beginning with FHL film #2283045 (Aaberg, Agnes - Akre, Emma).For a complete list of roll numbers and contents of each roll, see the online FHL catalog page for this title. See **https://familysearch.org/search/catalog/1122664.**

■ **1917-1918.** See ***South Dakota, World War I Selective Service System Draft Registration Cards, 1917-1918*** **[Microfilm],** from the originals at the National Archives, Washington, DC. The draft cards are arranged alphabetically by state, then alphabetically by county or city, and then alphabetically by surname of registrants. Filmed by the National Archives, 1987-1988, 22 rolls, beginning with FHL film #18k77785 (South Dakota: Aurora Co, Bon Homme Co, and Brown Co). For a complete list of roll numbers and contents of each roll, see the online FHL catalog page for this title. See **https://familysearch.org/search/catalog/747000.**

■ **1924-1928.** See ***Fox's Who's Who Among South Dakotans: A Biographical Directory of Citizens Who are Prominent in Professional, Political, Business and Civic Affairs of the State*** **[Book, Microfilm & Digital Version],** from the book edited by Lawrence K. Fox, publ. 1924-1928, 2 vols. Contents: Vol. 1: 1924-1925; Vol. 2: 1928, FHL book 978.3 D3f. Also on microfilm, FHL film 1000589. For a digital version of this 2-vol. book, see the online FHL catalog page for this title. See **https://familysearch.org/search/catalog/184399.**

■ *1925 South Dakota State Census* **[Microfilm],** from the original records at the SDSHS, Pierre, SD. Consists of cards containing statistical data for all individuals enumerated in the state. The cards are arranged alphabetically by surname. The last name on each roll is repeated as the first name on the next roll. Each card contains: name of person, county, post office where person received mail; town or township name (if in a town, ward number); person's age, occupation, whether owner or renter, place of birth, years living in SD, years living in US; if foreign born, whether naturalized; birthplace of father and birthplace of mother; extent of education; military service, including wars fought, state, company, regiment, and division; marital status, maiden name of wife, year married, church affiliation; sex, ethnicity (color); Misc. (read, write, blind, deaf, idiotic, insane); and the name of the enumerator. Filmed by the Genealogical Society of Utah, 2003, 213 rolls, beginning with FHL film #2368063 (Aabelson, Magnus - Afrank, Mollie). For a complete list of roll numbers and contents of each roll, see the online FHL catalog page for this title. See **https://familysearch.org/search/catalog/1130131.**

■ *1935 South Dakota State Census* **[Microfilm],** from the original records at the SDSHS, Pierre, SD. Consists of cards containing statistical data for all individuals enumerated in the state. The cards are arranged alphabetically by surname. The last name on each roll is repeated as the first name on the next roll. Each card contains: name of person, county, post office where person received mail; town or township name (if in a town, ward number); person's age, occupation, whether owner or renter, place of birth, years living in SD, years living in US; if foreign born, whether naturalized; birthplace of father and birthplace of mother; extent of education; military

service, including wars fought, state, company, regiment, and division; marital status, maiden name of wife, year married, church affiliation; sex, ethnicity (color); Misc. (read, write, blind, deaf, idiotic, insane); and the name of the enumerator. Filmed by the Genealogical Society of Utah, 2003, 733 rolls, beginning with FHL film #2369161 (Aaberg, Adoph – Adolph, Ina). For a complete list of roll numbers and contents of each roll, see the online FHL catalog page for this title. See
**https://familysearch.org/search/catalog/1143646.**

■ **1942.** See ***South Dakota, World War II 4th Draft Registrations Cards, 1942*** **[Microfilm & Digital Images],** from the originals at the National Personnel Records Center, St. Louis, MO. These cards represent older men, ages 45 to 65 in April 1942, that were registered for the draft. They had birth dates between 28 Apr 1877 and 16 Feb 1892. Includes name of individual, date and place of birth, address, age, telephone number, employer's name and address, name and address of person who would know where the individual can be located, signature, and physical description. Film located at the FHL was digitized in 2015. Access the images by the DGS numbers, beginning with DG #101549937. For a complete list of DGS numbers and contents of each, see the online FHL catalog page for this title. See
**https://familysearch.org/search/catalog/2624776.**

■ ***1945 South Dakota State Census*** **[Microfilm],** from the original records located at the SDSHS, Pierre, SD. Consists of cards containing statistical data for all individuals enumerated in the state. The cards are arranged alphabetically by surname. The last name on each roll is repeated as the first name on the next roll. Each card contains: name of person, county, post office where person received mail; town or township name (if in a town, ward number); person's age, occupation, whether owner or renter, place of birth, years living in SD, years living in US; if foreign born, whether naturalized; birthplace of father and birthplace of mother; extent of education; military service, including wars fought, state, company, regiment, and division; marital status, maiden name of wife, year married, church affiliation; sex, ethnicity (color); misc. (read, write, blind, deaf, idiotic, insane); and the name of the enumerator. The 1945 census cards were microfilmed by the Genealogical Society of Utah, completed in late 2004, 193 rolls, beginning with FHL film #2370848. For a complete list of roll numbers and contents of each roll, see the online FHL catalog page for this title. See
**https://familysearch.org/search/catalog/1174457.**

# Chapter 3C
# Central Southern
## Arkansas, Louisiana, Oklahoma & Texas

## ARKANSAS
### Censuses & Substitutes, 1686-2013

### Historical Timeline for Arkansas

**1539-1542.** Spanish Conquistador Hernando DeSoto embarked from Havana in 1539 with a total of nine ships, and landed on Florida's West Coast. He was on a quest for gold. DeSoto led his party of some 620 men, 400 horses, numerous beef cattle, and over 200 pigs into present-day Georgia, South Carolina, North Carolina, Tennessee, Alabama, Mississippi, and Arkansas. He seemed to like Arkansas, because he meandered within the land of the Osage and Quapaw for nearly a year. To gain dominance over the Quapaw Indians, DeSoto had tried to convince them that he was immortal, but when he died from fever in 1542, his men wrapped his body in blankets filled with sand and tossed him unceremoniously into the Mississippi to prevent his discovery. Hernando DeSoto's legacy in Arkansas lives on with the domestic pigs he intentionally released to run wild there. Their descendants are now called Razorbacks.

**1673.** French Jesuit Father Jacques Marquette and trader Louis Juliet were the first Europeans to see the Mississippi River. They floated down river from the Great Lakes area, and reached the Quapaw villages of Arkansae and Kappa.

**1682. Louisiana.** French explorer René-Robert Cavelier (Sieur de la Salle) erected a cross near the confluence of the Mississippi River and the Gulf of Mexico, after floating down river from the Great Lakes area. He claimed the entire Mississippi Basin for Louis XIV of France, for whom Louisiana was named.

**1686. Arkansas Post.** A son of an expatriated Italian, French soldier/trader Henri DeTonti founded Arkansas Post, near the point where the Arkansas River joins the Mississippi. Arkansas Post was the first white settlement in the Lower Mississippi River Valley. As an experiment, the French invited a group of German settlers to create farms around Arkansas Post.

**1702-1762. Louisiana.** The earliest jurisdiction of Louisiana ran from the Gulf of Mexico to the junction of the Arkansas River with the Mississippi River. The French administered Arkansas Post, Natchez, Baton Rouge, New Orleans, Biloxi, and Mobile as part of Louisiana. Fort Louis de la Louisiane (now Mobile), was the capital of Louisiana, 1702-1720. By 1720, The Illinois Country was separated from Quebéc and added to Louisiana. The original Louisiana area became known as *Lower Louisiana*. The capital of Lower Louisiana was at New Orleans, 1720-1762.

**1721.** Several hundred French and German colonists abandoned Arkansas Post. Some returned to France, but a group of Germans relocated along the Mississippi north of New Orleans. The fur trading fort at Arkansas Post remained and continued to be the focal point for trade with the Quapaw and Osage Indians in the region. As a failed farming community, Arkansas Post was typical of the French efforts to colonize Louisiana. They were much more interested in trading for furs with the Indians.

**1763. Treaty of Paris.** This was the end of the French and Indian war. In Europe it was called the Seven Years War. At the 1763 treaty, the French surrendered all their claims in North America. Spain acquired the former French areas west of the Mississippi, renamed *Spanish Louisiana*. Great Britain gained all of Québec, which they immediately renamed the Province of Canada. Britain also gained

Acadia, which they renamed Nova Scotia. Britain now controlled all of North America east of the Mississippi River. They named their entire area *British North America*.

**1800. Louisiana.** Napoleon acquired title of Louisiana from Spain. At the Third Treaty of San Ildefonso, the Spanish acknowledged that it was too costly to explore the country and could not see the rewards being worth the investment. Spain retroceded Louisiana to France in exchange for the Grand Duchy of Tuscany (now part of Italy).

**1803. Louisiana Purchase.** The United States purchased Louisiana from France. Sent by President Jefferson to attempt the purchase of New Orleans, the American negotiators (James Madison and Robert Livingston) were surprised when Napoleon offered the entire tract to them. The Louisiana Purchase was officially described as the "drainage of the Mississippi and Missouri River basins." Adding the area doubled the size of the United States.

**1804-1805**. In 1804, Congress divided the Louisiana Purchase into two jurisdictions: **Louisiana District** and **Orleans Territory**. The latter had north and south bounds the same as the present state of Louisiana, but did not include land east of the Mississippi River, and its northwestern corner extended on an indefinite line west into Spanish Tejas. For a year, Louisiana District was attached to Indiana Territory for judicial administration, but became Louisiana Territory with its own Governor on July 4, 1805.

**1812.** June 4th. Louisiana Territory was renamed **Missouri Territory**. This was to avoid any confusion after Orleans Territory became the State of Louisiana on April 30, 1812. The General Assembly of the Territory of Missouri met in St. Louis in October, and converted the first five original districts into counties: Cape Girardeau, New Madrid, St. Charles, St. Louis, and Ste. Genevieve. A year later, the territorial legislature created Arkansas County from lands ceded by the Osage Indians.

**1817.** Fort Smith was established on the Arkansas River (near the present Oklahoma state line).

**1818.** The Quapaw Indians ceded their lands between the Arkansas and Red Rivers, opening the area to white settlement.

**1819.** July. **Arkansas Territory** was created by Congress, taken from Missouri Territory. The territorial capital was at Arkansas Post. The area included all of present-day Arkansas and most of Oklahoma. Arkansas Territory misinterpreted the new boundary with Spanish Mexico, believing their southern line with Louisiana extended west on the same latitude. The confusion came from the language of the treaty with Spain, which described the lay of the Sabine River without maps, and the only maps available to the Arkansas territorial legislators had the Sabine River incorrectly located. A new survey of the area was not done until 1828, and during that time Arkansas Territory created counties that extended into Spanish Mexico.

**1820.** April. Old Miller County, Arkansas Territory was created in an area partly outside of the legal jurisdiction of Arkansas Territory, due to a misunderstanding of the 1819 Treaty with Spain. Old Miller County straddled the Red River with its northern portion well into present-day Oklahoma, an area legally part of Arkansas Territory; and its southern portion well into present-day Texas, which was still part of Spanish Mexico.

**1820.** June. Federal Census was taken in Arkansas Territory, but the original manuscripts were lost.

**1821.** The Arkansas territorial capital was moved from Arkansas Post to Little Rock.

**1821.** August. The southeastern portion of Missouri Territory became the State of Missouri. The large remaining area of the Louisiana Purchase was mostly uninhabited and Congress officially named the area *Unorganized Territory*.

**1821.** September. Mexico gained independence from Spain. The part of Old Miller County, Arkansas Territory, south of the Red River was now in Mexico.

**1824.** The Quapaw Indians were forced to cede their lands south of the Arkansas River, leaving them with just the reservation lands in the area of present-day Lincoln, Jefferson, and Cleveland counties, Arkansas.

**1825-1828.** In 1825, a small area north of the Red River was separated from Arkansas Territory. In 1828, a larger area of Arkansas Territory was added to the 1825 area and together, set aside by Congress as an "Indian Reserve," reducing Arkansas Territory to its present size and shape. The separated area was called the "Indian Territory" by everyone, but that name did not become official until it was mentioned in new treaty documents with the five civilized tribes after the Civil War.

**1828.** About half of Old Miller County, Arkansas Territory, lay north of the Red River, and was impacted dramatically by the creation of the Indian Territory. About 1,5000 inhabitants of Miller County north of the Red River were forced to move, and it could be the only time in U.S. history that whites were forced to leave their homes to make room for Indians. (It was usually the other way around). Meanwhile, people living in the part of old Miller County south of the Red River had not yet learned that they were actually living in Mexico.

**1830 Federal Census** was taken in Arkansas Territory, and the manuscripts survive for all twenty-three counties, including old Miller County, now entirely outside of the U.S. in Mexico's Province of Tejas.

**1836.** March. The Republic of Texas gained its independence from Mexico, and old Miller County tried in vain to reassert its position as an Arkansas county. When Texas created its Red River County in 1836, old Miller County effectively ceased to exist. Named to honor Arkansas Territory's first Governor, James Miller, another Miller County, Arkansas was created in 1874, with the county seat located at Texarkana, Arkansas.

**1836.** June $15^{th}$. Arkansas became the $25^{th}$ state. The state capital was at Little Rock.

**1875-1896.** Fort Smith's most famous resident was Judge Isaac Parker, who served as US District Judge from 1875-1896. He was nicknamed "The Hanging Judge" because in his first day after assuming his post he had tried eighteen people for murder, convicted fifteen of them, sentenced eight of those to die, and hanged six of them, all in one day.

## Arkansas Colonial, Territorial, and Statewide Censuses

**French Colonial Era, 1682-1762:** Lists of inhabitants of Arkansas Post in French Louisiana were identified in the French censuses of 1686, 1723, and 1749.

**Spanish Colonial Era, 1763-1802:** 1791 and 1802 name lists survive for Arkansas Post in Spanish Louisiana during this period.

**Arkansas County, Missouri Territory, 1813-1819:** Arkansas County had a countywide tax list taken in 1814 and another in 1816, which were the first American census substitutes for the area that became Arkansas Territory in 1819.

**Arkansas Territory, 1819-1835:** Several censuses were authorized by the territorial legislature, and a few surviving name lists exist for 1823, 1827, 1829, 1833, and 1835. The territorial legislative act required that the censuses be conducted by the sheriff of each county. As a result, many of these territorial censuses were referred to as "Sheriff's Censuses."

**State of Arkansas, 1836-Current:** Upon statehood in 1836, the Arkansas Constitution provided for enumerations of the inhabitants of the state every four years commencing in 1838 for the purpose of legislative apportionment. The General Assembly directed that a census be taken on January 1, 1842, and every four years thereafter. As was done in the territorial censuses, the Sheriffs of the various counties were to be in charge of conducting the state censuses. Although authorized, it can not be confirmed if all of them were actually taken. Only the state censuses of 1838, 1854, and 1865 have any extant manuscripts that can be found.

**AR Federal Censuses:** The first federal census taken under the name Arkansas was in 1820, but that census was lost. Beginning with the 1830 federal census through 1940, all of the censuses taken for Arkansas are complete, with the exception of the 1890 federal census which was lost due to a fire in Washington, DC in 1921.

## Online Resources at the Arkansas History Commission

With the combined resources of a state library and a state archives, the Arkansas History Commission (AHC) has become a genealogist's one-stop resource center for all of Arkansas. For example, there have been more copies of county records transferred to this state archives than any other state. Research in county records from all 75 Arkansas counties can be accomplished in one research room. The main facility is located in Little Rock near the state capitol building, and regional facilities are located at Powhatan (Northeast Arkansas Regional Archives) and Washington (Southeast Arkansas Regional Archives. Online resources are identified by visiting these resource centers:

**Arkansas Digital Ark-ives.** This online digital archive has documents, visuals, maps, broadsides, pamphlets, and three-dimensional objects significant to Arkansas history and culture. The collections are from the holdings of the Arkansas History Commission. For a Browse, Advanced Search, and more, see **http://cdm16790.contentdm.oclc.org.**

**Search Records.** From this page you can search for county records, military records, maps, newspapers, land records, church records, manuscript materials on microfilm, and the State Archives' vertical and printed ephemera files. Here you can also search for photographs located in several of the State Archives' extensive photographic collections, as well as search military and county records, newspapers, vertical files, and general microfilm collections held at the regional archives. These materials have not been digitized, but are available on-site in the research rooms. Some are available as original documents, while others are available only on microfilm. See **www.ark-ives.com/research/search-records.aspx.**

**The Arkansas Records Catalog (Ark-cat).** The Ark-cat is a state-wide project with numerous participating repositories. The archives, special collections, libraries, historical and genealogical societies, and museums across the state are devoted to providing the public access to their invaluable collections. See **www.ark-cat.com/.**

---

## Arkansas Databases Online at Ancestry.com

The Ancestry.com subscription website allows free access to all indexes, but to view any particular record requires a membership. Ancestry offers trial memberships and subscriptions for short periods and reduced rates. The following databases at the Ancestry.com website are unique statewide Arkansas databases under the categories of Census & Voter Lists, Vital Records, Military, Immigrations, and Wills & Probates. To review the complete list of Arkansas statewide and countywide databases, see **http://search.ancestry.com/Places/US/Arkansas/Default.aspx.**

■ **1779-1850.** See ***Arkansas Marriages to 1850* [Online Database],** indexed at the Ancestry.com website. Source: Jordan Dodd's Early American Marriages: Arkansas to 1850, publ. 1995. Each index record includes: Name, Spouse name, Marriage date, and Marriage county. This database has 18,173 records. See **http://search.ancestry.com/search/db.aspx?dbid=2082.**

■ **1779-1992.** See ***Arkansas Marriages, 1779-1992* [Online Database],** indexed at the Ancestry.com website. Source: Hunting for Bears records extracted from microfilmed county records at the Family History Library, Salt Lake City, UT. Each index record includes: Name, Age, Marriage date, Spouse, County, Spouse's age, and State (Arkansas). See This database has 202,790 records. See **http://search.ancestry.com/search/db.aspx?dbid=7845.**

■ **1818-1998.** See ***Arkansas, Wills and Probate Records, 1818-1998* [Online Database],** indexed at the Ancestry.com website. Source: Ancestry extracts from Arkansas county, district, and probate courts. This database includes images and index to various documents filed in probate court. Each index record includes: Name, Probate date, Probate place, Inferred Death year, Inferred death place, and Item description. This database has 120,624 records. See **http://search.ancestry.com/search/db.aspx?dbid=8638.**

■ **1819-1870.** See ***Arkansas, Compiled Census and Census Substitutes Index, 1819-1870* [Online Database],** indexed at the Ancestry.com website. Source: Accelerated Indexing Systems, Salt Lake City, UT, 1999. This collection contains the following indexes: 1819-1829 Tax Lists Index; 1820 Federal Census Index; 1823 Sheriff's Census Index; 1829 Sheriff's Census Index; 1830 Federal Census Index; 1830-1839 Tax Lists Index; 1840 Federal Census Index; 1840 Pensioners Index; 1850 Federal Census Index; 1850 Slave Schedule; 1860 Federal Census Index; and 1870 Federal Census Index. This database has 210,599 records. See **http://search.ancestry.com/search/db.aspx?dbid=3534.**

■ **1820-1949.** See ***Arkansas Marriages, 1820-1949* [Online Database],** indexed at the Ancestry.com website. Source: Hunting for Bears records extracted from microfilmed county records at the Family History Library, Salt Lake City, UT. Each index record includes: Name, Spouse, Marriage date, and County. This database has records. See 39,640 **http://search.ancestry.com/search/db.aspx?dbid=7841.**

■ **1837-1957.** See ***Arkansas, County Marriages Index, 1837-1957*** **[Online Database],** indexed at the Ancestry.com website. Source: FamilySearch extractions from microfilmed original records at various county courthouses in Arkansas. County clerks recorded marriages in Arkansas before statewide registration began in 1917. This database is an index to the original county marriage records (Marriage Books, Licenses, and Returns). This index may list the following: Name, Age, Residence (city, county, state), Spouse's name and age and residence, Marriage date, License date, Marriage county, and FHL film number. This database has 3,554,066 records. See
**http://search.ancestry.com/search/db.aspx?dbid=2548.**

■ **1845-1941.** See ***Arkansas, Washington County Marriage Records, 1845-1941*** **[Online Database],** digitized and indexed at the Ancestry.com website. Source: Washington County Archives, Fayetteville, AR. This database contains the images from the marriage record books. The index record includes: Name, Gender, Year, Place (Washington Co AR), and Spouse, Spouse Gender. This database has 60,721 records. See
**http://search.ancestry.com/search/db.aspx?dbid=60627.**

■ **1851-1900.** See ***Arkansas Marriages, 1851-1900*** **[Online Database],** indexed at the Ancestry.com website. Source: Liahona Research database, edited by Jordan Dodd, from county records on microfilm at the Family History Library in Salt Lake City, UT. Each indexed record includes: Name, Spouse, Marriage date, County, and State (Arkansas). This database has 142,055 records. See
**http://search.ancestry.com/search/db.aspx?dbid=4383.**

■ **1860-1907.** See ***Arkansas, Homestead and Cash Entry Patents, Pre-1908*** **[Online Database],** indexed at the Ancestry.com website. Source: BLM, General Land Office Automated Records Project. Each index record includes: Name, Land Office, Sequence, Document number, Total acres, Signature, Canceled document, Issue date, Mineral rights reserved, Metes and bounds, Statutory reference, Multiple warrantee and patentee names, Act or treaty, Entry classification, and Land description, This database has 157,594 records. See
**http://search.ancestry.com/search/db.aspx?dbid=2070.**

■ **1861-1866.** See ***Report of the Adjutant General of Arkansas, for the Period of the Late Rebellion, and to November 1, 1866*** **[Online Database],** digitized and indexed at the Ancestry.com website. Source: Book, same title, publ. 1867. This database contains images of the book text with an added OCR name index. This database has 279 pages.
**http://search.ancestry.com/search/db.aspx?dbid=29991.**

■ **1866-1900.** See ***Fort Smith, Arkansas, Criminal Case Files Index, 1866-1900*** **[Online Database],** indexed at the Ancestry.com website. Source: National Archives microfilm, Defendant Jacket Files, U.S. District Courts, Arkansas. This database consists of an index to criminal court cases of such famous outlaws as Wyatt Earp and "Cherokee Bill" Goldsby. Many of these 50,000 cases were heard by the famous "hanging" Judge Isaac C. Parker, appointed by President Grant to bring law and order to the territory of Arkansas. The descriptions provide the first and last name of the defendant, the type of crime, the year, the jacket number, and other information. This database has 49,892 records. See
**http://search.ancestry.com/search/db.aspx?dbid=3119.**

■ **1867-2010.** See ***Fort Smith, Arkansas, Fort Smith National Cemetery, 1867-2010*** **[Online Database],** digitized indexed at the Ancestry.com website. Source: Ancestry database. This database contains digital images of all gravestones in Fort Smith National Cemetery, located in Fort Smith, Arkansas. Fort Smith National Cemetery was established in 1867, and this collection includes burials through 2010 for more than 13,000 people. The cemetery section is provided for each image. Information on the markers varies. Some may contain only a number of initials; others may include facts such as name, birth date, death date, age, rank, and state of origin.
This database has 13,007 records. See
**http://search.ancestry.com/search/db.aspx?dbid=2301.**

■ **1868-2010.** See ***Little Rock, Arkansas, Little Rock National Cemetery, 1868-2010*** **[Online Database],** digitized and indexed at the Ancestry.com website. Source: Ancestry database. This database contains digital images of all gravestones in Little Rock National Cemetery, located in Little Rock, Arkansas. Little Rock National Cemetery was established in 1868, and this collection includes burials through 2010 for more than 21,000 people. The cemetery section is provided for each image. Information on the markers varies. Some may contain only a number of initials; others may include facts such as name, birth date, death date, age, rank, and state of origin. This database has 21,310 records. See
**http://search.ancestry.com/search/db.aspx?dbid=2304.**

■ **1891-1935.** See ***Arkansas, Confederate Pension Records, 1891-1935*** **[Online Database],** indexed at the Ancestry.com website. Source: AR History Commission. This database contains information extracted from records collected by the Arkansas State Pensions Board and includes the following details:
Name of veteran, Application number, Name of widow, Company, Regiment, State served from, Division, County where received pension, Veteran's death date, Widow's death date, Application year (veteran), comments (approved, widow application date, etc.). This database has 36,098 records. See
**http://search.ancestry.com/search/db.aspx?dbid=2281.**

■ **1901-1905.** See ***Polk County, Arkansas Marriages, 1901-1905*** **[Online Database],** indexed at the Ancestry.com website. Source: Book, same title, by Marilyn Brown, publ. 1998. Each record include: Name, Age, Residence of the bride and groom, and Date of marriage. In addition, the name, age, and residence of the witness is also given. This database has 1,147 records. See
**http://search.ancestry.com/search/db.aspx?dbid=3434.**

■ **1901-1929.** See ***Arkansas, Confederate Pensions, 1901-1929*** **[Online Database],** digitized at the Ancestry.com website. Source: FamilySearch. This is an image only database. Browse through the records, organized in alpha order. This database has 159,626 records. See
**http://search.ancestry.com/search/db.aspx?dbid=60237.**

■ **1906-1910.** See ***Polk County, Arkansas, Marriage Index, 1906-1910*** **[Online Database],** indexed at the Ancestry.com website. Source: Book, same title, by Marilyn Brown, publ. 1998. Each record, in addition to showing the date of marriage, contains the name, age, and residence of the bride and groom, and a source document reference. This database has 2,304 records. See
**http://search.ancestry.com/search/db.aspx?dbid=3439.**

■ **1907-1968.** See ***Arkansas, Naturalization Records, 1907-1968*** **[Online Database],** digitized and indexed at the Ancestry.com website. Source: National Archives microfilm from various district courts. This database includes images and index to Declarations, Petitions, and Naturalizations filed at various district courts in Arkansas. Each index record includes: Name, Record type, Date, and Place. This database has 2,083 records. See
**http://search.ancestry.com/search/db.aspx?dbid=2506.**

■ **1914-1950.** See ***Arkansas Death Index, 1914-1950*** **[Online Database],** indexed at the Ancestry.com website. Source: AR Vital Records, Dept of Health.
In addition to providing the name of the deceased, the index provides the date of death, county of death, gender, race, age at time of death, volume number, and certificate number. With this information, it will be possible to obtain a copy of the original death certificate from the AR Dept of Health, Little Rock. This database has 594,114 records. See
**http://search.ancestry.com/search/db.aspx?dbid=8771.**

■ **1933-1939.** See ***Arkansas Marriage Index, 1933-1939*** **[Online Database],** digitized and indexed at the Ancestry.com website. Source: AR Vital Records, Dept of Health. This database contains the scanned images of a computer print-out index. Each entry includes Groom's full name, Bride's full name, Marriage date, License date, County of marriage, Certificate number, and Volume number. This database has 421,079 records. See
**http://search.ancestry.com/search/db.aspx?dbid=8780.**

■ **1923-1939.** See ***Arkansas, Divorce Index, 1923-1939*** **[Online Database],** digitized and indexed at the Ancestry.com website. Source: AR Dept of Health, with scanned images from the computer print-out index on microfiche. This database is an index to divorces that were filed in Arkansas from 1923-1927 and 1934-1939. Information that may be found in this database includes plaintiff's name, defendant's name, date of divorce, county of divorce, and reference information for locating the divorce certificate, including a volume number, docket number, and certificate number (the certificate number will only be listed for the 1934-1939 divorces).This database has 108,392 records. See
**http://search.ancestry.com/search/db.aspx?dbid=8770.**

## Arkansas Databases Online at FamilySearch.org

The following databases are available for free at the FamilySearch.org website. To see the current list, visit the Arkansas Research Page for lists of Indexed and Image Only Databases. See
**https://familysearch.org/search/collection/location/48**.

■ **1812-1965.** See ***Arkansas Births and Christenings, 1812-1965*** **[Online Database],** indexed at the FamilySearch.org website. Source: FamilySearch extractions from county records on microfilm at the

Family History Library, Salt Lake City, UT. This database is an Index to birth, baptism and christening records from the state of Arkansas. Included are a few records of events predating the creation of Arkansas territory. Each index record includes: name, Gender, Birth date, Birthplace, Race, Father's name, Father's birthplace, Mother's name, and Mother's birthplace. This database has 10,642 records. See
**https://familysearch.org/search/collection/1674674.**

■ **1817-1979.** See ***Arkansas Probate Records, 1817-1979*** **[Online Database],** digitized at the FamilySearch.org website. This is an image only database. Browse through the records, organized by County, then Volume Title and Year. Many county records include index books to probates, or wills. This database has 939,415 records. See
**https://familysearch.org/search/collection/2061549.**

■ **1837-1944.** See ***Arkansas Marriages, 1837-1944*** **[Online Database],** indexed at the FamilySearch.org website. Source: FamilySearch extractions from microfilmed records at the Family History Library, Salt Lake City, UT. Each index record includes: Name, Birth date, Age, Spouse's name, Spouse's age, Event date, and Even place. This database has 1,001,777 records. See
**https://familysearch.org/search/collection/1674711.**

■ **1837-1957.** See ***Arkansas, County Marriages, 1837-1957*** **[Online Database],** digitized and indexed at the FamilySearch.org website. Source: original county records collected by members of the Arkansas Genealogical Society. This database include images and index to original marriage records. Each index record includes: Name, Event type, Even date, Event place, Registration place, Residence place, Gender, Spouse's name, Spouse's residence place (city, state), Spouse's gender, and Page number. This database has 1,785,018 records. See
**https://familysearch.org/search/collection/1417439.**

■ **1861-1865.** See ***Arkansas Civil War Service Records of Confederate Soldiers, 1861-1865*** **[Online Database],** indexed at the FamilySearch.org website. Source: National Archives microfilm series M317. Includes Confederate service records of soldiers who served in organizations from Arkansas. The records include a jacket-envelope for each soldier, labeled with his name, his rank, and the unit in which he served. The jacket-envelope typically contains card abstracts of entries relating to the soldier as found in original muster rolls, returns, rosters, payrolls, appointment books, hospital registers, Union prison registers and rolls, parole rolls, inspection reports; and the originals of any papers relating solely to one soldier. This database has 532,541 records. See
**https://familysearch.org/search/collection/1932365.**

■ **1861-1865.** See ***Arkansas Civil War Service Records of Union Soldiers, 1861-1865*** **[Online Database],** indexed at the FamilySearch.org website. Source: National Archives microfilm series M399. Includes Union service records of soldiers who served in organizations from Arkansas. Each index record includes: Name, Event type, Event year, Age, and Military unit. This database has 158,093 records. See
**https://familysearch.org/search/collection/1932392.**

■ **1864-1872.** See ***Arkansas, Freedmen's Bureau Field Office Records, 1864-1872*** **[Online Database],** digitized at the FamilySearch.org website. Source: National Archives microfilm series M1901. The Bureau of Refugees, Freedmen, and Abandoned Lands (often called the Freedmen's Bureau) was created in 1865 at the end of the American Civil War to supervise relief efforts including education, health care, food and clothing, refugee camps, legalization of marriages, employment, labor contracts, and securing back pay, bounty payments and pensions. These records include letters and endorsements sent and received, account books, applications for rations, applications for relief, court records, labor contracts, registers of bounty claimants, registers of complaints, registers of contracts, registers of disbursements, registers of freedmen issued rations, registers of patients, reports, rosters of officers and employees, special and general orders and circulars received, special orders and circulars issued, court trials, property restoration, and homesteads. This database has 23,972. See
**https://familysearch.org/search/collection/2328125.**

■ **1867-2013.** See ***Arkansas, Oakland and Fraternal Historic Cemetery Records, 1867-2013*** **[Online Database],** digitized and indexed at the FamilySearch.org website. Source: Oakland and Fraternal Historic Cemetery, Little Rock, AR. This database includes an index and images of the cemetery record books. Each index record includes: Name, Titles and terms, Event type, Even date, Event place, Burial place (Little Rock, AR), Burial place, Cemetery section and lot, Document type, Page Number, and Source reference. This database has 84,121 records. See
**https://familysearch.org/search/collection/2156084.**

■ **1877-1963.** See ***Arkansas, Sebastian County Births and Deaths, 1877-1963*** **[Online Database],** indexed at the FamilySearch.org website. Source: Sebastian County Clerk, Fort Smith, AR. Includes records of births and deaths from Sebastian County, Arkansas, 1877-1929. Also includes death records from Fort Smith, 1945-1963. This collection is part of a cooperative indexing project with the Central Arkansas Genealogical And Historical Society. This database has 32,250 records. See **https://familysearch.org/search/collection/1881199.**

■ **1882-1963.** See ***Arkansas Deaths and Burials, 1882-1929; 1945-1963*** **[Online Database],** indexed at the FamilySearch.org website. Source: FamilySearch extractions from records on microfilm at the Family History Library, Salt Lake City, UT. Each index record includes: Name, Gender, Death date, Age, Birth date, Birthplace, Occupation, Race, and Marital status. This database has 10,447 records. See **https://familysearch.org/search/collection/1674710.**

■ **1891-1939.** See ***Arkansas Ex-Confederate Pension Records, 1891-1939*** **[Online Database],** digitized and indexed at the FamilySearch.org website. Source: Arkansas State Auditor. This collection includes an index and images of pension records of former Confederate soldiers and widows who resided in the state of Arkansas. These records are the administrative records from the Arkansas State Auditor, which authorized and disbursed pension payments. Each index record includes: Name, Event type, Event date, Event place, and Page number. This database has 172,347 records. See **https://familysearch.org/search/collection/1921864.**

■ **1901-1929.** See ***Arkansas, Confederate Pensions, 1901-1929*** **[Online Database],** digitized at the FamilySearch.org website. Source: AR State Auditor's Office, Little Rock, AR. This is an image only database. Browse through the records, organized in alpha order. This database has 159,626 records. See **https://familysearch.org/search/collection/1837922.**

■ **1914-1950. See *Arkansas Death Index, 1914-1950* [Online Database],** indexed at the FamilySearch.org website. Source: AR Vital Records, Dept of Health. Each index record includes: name, Event type, Event date, Certificate number, Volume number, and film number. This database has 594,114 records. See **https://familysearch.org/search/collection/1940760.**

■ **1923-1939.** See ***Arkansas Divorce Index, 1923-1939*** **[Online Database],** indexed at the FamilySearch.org website. Source: Arkansas Genealogical Society. Each index record includes: Name, Event type, Event date, Spouse's name, Volume, and Court docket number. This database has 107,965 records. See **https://familysearch.org/search/collection/1967739.**

■ **1933-1939.** See ***Arkansas Marriage Index, 1933-1939*** **[Online Database],** indexed at the FamilySearch.org website. Source: AR Vital Records, Dept of Health. Each index record includes: Name, Event type, Event date, Gender, Spouse's name, Certificate number, and Volume number. This database has 421,079 records. See **https://familysearch.org/search/collection/1940215.**

■ **1940-1945.** See ***Arkansas First Draft Registration Cards, 1940-1945*** **[Online Database],** digitized and indexed at the FamilySearch.org website. Source: National Archives, Southwest Region, Ft. Worth, TX. Name index and images of draft registration cards (SSS-1 forms) covering a special classification of individuals born between 1897 and 1928. Each index record includes: Name, Event type, Registration date, Even place, and Gender. More information is on the card image. This database has 359,665 records. See **https://familysearch.org/search/collection/1875142.**

## Arkansas Databases Online At Various Websites

Several statewide databases for Arkansas are noted here, along with a selection of Arkansas countywide databases through 1840. Review more databases specific to certain Arkansas counties at the **www.censusfinder.com/arkansas.htm** website.

■ **1813-1900s Arkansas Original Land Owners.** See the ***Family Maps*** series for Arkansas counties, maps of all original land patents, compiled by Greg Boyd, publ. Arphax Publishing Co., Norman, OK. These privately-produced computer-generated maps show the first property owners for an entire county, produced as a book of maps, each map laid out on the federal township grid, and includes indexes to help you locate a person, place-name, or cemetery. Additional maps are added for each county to show roads, waterways, railroads, selected city centers, and cemeteries within a county. At this writing, *Family Maps* books have been published for the following Arkansas counties: Ashley, Benton, Boone, Bradley, Carrol, Clark, Cleburne, Cleveland, Columbia, Conway, Drew, Faulkner, Franklin, Fulton, Garland, Grant, Hempstead, Howard, Lawrence, Logan, Madison, Montgomery, Nevada, Newton, Ouachita, Pike, Polk, Pope, Pulaski, Saline, Scott, Searcy, Sebastian, Sevier, Sharp, Union, Van Buren, and Washington counties. Visit the publisher's information and ordering website for more details and updated county coverage. See **www.arphax.com.** Arphax's entire *Family Maps* series is also available as a subscription service online. See **www.historygeo.com.**

■ **1813-1900s.** See ***Arkansas US GenWeb Archives* [Online Databases],** name lists are available for all counties. Typical county records include Bibles, Biographies, Cemeteries, Censuses, Court, Death, Deeds, Directories, Histories, Marriages, Military, Newspapers, Obituaries, Photos, Schools, Tax Lists, Wills, and more. Links to all Arkansas counties and projects are located at the USGenWeb home page for Arkansas. See **http://usgwarchives.net/ar/arfiles.htm.**

■ **1813-1900s.** See ***Linkpendium – Arkansas: Family History & Genealogy, Census, Birth, Marriage, Death, Vital Records & More* [Online Databases].** Linkpendium is a genealogical portal site with links to state, county, town, and local databases. Currently listed are selected sites for Arkansas statewide resources (540), Renamed/Discontinued Counties (5), Arkansas County (220) Ashley County (187), Baxter County (162), Benton County (632), Boone County (199), Bradley County (187), Calhoun County (213) and 68 more Arkansas counties. See **www.linkpendium.com/ar-genealogy.**

■ ***1814 Territory Tax List, Missouri Territory, Arkansas County* [Online Database],** indexed at the USGenWeb Archives site for Arkansas. See **http://files.usgwarchives.net/ar/state/history/terr/1814.txt.**

■ ***1816 Territory Tax List, Missouri Territory, Arkansas County* [Online Database],** indexed at the USGenWeb Archives site for Arkansas. See **http://files.usgwarchives.net/ar/state/history/terr/1816.txt.**

■ **1818-1829.** See ***Lafayette Co Early Arkansas Territory Tax List – Before 1830* [Online Database],** indexed at the USGenWeb Archives site for Arkansas: **http://files.usgwarchives.net/ar/lafayette/taxlists/laftax1.txt.**

■ **1819-1999.** See ***Arkansas Newspaper Archives* [Online Databases],** digitized and indexed newspapers at the GenealogyBank website, for Camden, Denson, Forrest City, Fort Chaffee, Fort Smith, Heber Springs, Helena, Hot Springs, Jonesboro, Little Rock, McGehee, Pine Bluff, and Van Buren, Arkansas. See **www.genealogybank.com/explore/newspapers/all/usa/arkansas.**

■ ***1821 Hempstead-Miller Co. Index* [Online Database],** names of early Hempstead and Miller County (Arkansas Territory) settlers who signed an 1821 petition concerning the Choctaw treaty. These people were all caught in the area that was ceded to the Indians, and were being told they had to move: **www.rootsweb.ancestry.com/~txredriv/miller/Miller5.html.**

■ ***1828 Miller County, Arkansas: Petition Index of Names* [Online Database],** includes the list of petitioners and also the list of grand jurors, related to the treaty with the Delawares and Shawnees. These are some of the people forced to leave their homes after the creation of the Indian Territory. Their petitions went unanswered. (One juror on the list: Andrew Dollarhide). Indexed at the RootsWeb site for Miller Co AR. See **www.rootsweb.ancestry.com/~txredriv/miller/Miller2.html.**

■ ***1829 Sheriff Census, Johnson County, Arkansas* [Online Database],** indexed at the Johnson County Genealogy website. See **www.johnsoncountygenealogy.com/1829sheriffcensus.html.**

■ ***1829 Tax Census, Lawrence County, Arkansas* [Online Database],** indexed at the ArkansasGenealogy.com website. See **www.arkansasgenealogy.com/lawrence/1829tax.htm.**

■ **1830-1832.** See ***Miller County, Arkansas, Tax Records for 1830 and 1832, Arkansas Territory* [Online Database],** indexed at the USGenWeb Archives site for Miller Co AR. See **http://files.usgwarchives.net/ar/miller/taxlists/tax30.txt.**

■ ***1832 Tax Records, Hot Spring County, Arkansas* [Online Database].** indexed at the USGenWeb site for Hot Spring Co AR. See **http://files.usgwarchives.net/ar/hotspring/taxlists/tax1832.txt.**

■ *1832-1890 Divorces of Jackson County, Arkansas* **[Online Database],** indexed at the RootsWeb site for Jackson Co AR. See www.rootsweb.ancestry.com/~arjackso/divorces.htm.

■ *1833 Tax Records, Hot Spring County, Arkansas* **[Online Database],** indexed at the USGenWeb site for Hot Spring Co AR. See http://files.usgwarchives.net/ar/hotspring/taxlists/tax1833.txt.

■ *1834 Tax Records, Hot Spring County, Arkansas* **[Online Database],** indexed at the USGenWeb site for Hot Spring Co AR. See http://files.usgwarchives.net/ar/hotspring/taxlists/tax1834.txt.

■ *1834-1852 Tax Lists, Carroll County, Arkansas* **[Online Database],** indexed at the RootsWeb site for Carroll Co AR. See www.rootsweb.ancestry.com/~arcchs/Tax/1834_38_tax.html.

■ *1834-1853 Tax Records, Pike County, Arkansas* **[Online Database],** indexed at the Pike County Archives & History Society site. See www.pcahs.org/pcaolr/tax.htm.

■ *1834-1840 Tax Records, Greene County, Arkansas* **[Online Database],** indexed at the USGenWeb site for Greene Co AR. See www.argenweb.net/greene/COURTRECORDS/18341840.htm.

■ *1835 Poll Tax, Pope County, Arkansas* **[Online Database],** indexed at the USGenWeb site for Pope Co AR. See www.argenweb.net/pope/poll.html.

■ **1835.** See ***Federal Pension Roll of 1835 – Arkansas*** **[Online Database],** indexed at the USGenWeb Archives site for Arkansas. See http://files.usgwarchives.net/ar/state/military/revolution/index35.txt.

■ *1835 Tax Records, Hot Spring County, Arkansas* **[Online Database],** indexed at the USGenWeb site for Hot Spring Co AR. See http://files.usgwarchives.net/ar/hotspring/taxlists/tax1835.txt.

■ *1836 Tax Rolls, Saline County, Arkansas* **[Online Database],** indexed at the USGenWeb site for Saline Co AR. See www.argenweb.net/saline/newtxls.htm.

■ *1837-1839 Tax Records, Van Buren County, Arkansas* **[Online Database],** indexed at the RootsWeb site for Van Buren Co AR. See www.rootsweb.ancestry.com/~arvanbur/cocourt/1833tax.htm.

■ **1999-Current.** See ***Arkansas Recent Newspaper Obituaries*** **[Online Database],** digitized and indexed at the GenealogyBank.com website. Search Arkansas newspaper obituaries for Arkadelphia, Bella Vista, Benton, Bentonville, Booneville, Cabot, Camden, Carlisle, Charleston, Clinton, El Dorado, Farmington, Fayetteville, Fort Smith, Gravette, Greenwood, Heber, Springs, Helena & West Helena, Hope, Hot Springs, Jacksonville, Jonesboro, Little Rock, Lonoke, Magnolia, Malvern, Maumelle, Newport, North Little Rock, Paragould, Paris, Pea Ridge, Pine Bluff, Prescott, Rogers, Russellville, Searcy, Sherwood, Siloam Springs, Springdale, Springdale-Rogers, Stuttgart, Van Buren, and White Hall, Arkansas. See www.genealogybank.com/explore/obituaries/all/usa/arkansas.

---

## Arkansas Periodical Articles
### Censuses & Substitute Name Lists in Genealogical Periodicals

PERSI (PERiodical Source Index) is a digitized database project of the Allen County Public Library (ACPL), Fort Wayne, IN. Since 1986, the PERSI extractors have indexed article titles, places, and surnames from over 11,000 genealogical & historical periodicals. The PERSI database is currently available online through the **FindMyPast.com** subscription website. The Genealogy Center of the ACPL in Fort Wayne IN holds all 11,000 periodicals and will make copies of any article by special request. To obtain an order form for requesting a printed copy of any article indexed in the PERSI database, see http://genealogycenter.org/docs/default-source/resources/articlerequest.pdf?sfvrsn=2.

**Arkansas PERSI Search:** Using the FindMyPast.com website, the keywords "Arkansas Tax" had 577 results.; "Colonial" had 57 results. Examples of Arkansas articles available are shown below:

■ **"1723 Colonial French Census of Louisiana, Arkansas Colonists" [Printed Article].** Names listed in *Louisiana Genealogical Register*, Vol. 8, No. 2 (Jun 1961).

■ **"1749 Colonial French Census of Louisiana, Arkansas Colonists" [Printed Article].** Names listed in *White County Heritage*, Vol. 2, No. 3 (Jul 1964); and in *Genealogical and Historical Magazine of the South*, Vol. 3, No. 3 (Aug 1986).

■ **"1791 Colonial Spanish Census, Inhabitants of Arkansas Post" [Printed Article].** Name list in *Genealogical and Historical Magazine of the South*, Vol. 3, No. 2 (May 1986).

■ **"1827 Arkansas Territory Census, Phillips County" [Printed Article].** Name list published in *Tri-County Genealogy*, Vol. 9, No. 3 (Fall 1994).

■ **"1835 Arkansas Territory Census" [Printed Article].** Names listed in *Tracks and Traces*, Vol. 18, No. 2 (Nov 1996).

■ **"1838 Arkansas State Census, Madison County" [Printed Article].** Name list published in *Madison County Musings*, Vol. 1, No. 2 (Summer 1982).

■ **"1854 Arkansas State Census, Madison County" [Printed Article].** Name list published in *Madison County Musings*, Vol. 2, No. 1 (Spring 1983).

## Arkansas Books & Microfilms at the Family History Library

Important Arkansas statewide census substitutes are cited below in chronological order. Each item includes a FHL book number or FHL film number, which can be used to search the FHL catalog for more details. To review an item, start at the FamilySearch catalog search page. See https://familysearch.org/search/catalog/results. Select "Search by Place" then "United States, Arkansas" to see a list of catalog categories. Or, select "Call Number" then type an FHL book number; or select "Film/Fiche Number" to view a specific title.

■ **1808-1812.** See ***Probate Records, 1808-1812 (Louisiana Territory)*** **[Microfilm],** from an original manuscript, author/publisher not noted. The probates identified in this record are for all of old Louisiana Territory. Included are probates from Arkansas District, one of the five districts created in Louisiana Territory, 1805-1806. In 1812, the districts all became counties, and Louisiana Territory was renamed Missouri Territory. Filmed by the Genealogical Society of Utah, 1975, 1 roll, FHL film #978542.

■ **1811-1900.** See ***Index to Wills and Administrations of Arkansas From the Earliest to 1900*** **[Printed Book],** compiled and edited by Mrs. James Harold Stevenson, Honorary State Regent, and Mrs. Edward Lynn Westbrooke, Honorary State Regent, Daughters of the American Revolution. (Copyrighted by Corinne Cox Stevenson and Gilberta Wood Westbrooke). The index is organized by county, and shows a name, date of activity, and book and page number of the case. Published by C. Stevenson and G. Westbrooke, Jonesboro, AR, 1986, 748 pages, FHL book 976.7 P22st. For access to a digital version of this book, see the online FHL catalog page for this title. See https://familysearch.org/search/catalog/448242.

■ **1818-1900.** See ***Arkansas Pensioners, 1818-1900: Records of some Arkansas Residents Who Applied to the Federal Government for Benefits Arising From Service in Federal Military Organizations (Revolutionary War, War of 1812, Indian and Mexican Wars)*** **[Printed Book],** by Dorothy Payne. Includes muster rolls for Arkansas companies, 1836-1847. Published by Southern Historical Press, Easley, SC, 1985, 220 pages, FHL book 976.7 M2pa

■ **1819-1839.** See ***Arkansas Tax Lists, 1819-1839*** **[Printed Book],** edited by Ronald Vern Jackson, et al. Contents: Vol. 1: 1819-1829, Vol. 2: 1830-1839. Arranged in alphabetical order by surname. Published by Accelerated Indexing Systems, Salt Lake City, UT, 1980, 2 vols., FHL book 976.7 R48j.

■ **1819-1845.** See ***Arkansas Marriage Notices, 1819-1845*** **[Printed Book],** by James Logan Morgan, published by Arkansas Research, Conway, AR, 1992, 82 pages, FHL book 976.7 V2m.

■ **1819-1879.** See ***The Arkansas Gazette Obituaries Index, 1819-1879*** **[Printed Book],** by Stephen J. Chism. This Little Rock newspaper index includes 14,329 obituary entries for the years 1819-1879, plus 4,200 names under the heading "deaths." Published by Southern Historical Press, Greenville, SC, 1990, 109 pages, FHL book 976.77s/L1.V42c.

■ **1819-1950.** See ***Arkansas Biographical Card File Index*** **[Microfilm],** from the originals at the Arkansas History Commission, Little Rock, AR. Source listings include freedmen records, county histories, biographies, military records, newspapers, Bible records, land records, and church records. Filmed by the Genealogical Society of Utah, 1994, 53 rolls, beginning with FHL film #1926788 (unnamed Alston, Mrs. Robert B.). For a complete list of roll numbers and contents of each roll, see the online FHL catalog page for this title. See **https://familysearch.org/search/catalog/239800**.

■ **1819-1881.** See ***Arkansas Gazette Index: An Arkansas Index*** **[Printed Index],** by Shannon J. Henderson, From preface, "The Arkansas Gazette has long been considered the prime source for information on the social, cultural, and political affairs of the people of Arkansas." Contents: Vol. 1: 1819-1829; Vol. 2: 1830-1839; Vol. 3: 1840-1849; Vol. 4: 1850-1859; Vol. 5: 1860-1869; Vol. 6: 1870-1873; Vol. 7: 1874-1879; Vol. 8: 1880-1881. Published 1876, 8 vols., FHL book 976.7 B32.

■ **1819-1879.** See ***The Arkansas Gazette Obituaries Index, 1819-1879*** **[Printed Index],** by Stephen J. Chism. The newspaper is published in Little Rock, Pulaski County, Arkansas. From the Intro: "In this index, we have included 14,329 entries for the years 1819-1879, while the Arkansas Index for the same period lists 4,201 names under the heading 'deaths.' This can be attributed to our inclusive policy of listing every mention of death, whether it appears in an obituary column or in the text of an article on another subject.." Published by Southern Historical Press, Greenville, SC, 1990, 109 pages, FHL book 976.773/L1 V42c.

■ **1819-1839.** See ***Arkansas Tax List, 1819-1839*** **[Printed Index],** edited by Ronald Vern Jackson, et al. Arranged in alphabetical order by Surname. Contents: 1819-1829 – 1830-1839. Published by Accelerated Indexing Systems, Bountiful, UT, 1980, 2 vols., FHL book 976.7 R48j vol. 1 (1819-1829) & Vol. 2 (1830-1839).

■ ***1820 Census of the Territory of Arkansas (Reconstructed)*** **[Printed Book],** by James Logan Morgan, published by Arkansas Research, Conway, AR, 1992, 108 pages. FHL book 976.7 X2. The 1820 Arkansas Territory Federal Census was lost. A reconstruction was compiled from tax lists, voter lists, and other sources, first by Bobbie Jones McLane in 1965, and again in 1992 by James Logan Morgan.

■ **1820-1907.** See ***Index to the Arkansas General Land Office, 1820-1907*** **[Printed Book],** by Sherida K. Eddlemon. Organized by county. 7 Volumes, published by Heritage Books, Bowie, MD, 1998-2002, 7 vols., FHL book 976.7 R22e v.1-7.

■ **1821-1884.** See ***Arkansas, Tax Records 1821-1884*** **[Microfilm],** from the originals at the Arkansas History Commission, Little Rock, AR. Filmed by the Genealogical Society of Utah, 1994, 2002, 72 rolls, beginning with FHL film #1954757 (List of available county tax records, Arkansas-Yell County); and FHL film #1955034 (List of Arkansas county tax records (Revised), Arkansas-Yell County). For a complete list of roll numbers and contents of each roll, see the online FHL catalog page for this title: **https://familysearch.org/search/catalog/636459**.

■ ***1823 Arkansas County Sheriff's Census*** **[Printed Typescript],** a typescript of the name list, 3 pages. See FHL book 976.786 X2p. Also online, See **http://files.usgwarchives.net/ar/state/history/terr/sheriff1.txt**.

■ **1823-1829.** See ***Arkansas Sheriff's Censuses, 1823 & 1829*** **[Printed Index],** edited by Ronald Vern Jackson, et al, Accelerated Indexing Systems, Salt Lake City, UT. FHL book 976.7 X2s 1823, 1829.

■ **1829** See ***Lawrence County, Arkansas 1829 Sheriff's Census*** **[Printed Extract & Index],** transcribed by Marion Stark Craig, 1994, 30 pages. Includes photocopy of original records along with transcription and full-name index. See FHL book 976.725 X2c.

■ ***1833 Reconstructed Census of Scott County, Arkansas*** **[Printed Book],** researched and compiled by John Paul O'Nale, Scott County Historical & Genealogical Society, Waldron, AR, 19??, 20 pages, 2 maps. See FHL book 976.744 X2o 1833.

■ **1838-1916.** See ***Masonic Deaths in Arkansas, 1838-1916*** **[Printed Book],** abstracted and compiled by Arlene LaGrone. Extracted from the annual proceedings of Most Worshipful Grand Lodge of the State of Arkansas (F. & A. Masons). Includes supplements added by the society. Published by the Arkansas Genealogical Society, Hot Springs, AR, 1999, 183 pages, FHL book 976.7 C42L.

■ **1846-1847.** See ***Arkansas Mexican War Soldiers*** **[Printed Index],** compiled by Desmond Walls Allen. Contains a roster of 1,532 men who served in Arkansas units in the Mexican War, 1846-1847. The roster lists the soldier's name, rank, age, unit and company and remarks about death, discharge, prisoner status, enrollment date, desertion, transfer, and other comments found in the records. The roster is in alphabetical order. Published by Arkansas Research, Inc., 1988, 133 pages, FHL book 976.7 M22adwa.

■ **1861-1865.** See ***Index to Compiled Service Records of Confederate Soldiers Who Served in Organizations from the State of Arkansas*** **[Microfilm],** from the original records at the National Archives. Each index card contains the name of the soldier, his rank, and the unit in which he served. Filmed by the National Archives, 26 rolls, beginning with FHL film #821811 (Surnames starting with the letter A). For a complete list of roll numbers and the contents of each roll, see the online FHL catalog page for this title. See **https://familysearch.org/search/catalog/452498**.

■ **1861-1865.** See ***Index to Arkansas Confederate Soldiers*** **[Printed Index],** compiled by Desmond Walls Allen, published by Arkansas Research, Inc., 1990, FHL book 976.7 M22adwe.

■ **1861-1865.** See ***Index to Compiled Service Records of Volunteer Union Soldiers Who Served in Organizations from the State of Arkansas*** **[Microfilm],** from the original records at the National Archives. Each index card contains the name of the soldier, his rank, and the unit in which he served. Filmed by the National Archives, 4 rolls, beginning with FHL film #881488 (A-F). For a complete list of roll numbers and the contents of each roll, see the online FHL catalog page for this title. See **https://familysearch.org/search/catalog/314403**.

■ **1861-1865.** See ***Arkansas' Damned Yankees: An Index to Union Soldiers in Arkansas Regiments*** **[Printed Book],** by Desmond Walls Allen. Arranged in alphabetical order by surname. Published by Allen, Conway, AR, 1987, 220 pages, FHL book 976.M28.

■ **1861-1865.** See ***Arkansas Union Soldiers Pension Application Index*** **[Printed Index],** compiled by Desmond Walls Allen. The index contains the veteran, company, unit, and type of application. Includes death dates and places of Arkansas Union veterans. Published by Rapid Rabbit Copy, 1987, 180 pages, FHL book 976.7 M22a.

■ **1865.** See ***Washington County, Arkansas, Sheriff's Census for 1865*** **[Printed Book],** by Nancy Maxwell, published by Heritage Books, Bowie, MD, 1993, 74 pages. Includes surname index. FHL book 976.714 X2m. Note: This Washington Co AR name list is the only surviving countywide list from the 1865 Arkansas state census.

■ **1865-1874.** See ***Internal Revenue Assessment Lists for Arkansas, 1865-1874: Annual, Monthly and Special Lists*** **[Microfilm],** from the originals at the National Archives, Washington, DC, series 755. Filmed by the National Archives, 1968, 4 rolls, beginning with FHL film #1578509 (1st District, 1865-1866). For a complete list of roll numbers and contents of each roll, see the online FHL catalog page for this title. See **https://familysearch.org/search/catalog/577963**.

■ **1871-1955.** See ***Arkansas Donation Lands*** **[Printed Book],** compiled by Desmond Walls Allen. These books contain indexes to Arkansas Donation Land applications. The records were taken from donation land ledger books in the Arkansas State Land Commissioner's Office. Contents: vol. 1: 1871-1875, vol. 2: 14 December 1876 - 30 April 1880, vol. 3: 1 May 1880 - 30 June 1882, vol. 4: 3 July 1882 - 6 December 1887, vol. 5: 6 December 1887 - 21 December 1893, vol. 6: 21 December 1893 - 29 March 1902, vol. 7: 1 April 1902 - 30 December 1926, vol. 8: 1 January 1927 - 28 September 1938, vol. 9: 28 September 1938 - 21 March 1955. Published by Arkansas Research, Conway, AR, 2001, 9 vols., maps, FHL book 976.7 R22al v.1-9.

■ **1875-1890.** See ***20 Years in Miller County, Arkansas: 1875-1890: Tax & Census Record Index*** **[Printed Book],** by the Texarkana U.S.A. Genealogical Society, 200+ pages. Contains 1875 Miller County personal property tax assessment index, 1880 Miller County federal census index, 1885 Miller County personal property tax assessment index, 1890 Miller County personal property tax assessment index. See FHL book 976.756 R42.

■ ***1890 Census of Clark County, Arkansas*** **[Printed Book],** by William L. Newberry, Clark County Historical Association, Arkadelphia, Arkansas. The 1890 Federal census was completely destroyed for all of Arkansas. This book reconstructs the name lists from the Clark County Tax Receipt Book for 1890. FHL book 976.749 R48n.

■ ***1890 Census Reconstruction, Garland and Montgomery Counties, Arkansas*** **[Printed Book],** reconstructed from 1890 tax receipt books, compiled by Inez Halsell Cline, Bobbie Jones McLane, Wendy Bradley Richter, Typescript, 132 pages, map. Arranged in alphabetical order by surname. See FHL book 976.74 X2c 1890.

■ ***1890 Reconstructed Census of Grant County, Arkansas*** **[Printed Book],** compiled and published by Joan G. Threet, 72 pages. This reconstructed census was compiled by using personal property tax records, court minutes, marriage records & personal data from the compiler's husband's family. Also includes: list of post offices; Pine Grove (at Grapevine, Ark.) & Dogwood school photos (3 altogether); data on Threet & Moore families (1 page). Includes full-name index. Also includes index to 1890 marriages. See FHL book 976.771 X2t 1890.

■ ***1890 Reconstructed Census of Greene County, Arkansas*** **[Printed Book],** by the Greene County Historical and Genealogical Society, Paragould, AR, 1989, 50 pages. Includes surname index. Includes a 1930 map of school districts. This Greene County "census" was reconstructed through the use of tax records. See FHL book 976.7993 R4r.

■ ***1890 Census of Howard County, Arkansas*** **[Printed Book],** by Lucilee Westbrook,. This "census" was compiled from tax assessment records. The names are in alphabetical order by school district. FHL book 976.7483 R4w.

■ ***1890 Tax Book (Reconstructed 1890 Census) Logan County, Arkansas*** **[Printed Book],** compiled by Bill Hanks, Arkansas Ancestors, 1987, 118 pages. According to the transcriber, for the most part tax records are being used to reconstruct the 1890 census in Logan County, Arkansas. Names are listed in alphabetical order. See FHL book 976.737 X22h .

■ ***1890 Reconstructed Census of Mississippi County, Arkansas*** **[Printed Book],** compiled and published by Joan G. Threet, 132 pages. This "census" was reconstructed from court records, marriage records, newspapers and family records. Names are in alphabetical order. See FHL book 976.795 X2t 1890.

■ ***1890 Phillips County, Arkansas "Census" From Real Estate Tax Records*** **[Printed Book],** compiled by Carrie Davison and Rose Craig White of the Tri-County Genealogical Society, 1989, 84 pages, published by Ole English Press, Clarendon, AR. Includes surname index. See FHL book 976.788 X2.

■ ***1890 Census of Pike County, Arkansas*** **[Printed Book],** by Russell Pierce Baker. This "census" is a reconstruction of the destroyed-by-fire federal census of 1890 from the 1893 Pike County tax receipt book. FHL book 976.7485 X2b 1890.

■ ***1890 Census, Polk County, Arkansas*** **[Printed Book],** compiled by Wanda Tilley; typed and printed by Gypsie Cannon, Mena, AR, 198?, 21 pages. From preface: "Compiled from the 1888 real estate tax book; 1890 marriage records; and book of delinquent sales, 1878-1898, list of delinquent land sold on 10th day of June, 1890." Arranged in alphabetical order by surname. See FHL book 976.745 X2.

■ **1890.** See ***Prairie County, Arkansas 1890 Census Reconstruction: A Sesquicentennial Project*** **[Printed Book],** compiled by Margaret Harrison Hubbard, Hot Springs, AR, 1986, 105 pages, maps. This is a reconstruction made by using tax records and other records for that time period. Includes index. See FHL book 976.777 X2p 1890.

■ ***1890 Census of Randolph County, Arkansas as Constructed from the Personal Property Tax List*** **[Printed Book],** by Burton Ray Knotts. FHL book 976.724 R4k.

■ ***1890 Saline County, Arkansas Taxpayers: A Substitute for the Missing 1890 Census, with Full Name Index*** **[Printed Book],** compiled by Carolyn J. Billingsley, published by C. J. Billingsley, Alexander, AR, 1986, 103 pages. From preface: "This book was compiled from the 1889 Saline County tax book, the 1889 Saline County (paid) tax book, and the 1889 Saline County tax receipt book." Includes index. The names are arranged by school districts as they are on the tax books. See FHL book 976.772 R4b.

■ ***1890 Census (Reconstruction) of Sebastian County, Arkansas*** **[Printed Book],** compiled by members of the Frontier Researchers (Genealogical Society) of Fort Smith, AR,198?, 223 pages. Includes indexed names from the following books: (1) Lower District Real Estate Tax Record Book; (2) Lower District Personal Property Tax Record Book; (3) Upper District Real Estate Tax Record Book; (4) Upper District Voter Registration for 1892; (5) Fort Smith City Directory; (6) Fort Smith Marriages for 1890; (7) Birnie Brothers Funeral Home Records for 1890, Fort Smith; (8) First Lutheran Church Records, Fort Smith. See FHL book 976.736 X22c 1890.

■ **1890.** See ***Sevier County, Arkansas, 1890 Census Reconstructed From Tax Records: Sesquicentennial Project of State History Commission*** **[Printed Book],** compiled by Vinita Lovell Long, Martha Johnson, Mary McCrory, 1978, Arkansas, 83 pages. Includes index. See FHL 976.747 X28L 1890.

■ ***1890 White County, Arkansas "Census," Reconstructed From the 1890 Personal Property Tax Book*** **[Printed Book],** compiled by Wensil Marsh Clark, Arkansas Genealogical Society, Hot Springs, AR, published by W. M. Clark, Little Rock, AR, 1986, 98 pages, map. Includes surname index. See FHL book 976.776 R48c.

■ **1891-1936.** See ***Arkansas Confederate Veterans and Widows Pension Applications, 1891-1936*** **[Printed Index],** compiled by Frances T. Ingmire. Arranged in alphabetical order by surname of veteran. Published by F.T. Ingmire, St. Louis, MO, 1985, 442 pages, FHL book 976.7 M2B.

■ ***1892-1898 Voters Lists, Polk County, Arkansas*** **Printed Book],** compiled, typed, and printed by Shirley "Gypsie" Cannon, Mena, AR, 198?, 65 pages. Arranged in alphabetical order by surname. See FHL book 976.745 N48.

■ **1893-1939.** See ***Ex-Confederate Pension Records, 1893-1939*** **[Microfilm],** from the original Digest of the Statutes of Arkansas, with lists of pension claims allowed. Filmed by the Genealogical Society of Utah, 2000, 11 rolls, beginning with FHL film #2209370 (list of pension claims allowed 1893-1939; 1891-1896 pension listings, Arkansas-Cleveland counties). For a complete list of rolls and the contents of each roll, see the online FHL catalog page for this title. See **https://familysearch.org/search/catalog/722961**.

■ ***1901-1929 Arkansas Confederate Pension Records*** **[Microfilm],** from the originals of the State Auditor of Arkansas, now at the Arkansas History Commission, Little Rock, AR. Files are generally in alphabetical order, with some disruptions. Filmed by the Arkansas History Commission, c1980, 121 rolls, beginning with FHL film #1722443 (Aaron – Adams, John). For a complete list of rolls and contents of each roll, see the online FHL catalog page for this title. See **https://familysearch.org/search/catalog/598195**.

■ ***1911 Census of Confederate Veterans*** **[Printed Book],** an extract compiled by Bobbie Lee Jones McLane and Capitola Glazner. Complete for 44 counties. Includes the name of the veteran, address, date of birth, place of birth, where enlisted, names and birthplaces of the soldier's parents and grandparents, maiden name of wife, date and place of marriage, names of her parents, and names of children. Publ. Arkansas Ancestors, Hot Springs, AR, 1981, 3 vols., FHL book 976.7 X2m v.1-3. Indexed separately by Bobbie Lee Jones McLane, as An Index to the Three Volumes, Arkansas 1911 Census of Confederate Veterans [Printed Index], FHL book 976.7 X2m.

■ **1913-1970.** See ***Headstones, Hot Springs, Arkansas Monument Company*** **[Printed Book],** by Jimmie Lois Caton Jones. Contents: Vol. 1: 1913-1931, Vol. 2: 1934-1970. Includes names of purchasers, deceased, birth and death dates of deceased and the cemeteries where they are buried. Published by the author, 1990, 2 vols., FHL book 976.741/H1 U3J v.1-2.

■ **1914-1948.** See ***Arkansas Death Record Index*** **[Printed Index],** prepared for publication by Desmond Walls Allen. Contains an index to the death records filed with the Arkansas State Department of Health. Includes full name, county and date of death for each deceased. Contents: Vol. 1: 1914-1923; Vol. 2: 1934-1940; Vol. 3: 1941-1948; Vol. 4: 1924 – 1933. Published by Ark. Research, Conway, AR, 1996-1999, FHL book 976.7 V22ad, v.1-4.

■ **1915-1929, 1960, 1990-2005.** See ***Index of Death Notices Appearing in the Arkansas Gazette*** **[Printed Book],** by Oscar G. Russell. Published by the author, North Little Rock, AR, 1991-2006, FHL book 976.7 V42r pt. (year). Also on FHL CD No. 3510.

■ ***1926 Official List of Legal Voters of Howard County, Arkansas*** **[Printed Book],** published by Madigan's Books, Charleston, IL, 198?. See FHL book 976.7 A1 no. 137.

■ **1941-1990.** See ***Masonic Death Records from the Grand Lodge of Arkansas, 1941-1990*** **[Printed Book],** compiled by Desmond Walls Allen. Contains a compilation of death records taken from annual volumes of the Proceedings M.W. Grand Lodge F&A Masons of Arkansas. There are 44,634 death records, listing the member's name, death date, Masonic lodge number, and volume year of the Proceedings from which it was taken. Published by Arkansas Research, Conway, AR, 1999, 301 pages, FHL book 976.7 V2a.

# LOUISIANA
## Censuses & Substitutes, 1699-2001

### Historical Timeline for Louisiana

**1682. Louisiana Claim.** René-Robert Cavelier (Sieur de LaSalle) floated down the Mississippi River to its mouth at the Gulf of Mexico. He then claimed the entire Mississippi Basin for Louis XIV of France, for whom Louisiana was named.

**1702-1762. French Louisiana.** The earliest jurisdiction of Louisiana ran from the Gulf of Mexico to the junction of the Arkansas River with the Mississippi River. The French administered Arkansas Post, Natchez, Baton Rouge, New Orleans, Biloxi, and Mobile as part of Louisiana. Fort Louis de la Louisiane (now Mobile), was the capital of Louisiana, 1702-1720. By 1720, The Illinois Country was separated from Quebéc and became known as Upper Louisiana. The original Louisiana area became known as Lower Louisiana.

**1718-1720.** La Nouvelle-Orleans (New Orleans) was founded in 1718 by Jean-Baptiste Le Moyne (Sieur de Bienville). It was named for Philippe II, Duke of Orleans, the Regent of France. New Orleans became the seat of government for Lower Louisiana in 1720.

**1719.** Baton Rouge was established by the French as a military post.

**1721. German Coast.** A group of German immigrants, some who earlier had settled at Arkansas Post, acquired farmland on the east side of the Mississippi River north of New Orleans. Many of them were formerly of the German-speaking Alsace-Lorraine area of France. They easily adapted themselves to the French culture of Louisiana, and later intermarried with the French Acadians. Their main settlements were at Karlstein, Hoffen, Mariental, and Augsburg, all part of the German Coast. The farms they operated were to become the main source of food for New Orleans for decades.

**1755-1758 Expulsion of the Acadians.** When the British took over the area known as Acadia in 1713, they asked the French Acadians to swear allegiance to Britain or leave. Many of the Acadians left the Peninsula (now Nova Scotia), crossing the Bay of Fundy to areas of Acadia still under control of the French (now New Brunswick and Maine). They had a fairly peaceful coexistence with the British until 1755, when the British completed their conquest of Acadia. The British then began forcibly removing Acadians, at first by deporting them to the thirteen British colonies, but in 1758, they began transporting Acadians back to France. Some of the Acadians left voluntarily, making their way to other areas of North America held by the French.

**1763 Treaty of Paris.** The French and Indian War in colonial America ended. In Europe and Canada, it was called the Seven Years War. As the biggest loser in the war, France formally ceded all of its North American claims – Louisiana on the western side of the Mississippi was lost to Spain, the eastern side of the Mississippi and all of French Canada went to Britain. Soon after the treaty, all French military personnel left their North American posts. But, French civilian settlements continued in Lower Louisiana, such as New Orleans, Baton Rouge, Arkansas Post, and Natchez.

**1764-1765 Acadian Coast.** In 1764, British forces completed the deportation of French Acadians from their homes in present Nova Scotia, New Brunswick, and Maine. After a few initial families made their way to New Orleans via Mobile in early 1764, several shiploads of Acadians arrived in New Orleans in early 1765. Their first settlements were on the west side of the Mississippi River, near the present areas of St. James and Ascension Parishes. That first area became known as the Acadian Coast. Today there are 22 parishes of Louisiana considered part of Acadiana, a modern description of the region of southern Louisiana west of the Mississippi River first settled by French Acadians.

**1766.** Antonio de Ulloa became the first Spanish governor of Louisiana, headquartered at New Orleans. He was a brilliant scientist (discoverer of the element Platinum), highly regarded by Spanish Royalty, but rose to his highest level of incompetence as a military leader.

**1768.** The Louisiana Rebellion of 1768 was an attempt by a combined armed force of French Acadians, French Creoles and German Coast settlers around New Orleans to stop the handover of French

Louisiana to Spain. The rebels forced Spanish Governor de Ulloa to leave New Orleans and return to Spain, but his replacement Alejandro O'Reilly was able to crush the rebellion. O'Reilly, an Irishman turned Cuban, was responsible for establishing military rule in Spanish Louisiana.

**1777-1778.** During the Revolutionary War, a number of French-speaking Acadians from Louisiana joined their counterparts from the leftover French settlements of Kaskaskia and Vincennes. They were added to the Virginia Militia force commanded by General George Rogers Clark. General Clark later noted that the fiercely anti-British fighters he gained from the French communities contributed greatly to his monumental victories against the British in the conquest of the Old Northwest.

**1783. United States of America.** The treaty of Paris of 1783 first recognized the United States as an independent nation, with borders from the Atlantic Ocean to the Mississippi River, and from present Maine to Georgia. The treaty also reaffirmed the claims of Britain to present Canada; and Spain's claim to East Florida, West Florida, New Spain (including Nuevo Mexico & Tejas), and Louisiana west of the Mississippi River.

**1800. Louisiana.** Napoleon acquired title of Louisiana from Spain. At the Third Treaty of San Ildefonso, the Spanish acknowledged that it was too costly to explore the country and could not see the rewards being worth the investment. Spain retroceded Louisiana to France in exchange for the Grand Duchy of Tuscany (now part of Italy).

**1803. Louisiana Purchase.** The United States purchased Louisiana from France. Sent by President Jefferson to attempt the purchase of New Orleans, the American negotiators (James Madison and Robert Livingston) were surprised when Napoleon offered the entire tract to them. The Louisiana Purchase was officially described as the "drainage of the Mississippi and Missouri River basins." Adding the area doubled the size of the United States.

**1804-1805.** In 1804, Congress divided the Louisiana Purchase into two jurisdictions: Louisiana District and Orleans Territory. The latter had north and south bounds the same as the present state of Louisiana, but did not include land east of the Mississippi River, and its northwestern corner extended on an indefinite line west into Spanish Tejas. For a year, Louisiana District was attached to Indiana Territory for judicial administration, but became Louisiana Territory with its own Governor on July 4, 1805.

**1806.** A dispute between the U.S. and Spain over the Louisiana-Texas boundary was informally addressed by the two parties. Spain claimed east to the Red River; the U.S. claimed west to the Sabine River. In 1806, they made a temporary compromise with the so-called Neutral Ground, where neither exercised jurisdiction, creating a haven for fugitives. That lack of jurisdiction inspired the French Pirate, Jean Laffite, to use bayous within the Neutral Ground as a base of operations. The boundary issue was not resolved until the Adams-Onis Treaty, ratified in 1821.

**1810.** August. The 1810 Federal Census was taken in Orleans Territory. Although outside U.S. jurisdiction, the Neutral Ground was included in the enumeration. The population of Orleans Territory in 1810 was 76,556 people.

**1810.** September. A small group of Americans overcame the Spanish garrison at Baton Rouge, and unfurled the new flag of the Republic of West Florida.

**1810.** October. In a proclamation by President James Madison, the U.S. arbitrarily annexed Spain's West Florida from the Mississippi River to the Perdido River, an area that the U.S. believed should have been part of the Louisiana Purchase. The area included the existing towns of Baton Rouge, Biloxi, and Mobile. Spain disagreed that the area was ever part of Louisiana, refused to recognize the annexation, and continued their claim to West Florida in dispute with the U.S. for another ten years.

**1811.** The side-wheeler *New Orleans* was the first Mississippi steamboat. Launched in Pittsburgh, it was first used between Natchez and New Orleans. The port of New Orleans and other ports along the Mississippi River were to see dramatic increases in docking, warehousing, and manufacturing related to the huge increase in river traffic after the introduction of steamboats.

**1812.** January. Congress added to Mississippi Territory the portion of the West Florida annexation from the Perdido River to the Pearl River (an area that included Mobile and Biloxi); and the portion from the Pearl River to the Mississippi River was added to

Orleans Territory (an area that included Baton Rouge).

**1812**. April 30th. The same area as old Orleans Territory became Louisiana, the 18th state in the Union. New Orleans was the first state capital.

**1812.** June 4th. Louisiana Territory was renamed Missouri Territory. For about five weeks in 1812, a Louisiana Territory and a State of Louisiana existed at the same time.

**1815.** January. **Battle of New Orleans**. Major General Andrew Jackson commanded an American force of about 3,100 men that prevented an invading British Army with about 7,500 men from seizing New Orleans. Word of the December 1814 Treaty of Ghent officially ending the war had not reached New Orleans yet, and upon the retreat of the British Army, the Battle of New Orleans became the final American victory in the War of 1812.

**1820 Federal Census.** Louisiana had a population of 153,407 people.

**1821 Adams-Onis Treaty.** The treaty included the purchase of Florida, but also set the boundary between the U.S. and New Spain, from Louisiana to the Oregon Country. The treaty established the Sabine River and Red River borders with Spanish Tejas; ending any further claim by the U.S. to Texas as part of the Louisiana Purchase. The treaty also formalized the Arkansas River as the border with Nuevo Mexico; and established Latitude 42° North as the division between California and the Oregon Country. The treaty was named after John Quincy Adams, U.S. Secretary of State, and Luis de Onis, the Spanish Foreign Minister, the parties who signed the treaty at Washington in 1819. It was ratified by the U.S. Senate in 1821. John Quincy Adams was given credit for a brilliant piece of diplomacy by adding the western boundary settlements with Spain to the Florida Purchase.

**1860 Federal Census.** Louisiana had a diverse population of 708,002 people. The slave population of 331,726 was about 47% of the total, the largest percentage of any state. In 1860, the Acadians, German Coast settlers, and Creoles (descendants of colonial French, Spanish, or African settlers) outnumbered the Anglo-Americans, who were less than 20% of the population, the smallest number of any state.

**1861-1865.** Louisiana seceded from the Union in January 1861 and joined the Confederate States of America soon after. New Orleans was the largest city in the Confederacy, and was an early target by Union forces to control and maintain the flow of cotton on the Mississippi River to northern textile manufacturers. The city was captured in April 1862 and ruled by a Union Army General for the duration of the war.

## Louisiana's Colonial, State and Local, & Federal Censuses

**French and Spanish Colonial Eras:** Surviving original manuscripts of colonial French censuses and substitute name lists taken in North America reside in the Archives Nationales in Paris. For the Louisiana area, the earliest are for 1679, and all are available on microfilm. Most have been extracted and published, as noted in the bibliography. Original colonial Spanish censuses and name lists are located at the archives in Seville beginning with 1770, also available on microfilm. A number of colonial census compilations have been published for Louisiana areas from a variety of sources, the most impressive being the *Mississippi Valley Mélange, 1723-1791*, compiled by Winston DeVille. The Louisiana State Archives in Baton Rouge has name lists from various regions from 1759 to 1812.

**Orleans Territory**: In its first legislative session of 1806, Orleans Territory authorized a census for that year. Although statistical returns were transmitted to the federal government, there appears to be no name list associated with the census.

**State and Local Name Lists:** The constitution of 1812 provided for state censuses to be taken every four years commencing in 1813. Only the 1833 state census for St. Tammany Parish has been found. In 1898, Louisiana adopted the Federal decennial censuses as the means of apportionment of its state legislative districts. Although only one Parish-wide state census name list survives for Louisiana, there are many parish-wide substitute name lists found in local courthouses, including tax lists, voter lists, slave owner lists, and other local lists. A broad selection of parish lists are available, extracted or indexed in various genealogical periodicals or published online.

**Federal Censuses:** The U.S. Federal Census name lists open to the public begin with the 1810 Orleans Territory, followed by Louisiana 1820-1880, and 1900-1940. The LA 1890, like all other states, was lost in a fire in Washington, DC in 1921. A complete 1890 census name list for Ascension Parish, Louisiana is one of only two parishes/counties in the U.S. for which a copy was made and survived in the local courthouse (the other was Washington County, Georgia).

## Online Databases at the Louisiana State Archives

The Louisiana State Archives in Baton Rouge is administered by the Secretary of State of Louisiana. Online searchable databases include the Vital Records Index, Passenger Manifests, and the Confederate Pension Application Database:

**Vital Records Index.** Original vital records at the state archives are only available for births over 100 years old, and deaths and marriages over 50 years old. The archives will issue a birth, marriage, or death certificates for certain records for a small fee. Access the Vital Records Index at **www.sos.la.gov/HistoricalResources/ResearchHistoricalRecords/Pages/OnlinePublicVitalRecordsIndex.aspx**.

**New Orleans Ship Passenger List Online Index – January to July 1851.** This is an online index to a portion of the New Orleans ship passenger lists available on microfilm in the Research Library at the Louisiana State Archives. This index covers the roughly six-month period from January 1 to July 7, 1851. This online index is an attempt to fill in the previously unindexed two-year period of 1851 and 1852. Information provided in this database includes passenger name, date of arrival, name of ship and port of departure. See **www.sos.la.gov/HistoricalResources/ResearchHistoricalRecords/LocateHistoricalRecords/Pages/default.aspx.**

**Confederate Pension Application Index.** This index contains over 49,000 names that were included in the applications submitted to the Board of Pension Commissioners. The collection consists of alphabetically arranged pension applications for pensions that were granted to veterans and widows beginning in 1898, and are recorded on 152 reels of microfilm. The records were later transferred to the Archives after the last pension was paid in the 1950s. More than 18,000 applications were microfilmed and are available to researchers at the Archives Research Library. The pension applications may include service information, occupation, place of residence, and number of children. Other materials that may have been included with applications are letters, notes, copies of checks, newspaper clippings, court papers of various types, obituaries, and other miscellaneous papers. See **www.sos.la.gov/HistoricalResources/ResearchHistoricalRecords/LocateHistoricalRecords/Pages/ConfederatePensionDatabase.aspx**.

## Louisiana State Vital Records Registry

Birth records less than 100 years old and Death and Marriages less than 50 years old are located at the Vital Records Registry, State Registrar & Vital Records, Baton Rouge. For information, see **www.sos.la.gov/HistoricalResources/ResearchHistoricalRecords/Pages/OnlinePublicVitalRecordsIndex.aspx**.

## New Orleans Public Library's Louisiana Division, City Archives, & Special Collections

The Louisiana Division collects resources relating to the study of Louisiana and its citizens. Included are books by or about Louisianans; city, regional, and state documents; manuscripts, maps, newspapers, periodicals, microfilms, photographs, slides, motion pictures, sound recordings, video tapes, postcards, and ephemera of every sort. The Genealogy Collection contains books, periodicals, microfilms, and CD-ROMs with emphasis on the Southeast United States, Nova Scotia, France, and Spain. The City Archives is the official repository of the records of New Orleans municipal government, and the Special Collections maintained by the Division are the Rare Vertical File, the Carnival Collection, the Louisiana and New Orleans Photograph Collection, the Map Collection, the Menu Collection, the Postcard Collection, the Manuscript Collection, and the Rare Book Collection. See **http://nutrias.org/spec/speclist.htm**.

## Louisiana Databases Online at the New Orleans Public Library Website

The New Orleans Public Library is a main provider of online databases for anyone interested in genealogical research in Louisiana. The library has a strong Internet presence, using its own nutrias.org domain for preserving resources online. The various online genealogy indexes available are identified here, as follows:

■ **1837-1857.** See **New Orleans Newspaper Marriage Index, 1837-1857 – Daily Picayune [Online Database],** indexed online at the New Orleans Public Library's Louisiana Division website: **http://nutrias.org/~nopl/info/louinfo/newsmarr/newsmarr.htm.**

■ **1841-1846.** See ***Records of Interments in the Non-Municipal Cemeteries of New Orleans, 1841-1846, vol. 1 Protestant (Girod Street) Cemetery, July – December, 1841*** **[Online Database],** a compiled list of names, age, sex, birth, death, residence, marital status, and remarks. Online at the New Orleans Public Library's Louisiana Division website,. See **http://nutrias.org/~nopl/inv/prot1841.htm.**

■ **1844.** See ***New Orleans Second Municipal Council – List of Fire Victims and their Losses, 1844*** **[Online Database].** The records of the Second Municipality Council include a volume of the minutes of the 1844 "distribution committee," appointed to apportion a $1,000.00 appropriation for the relief of the victims of an October fire in the Fourth Ward. Also included among the Council's records is a separate volume, listing the names of the fire victims, along with a brief description of their families and losses, with the committee's appropriation toward their relief also recorded. See **http://nutrias.org/~nopl/inv/firevictims1844.htm.**

■ **1846-1880**. See ***Index to the Justices of the Peace Marriage Records, 1846-1880*** **[Online Database],** indexed online at the Louisiana Division website, New Orleans Public Library. From 1846 to 1870, the Justices of the Peace were the exclusive source for civil marriage licenses in Orleans Parish, which was divided into six districts, each of which was to elect a justice. Justices continued to function until 1880, when the judges of the newly established City Court assumed responsibility for issuance of civil marriage licenses. Indexed by alpha groups for Grooms and Brides. See **http://nutrias.org/~nopl/inv/jpmarrindex/jpmarrindex.htm.**

■ **1852-1893.** See ***New Orleans Office of the Mayor – Records of the Disposition of Destitute Orphans, 1852-1893*** **[Online Database],** transcriptions by year at the Louisiana Division website, New Orleans Public Library. See **http://nutrias.org/~nopl/inv/orphanstranscriptions.htm.**

■ **1862-1863.** See ***Orleans Parish Coroner's Office Reports of Deaths, 1862-1863*** **[Online Database],** extracted at the New Orleans Public Library's Louisiana Division website. The deaths listed here for the period November 29, 1862-December 5, 1863 were recorded in what appears to be a notebook used by the Coroner or someone in his office. Some, but not all, of the deaths also appear in the official record of Inquests and Views. These deaths are of special interest since they occurred during the period of Union occupation of New Orleans following the city's fall in April 1862. The data in the notebook were transcribed by members of NOVA (the New Orleans Volunteer Association) and made available to New Orleans Public Library for inclusion on its web site. Several of the reports are accompanied by links to newspaper accounts of the deaths. See **http://nutrias.org/~nopl/inv/coroner/th1862to1863.htm.**

■ **1875-1877.** See ***New Orleans City Insane Asylum Record of Next of Kin, 1875-1877, 1 vol.*** **[Online Database],** extracted at the Louisiana Division website, New Orleans Public Library. Includes the patient's name and the name and address of the person to be referred to--i.e., the next of kin. The volume is in very poor condition, with many pages either cut or torn out. Most of the entries are overwritten with "died," "removed," "released," etc. See **http://nutrias.org/~nopl/inv/next%20of%20kin.htm.**

■ **1879-1880.** See ***Louisiana 2nd District (Orleans Parish), Marriages, May 12, 1879 to April 12, 1880*** **[Online Database],** transcribed online at the Louisiana Division website, New Orleans Public Library. Judges in Louisiana have been authorized to celebrate marriages since 1820; only one volume of marriage records has survived from the Second District Court in New Orleans. See **http://nutrias.org/~nopl/inv/2dcmarriages.htm.**

■ **1880-1916.** See ***Orleans Parish Registrar of Voters - Index to Registrations of Foreign Born Persons, 1880-1916* [Online Database],** the index records for each registrant his name, address, ward, precinct, country of birth, age, place and date of naturalization, and date of registration. Each volume is divided into alphabetical sections with data entered in order more or less by ward and precinct. See **http://nutrias.org/~nopl/inv/vx/vx100.htm.**

■ **1882-1917**. See ***Registers of Patients Transported to the State Insane Asylum, 1882-1917* [Online Database],** indexed at the Louisiana Division website, New Orleans Public Library. The Civil Sheriff was responsible for transporting to the State Insane Asylum at Jackson persons judged by the Civil District Court to be insane. In three volumes the Sheriff recorded the number of the suit record ordering the patient to be sent to Jackson, the date that he took the patient into custody, the patient's name, age, sex, color, address, nativity, occupation, marital status, disease, duration and cause of insanity, and remarks. See **http://nutrias.org/~nopl/inv/civilsheriff/vf350.htm.**

■ **1882-1888.** *See* ***New Orleans City Insane Asylum Record of Patients, 1882-1884; 1888* [Online Database],** indexed at the Louisiana Division website, New Orleans Public Library. This volume contains information on insane patients visited by the City Physician and recommended to the State Asylum. For each patient, the record includes name, race, sex, age, place of birth (in general terms), type of insanity and sometimes a description of the patient's behavior. An index is included at the end of the volume. Transcription are by page numbers. See **http://nutrias.org/~nopl/inv/cityinsaneasylum.htm.**

## Louisiana Databases Online at Ancestry.com

The Ancestry.com subscription website allows free access to all indexes, but to view any particular record requires a membership. Ancestry offers trial memberships and subscriptions for short periods and reduced rates. The following databases at the Ancestry.com website are unique statewide databases under the categories of Census & Voter Lists, Vital Records, Military, Immigrations, and Wills & Probates. To review the complete list of Louisiana statewide and parish-wide databases, see **http://search.ancestry.com/Places/US/Louisiana/Default.aspx.**

■ **1695-1954.** See ***U.S., French Catholic Church Records (Drouin Collection), 1695-1954* [Online Database],** indexed at the Ancestry.com website. Source: In the 1940s the Institut Généalogique Drouin in Québec began microfilming records pertaining to French Canadians throughout French Canada and America. The entire Drouin Collection contains vital, notarial, and other miscellaneous records from Quebec, as well as French Catholic parish records from Ontario, Acadia, and the U.S. This database only contains the French Catholic parish records from the U.S., including areas of Louisiana. This database has 228,368 records. See **http://search.ancestry.com/search/db.aspx?dbid=1111.**

■ **1699-1732.** See ***The Census Tables for the French Colony of Louisiana from 1699 Through 1732* [Online Database],** digitized and indexed at the Ancestry.com website. Source: Book, same title, by Charles R. Maduell, Jr., publ. 1993. Includes the full text images and an OCR index. This database has 190 pages. See **http://search.ancestry.com/search/db.aspx?dbid=48009.**

■ **1718-1925.** See ***Louisiana, Marriages, 1718-1925* [Online Database],** indexed at the Ancestry.com website. Source: Hunting for Bears database, extracted from Parish courthouse records on microfilm at the Family History Library, Salt Lake City, UT. Each index record includes: Name, Spouse, Marriage date, and Marriage place. This database has 562,712 records. See **http://search.ancestry.com/search/db.aspx?dbid=7837.**

■ **1719-1820.** See ***Louisiana, Slave Records, 1719-1820* [Online Database],** indexed at the Ancestry.com website. Source: *Afro-Louisiana History and Genealogy, 1719-1820,* by Midlo Gwendolyn Hall, publ. 2009. This database is a compilation of information on over 100,000 slaves who came to Louisiana between 1719 and 1820. These descriptions of slaves were extracted from documents and records located in various places throughout Louisiana, as well as from some archives located in Texas, France, and Spain. Information in this database includes name of individual, name of master, gender, race, birthplace, age, family relationships including mate and children, selling information such as name of seller, name of buyer, selling currency, and selling value, as well as retrieval information for the original document in which this

information was found. This database has 100,666 records. See
http://search.ancestry.com/search/db.aspx?dbid=7383.

■ **1719-1820.** See ***Louisiana, Freed Slave Records, 1719-1820* [Online Database],** indexed at the Ancestry.com website. Source: *Afro-Louisiana History and Genealogy, 1719-1820,* by Midlo Gwendolyn Hall, publ. 2009. This database is a compilation of information on over four thousand slaves from Louisiana who were involved in manumission (the formal emancipation from slavery) between 1719 and 1820. Information contained in this database includes the means of manumission, the relationship of the freer to the freed when a third party bought the slave in order to free him, the name of the third party freer, reasons for manumission, whether a payment was made in order to free the slave and if so, how much it was, the conditions imposed in order to free the slave, and an indication as to whether the slave was likely actually freed. It also provides information on family relationships among the freed slaves, racial categories, ages, genders, birthplaces of mothers of slaves involved in manumission, and indications if an individual was possibly freed by a white father. This database has 4,064 records. See
http://search.ancestry.com/search/db.aspx?dbid=7382.

■ **1720s.** See ***The Settlement of the German Coast of Louisiana and Creoles of German Descent* [Online Database],** digitized and indexed at the Ancestry.com website. Source: Book, same title, by J. Hanno Deiler, publ. 1909. This great little history book gives a general chronology of events related to the French settlements of Louisiana, then a more detailed look at the group of German immigrants who settled along the Mississippi River just north of New Orleans. The full text of the book is digitized with an OCR index. This database has 158 pages. See
http://search.ancestry.com/search/db.aspx?dbid=48568.

■ **1720-1733.** See ***The New Orleans French, 1720-1733* [Online Database],** digitized and indexed at the Ancestry.com website. Source: Winston De Ville's, *The New Orleans French, 1720-1722: A Collection of Marriage Records Relating to the First Colonists,* publ. 1973. Includes the full text and OCR index. This database has 118 pages. See
http://search.ancestry.com/search/db.aspx?dbid=48051.

■ **1720-1770.** See ***Louisiana Troops 1720-1770* [Online Database],** digitized and indexed at the Ancestry.com website. Source: Book, same title, by Winston De Ville, publ. 1994. This is an indexed database of a book listing the Louisiana troops, mostly French, organized in alphabetical order. This database has 135 pages. See
http://search.ancestry.com/search/db.aspx?dbid=48043.

■ **1728-1850.** See ***Louisiana Marriages to 1850* [Online Database],** indexed at the Ancestry.com website. Source: Jordan Dodd, compiler, 1997. Each entry includes groom, bride, marriage date, county, and state. This database has 29,692 records. See
http://search.ancestry.com/search/db.aspx?dbid=2090.

■ **1756-1984.** See ***Louisiana, Wills and Probate Records, 1756-1984* [Online Database],** digitized and indexed at the Ancestry.com website. Source: Ancestry extractions from Louisiana parish, district, and probate courts, 2015. Probate records may include Letters of Administration, Inventories, Distribution and Accounting of Estates, Administrative Bonds, and Guardianships. Each index record includes: Name, Probate place, Inferred death place, and Item description. The documents may reveal information about heirs, witnesses, etc. This database has 222,207 records. See
http://search.ancestry.com/search/db.aspx?dbid=9067.

■ **1778-1783.** See ***The Canary Islands Migration to Louisiana, 1778-1783* [Online Database],** digitized and indexed at the Ancestry.com website. Source: Book, same title, by Sidney Louis Villeré, publ. 1972. During this period, the Canary Islands was Spanish territory, inhabited by Portuguese farmers. The King of Spain financed a group of Canary Island emigrants to Spanish Louisiana, giving them tools and clothing for two years. The emigrants settled on the west side of the Mississippi River, just north and just south of New Orleans. Over the years, their descendants were sometimes referred to as "Spanish Creoles," since most of the other native-born Louisiana colonial people (Creoles) were of French or African origin. The full text of the book was digitized with an OCR index. This database has 105 pages. See
http://search.ancestry.com/search/db.aspx?dbid=48007.

■ **1790-1915.** See ***New Orleans, Louisiana, Birth Records Index, 1790-1915* [Online Database],** indexed at the Ancestry.com website. Source: LA State Archives, Vital Records Indexes. New Orleans was one of the first cities to establish the keeping of vital records, which they began doing in 1790. The

early records were somewhat inconsistent. It was not until 1914 when the keeping of vital records became a state-wide mandate, and the records are virtually complete since. This index provides information such as the child's name, parent's names (including the mother's maiden name), birth date, child's sex and color, and a reference to the original record. This database has 1,082,167 records. See
**http://search.ancestry.com/search/db.aspx?dbid=6587**.

■ **1791-1890.** See ***Louisiana, Compiled Census and Census Substitutes Index, 1791-1890* [Online Database],** indexed at the Ancestry.com website. Source: Accelerated Indexing Systems, Salt Lake City, UT, 1999. This collection contains the following indexes: 1791 Census of New Orleans, 1810 Federal Census Index, 1820 Federal Census Index, 1830 Federal Census Index, 1840 Federal Census Index, 1840 Pensioners List, 1850 Federal Census Index, 1850 Slave Schedule, 1850-1860 Sugar Census Index, 1860 Federal Census Index, 1870 Federal Census Index, 1890 Veterans Schedules, and Early Census Index. This database has 188,900 records. See
**http://search.ancestry.com/search/db.aspx?dbid=3550**.

■ **1804-1846.** See ***Louisiana, Orleans Parish Estate Files, 1804-1846* [Online Database],** indexed at the Ancestry.com website. Source: FamilySearch database, from Probate Court Records at the New Orleans City Archives. In Louisiana, Probate Records are often called Succession Records, and include petitions, successions, inventories, accounts, decrees and other court documents. Information found in these records includes: Name of testator or deceased, Names of heirs such as spouse, children, and other relatives or friends, Name of executor, administrator, or guardian, Names of witnesses, Residence of testator, Document and recording dates. This database has 7,080 records. See
**http://search.ancestry.com/search/db.aspx?dbid=60297**.

■ **1804-1949,** See ***New Orleans, Louisiana, Death Records Index, 1804-1949* [Online Database],** indexed at the Ancestry.com website. Source: LA State Archives, Vital Records Index. This index provides the following information: name, age, sex, color, death date, and a reference to the original record. This database has 686,801 records. See
**http://search.ancestry.com/search/db.aspx?dbid=6606**.

■ **1807-1860.** See ***New Orleans, Louisiana, Slave Manifests, 1807-1860* [Online Database],** digitized and indexed at the Ancestry.com website. Source: National Archives microfilm series M1895. Though a law banned the trans-Atlantic slave trade to the United States as of January 1808, slaves could still be bought and sold (and transported) within the country. By law, masters of vessels carrying slaves in coastal waters had to provide a manifest detailing their slave cargo when leaving ("outward") or entering ("inward") a port. The required slave manifests, provided by ships entering or leaving from the port at New Orleans, make up the records in this database. Each index record includes: Name, Gender, Color, Estimated birth year, Ship name, Port of departure, Port of arrival, Date of arrival, Age, First shipper/owner, Second shipper/owner residence, and Record type. This database has 104,117 records. See
**http://search.ancestry.com/search/db.aspx?dbid=1562**.

■ **1812-1815.** See ***Louisiana, Soldiers in the War of 1812* [Online Database],** indexed at the Ancestry.com website. Source: Marion John Bennett Pierson's *Louisiana Soldiers in the War of 1812*, pub. 1963. Each entry includes the rank and company to which the soldier was attached. This database has 14,209 records. See
**http://search.ancestry.com/search/db.aspx?dbid=48042**.

■ **1812-1879.** See ***Louisiana, War of 1812 Pension Lists* [Online Database],** digitized at the Ancestry.com website. FamilySearch database. This is an image only database. The collection consists of images of pension lists for years 1812-1815, recorded between 1873- 1879. Some lists are arranged in alphabetical order by surname. Includes lists of veterans and lists of claimants. These lists were maintained by the Auditor of the State of Louisiana. Browse the images for details. This database has 149 pages. See
**http://search.ancestry.com/search/db.aspx?dbid=60300**.

■ **1813-1963.** See ***New Orleans, Passenger Lists, 1813-1963* [Online Database],** indexed at the Ancestry.com website. Source: National Archives microfilm (8 series titles and 750 rolls). This database includes WPA transcripts of passenger lists, departure lists, and crew manifests from the port of New Orleans. These transcripts include the following details: Ship name, Passenger name, Arrival date, and Port of embarkation. The transcripts may also include the captain's name. The passenger lists were required by law in 1820, but some captains kept lists before then. This database has 4,288,331 records. See
**http://search.ancestry.com/search/db.aspx?dbid=7484**.

■ **1815-1977.** See ***New Orleans, Louisiana, Deaths Index, 1815-1977* [Online Database],** indexed at the Ancestry.com website. Source: Gladys Stovall Armstrong, compiler, *New Orleans, Louisiana, Deaths Index, 1815-1977.* Taken from small local newspapers, some published over a century ago, this database lists deaths for over 2,700 residents of the area between 1840 and 1970. Many of these newspapers, like the *New Orleans Parish*, are obscure and contained printed obituaries for persons larger newspapers may not have printed. Information includes date of death and, in some cases, relatives still living. This database has 2,700 records. See http://search.ancestry.com/search/db.aspx?dbid=3528.

■ **1819-1964.** See ***Louisiana, Statewide Death Index, 1819-1964* [Online Database],** indexed at the Ancestry.com website. Source: LA State Archives, Vital Records Index. Each index record includes the following information: Name of deceased, Age of deceased, Date of death, Parish of death, Reference to the actual record (a volume number, a certificate number, and the year in which the certificate was issued). This database has 2,081,698 records. See http://search.ancestry.com/search/db.aspx?dbid=6697.

■ **1820-1875.** See ***New Orleans, Passenger List Quarterly Abstracts, 1820-1875* [Online Database],** indexed at the Ancestry.com website. Source: National Archives microfilm series M272. These are passenger lists from vessels coming from foreign ports. The abstracts are arranged chronologically by arrival date, and they typically contain: Arrival date, Vessel name, Port of embarkation, Master's name, Passenger's name, age, sex, occupation, country they left, country to which they intend to become inhabitants, and deaths (whether this passenger died). This database has 408,999 records. See http://search.ancestry.com/search/db.aspx?dbid=2860.

■ **1821-1907.** See ***Louisiana, Homestead and Cash Entry Patents, Pre-1908* [Online Database],** indexed at the Ancestry.com website. Source: BLM General Land Office Automated Records Project, 1993. This database is an index to land patents, the first-title deed and the true beginning of private ownership of the land. The patent describes in legal terms the land to which the title is given. Each index record includes: Name, Land Office, Sequence, Document number, Total acres, Signature, Canceled document, Issue date, Mineral rights reserved, Metes and bounds, Statutory reference, Multiple warrantee and patentee names, Act or treaty, Entry classification, and Land description. This database has 78,869 records. See http://search.ancestry.com/search/db.aspx?dbid=2074.

■ **1831-1964.** See ***New Orleans, Louisiana, Marriage Records Index, 1831-1964* [Online Database],** indexed at the Ancestry.com website. Source: LA State Archives, Vital Records Index. In addition to providing the names of the people who were married, the index provides their ages, sex, marriage date, and a reference to the original record. This database has 834,468 records. See http://search.ancestry.com/search/db.aspx?dbid=6500.

■ **1836-2001.** See ***Louisiana, Naturalization Records, 1836-2001* [Online Database],** digitized and indexed at the Ancestry.com website. Source: National Archives microfilm of district court records, ARC #592776 & #647811. Includes Declarations of Intentions and Oaths of Allegiance/Naturalization Records. Each index record includes: Name, Gender, Age, Birth date, Birthplace, Naturalization date, Court, Court city, Document type, and Petition number. The scanned documents give more information. This database has 109,707 records. See http://search.ancestry.com/search/db.aspx?dbid=2507.

■ **1840-1906.** See ***Southwest Louisiana, Deaths Index, 1840-1906* [Online Database],** indexed at the Ancestry.com website. Source: FamilySearch database, from Donald J. Hebert's *Southwest Louisiana Records, and St. Mary Parish Records.* Each index record may include: Name, Gender, Birthplace, Birth date, Age, Race, Occupation, Residence, Place of death, Date of death. Place of burial, Date of burial, Cemetery, Spouse's name, Father's name, Mother's name, Mother's birthplace, and FHL film number. This database has 6,016 records. See http://search.ancestry.com/search/db.aspx?dbid=2553.

■ **1851-1900.** See ***Louisiana Marriage Records, 1851-1900* [Online Database],** indexed at the Ancestry.com website. Source: Liahona Research, Jordan Dodd, compiler, 2000. Although official vital records registration began for Louisiana in 1914, many parishes kept records long before that date. This update adds the records for Bienville, Caldwell, Jackson, and Ouachita parishes to those of Bossier, Lincoln, and Sabine for the years 1851 through 1900.

Each entry lists, at a minimum, spouses' names and the date of the marriage. This database has 43,140 records. See
http://search.ancestry.com/search/db.aspx?dbid=5228.

■ **1854 History.** See ***History of Louisiana* [Online Database],** digitized and indexed at the Ancestry.com website. Source: Charles Gayarré's *History of Louisiana,* publ. 1854. This database has 2,274 records. See
http://search.ancestry.com/search/db.aspx?dbid=28137.

■ **1861-1865.** See ***Louisiana, Confederate Soldiers Index, 1861-1865* [Online Database],** digitized and indexed at the FamilySearch.org website. Source: Andrew B Booth's *Records of Louisiana Confederate Soldiers & Confederate Commands,* publ. 1920. This database constitutes 3 volumes of records of Louisiana Confederate soldiers and commands. This alphabetized roll contains the records of individuals, and also provides a brief history of Louisiana's 982 companies in the Confederate army. This database has 102,099 records. See
http://search.ancestry.com/search/db.aspx?dbid=3199.

■ **1861-1875.** See ***Louisiana Military Record* [Online Database],** indexed at the Ancestry.com website. Source: Barrett Napier's *Military Record of Louisiana: Including Biographical and Historical Papers Relating to the Military Organizations of the State*, publ. 1875. This database, contains a variety of documents relating to the state's military history. Some of the subjects include the Confederate dead buried in Virginia; battles in Virginia; biographical and historical papers relating to military organizations; and Washington artillery. This database has 459 pages. See
http://search.ancestry.com/search/db.aspx?dbid=8538.

■ **1864-2003.** See ***Chalmette, Louisiana, Chalmette National Cemetery, 1864-2003* [Online Database],** digitized and indexed at the Ancestry.com website. This database contains an index and digital images of all gravestones in Chalmette National Cemetery, established in 1864. The cemetery section is provided for each image. Information on the markers varies. Some may contain only a number of initials; others may include facts such as name, birth date, death date, age, rank, and state of origin. This database has 8,525 records. See
http://search.ancestry.com/search/db.aspx?dbid=2293.

■ **1872-1874.** See ***Rayville, Louisiana Newspaper Name Index, 1872-1874* [Online Database],** indexed at the Ancestry.com website. Source: Book, same title, by Becky Calvin. This database is a name index to the *Richland Beacon* newspaper between 1872 and 1874. Each entry contains the person's name, why their name appeared in print, issue date, and a concise summary of the newspaper article. This database has 3,036 records. See
http://search.ancestry.com/search/db.aspx?dbid=4187.

■ **1898-1950.** See ***Louisiana, Confederate Pensions, 1898-1950* [Online Database],** digitized at the Ancestry.com website. Source FamilySearch database. This is an image only database, organized by the names of veterans and widows in alphabetical order. Information found in applications submitted by the veteran may include: Applicant's name, Date application was filed, Date and place of birth, Current residence and length of residency, Company, regiment and branch of service, Dates and places of enlistment and discharge, Nature of wounds received, Sworn statements on proof of service by comrades, Names of witnesses, and War department service abstracts. If the application was submitted by a widow of a veteran it may also include the following: Wife's full name and age, Number of children and their gender, Date and place of marriage to the veteran, and Date and place of the veteran's death. This database has 199,883 records. See
http://search.ancestry.com/search/db.aspx?dbid=60295.

■ **1905-1910.** See ***Italian Passengers to Louisiana, 1905-1910* [Online Database],** indexed at the Ancestry.com website. Source: Database compiled, by Shirley Nichols, 2000. This database contains records of sixteen Italian passenger vessels arriving in New Orleans on various dates between May 1905 and February 1910. It includes lists from the following ships: SS Vincenzo Florio, 5 May 1905; SS Vincenzo Florio, 21 Jan 1906; SS Piemonte, 31 May 1907; SS Piemonte, 16 Oct 1907; SS Gerty, Oct 1907; SS Sofia, 3 Jan 1908; SS Liguria, 11 Mar 1908; SS Liguria, Oct 12, 1908; SS Giulia, Oct 1908; SS Liguria, 14 May 1909; and SS Liguria, 22 Feb 1910; Each index record includes: Name, Arrival date, Age, Gender, Marital status, Native country/town, Destination, Ship, and Occupation. This database has 10,276 records. See
http://search.ancestry.com/search/db.aspx?dbid=4742.

■ **1866-1963.** See ***Louisiana, State Penitentiary Records, 1866-1963*** **[Online Database],** indexed at the Ancestry.com website. Source: FamilySearch database, acquired from the LA State Archives. This is an image only database. Browse through the images, organized by 47 vols./date range. Most records include the following: Name of prisoner, Age, Height and weight, Physical description including color of eyes, hair and identifying marks, Marital status, Reason for entry in (offense) ledger, Term of imprisonment, Level of education, Literacy, Birth date and place, Death date, Burial date and place, Cause of death, Last residence prior to confinement, Discharge or transfer date, and Where transferred. This database has 38,041 records. See
**http://search.ancestry.com/search/db.aspx?dbid=60299**.

---

## Louisiana Databases Online at FamilySearch.org

The following databases are available for free at the FamilySearch.org website. To see the current list, visit the Louisiana Research Page for lists of Indexed and Image Only Databases. See
**https://familysearch.org/search/collection/location/37**.

■ **1804-1846.** See ***Louisiana, Orleans Parish Estate Files, 1804-1846*** **[Online Database],** digitized and indexed at the FamilySearch.org website. Source: FamilySearch extractions from Louisiana parish, district, and probate courts. Each index record includes: Name, Event place, Event (probate) year, Record type, Event type, Court type, First image number, Last image number, and Number of images. More information is usually given on the document images. This database has 7,080 records. See
**https://familysearch.org/search/collection/1388197**.

■ **1805-1920.** See ***Louisiana, Orleans Parish Will Books, 1805-1920*** **[Online Database],** digitized at the FamilySearch.org website. Source: New Orleans City Archives, Court Records. This is an image only database of the Will Books from Orleans Parish courts. Included are copies of all wills filed in Orleans Parish, 1805-1920. The will books comprise 39 bound volumes. Each volume is individually indexed at the front of each book. The will books were created in several courts including the Court of Probates (1805-1846), Second District Court (1846-1880) and Civil District Court (1880-1920). Volume 31, No. 11 is missing. Browse through the images, organized by Volume Title and Year Range. This database has 25,285 records. See
**https://familysearch.org/search/collection/2019728**.

■ **1811-1934.** See ***Louisiana Births & Christenings, 1811-1830 & 1854-1934*** **[Online Database],** indexed at the FamilySearch.org website. Source: FamilySearch extractions from records on microfilm at the Family History Library, Salt Lake City, UT. Each index record includes: Name, Gender, Christening date, Christening place, Birth date, Birthplace, and Mother's name. This database has 29,549 records. See
**https://familysearch.org/search/collection/1674847**.

■ **1812-1815, 1873-1879.** See ***Louisiana War of 1812 Pension Lists*** **[Online Database],** digitized at the FamilySearch.org website. Source: LA State Archives, Baton Rouge, LA. This is an image only database with images of pension lists for years 1812-1815, recorded between 1873 and 1879. Some lists are arranged in alphabetical order by surname. Includes lists of veterans and lists of claimants. Browse the images, organized by 1) List of Pensioners paid by State Auditor, 1876-1877; 2) List of Pensioners - Pensions to Veterans, 1878-1879; and 3) List of Pensioners under acts of 1873 & 1876. This database has 149 pages. See
**https://familysearch.org/search/collection/1527724**.

■ **1816-1906.** *See* ***Louisiana Marriages, 1816-1906*** **[Online Database],** indexed at the FamilySearch.org website. Source: FamilySearch extractions from records on microfilm at the Family History Library, Salt Lake City, UT. This database has 133,814 records. See
**https://familysearch.org/search/collection/1674881**.

■ **1820-1945.** See ***Louisiana, New Orleans Passenger Lists, 1820-1945*** **[Online Database],** digitized and indexed at the FamilySearch.org website. Source: National Archives microfilm series M259 & T905. Each index record includes: Name, Event type, Event date, Event place, Gender, Age, Birth year (estimated), Birthplace, and Ship name. This database has 1,233,573 records. See
**https://familysearch.org/search/collection/1916009**.

■ **1822-1880.** See ***Louisiana, Orleans Court Records, 1822-1880*** **[Online Database],** digitized at the FamilySearch.org website. Source: New Orleans City Archives, District Court Records. This is an image only database, including dockets and indexes for the Parish Court, 1822-1840; Commercial Court, 1839-

1846, First Judicial District Court, 1839-1842; Second, Third, Fourth and Fifth Judicial Court, 1846-1880 and the Sixth and Seventh Judicial District Courts, 1854-1880. Browse through the images, organized by Commercial Court, Parish Court, or District Court, then by Volume Title, and Date Range. This database has 48,176 records. See https://familysearch.org/search/collection/2030501.

■ **1831-1906.** See ***Louisiana Naturalization Records, 1831-1906*** **[Online Database],** indexed at the FamilySearch.org website. Source: National Archives Naturalization records. Each record includes: Name, Event type, Event place, and Birthplace. This database has 20,710 records. See https://familysearch.org/search/collection/1459894.

■ **1837-1957.** See ***Louisiana, Parish Marriages, 1837-1957*** **[Online Database],** digitized and indexed at the FamilySearch.org website. Source: FamilySearch extractions from all LA parish courthouses. (at this writing, about 20% complete). Each index record includes: Name, Event type, Event date, Event place, Age, Birth year (estimated), Father's name, Mother's name, Spouse's name, Spouse's birth year (estimated), Spouse's father's name, Spouse's father's titles, and Spouse's mother's name. This database has 1,107,552 records. See https://familysearch.org/search/collection/1807364.

■ **1838-1861.** See ***Louisiana, Eastern District Naturalization Petitions, 1838-1861*** **[Online Database],** indexed at the FamilySearch.org website. Source: National Archives microfilm series P2233. This database includes naturalization petitions filed in the U.S. District Court for the Eastern District of Louisiana, which was located in New Orleans. The set includes papers filed in naturalization proceedings including petitions for naturalization and oaths of the petitioner and two witnesses. Occasionally declarations of intention filed in other courts are included. The information given for each petition includes the name and residence of the petitioner, country of birth, city and date of arrival, and the names of two witnesses. This database has 1,450 records. See https://familysearch.org/search/collection/1854308.

■ **1846-1880.** See ***Louisiana, Orleans Parish Second District Judicial Court Case Files, 1846-1880*** **[Online Database]**, digitized at the FamilySearch.org website. Source: New Orleans City Archives, Second District Judicial Court Records. This is an image only database of civil case files. Browse the images, organized by Record Type, Date Range, and Volume. This database has 287,610 records. See https://familysearch.org/search/collection/1879925.

■ **1850-1956.** See ***Louisiana Deaths Index, 1850-1875, 1894-1956*** **[Online Database],** indexed at the FamilySearch.org website. Source: LA State Archives, Vital Records Indexes. The statewide records for all parishes cover 1911-1956. Coverage outside these dates for individual Parishes varies. This collection does not include records for deaths from 1875-1893 and has only a few entries for 1894-1904. Death records for 1850-1875 are for Jefferson Parish only. Each index record includes: Name, Event type, Event date, Gender, Age, Race, Birth year (estimated), Birthplace, Father's name, Mother's name, Spouse's name, and Certificate number. This database has 679,383 records. See https://familysearch.org/search/collection/1609793.

■ **1861-1865.** See ***Louisiana Civil War Service Records of Confederate Soldiers, 1861-1865*** **[Online Database],** indexed at the FamilySearch.org website. Source: National Archives microfilm series M320. Confederate service records of soldiers who served in organizations from Louisiana. The records include a jacket-envelope for each soldier, labeled with his name, his rank, and the unit in which he served. The jacket-envelope typically contains card abstracts of entries relating to the soldier as found in original muster rolls, returns, rosters, payrolls, appointment books, hospital registers, Union prison registers and rolls, parole rolls, inspection reports; and the originals of any papers relating solely to the particular soldier. This database has 778,925 records. See https://familysearch.org/search/collection/1932372.

■ **1861-1865.** See ***Louisiana Civil War Service Records of Union Soldiers, 1861-1865*** **[Online Database],** indexed at the FamilySearch.org website. Source: National Archives microfilm series M396. Union service records of soldiers who served in organizations from Louisiana. The records include a jacket-envelope for each soldier, labeled with his name, his rank, and the unit in which he served. The jacket-envelope typically contains card abstracts of entries relating to the soldier as found in original muster rolls, returns, rosters, payrolls, appointment books, hospital registers, prison registers and rolls, parole rolls, inspection reports; and the originals of any papers relating solely to the particular soldier. This database has 119,515 records. See **https://familysearch.org/search/collection/1932399**.

■ **1865-1872.** See ***Louisiana, Freedmen's Bureau Field Office Records, 1865-1872*** **[Online Database],** digitized at the FamilySearch.org website. Source: National Archives microfilm series M1905. This is an image only database. The Bureau of Refugees, Freedmen, and Abandoned Lands was created in 1865 at the end of the American Civil War to supervise relief efforts including education, health care, food and clothing, refugee camps, legalization of marriages, employment, labor contracts, and securing back pay, bounty payments and pensions. Browse through the images, organized by Freedmen's Bureau Office or Subordinate Field Office location. This database has 97,119 records. See **https://familysearch.org/search/collection/2333781**.

■ **1866-1963.** See ***Louisiana State Penitentiary Records, 1866-1963*** **[Online Database],** digitized at the FamilySearch.org website. Source: LA State Archives, Baton Rouge, LA. This is an image only database of 36 vols. of registers of convicts admitted to the prison. The index books to the registers were also digitized. Browse through the images, organized by Record Type, Volume, and Year Range. This database has 21,796 records. See **https://familysearch.org/search/collection/1931391**.

■ **1898-1950.** See ***Louisiana Confederate Pensions, 1898-1950*** **[Online Database],** digitized at the FamilySearch.org website. Source: LA State Archives, Baton Rouge, LA. This is an image only database with images of applications for pensions filed by Confederate veterans and widows living in the state of Louisiana. Browse the images, organized in alphabetical order. This database has 199,883 images. See **https://familysearch.org/search/collection/1838535**.

■ **1910, 1960.** See ***Louisiana, Orleans Parish Vital Records, 1910, 1960*** **[Online Database],** indexed at the FamilySearch.org website. Source: LA State Archives, Baton Rouge, LA. This collection includes birth records and index for 1910. It also includes marriage and death records and indexes for 1960. Each index record incudes: Event type, Event date, Event place, Gender, Age, Birth year, and Certificate number. This database has 13,283 records. See **https://familysearch.org/search/collection/1929995**.

■ **1917-1920.** See ***Louisiana World War I Service Records, 1917-1920*** **[Online Database],** digitized at the FamilySearch.org website. Source: LA State Archives, Baton Rouge, LA. This is an image only database of enlistment or induction records from World War I. A series of cards, about 3 cards per page, have a wealth of information about each enlistee, including events after enlistment, such as battles, wounds, promotions, etc. The collection is arranged alphabetically by parish name. Within a parish, the names are divided by alpha groups, but not a strict A to Z. This database has 27,210 records. See **https://familysearch.org/search/collection/2489920**.

■ **1940-1945.** See ***Louisiana First Registration Draft Cards, compiled 1940-1945*** **[Online Database],** digitized and indexed at the FamilySearch.org website. Source: National Archives, Selective Service System records. Each index record includes: Event type, Event date, Event place, Gender, and Birth date. The registration card images have more information. This database has 394,216 records. See **https://familysearch.org/search/collection/1916286**.

## Louisiana Databases Online At Various Websites

■ ***1731 Ursuline Orphanage, New Orleans, Louisiana*** **[Online Database],** indexed at the USGenWeb site for Orleans Parish LA. See **http://files.usgwarchives.net/la/orleans/history/schools/orphans.txt.**

■ ***1785 Census of Avoyelles Post, Avoyelles Parish, Louisiana*** **[Online Database],** indexed at the USGenWeb site for Avoyelles Parish LA. See **http://files.usgwarchives.net/la/avoyelles/census/avoy1785.txt.**

■ **1785.** See ***Spanish Baton Rouge Census of 1786*** **[Online Database],** indexed at the USGenWeb site for East Baton Rouge Parish LA. See **http://files.usgwarchives.net/la/eastbatonrouge/census/span1786.txt.**

■ **1785.** See ***Opelousas Militia 1785 Muster Roll, St. Landry Parish, Louisiana*** **[Online Database],** indexed at the USGenWeb site for St. Landry Parish LA. See **http://files.usgwarchives.net/la/stlandry/military/1785must.txt.**

■ *1788 Militia List, Post of Rapide, Rapides Parish, Louisiana* **[Online Database],** indexed at the USGenWeb site for Rapides Parish LA. See **http://files.usgwarchives.net/la/rapides/military/rapi1788.txt.**

■ *1790-1904 Birth Indexes, Orleans Parish, Louisiana* **[Online Database],** extracted from the State Archives Birth Index. Indexed at the USGenWeb site for Orleans Parish LA. See **www.usgwarchives.net/la/orleans/birth-index.htm.**

■ *1793 Tax List, Natchitoches Parish, Louisiana* **[Online Database],** extracted at the USGenWeb site for Natchitoches Parish LA. See **http://files.usgwarchives.net/la/natchitoches/taxlists/tax1793.txt.**

■ *1794 Militia List, Post of Rapide, Rapides Parish, Louisiana* **[Online Database],** indexed at the USGenWeb site for Rapides Parish LA. See **http://files.usgwarchives.net/la/rapides/military/rapi1794.txt.**

■ **1795-1799.** See *Militia List, Post of Rapide, Rapides Parish, Louisiana* **[Online Database**], indexed at the USGenWeb site for Rapides Parish LA: **http://files.usgwarchives.net/la/rapides/military/rapi1790.txt.**

■ *1796-1947 Index of Land Records, Rapides Parish, Louisiana* **[Online Database],** indexed at the USGenWeb site for Rapides Parish LA. See **http://files.usgwarchives.net/la/rapides/deeds/land-ind.txt.**

■ **1804-1972.** See *Louisiana Biography/Obituary Index* **[Online Database**], indexed at the New Orleans Public Library's Louisiana Division website. This database references obituaries and death notices published in New Orleans newspapers from 1804-1972 and biographical information published in older Louisiana collective biographies. The original index, housed in the Louisiana Division of New Orleans Public Library, is an alphabetical card file of more than 650,000 names. See **http://nopl.minisisinc.com/NOPL/SCRIPTS/MWIMAIN.DLL/144/obit_public?directsearch.**

■ *1805 New Orleans City Directory* **[Online Database],** extracted and indexed at the USGenWeb site for Orleans Parish LA. See **http://files.usgwarchives.net/la/orleans/history/directory/1805nocd.txt.**

■ *1805-1971 City Directories, New Orleans, Louisiana* **[Online Database],** includes separate indexes for 1805, 1811, 1822-1824, 1832, 1834, 1838, 1841, 1842-1843, 1846, 1849, 1859, 1861, 1866, 1867, 1868-1915, 1931-1935, 1938-1940, 1942, and 1971. Indexed at the USGenWeb site for Orleans Parish LA. See **www.usgwarchives.net/la/orleans/directry.htm.**

■ **1805-1991.** See *Louisiana Newspaper Archives (1805-1991)* **[Online Database],** digitized and indexed newspapers at the GenealogyBank website for the following cities: Abbeville, Alexandria, Amite, Ascension, Bastrop, Baton Rouge, Bogalusa, Bossier City, Covington, Crowley, De Ridder, Donaldsonville, Eunice, Fort Polk, Franklin, Gueydan, Hammond, Kaplan, L Place, Lafayette, Lake Arthur, Lake Charles, Leesville, Marksville, Minden, Morgan City, Natchitoches, New Iberia, New Orleans, Plaquemine, Rayne, Rayville, St. Francisville, St. Martinville, Sulphur, Vidalia, Ville Platte, and Zachary. See **www.genealogybank.com/gbnk/newspapers/explore/USA/Louisiana.**

■ *1811 New Orleans City Directory* **[Online Database],** indexed at the USGenWeb site for Orleans Parish LA. See **http://files.usgwarchives.net/la/orleans/history/directory/1811nocd.txt.**

■ *1824 New Orleans City Directory* **[Online Database],** indexed at the USGenWeb site for Orleans Parish LA. See **http://files.usgwarchives.net/la/orleans/history/directory/1824nocd.txt.**

■ *1832 New Orleans City Directory* **[Online Database],** indexed at the USGenWeb site for Orleans Parish LA. See **http://files.usgwarchives.net/la/orleans/history/directory/1832nocd.txt.**

■ **1842 New Orleans City Directory [Online Database],** indexed at the USGenWeb site for Orleans Parish. See **http://files.usgwarchives.net/la/orleans/history/directory/.**

■ **1986 - Current.** See *Louisiana Recent Newspaper Obituaries (1986-Current)* **[Online Database**], digitized and indexed newspaper obituaries at the GenealogyBank website, including newspapers from these cities: Abbeville, Amite, Ascension, Bastrop,

Baton Rouge, Bogalusa, Bossier City, Covington, Crowley, Rayne, De Ridder, Donaldsonville, Eunice, Fort Polk, Franklin, Gueydan, Hammond, Kaplan, La Place, Lafayette, Lake Arthur, Lake Charles, Leesville, Marksville, Minden, Morgan City, New Iberia, New Orleans, Plaquemine, Rayne, Rayville, St. Martinville, Sulphur, Ville Platte, and Zachary. See **www.genealogybank.com/gbnk/obituaries/explore/USA/ Louisiana.**

## Louisiana Periodical Articles

### Censuses & Substitute Name Lists in Genealogical Periodicals

PERSI (PERiodical Source Index) is a digitized database project of the Allen County Public Library (ACPL), Fort Wayne, IN. Since 1986, the PERSI extractors have indexed article titles, places, and surnames from over 11,000 genealogical & historical periodicals. The PERSI database is currently available online through the **FindMyPast.com** subscription website. The Genealogy Center of the ACPL in Fort Wayne IN holds all 11,000 periodicals and will make copies of any article by special request. To obtain an order form for requesting a printed copy of any article indexed in the PERSI database, see **http://genealogycenter.org/docs/default-source/resources/articlerequest.pdf?sfvrsn=2.**

**Louisiana PERSI Search:** Using the FindMyPast.com website, the keywords "Louisiana Tax" had 30 results.; "Colonial" had 172 results. Examples of Louisiana articles available are shown below:

■ **1706-1741**. See **"Early Census Tables, 1706-1741, Notes in French" [Printed Article],** in *Louisiana Historical Society Publications* (Louisiana Historical Society, New Orleans, LA), Vol. 5 (1911).

■ **1721.** See **"Census, 1721, Workers in Labor Force" [Printed Article],** in *Louisiana Genealogical Register* (Louisiana Genealogical & Historical Society), Vol. 27, No. 2 (Jun 1980).

■ **1724.** See "**1724 German Coast Census" [Printed Article],** in *Bean Stalk* (Southern Bean Association, Norman, OK),Vol. 35, Nos. 1 & 2 (Mar –June 2006). For access to a digital version of this article, see the online FHL catalog page. See **https://familysearch.org/search/catalog/1842321.**

■ **1726.** See **"Residents, 1726, Natchitoches Post" [Printed Article],** in *Louisiana Genealogical Register* (Louisiana Genealogical & Historical Society, Baton Rouge, LA), Vol. 8, No. 3 (Sep 1961).

■ **1728.** See **"Directory of New Orleans Inhabitants, 1728" [Printed Article],** in *Louisiana Genealogical Register* (Louisiana Genealogical & Historical Society, Baton Rouge, LA), Vol. 6, No. 4 (Aug 1959).

■ **1749.** See **"German Coast of LA, 1749: Reconstructed Families" [Printed Article]** in *Louisiana Genealogical Register* (Louisiana Genealogical and Historical Society, Baton Rouge, LA), Vol. 29, No. 4 (Dec 1982).

■ **1766.** See **"1766 Spanish Census, Pointe Coupee Parish, Louisiana" [Printed Article],** in *Louisiana Genealogical Register* (Louisiana Genealogical & Historical Society, Baton Rouge, LA), Vol. 7, No. 3 (Sep 1960); and Vol. 7, No. 4 (Dec 1960).

■ **1767.** See **"Acadian Records, St. Gabriel, 1767" [Printed Article],** in *New Orleans Genesis* (Genealogical Research Society of New Orleans), Vol. 10, No. 39 (Jun 1971).

■ **1773-1785.** See ***The Acadian Exiles in Chatellerault, 1773-1785*** **[Printed Book],** by Albert J. Robichaux, Publ. Herbert Pub., Eunice, LA, 190 pages, FHL book 944.63/C1 D2r.

■ **1770.** See **"Militia Lists, Acadian Coast, 1770" [Printed Article]**, in *Louisiana Genealogical Register* (Louisiana Genealogical & Historical Society, Baton Rouge, LA), Vol. 9, No. 2 (Jun 1962).

■ **1774.** See **"Recensements General des Attakapas, 1774" [Printed Article],** in *Louisiana Genealogical Register* (Louisiana Genealogical & Historical Society, Baton Rouge, LA), Vol. 13, No. 4 (Dec 1966).

■ **1777.** See **"New Orleans Census, 1777" [Printed Article],** in *New Orleans Genesis* (Genealogical Research Society of New Orleans), Vol. 21, No. 81 (Jan 1982).

■ **1781.** see **"Census and Tax List for Church at Attakapas, 1781" [Printed Article],** in *Attakapas Gazette* (Attakapas Historical Association, Lafayette, LA), Vol. 20, No. 1 (Spring 1985).

■ **1782.** See **"Census, 1782, Baton Rouge" [Printed Article],** in *Louisiana Genealogical Register* (Louisiana Genealogical & Historical Society), Vol. 8, No. 4 (Dec 1961).

■ **1796.** See **"Persons Residing Along Ouachita River, 1796" [Printed Article],** in *New Orleans Genesis* (Genealogical Research Society of New Orleans), Vol. 16, No. 63 (Jun 1977).

■ **1803.** See **"Appraisement of Property, 1803, Ouachita Parish, Louisiana" [Printed Article],** in *Northeast Louisiana Genealogical Society Quarterly* (NLGS, Monroe, LA), Vol. 2, No. 3 (Jul 1976).

■ **1806.** See **"1806 Tax Roll, Iberville Parish, Louisiana" [Printed Article],** in *Baton Rouge Newsletter* (Baton Rouge Genealogical & Historical Society, Baton Rouge, LA), Vol. 5, No. 3 (Aug 1985).

■ **1808.** See **"1808 Taxpayers, Ouachita Parish, Louisiana" [Printed Article],** in *Louisiana Genealogical Register* (Louisiana Genealogical & Historical Society, Baton Rouge, LA), Vol. 9, No. 4 (Dec 1962).

■ **1808.** See **"Militia Officers, 1808" [Printed Article],** in *New Orleans Genesis* (Genealogical Research Society of New Orleans), Vol. 1, No. 3 (Jun 1962).

■ **1810.** See **"1810 Delinquent Taxpayers, Attakapas Parish, Louisiana" [Printed Article],** in *Attakapas Gazette* (Attakapas Historical Association, Lafayette, LA), Vol. 10, No. 4 (Winter 1975).

■ **1810.** See **"1810 Land Owners and Slave Owners, Attakapas Parish, Louisiana" [Printed Article],** in *Attakapas Gazette* (Attakapas Historical Association, Lafayette, LA), Vol. 11, No. 2 (Summer 1976).

■ **1811-1812.** See **"1811-1812 Tax List, St. Tammany Parish, Louisiana," [Printed Article]** in *Louisiana Genealogical Register* (Louisiana Genealogical & Historical Society, Baton Rouge, LA), Vol. 14, No. 4 (Dec 1967).

■ **1813.** See **"Census of 1813 - Territory of Louis Carriere" [Printed Article],** in *Louisiana Genealogical Register* (Louisiana Genealogical & Historical Society, Baton Rouge, LA), Vol. IIV, No. 2 (Jun 1967).

■ **1813.** See **"1813 Tax List, St. Mary Parish, Louisiana" [Printed Article],** in *Attakapas Gazette* (Attakapas Historical Association, Lafayette, LA), Vol. 12, No. 4 (Winter 1977).

■ **1825.** See **"1825 Voter Registration, Iberville Parish, Louisiana" [Printed Article],** in *Le Raconteur* (Le Comité des Archives de la Louisiana, Baton Rouge, LA), Vol. 14, No. 1 (Apr 1994).

■ **1837.** See **"1837 Voters, St. Tammany Parish, Louisiana" [Printed Article],** in *New Orleans Genesis* (Genealogical Research Society of New Orleans), Vol. 25, No. 103 (Jul 1987). This same database was indexed online at the USGenWeb site for St. Tammany Parish LA. See **http://files.usgwarchives.net/la/sttammany/court/vote1837.txt.**

■ **1837.** See **"1837 Census of Voters, Ascension Parish, Louisiana" [Printed Article],** in *Le Raconteur* (Le Comité des Archives de la Louisiana, Baton Rouge, LA), Vol. 22, No. 3-4 (Dec 2002).

■ **1841.** See **"1841 Voters, West Baton Rouge Parish, Louisiana" [Printed Article]**, in *West Baton Rouge Genealogical Society Newsletter* (Port Allen, LA), Vol. 10, No. 1 (Jan 1995).

■ **1845.** See **"1845 List of Voters, Lafourche Parish, Louisiana" [Printed Article],** in *Terrebonne Life Lines* (Terrebonne Genealogical Society, Houma, LA), Vol. 27, No. 3 (Fall 2008).

## Louisiana Books & Microfilms at the Family History Library

Important Louisiana statewide census substitutes are cited below in chronological order. Each item includes a FHL book number or FHL film number, which can be used to search the FHL catalog for more details. To review an item, start at the FamilySearch catalog search page. See **https://familysearch.org/search/catalog/results**. Select "Search by Place" then "United States, Louisiana" to see a list of catalog categories. Or, select "Call Number" then type an FHL book number; or select "Film/Fiche Number" to view a specific title.

■ **1679-1804.** See ***Name Card Index to Records of the French Superior Council, 1679-1803; & Judicial Records of the Spanish Cabildo, 1769-1804* [Microfilm],** from the originals at the Louisiana Historical Center, New Orleans. Filmed by the Genealogical Society of Utah, 1981, 9 rolls, beginning with FHL film #1276244 (Abad, Juan – Azurto, Pablo). For complete list of roll numbers and contents of each roll, see the online FHL catalog page for this title. See **https://familysearch.org/search/catalog/251081**.

■ **1696-1781.** See ***Recensements et Correspondence Général, 1696-1781*** **[Microfilm],** from the French language originals of the Governor-Generals of La Louisiane Française located at les Archives Nationales, Paris. Includes correspondence, passenger lists, censuses, and land grants during the French administration of Louisiana. Filmed by the Genealogical Society of Utah, 1974, 2 rolls, FHL film #1080001 (1696-1781) & FHL film #1080002 (1706-1732).

■ **1699-1820.** See ***Early Louisiana Settlers, 1600s-1800s*** **[CD-ROM].** This is CD No. 525 produced for the Family Tree Maker (Broderbund) archives in collaboration with Genealogical Publishing Co., Inc., Baltimore, 2000. Contents: *The Canary Islands Migration to Louisiana, 1778-1783*: the *History and Passenger Lists of the Islenos Volunteer Recruits and their Families,* compiled and written by Sidney Louis Villeré; *The Settlement of the German Coast of Louisiana and the Creoles of German Descent,* by J. Hanno Deiler; *The Census Tables for the French Colony of Louisiana from 1699 through 1732*, compiled and translated by Charles R. Maduell; *Louisiana Census Records, 1810 & 1820*; compiled by Robert Bruce L. Ardoin (vols. I-II*); Gulf Coast Colonials: A Compendium of French Families in early Eighteenth Century Louisiana*, by Winston De Ville: *The New Orleans French, 1720-1733: A Collection of Marriage Records Relating to the First Colonists of the Louisiana Province*, by Winston De Ville; *Old Families of Louisiana,* by Stanley Clisby Arthur, editor and compiler, George Campbell Huchet de Kernion, collaborator and historian; *Louisiana Troops, 1720-1770,* by Winston De Ville; *Louisiana Colonials: Soldiers and Vagabonds,* translated and compiled by Winston De Ville; and *Louisiana Soldiers in the War of 1812*; by Marion John Bennett Pierson. See FHL CD No. 9, part 525.

■ **1699-1769.** See ***France's Forgotten Legion, a CD-ROM Publication: Service Records of French Military and Administrative Personnel Stationed in the Mississippi Valley and Gulf Coast Region, 1699-1769*** **[CD-ROM],** by Carl A. Brasseaux, publ. LSU Press, Baton Rouge, 2000. See FHL CD No. 1400.

■ **1699-1803.** See ***The First Families of Louisiana: An Index to Glenn R. Conrad's 2-Volume Series of 1970*** **[Printed Index],** compiled by Donna Rachal Mills, publ. by Mills Historical Press, 1992, 89 pages, FHL book 976.3 D2c. For access to a digital version of this title, see the FHL catalog page. See **https://familysearch.org/search/catalog/568996**.

■ **1699-1860. See** ***Databases for the Study of Afro-Louisiana History and Genealogy, 1699-1860*** **[CD-ROM],** compiled by Gwendolyn Midlo Hall, published by Louisiana State University, Baton Rouge, LA, 2000. Contains computerized information from original manuscript sources, including Louisiana slave database 1719-1820, Louisiana free database 1720-1820, Louisiana censuses 1699-1860, and censuses 1784-1850 for New Orleans, Louisiana; Pensacola, Florida; and Mobile, Alabama. See FHL CD No. 1380.

■ **1718-1724.** See ***Passage Index, Louisiana, 1718-1724*** **[Microfilm],** from the originals at the Louisiana State Museum in New Orleans. Text in French. Index to arrivals by ship in Louisiana. Filmed by the museum, 1980, 2 rolls, FHL film # 1292185 (Index, A-L) & FHL film #1292296 (Index, L-Z).

■ **1718-1900.** See ***Marriage Records Index and Contracts (Louisiana), 1718-1900*** **[Microfilm],** from originals at the State Museum of New Orleans, a card file index of marriages records and contracts in various newspapers in Louisiana. Filmed by the museum, 1980, 1 roll, FHL film #1292185.

■ **1719-1720.** See ***Louisiana Colonials: Soldiers and Vagabonds*** **[Printed Book],** by Winston De Ville. Descriptive list for 1719-1720, from originals in the Archives des Colonies, Paris. Publ. Mobile, AL, 1963, FHL book 976.3 M23d.

■ ***1722-1803 Natchitoches Colonials: Censuses, Military Rolls, and Tax Lists*** **[Printed Book],** Vol. 5 of Cane River Creole Series, by Elizabeth Shown Mills, published by Adams Press, Chicago, 1981, 161 pages. This is a very good listing of colonial name lists for the areas of Louisiana north and west of New Orleans. See FHL book 976.365 X2.

■ **1722-1803.** See ***German Ancestors and Patriots of Louisiana, 1722-1803*** **[Printed Book],** by Leroy E. Willie. Includes 1724 census & other name lists. FHL book 976.3 D2w.

■ **1723-1791.** See ***Mississippi Valley Mélange: A Collection of Notes and Documents for the Genealogy and History of the Province of Louisiana and the Territory of Orleans*** **[Printed Book],** compiled by Winston De Ville, 6 vols., publ. Ville Platte & Baton Rouge, LA, 1996-2009. Includes indexes. **Vol. 1 includes:** Illinois church records,

1723-1724; the French fort in the Tombigbee, 1729; on the founding of Pointe Coupée Post, 1729-1732; French troops of Illinois in 1752; Fuselier de la Claire and the lands of Attakapas and Opelousas in 1770; the census of Opelousas Post, 1774; Joachin de Ortega on the Texas Frontier--the Galvez correspondence of 1779; building Fort Miró in the Ouachita Valley of Spanish Louisiana, 1790-1791; slave owners of Pointe Coupée & False River in 1795; Metairie, Louisiana census of 1796; Bayou Sarah settlers in 1797; a Rapides Post petition of 1797 with 38 transcribed signatures; Southwest Louisiana ranchers, a ca. 1810 tax list. **Vol. 2 includes:** knighthood in colonial Louisiana; Juchereau de St. Denys and the Order of St. Louis; Louisiana officers in 1740—the Bienville recommendations; French troops in New Orleans, 1745; land owners below New Orleans in 1751; Acadians in Philadelphia; a prospective first militia of Attakapas Post—the roll of 1773; the D'Hauterive land grant of 1775—aristocratic perquisite in southwest Louisiana; Galvez rosters of 1779—soldier selection at the German and Acadian coasts during the American Revolution; southwest Louisiana militiamen during the American Revolution—the rosters of Attakapas and Opelousas posts in 1780; Louisiana loyalists in 1781; of clavinette and violin in colonial Louisiana—questions on Acadian music in 1785; Attakapas Post petitioners of 1791—an Acadian and Creole defense of a commandant; the greening of New Orleans in 1792—Governor Carondelet as environmentalist; lost in the Latin South—a petition of some Anglo-Americans, ca. 1792; turmoil in Spanish Louisiana—a public notice of 1793. **Vol. 3 includes:** The Bermudez Manuscript of 1612; Louisiana officers in 1714; Military deserters of Louisiana in 1716; Constructing a future cathedral, 1724; A Natchitoches narrative of 1732; Four letters of 1734; on the family Fontenette; Anglo-Americans in British West Florida; The loyalist military in colonial Mississippi, 1779; Terre aux Boeufs militia men in 1779; Anglo-Americans in early Mobile, 1780; Public balls of New Orleans in 1792; the Ursuline convent in 1795; and Militia officers of Orleans Territory in 1808. **Vol. 4 includes:** Bienville's cadets - The Order of St. Louis - Indians and Louisiana forts in 1732 - French troops in the province of Louisiana, 1758 - Naval officers of the Company of the Indies, 1769 - On obtaining French military service records - Opelousas District papers, 1777-1800 - Oaths of allegiance at Natchez, 1787 - St. Landry Catholic church of Opelousas, building materials for the 1827-1828 construction - Some petitions for Spanish land grants at Rapides Post 1800-1801. **Vol. 5 includes:** Colonial naval infantry ranks - French Colonial administration to 1763 - Louisiana officers & workers, 1715-1716 - The soldiers of Plantin's Company (1723-1730) - The 1759 log of personnel transfers - Observations on translations. **Vol. 6 includes:** Duplessis' Report on Conditions in Louisiana: 1758; Louisiana Officers in 1759; Denis Braud: Louisiana's First Publisher; Louisiana's Half-Pay Officers in 1769; De Mezière's Misery – evidence that he did not die from falling off a horse; General Inventory of the Property Belonging to the King…at Natchitoches; a very rare ship-list from Philadelphia to New Orleans in 1788, with many well-known American family members named, and their ages; a 1792 letter from General James Wilkinson to Governor Gayoso de Lemos; the 1792 origin of Juschereau de St. Denys' "painted leg," a long letter of 1796 from "the ladies of Illinois" complaining of new immigrants; Babé, Free Negress vs Widow Lebleu: A Struggle for Freedom in Colonial Louisiana; Independence and Bastille Days in Territorial Louisiana; Jean Laffite's Crew in 1813. See FHL book 976.3 D2de, vol. 1-6.

■ **1724-1837.** See ***Guide to the Louisiana Miscellany Collection, 1724-1837*** **[Printed Book],** compiled, translated, and edited by Judy Riffel, published Comité des Archives de la Louisiane, Baton Rouge, LA, 2006, 248 pages. From intro: "Abstracts of documents containing genealogical information found in the Louisiana section of Records of the states of the United States (four reels of microfilm) and Louisiana miscellany 1724-1837 (five reels of microfilm). Includes "Baton Rouge district land concessions, 1785-1798, in one volume, and regulations concerning general police, June, 1795, also in one volume. Other materials include Jean-Baptiste Bénard de la Harpe's journal historique, 1724; documents on French and Spanish management of Louisiana, 1731-1799; manuscripts of 1780 on Louisiana and Florida; surveyors' records, including correspondence of François Gonsolin, Louis LeBlanc, Carlos Laveau Trudeau, on the Attakapas district; a record book of Spanish land grants, 1785-1799, of 186 pages; a surveyor's notebook, 1795-1797; thirty-six manuscript plats for land grants located mostly in the Baton Rouge district; vital statistics from a Bible and other sources; and a few papers each for Bernardo de Gálvez, 1776-1786, and Manuel Gayoso de Lemos, 1794-1797; correspondence of American and French officials relating to the purchase of Louisiana, 1803-1804 ... " See FHL book 976.3 A3rj.

■ **1745.** See ***French Troops in the Mississippi Valley and on the Gulf Coast, 1745*** **[Printed Book],** by Winston De Ville, publ. Ville Platte, LA, 1986, 42 pages, FHL book 976.3 M2dvw.

■ **1755-1800.** The ***Cajuns: From Acadia to Louisiana*** **[Printed Book],** by William Faulkner Ruston, publ. Farrar, Straus and Giroux, New York, 1979, 342 pages, FHL book 976.3 F2ru.

■ **1758-1796.** See ***Some Late Eighteenth Century Louisianans, 1758-1796*** **[Printed Book],** by Jacqueline K. Voorhies, publ. Lafayette, LA, 1973. (Book not at FHL, check New Orleans Public, LSU, or LA state archives).

■ **1759-1812.** See ***Calendar of the Natchez Trace Collection, Provincial & Territorial Documents, 1759-1813*** **[Printed Book],** compiled by Judy Riffel, a description of the Natchez Trace Collection. From the intro: "…the documents are primarily from the colonial and territorial period of Louisiana and Mississippi and include civil records such as marriage contracts, conveyances, probates, and land surveys. Other types of documents such as receipts, letters, and journals were also found. The order of the entries in this calendar corresponds to the order in which the documents appear on the microfilm, which includes a full-name index. Publ. Comité des Archives de la Louisiane, Baton Rouge, LA, 1999, 217 pages, FHL book 976.R2 The original records of the Natchez Trae Collection reside at the University of Texas, Austin. A copy of the 10-roll set of microfilm is at the Louisiana State Archives.

■ **1759-1812.** See ***Inside the Natchez Trace Collection: New Sources for Southern History*** **[Printed Book],** by Katherine J. Adams and Lewis L. Gould, University of Texas at Austin, Center for American History. Publ. LSU Press, Baton Rouge, LA, 1999, 207 pages, FHL book 976.3 H29ak.

■ **1765-1803.** See ***The Founding of New Acadia: The Beginnings of Acadian Life in Louisiana, 1765-1803*** **[Printed Book],** by Carl A. Brasseaux, publ. LSU Press, Baton Rouge, LA, 1987, 229 pages, FHL book 976.3 F2b.

■ **1765-1803.** See ***French, Cajun, Creole, Houma: A Primer on Francophone Louisiana*** **[Printed Book],** by Carl A. Brasseaux, publ. LSU Press, Baton Rouge, LA, 2005, 159 pages, FHL book 976.3 H2bcr

■ **1766, 1769, 1777.** See ***Louisiana's Acadian Coast Census Index, 1766, 1769, 1777: With Annotations*** **[CD-ROM],** by Phoebe Chauvin Morrison. CD-ROM Publication, published Houma, LA, 2001. Index indicates both husbands and wives by family numbers, with annotated census records citing the sources of location: Fam. No., Name, Born, Married, Spouse, Parents, & Notes. See FHL CD-ROM no. 684.

■ **1770-1789.** *See* ***Louisiana Census and Militia Lists, 1770-1789, Volume I : German Coast, New Orleans, Below New Orleans and Lafourche*** **[Printed Book & Microfiche],** from the book compiled, translated and edited by Albert J. Robichaux, Jr., original published: Harvey, LA, 1973, 170 pages. Census records acquired from the Papeles Procedentes de Cuba deposited in the General Archives de Indies in Seville, Spain. Includes: 1770 militia lists of New Orleans; 1777 general census of the city of New Orleans; 1770 militia of the German Coast; 1784 general census of the second German Coast; 1785 militia list of St. Charles Parish; 1770 general census below New Orleans; 1789 general census of Lafourche. Includes index. See FHL book 976.3 X2pr. Filmed by the Genealogical Society of Utah, 1991, FHL microfiche #6088510.

■ **1770-1804.** See ***Marriage Contracts, Wills and Testaments of the Spanish Colonial Period in New Orleans, 1770-1804*** **[Printed Book],** compiled and indexed by Charles R. Maduell, Jr., publ. New Orleans, 1969, FHL book 976.335/N1 V25mc.

■ **1773-1785.** See ***The Acadian Exiles in Chatellerault, 1773-1785*** **[Printed Book],** by Albert J. Robichaux, Publ. Herbert Pub., Eunice, LA, 190 pages, FHL book 944.63/C1 D2r.

■ **1778-1783.** See ***The Canary Islanders of Louisiana*** **[Printed Book],** by Gilbert C. Din, publ. LSU Press, Baton Rouge, LA, 256 pages, FHL book 976.3 F2d.

■ **1779.** See ***The Acadian Coast in 1779: Settlers of Cabanocey and La Fourche in the Spanish Province of Louisiana During the American Revolution*** **[Printed Book],** by Winston De Ville, pub. 1993, Ville Platte, LA. Includes index. FHL book 976.3 X29d.

■ **1781-1797.** See ***Anglo-Americans in Spanish Archives: Lists of Anglo-American Settlers in the Spanish Colonies of America; A Finding Aid*** **[Printed Book],** by Lawrence H. Feldman. Published by Genealogical Publishing Co., Inc., 1991, 349 pages. Abstracted from original census documents, includes genealogical data about individuals and families who settled in the French territories of Louisiana and the Floridas after they came under Spanish rule in 1766. Includes an index of personal names. FHL book 973 X2fe.

■ **1782, 1786 & 1793.** See ***Baton Rouge & New Feliciana: Census Reports for Louisiana's Florida Parishes in 1782, 1786, & 1793*** **[Printed Book],** by Albert J. Tate and Winston De Ville, publ. by Provincial Press, Lafayette, LA, 2000, 90 pages. Louisiana's "Florida Parishes" include the following parishes of today: East Baton Rouge, West Feliciana, East Feliciana, St. Helena, Livingston, Tangipahoa, Washington and St. Tammany. See FHL book 976.3 X2t.

■ **1784.** See ***Valenzuela in the Province of Louisiana: A Census of 1784*** **[Printed Book],** by Winston De Ville, publ. 1987, LA. The settlers were natives of the Canary Islands who arrived between 1778 and 1783. Includes surname index. FHL book 976.3 A1 no. 56.

■ **1784-1785.** See ***Acadian Emigrants to Louisiana, 1784-1785*** **[Microfilm],** from the originals at the Louisiana Historical Center, New Orleans. Text in French. Filmed by the Genealogical Society of Utah, 1981, 1 roll, FHL film # 1305383. For a digital version of this title, see the FHL catalog page. See **https://familysearch.org/search/catalog/248803**.

■ **1785.** See ***De Nantes à la Louisiane: en 1785, 1600 Acadiens quittent le vieux continent, à destination de la Nouvelle-Orléans: l'histoire de l'Acadie, l'odyssée d'un peuple exilé*** [Printed Book], by Gérard-Marc Braud. Covers the history of Acadia and those who took refuge in France after the English deported them in 1755 from what is now eastern Canada. It focuses on the 1,600 Acadians who left Nantes, France for New Orleans in 1785 and settled in various areas of Louisiana. Publ. Quest Editions, Nantes, France, 1994, 156 pages, FHL book 976.3 W2b.

■ **1785.** See ***The Crew and Passenger Registration Lists of the Seven Acadian Expeditions of 1785: A Listing by Family Groups of the Refugee Acadians Who Migrated From France to Spanish Louisiana in 1785*** **[Printed Book],** compiled and edited by Milton P. Rieder, Jr. and Norma Gaudet Rieder, Publ. Metairie, LA, 1965, 103 pages, FHL book 976.3 W3r.

■ **1789-1841.** See ***Index of New Orleans Confirmations, 1789-1841*** **[Printed Book],** by Donald J Hebert, publ. Claitor's, Baton Rouge, LA, 1984, 119 pages, FHL book 976.3 K2f.

■ ***1790 Census Index, Miscellaneous Sources*** **[Printed Book],** a census substitute compiled from tax lists, "Vol. 13, Bicentennial Edition" of an attempt to replace the lost 1790 censuses with tax records from CA, FL, IL, LA, MS, OH, & NJ, edited by Ronald Vern Jackson, publ. Accelerated Indexing Systems, North Salt Lake, UT, 1990, FHL book 973 X22j.

■ **1790-1804.** See ***Law Suits, Court of Louisiana, 1790-1804; Book No. 4078*** **[Microfilm],** from originals at the New Orleans Public Library. Text in French and Spanish with synopsis in English. Filmed by the Genealogical Society of Utah, 1972, 1 roll, FHL film #906355.

■ ***1791 Colonial Spanish Census of New Orleans*** **[Printed Book].** An English translation, made by the City Archives Department, is filed under call number AA840, New Orleans Public Library. The census is indexed in New Orleans Genesis, vol. 1; the original index to the census is housed at the Louisiana State Museum. This census, dated November 6, 1791, is arranged by street of residence of the enumerated individuals, apparently the heads of households. In addition to the named individuals, each entry also records the numbers of other members of the household by category as follows: white men, white women, free men of mixed blood, free women of mixed blood, free negro men, free negro women, male slaves of mixed blood, female slaves of mixed blood, negro male slaves, and negro female slaves.

■ **1793.** See ***New Feliciana in the Province of Louisiana: A Guide to the Census of 1793*** **[Printed Book],** by Winston De Ville, publ. 1987, 32 pages. Includes index. See FHL book 976.3 A1 No. 57.

■ ***1795 Chimney Tax of New Orleans: A Guide to the Census of Proprietors and Residents of the Vieux Carré*** **[Printed Book],** compiled by Winston De Ville, publ. Ville Platte, LA, 1995, 31 pages, FHL book 976.335/N1 R4d.

■ **1795-1808.** See ***Law Suits in New Orleans, 1795-1808*** **[Microfilm],** from the originals at the New Orleans Public Library. Filmed by the Genealogical Society of Utah, 1972, 1 roll, FHL film #906356.

■ **1803-1877.** See **Acadian to Cajun: Transformation of a People, 1803-1877 [Printed Book],** by Carl A. Brasseaux, publ. University Press of Mississippi, Jackson, MS, 1992, 252 pages, FHL book 976.3 F2bc.

■ **1804.** See ***Mayor's Office, Census of the City of New Orleans, 1804*** **[Microfilm],** from the originals at the New Orleans Public Library, filed under call number TK840 1804. Contains a record in English and French, giving names of male residents and their wives or other adult women living in the household, the profession and employment of the male, the age of males and females, the number of boys and girls living in the household, and, usually, their ages. The number of male and female adult and juvenile slaves in each household is also tallied; no names are recorded for slaves. A final column, labeled "Observations," indicates the head of household's military status, listing the company in which he served. FHL film 1309932.

■ **1804-1820.** See ***New Orleans Marriage Contracts, 1804-1820: Abstracted From the Notarial Archives of New Orleans*** **[Printed Book],** by Charles R. Maduell, Jr., publ. Polyanthos, New Orleans, 1977, 137 pages, FHL book 976.335/N1 V25md.

■ **1804-1899.** See ***Newspaper Marriage Index (New Orleans, Louisiana), 1804-1899*** **[Microfilm],** from the originals at the New Orleans Public Library. Filmed by the Genealogical Society of Utah, 2005-2006, 4 rolls, beginning with FHL film #2397871 (Abbatt, Robert – Byrnes, Wm. J.). For a complete list of roll numbers and contents of each roll, see the online FHL catalog page for this title. See **https://familysearch.org/search/catalog/1333348**.

■ **1805.** See ***New Orleans in 1805: A Directory and a Census Together with Resolutions Authorizing Same, Now Printed for the First Time from the Original manuscript; Facsimile*** **[Digitized Book],** by Charles Louis Thompson, Mathew Flannery, and Dolley Madison Heartman, publ. Pelican Gallery, New Orleans, 1936, 107 pages. For access to a digital version of the book, see the online FHL catalog page: **https://familysearch.org/search/catalog/2204410**.

**1805-1940.** See ***New Orleans (Louisiana) City Directories*** **[Microfilm],** from the originals of various publishers, filmed by Research Publications, Woodbridge, CT, 1980-1984, 158 microfiche, 389 microfilm rolls. FHL has the following years: 1805, 1807, 1809, 1811, 1822-1824, 1832, 1834, 1838, 1841-1843, 1846, 1851-1852, 1854-1855, 1857-1859, 1860-1861, 1866-1933, 1935, and 1940. FHL fiche #60442250 (1805- ). For a complete list of fiche and roll numbers, see the online FHL catalog for this title: **https://familysearch.org/search/catalog/543152**.

■ **1808, 1814-1828.** See ***Miscellaneous Louisiana Militia Records, 1808, 1814-1828*** **[Microfilm],** from the originals at the Jackson Barracks Military Library, New Orleans, LA. Filmed by the Genealogical Society of Utah, 1990, 1 roll, FHL film #1704156.

■ **1811-1893.** See ***Death Notices From Louisiana Newspapers*** **[Printed Book]**, compiled by Brenda Lagroue Mayers and Gloria Lambert Kerns. Contents: Vol. 1: Indexes obituaries from Ascension, East Feliciana, Livingston, St. Helena, Tangipahoa, and West Feliciana parishes, 1811-1819; Vol. 2: Indexes obituaries from Ascension, East Baton Rouge, and Pointe Coupee parishes, 1822-1914; Vol. 3: Indexes obituaries from Ascension, East Baton Rouge, Iberville, and Washington parishes, 1833-1917; Vol. 4: Indexes obituaries from East Baton Rouge, St. Charles, St. John the Baptist, St. Tammany, 1847-1893; Vol. 5: Indexes obituaries from Assumption, East Baton Rouge, Iberia, Lafourche, Orleans, St. John the Baptist, St. Martin, and St. Mary parishes, 1824-1887; and Vol. 6: Indexes obituaries from Acadia, Iberia, Rapides, St. Landry, St. Mary parishes, 1836-1887. Publ. Folk Finders, Baker, LA, 1984, 6 vols., FHL book 976.31 V4m.

■ **1812-1815.** See ***Louisiana Soldiers in the War of 1812*** **[Printed Book],** compiled by Marion John Bennett Pierson, publ. Louisiana Genealogical & Historical Society, Baton Rouge, LA, 1963, 124 pages, FHL book 976.3 M23p. For access to a digital version of this title, see the online FHL catalog page: **https://familysearch.org/search/catalog/154087**.

■ **1820-1830.** See ***Marriages and Family Relationships of New Orleans, 1820-1830*** **[Printed Book],** by Charles R. Maduell, publ. New Orleans, 1969, 153 pages, FHL book 976.335/N1 V2m. For access to a digital version of this title, see the online FHL catalog page. See **https://familysearch.org/search/catalog/149846**.

■ **1820-1852.** See ***The "Foreign French:" Nineteenth Century French Immigration into Louisiana*** **[Printed Book],** by Carl A. Brasseaux, published by the Center for Louisiana Studies, University of Southwestern Louisiana, Lafayette, LA , 1990-1993. Contents: Vol. 1: 1820-1839; Vol. 2: 1840-1848; Vol. 3: 1849-1852. 3 vols, FHL book 976.3 W3b v. 1-3.

■ **1830-1840.** See ***Marriages and Family Relationships of New Orleans, 1830-1840*** **[Printed Book],** by Charles R. Maduell, Jr. Publ. Hebert Publications, 1980, 255 pages, FHL book 976.335/N1 V2mm.

■ **1837.** See ***Assessment of Property and Census of Slaves and their Owners, 1837.*** **[Microfilm].** Originals at Orleans Parish Courthouse, filmed by the Genealogical Society of Utah, 1972, FHL film #906708.

■ **1849-1899.** See ***Naturalization Records [2nd District Court, Orleans Parish], 1849-1899*** **[Microfilm],** from originals at the New Orleans Public Library. Each volume indexed. Filmed by the Genealogical Society of Utah, 1981, 20 rolls, beginning with FHL film #1306172 (Declarations of Intention, 1849-1853). For a complete list of roll numbers and contents of each roll, see the online FHL catalog page for this title. See **https://familysearch.org/search/catalog/282887**.

■ ***1854-1857 Census, City of Carrollton*** **[Microfilm],** from original records at the New Orleans Public Library. The City of Carrollton was incorporated in 1845 as part of Jefferson Parish and, in 1874, was annexed to the City of New Orleans. The boundaries of Carrollton were the River, the present Jefferson Parish line, the shore of Lake Pontchartrain, and Lowerline Street (and its projected extension to the Lake). This census gives the name and occupation of householders in the City of Carrollton and tallies the number of males and females in each household, and the number of children in general age groups. The names are grouped alphabetically by first letter of the name only. Original records at the New Orleans Public Library, Volume 1 (1854-1855) is not filmed. Volume 2 is filed under call number IV TK840 1854-1857.

■ ***1855-1856 New Orleans Census of Merchants and Persons Following Professions Requiring Licenses,*** **[Original Bound Volumes],** 3 vols., original records at the New Orleans Public Library, filed under call number LC840. These volumes give name, residence or place of business, callings or professions, number of license, amount paid, and remarks; individuals are listed together by square of property occupied; related forms are also included at the front of each volume. Volume one (1855) is for the Second Ward; volume two (1855) covers the Third Ward; and volume three (1856) is for the Third Municipal District. Indexed.

■ **1861-1865.** See ***Index to Prisoners of War Compiled From Various Union Prisons*** **[Microfilm],** from the originals located at the Jackson Barracks Military Library, New Orleans, LA. Filmed by the Genealogical Society of Utah, 1990, 1 roll, FHL film #1685402.

■ **1862-1863, 1926.** See ***Miscellaneous Death Reports and Indexes, 1862-1863, 1926*** **[Microfilm],** from originals at a location not noted, but probably New Orleans Public Library (based on year of filming). Filmed by the Genealogical Society of Utah, 1972, 1 rolls, FHL film #906706.

■ **1862-1865.** See ***Deaths and Burials of Confederate Soldiers in New Orleans, Louisiana*** **[Microfilm],** from the originals at the Jackson Barracks Military Library, New Orleans. Includes register of Confederate soldiers who died in Camp Douglas, 1862-65 and lie buried in Oakwoods Cemetery, Chicago, IL, 1892, newspaper articles, register of the Confederate dead buried on Johnson's Island, correspondence, and manuscript listings of confederate deaths. Filmed by the Genealogical Society of Utah, 1990, 1 roll, FHL film #1704156.

■ ***1863-1866 Internal Revenue Assessment Lists for Louisiana, Bureau of Internal*** **Revenue [Microfilm],** from the originals at the National Archives, Central Plains Region, series M769. District 1: Ascension, Jefferson, Lafourche, Livingston, Orleans, Plaquemines, St. Bernard, St. Charles, St. Helena, St. James, St. John the Baptist, St. Tammany, Terrebonne, & Washington parishes. District 2: Assumption, Avoyelles, Calcasieu, East Baton Rouge,

East Feliciana, Iberville, Lafayette, Natchitoches, Pointe Coupee, Rapides, Sabine, St. Landry, St. Martin, St. Mary, Vermilion, West Baton Rouge, & West Feliciana parishes. District 3: Bienville, Bossier, Caddo, Caldwell, Carroll, Catahoula, Claiborne, Concordia, De Soto, Franklin, Jackson, Madison, Morehouse, Ouachita, Tensas, Union, & Winn parishes. Filmed by the National Archives, 1985, beginning with FHL film #1578469 (District 1: 1863-1864). For a complete list of roll numbers and contents of each roll, see the online FHL catalog page for this title. See **https://familysearch.org/search/catalog/577907**.

■ **1865.** See ***The Civil War Tax in Louisiana, 1865: Based on Direct Tax Assessments of Louisianans, original printed 1892 with the title, List of Names of Citizens of Louisiana From Whom the United States Direct Tax was Collected in 1865, Together with the Amounts Paid by Each*** **[Printed Book].** Reprinted 1975 by Polyanthos, Inc., New Orleans, 363 pages. See FHL book 976.3 R4c. For access to a digital version of this title, see the FHL catalog page: **https://familysearch.org/search/catalog/153997**.

■ **1866-1872.** See ***District Court Cases, 1866-1872*** **[Microfilm],** from the originals at the New Orleans Public Library. Selected suits were microfilmed, including interdictions, divorces, authorizations, separations of bed and board, successions, emancipations, separations of property and tutorships. Filmed by the Genealogical Society of Utah, 1991, 2 rolls, FHL film #1822282 (1870-1871) & FHL film #1822283 (1866-1872).

■ ***1869-1870 Orleans Parish Poll Tax Rolls*** **[Printed Book],** compiled by Judy Riffel, et al., publ. Baton Rouge, LA, 1996, 258 pages. An index to the original tax records for the city of New Orleans, Louisiana. The original microfilm reels are located at the Louisiana State Archives (accession numbers: P1978-170 for 1869; P1978-172 for 1870). Index book only at FHL, book 976.335/N1 R42r.

■ **1884-1944.** See ***Register Books, 1884-1934 (Soldiers' Home of Louisiana-New Orleans); Index, 1905-1944*** **[Microfilm],** from the originals at the Jackson Barracks Military Library, New Orleans. The Soldiers' Home was also known as Camp Nichols. Filmed by the Genealogical Society of Utah, 1990, 5 rolls, beginning with FHL film #1685399 (Index to registers, 1905-1944). For a complete list of roll numbers and contents of each roll, see the online FHL catalog page for this title. See **https://familysearch.org/search/catalog/581318.**

■ **1892-1899.** See ***Rosters and Applications (United Confederate Veterans), 1892-1896; and Rosters, 1895-1899*** **[Microfilm],** from the originals at the Jackson Barracks Military Library, New Orleans, LA. The United Confederate Veterans (UCV) organization began in 1889 in New Orleans, where the national headquarters was located until the UCV disbanded in the early 1950s. One of the early Commanders-in-Chief of the UCV was also the Adjutant General of the State of Louisiana, a former Confederate officer, and keeper of the records for the national organization. These records of the rosters of the various UCV Camps from all over the country, and the original applications for membership ended up in the Jackson Barrack Military Library, the site of the National Guard of Louisiana. Filmed by the Genealogical Society of Utah, 1990, 8 rolls, FHL film #1685778, 1685779, 16857780, 1703671, 1703672, and 1703673 (Rosters, Applications, 1892-1896); and FHL film #1710607-171608 (Rosters, 1895-1899).

■ ***1892-1898 Registers of Direct Tax Payers*** **[Microfilm],** from the original records located at the State Archives and Records Service, Baton Rouge, Louisiana. Does not include Acadia, Calcasieu, Cameron, Grant, Iberia, Lincoln, Red River, Richland, Tangipahoa, Union, Vermilion, Vernon, or Webster parishes. Filmed by the Genealogical Society of Utah, 1985. 5 rolls, FHL film 1412744-1412748.

■ **1898.** See ***Louisiana Volunteers in the War of 1898*** **[Printed Book],** compiled by Nancy Lowrie Wright and Cathy Dantin Shannon, publ. Wright Shannon Publications, Houma, LA, 1989, 94 pages, FHL book 976.3 M2w.

■ **1898.** See ***Index to Compiled Service Records of Volunteer Soldiers Who Served During the War With Spain in Organizations from the State of Louisiana*** **[Microfilm],** from originals at the National Archives, Washington, DC. From intro: "This microfilm publication reproduces an alphabetical card index to the compiled service records of volunteer soldiers of the War with Spain belonging to units from the state of Louisiana. The cards give the name of the soldier, his rank, and the unit in which he served." Filmed by the archives, series M240, 1957, 1 roll, FHL film #880013.

■ **1911.** See ***Enumeration of Ex-Confederate Soldiers and Widows of Deceased Soldiers of Louisiana*** **[Microfilm],** from the original records located at the Louisiana State Archives, Baton Rouge, LA. Filmed by the Genealogical Society of Utah, 1985, 1 roll, FHL film #1412742.

■ **1911.** See ***An Index to the Census of 1911 of Confederate Veterans or their Widows, Pursuant to Act 71 of 1908*** **[Printed Index],** by Houston C. Jenks, Index lists, alphabetically, names of soldiers or their widows, and includes their parish, age, state where he enlisted for service, his regiment and company in which he served, an assessment and a valuation of property, any infirmities the soldier or widow might have, the date of their marriage, and the reel number where the data was found at the Louisiana State Archives. Publ. H.C. Jenks, Baton Rouge, LA, 1989, 115 pages, FHL book 976.3 M22j.

■ ***1920-1940 New Orleans Voter Registration Cards, New Orleans Registrar of Voters*** **[Microfilm],** from the original records located at the New Orleans Public Library's Louisiana Division. Contains names, birthplace, age, date of birth, sex, race, and political persuasion. Filmed by the New Orleans Public Library, Louisiana Division, 1983, 11 rolls. Also available at the FHL as Voter registration cards, 1920-1940, second series, FHL film #1412334-1412343, and 1689670.

# OKLAHOMA
## Censuses & Substitutes, 1828-2012

### Jurisdictional History of the Indian Territory, Oklahoma Territory, and Oklahoma

The term *Indian Country* was used to describe the western areas encompassing several Indian tribes, whether nations, reservations, or those roaming free over the Great Plains. The evolution of the Indian Country into an official Indian Territory took place over the whole of the 19th Century. However, Indian Territory was never a territory in the official sense of the term. For the entire period of its existence, it never had a combined territorial government or a federally appointed territorial governor.

- Soon after the 1803 Louisiana Purchase, Thomas Jefferson urged the resettling of tribes of the eastern United States on the new lands west of the Mississippi. In 1804, Congress passed legislation authorizing the negotiation of removal treaties with the eastern tribes, and over the next twenty years, several tribes or portions of tribes moved west.

**This first phase of removal** was mostly voluntary, and often conflicted with white settlers moving west of the Mississippi at the same time. For example, when Arkansas Territory was established in 1819, it included most of the area of present-day Oklahoma. And in 1821, Missouri was admitted to the Union, further reducing the perceived range of land that was to be dedicated to the relocation of eastern Indian tribes.

- In 1828, the present western boundary of Arkansas was drawn, and for the first time, the law described the area west of that line as the exclusive domain of Indian tribes. But, its jurisdiction was still part of the larger area officially called *Unorganized Territory*.
- Due to a misunderstanding of the Arkansas boundary, early white settlers north of the Red River (in present-day McCurtain County, Oklahoma) thought they were living in old Miller County, Arkansas Territory. In 1828, several hundred families were moved to areas south of the Red River to vacate the newly defined Indian domain. This was a rare case in American history where whites were relocated to make room for Indians – it was usually the other way around.
- In the 1830s, forced removal of eastern Indian tribes began, the most notorious being the Cherokee removal, which history remembers as the "trail of tears."
- In 1834, legislation defined "Indian Country" as any portion of the western United States that was not part of a state or territory, thus, Indian Country was the same as Unorganized Territory. The new law also regulated certain activities of non-Indians within the region and established judicial boundaries: the northern portion of the region (modern Kansas) was to be under the control of the federal courts of Missouri; the southern portion (modern Oklahoma), under the federal courts of Arkansas. Federal censuses in the Indian Country taken from 1820 through 1870 for non-Indians were under the jurisdiction of the Missouri and Arkansas federal marshals. (Indians were specifically excluded from the federal censuses, except those who lived off reservations and subject to taxes like non-Indians).

- In the Indian Country, the most populous of the tribes were located in the southern portion, namely, the relocated Choctaw, Cherokee, Chickasaw, Creek, and Seminole Nations (the so-called Five Civilized Tribes). To the north in present-day Kansas were the reservations of numerous small Midwestern and Plains tribes.

**A second removal** and concentration of Indian populations took place in 1854, when twelve treaties were negotiated with tribes living in the northern part of the Unorganized Territory Together, these agreements opened most of present-day Kansas for white settlement. That same year Congress created Kansas Territory, which encompassed the remaining tribes and their diminished reservations. As a result, the Indian Country was reduced to the area of present-day Oklahoma (except for the Panhandle) with most of the land owned by the Five Civilized Tribes.
- Evidence of non-Indians living in the Indian Country can be seen in the 1860 federal census, where whites, blacks, adopted, or intermarried persons living on "Indian Lands West of Arkansas" were named and listed at the end of the Arkansas census schedules.
- In 1865, because the governments of the Five Civilized Tribes had supported the South during the Civil War, the federal government declared void its existing treaties with the five tribes. New treaties were negotiated the following year, in which the tribes either ceded the western portions of their lands to the federal government for the resettlement of more Indians, or, in the case of the Cherokees, provided for the sale of their western lands (the Cherokee Outlet).

**A third wave of removals** took place between 1866 and 1885, as the government started moving remaining tribes from Texas, Kansas, Nebraska, and elsewhere into the southern region. This is where the newly ceded western lands of the Five Civilized Tribes were now available for Indian settlement. During this time, the Cheyenne and Arapaho, the Comanche, Kiowa, and Apache, the Wichita and Caddo, the Potawatomi and Shawnee, the Kickapoo, the Iowa, the Sauk and Fox, the Pawnee, the Oto and Missouri, the Ponca, the Tonkawa, the Kaw, the Osage, the Peoria, the Wyandot, the Eastern Shawnee, the Modoc, and the Ottawa reservations were established in the Indian Country.
- In the Osage Reservation Act of 1872, the law stated that the reservation was located in *Indian Territory*, and all subsequent tribal agreements, executive orders, and other federal actions relative to the region now referred to the area officially as Indian Territory.
- In 1887, Congress passed the General Indian Allotment Act, which initiated the process of dividing tribal property and dissolving tribal agreements. Subsequent allotment acts by 1906 had essentially ended tribal land ownership in present-day Oklahoma, with allotments of land divided among individual Indians. Records of the allotments, including a final "census" of the families involved, provides the most complete list of inhabitants of the Indian Territory for that time period.
- In 1889, Congress established a separate federal court at Muskogee for Indian Territory, and for the first time it officially defined the area's boundaries: Indian Territory was the area bounded by the states of Kansas, Missouri, Arkansas, and Texas and the Territory of New Mexico. On April 22 the Unassigned Lands were opened to settlement by non-Indians in the first of the famous land runs. Over fifty thousand homesteaders settled in the region on that day.
- In May 1890 Indian Territory was divided into Oklahoma Territory and Indian Territory. Oklahoma Territory was defined as incorporating the Unassigned Lands and all reservations, with the exception of those of the Five Civilized Tribes and a few small reservations. While all of the reservations in the Cherokee Outlet were to be part of Oklahoma Territory, that portion of the Outlet still owned by the Cherokee Nation would remain as part of Indian Territory until purchased by the government. Almost immediately a special commission was organized to negotiate the allotment of the reservations in Oklahoma Territory and the sale of unallotted lands so that they could be opened for non-Indian settlement.
- Special censuses were taken periodically for Indians, and in the 1890 and 1900 federal censuses, Indian tribes were enumerated with population schedules added to the regular schedules for each territory or state (1890 lost, 1900 extant).
- In 1893 the Cherokees sold their remaining portion of the Outlet, which was immediately incorporated into Oklahoma Territory and opened for settlement. Thus by 1893 Indian Territory had been reduced to just the reservations of the Five Civilized Tribes proper and the small reservations in the northeast.
- Later in 1893, the Dawes Commission was created by Congress to negotiate agreements with the Five Civilized Tribes to allot their lands, and in 1898 the allotment process began in what remained of Indian Territory.

- In a futile attempt to maintain some semblance of continued Indian separation, leaders of the Five Civilized Tribes organized a constitutional convention in 1905, drew up a constitution, and asked to be admitted to the Union as the state of Sequoyah. Congress rejected the plan and in 1907 approved a statute that joined Indian Territory with Oklahoma Territory to create the new state of Oklahoma.

## Censuses & Substitutes for Indian Territory, Oklahoma Territory, and Oklahoma

Several censuses were taken by the Five Civilized Tribes separate from the federal censuses or those taken by Oklahoma Territory. This included censuses taken in 1880 and 1890 by the Cherokee government; an 1885 Choctaw census; and an 1890 census by the Chickasaw tribe. The Indian censuses identify both Indians and non-Indians living on their reservations.
- The 1890 federal census included population schedules for the newly formed Oklahoma Territory, and added the Indian tribes of Indian Territory on separate schedules. Unfortunately, most of the 1890 federal censuses were burned or destroyed after a fire in the Commerce Building in Washington, DC in 1921. But some relief to the 1890 disaster exists, since Oklahoma Territory took a special territorial census in 1890 for its original seven counties (Beaver, Canadian, Cleveland, Kingfisher, Logan, Oklahoma, and Payne), which all survive.
- The 1900 federal census for Oklahoma Territory included separate population schedules for Indians.
- Just prior to statehood in 1907, the federal government sponsored a census for Indian and Oklahoma territories. However, of the 75 counties enumerated, only the name list for Seminole County survives at the National Archives.

## Online Resources at the Oklahoma Historical Society

The OHS in Oklahoma City has many databases of interest to genealogists, whether for the Indian Country, Indian Territory, Oklahoma Territory, or the State of Oklahoma. See their Genealogical Resources page. See **www.okhistory.org/research/genealogy.**

**Online Catalog:** includes many resources pertaining to genealogical research, including cemetery books, birth, death and marriage indexes, and county histories.

**American Indian Ancestry:** databases with online searching include the following:
- 1896 Applications for Enrollment.
- Dawes Final Rolls of the Five Civilized Tribes
- Hastain's Township Plats of the Creek Nation
- Moore's Seminole Roll and Land Guide
- Individual Indian Files
- Official Register of the United States Indian Agency Employees & Officials
- Finding Your American Indian Ancestors (PDF)

**Oklahoma Genealogical Resources:** Databases with online searching include the following:
- US Census Records. Search the 1933 Unemployment Relief database with more than 100,000 names listed. The complete 1890 OK Territorial Census is indexed here as well. Censuses on microfilm are identified here as the 1860 Lands West of Arkansas, 1890 Veterans & Widows; and 1900 Federal Census of Oklahoma Territory
- 1889 Oklahoma County Land Database & Map. This index includes names extracted from U.S. land patents homesteads: Oklahoma County, Oklahoma Territory Land Run of April 22, 1889
- 1901 El Reno Land Lottery - individuals whose names were drawn
- 1901 El Reno and Lawton land lottery tickets (partial listing)
- Biographical & Topical Vertical Files
- City Directories, Phone Books, Yearbooks
- Daughters of Union Veterans Application Index
- Divorce records from Oklahoma County
- Deaths found in OKC City Directories, 1918, 1920-23
- Family Histories
- Gateway to Oklahoma History - Newspapers and Photos Online
- Grant County, Mills Funeral Home
- Grant County, Wilson Funeral Home
- Indian Pioneer Histories (Available online through the University of Oklahoma)
- Marriage Records Collection Updated
- Newspaper Archives
- Official Register of the United States Indian Agency Employees & Officials
- Oklahoman Obituary Index
- Oklahoma City Death Register, 1908-1926
- Oklahoma Military Casualties Database Online Exhibit
- Oklahoma Military Hall of Fame Online Exhibit
- Oklahoma Military Deaths - WWI, WWII, Vietnam and Korea
- Oklahoma State Penitentiary Records, 1930s
- Probate Records from Oklahoma County, 1890-1928
- Teacher's Reports from the Dawes Commission Records
- Smith's First Directory of Oklahoma Territory
- United Daughters of the Confederacy Applications

## Oklahoma Databases Online at Ancestry.com

The Ancestry.com subscription website allows free access to all indexes, but to view any particular record requires a membership. Ancestry offers trial memberships and subscriptions for short periods and reduced rates. The following databases at the Ancestry.com website are unique Indian Territory & Oklahoma Territory & Oklahoma databases under the categories of Census & Voter Lists, Vital Records, Military, Immigrations, and Wills & Probates. To review the complete list of Oklahoma statewide and countywide databases, see **http://search.ancestry.com/Places/US/Oklahoma/Default.aspx**.

■ **1841-1927.** See ***Oklahoma and Indian Territory, Marriage, Citizenship and Census Records, 1841-1927*** **[Online Database],** digitized and indexed at the Ancestry.com website. Source: Oklahoma Historical Society, Oklahoma City. Each index record includes; Name, Gender, Marriage age, Marriage date, Event date, Spouse, Spouse gender, Spouse age, and Marriage place. The document images may have more information. This database has 32,299 records. See **http://search.ancestry.com/search/db.aspx?dbid=9026**.

■ **1851-1959.** See ***Oklahoma and Indian Territory, Indian Censuses and Rolls, 1851-1959*** **[Online Database],** digitized and indexed at the Ancestry.com website. Source: Selected Tribal Records, National Archives. This collection includes a variety of tribal rolls, censuses, and other records created by the Bureau of Indian Affairs. Records in the collection relate to the Arapaho, Cherokee, Eastern Cherokee, Cheyenne, Chickasaw, Choctaw, Creek, Delaware, Kickapoo, Miami, Muskogee, Osage, Potawatomi, Sac and Fox, Seminole, and Shawnee tribes. Each index record includes: Name, Gender, Birth date, Residence date, Age, and Native American tribe. This database has 640,670 records. See **http://search.ancestry.com/search/db.aspx?dbid=8810**.

■ **1856-1933.** See ***Oklahoma, Historical Indian Archives Index, 1856-1933*** **[Online Database],** indexed at the Ancestry.com website. Source: OK Historical Society, Oklahoma City, OK. This database is an index to a collection of titles held by the Oklahoma Historical Society, whose staff created the index on cards over the years. Most of the cards deal with subjects rather than individuals. They include censuses, missionaries, permits for doctors, Indians in specific tribes, elections, legislators, chiefs, teachers, businesses, trading posts, schools, and the Cherokee Nation. Search this database by keyword or subject. This database has 80,327 records. See **http://search.ancestry.com/search/db.aspx?dbid=9205**.

■ **1870-1930.** See ***Oklahoma, Select Marriages, 1870-1930*** **[Online Database],** indexed at the Ancestry.com website. Source: FamilySearch extractions from records on microfilm at the Family History Library, Salt Lake City, UT. Each index record includes: Name, Gender, Age, Birth date, Marriage date, Marriage place, Father, Mother, Spouse, and FHL film number. This database has 24,708 records. See **http://search.ancestry.com/search/db.aspx?dbid=60105**.

■ **1884-1934.** See ***Oklahoma and Indian Territory, Land Allotment Jackets for Five Civilized Tribes, 1884-1934*** **[Online Database],** digitized and indexed at the Ancestry.com website. Source: National Archives, Records of the Bureau of Indian Affairs. This collection includes the allotment records for those who were listed on the final membership rolls. The records include original applications for allotment submitted on printed forms, transcripts of hearings held by the Commission pertaining to the selection of tracts, printed plat maps (form 59) annotated to show the location of selections, notices of contested allotment selections, and some related correspondence. The files often include receipts for allotment certificates and certificates of eligibility for allotment. Applications for minor children generally include letters of guardianship or administration. Each index record includes: Name, Tribe, Allotment category, Roll number, and Card number. The document images have more information. This database has 204,413 records. See **http://search.ancestry.com/search/db.aspx?dbid=3999**.

■ **1885-1940.** See ***U.S., Indian Census Rolls, 1885-1940*** **[Online Database],** digitized and indexed at the Ancestry.com website. Source: National Archives microfilm series M595, Records of the Bureau of Indian Affairs. This database has the full image census pages for every Indian census taken in the U.S., 1885 through 1940. Included on the rolls are the largest concentrated group of Indians in the U.S., those living in the jurisdictions of the Indian Territory, Oklahoma Territory, or within the state of Oklahoma. Each index record includes: Name, Date of birth, Age, Gender, Marital status, Relation to head of household,

Tribe, Reservation, Agency, Last census number, Census date, and Neighbors (view others on page). The census page images include more information about place of enrollment, residence, degree of blood, etc. This database has 7,559,854 records. See **http://search.ancestry.com/search/db.aspx?dbid=1059**.

■ **1889-1926.** See ***Oklahoma, Land Run and other Land Records, 1889-1926*** **[Online Database],** digitized and indexed at the Ancestry.com website. Source: Federal Tract Books of Oklahoma Territory, microfilm at the Oklahoma Historical Society, Oklahoma City. This is an image only database containing the images to the federal tract books in which Oklahoma land grants were recorded. The various openings and land runs relate to specific dates in the tract book entries. Individual land ownership in Oklahoma began in 1902 with the allotment of lands by the Dawes Commission. Prior to that time, land in the Indian Territory belonged to the respective Indian Nation in which the individual lived. In Oklahoma Territory, with the exception of Indian allotments, ownership began in 1889. Land ownership in the Panhandle was possible after the first official survey for the area was completed in the 1890s. There were eight land openings total: five were done by land runs, two by land lotteries, and one by sealed bid. Browse through the images, organized by Roll number and Vol. number (in chronological sequence). See **http://search.ancestry.com/search/db.aspx?dbid=9244**.
**Note:** For more information about the Oklahoma Land Runs, refer to the **Land Run of 1889** and related articles from the *Encyclopedia of Oklahoma History & Culture,* online at the Oklahoma Historical Society's website.

■ **1889-1951.** See ***Web: Oklahoma County, Oklahoma, Marriage Index, 1889-1951*** **[Online Database],** indexed at the Ancestry.com website. This database is also accessible at the Oklahoma Historical Society website. Each index record includes: Name, Spouse's name, Marriage date, Marriage place, and Notes. This database has 205,434 records. See **http://search.ancestry.com/search/db.aspx?dbid=9233**.

■ **1889-1991.** See ***Oklahoma, Naturalization Records, 1889-1991*** **[Online Database],** digitized and indexed at the Ancestry.com website. Source: National Archives, Records of District Courts (Declarations & Petitions). Each record index includes: Name, Gender, Petition age, Record type, Birth date, Birth place, Petition date, Petition place, Petition number, and Court district. The document image has much more information. This database has 34,261 records. See **http://search.ancestry.com/search/db.aspx?dbid=2508**.

■ **1890-1893.** See ***U.S., Wallace Roll of Cherokee Freedmen, 1890-1893*** **[Online Database],** indexed at the Ancestry.com website. In accordance with an 1866 treaty, in 1888 the Congress of the United States appropriated $75,000 to be shared between the Cherokee, Shawnee and Delaware Indian tribes. This database is a transcription of the Wallace Roll of Cherokee Freedmen intended to identify those Cherokee entitled to a share of this money. Compiled by Special Agent John Wallace, it includes authenticated freedmen, admitted freedmen, those who died between 1883 and 1890, and "Free Negroes" associated with the tribe. Researchers will find information on over 3,800 Cherokee including age, sex, and residence. The Wallace roll was set aside as "fraudulent" by a decree of 8 May 1895 of the United States Court of Indian Affairs. Each record includes: Last name, Office #, Wallace #, First name, Age, Sex, Residence, and Record type. This database has 3,806 records. See **http://search.ancestry.com/search/db.aspx?dbid=3912**.

■ **1890 & 1907.** See ***Oklahoma, Territorial Census, 1890 and 1907*** **[Online Database],** digitized and indexed at the Ancestry.com website. Source: National Archives microfilm series M1811 (1890) and M1814 (1907). In June 1890 a territorial census of Oklahoma was taken. It enumerated the following seven counties: Beaver, Canadian, Cleveland, Kingfisher, Logan, Oklahoma, and Payne Co OK Territory. In 1907 a census of Indian and Oklahoma territories, comprising the proposed state of Oklahoma, was also taken. However, only the schedules for Seminole County exist. Information available in this database includes: Enumeration place (town, county, state), Name of individual, Relationship to the head of household, Race, Gender, Age, Place of birth (1890 only), Number of years in the U.S. (1890 only). Additional information about an individual may be listed on the original record. This information can be obtained by viewing the census image. This database has 65,696 records. See **http://search.ancestry.com/search/db.aspx?dbid=8925**.

■ **1890s-2008.** See ***Oklahoma, Wills and Probate Records, 1801-2008*** **[Online Database],** indexed at the Ancestry.com website. Source: Ancestry extractions from Oklahoma county, district, and probate courts. The 1801 title starting date comes from an uncorrected record dated 1891. This database includes Wills, Letters of Administration, Inventories, Distribution and Accounting, Bonds, and Guardianships. The contents of a probate file can vary from case to case, but certain details are found in most probates. Most importantly, the names and residences of beneficiaries and their relationship to the decedent may be found. An inventory of the estate assets can reveal personal details about the deceased's occupation and lifestyle. There may also be references to debts, deeds, and other documents related to the settling of the estate. It is possible to browse through the images, organized by county, then type of record. Each index record includes: Name, Probate date, Probate place, Inferred death year, Inferred death place, Case number, and Item Description (type of record). This database has 250,454 records. See **http://search.ancestry.com/search/db.aspx?dbid=9077**.

■ **1895-1914.** See ***U.S., Native American Citizens and Freedmen of Five Civilized Tribes, 1895-1914* [Online Database],** indexed at the Ancestry.com website. Source: National Archives microfilm series T529-Final Rolls of Citizens. This database contains the federal government's official tribal rolls (the "**Dawes Rolls**") for the Five Civilized tribes. The rolls provide details on Indians who could claim tribal membership by blood or marriage. They are organized by tribe and can be further broken down by claims by blood, marriage, minor children, newborns, and freedmen, which were former slaves held by Indians. They may list Name, Age, Gender, and Census card number. Rolls include both approved and disapproved names. This database has 104,657 records. See **http://search.ancestry.com/search/db.aspx?dbid=2976**.

■ **1896.** See ***U.S., Native American Applications for Enrollment in Five Civilized Tribes (Overturned), 1896* [Online Database],** digitized and indexed at the Ancestry.com website. Source: National Archives microfilm series M1650, Records of the Bureau of Indian Affairs. The index record includes: Name, Tribe, Application number, Roll number, and Roll description. The corresponding image record is a typescript index with the same information. It appears that this database is an index to Roll 1 only (Master Index). The microfilm series M1650 has 54 rolls, with many different types of documents related to the application process, all part of the enrollments by the Dawes Commission, but the textual portion is not evident here. Also, there is no explanation of the meaning of "Overturned." This database has 13,848 records. See **http://search.ancestry.com/search/db.aspx?dbid=1238**.

■ **1896.** See ***Dawes Commission Index (Overturned), 1896* [Online Database],** indexed at the Ancestry.com website. Source: National Archives, Applications from the Bureau of Indian Affairs Relating to Enrollment of the Five Civilized Tribes. Ancestry's description: "This is an index to over 14,000 records of individuals in the Five Civilized Tribes that applied for citizenship under the Act of 1896. The Five Civilized Tribes include the Cherokee, Choctaw, Chickasaw, Creek and the Seminole. Each record includes the individual's name tribe, and case number. This compilation, in effect an Indian census, was also used as the basis for the allotment of tribal lands to individual Indians." There is no explanation for the meaning of "overturned" in the title. Each index record includes: Name, Residence, Tribe, and Case number. This database has 13,980 records. See **http://search.ancestry.com/search/db.aspx?dbid=3075**.

■ **1896-1897.** See ***U.S., Citizenship Case Files in Indian Territory, 1896-1897* [Online Database],** digitized and indexed at the Ancestry.com website. Source: National Archives microfilm series P2293. This database contains court case files from the U.S. Court in Indian Territory regarding applicants seeking enrollment in the Cherokee and Creek tribes. Each index record includes: Name, Case name, and Case number. The digitized images may have more information. This database has 9,494 records. See **http://search.ancestry.com/search/db.aspx?dbid=2136**.

■ **1898-1914.** See ***Oklahoma and Indian Territory, Dawes Census Cards for Five Civilized Tribes, 1898-1914* [Online Database],** digitized and indexed at the Ancestry.com website. Source: National Archives microfilm series M1186. This database contains the citizenship enrollment cards, sometimes referred to as census cards, which were prepared by the Dawes Commission. Individuals were enrolled as citizens of tribes according to the following categories: By blood, By marriage; Newborns, by blood; Minors, by blood; Freedmen (former black slaves of Indians); Newborn freedmen; Minor freedmen; and Delaware Indians adopted into the Cherokee tribe. Each index record includes: Name, Gender, Age, Father name, Mother name, Census card number, Tribe, and Enrollment category. This database has 197,656 records. See **http://search.ancestry.com/search/db.aspx?dbid=60543**.

■ **1898-1914.** See ***U.S., Native American Applications for Enrollment in Five Civilized Tribes, 1898-1914* [Online Database],** digitized and indexed at the Ancestry.com website. Source: National Archives microfilm series M1301. This collection includes enrollment applications of members of the Five Civilized tribes in what was Indian Territory, now Oklahoma. The applications are primarily from the years 1898–1906, although some were added in 1914. Application packets vary in size and scope but typically include an affidavit from the applicant and supporting documentation that proved his or her eligibility for tribal membership. The packets are arranged by tribe and status (member by blood, marriage, freedmen, minors, etc.). Applicants who had blended backgrounds typically chose tribal affiliation based on the heritage of the mother. Each index record includes: Name, Application date, Place, Tribe, Enrollment category, and Census card number. This database has 68,500 records. See
http://search.ancestry.com/search/db.aspx?dbid=2397.

■ **1898-1914.** See ***U.S., Native American Enrollment Cards for the Five Civilized Tribes, 1898-1914* [Online Database],** digitized and indexed at the Ancestry.com website. Source: National Archives microfilm series M1186, Records of the Bureau of Indian Affairs. This database contains the citizenship enrollment cards, sometimes referred to as census cards, which were prepared by the Dawes Commission. Individuals were enrolled as citizens of tribes according to the following categories: By blood, By marriage; Newborns, by blood; Minors, by blood; Freedmen (former black slaves of Indians); Newborn freedmen; Minor freedmen; and Delaware Indians adopted into the Cherokee tribe. Each index record includes: Name, Gender, Age at census enrollment, Enrollment date, Tribal affiliation, Census card number, and Dawes Roll number. This database has 101,523 records. See
http://search.ancestry.com/search/db.aspx?dbid=1241.

■ **1908-1910.** See ***U.S., Records Related to Enrollment of Eastern Cherokee by Guion Miller, 1908-1910* [Online Database],** indexed at the Ancestry.com website. Source: National Archives microfilm series M665. In 1906, the U.S. Court of Claims appointed Guion Miller from the Interior Department to determine who was eligible for funds under the treaties of 1835-1836 and 1845 between the United States and the Eastern Cherokee. In certifying the eligibility of the Cherokees, Miller used earlier census lists and rolls that had been complied by Hester, Chapman, Drennen, and others between 1835 and 1884. Copies of some of these rolls and the indexes to them are filed with the Guion Miller records and are part of this publication. There are an estimated 90,000 individual applicants from throughout North America included within this publication. Many are from people with Cherokee blood living in Oklahoma. Applications typically include the applicant's name, Indian name, residence, date and place of birth, marriage status, and name of spouse. Also included are the names of siblings, parents, aunts and uncles, grandparents, and great-grandparents, further establishing family relationships vital to affirming tribal connections. This database has 79,496 records. See
http://search.ancestry.com/search/db.aspx?dbid=60555.

■ **1908-1927.** See ***Oklahoma, Indian Land Allotment Sales, 1908-1927* [Online Database],** digitized and indexed at the Ancestry.com website. Source: National Archives, Records of the Bureau of Indian Affairs. Land distributed to Native Americans through government allotment (such as via the Dawes Commission) came with many restrictions governing its sale or lease. An act passed in May 1908 removed many of these restrictions. In particular, this allowed Indians to sell or lease, and incoming settlers to obtain allotment lands. This series contains records of actions taken on applications for removal of restrictions. Records include the applicant's name, enrollment number, tribe, degree of Indian blood, address, legal description of the land to be sold, date petition was filed, date approved, and date of sale. Each index record includes: Name, Residence year, Residence place, Filed date, Tribe, Enrollment number, and Application number. This database has 26,700 records. See
http://search.ancestry.com/search/db.aspx?dbid=60544.

■ **1912-1921.** See ***Oklahoma, Creek Equalization Records, 1912-1921* [Online Database],** indexed at the Ancestry.com website. Source: National Archives microfilm, Bureau of Indian Affairs. This collection contains applications to prove heirship by descent among members of the Creek nation. Many of the files include Proof of Heirship forms which contain the name of the deceased allottee, date and place of death, name of spouse, and the names of the allottee's children and the heirs of deceased children. There are numerous gaps. Forms may include other details as well, including: age, tribal affiliation, whether spouse

is alive or deceased, names of other spouses, number of children, post office, and names of informants. This database has 3,634 records. See
**http://search.ancestry.com/search/db.aspx?dbid=60542**.

■ **1915-1955.** See ***Web: Oklahoma, Confederate Pension Index, 1915-1955* [Online Database],** indexed at the Ancestry.com website. This database is also accessible at the OK Dept of Library's Digital Prairie website. Each index record includes: Name, Residence, Spouse, and a link to the OK Dept of Libraries site. This database has 8,029 records. See
**http://search.ancestry.com/search/db.aspx?dbid=9236**.

■ **1921.** See ***Oklahoma Osage Tribe Roll, 1921* [Online Database],** indexed at the Ancestry.com website. Original data: Electronic reproduction of a report submitted by the Osage Indian Agency in Pawhuska, Oklahoma to the Secretary of the Interior in Washington, D.C. in 1921. By an Act of Congress in 1906, the lands of the Osage Nation in what is now Osage County, Oklahoma were divided among the 2,229 members of the tribe. Each member received an allotment of 657 acres of surface rights. This database is a census of the tribe conducted in 1908 and certified by the Osage Indian Agency in 1921. In addition to providing the tribe member's name, each record also includes birth information, sex, and relationship to the head of the household. Affidavit numbers are provided for those who applied for proof of Indian blood and to what degree. This database has 2,348 records. See
**http://search.ancestry.com/search/db.aspx?dbid=4663**.

■ **1923-1942.** See ***Web: Oklahoma County, Oklahoma, Divorce Index, 1923-1942* [Online Database],** indexed at the Ancestry.com website. This database is also accessible at the Oklahoma Historical Society website. Each index record includes: Name, Spouse name, Divorce date, Divorce place, and Notes (record type, source). This database has 44,010 records. See
**http://search.ancestry.com/search/db.aspx?dbid=9234**.

■ **1923-1942.** See ***Web: Oklahoma County, Oklahoma, Divorce Index, 1923-1942* [Online Database],** indexed at the Ancestry.com website. This database is also accessible at the Oklahoma Historical Society website. Each index record includes: Name, Spouse's name, Divorce date, Divorce place, and Notes. This database has 44,010 records. See
**http://search.ancestry.com/search/db.aspx?dbid=9234**.

■ **1924-1929.** See ***U.S., Cherokee Baker Roll and Records, 1924-1929* [Online Database],** digitized and indexed at the Ancestry.com website. Source: National Archives microfilm series M2104, Records of the Bureau of Indian Affairs. The Baker Roll was the final roll compiled for determining membership in the Eastern Band of Cherokees. Documents include applications for tribal membership, correspondence regarding applications and other matters, transcripts of testimony, copies of decisions and findings by the Enrolling Commission, and indexes created for some of the document collections. This database has 20,005 records. See
**http://search.ancestry.com/search/db.aspx?dbid=2398**.

■ **1937.** See ***Oklahoma and Indian Territory, Indian and Pioneer Historical Collection, 1937* [Online Database],** digitized and indexed at the Ancestry.com website. Source: Indian Pioneer History Collection, edited by Grant Foreman, Indian Archives Division, Oklahoma Historical Society, Oklahoma City. This collection contains transcripts of oral histories about pioneer life in Oklahoma in the early twentieth century. The project was funded by the WPA in 1937. The original collection was made up of some 80,000 entries and contains 116 volumes. The information may include names, residence, birth date and place, interview date, death date, age at death, burial place. Interviews may also mention names of neighbors, family members, doctors, teachers, missionaries, and others. The collection also includes lists of many old cemeteries, some of which no longer exist. This database has 46,724 records. See
**http://search.ancestry.com/search/db.aspx?dbid=9025**.

■ **1972-2012.** See ***Web: Oklahoma, Oklahoman Obituary Index, 1972-2012* [Online Database],** indexed at the Ancestry.com website. This database is also accessible at the Oklahoma Historical Society website. Each index record includes: Name, Death year, Death country (USA), Publication date (of the obituary), and Publication place. This database has 241,026 records. See
**http://search.ancestry.com/search/db.aspx?dbid=9235**.

## Oklahoma Databases Online at FamilySearch.org

The following databases are available for free at the FamilySearch.org website. To see the current list, visit the Oklahoma Research Page for lists of Indexed and Image Only Databases. See
**https://familysearch.org/search/collection/location/44**.

■ **1870-1930.** See ***Oklahoma Marriages, 1870-1930* [Online Database],** indexed at the FamilySearch.org website. Source: FamilySearch extractions from marriage registers on microfilm at the Family History Library, Salt Lake City, UT. Each index record includes: Name, Spouse's name, Event place, and Event date. This database has 9,655 records. See **https://familysearch.org/search/collection/1681007**.

■ **1887-2008.** See ***Oklahoma Probate Records, 1887-2008* [Online Database],** indexed at the FamilySearch.org website. Source: FamilySearch extractions from Oklahoma county courthouses. This image only database includes Wills, Letters of Administration, Inventories, Distribution and Accounting, Bonds, and Guardianships. The contents of a probate file can vary from case to case, but certain details are found in most probates. Most importantly, the names and residences of beneficiaries and their relationship to the decedent may be found in the file. An inventory of the estate assets can reveal personal details about the deceased's occupation and lifestyle. There may also be references to debts, deeds, and other documents related to the settling of the estate. Browse through the images, organized by county, then Volume Title, and Year. This database has 6,044,798 records. See **https://familysearch.org/search/collection/2063710**.

■ **1890-1995.** See ***Oklahoma, County Marriages, 1890-1995* [Online Database],** digitized and indexed at the FamilySearch.org website. Source: FamilySearch extractions from original county records on microfilm at the Family History Library, Salt Lake City, UT. The images are from the record copy of an Application for Marriage License, Marriage License, and Certificate of Marriage. Each index record includes: Name, Event type (Marriage), Event date, Event place, Gender, Age, Birth year (estimated), Spouse's name, Spouse's gender, Spouse's age, Spouse's birth year (estimated), Spouse's father's name, and Page number. This database has 1,189,809 records. See **https://familysearch.org/search/collection/1709399**.

■ **1895-1936.** See ***Oklahoma, School Records, 1895-1936* [Online Database],** digitized and indexed at the FamilySearch.org website. FamilySearch indexing project, with cooperation from the Northwest OK Gen. Soc. for Woodward Co OK records. Each index record includes: Name, Event type, Event date, Event place, Gender, Birth date, and Parent name. The document images have more information. This database has 90,912 records. See **https://familysearch.org/search/collection/1926701**.

■ **1898-1914.** See ***Oklahoma Applications for Enrollment to the Five Civilized Tribes, 1898-1914* [Online Database],** indexed at the FamilySearch.org website. Source: National Archives microfilm series M1301. These records list the individuals who were accepted as eligible for tribal membership in the Five Civilized Tribes: Cherokees, Creeks, Choctaws, Chickasaws, and Seminoles. This record set is also known as the *Final Rolls of Citizens and Freedmen of the Five Civilized Tribes: Applications for Enrollment of the Commission to the Five Civilized Tribes, 1898-1914*. The records include 101,000 names from 1898-1914 (primarily from 1899-1906) and provide the enrollee's name, sex, blood degree, and census card number. This database has 882,272 records. See **https://familysearch.org/search/collection/1852353**.

■ **1899-1907.** See ***Oklahoma Applications for Allotment, Five Civilized Tribes, 1899-1907* [Online Database],** indexed at the FamilySearch.org website. Source: National Archives, Records of the Bureau of Indian Affairs. This is an image only database with digital images of land allotment records for the Five Civilized Tribes in Indian Territory. Under the terms of the 1887 Dawes Act, Indian reservations were surveyed and lands held in common by the tribes were allotted in smaller parcels to individual members of the tribe. These records describe the parcels of land and name the tribal member to whom each parcel was allotted. Records are arranged by name of tribe (Cherokee, Choctaw, Chickasaw, Creek and Seminole), by membership designation (member by blood, by intermarriage or freedmen), application number and according to age group – newborn and minor children are listed separately. The application files numbered 237, 5695, 7680, 7946, 16807, 19289-19290, 21336, 22017, 24261-24265, 28705 of Cherokee by Blood were missing at the archive. Files numbered 2260-2264 of Creek Freedmen and 6581 of Creek by Blood were also missing. Browse through the images, organized by Tribe membership designation (Cherokee by blood, Choctaw by marriage, etc.), then chronologically by Application number. An index for this database is in progress and will be published when completed. This database has 1,406,867 records. See **https://familysearch.org/search/collection/1390101**.

## Oklahoma Databases Online At Various Websites

■ **1800s-1900s Arkansas Original Land Owners.** See the ***Family Maps*** series for Oklahoma counties, maps of all original land patents, compiled by Greg Boyd, publ. Arphax Publishing Co., Norman, OK. These privately-produced computer-generated maps show the first property owners for an entire county, produced as a book of maps, each map laid out on the federal township grid, and includes indexes to help you locate a person, place-name, or cemetery. Additional maps are added for each county to show roads, waterways, railroads, selected city centers, and cemeteries within a county. At this writing, Family Maps books have been published for Canadian County, Cleveland County, Harper County, and Tillman County, Oklahoma. Visit the publisher's information and ordering website for more details. See www.arphax.com.

■ **1800s-1900s.** See ***Oklahoma US GenWeb Archives*** **[Online Databases],** name lists are available for all counties. Typical county records include Bibles, Biographies, Cemeteries, Censuses, Court, Death, Deeds, Directories, Histories, Marriages, Military, Newspapers, Obituaries, Photos, Schools, Tax Lists, Wills, and more. Links to all Oklahoma counties and projects are located at the USGenWeb website for Oklahoma. See http://usgwarchives.net/ok/okfiles.htm.

■ **1800s-1900s.** See ***Linkpendium – Oklahoma: Family History & Genealogy, Census, Birth, Marriage, Death, Vital Records & More*** **[Online Databases].** Linkpendium is a genealogical portal site with links to state, county, town, and local databases. Currently listed are selected sites for Oklahoma statewide resources (539), Renamed/Discontinued Counties (19), Adair County (132) Alfalfa County (127), Atoka County (151), Beaver County (134), Beckham County (170), Blaine County (144), Bryan County (257) and 70 more Oklahoma counties. See www.linkpendium.com/ok-genealogy.

■ **1845-1923.** See ***Oklahoma Newspaper Archives*** **[Online Database],** digitized and indexed at the GenealogyBank website. Search newspapers for Caddo, Doaksville, Eufaula, Fort Washita, Guthrie, Hobart, Langston, Miami, Oklahoma City, Perry, Tahlequah, and Tulsa, Oklahoma. See www.genealogybank.com/explore/newspapers/all/usa/oklahoma.

■ **1851-1902. See Oklahoma (Western) Cherokee Rolls/Censuses, 1851-1902 [Online Database],** an essay on the types of censuses taken for the western Cherokees who first started moving into the area of present southern Missouri as early as the 1790s. Each of Cherokee Rolls/Censuses are identified by year and locations, 1851-1902. See http://files.usgwarchives.net/ok/adair/census/cherokee/cherwest.txt.

■ ***1860 Index of Indian Lands West of Arkansas*** **[Online Database],** list of names of whites, blacks, adopted, or intermarried persons living on Indian Country lands west of Arkansas. See http://us-census.org/pub/usgenweb/census/ar/indianlands/1860.

■ ***1890 Oklahoma Territorial Census*** **[Online Database],** indexed at the Oklahoma Historical Society website. The 1890 Oklahoma Territorial Census lists individuals residing in the seven counties, often listed only by number on the census. The counties and their accompanying numbers are: County No. 1: Logan County; No. 2: Oklahoma County; No. 3: Cleveland County; No. 4: Canadian County; No. 5: Kingfisher County; No. 6: Payne County; and No. 7: Beaver County. The 1890 Oklahoma Territorial Census recorded the individual's name, age at nearest birthday, relationship to the head of the family, birthplace, sex, color, number of years in the United States, length of residence in the territory, if they were a soldier, if they had been naturalized, and if they were able to read or write. The county and town were also listed. See www.okhistory.org/research/1890.php.

■ **1890 Oklahoma Territorial Census [Online Database],** indexed at the Genealogy Trails website: http://genealogytrails.com/oka/1890OKTerritorycensus.html.

■ **1981-Current.** See ***Oklahoma Recent Newspaper Obituaries*** **[Online Database],** digitized and indexed at the GenealogyBank.com website. Search Oklahoma newspaper obituaries for Ada, Altus, Alva, Antlers, Ardmore, Bartlesville, Bethany, Broken Arrow, Chickasha, Claremore, Coweta, Duncan, Durant, Edmond, Enid, Fairland, Frederick, Grove, Guymon, Lawton, McAlester, Miami, Midwest City, Moore, Muskogee, Norman, Nowata, Oklahoma City, Owasso, Pauls Valley, Pawhuska, Perry, Poteau, Pryor, Sand Springs, Shawnee, Skiatook, Stillwater, Tahlequah, Tulsa, Tuttle, Vinita, Wagoner, Waurika, Weatherford, and Woodward, Oklahoma. See www.genealogybank.com/explore/obituaries/all/usa/oklahoma.

## Census Records Online for the Five Civilized Tribes

The following selected list of databases of the Five Civilized Tribes are listed at the CensusFinder website. Each database listed under the Tribe name has a direct link to an online census website.

**Cherokee Nation Censuses:**
- 1851 Chapman Roll Eastern Cherokees
- 1851 Siler Rolls - Cherokees East of the Mississippi
- 1854 Act of Congress Roll
- 1860 Federal Census Index of Indian Territory
- 1860 Federal Census Index of Indian Territory Slave Schedules
- 1860 Federal Census Slave Schedule
- 1880 & 1890 Canadian District Cherokee Nation Census Names
- 1900 Federal Census of Cherokee Nation - White
- 1900 Federal Census of Cherokee Nation -Indian
- Chilocco School Yearbooks 1931, 1939 & 1946
- Early Cherokee Nation Birth Records
- Miscellaneous Indian Territory Citizenship Testimonies
- 1805 Cherokee Nation Baptisms
- 1896 City Directory of Tahlequah, IT
- 1900 Arcadia School Report - Rose, IT (Saline District)
- 1903 Cherokee Baptist Academy Roster

**Chickasaw Nation Censuses:**
- 1860 Federal Census Index of Indian Territory
- 1860 Federal Census Index of Indian Territory Slave Schedules
- 1860 Federal Census Slave Schedule
- 1900 Federal Census Pages 101A-112B
- 1895-1907 Chickasaw Nation Marriage Records

**Choctaw Nation Censuses:**
- 1860 Federal Census Index of Indian Territory
- 1860 Federal Census Index of Indian Territory Slave Schedules
- 1902 Choctaw Indian Census Cards
- Black Choctaws of the Choctaw Freedmen from Oklahoma
- Choctaw Freedmen Enrollment Card Numbers Index
- Choctaw Freedmen of Oklahoma
- Choctaw Full Blood Docket - Case files in the Pushmataha County Courthouse.
- Estate Records of Full Blood Choctaw Indians 1908-1911

**Creek Nation Censuses:**
- 1832 Census Images of Creek Census
- 1860 Federal Census Index of Indian Territory Slave Schedules
- 1900 Federal Census of Creek Nation. White
- 1900 Federal Census of Creek Nation. Indian
- Bounty Land Applications
- Creek Emigration Letters
- 1833? Valuation of Improvements

**Seminole Nation Censuses:**
- 1860 Federal Census Index of Indian Territory
- 1860 Federal Census Index of Indian Territory Slave Schedules
- 1898 Moore's Seminole Roll and Land Guide.
- Dawes Seminole Rolls All Surnames Index
- Dawes Seminole Roll - Indians by Blood
- Dawes Seminole Roll - Freedmen
- Dawes Seminole Roll - Citizens by Blood, Newborn & Freedmen

See **www.censusfinder.com/indian-census.htm**.

## Oklahoma Periodical Articles
### Censuses & Substitute Name Lists in Genealogical Periodicals

PERSI (PERiodical Source Index) is a digitized database project of the Allen County Public Library (ACPL), Fort Wayne, IN. Since 1986, the PERSI extractors have indexed article titles, places, and surnames from over 11,000 genealogical & historical periodicals. The PERSI database is currently available online through the **FindMyPast.com** subscription website. The Genealogy Center of the ACPL in Fort Wayne IN holds all 11,000 periodicals and will make copies of any article by special request. To obtain an order form for requesting a printed copy of any article indexed in the PERSI database, see **http://genealogycenter.org/docs/default-source/resources/articlerequest.pdf?sfvrsn=2.**

**Oklahoma PERSI Search:** Using the FindMyPast.com website, the keywords "Oklahoma Territorial Census" had 96 results.; "Oklahoma Tax" had 202 results. A selection of Indian Territory, Oklahoma Territory, and Oklahoma census substitute articles available are shown below:

■ **"1874 Canadian District Per Capita Tax, Cherokee Nation" [Printed Article]**, in *The Cherokee Tracer* (Marybelle W. Chase, Tulsa, OK), Vol. 6, No. 3 (Summer 1996).

■ **"1874 Cherokee Nation Receipt Roll" [Printed Article]**, in *The Cherokee Tracer* (Marybelle W. Chase, Tulsa, OK), Vol. 7, No. 1 (Winter 1997).

■ **"1874 Tahlequah Receipt Roll, Cherokee Nation: [Printed Article]**, in *The Cherokee Tracer* (Marybelle W. Chase, Tulsa, OK),, Vol. 10, No. 1 (Winter 2000).

■ **"1880-1895 Tax Lists, Greer County, Texas (now Oklahoma)" [Printed Article]**, in *Oklahoma Genealogical Society Bulletin* (Oklahoma City, OK), Vol. 35, No. 4 (1990).

■ **"1881-1886 Tax Records, Greer County, Texas (now Oklahoma)" [Printed Article],** in *Western Trails Newsletter,* (Western Trails Genealogical Society, Altus, OK), Vol. 2, No. 4 (Oct 1989).

■ **"1887 Personal Property Tax Warrants, Garfield County, Oklahoma" [Printed Article],** in *Four States Genealogist* (Tulsa, OK), Vol. 2, No. 2 (Jan 1970).

■ **"1892 Canadian County Tax Rolls" [Printed Article],** in *Canadian County Connections*, published serially beginning with Vol. 1, No. 1 (Feb 1978).

■ **"1895 Tax Receipts, Beaver County, Oklahoma" [Printed Article],** in *Beaver County Heritage News*, Vol. 4, No. 4 (Oct 1996); and Vol. 5, No. 1 (Jan 1997).

■ **"1896 Tax List, Greer County, Oklahoma" [Printed Article],** published serially in *Western Trails Newsletter,* (Western Trails Genealogical Society, Altus, OK), Vol. 10, No. 1 (Jan 1998) through Vol. 11, No. 3 (Jul 1998).

■ **"1897 Tax List, Washington County, Oklahoma" [Printed Article],** in *Bartlesville Genealogical Society Newsletter*, July 1999 issue.

■ **"1897 Tax Roll, Greer County, Oklahoma" [Printed Article],** in *Tree Tracers*, (Southwest Oklahoma Genealogical Society, Lawton, OK), Vol. 5, No. 2 (Winter 1980).

■ **"1897 Occupation Tax, Osage County, Oklahoma" [Printed Article],** in *Bartlesville Genealogical Society Newsletter*, July 1999 issue.

■ **"1898 Assessment Roll, Greer County, Oklahoma" [Printed Article],** in *Oklahoma Genealogical Society Bulletin,* (Oklahoma City, OK), Vol. 16, No. 2 (Jun 1971).

■ **"1898 Tax Assessment Roll, Jackson County, Oklahoma" [Printed Article],** in *Oklahoma Genealogical Society Bulletin,* (Oklahoma City, OK), Vol. 15, No. 1 (Mar 1970) through Vol. 16, No. 1 (Jan 1971).

■ **1900 Personal Property Tax, Canadian County, Oklahoma" [Printed Article],** in *Oklahoma Genealogical Society Bulletin,* (Oklahoma City, OK), Vol. 17, No. 1 (Jan 1972); and Vol. 17, No. 2 (Jun 1972).

■ **"1900-1906 Tax Rolls, Logan County, Oklahoma" [Printed Article],** in *Logan County Genealogical Society News,* (Guthrie, OK), Vol. 5, No. 2 (Jan 1986) and Vol. 5, No. 4 (Jul 1986).

■ **"1902-1903 Tax Rolls, Kiowa County, Oklahoma" [Printed Article],** published serially in *Kiowa County Genealogical Society Newsletter,* (Hobart, OK), beginning with Vol. 7, No. 1 (Feb 2000).

■ **"1903 Tax List, Garfield County, Oklahoma" [Printed Article],** published serially by township in *Garfield County Roots and Branches*, (Geary, OK), beginning with Vol. 9 No. 4 (Fall 1986).

■ **"1905-1914 Tax Lists, Wagoner County, Oklahoma" [Printed Article],** published serially in *Wagoner Genealogist,* (Wagoner, OK), beginning with Vol. 7, No. 2 (Jun 1987).

■ **"1906 Tax List, Okmulgee County, Oklahoma" [Printed Article],** in *Okmulgee County Genealogical Society Newsletter,* (Okmulgee, OK), (Vol. 9, No. 2 (May 1994).

■ **"1907 Tax List, Garfield County, Oklahoma" [Printed Article],** in *Garfield County Roots and Branches,* (Geary, OK), (1990 issue).

■ **"1907 Tax List, Stephens County, Oklahoma" [Printed Article],** published serially in *Foot Steps*, (Stephens Co Genealogical Society, Duncan, OK), beginning with Vol. 1, No. 1 (Jan1986).

■ **"1908 Tax List, Bryan County, Oklahoma" [Printed Article],** in *Bryan County Heritage Quarterly,* (Calera, OK), Vol. 1, No. 3 (Feb 1985); May, August, and November issues, 1994; and Feb 1997 – Feb 2000).

■ **"1908 Taxpayers, Coal County, Oklahoma" [Printed Article],** in *Oklahoma Genealogical Society Bulletin*, (Oklahoma City, OK), Vol. 28, No. 2 (1983).

■ **"1908 Assessment Roll, Logan County, Oklahoma" [Printed Article],** in *Logan County Genealogical Society News*, (Guthrie, OK), Vol. 20, No. 2 (Spring 2001).

■ **"1908 Personal Property Tax List, Pontotoc County, Oklahoma" [Printed Article],** published serially in *Pontotoc County Quarterly*, (Ada,. OK), beginning with Vol. 4, No. 2 (Feb 1973).

## Oklahoma Books & Microfilms at the Family History Library

Important censuses and census substitutes for the area are cited below in chronological order. Each item includes a FHL book number or FHL film number, which can be used to search the FHL catalog for more details. To review an item, start at the **FamilySearch Catalog Search Page**. Select "Search by Place" then "United States, Oklahoma" to see a list of catalog categories. Or, select "Call Number" then type an FHL book number; or select "Film/Fiche Number" to view a specific title.

■ **1828-1900s.** See ***Cherokee Nation*** **[Microfilm],** from the originals in the Oklahoma Historical Society, Indian Archives Division, Oklahoma City, OK. Includes correspondence, census records, enrollment records, laws and acts, journals, national council and senate records, court records, vital records, probate records, land and property records, school records, and other miscellaneous documents. Includes Register of Persons... Under Treaty of 1817, Cherokee (Tahlequah) Census; Includes Cherokee Nation East, Roll of 1835; Cherokees Census of Flint District, With a Complete List of Names of Emigrants, 1855; Includes Enrollments and Censuses, 1867-1920; Supplemental Roll of Those Left Off the Rolls of 1880, Cherokee (Tahlequah), Per Capita; and the Hester Roll of Eastern Cherokees (those living east of the Mississippi River in 1884). Filmed by the Oklahoma Historical Society, 1976, 129 rolls, beginning with FHL film #1666294. For a complete list of roll numbers and contents of each roll, see the online FHL catalog page for title. See **https://familysearch.org/search/catalog/529945**.

■ **1828-1900s.** See ***Choctaw Nation*** **[Microfilm],** from the originals at the Oklahoma Historical Society, Indian Archives Division, Oklahoma City, OK. Includes census, Choctaw Indians, government records, correspondence, occupations, vital statistics, probate records, land and property, court records, military records, schools and other miscellaneous information. Filmed by the Oklahoma Historical Society, 90 rolls, beginning with FHL film #1666451 (Census and citizenship: Mississippi Choctaw census and citizenship 1830-1899). For a complete list of roll numbers and contents of each roll, see the online FHL catalog page for this title. See **https://familysearch.org/search/catalog/544264**.

■ **1828-1900s.** See ***Sac and Fox, and Shawnee Nations*** **[Microfilm],** from the originals in the Oklahoma Historical Society, Indian Archives Division, Oklahoma City, OK. Includes correspondence, census records, enrollment records, laws and acts, journals, national council and senate records, court records, vital records, probate records, land and property records, school records, and other miscellaneous documents. Filmed by the Oklahoma Historical Society, 1971, 64 rolls, beginning with FHL film #1671001. For a complete list of roll numbers and contents of each roll, see the online FHL catalog page for this title. See **https://familysearch.org/search/catalog/544287**.

■ **1828-1900s.** See ***Indians and Intruders*** **[Printed Book],** compiled by Sharron Standifer Ashton, published by Ashton Books, Norman, OK, 1996-2002, 5 vols., index included in each volume. Contents: **Vol. 1:** White intruders in the Old Creek Nation, 1831; intruders in the Choctaw Nation, 1882; 1860 Indian Territory slave schedules, Chickasaw District and Choctaw Nation; records of burials, baptisms, marriages and deaths at Fort Supply, Indian Territory; evidence of marriage in the Creek national records; Chickasaw traders in 1766; Cherokee Nation permits; intruders and non-citizens in the Creek Nation; **Vol. 2:** Cherokee voters in the Old Cherokee Nation, 1835; Creek nation licenses and permits, 1875-1895; Choctaw Nation divorce records, 1875-1905; records of marriage in the Cherokee Nation, 1869-1895 and undated; Choctaw Nation marriages, 1889-1898; **Vol. 3:** Creek Indian light horseman; Cherokee Civil War claims index; Chickasaw Nation citizenship records; Our brother in red, Indian Territory news, January 1890-May 1891; early Choctaw Mission students, 1823; map of Pushmataha District, Choctaw Nation; Choctaw Nation Court records, Blue County, 1852-1858; Peter James Hudson; Indian captives in the Southwest, 1870-1872; **Vol. 4:** List of valuations of Cherokee improvements, 1835; roll of Pickens County, Chickasaw Nation, 1866; murder in the Choctaw Nation; Choctaw deaths, 1837-1854; Our brother in red, Indian Territory news, June 1891-August 1891; index to Chickasaw Nation record book, 1837-1855; abstracts from The Cherokee advocate, 1878; murders in the Cherokee and Choctaw Nations; register of Cherokee claims, 1842. Family History Library has bound v. 3-4 as one volume. FHL book 970.3 C424as, vols. 1-5, and FHL fiche #6002360-6002361.

■ **1831-1832.** See ***Register of Choctaw Emigrants to the West, 1831 and 1832*** **[Printed Book],** compiled by Betty C. Wiltshire, published by Pioneer Publ., Carrollton, MS, 199? 160 pages. FHL book 970.3 C451wb.

■ **1831-1847.** See ***Choctaw and Chickasaw Early Census Records*** **[Printed Book],** compiled by Betty Wiltshire, published by Pioneer Publ., Carrollton, MS, 199?, 173 pages. Includes index. Includes census of Choctaws, 1831 (Armstrong rolls) for the districts of Mushuluatubbee, Leflore and Natachache; muster rolls of Chickasaws, 1847; and rolls of Chickasaws, 1839. FHL book 970.1 W712c.

■ ***1837-1847 Chickasaw Indians Census Rolls, Indian Territory*** **[Printed Book],** abstracted and edited by Bennie Coffey Loftin and Johnny Cudd, published by the Pittsburg County Genealogical and Historical Society, McAlester, OK, 199?, 120 pages. FHL book 970.3 C432ci.

■ **1832-1900s.** See ***Creek Nation*** **[Microfilm],** from the originals at the Oklahoma Historical Society, Indian Archives Division, Oklahoma City, OK. Includes census, correspondence, Creek Indians, Shawnee Indians, court records, government records, military records, land and property, vital statistics, schools, and other miscellaneous records. Filmed by the Oklahoma Historical Society, 1971, 51 rolls, beginning with FHL film #1666121. For a complete list of roll numbers and contents of each roll, see the online FHL catalog page for this title. See **https://familysearch.org/search/catalog/544270**.

■ ***1851 Cherokee Old Settlers' Annuity Roll*** **[Printed Book],** transcribed by Marybelle W. Chase, published by the author, Tulsa, OK, 1993, 132 pages. Includes Index. FHL book 970.3 C424cha. See also ***Cherokee Old Settler Roll, 1851*** **[Printed Book],** compiled and indexed by Larry S. Watson, published by Histree, Yuma, AZ, 1993, 103 pages. FHL book 970.3 C424wa.

■ **1854-1934.** See ***Kiowa Nation*** **[Microfilm],** from the originals at the Oklahoma Historical Society, Indian Archives Division, Oklahoma City, OK. Includes census, enrollments, correspondence, court records, government relations, military history, history and culture, probate records, vital statistics, land and property, schools, Kiowa Indians, Comanche Indians, Apache Indians, Wichita Indians and affiliated bands, Caddo Indians, Delaware Indians, information on Quanah Parker and Cynthia Ann Parker, and other miscellaneous information. Filmed by the Oklahoma Historical Society, 1971, 116 rolls, beginning with FHL film #1666146 (Kiowa Agency census and enrollment... ). For a complete list of roll numbers and contents of each roll, see the online FHL catalog page for this title. See **https://familysearch.org/search/catalog/544279**.

■ ***1855 Census of Choctaw Nation, Indian Territory (Oklahoma)*** **[Printed Book],** by Alma Mason, published by the author, McAlester, OK, c1995, 107 pages. Includes Apukshunnubbee District which is Cedar, Boktucklo, Eagle, Nashoba, Red River, Towson and Wade counties; Moshulatubbee District which is Gaines, San Bois, Skullyville, Sugar Loaf, and Tobucksy counties; and Pushmataha District which is Atoka, Blue, Jack's Fork, Kiamichi and Pushmataha counties. FHL book 976.6 X2m.

■ ***1860 Census of the Free Inhabitants of Indian Lands West of Arkansas*** **[Printed Book],** compiled by Carole Ellsworth and Sue Emler, publ. Oklahoma Roots Research, Gore, OK, 1984, 48 pages. Includes index. From intro: "Compiled from original microfilmed census published by the National Archives. This census is at the end of the 1860 census of Yell County, Arkansas. Film number M653-roll number 52." This census was taken of the free inhabitants of the following Indian Nations: Creek, Cherokee, Chickasaw, Choctaw and Seminole. Enumeration includes whites, and those blacks who were considered free, living in the Indian Nation. Included are surnames when given, age and sex, occupation and country or state of birth. In the Creek Nation, the census taker noted those citizens who were married to natives (Indians), and whether they had been adopted by one of the tribes. FHL book 976.6 X2e.

■ **1860-1900.** See ***Notes on the Wyandotte's From Ohio to Indian Territory*** **[Printed Book],** by Toni Jollay Prevost, published by the author, Lake Mary, FL, 1992, 19 pages. Contains information about the Treaty of the 6th of April 1816 in Ohio concerning the Wyandottes; the Wyandotte land improvements in Ohio in 1843; Wyandotte children enrolled in the Shawnee Methodist Mission school in Kansas in 1851; Wyandottes who served in the Civil War from Wyandotte County, Kansas; Wyandottes on the 1860 and 1870 federal census of Wyandotte County,

Kansas; abstracted index of the Wyandottes on the 1900 federal census in Indian Territory from Canada, Ohio, and Kansas; and biographical reference information on prominent Wyandotte families. FHL book 970.1 A1 No. 166 and FHL film #1697876.

■ **1864-1909.** See ***Quapaw Nation*** **[Microfilm],** from the originals at the Oklahoma Historical Society, Indian Archives Division, Oklahoma City, OK. Includes census; vital statistics; correspondence; Chippewa, Munsee or Christian Indians; Citizen Potawatomi Indians; Delaware Indians; Kansas or Kaw Indians; Miami Indians; New York Indians; Nez Perce Indians; Oneida Indians; Modoc Indians; Ottawa Indians; Ponca Indians; Seneca Indians, Shawnee Indians; Tonkawa Indians: Peoria and Confederated tribes; Wyandot Indians; military history; court records; history; land and property; schools and other miscellaneous information. Filmed by the Oklahoma Historical Society, 25 rolls, beginning with FHL film #1671120 (Census and Enrollment). For a complete list of roll numbers and contents of each roll, see the online FHL catalog page for this title. See https://familysearch.org/search/catalog/544282.

■ **1863-1886.** See ***Executive Department, Cherokee Nation G.W. Ross Sec'ty, October 24, 1865: Rebound Title Acts and Resolutions 1863-1886 Cherokee Nation*** **[Microfilm],** from the originals at the Oklahoma Historical Society, Indian Archives Division, Oklahoma City, OK. Some text written in the Cherokee language. From intro: "This group of records includes various census rolls from 1835 through 1868, Civil War rosters of Indian Home Guards, claims for Civil War service being made in 1899, list of potential claimants who were supposed to be living in Indian Territory and some marriages (in the Cherokee language) performed by Reverend George Swimmer from 1864 to 1895. Also in the group are receipt rolls for a per capita payment under an act dated November 19, 1874 for Canadian and Tahlequah Districts and a census fragment 190-". Filmed by the Oklahoma Historical Society, 1976, 1 roll, FHL film #1666301.

■ **1867-1896.** See ***List of Shawnee: Registered Members of the Shawnee Tribe 1867-1881 and Rolls of the Shawnee Tribe, 1896 Census*** **[Printed Book],** transcribed by Bobbie Dunbar, published by the author, Richland, MO, 1990, 24 pages. From intro: "Register of the name of the members of the Shawnee Tribe of Indians who have moved to and located in Cherokee Nation Indian Territory prior to the 10th day of June 1871 within two years from the 9th day of June 1869, in accordance with an agreement between the Shawnee Tribe Indians and the Cherokee Nation of Indians, by their delegations in Washington City, DC." FHL book 970.3 Sh28db.

■ **1869-1933.** See ***Cheyenne and Arapaho Nations*** **[Microfilm],** from the originals at the Oklahoma Historical Society, Indian Archives Division, Oklahoma City, OK. Includes census, correspondence, Cheyenne Indians, Arapaho Indians, Concho Indians, government relations, court records, military history, history and culture, probate records, land and property, schools and other miscellaneous information. Filmed by the Oklahoma Historical Society, 1971, 115 rolls, beginning with FHL film #1670886 (Census, Letters sent). For a complete list of roll numbers and contents of each roll, see the online FHL catalog page for this title. See https://familysearch.org/search/catalog/544274.

■ **1870-1930.** See ***Pawnee Agency*** **[Microfilm],** from the originals at the Oklahoma Historical Society in Oklahoma City, OK. Includes Pawnee, Kaw, Ponca, Nez Perce, Oto, Missouri, and Tonkawa-Lipan Apache. Includes census, enrollments, council minutes, correspondence, court records, military records, history, cultural information, land and property, schools and other miscellaneous information. Filmed by the Oklahoma Historical Society, 55 rolls, beginning with FHL film #1671065 (Census and enrollment, letters and documents sent and received 4 June, 1894 through March 28, 1927; Census volumes and lists for the Nez Perce, Kaw, Tonkawa, Pawnee and Oto and Missouri 1880-1926). For a complete list of roll numbers and contents of each roll, see the online FHL catalog page for this title. See https://familysearch.org/search/catalog/538241.

■ **1874-1881.** See ***Expanded Index of the Peoria Census, Annuity Rolls and Administrations, 1874-1881: With Undated Material, Quapaw Agency, Indian Territory*** **[Printed Book]**, extracted from original records at the Oklahoma Historical Society, Indian Archives Division, Oklahoma City, OK, published by Gregath, Wyandotte, OK, c1995, 32 pages. FHL book 970.1 A1 No. 198.

■ **1878-1883.** See ***Expanded Index of the Ottawa Census, Annuity Rolls and Administrations: 1878-1883, With Undated Material, Quapaw Agency, Indian Territory*** **[Printed Book],** extracted from original records at the Oklahoma Historical Society, Indian Archives Division, Oklahoma City, OK, published by Gregath, Wyandotte, OK, 199?, 18 pages. FHL book 970.1 A1 No. 196.

■ ***1878 Annuity Rolls and 1890 Census of Chickasaw Nation, Indian Territory*** **[Printed Book],** compiled by Joyce A. Rex, published McClain County Historical Society, Purcell, Oklahoma, 1990, 3 vols. Contents: vol. 1: 1878 annuity rolls and 1890 census of Pontotoc County now McClain County and portions of Grady, Garvin, Murray, Pontotoc, Johnston and Coal counties, Oklahoma; vol. 2: Pickens County now Carter, Love, Marshall counties, and portions of Garvin, Grady, Stephens, Jefferson, Murray, and Johnston counties, Oklahoma; vol. 3: Tishomingo and Panola counties, now Bryan county and portions of Johnston, Pontotoc and Murray counties, Oklahoma. FHL book 970.3 C432rj v. 1-3. Also available on 11 microfiche, FHL film #6125933-6125935.

■ ***1880 Cherokee Nation Census, Indian Territory (Oklahoma)*** **[Printed Book, CD-ROM & Microfilm],** from microfilmed originals at the National Archives, Ft. Worth, TX, both a book and CD-ROM publication, transcribed by Barbara Benge, published by Heritage Books, Bowie, MD, 2000, 596 pages. Includes index. Contains transcriptions of the original 1880 census of the Cherokee Nation, which is also available on FHL film #989204. Transcribed publication: FHL CD-ROM No. 1682 and FHL book 970.3 C424vLb.

■ ***1880 and 1890 Census, Canadian District, Cherokee Nation, Indian Territory*** **[Printed Book],** transcribed by Sharron Standifer Ashton, published by Oklahoma Genealogical Society, Oklahoma City, 1978, 90 pages. The Canadian District of the Cherokee Nation covered the area that is now Muskogee and McIntosh Counties, Oklahoma. FHL book 970.3 C424ash.

■ ***1885 Choctaw Census, Indian Territory*** **[Printed Book],** transcribed by Monty Olsen, published by the Bryan County Heritage Association, 1996-2000, 4 vols. Index included in each volume. Contents: vol. 1: Blue County; vol. 2: Kiamitia County; vol. 3:. Pushmataha District: Atoka County [and] Jacks Fork County; vol. 4: Apukshunnubbee District: Cedar County, Wayne County, Boktoklo County, Towson County, Nashoba County, Eagle County and Red River County. The FHL has bound together all of Apukshunnubbee District including Eagle, Boktoklo, Towson, Nashoba, Eagle, Red River, Wade and Cedar Counties as one volume, and has bound together Atoka and Jacks Fork Counties. FHL book 970.3 C451 v. 1-4. See also ***Index to the 1885 Choctaw Census [Microfilm],*** from the original manuscript at the National Archives branch at Ft. Worth, TX. Filmed by the National Archives, 198?, series 75, 1 roll, FHL film #505975. See also ***The 1885 census of Atoka County, Choctaw Nation, Indian Territory*** **[Printed Book],** by James P. Cummings, published by the author, Mesquite, TX, 1976, 39 pages. FHL book 970.1 A1 No. 86.

■ ***1885-1940 Indian Census Rolls*** **[Microfilm],** from the original records of the Bureau of Indian Affairs, now located at the National Archives, Washington, DC, Series M-595, 692 rolls. Contains census lists that were usually submitted each year by agents or superintendents in charge of Indian reservations, as required by an act of 1884. Usually given are the English and/or Indian name of the person, roll number, age or date of birth, sex, and relationship to head of family. Beginning in 1930, the rolls also show the degree of Indian blood, marital status, ward status, place of residence, and sometimes other information. For certain years (including 1935, 1936, 1938, and 1939) only supplemental rolls of additions and deletions were compiled. Most of the 1940 rolls have been retained by the Bureau of Indian Affairs and are not included in this publication. The FHL has the entire collection, but cataloged by the various Indian agencies or tribes that originally generated the census name lists. (Several tribe lists are included in this bibliography). A descriptive bulletin was published by the National Archives, FHL's copy titled, ***Indian Census Rolls, 1885-1940: National Archives Microfilm Publications, Pamphlet Describing M595***, 34 pages. FHL book 973 J53m no. 595.

**Note:** To compensate for the lack of a roll list for all 692 rolls of microfilm for series M595, check out the digitized version at the Ancestry.com website, a database with 7,559,854 records. For Ancestry's title, ***U.S., Indian Census Rolls, 1885-1940***, see **http://search.ancestry.com/search/db.aspx?dbid=1059**

■ ***1886-1927 Indian Census Rolls, Ponca Agency,* [Microfilm],** from the originals of the Bureau of Indian Affairs, now at the National Archives, Washington, DC., Includes the following: 1886: Ponca, Oto, Tonkawa 1887: Pawnee, Ponca, Tonkawa, Oto 1888: Ponca, Oto, Missouri, Tonkawa 1889-1890: Pawnee, Ponca, Oto, Tonkawa (not always in this order) 1891-1901: Ponca, Pawnee, Oto, Missouri, Tonkawa (not always in this order) 1902-1903: Tonkawa, Oto, Missouri, Ponca (not always in this order) 1904-1912: Ponca, Tonkawa (not always in this order) 1913: Ponca, Tonkawa, Kaw 1914: Ponca, Tonkawa 1915-1919: Ponca, Tonkawa, Kaw 1922-1924: Ponca, Tonkawa, Oto, Missouri (not always in this order) 1925-1927: Ponca, Oto, Tonkawa. Filmed by the National Archives, 1965, 6 rolls, beginning with FHL #580765 (Ponca 1886-1890). For a complete list of roll numbers and contents of each roll, see the online FHL catalog page for this title. See **https://familysearch.org/search/catalog/746171**.

■ ***1887-1939 Indian Census rolls, Cheyenne and Arapaho* [Microfilm],** from the originals at the National Archives, Washington, DC. (part of series M595). Includes the following: 1887: Cheyenne, enlisted scouts, Arapaho 1888: Arapaho, Cheyenne, Fort Reno scouts, Cheyenne (other areas) 1889-1890: Missing 1891-1927: Arapaho, Cheyenne (not always in this order) 1928-1934: Alphabetical 1931: Supplemental rolls for births, deaths, adjustments 1932: Supplemental rolls for births, additions, deaths, adjustments 1933: Supplemental rolls for additions, deductions, adjustments, deaths 1934: Supplemental rolls for adjustments, additions, deductions, births, deaths, stillbirths 1935: Supplemental rolls only for adjustments 1936: Supplemental rolls only for adjustments, marriages 1937: Census rolls with supplemental rolls for births, deaths 1938: Supplemental rolls only for births, deaths, deductions, additions 1939: Supplemental rolls only for births, stillbirths, deaths, deduction, and adjustments. Filmed by the National Archives, 1965, 6 rolls, beginning with FHL film #574191. Selected census rolls extracted and published as ***Cheyenne Indian Census Rolls, Indian Territory, 1895-1900* [Printed Book],** compiled by Valorie Millican, publisher not noted, 2003, 226 pages. Includes a transcription of the census arranged alphabetically by name of individual, followed by a transcription arranged by household for each census year. FHL book 970.3 C429mv.

■ **1890. See First Territorial Census of Oklahoma, 1890 [Microfilm],** from the original schedules at the Oklahoma Historical Society, Oklahoma City, OK. Contains population schedules for the seven original counties of Logan, Oklahoma, Cleveland, Canadian, Kingfisher, Payne, and Beaver. Filmed by the Historical Society of Oklahoma, 1961, 1 roll, FHL film #227282.

■ **1890.** See ***Smith's First Directory of Oklahoma Territory, For the Year Commencing August 1st, 1890* [Printed Book],** by James W. Smith, originally published by the author, Guthrie, OK, 1890, 331 pages. FHL book 976.6 E4s 1890. Indexed in ***Basore's Name Finding List for Smith's First Directory of Oklahoma Territory August 1, 1890-1* [Printed Book],** by Brian Basore, published by the Oklahoma Historical Society, 2002, 128 pages. FHL book 976.6 E42b.

■ ***1890 Census of Chickasaw Nation, Indian Territory: And Other Records* [Printed Book],** by Joyce A. Rex, published by McClain County Historical & Genealogical Society, Purcell, OK, 1993, 3 vols., full-name index included in each volume. Contents: vol. 1: Pontotoc County (now McClain County and portions of Grady, Garvin, Murray, Pontotoc, Johnston and Coal Counties); vol. 2: Pickens County (now Carter, Love and Marshall Counties and portions of Garvin, Grady, Stephens, Jefferson, Murray and Johnston Counties); vol. 3: Tishomingo and Panola Counties (now Bryan County and portions of Pontotoc and Murray Counties). FHL book 970.3 C432 v.1-3.

■ ***1890 Census of the Cherokee Nation, Tahlequah District* [Microfilm],** from the originals at the Oklahoma Historical Society, Indian Archives Division, Oklahoma City, OK. Some text written in the Cherokee language. Includes Tahlequah District census, schedule 1 in 7 volumes. In each volume abbreviations in columns 2 and 3 are "C" for Cherokee, "N" for native, "A" for adopted, "W" for white, "Col." for Colored, "D" for Delaware, "S" for Shawnee and "NC" for Native Cherokee. Filmed by the Oklahoma Historical Society, 1976, 2 rolls, as follows:

- **Tahlequah District Census**, schedule 1 1890 book 1 A-C, FHL film #1666299.
- **Tahlequah District Census,** schedule 1, 1890, book 2, C-F; book 3 F-H; book 4, H-M; book 5, N-R; book 6, R-T; book 7, T-Y; FHL film #1666300.

■ ***1890 Census of the Cherokee Nation, Sequoyah District*** **[Microfilm],** from the originals at the Oklahoma Historical Society, Indian Archives Division, Oklahoma City, OK. Some text written in the Cherokee language. Includes Sequoyah District census. Schedule 1 is in 2 volumes. In each volume abbreviations in columns 2 and 3 are "C" for Cherokee, "N" for native, "A" for adopted, "W" for white, "Col." for colored, "D" for Delaware, "S" for Shawnee, and "NC" for native Cherokee. Filmed by the Oklahoma Historical Society, 1976, 1 roll, FHL film #1666299.

■ ***1890 Census of the Cherokee Nation, Saline District*** **[Microfilm],** from the originals at the Oklahoma Historical Society, Indian Archives Division, Oklahoma City, OK. Some text written in the Cherokee language. Includes Saline District census, schedule 1 is in 2 volumes. In each volume abbreviation in columns 2 and 3 are "C" for Cherokee, "N" for native, "A" for adopted, "W" for white, "Col" for colored "D" for Delaware and "S" for Shawnee, "NC" for Native Cherokee. Filmed by the Oklahoma Historical Society, 1976, 1 roll, FHL film #1666299.

■ ***1890 Census of the Cherokee Nation, Canadian District*** **[Microfilm],** from the originals at the Oklahoma Historical Society, Indian Archives Division, Oklahoma City, OK. Some text written in the Cherokee language. Includes Canadian District census, schedule 1 is in 4 volumes. In each volume Abbreviations in columns 2 and 3 are "C" for Cherokee, "N" for native, "A" for adopted, "W" for white, "Col." for colored, "D" for Delaware and "S" for Shawnee, "NC" for Native Cherokee. Filmed by the Oklahoma Historical Society, 1976, 1 roll, FHL film
#1666296.

■ ***1891 Census Roll of Citizen Band of Potawatomi Indians Residing in Oklahoma, Indian Territory, Kansas, and Elsewhere*** **[Microfilm],** from the handwritten records made by Samuel L. Patrick, U.S. Indian Agent, filmed by the Genealogical Society of Utah, 1979, 1 roll, FHL film #1036363.

■ ***1891-1895 Tax rolls, Cleveland County, Oklahoma*** **[Microfilm],** from the original manuscripts at the Cleveland County Genealogical Society, Norman, OK. Lists are arranged by township and then alphabetically by surname. Filmed by the Genealogical Society of Utah, 1999, 2 rolls, FHL film #2168965 (vol. 1, 1891; vol. 2, 1892; vol. 3, 1893; and vol. 4, 1894) and FHL film #2168966 (vol. 5, 1895; and vol. 6, 1895). See also ***Cleveland County, Oklahoma Census of Taxpayers, 1891*** **[Microfilm],** compiled by the Cleveland County Genealogical Society, manuscript microfilmed by the Genealogical Society of Utah, 1977. Part one contains an alphabetical list of taxpayers which gives name, page number in original tax rolls, town or township where the property was located and a brief legal description of the property. Part two contains the same information transcribed in the order it appeared in the tax rolls. See FHL film #2168969.

■ **1893-1966 Kay County.** See ***Old Census Records, Petition to Incorporate, 1893-1966*** **[Microfilm],** from the originals at Kay County Clerk's Office, Newkirk, OK. Filmed by the Genealogical Society of Utah, 1996, 2 rolls: FHL film #2048208 (old census records, Town of Blackwell, 1893; Town of Braman, 1898; Town of Cross 1893; Town of Dilworth, 1917; Town of Kardy, 1906; Town of Kildare, 1902; Town of Nardin, 1898; Town of Kildare Census, 1894; Town of Newkirk, 1893; Town of Parker, 1893) and FHL film #2048209 (Town of Peckham, 1902; Town of Ponca city, 1893; Town of Tonkawa, 1894; Town of Washunga, 1923; Town of Uncas, 1966).

■ ***1894-1907 Election Returns, Greer County, Texas (to 1896); Greer County, Oklahoma (after 1896)*** **[Microfilm],** from the originals at the Greer County courthouse, Mangum, OK. Filmed by the Genealogical Society of Utah, 1994, 1 roll, FHL film #1954679.

■ ***1894-1922 Tax Records, Kay County, Oklahoma,*** **[Microfilm],** from the originals at the Kay County Courthouse, Newkirk, OK. Filmed by the Genealogical Society of Utah, 1996, 8 rolls, beginning with FHL film #2048694 (Personal Tax Rolls, 1894-1922).

■ ***1895-1930 Indian Census Rolls*** **[Microfilm],** from the originals of the Bureau of Indian Affairs, now located at the National Archives, Washington, DC. Census rolls available for the following years and tribes:

- **1897-1898** Kechai Indian Census at Anadarko Agency, Oklahoma Territory, FHL film #5765900.
- **1897-1898** Wacoe Indian Census at Anadarko Agency, Oklahoma Territory, FHL film # 576900.
- **1897-1898** Tawakoni Indian Census at Anadarko Agency, Oklahoma Territory, FHL film #576900.

- **1897-1898** Delaware Indian Census at Kiowa Agency, Oklahoma Territory, FHL film # 576900.
- **1895-1934** Kiowa Indian Census at Kiowa Agency, Oklahoma Territory, 7 rolls, beginning with FHL film #576900 (census of 1895).
- **1895-1915** Comanche Indian Census at Anadarko Agency, Oklahoma Territory, 6 rolls, beginning with FHL film #576900 (census of 1895). Selected census years extracted and published as Comanche Indian Census Rolls, Indian Territory, 1900-1903, compiled by Valorie Millican, publisher not noted, 2003, 117 pages. Includes a transcription of the census arranged alphabetically by name of individual, followed by a transcription arranged by household for each census year. FHL book 970.3 C73m.
- **1896-1930** Apache Indian Census at Kiowa Agency, Oklahoma Territory, 8 rolls, beginning with FHL film #576900 (census of 1896).
- **1895-1899** Caddo Indian Census at Kiowa Agency, Oklahoma Territory, 6 rolls, beginning with FHL film #576900 (census of 1895).
- **1895-1924** Wichita Indian Census at Anadarko, Oklahoma Territory, 6 rolls, beginning with FHL film #576900 (census of 1895).

■ ***1896-1916 Tax Rolls, Greer County, Oklahoma* [Microfilm],** from the originals at the office of the County Clerk, Lawton, OK. Filmed by Southwest Oklahoma Genealogical Society, 198?, 20 rolls, beginning with FHL film #1324619 (1896). For a complete list of roll numbers and contents of each roll, see the online FHL catalog page for this title. See **https://familysearch.org/search/catalog/78235**.

■ **1896.** See ***Index to Payment Roll For Old Settlers Cherokee, 1896* [Printed Book],** transcribed by Marybelle W. Chase, published by the author, Tulsa, OK, 198?, 41 pages. Living persons were indexed separately from those who were dead at the date of payment. The payment roll of 1896 was prepared in accordance with an 1846 treaty which provided for payment of shares from funds established by the treaty to Cherokee Old Settlers in Indian Territory as original beneficiaries or as their legal heirs. The Old Settlers were Cherokees who began voluntary migration to land in what is now Arkansas after an 1817 treaty between the Cherokee Tribe and the United States. FHL book 970.3 C424cmwin. Also on microfiche, filmed by the Genealogical Society of Utah, 1993, 2 microfiche, #6101765.

■ ***1896 Tobucksy County, Choctaw Nation, Indian Territory* [Printed Book],** copied by Alma Burke Mason; typed by Bennie Lou Coffey Loftin, published by Pittsburg County Genealogical Society, McAlester, OK, 1988, 28 pages. FHL book 970.3 C451ma.

■ ***1896 Census of Citizens of Tahlequah District, Cherokee Nation* [Microfilm],** from the original records in Tahlequah, OK. Alphabetically arranged by first letter of surname. Most of Tahlequah District, Cherokee Nation is now Cherokee County, Oklahoma. Filmed by the Genealogical Society of Utah, 1976, 1 roll, FHL film #989203.

■ **1896-1950 Seminole County, Konawa Area.** See ***They Came From Everywhere* [Printed Book],** by Arthur Ward Kennedy, published by Rapid Rabbit Copy, Conway, AR, 1993, 3 vols. Contents: vol. 1: The people: census of Konawa and Avoca townships, 1896-1920; vol. 2: Part one of history, introduction, background and story of the Konawa area through 1930; vol. 3: Part two of history, the Konawa area during two decades of crises 1930-1950. FHL book 976.671 X2k, vol. 1-3.

■ **1896-1909.** See ***Applications for Enrollment of the Five Civilized Tribes, Dawes Commission, 1896-1909* [Microfilm],** from the original Bureau of Indian Affairs records now at the National Archives, Washington, DC. From introduction: "An act of Congress approved March 3, 1893 authorized the establishment of the Commission to negotiate agreements with the Cherokee, Choctaw, Chickasaw, Creek, and Seminole tribes providing for the dissolution of the tribal governments and the allotment of land to each tribal member. Senator Henry L. Dawes of Massachusetts was appointed Chairman of this Commission on November 1, 1893, after which it has commonly been referred to as the Dawes Commission. The Commission was authorized by an act of Congress approved June 28, 1898 to prepare citizenship (tribal membership) rolls for each tribe. These final rolls were the basis for allotment. Under this act, subsequent acts, and resulting agreements negotiated with each tribe, the Commission received applications for membership covering more than 250,000 people and enrolled more than 101,000. The Commission enrolled individuals as "citizens" of a tribe under the following categories: citizens by blood, citizens by marriage, new born citizens by blood, minor citizens by blood, freedmen (former black slaves of Indians, later freed and admitted to tribal citizenship), new born freedmen, and minor freedmen. Delaware Indians adopted by the Cherokee tribe were enrolled as a separate group within the Cherokee.

Within each enrollment category, the Commission generally maintained three types of census cards: 'Straight' cards for persons whose applications were approved, 'D' cards for persons whose applications were considered doubtful and subject to question, and 'R' cards for persons whose applications were rejected. Persons listed on 'D' cards were subsequently transferred to either 'Straight' or 'R' cards depending on the Commission's decisions. All decisions of the Commission were sent to the Secretary of the Interior for final approval. Filmed by the National Archives, 1983, series M1301, 468 rolls, beginning with FHL film #1439798 (Choctaws by blood 1-148). For a complete list of roll numbers and contents of each roll, see the online FHL catalog page for this title. See **https://familysearch.org/search/catalog/361915**.

■ **1896-1909 Dawes Commission, Published Report.** See ***The Final Rolls of Citizens and Freedmen of the Five Civilized Tribes in Indian Territory, prepared by the Dawes Commission and Commissioner to the Five Civilized Tribes, 1907*** **[Printed Book],** Government Printing Office, 2 vols., 1,267 pages. Reprinted by Genealogical Publishing Co., Inc., Baltimore, 2003, 2 vols., 633 & 635 pages. Includes Creek, Seminole, Cherokee, Choctaw, and Chickasaw Indian Rolls, vol. 1 is a combined index, "Index to the Final Rolls." FHL has the original book, FHL book 970.1 Un3c v. 1-2 and FHL film #962366 (vol. 1); FHL film #908371 (vol. 2). The index can be used as a finding aid to the Dawes Commission Allotments, 1896-1909, which includes a complete census listing of all Indian families involved in the allotments (over 250,000 applications and over 101,000 individuals enrolled). Look up a name and find their roll number in vol. 1, "Index to the Final Rolls of the Five Civilized Tribes." Then go to vol. 2, the "Final Rolls of the Five Civilized Tribes," to look up a membership roll number to get a census card number. To find the census cards see the "**Dawes Rolls**," Applications for Enrollment of the Five Civilized Tribes, Dawes Commission, 1896-1909.

■ **1898-1914.** See ***Indian Records, Choctaw by Blood: Choctaw Nation, Indian Territory, Final Rolls*** **[Printed Book],** transcribed, indexed and published by Arlene LeMaster, Family Heritage Resources, Poteau, OK, 1990, 3 vols. This is an extraction of the Choctaw applications for enrollment from the **Dawes Rolls**. FHL book 970.3 C451 vol. 1-3.

■ **1898-1914.** See ***Campbell's Abstract of Seminole Indian Census Cards and Index*** **[Printed Book],** compiled by John Bert Campbell, published by Oklahoma Print, Muskogee, OK, 1925, 120 pages. Appears to be an extract of Seminole census cards from the "Index to the Final Rolls." FHL book 970.3 Se52c. Also on microfiche, filmed by the Genealogical Society of Utah, 1995, 2 microfiche, FHL film #6111030.

■ ***1897-1914 Tribal Census for Annuity Rolls*** **[Microfilm],** from the originals at the Regional National Archives, Ft. Worth, TX. Filmed by the National Archives, 1978, 1 roll, FHL film #1028501.

■ **1898.** See ***Complete Delaware Roll 1898*** **[Printed Book],** by Dorothy Tincup Mauldin and Jeff Bowen, published by Native American Genealogical Research & Publishing, Hixson, Tennessee, 2001, 100 pages. Includes every name index. In 1867, Delaware tribal members who wished to preserve tribal membership when they were removed from Kansas to Indian Territory purchased 157,000 acres from the Cherokee in Indian Territory. This tract of land was large enough to provide 160 acres for each of the 985 members on the roll taken in Kansas. This 1898 roll was a list of the 1867 enrollees who were still living or their heirs and a list of their holdings. FHL book 970.3 D376m.

■ ***1900 Creek Nation Census*** **[Printed Book],** compiled by Carole Ellsworth and Sue Emler, published by Oklahoma Roots Research, 1984, FHL book 970.3 C861e and FHL film #6101319.

■ ***1901-1907 Native American Census: Seneca, Eastern Shawnee, Miami, Modoc, Ottawa, Peoria, Quapaw, and Wyandotte Indians (under Seneca School, Indian Territory)*** **[Printed Book],** compiled by Jeff Bowen, published Mountain Press, Signal Mountain, TN, 199?, 223 pages. Includes index. These censuses were taken at the Seneca School in Indian Territory. Wyandotte (or Wyandot) Indians are included with the Huron Indian materials. FHL book 970.1 B675ba.

■ **1901-1920 Kay County.** See ***Treasurer's Tax rolls, 1901-1920*** **[Microfilm],** from the original records at the Kay County Courthouse in Newkirk, OK. Includes some Kaw Indians, also known as the Kansa Indians, who lived on a reserve in the eastern portion of what is now Kay County. Filmed by the Genealogical Society of Utah, 1996, 37 rolls, beginning with FHL film #2056845 (Treasurer's tax rolls Ponca City, Parker, Waltham, Weston, 1901 Blackwell, Cross Cities; and railroads). For a complete list of roll numbers and contents of each roll, see the online FHL catalog page for this title. See **https://familysearch.org/search/catalog/679511**.

■ ***1904-1915, Kiowa Indian Census*** **[Microfilm],** from the original records at the Anadarko Philamanthic Museum, Anadarko, OK. Also contains records for Wichita, Caddo, Apache and Comanche tribes that were under the Kiowa Agency. Filmed by the Genealogical Society of Utah, 1996, 1 roll, FHL film #2031240.

■ **1905.** See ***Census of the Comanche Tribe of Indians, Kiowa Indian Agency, O. T., June 30, 1905*** **[Printed Book],** extracted from FHL film #576902, by Faye Riddles Washburn, published by Southwest Oklahoma Genealogical Society, 1990, 57 pages. FHL book 970.1 A1 no. 192.

■ **1905-1917.** See ***Garfield County, Oklahoma Taxpayers*** **[Printed Book],** compiled by Garfield County Genealogists, Inc., Enid, OK, 2000, 2 vols. Contains indexes to county tax records for 1905-1907 and an alphabetical list of taxpayers and their post office addresses copied from the R.L. Polk City directory of Enid, Oklahoma, 1917. FHL book 976.628 R4g v. 1-2.

■ ***1905-1906 Oklahoma City Directory*** **[Printed Book],** R. L. Polk and Co., Dallas, TX. FHL book 976.638 E4p (book includes directories for 1916, 1941, 1960, 1969, 1975, and 1986, by various publishers. See also, FHL film #928379 (1905-1906 directory only).

■ ***1908 Tax Roll, Muskogee County, Oklahoma*** **[Microfilm],** from the originals at the Muskogee County courthouse, Muskogee, OK. Filmed by the Genealogical Society of Utah, 1993, 1 roll, FHL film #1902077.

■ ***1908 Craig County, Oklahoma, First Tax List After Statehood: Beginning with 1908, roll books I, II, III, IV*** **[Printed Book],** copied & indexed by Alta Mae Bowman and Mary Nell Bowman, published by the Craig County Genealogical Society, 1995, 96 pages. This index covers four volumes of Craig County tax records now in the Archives of the Vinita Public Library. FHL book 976.698 R42b.

■ ***1908 Indian Tax Rolls, McCurtain County, Oklahoma*** **[Printed Book],** compiled and published by the McCurtain County Genealogical Society, Idabel, OK, 1987, 10 pages. Includes history of the county and a list of cemeteries in the county. This is an index to taxation of Choctaw Indians in McCurtain County, Oklahoma, in 1908. FHL book 970.1 A1 no. 135.

■ **1910.** See ***McAlister, Pittsburg County, Oklahoma, an Extraction of Records From the Oklahoma State Prison in 1910: Copied From the Census Records of 1910, Indexed by Volume*** **[Printed Book],** extracted by John D. Woods, published by the author, Pleasant View, UT, 1993, 6 vols. FHL book 976.675 X28W 1910, vol. 1-6 and FHL film #1750784.

■ ***1911 Index to Tax Lists of Comanche County, Oklahoma, and Tax Information Extracted from R. L. Polk & Co.'s Lawton City Directory, 1911*** **[Printed Book],** compiled by Jewell (Rone) Tankersley, published by the author, Lawton, OK, 1984, 111 pages. FHL book 976.648 R4t.

■ **1912-1936 Dewey County, Oklahoma.** See ***Scholastic Census, 1912-1936; and Pupil's High School Credit Records, 1901-1952*** **[Microfilm],** from the original records of the Dewey County Superintendent of Schools, Taloga, OK. Most names arranged alphabetically within districts. Filmed by the Genealogical Society of Utah, 1989-1990, 25 rolls, beginning with FHL film #1664668 (1912).

■ ***1912-1936 School District Enumeration Reports, Ellis County, Oklahoma*** **[Microfilm],** from the originals of the Office of the County Superintendent at the Ellis County courthouse in Arnett, Oklahoma. Ellis County was organized in 1907 from Woodward County and half of Day County (formerly known as "E" County in Oklahoma Territory). Filmed by the Genealogical Society of Utah, 1990, 12 rolls, beginning with FHL film #1065158 (1912-1914). For a complete list of roll numbers and contents of each roll, see the online FHL catalog page for this title. See **https://familysearch.org/search/catalog/367110**.

■ ***1912-1934 Scholastic Enumeration Records, Major County, Oklahoma*** **[Microfilm],** from the originals at the Major County courthouse in Fairview,

OK. Some books and years missing. Filmed by the Genealogical Society of Utah, 1991, 12 rolls, beginning with FHL film #1787502 (Enumeration records, 1912). For a complete list of roll numbers and contents of each roll, see the online FHL catalog page for this title. See
**https://familysearch.org/search/catalog/519319**.

■ ***1912-1926 School Censuses, Woodward County, Oklahoma* [Microfilm],** from the original records at the Woodward County Courthouse, Woodward, OK. Most volumes individually indexed. Filmed by the Genealogical Society of Utah, 1989, 11 rolls, beginning with FHL film #1639863 (1912-1913 enumerations). For a complete list of roll numbers and contents of each roll, see the online FHL catalog page for this title. See
**https://familysearch.org/search/catalog/521441**.

■ ***1916 County Register of Electors, Latimer County, Oklahoma* [Microfilm],** from the original records at the Latimer County Courthouse, Wilburton, OK. Contains an alphabetical list of registered voters including name, school district number, date of registration, age, residence, occupation, race, political affiliation, and registration certificate number. Filmed by the Genealogical Society of Utah, 1998, 1 roll, FHL film #2129955.

■ ***1916-1946 Precinct Registers, Alfalfa County, Oklahoma* [Microfilm],** from the originals at Alfalfa County Museum, Cherokee, OK. Names in the register are listed alphabetically under each town. Information for each person listed in the register includes name, school district, date of registration, age, residence, occupation, race, color and political party. Precinct registers are not numbered. Filmed by the Genealogical Society of Utah, 1999, 1 roll, FHL film #2134766.

■ ***1916-1920 County Register of Electors, Cotton County, Oklahoma* [Microfilm],** from the original records at the Cotton County Courthouse in Walters, OK. Names are listed under the first letter of the last name. Information includes name of voter; school district; date of registration; age, address and occupation of voter; occupation, race, color and political affiliation of voter and registration certificate number. Filmed by the Genealogical Society of Utah, 1998, 1 roll, FHL film #2109807.

■ **1916-1948.** See ***Precinct Registers, 1916-1948; Register of Electors, 1916-1918, Greer County, Oklahoma* [Microfilm],** of originals in the Greer County courthouse in Mangum, OK. Most volumes individually indexed (formatted in the "ABC self-indexing format"). Some of the registers give birth dates as early as 1856. Filmed by the Genealogical Society of Utah, 1994, 1 roll, FHL film #1954680.

■ ***1916-1922 Precinct Voting Registers, McClain County, Oklahoma* [Microfilm],** from the original records at the McClain County Clerk's office in Purcell, OK. Filmed by the Genealogical Society of Utah, 1997, 1 roll, FHL #2108408.

■ ***1916-1920 Census Records, Pawnee Agency* [Microfilm],** from the originals at the Regional National Archives, Ft. Worth, TX. Filmed by the National Archives, 1978, 1 roll, FHL film #1249780.

■ ***1916-1933 Voter Registration Records, Canadian County, Oklahoma* [Microfilm],** from the original records at the Canadian County Courthouse in El Reno, OK. Volume 2 is indexed. Index is at beginning of volume. Filmed by the Genealogical Society of Utah, 2001, 1 roll, FHL film #2257892.

■ ***1917 Comanche Indian Census, Kiowa Indian Agency, Anadarko, Caddo County, Oklahoma* [Printed Book],** compiled by Polly Lewis Murphy, et al, published by the authors, Anadarko, OK, 1990, 71 pages. FHL book 970.3 C73c.

# TEXAS
## Censuses & Substitutes, 1700s-2012

### Texas Jurisdictions, 1691-1896

Texas was closely linked with Coahuila Province during all of the years of the Spanish era of Mexico, 1691-1820. The earliest populations in the region began when troops from Coahuila established Nacogdoches in 1716, San Antonio de Bexar in 1718, and La Bahia del Espiritu Santo in 1722, the last mentioned post being moved in 1749 to what is now Goliad. The Medina River just west of San Antonio became the western boundary of the "Texas" command, while the lower Nueces River marked the boundary with New Santander province.

- Texas became a separate province about 1726, with San Antonio as its capital from 1773. The Spanish government in Madrid in 1805 formally defined the west boundary (a northwestern trace from the Medina River to the southeastern corner of present-day New Mexico, and from that point to the Red River, at the southwestern corner of present-day Oklahoma). West of that line was the colonial Spanish province of Nuevo Mexico.
- At the end of the Spanish era in 1820, Texas was a moribund province, its few thousand Hispanics living mainly in San Antonio, LaBahia (Goliad), and Nacogdoches. The ruins of destroyed and abandoned settlements and missions dotted this Indian besieged province barely maintaining its population in the years 1790-1820. To the east, American frontier families were beginning to cross the Sabine, while in the extreme northeast the Americans along the Red River were a de facto part of Miller County, Arkansas Territory. To the west in 1820, the Rio Grande valley contained a few towns such as Laredo, Presidio del Rio Grande and Paso del Norte, this latter town being on the south bank opposite El Paso. But the valley was not part of Texas until 1848.
- The Louisiana Purchase of 1803 by the United States forced a formal clarification of the eastern boundary of Texas. Spain claimed east to the Red River; the U.S., west to the Sabine. They compromised in 1806 with the so-called Neutral Ground, a buffer zone where neither would exercise jurisdiction in what was to be a no-man's land. But actually, it became a haven for pirates, outlaws, fugitives, and others enjoying freedom from government. The Neutral Ground was bounded west by the Sabine and east by Louisiana's Calcasieu River and Bayou Pierre. Finally, the Spanish-American treaty of 1819 (ratified by the parties in 1821 and by Mexico in 1828) set the east Texas border to run up the Sabine to the 32$^{nd}$ parallel and then due north to the Red River. This is the modern Texas line with Louisiana and Arkansas, but it took nearly two decades to clarify just where that due-north line met the Red River. This uncertainty made it possible for Arkansas Territory in April 1820 to create Miller County partly in what is now northeast Texas.
- Mexico became independent in 1821. It renamed New Santander province as the state of Tamaulipas and in 1824 joined Texas to Coahuila as the state of *Coahuila y Texas*.
- Mexico in the 1820s tried to build a barrier against on-coming Americans by encouraging "fit" Anglo settlers to take up land. This began in earnest with an 1823 contract with Stephen Austin to bring in 300 families, giving Austin authority to grant these families land. In 1824 a similar contract was made with Green DeWitt for 400 families. Further such empresario grants were made until by 1830 most of present-day Texas was covered by such grants, although the grants along the Red River and in the Texas panhandle never functioned.
- Politically, Texas in 1830 was the department of Bexar within the state of Coahuila and Texas. The western boundary remained unchanged from 1805, though common usage and contemporary maps increasingly marked the whole Nueces River as the boundary. Within the department of Bexar were four jurisdictions called municipalities. These were headquartered at San Antonio, LaBahia (Goliad), San Felipe de Austin (Austin's colony), and Nacogdoches.
- As American population rapidly increased in east Texas and in the empresario colonies south and southeast of San Antonio, more municipalities were created and some of these were subdivided into districts. By 1828, Austin's colony had seven such districts.
- The Mexican congress by act of 6 April 1830 barred further American immigration into Texas. Mexican troops were stationed around east Texas to enforce the ban, though Austin and DeWitt were allowed to bring in a few families in fulfillment of their contracts. Significant legal immigration from the U.S. resumed only in 1834. The last two years of Mexican government in Texas saw a typical American scramble for land.
- By 1834, new departments of Brazos and Nacogdoches were carved from Bexar and four new municipalities were created: Bastrop, Matagorda, San Augustine, and San Patricio. By the end of the Mexican era in 1835, the entity called Texas was composed of three departments, each with representation in the state legislature of Coahuila and Texas. These departments were subdivided into municipalities and some further into districts. Add the empresario grants, new towns, and clusters of farms informally called "settlements" and Texas was a mosaic of jurisdictions, with a population of about 24,000 Americans and 6,000 Hispanics. Maps in William Pool's *Historical Atlas of Texas* (Encino Press, Austin, TX, 1975) may be the best source for locating places in Texas at the time of independence.
- The Texas war for independence began in October 1835 at Gonzales and climaxed on 21 April 1836 with the battle of San Jacinto, where the Mexican president-dictator Gen. Antonio Lopez de Santa Ana was captured. He agreed (at least while a prisoner) to

Texas independence and to the withdrawal of Mexican forces across the Rio Grande.
- The Texas provisional government in December 1835 proceeded to claim the Rio Grande for a western boundary, even up in New Mexico, but the Republic of Texas could never assert its authority west of the Nueces. The Mexican congress refused to confirm the Santa Ana agreement, never recognized the Texas republic, and treated it as a province in rebellion. Mexican forces in 1841 crossed the Nueces and briefly occupied San Antonio, thereby pushing Texas another step toward eventual annexation by the United States in 1845.
- With the annexation of Texas came the claim to the Rio Grande and in 1846 U.S. troops crossed the Nueces, bringing war with Mexico and the American capture of the Rio Grande Valley in 1847-1848.
- Having given credence to the Texas claim, the U.S. now bought out that claim to New Mexico, paying ten million dollars to Texas by act of 9 September 1850, ratified by Texas 25 November 1850. This act established the present Texas boundaries.
- A later claim by Texas in 1860 for the northern branch of the Red River as its boundary, allowed Greer County to be created and settled by Texans – but the U.S. government forced Texas to transfer old Greer County to Oklahoma Territory in 1896.

## Texas Censuses & Substitutes

**Spanish Era, 1716-1821.** The elaborate Spanish bureaucracy required detailed reports from its frontier posts. This included population data, especially after a royal order of 1776 from Madrid commanded periodic censuses from its American colonies. A good many Texas censuses survive for towns, missions, and their environs, and some have been published, such as for Nacogdoches 1792 and Salcedo 1805. Others can be found in the microfilmed archives for San Antonio de Bexar, Nacogdoches, and Laredo, now located at the State Archives in Austin.

**Mexican Era, 1821-1836.** There are lists of American settlers, such as the Austin and DeWitt colony lists of 1826-1828 and the published lists for what seems to be the department of Nacogdoches. An inventory of extant Spanish and Mexican censuses for Texas does not at present exist but would be valuable.

**Republic of Texas, 1836-1845**, took no known national census. Publications purporting to be such "censuses" are usually the tax lists required yearly from Jan 1837 as compiled by the county assessors. Such ad valorem tax lists (containing real, personal, and poll/head tax information) were made in two copies, one sent to the Texas capital. The state's thousands of lists have been microfilmed, those from 1837 through the late 1970s.

**State Censuses.** Texas was annexed to the U.S. as the 26th state in the Union in 1845. References were found to possible state censuses in 1847-1848, 1851, 1858, and 1887. It seems likely the county assessors doing the enumeration were required only to tally the population by several age/sex/race categories and send the counts to Austin. The state and university libraries and archives in Austin could produce no actual name lists for any of the state censuses, except one county list for 1858 Austin County.

**Federal Censuses.** The first U.S. federal census in Texas were those for Miller County, Arkansas Territory. The 1820 Miller census (lost) included the parts of present-day Oklahoma, Texas, and Arkansas where those states now corner. In 1828, the Indian boundary was established at the present Oklahoma-Arkansas line and Arkansas Territory adjusted its counties so that the Miller 1830 census (extant) was totally south of the Red River in what is now Texas.
- The U.S. federal censuses, 1850-1940 are complete for all Texas counties, except for the 1890, lost for all states. The orderly way large areas of north and northwest Texas were sectioned into counties with little or no population does mean that the 1860 and 1870 censuses have many unorganized counties without population.

## Online Resources at the Texas State Library & Archives Commission

**Republic Claims**. This series is now available in digital form as well as microfilm. It includes claims for payment, reimbursement, or restitution submitted by citizens to the Republic of Texas government from 1835 through 1846. It also includes records relating to Republic pensions and claims against the Republic submitted as public debt claims after 1846.

**Republic of Texas Passports**. The collection of 55 documents has been digitized and a complete listing of names is available. Added to the lists are 287 names as part of the Sutherland Passport.

**County Records Available on Microfilm** is available online, along with instructions for borrowing rolls through Interlibrary loan. County records include vital records, court records, and tax rolls. Most of the microfilm is housed in depository libraries throughout Texas. Select a county and see a list of records and years available, e.g., Bowie County Records (Available from Texas A&M University-Commerce), includes Death records, Deeds, Marriages, Medical register, Probates, Civil court cases, Divorces, Naturalizations, School censuses, and more.

**Texas Adjutant General Service Records, 1836-1935.** The Service Records Series combines both official service record files from the Adjutant General's Office and alphabetical files created by other agencies which contain records related to an individual's service in a military unit.

**Confederate Indigent Families Lists, 1863-1865.** View the names of families that received aid through the 1863 "Act to Support the Families and Dependents of Texas Soldiers."

**Confederate Pension Applications** provides the names, county of residence, and pension number for some 54,634 approved, rejected, and home pensions issued by the Texas government between 1899 and 1975.

**Frequently Asked Questions About Texas Vital Statistics Indexes.** Includes information about what records are available, births, marriages, divorces, deaths, and copies of certificates.

**Texas County Tax Rolls.** Microfilmed copies of the Texas county tax rolls are available for on-site use in the Genealogy Collection of the Texas State Library. This online inventory identifies each county and the tax rolls available for all 254 Texas counties. **Note:** see the FHL Books & Microfilms listing, *1837-1910 Texas County Tax Rolls.*

**Texas City Directories** from the past are available for on-site use. This online list identifies the cities and years.

**Newspapers Available on Microfilm.** The microfilm is available for on-site viewing or to be borrowed through interlibrary loan. An alpha list of newspapers is here for locating one of interest.

**1867 Voters' Registration.** The U.S. Congress passed legislation that called for a registration of qualified voters in each of the former Confederate states. These lists would be used to determine all who would be eligible to vote for any proposed Constitutional Convention in the state. This is an information page and list of microfilm available. **Note:** TX 1867-1869 Voter Registration database was digitized and indexed at the Ancestry.com website.

**Texas Convict Record Ledgers and Indexes.** The record ledgers are excellent sources of individual convict descriptions and information regarding their incarceration. Although the original records are too fragile to be used, they have been microfilmed and may be viewed on-site or borrowed through the interlibrary loan program. This site has a table with the volume number, years of coverage, and roll number.

## Texas Databases Online at Ancestry.com

The Ancestry.com subscription website allows free access to all indexes, but to view any particular record requires a membership. Ancestry offers trial memberships and subscriptions for short periods and reduced rates. The following databases at the Ancestry.com website are unique Texas databases under the categories of Census & Voter Lists, Vital Records, Military, Immigrations, and Wills & Probates. To review the complete list of Texas statewide and countywide databases, see
**http://search.ancestry.com/Places/US/Texas/Default.aspx.**

■ **1700s-2008.** See ***Texas, Land Title Abstracts, 1700-2008*** **[Online Database],** indexed at the Ancestry.com website. This database contains abstracts of original titles located in the archives of the Texas General Land Office in Austin, Texas. The records provide information about lands granted and transferred within the state of Texas including those dated in the 1700s. Fields of information include the district name (a three-letter code) the county, page in original document, grantee, patentee, date, volume, description/location, acreage, class, file, and any additional data found in the record. This database has 442,615 records. See
**http://search.ancestry.com/search/db.aspx?dbid=5112.**

■ **1800-1900.** See ***Texas, Index Card Collections, 1800-1900*** **[Online Database],** digitized and indexed at the Ancestry.com website. Source: TX State Archives. This collection contains a card catalog pertaining to people and organizations which were

influential to Texas history, organized by the following: **Biographical index Cards** are arranged alphabetically by subject. Individual people are listed on the cards, as well as schools, business and other non-human entities. Each card contains the name of the person or organization, as well as a reference to a book in the biographical collection (not included in this collection). Cards may also contain a date, or location reference. The **Ships at Texas Ports** collection is arranged chronologically and lists the date the ship arrived or departed from a Texas port. These cards include the years 1836 – 1843. These cards do not refer to a specific person, and are not searchable by any names. **Colonial Ship Lists and Customs House Ship Lists** may contain the name of the person on the card, the name of the colony and ship, date they arrived or departed, age, occupation, and point of origin. This database has 102,875 records. See
**http://search.ancestry.com/search/db.aspx?dbid=2265**.

■ **1800-2012.** See ***Tarrant County, Texas, Probate Index, 1800-2012*** **[Online Database],** indexed at the Ancestry.com website. Source: Tarrant County Clerk Office, Fort Worth, TX. Each index record includes: Name, Address, File date, Party type, Case type description, Case number, Case status, and Style (notes). This database has 408,124 records. See
**http://search.ancestry.com/search/db.aspx?dbid=7004**.

■ **1820-1890.** See ***Texas, Compiled Census and Census Substitutes Index, 1820-1890*** **[Online Database],** indexed at the Ancestry.com website. Source: Accelerated Indexing Systems, Salt Lake City, UT, 1999. This collection contains the following indexes: 1850 Federal Census Index; 1850 Slave Schedule; 1860 Federal Census Index; 1860 Slave Schedule; 1870 Federal Census Index; 1880 Federal Census Index; 1890 Veterans Schedule; Tax List Indexes 1820-1829; Tax List Indexes 1830-1839; Tax List Indexes 1840-1849. Each index record includes: Name, State (TX), County, year, and Database (census, tax list, etc.). This database has 79,060 records. See
**http://search.ancestry.com/search/db.aspx?dbid=3575**.

■ **1824-1881.** See ***Marriage Records of Nacogdoches County, Texas, 1824-1881*** **[Online Database],** digitized and indexed at the Ancestry.com website. Source: Book, same title, by Pauline Shirley Murrie, publ. 1968. The book text was scanned, with an OCR index. This database has 172 pages. See
**http://search.ancestry.com/search/db.aspx?dbid=29465**.

■ **1825-1835.** See ***Character Certificates in the General Land Office of Texas*** **[Online Database],** digitized and indexed at the FamilySearch.org website. Source: Book, same title, by Clifford White, publ. 1989. An immigrant into Mexican Texas between 1825 and 1835 had to meet specific requirements before becoming eligible to receive land. He was required to apply to the officials of the municipality or to the Commissioner where he proposed to settle and to prove his good character by binging credentials from his place of origin, or by two creditable witnesses. This book identifies the immigrants and details about each. The complete book text was digitized with an OCR index. There is an index to names included in the book as well. This database has 265 pages. See
**http://search.ancestry.com/search/db.aspx?dbid=48419**.

■ **1833-1974.** See ***Texas, Wills and Probate Records, 1833-1974*** **[Online Database],** digitized and indexed at the Ancestry.com website. Source: Ancestry extractions from TX county, district, and probate courts. Probate records may include Wills, Letters of Administration, Distribution and Accounting Records, Bonds, and Guardianships. The contents of a probate file can vary from case to case, but certain details are found in most probates. Most importantly, the names and residences of beneficiaries and their relationship to the decedent may be found in the file. An inventory of the estate assets can reveal personal details about the deceased's occupation and lifestyle. There may also be references to debts, deeds, and other documents related to the settling of the estate. This database has 110,887 records. See
**http://search.ancestry.com/search/db.aspx?dbid=2115**.

■ **1837-1965.** See ***Texas, Select County Marriage Index, 1837-1965*** **[Online Database],** indexed at the Ancestry.com website. Source: FamilySearch extractions from records on microfilm at the Family History Library, Salt Lake City, UT. This database is an index to a variety of marriage records (registers, licenses, intentions to marry, etc.) from select counties in Texas - from 183 of the 254 counties in Texas. Each index record includes: Name, Gender, Marriage date, Marriage place, Spouse, and FHL film number. This database has 3,185,816 records. See
**http://search.ancestry.com/search/db.aspx?dbid=60183**.

■ **1837-2011.** See ***Texas, Marriage Collection, 1814-1909 and 1966-2011*** **[Online Database],** indexed at the Ancestry.com website. Source: Liahona, Hunting

for Bears, et al, extracted from records on microfilm at the Family History Library, Salt Lake City, UT. No record before 1837 could be found in this database. Each index record includes: Name, Marriage Place, Spouse, and Source. (no date of marriage, except as part of the range 1814-1909, or 1966-2011. This database is not useless, but it is not very useful without a date of marriage to confirm the right couple). This database has 16,016,525 records. See
**http://search.ancestry.com/search/db.aspx?dbid=8795**.

■ **1838-1900.** See ***Texas, Muster Roll Index Cards, 1838-1900* [Online Database],** indexed at the Ancestry.com website. Source: TX State Archives. This database includes records of enlistments to Texas militia units of the Texas State Rangers, Confederate Army, and Union Army. Each index record includes: Name, Age, Estimated birth year, Enlistment date, Enlistment place, and Record type. The image of a card may have more information, depending on the type of record. This database has 116,060 records. See
**http://search.ancestry.com/search/db.aspx?dbid=2059**.

■ **1844-1847.** See ***A New Land Beckoned: German Immigration to Texas, 1844-1847* [Online Database],** indexed at the Ancestry.com website. Source: Book, same title, by Chester W. Geue, publ. 1982. Includes an indexed list of 4,200 German immigrants. This database has 192 pages. See
**http://search.ancestry.com/search/db.aspx?dbid=48470**.

■ **1846.** See ***Republic of Texas Poll Lists for 1846* [Online Database],** indexed at the Ancestry.com website. Source: Book, same title, by Marion Day Mullins, publ. 1974, 1982. The title "Republic of Texas" may come from the Poll Tax collection at the TX State Archives, from where this database was extracted, but this 1846 list was prepared after Texas was annexed to the U.S. as a state in 1845. This is an image only database, but the entire book is an index to the names of taxpayers, listed in alphabetical order. This list of names is the closest thing to a census for the first years of Texas statehood. Browse the collection, organized by Title Page, Forward, and Surname groups A-B through Y-Z. This database has 193 pages. See
**http://search.ancestry.com/search/db.aspx?dbid=48427**.

■ **1846-1910.** See ***Texas, County Tax Rolls, 1846-1910* [Online Database],** indexed at the Ancestry.com website. Source: TX State Archives. Information in the tax records may include: Name of owner, Assessment number, Original grantee, Number of acres of land, Value, Town plot description, Name of city or town, Kind, number, and value of livestock, Kind, quantity, and value of farm commodities, Amount of state taxes, and Amount of county taxes. This database has 3,852,784 records. See
**http://search.ancestry.com/search/db.aspx?dbid=60184**.

■ **1847-1861.** See ***A New Land Beckoned: German Immigration to Texas, 1847-1861* [Online Database],** indexed at the Ancestry.com website. Source: Book, same title, by Chester W. Geue, publ. 1982. Includes an indexed list of German immigrants. This database has 173 pages. See
**http://search.ancestry.com/search/db.aspx?dbid=48471**.

■ **1861-1938.** See ***Texas, Prison Employee Ledgers, 1861-1938* [Online Database],** digitized and indexed at the Ancestry.com website. Source: TX State Archives. This collection is comprised primarily of payrolls for employees who worked in the Texas State Penitentiary System, including guards, physicians, sergeants, and others. You will also find some guard ledgers, with details on guards' service, and discharge records. Payroll records typically provide a name, date, pay, and occupation. Ledgers include name, prison assigned, date of assignment, and discharge, resignation, or suspension. Reasons for the discharge or suspension are often noted. This database has 207,611 records. See
**http://search.ancestry.com/search/db.aspx?dbid=1991**.

■ **1867-1869.** See **Texas, Voter Registration Lists, 1867-1869 [Online Database],** digitized and indexed at the Ancestry.com website. Source: TX State Archives, Austin, TX. The Reconstruction Acts of 1867 required Southern states to ratify the 14th Amendment, draft new state constitutions, and register voters, both black and white, to vote in state constitutional conventions. In order to vote, men had to swear an oath of allegiance to the United States, and some were disqualified because of their participation in Confederate government posts. These records list the names of more than 139,000 men age 21 and over who registered to vote in Texas between 1867 and 1869. Each index record includes: Name, Birthplace, Registry date, County, and database IDs. The digitized images have more information about a person. This database has 140,267 records. See
**http://search.ancestry.com/search/db.aspx?dbid=2274**.

■ **1870-2012.** See ***Texas, County Marriage Records, 1870-2012*** **[Online Database],** indexed at the Ancestry.com website. Source: Bexar and Brazoria County, TX, from records at the Co Clerk's office, both counties. Each index record includes: Name, Gender, Marriage date, Recording date, Spouse, and Document number. This database has 3,829,639 records. See
**http://search.ancestry.com/search/db.aspx?dbid=9168**.

■ **1875-1945.** See ***Texas, Convict and Conduct Registers, 1875-1945*** **[Online Database],** digitized and indexed at the Ancestry.com website. Source: TX State Archives. Each index record includes: Name, Birth year, Birth place, Record date, Place of residence, Prison location, Age, and Convict number. The document images have more information about a prisoner. This database has 263,765 records. See
**http://search.ancestry.com/search/db.aspx?dbid=2143**.

■ **1882-1888.** See ***Texas, Capitol Building Payroll, 1882-1888*** **[Online Database],** indexed at the Ancestry.com website. Source: TX State Archives. This database contains a collection of cards listing people on the payroll of the Texas State Capitol during the 1880s. Each card shows the person's name, occupation, and year of employment. Cards are arranged alphabetically by surname. This database has 6,906 records. See
**http://search.ancestry.com/search/db.aspx?dbid=2176**.

■ **1884-1958.** See ***Alabama, Texas and Virginia, Confederate Pensions, 1884-1958*** **[Online Database],** digitized and indexed at the Ancestry.com website. Source: AL, TX, and VA State Archives. Each index record includes: Name, Application place, Birth place, Age, and Application type. The document images and the information on them vary from state to state. This database has 219,155 records. See
**http://search.ancestry.com/search/db.aspx?dbid=1677**.

■ ***1890 Census Substitute*** **[Online Database],** indexed at the Ancestry.com website. This is Ancestry's collection of city directories (and other name lists) from all over the U.S. for the time of the lost 1890 federal census. Included are city directories for **Austin,** 1887-1992; **Dallas**, 1889-1894; **Galveston**, 1888-1891; **Houston**, 1882-1895; **San Antonio**, 1891-1894; and **Waco**, 1890. Go to *View All Collections Included in this Search* for a complete list of databases, alphabetically by place (county, city, state, etc.), and year. See
**http://search.ancestry.com/search/group/1890census#databases**.

■ **1892-1947.** See ***Texas, Court of Criminal Appeal Indexes, 1892-1947*** **[Online Database],** digitized and indexed at the Ancestry.com website. Source: TX State Archives. This database contains a list of appellants and appellees involved in criminal court cases in the state of Texas (1892–1947). These records are an index to case records and so typically contain only the names of the appellant and appellee (which may be the state) and county. They may also indicate how a case was disposed of, who offered the opinion, and (beginning in 1909) docket number. This database has 42,793 records. See
**http://search.ancestry.com/search/db.aspx?dbid=2147**.

■ **1893-1963.** See ***Texas, Passenger Lists, 1893-1963*** **[Online Database],** digitized and indexed at the Ancestry.com website. Source: National Archives microfilm, Selected Passenger and Crew Lists and Manifests. These passenger and crew lists from both ships and aircraft were recorded a variety of forms, and usually include the name of the vessel and arrival date, ports of departure and arrival (as well as future destinations on a ship's itinerary), dates of departure and arrival, shipmaster, full name, age, gender, physical description, military rank (if any), occupation, birthplace, citizen of what country, and residence. This database has 1,027,708 records. See
**http://search.ancestry.com/search/db.aspx?dbid=8722**.

■ **1895-1964.** See ***Border Crossings: From Mexico to U.S., 1895-1964*** **[Online Database],** digitized and indexed at the Ancestry.com website. Source: National Archives microfilm, publications from CA, AZ, NM, and TX ports of entry. This database includes records of border crossing in the Texas ports of entry at Brownsville, Del Rio, Eagle Pass, El Paso, Fabens, Fort Hancock, Hidalgo, Laredo, Presidio, Rio Grande City, San Antonio, Yseleta, and Zapata. Each index record includes: Name, Gender, Arrival age, Birth date, Arrival date, Arrival place, Record has photo (y/n), and Record type. The image of the records may have more information about a person. This database has 5,878,615 records. See
**http://search.ancestry.com/search/db.aspx?dbid=1082**.

■ **1901-1905.** See ***Houston Chronicle Obituaries, 1901-1905*** **[Online Database],** indexed at the Ancestry.com website. Source: *Index to Obituary Notices in the Houston Chronicle,* compiled by Linda Bennett. This index not only provides the name of the deceased, but also the date of death, age at time of death, obituary date, and section and page number the obituary is found on. Dates are given in the

month/day/year format. This database has 4,023 records. See
**http://search.ancestry.com/search/db.aspx?dbid=7291**.

■ **1903-1932.** See ***Texas, Birth Certificates, 1903-1932*** **[Online Database],** indexed at the Ancestry.com website. Source: Vital Statistics Bureau, TX Dept of health. Each index record includes: Name, Birth date, Gender, Birth place, Father, Father birth place, Mother, Mother birth place, and Mother residence. The certificate image has more information. This database has 2,285,123 records. See
**http://search.ancestry.com/search/db.aspx?dbid=2275**.

■ **1903-1982.** See ***Texas, Death Certificates, 1903-1982*** **[Online Database],** digitized and indexed at the Ancestry.com website. Source: Vital Statistics Bureau, TX Dept of Health. Each index record includes: Name, Birth date, Birth place, Gender, Race, Residence, Father, Age at death, Death date, and Death place, The document image has more information. This database has 4,814,886 records. See
**http://search.ancestry.com/search/db.aspx?dbid=2272**.

■ **1903-1997.** See ***Texas Birth Index, 1903-1997*** **[Online Database],** digitized and indexed at the Ancestry.com website. This database is original computer print-out prepared as an index by the Texas Dept of Health, Bureau of Vital Statistics. Ancestry's index record includes: Name, Date of birth, Gender, Birth county, Father's name, Mother's name, and Roll number. This database has 17,102,156 records. See
**http://search.ancestry.com/search/db.aspx?dbid=8781**.

■ **1903-2000.** See ***Texas Death Index, 1903-2000*** **[Online Database],** indexed at the Ancestry.com website. Source: Vital Statistics Bureau, TX Dept of Health. Each Index record includes: Name of deceased, Death county, Death date, Death certificate number, Gender, and Marital status. This database has 7,256,189 records. See
**http://search.ancestry.com/search/db.aspx?dbid=4876**.

■ **1906-1989.** See ***Texas, Naturalization Records, 1906-1989*** **[Online Database],** digitized and indexed at the Ancestry.com website. Source: National Archives, Records of District Courts. Includes Declarations of Intentions and Oaths of Allegiance/Naturalization Records. Each index record includes: Name, Gender, Age, Birth date, Birthplace, Record date, Court district, Court place, Record type, and Petition number. The document images give more information. This database has 91,013 records. See
**http://search.ancestry.com/search/db.aspx?dbid=60189**.

■ **1917.** See ***Houston, Texas City Directory, 1917*** **[Online Database],** indexed at the Ancestry.com website. Source: R. L. Polk's Houston City Directory, 1917. Each index record includes: Name, Trade, Business (name), Residence address, and Comments. This database has 77,8881 records. See
**http://search.ancestry.com/search/db.aspx?dbid=4398**.

■ **1956-2009.** See ***Web: El Paso County, Texas, Death Index, 1956-2009*** **[Online Database],** indexed at the Ancestry.com website. This database is also accessible at the El Paso County Clerk's website. Each index record includes: Name, Death date, Death location, and a link to the El Paso County Clerk's website. This database has 125,547 records. See
**http://search.ancestry.com/search/db.aspx?dbid=70089**.

■ **1968-2011.** See ***Texas, Divorce Index, 1968-2011*** **[Online Database],** indexed at the Ancestry.com website. Source: Vital Statistics Bureau, TX Dept of Health. Each index record includes: Name, Estimated birth year, Age, Spouse's name, Spouse's age, Marriage date, Number of children, Divorce date, and Divorce place. This database has over 3,680,000 divorces. See
**http://search.ancestry.com/search/db.aspx?dbid=8794**.

■ **1981-1992.** See ***Texas, Naturalization Records, 1981-1992*** **[Online Database],** digitized and indexed at the Ancestry.com website. Source: National Archives, Records of District Courts. Includes Declarations of Intentions and Oaths of Allegiance/Naturalization Records. Each index record includes: Name, Gender, Age, Birth date, Birthplace, Record date, Court district, Court place, Record type, and Petition number. The document images give more information. This database has 219,151 records. See
**http://search.ancestry.com/search/db.aspx?dbid=2509.**

## Texas Databases Online at FamilySearch.org

The following databases are available for free at the FamilySearch.org website. To see the current list, visit the Texas Research Page for lists of Indexed and Image Only Databases. See
**https://familysearch.org/search/collection/location/26**.

■ **1800-1990.** See ***Texas Probate Records, 1800-1990*** **[Online Database],** digitized at the FamilySearch.org website. Source: FamilySearch extraction from county records on microfilm at the Family History Library, Salt Lake City, UT. This is an image only database. Browse through the records, organized by County, then Volume Title and Year. Many county records include index books to probates, or wills. This database has 1,164,427 records. See
https://familysearch.org/search/collection/2016287.

■ **1800s-1900s.** See ***Texas, Gonzalez de la Garza Genealogy Collection*** **[Online Database],** indexed at the FamilySearch.org website. digitized at the FamilySearch.org website. This is an image only database of a genealogical card file containing some 270,000 cards, compiled by Rudolfo Gonzalez de la Garza. The card file indexes thousands of families of Southern Texas and Northern Mexico. The original card file is at the Laredo Public Library. Browse the images of the cards, organized in alpha order. This database has 270,253 records. See
https://familysearch.org/search/collection/1918470.

■ **1837-1910.** See ***Texas, County Tax Rolls, 1837-1910*** **[Online Database],** digitized and indexed at the FamilySearch.org website. Source: Microfilm at the TX State Archives. The State Archives microfilm collection is identified with the contents of 424 rolls at their information page. See **Texas County Tax Rolls.** Texas may not have state censuses, but there are thousands of name lists available from the tax rolls for 231 of the 254 Texas counties. The tax rolls are a boon for finding the name of an ancestor living in Texas, because the name of every taxpayer is shown, including real or personal property holders. Therefore, the tax rolls provide a good list of the adult residents of a county, often more so than a head of households census list. Each index record includes: Name Event type, Event year, and County. The images of the registers have much more information. This database has 4,575,333 records. See
https://familysearch.org/search/collection/1827575.

■ **1837-1965.** See ***Texas, County Marriage Records, 1837-1965*** **[Online Database],** digitized and indexed at the FamilySearch.org website. Source: Records of various county clerks at the TX State Archives. This database consists of various types of marriage records (registers, licenses, intentions to marry, etc.) from 183 of the 254 counties in Texas. Each index record includes: Name, Event type, Event date, Event place, Gender, Spouse's name, and Spouse's gender. The original document has more information. This database has 1,724,715 records. See
https://familysearch.org/search/collection/1803985.

■ **1837-1973.** See ***Texas Marriages, 1837-1973*** **[Online Database],** indexed at the FamilySearch.org website. Source: FamilySearch extractions from records on microfilm at the Family History Library, Salt Lake City, UT. Each index record includes: Name, Spouse's name, and Event place. This database has 1,695,783 records. See
https://familysearch.org/search/collection/1681052.

■ **1837-1977.** See ***Texas, County Marriage Index, 1837-1977*** **[Online Database],** indexed at the FamilySearch.org website. Source: FamilySearch extractions from county records on microfilm at the Family History Library, Salt Lake City, UT. Each index record includes: Name, Event type, Event date, Event place, and Spouse's name. This database has 1,575,573 records. See
https://familysearch.org/search/collection/1803987.

■ **1840-1981.** See ***Texas Births and Christenings, 1840-1981*** **[Online Database],** indexed at the FamilySearch.org website. Source: FamilySearch extractions from records on microfilm at the Family History Library, Salt Lake City, UT. Each index record includes: Name, Gender, Birth date, Birthplace, Race, Father's name, and Mother's name. This database has 515,974 records. See
https://familysearch.org/search/collection/1681015.

■ **1841-1985.** See **Texas, Mills County Clerk Records, 1841-1985 [Online Database],** digitized at the FamilySearch.org website. Source: Mills Co Clerk's Office, Goldthwaite, TX. This is an image only database, with Mills Co TX births, marriages, deaths, court records, deed records, divorce records, naturalization records, probate records, and indexes for each of the record types. Browse through the images, organized by Record Category, then Record Description. This database has 153,275 images. See
https://familysearch.org/search/collection/1837923.

■ **1861-1865.** See ***Texas, Civil War Service Records of Confederate Soldiers, 1861-1865*** **[Online Database],** indexed at the FamilySearch.org website. Source: National Archives microfilm series M323. The records include a jacket-envelope for each soldier, labeled with his name, rank, and unit; and

card abstracts of entries relating to the soldier as found in original muster rolls, returns, rosters, payrolls, appointment books, hospital registers, Union prison registers and rolls, parole rolls, or inspection reports. This database has 956,501 records. See
**https://familysearch.org/search/collection/1932381**.

■ **1861-1865.** See ***Texas, Civil War Service Records of Union Soldiers, 1861-1865*** **[Online Database],** indexed at the FamilySearch.org website. Source: National Archives microfilm series M402. The records include a jacket-envelope for each soldier, labeled with his name, rank, and unit; and card abstracts of entries relating to the soldier as found in original muster rolls, returns, rosters, payrolls, appointment books, hospital registers, prison registers and rolls, parole rolls, or inspection reports. This database has 33,955 records. See
**https://familysearch.org/search/collection/1932425**.

■ **1865-1870.** See ***Texas, Freedmen's Bureau Field Office Records, 1865-1870*** **[Online Database],** indexed at the FamilySearch.org website. digitized at the FamilySearch.org website. Source: National Archives microfilm series M1912. The Bureau of Refugees, Freedmen, and Abandoned Lands (often called the Freedmen's Bureau) was created in 1865 at the end of the American Civil War to supervise relief efforts including education, health care, food and clothing, refugee camps, legalization of marriages, employment, labor contracts, and securing back pay, bounty payments and pensions. These records include letters and endorsements sent and received, account books, applications for rations, applications for relief, court records, labor contracts, registers of bounty claimants, registers of complaints, registers of contracts, registers of disbursements, registers of freedmen issued rations, registers of patients, reports, rosters of officers and employees, special and general orders and circulars received, special orders and circulars issued, court trials, property restoration, and homesteads. This database has 29,370 records. See
**https://familysearch.org/search/collection/1989155**.

■ **1890-1976.** See ***Texas Deaths, 1890-1976*** **[Online Database],** digitized and indexed at the FamilySearch.org website. Source: Vital Statistics Bureau, TX Dept of Health. This database includes images of death certificates and an index. Each index record includes: name, Event type, Event date, Gender, Marital status, Birth date, Father's name, Mother's name, and Certificate number. The certificate image has more information. This database has 4,543,234 records. See
**https://familysearch.org/search/collection/1983324**.

■ **1892-2010.** See ***Texas, Daughters of the Republic of Texas, Membership Applications, 1892-2010*** **[Online Database]**, digitized at the FamilySearch.org website. Source: Daughters of the Republic of Texas, Austin, TX. This is an image only database with documents from the lineage society dedicated to preserving the memory of Texas pioneer families. Membership is limited to descendants of those who "rendered loyal service for Texas" prior to Feb 1846. These records consist of 1,525 booklets containing membership applications and their attendant documentation. Browse through images, organized by Vol. and Application No. Range. This database has 386,880 records. See
**https://familysearch.org/search/collection/1918480**.

■ **1893-2007.** See ***Texas, Bexar County, San Antonio Cemetery Records, 1893-2007*** **[Online Database],** digitized at the FamilySearch.org website. Source: San Antonio Parks & Recreation Dept. This is an image only database with records from Odd Fellows Cemetery, Old City Cemetery, and San Jose Burial Park. Browse through the images, organized by Cemetery/Record type, Volume, and Year range. Some cemetery card files are in alphabetical order. This database has 38,892 images. See
**https://familysearch.org/search/collection/1828544**.

■ **1895-2008.** See ***Texas, Houston, Historic Hollywood Cemetery Records, 1895-2008*** **[Online Database],** digitized at the FamilySearch.org website. Source: Historic Hollywood Cemetery, Houston, TX. This is an image only database with burial applications, obituaries, lot books, interment documents, mausoleum records, and plot maps from the Historic Hollywood Cemetery, near downtown Houston. Browse the images, organized by Record type, Date range, and Volume. This database has 41,543 images. See
**https://familysearch.org/search/collection/2040173**.

■ **1903-1910.** See ***Texas and Arizona Arrivals, 1903-1910*** **[Online Database],** digitized and indexed at the FamilySearch.org website. Source: National Archives microfilm series A3365. This collection contains Lists of Aliens Arriving at Brownsville, Del Rio, Eagle Pass, El Paso, Laredo, Presidio, Rio Grande City and Roma, Texas, May 1903-June 1909, and at Aros

Ranch, Douglas, Lochiel, Naco and Nogales, Arizona, July 1906-December. The records are arranged in order by the port city, then by date and usually contain the date of arrival, full name, age, gender, marital status, occupation, ability to read and write, nationality, race, town and country of last residence, birthplace, and final destination. Other forms might also include a physical description of the person. This database has 54,357 records. See **https://familysearch.org/search/collection/2423050**.

■ **1903-1929.** See ***Texas, Laredo Index of Arrivals, 1903-1929*** **[Online Database],** digitized and indexed at the FamilySearch.org website. Source: National Archives microfilm series A3379 (Index). Each index record includes: Name, Even type, Event date, Event place, Gender, Age, Birth year (estimated), and Birth country. The index card image may have more information. This database has 616,001 records. See **https://familysearch.org/search/collection/2304686**.

■ **1903-1935.** See ***Texas Birth Certificates, 1903-1935*** **[Online Database],** digitized and indexed at the FamilySearch.org website. Source: Vital Statistics Bureau, TX Dept of Health. Each index record includes: Name, Event type, Event date, Event place, Gender, Father's name, and Mother's name. The certificate images have more information about a person. This database has 2,278,910 records. See **https://familysearch.org/search/collection/1803956**.

■ **1903-1955.** See ***Texas, Laredo Arrival Manifests, 1903-1955*** **[Online Database],** digitized and indexed at the FamilySearch.org website. Source: National Archives microfilm series A3437. Each index record includes: Name, Event type, Event date, Event place, Gender, Age, Birth year (estimated), and Birth country. The original image has much more information about a person. This database has 533,162 records. See **https://familysearch.org/search/collection/2038112**.

■ **1903-1973.** See ***Texas Deaths and Burials, 1903-1973*** **[Online Database],** indexed at the FamilySearch.org website. Source: FamilySearch extractions from records on microfilm at the Family History Library, Salt Lake City, UT. This database has 271,140 records. See **https://familysearch.org/search/collection/1681049**.

■ **1903-1997.** See ***Texas Birth Index, 1903-1997*** **[Online Database],** indexed at the FamilySearch.org website. Source: Vital Statistics Bureau, TX Dept of Health. Each index record includes: Name, Event type, Event date, Event place, and Certificate number. This database has 17,102,196 records. See **https://familysearch.org/search/collection/1949342**.

■ **1903-2000.** See ***Texas Death Index, 1903-2000*** **[Online Database],** indexed at the FamilySearch.org website. Source: Vital Statistics Bureau, TX Dept of Health. Each index record includes: Name, Event type, Event date, Event place, Gender, and Marital status. This database has 7,255,830 records. See **https://familysearch.org/search/collection/1949337**.

■ **1905-1927.** See ***Texas, El Paso Manifests of Arrivals at the Port of El Paso, 1905-1927*** **[Online Database],** digitized and indexed at the FamilySearch.org website. Source: National Archives microfilm series A3406. Includes manifests and index cards of alien arrivals. Each index record includes: Name, Event type, Event date, Even place, Gender, Age, Birth year (estimated), and Birthplace. The image of the card has more information. This database 294,100 records. See **https://familysearch.org/search/collection/2120714**.

■ **1905-1954.** See ***Texas, Eagle Pass Arrival Manifests and Indexes, 1905-1954*** **[Online Database],** digitized and indexed at the FamilySearch.org website. Source: National Archives microfilm series M1755 and M2040. This collection contains arrival manifests and an index to a portion of the arrivals. The index only covers 1929-1954, while the manifests cover from 1905 to 1954. Each index record includes: Name, Event type, Event date, Event place, Age, Birthplace, and Birth year (estimated). The images of the documents have much more information about a person. This database has 122,918 records. See **https://familysearch.org/search/collection/1916041**.

■ **1906-1953.** See ***Texas, Indexes and Manifests of Arrivals at the Port of Del Rio, 1906-1953*** **[Online Database],** digitized and indexed at the FamilySearch.org website. Source: National Archives microfilm series A3395. Each index record includes: Name, Event type, Event date, Event place, Gender, Age, and Birth year (estimated). The card image may have more information. This database has 104,679 records. See **https://familysearch.org/search/collection/2141027**.

■ **1906-1989.** See ***Texas Naturalization Records, 1906-1989*** **[Online Database],** digitized and indexed at the FamilySearch.org website. Source: National Archives microfilm. Includes Indexes, Declarations, and other Naturalization papers. Each index record includes: Name, Event type, Event date, Event place, Birth date, and Source reference. The images of the index cards have more information. This database has 88,140 records. See **https://familysearch.org/search/collection/1389983**.

■ **1917-1920.** See ***Texas, World War I Records, 1917-1920*** **[Online Database],** digitized and indexed at the FamilySearch.org website. Source: Texas Military Forces Museum, Austin, TX. Each index record includes: Name, Event type, Event date, and Event place. The original document image has more information. This database has 209,675 records. See **https://familysearch.org/search/collection/2202707**.

■ **1923-1946.** See ***Texas, Matagorda County, School Census Records, 1923-1946*** **[Online Database],** digitized and indexed at the FamilySearch.org website. Source: Matagorda Co Judge's office, Bay City, TX. Each index record includes: Name, Event type, Event date, Event place, Residence, Gender, Age, Birth date, and Parent name. The images of the original records have much more information. This database has 372,298 records. See **https://familysearch.org/search/collection/1390096**.

■ **1924-1952.** See ***Texas, El Paso Alien Arrivals, 1924-1952*** **[Online Database],** digitized and indexed at the FamilySearch.org website. Source: National Archives microfilm series A3396 (Index). Each index record includes: Name, Event type, Event date, Event place, Gender, Age, Birth year (estimated), and Birth country. The card image has more information about a person. This database has 200,315 records. See **https://familysearch.org/search/collection/2141040**.

■ **1924-1954.** See ***Texas, Manifests of Aliens Granted Temporary Admission at El Paso, ca. July 1924-1954*** **[Online Database],** digitized and indexed at the FamilySearch.org website. Source: National Archives microfilm series M1757. Each index record includes: Name, Event type, Event date, Event place, Gender, Age, Nationality, and Birth year (estimated). The images of the record has more information. This database has 117,170 records. See **https://familysearch.org/search/collection/2299398**.

■ **1943-1964.** See ***Texas, Brownsville Passenger and Crew List of Airplanes, 1943-1964*** **[Online Database],** digitized and indexed at the FamilySearch.org website. Source: National Archives microfilm series A3423. Each index record includes: Name, Event type, Event date, Event place, Gender, Age, Birth year (estimated), and Birth country. The images of the registers have more information. This database has 190,879 records. See **https://familysearch.org/search/collection/2141045**.

■ **1944-1952.** See ***Texas, San Antonio, Alien Arrivals, May 1944-March 1952*** **[Online Database],** digitized and indexed at the FamilySearch.org website. Source: National Archives microfilm series M1973. Each index record includes: Name, Event type, Even date, Event place, Gender, and Birth country. The image card has more information. This database has 4,445records. See **https://familysearch.org/search/collection/2299368**.

■ **1946-1954.** See ***Texas, Houston Arrival Manifests of Airplanes, 1946-1954*** **[Online Database],** digitized at the FamilySearch.org website. Source: National Archives microfilm series A4025. This image only database contains arrival manifests which usually include full name, age, gender, marital status, citizenship, last permanent residence, birthplace, and final destination. Browse through the images, organized by date of arrival. This database has 4,360 images. See **https://familysearch.org/search/collection/2443353**.

■ **1964-1998.** See ***Texas Death Index, 1964-1998*** **[Online Database],** indexed at the FamilySearch.org website. Source: Vital Statistic Bureau, TX Dept of Health. Each index record includes: Name, Gender, Event date, County, and Event place. This database has 4,113,934 records. See **https://familysearch.org/search/collection/1375599**.

■ **1966-2010.** See ***Texas Marriages, 1966-2010*** **[Online Database],** indexed at the FamilySearch.org website. Source: Vital Statistics Bureau, TX Dept of Health. Each index record includes: Name, Name suffix, Event type, Event date, Event place, Age, Birth year (estimated), Spouse's name, Spouse's age, Spouse's birth year (estimated), Certificate number, and Affiliate county code. This database has 7,606,159 records. See **https://familysearch.org/search/collection/2031191**.

■ **1968-2010.** See ***Texas Divorce Index, 1968-2010* [Online Database],** indexed at the FamilySearch.org website. Source: Vital Statistics Bureau, TX Dept of Health. Each index record includes: Name, Name suffix, Event type, Event date, Event place, Age, Marriage date, Birth year (estimated), Spouse's name, Spouse's birth year (estimated), Number of children under age 18, File number, and Affiliate county code. This database has 3,599,300 records. See **https://familysearch.org/search/collection/2038378**.

■ **1977-1986.** See ***Texas Deaths, 1977-1986* [Online Database],** digitized and indexed at the FamilySearch.org website. Source: Vital Statistics Bureau, TX Dept of Health. This database includes images of death certificates and an index. Each index record includes: Name, Event type, Even date, Event place, Gender, Age, Birth year (estimated), Father's name, Mother's name, and Certificate number. The certificate image has more information. This database has 108,598 records. See **https://familysearch.org/search/collection/1930157**.

## Texas Databases Online At Various Websites

■ **1782-1880.** See ***Texas Censuses, 1782-1880* [Online Database],** indexed at the USGenWeb site for Texas. Includes separate databases for 1782, 1790, 1792, 1810, 1831, 1832, 1833, 1834, 1835, 1850, and 1880. See **http://files.usgwarchives.net/tx/census**.

■ **1813-1900s.** See ***Linkpendium – Texas: Family History & Genealogy, Census, Birth, Marriage, Death, Vital Records & More* [Online Databases].** Linkpendium is a genealogical portal site with links to state, county, town, and local databases. Currently listed are selected sites for Texas statewide resources (1,012), Renamed/Discontinued Counties (15), Anderson County (309) Andrews County (109), Angelina County (270), Aransas County (129), Archer County (143), Armstrong County (187), Atascosa County (195) and 247 more Texas counties. See **www.linkpendium.com/tx-genealogy**.

■ **1813-1900s Texas Original Land Owners.** See the ***Family Maps*** series for Arkansas counties, maps of all original land patents, compiled by Greg Boyd, publ. Arphax Publishing Co., Norman, OK. These privately-produced computer-generated maps show the first property owners for an entire county, produced as a book of maps, each map laid out on the federal township grid, and includes indexes to help you locate a person, place-name, or cemetery. Additional maps are added for each county to show roads, waterways, railroads, selected city centers, and cemeteries within a county. At this writing, *Family Maps* books have been published for the following Texas counties: Angelina, Austin, Bastrop, Bell, Bosque, Bowie, Burnet, Caldwell, Cameron, Collin, Colorado, Comal, Cooke, Dallas, Denton, Duval, Ellis, Fannin, Foard, Grayson, Gregg, Grimes, Hall, Hardin, Harrison, Henderson, Hopkins, Hunt, Lamar, Lavaca, Leon, Mason, McLennan, Medina, Montague, Montgomery, Nacogdoches, Navarro, Red River, Roberts, Rusk, Smith, Stephens, Tarrant, Taylor, Tom Green, Upshur, Uvalde, Washington, Wise, Wood, and Young County, Texas. Visit the publisher's information and ordering website for more details and updated county coverage. See **www.arphax.com.** Arphax's entire *Family Maps* series is also available as a subscription service online. See **www.historygeo.com.**

■ **1813-1993.** See ***Texas Newspaper Archives* [Online Databases],** digitized and indexed newspapers at the GenealogyBank website, for Austin, Beaumont, Beeville, Brazoria, Brownsville, Clarksville, Cleburne, Corpus Christi, Corsicana, Dallas, Denison, Edinburg, El Paso, Fort Worth, Galveston, Henderson, Houston, Huntsville, Kingsville, Laredo, Marshall, Nacogdoches, Palestine, Paris, Pittsburg, Richardson, Rusk, San Antonio, San Augustine, San Luis, Taft, Victoria, Waco, and West Columbia, Texas. See **www.genealogybank.com/explore/newspapers/all/usa/texas**.

■ **1829-1845.** See ***The First Census of Texas, 1829-1836, to Which are Added Texas Citizenship Lists, 1821-1845, and Other Early Records of The Republic of Texas* [Online Database],** an index to the book, same title, by Marion Day Mullins, publ. Washington, DC, 1962. See **www.rootsweb.ancestry.com/~txjacks2/Index_First_Census.htm**.

■ **1835. See Index of Texas Statewide Census, 1835 [Online Database],** indexed at the USGenWeb site for Texas. See **http://files.usgwarchives.net/tx/census/1835**.

■ **1837-1900s.** See ***Texas US GenWeb Archives* [Online Databases],** name lists are available for all counties. Typical county records include Bibles,

Biographies, Cemeteries, Censuses, Court, Death, Deeds, Directories, Histories, Marriages, Military, Newspapers, Obituaries, Photos, Schools, Tax Lists, Wills, and more. Links to all Texas counties and projects are located at the USGenWeb home page for Texas. See **www.txgenweb.org**.

■ **1837-Current.** See ***Surname Index - Texas General Land Office*. [Online Database],** an important resource for genealogists. Established in 1837, the Archives consist of land grant records and maps dating to the 16th century that detail the passage of Texas public lands to private ownership. The Texas General Land Office Archives Surname Index contains alphabetical listings of grantees and patentees that were issued land grants by the Republic and State of Texas. The index also lists grantees for Spanish and Mexican land grants filed in the Spanish Collection. See **www.glo.texas.gov/history/archives/surname-index**.

■ **1837-Current.** See ***Briscoe Center for American History, Texas Newspaper Collection at the University of Texas at Austin* [Online Database].** The Briscoe Center's Newspaper Collections contain more than 4,500 Texas, Southern, U.S., and non-U.S. titles and is the largest collection of its kind in Texas. For more information about a specific geographic focus at the Briscoe Center home page. See **www.cah.utexas.edu/research/newspapers.php**.

■ **1851-Current.** See ***Texas State Cemetery* [Online Database],** indexed at the Cemetery.state.tx website. See **www.cemetery.state.tx.us**.

■ **1877-1922.** See ***Sanborn Fire Insurance Maps – Texas* [Online Database],** images at the Perry-Castañeda Library Map Collection – University of Texas, Austin, TX. See **www.lib.utexas.edu/maps/sanborn/texas.html**.

■ **1984-Current.** See ***Texas Recent Newspaper Obituaries* [Online Database],** digitized and indexed at the GenealogyBank.com website. Search Texas newspaper obituaries for Abilene, Alice, Allen, Alvarado, Amarillo, Angleton, Arlington, Athens, Atlanta, Austin, Bay City, Baytown, Beaumont, Bellaire, Big Sandy, Big Spring, Blanco, Bonham, Borger, Breckenridge, Brownsboro, Brownsville, Brownwood, Bryan-College Station, Buda, Bullard, Burleson, Burnet, Carrollton, Carthage, Celina, Cleburne, Cleveland, Clifton, Clute, Commerce, Conroe, Coppell, Corpus Christi, Corsicana, Cuero, Cypress, Daingerfield, Dallas, Dayton, Deer Park, Del Rio, Denton, Edinburg, Edna, El Paso, Ennis, Fairfield, Flower Mound, Fort Worth, Fredericksburg, Freer, Friendswood, Frisco, Gainesville, Galveston, Gladewater, Glen Rose, Graham, Grand Saline, Greenville, Gun Barrel City, Hallsville, Harlingen, Hearne, Hempstead, Highland Park-University Park, Houston, Humble, Huntsville, Ingleside, Irving, Jacksboro, Jacksonville, Jasper, Katy, Keller, Kerrville, Kilgore, Laredo, Lewisville, Lexington, Lindale, Linden, Little Elm, Llano, Longview, Lubbock, Lufkin, Lumberton, Magnolia, Mansfield, Marble Falls, Marlin, Marshall, McAllen, McKinney, Meridian, Mesquite, Mexia, Midland, Midlothian, Mineola, Mineral Wells, Mount Pleasant, Nacogdoches, New Boston, New Braunfels, Odessa, Olney, Orange, Overton, Palestine, Paris, Pasadena, Pearland, Pittsburg, Plainview, Plano, Port Arthur, Quitman, Red Oak, Robstown, Rowlett, Royse City, San Angelo, San Antonio, San Marcos, Seguin, Sherman, Southlake, Stephenville, Sugar Land, Sweetwater, Texarkana, Texas City, The Woodlands, Tomball, Travis County, Van Alstyne, Victoria, Waco, Waxahachie, Weatherford, Webster, West University Place, Whitehouse, Wichita Falls, and Yorktown, Texas. See **www.genealogybank.com/explore/obituaries/all/usa/texas**.

## Texas Books & Microfilms at the Family History Library

Important censuses and census substitutes for the area are cited below in chronological order. Each item includes a FHL book number or FHL film number, which can be used to search the FHL catalog for more details. To review an item, start at the **FamilySearch Catalog Search Page**. Select "Search by Place" then "United States, Texas" to see a list of catalog categories. Or, select "Call Number" then type an FHL book number; or select "Film/Fiche Number" to view a specific title.

■ **1700s-1800s.** See ***Early Texas Settlers, 1700s-1800s* [CD-ROM],** originally published by Broderbund , Family Tree Maker's Family Archives, Genealogical Records No. 514, published 2000, in collaboration with Genealogical Publishing Co., Inc., Baltimore. Contents: *Austin Colony Pioneers: Including History of Bastrop, Fayette, Grimes, Montgomery and Washington Counties, Texas and*

*Their Earliest Settlers*, by Worth S. Ray; *Ancestor Lineages of Members Texas Society, National Society Colonial Dames Seventeenth Century*, compiled by Jeanne Mitchell Jordan Tabb; *Stephen F. Austin's Register of Families*, edited by Villamae Williams from the originals in the General Land Office, Austin, Texas; *Character Certificates in the General Land Office of Texas*, edited by Gifford White from the files of the General Land Office, Austin, Texas; *Kentucky Colonization in Texas: A History of the Peters Colony*, by Seymour V. Connor; *Republic of Texas: Poll Lists for 1846*, by Marion Day Mullins; *A New Land Beckoned: German Immigration to Texas, 1844-1847*, compiled and edited by Chester W. and Ethel H. Geue; and *New Homes in a New land: German Immigration to Texas, 1847-1861*, by Ethel Hander Geue.

■ **1736-1838.** See ***Bexar County Spanish Archives (San Antonio, Texas)*** **[Microfilm],** from the original records at the Bexar County courthouse. Includes index compiled by Richard G. Santos. Filmed by the Genealogical Society of Utah, 1977, 13 rolls, beginning with FHL film #1019360 (Index to Bexar County Spanish archives, 1736-1838; wills and estates No. 1-9, 1736-1838). For a complete list of roll numbers and contents of each roll see the online FHL catalog page for this title. See **https://familysearch.org/search/catalog/414789**.

■ **1749-1872.** See ***Indexes to the Laredo Archives*** **[Printed Book],** compiled by Robert D. Wood, published by Burke Pub., 1993, 138 pages. Includes a chronological, topical/subject, person name (surname) and place name index. Index to records referred to as the Laredo Archives that document early government in the town of Laredo, Texas. Those records in the archives of interest to genealogists consist mainly of court records, with some references to probate and tax matters. FHL book 976.4462/L1 N22w.

■ **1756-1830s.** See ***Lost Spanish Towns: Atascosito and Trinidad de Salcedo*** **[Printed Book],** by Jean L. Epperson, published by Dogwood Press, Woodville, TX, 1996, 118 pages. This book covers a part of the history of Southeast Texas from 1756 to the 1830s. From introduction: "Atascosito, located near the lower Trinity River, was a recognized geographical place in 1756, a small rancho in 1766, a temporary Indian mission in 1785, and a Spanish military post from 1805 through 1812. "The villa and military post of Santisima Trinidad de Salcedo was founded in January 1806 on the east side of the Trinity River... The Spanish Royalist Army destroyed Salcedo in September 1813." FHL book 976.4 H2ej.

■ **1767-1835.** See ***Index to Spanish and Mexican Land Grants in Texas*** **[Printed Book],** by Virginia H. Taylor, published by Lone Star Press, Austin, TX, 1995, 258 pages. FHL book 976.4 R22t.

■ **1782-1836.** See ***Residents of Texas, 1782-1836*** **[Printed Book],** compiled by the Institute of Texan Cultures, University of Texas, published by the Institute, San Antonio, TX, 1984, 3 vols. Each volume includes an index. Consists chiefly of names of residents and information concerning their wives and children. Vol. 3 contains transcriptions of proceedings involving land and property and other matters. Vol. 1 has period dates 1782-1806. FHL book 976.4 D2rte vol. 1-3.

■ **1809-1836.** See ***Citizens & Foreigners of the Nacogdoches District, 1809-1836*** **[Printed Book],** by Carolyn Reeves Ericson, published by the author, Nacogdoches, TX, 1981, 2 vols., FHL book 976.4 H2e, v.1-2.

■ **1820-1829.** See ***Texas, 1820-1829, Index of County Tax Lists*** **[Printed Book],** edited by Ronald Vern Jackson, et al, published by Accelerated Indexing Systems, North Salt Lake, UT, 1981, 55 pages. FHL book 976.4 X2j 1820-1829.

■ **1820s-1846.** See ***Red River County Deed Abstracts*** **[Printed Book],** by Joyce Martin Murray, published by the author, Dallas, TX, 1986, 2 vols. Includes index of names, index of places, and index of slave names. Contents: Vol. 1: Republic of Texas and state of Coahuila and Texas (Mexico); Abstracts of deed record books A-B, A-B-C, D, F, to 19 Feb. 1846, annexation to United States; Vol. 2: Red River County, Texas, abstracts of deed record books F, G, H, I, J, and part of K. FHL book 976.4212 R28m.

■ **1821-1846.** See ***Coahuila y Texas: Desde la Consumación de la Independencia Hasta el Tratado de Paz de Guadalupe Hidalgo, (A historical unfolding of Coahuila and Texas from Independence to the Treaty of Guadalupe Hidalgo)*** **[Printed Book],** by Vito Alessio Robles, published in Mexico, D.F., Editorial Porrea, 2 vols., 1,082 pages. Includes indexes and bibliographical references. FHL book 972.14 H2r v.1-2.

■ **1821-1846.** See ***Apellidos de Tamaulipas, Nuevo León, Coahuila y Texas, (Surnames of Tamaulipas, Nuevo León, Coahuila and Texas)*** **[Printed Book],** by Rudolfo Gonzales de la Garza, published by Nuevo Laredo, Mexico, 1980, 351 pages. FHL book 972 D4g.

■ **1823-1835.** See ***Stephen F. Austin's Register of Families*** **[Printed Book],** edited by Villamae Williams from the originals in the General Land Office, Austin, Texas. Originally published: St. Louis, MO. Reprint by Genealogical Publishing Co., Inc., Baltimore, MD, 1989. Includes index. Includes land records. FHL book 976.4 W2au 1989.

■ **1826.** See ***The Atascosito Census of 1826*** **[Printed Book],** transcription from a photostatic copy of an original document in the Library of Congress. From introduction: "The Atascosito District is bounded as follows viz. On the west by the Colony of San Felipe de Austin on the north by the District of Nacogdoches, on the east by the reserved lands on the Sabine, on the south by the Gulf of Mexico including all Islands and Bays within three leagues of the Sea Shore." FHL book 976.4 A1 no. 149; also on microfiche, FHL film #6089073.

■ ***1826-1835 Colonial Deeds, San Felipe de Austin (Texas)*** **[Microfilm],** from a copy of photocopied loose deeds at the Austin County courthouse, Bellville, Texas. Filmed by the Genealogical Society of Utah, 1977, 3 rolls, as follows:
- Index to Colonial Deeds, 1826-1860; Vol.1, A1-C35; Vol. 2, C36-G34, FHL film #1019280.
- Vol. 3, G35 – L12, Vol. 4, L13- P83, FHL film #1019281.
- Vol. 5, P84-T34; Vol. 6, T35-Y7, FHL film #101982.

■ ***1826-1836 Index of Documents, Department of Nacogdoches*** **[Printed Book],** compiled and published by Carolyn Ericson, Nacogdoches, TX, 39 pages, FHL book 976.4182 P22i. To access a digital version of this book, see the online FHL catalog page for this title. See **https://familysearch.org/search/catalog/611776**.

■ **1829-1845.** See ***The First Census of Texas, 1829-1836: To Which Are Added Texas Citizenship Lists, 1821-1845 And Other Early Records of the Republic of Texas*** **[Microfilm],** by Marion Day Mullins, from a reprint of the Special Publication of the National Genealogical Society, No. 22, 1962, 61 pages. Includes census, 1820-1836; citizenship lists, 1821-1845; certificates of entrance into Texas in 1835; election in San Augustine in November 1834. Filmed by the Genealogical Society of Utah, 1971, 1 roll, FHL film #844966. Another filming, FHL film #1000607. To access a digital version of this book, see the online FHL catalog page for this title. See **https://familysearch.org/search/catalog/738730**.

■ ***1830 Citizens of Texas: A Census of 6,500 Pre-Revolutionary Texas*** **[Printed Book],** by Gifford White, published by Eakin Press, Austin, TX, 1983, 282 pages. Includes index and list of registered voters of 1867. FHL book 976.4 X2wh.

■ **1830-1839.** See ***Texas, 1830-1839, Index of County Tax Lists*** **[Printed Book],** edited by Ronald Vern Jackson, et al, published by Accelerated Indexing Systems, North Salt Lake, UT, 1982, 39 pages. FHL book 976.4 X2j 1830-1839.

■ **1830-1900.** See ***Texas Ranger Service Records, ca. 1830-1900*** **[Microfilm],** from the originals at the Texas State Archives, Austin, TX. Filmed by the TX State Archives, 1971, 2 rolls, as follows:
- Texas Ranger Service records, ca. 1830-1846 - Texas Ranger Service records, Minute men, (primarily), 1841 Acklin, John - Villareal, Juan, FHL film #2282494.
- Texas Ranger Service records, Minute men, (primarily), 1841 Waddock, Bryan - York, H. - Texas Ranger Service records, (et al) 1847-1900, companies: Frontier Battalion companies, Minute men companies, Misc. units companies. Companies are listed alphabetically within each of these groups - Minute men, commanding officers; Counties, Frontier battalions, commanding officers. These groups are listed alphabetically within county order - Ranger index, ca. 1847-1900 Abercrombie, J.W. - Zurcher, L., FHL film #2282495

■ ***1835 Entrance Certificates, Nacogdoches District*** **[Printed Book],** compiled by Betty Fagan Burr, published by Frances Terry Ingmire, St. Louis, MO, 1982, 40 pages. From bibliography: "From the R.B. Blake translation of the original Spanish certificates." Includes index. FHL book 976.4 P4n.

■ ***1835 Sabine District, Texas, Census*** **[Printed Book],** compiled by Mrs. Helen Gomer Schluter, published by Ericson Books, Nacogdoches, TX, 1983, 56 pages. From Introduction: "This 1835 Sabine District, Texas, census was copied from the original Nacogdoches Archives, Austin, Texas, by Mr. R. B. Blake." Includes additions to the original census records and a comprehensive index by Mrs. Helen Gomer Schluter. FHL book 976.4177 X2sh.

■ **1836.** See ***A Brief Account of the Origin, Progress and Present State of the Colonial Settlements of Texas: Together With an Exposition of the Causes Which Have Induced the Existing War With Mexico*** **[Printed Book],** by William H. Wharton, extracted from a work entitled *A Geographical, Statistical and Historical Account of Texas*, originally published by S. Nye, Nashville, TN, 1836, 16 pages. Reprint published by Pemberton Press, Austin, TX, 1964. Filmed by the Genealogical Society of Utah, 1972, FHL film #874251.

■ **1836-1935.** See ***Guide and Index to the Texas Adjutant General Service Records, 1836-1935*** **[Printed Book],** by Anthony Black and the Texas State Archives; edited by Robert de Berardinis, Contents: Vol. 1: Cumulative Index; Vol. 2: Separate Indexes, publ. Heritage Books, Westminster, MD, 2009, 2 vols., FHL book 976.4 M22ba v. 1-2.

■ **1837-1910.** See ***Texas County Tax Rolls, 1837-1910*** **[Microfilm],** from the originals at the Texas State Archives, Austin, TX. filmed by the TX State Archives, 424 rolls, 1974-1975. A complete set is also located at the Family History Library in Salt Lake City. Texas may not have state censuses, but there are thousands of name lists available from the tax rolls for all 254 Texas counties. The tax rolls are a boon for finding the name of an ancestor living in Texas, because the name of every taxpayer is shown, including real or personal property holders. Therefore, the tax rolls provide a good list of the adult residents of a county, often more so than any head of households census list. The TX State Archives microfilm collection is identified at their information page. See **www.tsl.texas.gov/arc/taxrolls.html**. The 424 FHL rolls begin with FHL film #2282072 (Anderson Co, 1846-1881, A-C). For a complete list of roll numbers and contents of each roll, see the online FHL catalog page for this title. See **https://familysearch.org/search/catalog/986276**.

■ **1840-1849.** See ***Texas, 1840-1849, Index of County Tax Lists*** **[Printed Book],** edited by Ronald Vern Jackson, et al, published by Accelerated Indexing Systems, North Salt Lake, UT, 1982, 69 pages. FHL book 976.4 X2j 1840-1849.

■ ***1840 Census of the Republic of Texas*** **[Printed Book],** edited by Gifford White, published by Pemberton Press, Austin, TX, 1966, 236 pages. In spite of the title – there was no census in Texas in 1840 – the names apparently were taken from the *First Settlers* book below. FHL book 976.4 X2w 1840.

■ **1840.** See ***First Settlers of the Republic of Texas: Headright Land Grants Which Were Reported as Genuine and Legal by the Traveling Commissioners, January, 1840*** **[Printed Book],** 2 vols., originally published by Cruger & Wing, Austin, Texas, 1841; reproduced and indexed by Carolyn Reeves Ericson and Frances T. Ingmire, Nacogdoches, TX, 1982. Contents: Vol. 1: Counties of Austin, Bastrop, Bexar, Brazoria, Colorado, Fannin, Fayette, Fort Bend, Galveston, Goliad, Gonzales, Harris, Harrison, Houston, Jackson, and Jasper; Vol. 2: Counties of Jefferson, Liberty, Matagorda, Milam, Montgomery, Nacogdoches, Red River, Refugio, Robertson, Sabine, San Augustine, Shelby, Victoria, and Washington. FHL book 976.4 R2er v. 1&2.

■ **1840s.** See ***Early Settlers and Indian Fighters of Southwest Texas: Facts Gathered From Survivors of Frontier Days*** **[Printed Book],** by A. J. Sowell, originally published by B. C. Jones, printers, 1900; facsimile reproduction, including new index, published by State House Press, Austin, TX, 1986, 861 pages. FHL book 976.4 H2saj 1986.

■ **1846.** See ***Republic of Texas: Poll Lists For 1846*** **[Printed Book],** by Marion Day Mullins, published by Genealogical Publishing Co., Inc., Baltimore, 1974, 189 pages. FHL book 976.4 R4m.

■ **1846.** See ***Taxpayers of the Republic of Texas: Covering 30 counties and the District of Panola*** **[Printed Book],** compiled by Beth and Emily Dorman. Published by the authors, 1988, Grand Prairie, TX, 275 pages. Includes index. FHL book 976.4 R4d. Also on microfiche, FHL film #6007392.

■ **1846-1848.** See ***Compiled Service Records of Volunteer Soldiers Who Served During the Mexican War in Organizations From the State of Texas*** **[Microfilm],** from the originals at the National Archives, Washington, DC. Filmed by the National Archives, 1959, 19 rolls, beginning with FHL film #471519 (First Texas Mounted Rifles A-S). For a complete list of roll number and contents of each roll, see the online FHL catalog page for this title. See **https://familysearch.org/search/catalog/316485**.

■ ***1858 State Census of Austin County, Texas, Copied Under the Supervision of the Littlefield Fund and Assisted by Project No. 43 of the Bureau of Research in the Social Sciences at the University of Texas From Original Manuscripts Located in the Courthouse at Bellville, Texas* [Microfilm],** from the originals at the Austin County courthouse in Bellville, Texas. Filmed by the Genealogical Society of Utah, 1992, 1 roll, FHL film #1838537.

■ **1861-1865.** See ***Texas Confederate Index: Confederate Soldiers of the State of Texas* [Microfilm],** source not noted. Includes name, rank, commission, enlistment date and place, discharge date and place, company, description (age, residence, etc.). Filmed by Microfilm Service and Sales, Dallas, TX, 1961, 14 rolls, beginning with FHL film #227483 (Confederate Index, A-Bradford). For a complete list of roll numbers and contents of each roll, see the online FHL catalog page for this title. See **https://familysearch.org/search/catalog/424572**.

■ **1861-1865.** See ***Index to Compiled Service Records of Confederate Soldiers Who Served in Organizations From the State of Texas* [Microfilm],** from the original records at the National Archives, Washington, DC, an alphabetical card index to the compiled service records of Confederate soldiers belonging to units from the State of Texas, series M323, 41 rolls, beginning with FHL film #880014 (Surnames A – As). For a complete list of roll numbers and contents of each roll, see the online FHL catalog page for this title. See **https://familysearch.org/search/catalog/98127**.

■ **1861-1865.** See ***Index to Compiled Service Records of Union Soldiers Who Served in Organizations From the State of Texas* [Microfilm]**, from the original records at the National Archives, Central Plains Region, Kansas City, MO, series M402, 2 rolls, FHL film #881592 (Index, A-Ma, 1861-1865), and #881593 (Index, Mc-Z, 1861-1865).

■ ***1865-1866 Internal Revenue Assessment Lists for Texas* [Microfilm],** from the original records at the National Archives in Washington, DC. Contents: District 2: Atascosas, Austin, Bee, Calhoun, Cameron, Colorado, De Witt, Duval, Encinal (no longer exists), Fayette, Fort Bend, Frio, Goliad, Gonzales, Hidalgo, Jackson, Karnes, La Salle, Lavaca, Live Oak, McMullin, Matagorda, Maverick, Nueces, Refugio, San Patricio, Starr, Victoria, Washington, Webb, Wharton, Zapata, and Zavala counties. District 3: Archer, Bandera, Bastrop, Baylor, Bill, Bexar, Blanco, Bosque, Brown, Buchanan (no longer exists), Burleson, Burnet, Caldwell, Clay, Colahan (Callahan), Comal, Comanche, Concho, Cooke, Coryell, Dawson, Denton, Eastland, Edwards, El Paso, Erath, Falls, Gillespie, Guadalupe, Hamilton, Hardeman, Haskell, Hays, Hill, Jack, Johnson, Jones, Kemble (Kimble), Kerr, Kinney, Knox, Lampasas, Llano, McCulloch, Mason, Medina, Menard, Milam, Montague, Palo Pinto, Parker, Presidio, Runnels, San Saba, Shackelford, Tarrant, Taylor, Throckmorton, Travis, Uvalde, Wichita, Wilbargar (Wilbarger), Williamson, Wise, and Young counties. District 4 pt 1: Anderson, Bowie, Cass, Cherokee, Collin, Dallas, Ellis, Fannin, Freestone, Grayson, Harrison, Henderson, Hopkins, Hunt, Kaufman, Lamar, Limestone, Marion, Navarro, Panola, Red River, Rusk, Smith, Titus, Upshur, Van Zandt, and Wood counties. District 4 pt 2: Ellis, Freestone, Limestone, and Navarro counties. Names are arranged by collection district and thereunder by division. Filmed by the archives, 1987, 2 rolls, FHL film #1578479 (District 2) and film #1578480 (Districts 3-4).

■ **1867.** See ***Texas 1867 Special Voters' Registration* [Microfilm],** from the originals at the Texas State Library & Archives Commission, Austin, Texas. Available through Interlibrary loan from the TX archives. (FHL has microfilm, but not for circulation). The Reconstruction Act of March 13, 1867 required the commanding officer in each military district to have, before September 1, a registration of all qualified voters in each county. These lists would be used to determine all who would be eligible to vote for any proposed Constitutional Convention in the state. Forms include the following information: date of registration; county and precinct of residence; years resided in state; years resided in county; years resided in precinct; native of what state or county; how, when and where naturalized; signature; general remarks. Not all forms are completely filled out. Filmed by the Texas State Library, 1984, FHL has 7 rolls, as follows:

- Anderson - Caldwell counties, 1867, FHL film #1929135.
- Calhoun - Falls counties, 1869, FHL film #1929136.
- Erath - Hamilton counties, FHL film #1929137.
- Hardin - Kinney counties, FHL film #1929138.
- Lamar - Orange counties, FHL film #1929139.
- Navarro - Tyler counties, FHL film #1929140.
- Tarrant - Zapata counties, FHL film #1929141.

■ **1867.** See ***An index to the 1867 Voters Registration of Texas* [CD-ROM],** compiled by Donaly E. Brice & John C. Barron, published by Heritage Books, Bowie, MD, 2000. Lists voters arranged by county including name, date of registration, voting precinct, years of residence, state or country of birth. This is the first statewide listing of freed slaves in Texas. See FHL CD-ROM No. 898.

■ **1870-1930.** See ***Confederate Pensions (Texas): Applications Approved and Rejected* [Microfilm],** from the originals at the TX Comptroller's Office, Austin, TX. Filmed by the Genealogical Society of Utah, 1974, 700 rolls, beginning with FHL film #960279 (Index to Applications Approved, Rejected, and Inmates of the Confederate Home). For a complete list of roll numbers and contents of each roll, see the online FHL catalog page for this title. See **https://familysearch.org/search/catalog/70567**.
See also ***Confederate Pension Index for Texas, 1870-1930* [Microfilm],** from the original records at the TX State Archives, Austin, TX. Filmed by the Genealogical Society of Utah, 1996, 1 roll, FHL film #2031526

■ **1874 History.** See ***A Texas Scrap-Book: Made up of the History, Biography, and Miscellany of Texas and its People* [Printed Book],** compiled by D. W. C. Baker, original published by A.S. Barnes and Co., New York, 1874, 657 pages. Filmed by W. C. Cox, Tucson, AZ, 1974, FHL film #1000596. Indexed in ***Index to D. W. C. Baker's A Texas Scrapbook***, by Richard Morrison, published by the author, Austin, Texas, 1984, 153 pages. Includes name index, and index to sources and authors. FHL book 976.4 H2mr index.

■ **1884 History.** See ***Rangers and Pioneers of Texas: With a Concise Account of the Early Settlements, Hardships, Massacres, Battles, and Wars, by Which Texas Was Rescued From the Rule of the Savage and Consecrated to the Empire of Civilization* [Microfilm],** from the book by A.J. Sowell, originally published by Shepard Bros. & Co., San Antonio, TX, 1884, 411 pages. Filmed for the FHL by the Library of Congress, 1991, 1 roll, FHL film #1730711.

■ ***1890 Reconstructed Census for Selected Texas Counties* [Printed Books],** name lists compiled from local tax and other records, by Mary C. Moody and others, published for the following Texas counties:

- **Bexar County**, (tax rolls of 1890), FHL book 976.435 R4a.
- **Caldwell County**, FHL book 976.433 X2m.
- **Limestone County**, FHL book 976.4285 X2m.
- **Montgomery County**, FHL book 976.4153 X2m.
- **Nacogdoches County** (index to 1890 tax list), FHL book 976.4182 R42e.
- **Smith County** (index to 1890 tax book), FHL book 976.4225 R48e.
- **Travis County**, FHL book 976.431 X2m, pt. 1 & pt 2 (index).
- **Walker County**, FHL book 976.4169 X2m.
- **Cass County**, FHL book 976.4195 X28m.
- **Hamilton County**, FHL book 976.4549 X2m.
- **Kerr County**, FHL book 976.4884 X2d.
- **Leon County**, FHL book 976.4233 X28m.

■ **1914 History. See *History of the Cattlemen of Texas: A Brief Résumé of the Live Stock Industry of the Southwest and a Biographical Sketch of Many of the Important Characters Whose Lives are Interwoven Therein* [Printed Book],** with an introduction by Harwood P. Hinton; series editor, David Farmer, originally published by Johnston Printing & Advertising Co., 1914, 350 pages. Reprint by Texas State Historical Association in cooperation with the Center for Studies in Texas History at the University of Texas at Austin. Includes index and bibliographical references. FHL book 976.4 U2h. See also ***The Trail Drivers of Texas: Interesting Sketches of Early Cowboys and Their Experiences on the Range and on the Trail During the Days That Tried Men's Souls, True Narratives Related by Real Cow-punchers and Men Who Fathered the Cattle Industry in Texas* [Printed Book],** originally compiled and edited by J. Marvin Hunter; introduction by B. Byron Price, published by the University of Texas Press, Austin, TX, 1985, 1,085 pages. Includes index. FHL book 976.4 H2hj.

■ **1917-1918.** See ***Texas, World War I Selective Service System Draft Registration Cards, 1917-1918* [Microfilm],** from the original records at the National Archives in East Point, Georgia. The draft cards are arranged alphabetically by state, then alphabetically by county or city, and then alphabetically by surname of registrants. Cards are arranged in a rough alphabetical order by surname. Filmed by the National Archives, 1987-1988, 183 rolls, beginning with FHL film #1927189 (Texas, Anderson County, A-I). For a complete list of roll numbers and contents of each roll, see the online FHL catalog page for this title. See **https://familysearch.org/search/catalog/747002**.